LISTVERSE

EPIC BOOK *of*

(MIND-BOGGLING)

TOP 10 LISTS

Unbelievable Facts and Astounding Trivia on Movies, Music, Crime, Celebrities, History and More

JAMIE FRATER

Ulysses Press

Published by:
ULYSSES PRESS
P.O. Box 3440
Berkeley, CA 94703
www.ulyssespress.com

ISBN: 978-1-61243-297-7
Library of Congress Control Number: 2013957414

Acquisitions Editor: Keith Riegert
Managing Editor: Claire Chun
Editor: Lauren Harrison
Proofreader: Elyce Berrigan-Dunlop
Production: Lindsay Tamura
Cover photos: octopus © Morphart Creation/shutterstock.com; glider © Hein Nouwens/shutterstock.com; scorpion © Hein Nouwens/shutterstock.com; eye © Morphart Creation/shutterstock.com; skeleton © Morphart Creation/shutterstock.com
Interior photos: see page 719

10 9 8 7 6 5 4 3 2 1

Printed in Canada by Marquis Book Printing

Distributed by Publishers Group West

CONTENTS

CHAPTER 1

MYSTERIES

1. Top 10 Mysterious Artifacts That Are Allegedly Alien
2. Top 10 Real-Life Hidden Treasures You Could Still Find
3. Top 10 People Who Vanished into Thin Air
4. Top 10 Creepy Mysteries Involving Unidentified People
5. Top 10 Mysterious Urban Legends Based on Video Footage
6. Top 10 Places as Mysterious as the Bermuda Triangle
7. Top 10 Mysteries That Hint at Forgotten Advanced Civilizations
8. Top 10 Mysterious Letters
9. Top 10 Strange Unsolved Mysteries
10. Top 10 Mysterious Mass Animal Deaths
11. Top 10 Mysterious Prehistoric Sites from Around the World
12. Top 10 Entertainment Careers Cut Short by Unsolved Mysteries
13. Top 10 Secretly Connected Topics

TOP 10 Mysterious Artifacts That Are Allegedly Alien

by **Pauli Poisuo**

10 The Russian UFO Tooth Wheel

A Russian man found a strange piece of machinery from Vladivostok, the administrative capital of the Primorsky Krai area. The object resembled a piece of tooth wheel and was embedded in a piece of coal the man was using to light a fire. Although discarded pieces of old machines are not uncommon in Russia, the man became curious and showed his find to some scientists. Testing revealed that the toothed object was almost pure aluminum and almost certainly artificially made.

Also, it was 300 million years old. This raised some interesting questions, as aluminum of this purity and shape can't form naturally and humans didn't figure out how to make it until 1825. Curiously, the object also resembles parts that are used in microscopes and other delicate technical devices.

Although conspiracy theorists have been quick to declare the find a part of an alien spaceship, the scientists researching it are not willing to jump to conclusions and wish to run further tests in order to learn more about the mysterious artifact.

9 The Guatemala Stone Head

In the 1930s, explorers found an enormous, elegantly made sandstone statue in the middle of a Guatemalan jungle. The face carved in the stone didn't resemble the facial features of the Maya or any of the other people known to have populated the lands. In fact, its elongated cranium and fine features didn't seem to belong in the history books at all.

Researchers have claimed that the statue's unique features depict a member of an ancient alien civilization that was far more advanced than any of the pre-Hispanic races of America we know about. Some even speculated the head might just be a part of a much larger construct underneath (this was found to be untrue). Of course, there's a chance that the statue might be the work of a more recent artist or even a complete hoax. Sadly, we will probably never find out for sure: The head was used for target practice by revolutionary troops and its features have been destroyed to near obscurity.

8 The Williams Enigmalith

In 1998, a hiker named John J. Williams noticed an odd metallic protrusion in the dirt. He dug up a strange-looking rock which, upon cleaning, turned out to have a weird electrical component attached to it. The electric device was clearly man-made and somewhat resembled an electrical plug.

The rock has since become a well-known mystery in UFO enthusiast circles. It was featured in *UFO Magazine* and (according to Williams) *Fortean Times*, a famed magazine devoted to mysterious phenomena. Williams, an electrical engineer, says the electronic component embedded in the stone has not been glued or welded into the granite. In fact, the rock probably formed around the device.

Many believe that the so-called Williams Enigmalith is a hoax, as Williams refuses to break it (but is willing to sell it for $500,000). Also, the stone device does bear a certain resemblance to heat rocks that are commonly used to keep tropical pet lizards warm. Still, geological analysis has apparently determined that the stone is around 100,000 years old, which (if true) would mean the device inside can't possibly be of human creation. Williams is confident enough to let anyone research the Enigmalith on three conditions: He must be present, the rock must remain unharmed, and he will not have to pay for the research.

7 Ancient Aeroplanes

Incas and other pre-Columbian people left behind some extremely puzzling trinkets. Some of the strangest are probably the so-called ancient aeroplanes, which are small, golden figures that closely resemble modern jet planes. Originally thought to be zoomorphic (meant to resemble animals), the statues were soon found to have features that look very much like a fighter plane's wings, stabilizing tails, and even landing gears. They were aerodynamic enough that when ancient astronaut believers allegedly made model planes with their proportions and fitted them with propellers and (again, allegedly) jet engines, they flew perfectly. All of this has led to speculation that the Incas may have been in contact with—likely extraterrestrial—people who were able to build advanced jet planes, and who perhaps even possessed the technology themselves.

Well, that, or these wonderful statuettes might just be artistic representations of bees, flying fish, or other winged creatures. As always, the beauty is in the eye of the beholder.

6 The Ubaid Lizard Men

The Al-Ubaid archaeological site in Iraq is a gold mine for archaeologists and historians. It has yielded numerous objects from a pre-Sumerian time called the Ubaid period (5900–4000 BC). However, some of these objects are quite disturbing. A number of Ubaid statues depict strange, lizardlike humanoid figures in unique, unceremonious poses that seem to indicate they were not gods (such as the animal-headed deities of Egypt), but rather a race of lizard people.

Of course, the statues have been drawn into stories and theories of reptilian aliens that used to roam the earth (and perhaps still do, according to conspiracy theorists). Although this seems unlikely, their true nature remains a mystery.

5 The Sri Lanka Meteorite Fossils

Researchers who analyzed the remains of a meteorite that fell in Sri Lanka found that their subject was something more than just pieces of space rock. It was an alien artifact in the most literal sense: an artifact made of actual aliens. Two separate studies have found that the meteorite contains fossils and algae that are clearly of extraterrestrial origin.

Professor Chandra Wickramasinghe, the leading researcher on the first study, says the fossils provide compelling evidence of panspermia (the hypothesis that life exists throughout the universe and is spread by meteorites and other solid space debris). However, he is not without his critics. Wickramasinghe just happens to be a noted panspermia enthusiast with a tendency to claim that almost everything is of extraterrestrial origin. What's more, the traces of life the meteorite contains are actually freshwater species commonly found on Earth, which seems to indicate the object has been contaminated during its time on our planet.

4 The Summer's Triumph Tapestry

The tapestry known as "Summer's Triumph" was created around 1538 in Bruges, the capital of West Flanders province in the Flemish Region of Belgium. Currently, it resides in the Bayerisches National Museum.

"Summer's Triumph" is famous (or infamous) among conspiracy theorists because it clearly depicts a number of distinctly UFO-like objects flying in the skies. Although their presence is baffling, some speculate they may have been added to the tapestry (which depicts a victorious ruler's ascension to power) in order to connect the UFOs to the ruler as a symbol of divine intervention. This, of course, raises more questions than answers, such as, Why would the 16th-century Belgians recognize flying saucers and mentally connect them with divinity?

3 The Glorification of the Eucharist

An Italian painter named Ventura Salimbeni is responsible for one of the most mysterious altar paintings in history. "Disputa of the Eucharist," a 16th-century painting also known as "The Glorification of the Eucharist" (Eucharist is an alternate term for the Holy Communion), is a three-part work. The bottom two parts are relatively normal: They depict a number of religious authorities and an altar. However, the top part shows the Holy Trinity (Father, Son, and a dove depicting the Holy Ghost) looking upon them…and holding what seems to be a space satellite. The object is large and spherical, with a metallic finish, telescopic antennas, and strange lights. In fact, it heavily resembles an old Sputnik satellite.

Although UFO enthusiasts and ancient astronaut theorists have often claimed the "Disputa" as proof of extraterrestrial life (or perhaps time travel), experts have been quick to debunk such notions. According to them, the orb is a Sphaera Mundi, a globelike representation of the universe that used to be common in religious art. The strange lights on the "satellite" are merely the sun and the moon, and its antennas are actually scepter wands that act as symbols of authority for the Father and the Son.

2 The Mexican Government's Maya Artifacts

The story goes like this: In 2012, the Mexican government released a number of Maya artifacts they had been protecting for 80 years as state secrets.

These objects were retrieved from an unexplored pyramid that was found under another pyramid in Calakmul, the site of one of the most powerful ancient Maya cities. A government-sanctioned documentary by Raul Julia-Levy (the son of famous actor Raul Julia) and financier Elisabeth Thieriot (ex-wife of a former publisher of the *San Francisco Chronicle*) featured a number of these finds, most of which clearly depict UFOs and alien visitors.

The case may seem fairly enticing, but once you look closer, a strange pattern of fraud begins to emerge. Both of the documentarians seem to be lying about something. Julia-Levy doesn't appear to be whom he claims to be; Raul Julia's widow has publicly called out a conman named Salvador Alba Fuentes as lying about his identity. According to her, Salvador is attempting to ride on her late husband's fame and is going around telling everyone his name is, yes, Raul Julia-Levy. Meanwhile, Thieriot has shut down the production of the documentary and sued her partner, accusing "Julia-Levy" of stealing her documentary and misusing filming equipment (a statement "Julia-Levy" vehemently opposes). What's more, there seems to be very little scientific proof of the authenticity of the artifacts, and pictures that have emerged online are less than concrete evidence.

Perhaps the artifacts were cheap fakes manufactured by a local artisan. Perhaps the officials had second thoughts about the documentary and ordered Thieriot to shut it down by any means necessary. Whatever the truth behind these strange artifacts, their case is far from convincing.

1 The Betz Mystery Sphere

When the Betz family was examining the damage of a strange fire that had decimated 88 acres of their woodland, they made a strange discovery: a silvery sphere, about eight inches (20 centimeters) in diameter, completely smooth except for a strange, elongated triangle symbol. Initially they thought it might be a NASA gadget or even a Soviet spy satellite, but they eventually decided it was most likely just a souvenir. On a moment's whim, they decided to take it with them.

Two weeks later, the family's son was strumming a guitar in the same room as the sphere. Suddenly, the sphere started reacting to his tunes, emitting a strange throbbing sound and a resonance that deeply disturbed the family's dog. Soon, the Betz family found the orb had other strange properties. It could stop and change directions when pushed across the floor, eventually returning to the person who pushed it like a faithful dog. It seemed to draw power from solar energy, becoming noticeably more active on bright days.

It started looking like something (or someone) was controlling the sphere: It would occasionally emit low-frequency rattling and vibrations, like there was a motor running inside. It seemed to avoid falling and crashing at all costs, as if to protect something inside it. It even managed to completely defy the laws of gravity and climb up a slanted table to avoid falling.

A media frenzy ensued. Respected papers such as the *New York Times* and the *London Daily* sent reporters to witness the miracle sphere, which repeated its tricks to countless people. Even scientists and representatives of the military were impressed, although the Betz family wouldn't let them take the sphere for closer examination. However, that soon changed as the sphere took a turn for the worse. It started exhibiting poltergeistlike behavior: doors started slamming shut at night and strange organ music would fill the house out of the blue. At that point, the family decided to find out what the sphere really was. The Navy analyzed it and found it was…a perfectly ordinary (if high-quality) stainless steel ball.

To this day, it's not entirely clear what the mysterious sphere is. However, there have been many theories attempting to explain its possible nature. The most plausible of these is the most mundane: Three years before the Betz family found the orb, an artist named James Durling-Jones was driving in the area where it was found. On the luggage rack on his car roof were a number of stainless steel balls meant for a sculpture he was making, some of which dropped off during the bumpy ride. These balls matched the exact description of the Betz sphere, and were balanced enough to roll around at the slightest provocation (the Betz family lived in an old house with uneven floors, so such a ball would appear to behave erratically). These balls could even emit a rattling sound, thanks to tiny metal shavings stuck inside during the manufacturing process.

Although this doesn't explain all of the reported phenomena, it certainly casts a shadow over the "mysterious ghost ball from outer space" theory.

TOP 10 Real-Life Hidden Treasures You Could Still Find

by Corey Gibson

10 Forrest Fenn Hidden Treasure

Forrest Fenn wants you to have all of his money when he dies.

When Fenn was only nine years old, he found an arrowhead near his home in Texas—an arrowhead that would shape the rest of his life. Fenn fell in love with ancient artifacts. After becoming a pilot in the air force in the 1960s, Fenn regularly flew his plane to Pompeii to look for artifacts, of which he found plenty.

In the 1980s, Fenn was diagnosed with kidney cancer and told he would only have a few years to live. With his mortality looking him right in the face, Fenn decided to hide his most beloved artifacts and give everyone the clues to find his treasure, which he estimates to hold $1–3 million worth of gold, jewelry, and other valuable artifacts.

9 Treasure at Little Bighorn

For many Americans in the late 1800s, traveling West and striking it rich by finding gold didn't seem like an absurd idea. Some didn't even make it all the way to the Pacific. A few men struck it rich when they found gold in Montana. When fewer and fewer men dug up gold in that area, though, more and more of them continued west. But they probably should have kept looking.

According to some experts, Captain Grant Marsh was in charge of the *Far West*, a steamboat making its way up the Bighorn River, which runs through Wyoming and Montana, to resupply General George Custer in his fight against the Indians. When Captain Marsh heard of General Custer's defeat and found out he would have to take injured men away from the battlefield, the only thing he could do to keep the ship from sinking under the weight of so many wounded men was to bury the $375,000 worth of gold bars he had on board on the shores of the Bighorn River. Some say that Marsh had collected the gold bars from worried gold miners who didn't want to be attacked by the Sioux.

8 Treasure in the Mojave Desert

It may sound crazy that an oceangoing ship sunk 100 miles inland of the Pacific Ocean—in the Mojave Desert no less—but if it is true, there are mil-

lions of dollars worth of pearls in the Salton Sea, a shallow lake in inland Southern California.

Experts believe a large tide from the Gulf of California collided with runoff from the Colorado River. Enough water runoff developed that the ship (presumed to be Spanish) was carried into the Salton Sea. The ship would have been forgotten forever if it weren't for the abundance of pearls on board.

Surprisingly, there is a twist to the story. In 1870, the *Los Angeles Star* produced a story about a man named Charley Clusker who went out in search of the ship and actually found the treasure. But since the date the story ran, no other mention of Clusker or the ship he "found" has been dug up, leading many people to believe the ship and its pearls are still out there.

7 Mosby's Treasure in Virginia

Confederate Commander Colonel John Singleton Mosby was one sneaky fighter during the Civil War. He and his men were known as Mosby's Raiders for their lightning-quick raids of Union camps and their ability to elude the Union Army by blending in with the local townspeople. Mosby was essentially like Mel Gibson's character in *The Patriot*, but without all the drama.

After one of his many raids, which took place about 45 miles south of the Confederate line at Culpeper, Virginia, Mosby took Union General Edwin Stoughton prisoner, as well as a burlap sack containing $350,000 worth of gold, silver, and family heirlooms. The problem was, Mosby had also captured 42 other men during the raid and had to take them back through Union territory and across the Confederate line.

Following a route that parallels today's U.S. Route 211, Mosby's Raiders traveled south until they ran into a large contingency of Union soldiers. Unwilling to part with his treasure, Mosby instructed his men to bury the treasure between two large pine trees in case of a battle. Mosby marked the trees with his knife, and the Raiders headed back along their route and across the Confederate line without any trouble from the Union.

Unfortunately for Mosby, when he sent back seven of his most trusted men, they were all caught and hanged by the Union Army. Mosby never returned to look for the treasure.

6 $63 Million Hidden in Bedford County, Virginia

Thomas Beale must have been a strange man. Legend has it that in 1816, Beale and a few men he was traveling with came into a large sum of gold and silver while mining somewhere in the Rocky Mountains. With such a large fortune, estimated to be around $63 million in today's currency, all of the men wanted to make sure their next of kin would get the money should they perish. So Beale wrote three ciphers: One described the exact location of the treasure, the second described the contents of the treasure, and the third was a list of the men's names and their next of kin. Beale then entrusted Robert Morriss, a Lynchburg, Virginia, innkeeper with the safekeeping of a box containing the ciphers.

Morriss was supposed to wait ten years before opening it. At this point, if Beale did not return for the box, a key to the cipher was supposed to be mailed to Morriss. But it never arrived. For years, Morriss and a friend tried to decode the three ciphers, but they could only manage the second cipher (the one describing the contents of the treasure).

5 Treasure of Jean LaFitte

Jean LaFitte, along with his brother Pierre, were French pirates who made their living attacking merchant ships in the Gulf of Mexico and then selling the goods at one of their many ports or through a warehouse they owned. Apparently, the two brothers were so good at smuggling and pirating that they amassed enough wealth that they had to resort to burying some it.

After LaFitte died sometime between 1823 and 1830, legend of his treasures began circulating around Louisiana. Claims have been made that there are large caches of treasure buried somewhere in Lake Borgne, right off the coast of New Orleans, and another about 3 miles east of the Old Spanish Trail near the Sabine River in a gum tree grove.

4 Butch Cassidy's $20,000 Treasure

Butch Cassidy is arguably one of the most notable outlaws of the Wild West. He was such an outlaw that he even formed an outlaw group, called the Wild Bunch, to travel with him, robbing whomever they felt like. Before the law was hot on his tail, Cassidy and the Wild Bunch actually buried $20,000 somewhere in Irish Canyon, located in the northwestern part of Colorado in Moffat County.

3 John Dillinger's Buried Treasure

Being an outlaw means you have money, and everyone knows John Dillinger had a lot of it. Only months before he died, he buried $200,000 in Wisconsin.

Dillinger was hiding out with a few of his outlaw buddies in April 1934. FBI agents found out they were hiding in the Little Bohemia Lodge in Mercer, Wisconsin, and they surrounded Dillinger, along with infamous bank robber "Baby Face" Nelson and the other men. The FBI shot the first three men walking out the door, all three of whom happened to be civilians. Amid all the confusion, the gangsters were able to escape out a back entrance. It is said that Dillinger ran a few hundred yards north of the roadhouse, where he buried $200,000 in small bills inside a suitcase.

Just two months later, Dillinger was shot to death in Chicago, never getting the chance to go back to find the money.

2 $200 Million off the Coast of Key West

In 1622, the Spanish galleon *Nuestra Senora de Atocha* was heading back to Spain when it was caught in a hurricane off the coast of Key West. Many ships perished in the hurricane, and all of them were carrying an enormous cargo of gold, silver, and gems that has been valued to be worth around $700 million today.

Most of the loot has already been found. In 1985, treasure hunter Mel Fisher found $500 million of the buried treasure less than 100 miles off the coast of Key West.

Experts believe there is still plenty of treasure to find. The original captain's manifest states there are still about 17 tons of silver bars, 128,000 coins of different values, 60 pounds of emeralds, and 35 boxes of gold.

1 The Treasure of San Miguel

In 1712, Spain assembled one of the richest treasure fleets ever at that time. By 1715, Spain had amassed a fleet of 11 ships, all filled to the brim with silver, gold, pearls, and jewels, which are estimated to be worth about $2 billion by today's standards.

The plan for the ships was to leave from Cuba for the mainland just before hurricane season hit, hoping the foul weather would be a deterrent to pirates and privateers. It turned out that leaving so close to hurricane season was a mistake. Just six days after departing the shores of Cuba, all of the ships had sunk, thousands of sailors had died, and every bit of gold, silver, and jewelry was doomed to lay at the bottom of the sea.

Since then, seven of the ships have been recovered, but experts believe only a small amount of the valuables on board has been found.

The one ship that has yet to be found is the *San Miguel*—the ship that experts believe contains most of the treasure.

But where is it? Well, most of the ships that have been found have been located off the eastern shores of Florida, although some may have made it farther out to sea before sinking.

TOP 10 People Who Vanished into Thin Air

by **Robin Warder**

10 Maura Murray

On February 9, 2004, 21-year-old University of Massachusetts student Maura Murray e-mailed her professors and employer to tell them she was going away because of a (fabricated) death in the family. That night, she got into an accident by crashing her car into a tree near Woodsville, New Hampshire. Strangely, Maura had wrecked another car in an accident only a couple days earlier. A bus driver came by and asked Maura if she needed to call the police. Maura said no, but the driver called them anyway once he got to the nearest phone. When the police showed up ten minutes later, Maura had vanished.

There were no signs of any footprints or struggle at the scene, so it's possible Maura got a ride from someone. The next day, Maura's fiancé in Oklahoma received a voicemail which may have been from her, but he only heard sobbing on the other end of the line. While Maura had displayed some strange behavior in the days before she vanished, her family does not believe she disappeared willingly. After nine years, there is still no trace of what happened to her.

9 Brandon Swanson

Nineteen-year-old Brandon Swanson was heading back to his hometown of Marshall, Minnesota, on the evening of May 14, 2008, when he crashed his car into a ditch while driving on a rural gravel road. Brandon called his parents on his cell phone and asked them to come pick him up. They went looking for Brandon but were unable to find him. When Brandon's father called him back, Brandon said he would try heading toward the nearby town of Lynd. In the middle of their conservation, Brandon suddenly swore and the call was abruptly cut off.

Brandon's father tried calling him back several more times, but he never got an answer and was unable to find him. After police were notified, they found Brandon's car, but they were unable to locate him or his cell phone. One theory is that he might have accidentally stumbled into a nearby river and drowned, but searches turned up no trace of his body. No one knows what prompted Brandon to swear during that phone call, and it's the last anyone ever heard from him.

8 Louis Le Prince

Louis Le Prince was a French inventor who is renowned for having shot the world's first moving pictures on film. Strangely, "the father of cinematography" is also remembered for being the subject of one of the strangest disappearances of all time. On September 16, 1890, Le Prince was visiting his brother in Dijon, France, before boarding a train to Paris. When the train arrived at its destination, Le Prince had completely vanished.

The last time anyone saw Le Prince he was entering his cabin after having checked his luggage into a separate compartment. Neither Le Prince nor his luggage was ever seen again. There had been no signs of foul play or anything suspicious during the trip, and no one could recall seeing Le Prince outside his cabin. The windows were tightly closed, so it would have been difficult for him to jump off the train, but suicide seemed like an unlikely option since Le Prince was planning to travel to America to get patents for his new inventions. Because Le Prince was unable to get those patents, Thomas Edison took credit for the invention of motion pictures. As for Le Prince, his ultimate fate still remains a mystery.

7 Michael Negrete

At 4 a.m. on December 10, 1999, an 18-year-old UCLA freshman named Michael Negrete logged off his computer after playing video games with his friends all night. At 9 a.m., Michael's roommate woke up and noticed that he was gone but had left behind all his possessions, including his keys and wallet. He was never seen again.

The most curious aspect of Michael's disappearance is that his shoes were also left behind. Investigators used search dogs to track Michael's scent to a bus stop a couple miles away from campus, but would he really have walked that far without any shoes on? The only potential lead is an unidentified man who was seen in Dykstra Hall around 4:35 a.m. that day, but no one knows if he has any connection with Michael's disappearance. There's nothing in Michael's background to suggest he might have disappeared willingly, so the trail on him has remained completely cold for over a decade.

6 Barbara Bolick

On July 18, 2007, Barbara Bolick, a 55-year-old woman from Corvallis, Montana, went on a hiking trip in the Bitterroot Mountains with Jim Ramaker, a friend who was visiting from California. They were heading toward Bear Creek Overlook when Jim stopped to look at a scenic view. Barbara had been 20–30 feet behind him at the time, but Jim claimed that after turning away from her for less than a minute, he looked back to see that she had completely vanished. After authorities were notified, an extensive search of the area turned up no trace of Barbara.

On the surface, Jim Ramaker's story sounds pretty unbelievable. However, he was reportedly very cooperative with the authorities, and since there is no evidence that he did anything to Barbara, they do not consider him a suspect in her disappearance. It seemed likely that a guilty person would attempt to dream up a much better story than his victim simply vanishing into thin air. As of this writing, authorities haven't found any trace of foul play or any hint of what may have happened to Barbara Bolick.

5 Michael Hearon

On August 23, 2008, 51-year-old Michael Hearon traveled from his condo to his farm in Happy Valley, Tennessee, with plans to mow the lawn. That morning, neighbors saw Michael leaving the farm on his ATV—the last known sighting of him. The next day, Michael's friends visited the farm and saw his truck parked on the road with the windows rolled down. Michael's trailer was also attached to the vehicle with his lawnmower loaded on top of it, but the farm's lawn had not been mowed. His friends returned the next day and became concerned when they saw his truck parked in the same location and noticed that his keys, cell phone, and wallet were still inside.

Three days after Michael's disappearance, investigators uncovered their only clue when they found Michael's ATV on a steep hill about one mile from his home, a location he was never known to visit. Other than that, no major leads have surfaced and authorities could find no physical evidence to suggest foul play. Michael was not known to have any enemies or any reason to disappear on his own, so his whereabouts are a truly baffling mystery.

4 April Fabb

One of the most famous disappearances in British history took place in Norfolk, England, on April 8, 1969. A 13-year-old schoolgirl named April Fabb left her home in Metton to visit her sister in the nearby village of Roughton. She was taking the trip on her bicycle and was last seen riding down a country road by a truck driver at approximately 2:06 p.m. At 2:12 p.m., her bicycle was found lying in the middle of a field a few hundred yards away, but there was no sign of April.

Abduction seemed like a probable scenario in April's disappearance, but the perpetrator would have had a very narrow window to work with. They had only six minutes to abduct April and disappear from the area without any witnesses seeing anything. An extensive search was made for April, but there was no hint of her whereabouts. Authorities found April's case to be similar to the disappearance of another young British girl named Genette Tate in 1978, so notorious child murderer Robert Black was considered as a possible suspect. However, there's nothing to conclusively link him to April's disappearance, so it remains unsolved.

3 Brian Shaffer

Brian Shaffer was a 27-year-old medical student from Ohio State University who went to a bar called the Ugly Tuna Saloona on the evening of April 1, 2006. Sometime between 1:30 and 2 a.m., he mysteriously vanished. He had been drinking heavily that night and, after talking to his girlfriend on his cell phone, was last seen speaking to two young women. However, no one at the bar could remember seeing him after that.

The most baffling unanswered question in this case is how Brian exited the bar. The establishment's surveillance footage clearly showed him arriving, but no footage could be found of his exit! None of his friends or family believed that he disappeared on his own. While he had been upset about his mother passing away three weeks before, he was doing well in school and had plans to go on vacation with his girlfriend. But if Brian was abducted and met with foul play, how did the perpetrator get him out of the bar without being seen by any witnesses or the security cameras?

2 Jason Jolkowski

On the morning of June 13, 2001, 19-year-old Jason Jolkowski was called in early to his job in Omaha, Nebraska. He asked a friend to pick him up at a nearby high school, but never showed up.

The last confirmed sighting of Jason was about a half hour before he was supposed to meet his friend, when a neighbor saw Jason carrying trash cans into his garage. Surveillance cameras from the high school show that he never made it there. Jason had no personal problems or reason to disappear on his own, and there is no evidence to suggest what may have happened to him. His fate remains a true unsolved mystery at the time of this writing.

In 2003, Jim and Kelly Jolkowski memorialized their son by founding Project Jason, a nonprofit organization that has become one of the most prominent resources for the families of missing persons.

1 Nicole Morin

On July 30, 1985, eight-year-old Nicole Morin left her mother's penthouse apartment at the West Mall apartment building in Toronto, Ontario. After picking up the mail from the lobby at 10:30 a.m. that day, Nicole made plans to go swimming with her friend in the building's pool. She said goodbye to her mother and left the apartment, but 15 minutes later, her friend buzzed the apartment again to ask why Nicole hadn't arrived.

Nicole's disappearance led to one of the largest police investigations in Toronto's history, but they could find no trace of her. The most likely theory was that someone could have abducted Nicole right after she left her apartment, but the building was 20 stories high, so it would have been very difficult to get her out of there undetected. One tenant did say they saw Nicole make it to the elevator, but no one else reported hearing or seeing anything. Nearly 30 years later, authorities have still never turned up any solid evidence to determine what happened to Nicole Morin.

TOP 10 Creepy Mysteries Involving Unidentified People

by **Robin Warder**

10 Benjaman Kyle

On the morning of August 31, 2004, a nude man was found between two dumpsters behind a Burger King in Richmond Hill, Georgia. He appeared to be in his fifties and sported three depressions in his head, which seemed to indicate that he had been struck with a blunt object. He had no identification and could not remember his name or where he was from. When examined by doctors, they determined that the man had retrograde amnesia and was unlikely to regain his memory.

Since he was found behind a Burger King, the man was nicknamed "B. K." and he soon chose "Benjaman Kyle" as his new name. He seems to think that the unusually spelled "Benjaman" is his real first name. Benjaman does have memory fragments of a distant past, which could provide clues about his true identity. He believes that he hails from Indianapolis and lived in Colorado for a time. Benjaman is also convinced that his birth date is August 29, 1948, and he seems to have a detailed knowledge of the restaurant business. Investigators have used many avenues to figure out who Benjaman really is, such as DNA testing, fingerprint checks, and numerous media appearances. But Benjaman Kyle remains a man without an identity.

9 Bella in the Wych Elm

On April 18, 1943, four boys from Stourbridge, England, were playing in Hagley Woods when they came across a large witch hazel tree. When one

of the boys climbed the tree, he discovered a human skull in the hollow trunk. After police were notified, they found an entire skeleton concealed in the tree, along with a shoe, gold wedding ring, and fragments of clothing. A severed human hand was also buried next to the tree. A piece of taffeta was found in the skull's mouth, indicating that the victim had died from asphyxiation. A forensic examination determined that the victim was female and had been dead at least 18 months. Coincidentally, a resident had reported hearing a female scream in Hagley Woods about 18 months beforehand.

Though the woman was never identified, her legend grew months later after mysterious graffiti messages started appearing on walls, which often read, "Who put Bella in the Wych elm?" These messages all appeared to be written by the same unknown person, who may have had knowledge about what happened. This message last appeared in 1999 when it was sprayed on the 200-year-old Wychbury Obelisk. It was theorized that the unidentified woman might have been the victim of black magic, or that she was a member of a spy ring and was giving secrets to the Luftwaffe about local munitions factories. After 70 years, there are still no answers about who "Bella" was or who put her in the Wych elm.

8 Perseus

Over the course of several decades, the United States and the Soviet Union had no shortage of spies passing information to the other side, but one of the most prominent was never discovered. During World War II, the U.S. worked on the Manhattan Project, where they developed and produced the world's first atomic bombs. At least three people who worked on the project—Klaus Fuchs, David Greenglass, and Theodore Hall—were exposed as spies for the Soviet Union. However, in 1991, a Russian intelligence colonel named Vladimir Chikov published a series of articles claiming that the Soviets received important information about the project from an unidentified spy code-named "Perseus." According to Chikov, Perseus was a high-level scientist who worked at the White Sands Missile Range and the Los Alamos National Laboratory in New Mexico. He supposedly came aboard the Manhattan Project over a year before any of the other known spies, and the secrets he provided helped give the Soviets a head start in developing their own nuclear program. In 1999, Philip Morrison, a well-respected MIT physicist who had worked on the project, was publicly accused of being Perseus, but Morrison was able to produce a lot of credible evidence supporting his innocence. Some have speculated that Perseus did not exist, but if he was real, he has successfully gotten away with espionage for 70 years.

7 John Doe No. 24

On the morning of October 11, 1945, police found an unidentified African-American teenager wandering the streets of Jacksonville, Illinois. The young man was mute and deaf and was unable to communicate. He was eventually brought before a judge, who sentenced him to the Lincoln State School and Colony. Because he was the 24th unidentified man to be put into the state's mental health system, he forever became known as "John

Doe No. 24." At the time, state institutions were notorious for being brutal and dehumanizing, so John was subjected to many years of abuse.

To add to his hardships, he eventually went blind. However, in spite of his rough existence, John Doe No. 24 somehow managed to maintain a positive attitude and sense of humor. After remaining in the mental healthcare system for over 30 years, he was eventually transferred to a nursing home in Peoria. John often scribbled down the name "Lewis," providing a possible clue to his true identity, but no one discovered who he really was. He was believed to be 64 years old when he died of a stroke on November 28, 1993. After learning of his story, musician Mary Chapin Carpenter decided to purchase a headstone for his unmarked grave and immortalized him in a song called "John Doe No. 24."

6 The Rodney Alcala Photos

Notorious serial killer Rodney Alcala currently sits on death row at San Quentin State Prison. He became known as the "Dating Game Killer" after appearing as a contestant on *The Dating Game* during the midst of his murder spree. After he won the show, his potential date made the wise decision to not go out with him. Alcala was convicted of seven murders, but authorities have always suspected there were more. The mystery was heightened after Alcala's arrest in 1979 when investigators searched a storage locker he had rented in Seattle and found trophies of his crimes, along with over 1,000 disturbing photographs.

These photos feature numerous unidentified young women and teenage boys, most of whom are pictured nude or in sexually explicit poses. Alcala often passed himself off as a professional fashion photographer in order to lure people into his home to pose for him, and authorities fear that some of the individuals in his photos might be undiscovered victims. Most of the photos are too sexually explicit to be published, but in 2010, 120 of them were released to the public in order to seek their assistance. Thus far, over 20 women have been identified. Some people believe they have recognized a missing loved one in the photos. While none of these individuals has been positively identified as a missing person or unsolved homicide victim, there may come a time when they are realized as casualties of the Dating Game Killer.

5 The Persian Princess

While conducting a murder investigation, Pakistani authorities questioned a man named Ali Akbar, who had made a videotape showcasing that he had a mummy on sale for 600 million rupees ($11 million). On October 19, 2000, the mummy was located inside a gilded wooden coffin at the home of a tribal leader named Wali Mohammed Reeki, who claimed he had received the mummy from an Iranian who found it after an earthquake in Quetta, Pakistan. One week later, a press conference was held to announce that the mummy had been identified as a Persian princess from around 600 BC.

However, suspicions were immediately aroused when American archaeologist Oscar White Muscarella claimed he had previously been sent photographs of this mummy on behalf of a Pakistani dealer who was attempting to sell it. A piece of the mummy's coffin had been sent to a carbon-dating lab for analysis and was discovered to be only 250 years old.

Upon further investigation, it was eventually determined that this so-called Persian princess was actually a female in her twenties who had died in 1996. She had possibly been murdered after a blow to the neck with a blunt instrument, and her body had been filled with powder after her organs were removed. The whole thing was exposed as a hoax and the woman finally received a proper burial in 2008, but her true identity is still a mystery.

4 The Batman Rapist

Britain's longest-running rape investigation is code-named "Operation Eagle" and has been going on for 22 years. Authorities have spent that time attempting to catch an unidentified sexual predator who is responsible for at least 17 attacks, all but one of which have taken place within the city of Bath. The assailant first struck on May 21, 1991, when he attacked a 36-year-old woman returning home in her car. His modus operandi consists of attacking women in their vehicles and forcing them to drive to a secluded area at knifepoint, where he then proceeds to rape them. After one unsuccessful attack in 1999, the assailant left behind a hat with the Batman logo on it, which led to him being dubbed the "Batman Rapist."One of the rapist's most bizarre characteristics is an apparent tights fetish. He will often force the victim to remove their underwear and put their tights back on, so that he can rip through them to rape her. On one occasion, the victim wasn't wearing tights, so he forced her to put on a pair he had brought with him. In 2000, he even attempted to abduct a woman who had her seven-year-old daughter in the car, but she managed to get away. During the mid-'90s, there were a few long gaps when the rapist was inactive, leading authorities to suspect that he has attacked other victims who never came forward. There is currently a substantial reward for the capture of the Batman Rapist, but his identity still remains unknown.

3 Joseph Newton Chandler III

On July 30, 2002, Joseph Newton Chandler III, an elderly hermit from Eastlake, Ohio, committed suicide with a self-inflicted gunshot wound to the head. An autopsy discovered the presence of colon cancer in his body, which likely motivated his decision to take his own life. When probate courts attempted to work out the man's estate, they tracked down his surviving relatives. They were shocked to discover that nine-year-old Joseph Newton Chandler III had actually been killed in a car crash in Texas in 1945!

It turned out this unidentified man had been using Chandler's identity for decades. In 1978, he had requested a copy of Chandler's birth certificate and used it to apply for a Social Security card. Many theories were formed about who this man really was. Crime buffs began to speculate that "Chandler" might have been the Zodiac Killer since he bore a resemblance to the suspect's composite sketch. They also noted that "Joseph Chandler" happened to be the name of an investigator who found one of Jack the Ripper's victims. The man also bore a striking resemblance to Stephen Craig Campbell, a fugitive who had been wanted for attempted murder since 1982 and was never caught. However, there is no conclusive evidence to prove any of these theories, so no one knows the real story behind the man who stole the identity of Joseph Newton Chandler III.

2 Roland Doe/Robbie Mannheim

In 1973, William Peter Blatty's best-selling novel *The Exorcist* was adapted into one of the most successful movies of all time. It told the story of a young

girl being possessed by a demon, and believe it or not, it was actually inspired by a real-life incident. In 1949, a 13-year-old boy from Cottage City, Maryland, was supposedly possessed by a demon and subject to an exorcism. To protect his identity, he has only been publicly referred to as "Roland Doe" or "Robbie Mannheim." After the death of his spiritualist aunt, Roland reportedly became obsessed with using a Ouija board to contact her. Soon afterward, the family's home was plagued by strange noises and unexplained supernatural activity.

The family's Lutheran minister feared that Roland might be possessed, so two Catholic priests—Father Raymond J. Bishop and Father William J. Bowdern—were brought in to perform an exorcism on him at Georgetown

University Hospital. The exorcism was performed 30 times over the course of several weeks. Roland reportedly exhibited violent behavior and often spoke Latin in a demonic voice while words like "evil" and "hell" mysteriously appeared on his body. After the exorcism was complete, the family experienced no more problems and Roland grew up to live a normal life. There has been much debate about whether Roland was actually possessed or if a lot of these stories have been fabricated and the boy was merely experiencing psychological problems. Since his true identity is still a secret after all these years, the full truth may never be known.

1 Suzanne Davis/Sharon Marshall/ Tonya Dawn Tadlock

In April 1990, a young woman named Tonya Dawn Tadlock was killed in a mysterious hit-and-run accident in Oklahoma. The prime suspect was her much older husband, Clarence Hughes, but it turned out they were both living under pseudonyms. Hughes was actually a former convicted felon named Franklin Delano Floyd. However, no one could uncover the young woman's identity. Floyd claimed to have taken her in as a child in the early 1970s after she was abandoned by her real family, though authorities have always suspected she was abducted. Before they were married in 1989, Floyd raised the girl as his daughter, subjecting her to constant abuse. Over the years, they lived in different states under different names and she was also known as "Suzanne Davis" and "Sharon Marshall."On March 21, 1988, she had given birth to a son named Michael. Shortly after her death, Floyd was arrested and Michael was placed in foster care. A blood test would later reveal that Floyd was not Michael's biological father. After being released from jail in 1994, Floyd abducted Michael from his school in Oklahoma. When he was arrested two months later, Michael was nowhere to be found, though it is believed that Floyd murdered him. Floyd would be convicted of Michael's kidnapping and another unrelated murder and currently sits on death row in Florida. To this day, he refuses to divulge any information about what happened to Michael, who Michael's real father may be, or the true identity of the mysterious girl he raised as his daughter.

TOP 10 Mysterious Urban Legends Based on Video Footage

by Bryan Johnson

10 The Grifter

The Grifter is an urban legend that began to circulate on the Internet in 2009. The video is said to show horrifying images of people being tortured and killed. Viewers of the movie can experience nausea, trauma, night terrors, clinical depression, and even commit suicide. The content shows the human sacrifice of small babies and images of Satanic ritual abuse. In some cases, people have attempted to make a copy of the film, but all attempts have failed.

It has been said that the video was recorded in the 1930s and portrays a collection of strange pictures and sounds. In one part of the movie, the words "Your race is the one that is dying" appear while a picture of a rotting plant is seen. The footage displays close-up shots of corpses and people who have been possessed by demons. It has been described as the most disturbing video available on the Internet. However, many feel the tape is a hoax and nothing more than an urban legend. The story of the Grifter has spawned an Internet meme in which threads that discuss hoax videos are considered to be trolling for information on bizarre clips.

9 Garden City Ghost Car

A few years back a video surfaced on the Internet of a police chase in Garden City, Georgia, that has been dubbed the Ghost Car. In the video, officers can be seen attempting to pull over a white vehicle that is driving erratically. After a while, the driver swerves and makes a U-turn. The car moves off the highway, hits a dirt road, and comes to a dead end. It then moves to the left and disappears behind a chain-link fence.

The driver was never captured and it was revealed that the area beyond the fence was wooded with no roads. After examining the footage, many people have commented that the car traveled under the fence. However, this doesn't explain what happened to the driver and why the police ended the pursuit. After the area was searched, the officers recovered the video and were shocked. The clip was featured on the television show *Fact or Faked: Paranormal Files*, in which a stunt driver re-created the footage by driving through a chain-link fence that was weakened at the base. The stunt showed that a car is capable of traveling through a fence without knocking it over. However, it wasn't filmed on location. To date, the original Garden City surveillance video continues to baffle watchers.

8 Red Mist

SpongeBob SquarePants is a television show that is extremely popular around the world and has earned more than $8 billion in merchandising revenue for Nickelodeon. The cartoon features a wide variety of characters that live in the underwater city of Bikini Bottom. One of these characters is named Squidward Tentacles. The show is made for kids, but in 2004 an urban legend emerged surrounding a lost episode of the show that is said to display Squidward's suicide.

As the story goes, a disgruntled Scottish animator named Andrew Skinner developed an episode of *SpongeBob SquarePants* in 2004 called "Red Mist." He tried to pass off the episode as the official season 4 premiere and sent it to Hollywood for approval. In California, animators watched the tape and discovered a dark secret. The video starts with the picture of a salesman at Squidward's house. He knocks on the door and says, "The red mist is coming"; Squidward is confused. The tape flashes to a picture of Squidward playing the clarinet in front of a large crowd and SpongeBob can be seen violently booing the performance.

Squidward's body language is depressed. He returns to his house and sits in a chair with a blank look on his face. The audio turns scratchy, Squidward starts to cry and the tape begins to flash. At this point a series of real pictures come to view. The images show the body of a dead boy with his face mangled and entrails exposed. The shadow of the photographer is visible and the tape shows pictures of a deceased girl. The song "Amazing Grace" plays and the video goes into a sequence of frames in which the boy is mutilated. The words "do it" can be heard while Squidward pulls out a shotgun and commits suicide.

The event was so horrifying that three of the animators were hospitalized, including Barry O'Neill, Grant Kirkland, Jr., and Alyssa Simpson. One editor named Fernando de la Peña retired and an intern named Jackie McMullen committed suicide. It was reported that the tape was later tracked to Andrew Skinner, who was arrested for nine counts of murder, including the two children seen in the video.

After viewing the tape, a copy of the footage was made by an intern at Paramount Studios and released on the Internet. However, it was quickly removed by police and only a screenshot of Squidward's red eyes remains. Research on the story doesn't bring many results except for one article from 2002 that briefly mentions a man from Fife, Scotland, named Andrew Skinner who was arrested for attempted murder.

7 Chaplin Time Travel Video

The Circus is a silent film that was written and directed by Charlie Chaplin. The film was a box office success and raised $3.8 million in 1928. In 2004, a copy of the movie was released on DVD with bonus footage. The footage shows pictures of the public attending the film, including a premiere at Grauman's Chinese Theatre in Los Angeles. After looking over the material, an Irish filmmaker named George Clarke noticed something out of the ordinary in a clip of the public entering the premiere.

The footage shows a woman dressed in a heavy coat and hat holding what looks like a black object to her head. As she walks, it appears she is talking on a cell phone, which would be impossible in 1928. Toward the end of the footage, the woman can be seen stopping and chatting in a fashion similar to modern day cell phone users. She is wearing large shoes and has big hands.

After zooming in on the video, it is clear the woman is holding a black object to her head, which caused Clarke to post a video on YouTube questioning whether she might be a time traveler sent back in time to watch Chaplin's performance. In response, the story made headlines all over the world. It has since been discovered that the woman could be using a pocket-sized carbon microphone called the Siemens 1924 hearing aid. Others feel she is holding an ear trumpet. However, the explanation hasn't addressed why she is talking.

6 Groupie

Marilyn Manson (Brian Warner) is a controversial rock star who has sold over 50 million albums worldwide. He gained mainstream attention in the 1990s after media reports surfaced that described his shocking behavior on and off stage. Over the years, Manson has been the target of multiple attacks by the press who view his music as detrimental to children. Manson has produced some of the most disturbing videos on the Internet. In 2011, he collaborated with actor Shia LaBeouf to make a movie called *Born Villain*, which is said to contain shocking and violent images.

However, the most controversial video attributed to Marilyn Manson is called *Groupie*. The legend of the tape says that it was recorded by his band during their Antichrist Superstar Tour (1996–1998) and shows a fan being tortured by Marilyn and bass player Twiggy (Jeordie White). According to the story, the footage was captured on a handheld camcorder and shows Manson ordering the groupie to perform various acts.

The film starts out with Marilyn informing his guests that the girl will be taped. When she arrives, the party takes a weird turn.

After a short while, the girl is ordered to do things like drink a glass of urine with keyboard player Stephen Bier. The tape then turns dark while Manson ties the woman up and taunts her. As the video progresses, the members of the party become uneasy, as they are unclear if the events are staged or not. The video involves torture, weapons, and bloodshed.

Officially, there are only three people who have viewed *Groupie*: Manson, Tony Ciulla, and Andy Dick. However, evidence of the film can be found at the end of the band's "Dead to the World" video series in which an obscured shot of a tied-up woman can be viewed. During the scene, Marilyn is heard taunting the girl with the phrase "Jesus loves me because the Bible says so." The footage might have come from *Groupie*.

5 Texas Chupacabra

The Chupacabra (goat sucker) is a cryptid that has been identified in certain parts of the Americas. The creature is known for killing livestock and drinking their blood. The Chupacabra has a wide range of physical characteristics; some people have identified it as being a lizard-type creature with a long spine, while others say it is a smaller animal that looks like a bald coyote with sharp fangs, or a type of coyote, wolf, and dog hybrid.

Despite discrepancies in the creature's appearance, the Chupacabra is known to kill by stealthily attacking its prey and inflicting a series of three small puncture wounds to the chest and neck of its victim. The puncture wounds resemble an upside-down triangle, and the animal is then killed and drained of blood. The death is usually reported because of the bizarre circumstances. Currently, there are no large animals that practice hematophagy, or the act of drinking blood for food.

A large number of Chupacabra sightings have been made in Mexico and Texas. In most cases, a coyote-type creature has been blamed for killing livestock. One such example was the Elmendorf Beast, a hairless animal that was killed in 2004 and thought to be a wolf-coyote cross. One of the features of the creature was a long snout, which has come to characterize the beast. On August 8, 2008, Brandon Riedel, a police offer in DeWitt County, Texas, filmed a strange animal from his dash camera in the town of Cuero. In the video, the creature can be seen running away from the car and looks like a hairless coyote-type creature with a long snout and big ears. The snout of the creature has baffled many experts.

The footage was featured on the television show *Fact or Faked: Paranormal Files* where experts attempted to re-create the tape with a miniature horse. As you would expect, the horse looked nothing like the creature in the video and the footage has helped grow the legend of the Chupacabra. Many have suggested the animal could be an unknown coyote or a government experiment gone horribly wrong. The legend was potentially developed around the real events of cattle mutilation.

4 Cervine Birth

The legend surrounding the Cervine Birth footage started in 2009 with the posting of a bizarre video. The story says the clip was put on YouTube by an unidentified amateur artist studying in the UK. After a short time online, the movie was removed because of the disturbing content. The video starts with the scene of a foggy meadow and zooms in on a sick-looking albino deer lying on the ground. After the camera focuses on the deer's eye, it pans away to a vanity mirror and shows the animal's reflection flopping in an unnatural manner.

At this point, a dark fluid is excreted from the deer's tail, which indicates it might be giving birth. After several minutes, a stillborn humanoid infant is dropped from the deer's body. The creature is covered with a dark, tarlike substance, so it is difficult to identify. It has been claimed the artist put together a model of a human-animal hybrid to use in the film. The video then moves to a close-up blurry shot of the creature's face, and shows stock footage of an audience applauding in slow motion.

In 2009, a collection of people claimed to have watched the Cervine Birth video. However, the footage has become extremely difficult to locate, which has spawned an urban legend that the video might show an actual humanoid stillborn birth.

3 Munchkin Suicide

One of the most talked-about urban legends comes from the 1939 movie *The Wizard of Oz*. The legend says that an actor can be seen hanging himself in the film. The controversial scene appears at the very end of the Tin Man section of the movie when Dorothy, Toto, the Scarecrow, and the Tin Man start walking toward the Emerald City. In the sequence, an object can be seen for a brief second between two trees in the forest. The camera is not zoomed in, but it looks like a person swinging in the trees. For this reason, the urban legend suggests a munchkin can be seen committing suicide.

In the 1980s, the suicidal munchkin legend became popular when people started to watch the sequence on VHS tapes. As the Internet expanded, some have taken to posting detailed examinations of the footage online, which includes zoomed-in examples of what looks like a hanging human. This has caused people who worked on *The Wizard of Oz* film to claim the object is a large bird. Apparently, the movie borrowed several birds from the Los Angeles Zoo to make the forest appear more realistic. One of these birds, thought to be an emu or large crane, was captured on film during the scene in question.

The explanation hasn't stopped the urban legend from spreading, and people have wondered why other birds are not visible in the movie. Some have suggested the original footage was edited on DVD to make it look more like a bird. The claim says that there are multiple different copies of the scene available online. The DVD version is widespread and shows the bird more clearly, which has been attributed to advancements in high-definition TV.

2 Satan's Sphinx

"Satan's Sphinx" is an urban legend video that is said to cause the viewer to experience suicidal tendencies, homicidal thoughts, hysteria, insanity, and self-abuse. It was uploaded to the Internet in 2006 by government officials who were testing subliminal messaging and human reaction to violent images. Soon after the release of the clip, the experiment spiraled out of control and people complained that the video was making them depressed.

The urban legend says that the "Satan's Sphinx" video contains a high-pitched audio track that will irritate the viewer. Images of blood, death, and murder continually run across the screen. The pictures rotate so fast that it becomes impossible for people to individually identify them. At this point, incoherent whispering is heard and the screen begins to flash. Viewers get dizzy, but don't want to turn the movie off. The footage is said to last 3:49 and will cause the viewer to become depressed and sleepless. After the experiment, the clip was banned by the U.S. government, and all traces were removed from the Internet.

Some versions of the legend say the video is a Satanic ritual with subliminal messaging that was used by the U.S. government to recruit members for mind-control projects. Whatever the case, the underlying theme in the urban legend is that those who watch the video will commit suicide. It has been said that a screenshot from the video is available and shows a scared boy being held captive by two people in weird masks. The legend holds that if you find yourself watching the "Satan's Sphinx" video, you were meant to.

1 The McPherson Tape

The McPherson Tape is a real movie that has spawned a collection of urban legends. Officially, the film is called *UFO Abduction* and was created by Dean Alioto in 1989 for $6,500. The movie is one of the first examples of a "found-footage film" and follows the story of a Connecticut family named the Van Heeses who are abducted by extraterrestrials. The movie was made to look like a genuine home video recording that was taken in 1983 and recovered years later.

The film starts out with a birthday party of a five-year-old child at the Van Heeses' house. After a brief period of time, the group experiences a power outage and a bright flash of red light is seen. The men go outside to explore the area and find a plane crash over the hill. At the crash site, they witness a collection of extraterrestrials. The aliens scare the group and the men run back to the house in disbelief. Along the way, they use profanity and it becomes clear the movie is not scripted, but rather improvised. In many scenes the actors can be heard yelling over each other.

For over an hour, the family attempts to fight off the creatures, but the movie ends abruptly with the aliens entering the house and abducting the Van Heeses. At one point in the film, the men bring the body of one of the aliens into the house, but it soon disappears. Throughout the movie, the actors do a great job showing terror and fear. Some viewers have suggested the appearance of the aliens is quite convincing as they have long and slender limbs. However, others have complained about the unrealistic clothing on the creatures.

It has become extremely hard to find a copy of *UFO Abduction*. Sections of the movie can be seen on the Internet, but the entire footage from start to end is not available. In 1998, a remake of the 1989 movie was created by Dean Alioto and aired on UPN. The footage in the remake is much less convincing and clearly scripted. Since its release, the original footage has been called *The McPherson Tape* because it is said to show the actual abduction of the McPherson family. The 1989 footage has been added to a collection of videos that claim to show human contact with aliens. Another example is the "5 Hour Video," which shows military personnel from the U.S. and China fighting underground aliens. Very little information is available on the "5 Hour Video," which is one reason it has not been featured on this list.

TOP 10 Places as Mysterious as the Bermuda Triangle

by Michael Alba

10 Superstition Mountains

The Superstition Mountains are a mountain range located east of Phoenix, Arizona. According to legend, sometime in the 1800s a man named Jacob Waltz discovered a huge gold mine within the mountains that has since been dubbed the Lost Dutchman's Gold Mine. Waltz kept the location a secret until he was on his deathbed, upon which he may or may not (depending on which version of the story you're reading) have told a single person the secret. Regardless, the mine has never been found, in spite of many

expeditions. Some say the spirits of people who've lost their lives in search of the gold still haunt the mountains.

One reportedly Native American legend goes that the treasures of the mountains are guarded by creatures called Tuar-Tums ("Little People") that live below the mountains in caves and tunnels. Some Apaches believe that the entrance to hell is located in the mountains.

9 South Atlantic Anomaly

Did you ever wonder if there was a Bermuda Triangle in space? No? Well you're probably wondering it now, and you're in luck! Because there totally is, and it's called the South Atlantic Anomaly. The SAA is the area where the band of radiation known as Earth's inner Van Allen belt comes closest to the Earth's surface.

It's an area centered just a bit off the coast of Brazil, and it's responsible for numerous problems with satellites and spacecraft, from messing up their programs to actually shutting down their function. The Hubble Telescope is actually turned off from taking observations when passing through the Anomaly, and the International Space Station avoids scheduling spacewalks when passing through it (which happens up to five times a day). It's doesn't just cause technical problems, either—some astronauts report seeing "shooting stars" in their visual field as they pass through the area.

The cause of all these problems isn't fully understood. The main suspect is the high levels of radiation that accumulate at the Anomaly, but scientists aren't sure exactly how or why the effects occur.

8 Lake Anjikuni

Not content with just a few individuals disappearing, Lake Anjikuni in Canada decided to take things to the next level and provide the locale for the disappearance of an entire village. It all happened in November 1930, when a trapper named Joe Labelle was looking for shelter for the night. Labelle was familiar with the Inuit village, whose population ranges from 30 to 2,000, depending on who you believe. He made his way there and found quite an eerie scene—the villagers were nowhere to be found. Everything else, including food and rifles, had been left behind.

Labelle telegraphed the Royal Canadian Mounted Police (RCMP) and an investigation began. In the village burial ground it was discovered that at least one (sources vary) grave had been opened, clearly not by animals, and emptied. Furthermore, about 300 feet from the village, the bodies of around seven sled dogs were found, having starved to death despite open stores of food at the village. Some versions of the story even report strange lights being seen above the lake around the time of the disappearance.

So what really happened? There have been all sorts of claims about why the villagers disappeared, including aliens, ghosts, and even vampires. The RCMP's own website disregards the story as an urban legend, but with so many versions of it floating around from so many years ago, it's hard to be certain.

7 The Devil's Sea

The Devil's Sea (also called the Dragon's Triangle) is an area of the Pacific Ocean as riddled with strange happenings as its Atlantic counterpart near Bermuda. Located off the coast of Japan, it's been the site of countless claims of unexplained phenomena, including magnetic anomalies, inexplicable lights and objects, and of course, mysterious disappearances. The area is even considered a danger by Japanese fishing authorities.

One story has it that in 1952, the Japanese government sent out a research vessel, the *Kaio Maru No. 5*, to investigate the mysteries of the Devil's Sea. The *Kaio Maru No. 5* and its crew of 31 people were never seen again. Another story tells of Kublai Khan's disastrous attempts to invade Japan by crossing the Devil's Sea, losing at least 40,000 men in the process.

The usual theories abound for what's really going on, from aliens to gates to parallel universes, even to the lost city of Atlantis. Some suggest that high volcanic activity in the region is responsible for some of the disappearances (the *Kaio Maru No. 5* may have been caught in an eruption).

6 Bigelow Ranch

Bigelow Ranch (formerly known as Skinwalker Ranch and Sherman Ranch) is a 480-acre property in northwest Utah that is home to countless UFO sightings, animal mutilations, and other strange occurrences. Though mysterious happenings there have been documented since the 1950s, some of the most bizarre stories happened to a pair of ranchers named Terry and Gwen Sherman after they bought the ranch in 1994.

The first day they moved to the property, they saw a large wolf out in the pasture. They even went to pet the wolf because it seemed tame. It was docile with the Shermans, but ended up grabbing a calf by the snout through the bars of its enclosure. When Terry shot at the wolf with a pistol, the bullets had no effect. It finally left after Terry brought out the shotgun, though even that didn't do any actual damage. The Shermans tried tracking the wolf, but it's tracks stopped abruptly as if it had vanished.

And that wasn't the end of things. The Shermans were constantly plagued by such events as UFO sightings, intelligent floating orbs (reputed to have incinerated three of their dogs), inexplicable cryptids, and gruesome cattle mutilations. It got so bad that the Shermans actually sold their ranch to Robert Bigelow in 1996. Bigelow is the founder of the National Institute for Discovery Science (NIDS), and he wanted to study the mysteries surrounding the ranch. Bigelow owns the ranch to this day and NIDS keeps a tight lid on their findings.

5 Point Pleasant

Point Pleasant was probably aptly named at one point, but it is now so shrouded in tales of mysterious and creepy events as to be nothing but an ironic alliteration. The most famous of these occurrences involves a creature known as Mothman, who reputedly terrorized the small West Virginia community from November 1966 to December 1967. Over 100 different citizens of Point Pleasant are eyewitnesses to this creature, a seven-foot-tall broad-chested man with hypnotic, glowing red eyes and wings that stretch ten feet long and drag behind him on the ground.

The Mothman, who's been the subject of both a book and a movie (and who has his own statue in Point Pleasant), has many possible explanations. Some believe him to be an extraterrestrial, others that he is a mutant or a cryptid, and some suggest the people of Point Pleasant were actually being scared by owls or a Sandhill Crane. Whatever the case, reports of Mothman stopped after the Silver Bridge collapsed on December 15, 1967, killing 46 people and leading many to believe that the two events were somehow connected.

In addition to Mothman, several other paranormal tales from Point Pleasant include UFO sightings and reports of so-called Men in Black—human-looking creatures who unnerve others by the sheer abundance of peculiarities in their speech, appearance, and mannerisms. These "men" supposedly appear looking for information about the paranormal (or rather, people who have this information).

4 Michigan Triangle

The Michigan Triangle is another geographical triangle, located in the middle of Lake Michigan. It, too, is the site of mysterious disappearances of both land and sea craft. Some of the more famous ones include:

Captain Donner: On April 28, 1937, Captain George R. Donner of the *O.M. McFarland* was on his way from Erie, Pennsylvania, to Port Washington, Wisconsin, and had to pass through the triangle. As the story goes, he was exhausted and retired to his cabin, leaving the second mate to wake him when they neared their destination. About three hours later, when the second mate went to do so, Donner was not there. Nor was he in the galley. An exhaustive search of the ship was conducted, but he was never found.

Flight 2501: On June 23, 1950, Northwest Airlines Flight 2501 was on its way from New York to Minneapolis at the hands of experienced pilot Robert C. Lind and was carrying 58 passengers. Due to bad weather, when the flight was near Chicago it changed course and turned over Lake Michigan. Around midnight, Lind requested permission to drop altitude from 3,500 feet–2,500 feet without ever specifying a reason. His request was denied, and that was the last communication Flight 2501 ever had. Its last known position was supposedly within the Michigan Triangle.

While sources vary as to what amount of wreckage from Flight 2501 has been found (some say none, whereas others specify assorted floating debris such as seat cushions), it seems clear that the plane crashed into the water. Mysterious, however, is that the plane was in perfectly good condition and in capable hands at the time of the disappearance. What's more, despite searches still being conducted annually, neither the body of the plane nor complete human remains have ever been recovered.

3 San Luis Valley

San Luis Valley in southern Colorado is an area high in inexplicable phenomena, including UFO sightings and hundreds of unexplained farm animal mutilations. UFO sightings are so common that a woman named Judy Messoline has even set up a UFO watchtower on her property, which has witnessed over 50 UFO sightings since 2000 alone. Some of these are observed by dozens of people at a time.

For the UFO skeptics out there, far more chilling are the tales of animal mutilations from the region. They began in 1967 with a horse named Snippy. Snippy was found one morning with her brain missing and her neck bones completely cleaned. Since then, hundreds if not thousands of inexplicable animal mutilations have occurred in the region, sharing several things in common: There is never a trace of blood around the animals, and the animals are all damaged with precise cuts, distinctly not the work of predators. Finally, all of the mutilations happen overnight to otherwise healthy creatures.

Investigations into the incidents haven't yielded any results, yet they continue to this day. Some farmers report seeing strange lights in the sky on the nights before finding a carcass, leading some to believe that extra-terrestrials are involved. The alternative isn't much more appealing—that humans are the so-called "Phantom Surgeons of the Plains."

2 Bennington Triangle

This mysterious triangle is found in southwestern Vermont and is the site of a string of five mysterious disappearances between 1945 and 1950, related in no way but geographic location. These include:

Middie Rivers, 75 years old, was out leading a group of hunters on November 12, 1945. On their way back, he got ahead of his group and was never seen again. Only a single rifle shell found in a stream was recovered as evidence.

Paula Welden was an 18-year-old sophomore of Bennington College who was out hiking on December 1, 1946. She never returned and no trace of her was ever found.

Exactly three years later, on December 1, 1949, a veteran named James E. Tetford was taking a bus back to his home at the Bennington Soldier's Home, returning from a visit with relatives. Witnesses saw him on the bus at the stop before his, but when the bus arrived at his destination he was nowhere to be seen. His luggage was still on the bus.

Eight-year-old Paul Jepson disappeared on October 12, 1950, while his mother was busy feeding the pigs. Despite the boy having a highly visible red jacket, none of the search parties formed were able to find him.

The last disappearance was a woman named Frieda Langer. On October 28, 1950, she was hiking with her cousin on Glastenbury Mountain when she slipped in a stream. She decided to go back quickly and change her clothes, and, of course, she was never seen again. Well, not exactly—she's the only victim whose body was ever recovered, though it was found on May 12, 1951 (about six months later), in an area that had been thoroughly searched after her disappearance. The body was in such a mangled shape that no cause of death could be determined.

Though many theories abound, including aliens, bigfootlike monsters, or some unknown serial killer.

1 Bridgewater Triangle

The Bridgewater Triangle, an area of about 200 square miles in southeastern Massachusetts, just south of Boston, is like an all-you-can-eat buffet of the supernatural.

Among other things, the area has been subject to numerous cryptozoological sightings. Since the 1970s, there have been several reports of tall, hairy, apelike creatures roaming the swamp. There have also been numerous sightings of Thunderbirds, giant Pterodactyl-like creatures that have been seen fighting in midair. In 1976, there was a report of a man who saw a giant, ghostly, red-eyed dog rip the throats out of two of his ponies.

Besides these cryptids, there have been numerous reports of mutilated animals (mainly cows and calves) in the region. Some credit these mutilations to Satanic cults, but no one has come forward and no one even knows where the animals came from.

As if all this weren't enough, the Bridgewater Triangle is a hotbed of UFO sightings dating all the way back to 1760, when a "sphere of fire" was reportedly seen hovering over New England. Since then there have been numerous sightings of unexplained objects in the sky, including mysterious black helicopters. One from 1976 describes two UFOs landing along Route 44 near the city of Taunton, and another from 1994 recounts a strange triangular object with red and white lights seen by a Bridgewater Law Enforcement Officer. In 1908 on Halloween night, two undertakers who were traveling to Bridgewater noticed in the sky what looked like a "giant lantern." They watched it for almost 40 minutes before it disappeared.

TOP 10 Mysteries That Hint at Forgotten Advanced Civilizations

by **Hestie Barnard Gerber**

10 Ancient Devices

Ancient knowledge was a lot more refined and developed than we have been taught. From batteries to planispheres, an assortment of gadgets has been found and excavated. Two notable finds were the Nimrud lens and the famous Antikythera mechanism. The 3,000-year-old Nimrud lens was discovered at the palace of Nimrud in Iraq. Some experts believe the lens was part of an ancient telescope the Babylonians used, hence their advanced knowledge of astronomy. And the famous Antikythera mechanism (200 BC) was created to calculate the movements of the sun, moon, and planets to predict celestial events. Unfortunately, we can only speculate on the ways many of these devices were created and used, and why the ancient knowledge pertaining to them disappeared for millennia afterward.

9 The Rama Empire

Despite wars and several invasions, India's ancient history was largely preserved. Long believed to date from about 500 BC, discoveries in the past century have pushed back the origins of Indian civilization thousands of years. In the Indus Valley, the cities of Harappa and Mohenjo Daro were discovered. The cities were so sophisticated and well planned that archaeologists believe they were conceived as a whole before construction on them begun. The Harappa culture also remains an enigma. Its origins and deterioration are hidden, its dialect is unknown, and their writing is completely indecipherable. At the site, no differences in social class can be discerned and there are no temples or religious buildings. No other culture, including those of Egypt and Mesopotamia, has revealed the same degree of planning and development.

8 The Longyou Caves

They are considered by the Chinese to be the "Ninth Wonder of the Ancient World" but the origin of the 24 caves thus far uncovered is an unfathomable mystery. Discovered in 1992, no historical record or evidence of the work involved to excavate the almost one million cubic meters of stone exists. The chiseling was done in such a way that it left a consistent pattern throughout the caves, which some experts believe to be symbolic. The patterns are similar to those found on pottery that has been dated between 500 and 800 BC. Stone carvings and pillars can be viewed in the cave that has been opened up for public viewing. There is also a rumor that seven of the caves have a distribution pattern that matches the seven stars of the Big Dipper.

7 Nan Madol

Off the island of Pohnpei in Micronesia lies the ancient city of Nan Madol. Built on a coral reef exclusively from colossal basalt rocks (some weighing up to 50 tons), the city is intercrossed by a multitude of canals and connected via submerged tunnels. Its scale has been compared to the Great Wall of China and the Great Pyramid, even though the Pyramid stones only weigh about three tons each. No records exist as to who built the city, when it was built, or for what reason. Radiocarbon dating has placed its construction in 200 BC. The origin of the basalt rocks that make up the city is unknown, as are the methods used to transport them there and stack them as high as 50 feet and as thick as 17 feet. Human bones uncovered by archaeologists are remarkably larger than the local Micronesians of the area today.

6 The Stone Age Tunnels

From Scotland to Turkey, underneath hundreds of Neolithic settlements, archaeologists have uncovered evidence of an extensive network of underground tunnels. From almost 2,300 feet (700 meters) in Bavaria, Germany, to 1,200 feet (350 meters) in Austria, the tunnels are a man-made marvel.

The fact that they survived for 12,000 years is a testimony to the skill of the builders and of the sheer size the original network must have been. Even though they do not all link up, experts believe people used these tunnels to travel safely regardless of what danger they were facing. Throughout the system there also appear to be storage rooms and seating.

5 Pumapunku and Tiwanaku

Pumapunku is one of four structural arrangements in the ancient pre-Inca city of Tiwanaku in South America. The age of the megalithic ruins is extremely controversial as they have been prodded, excavated, and looted since they were discovered, and as such, experts say they have been contaminated in every way possible. The consensus is that they are older than the pyramids, with claims of up to 15,000 years. Even the Incas didn't know the ruins' history. The massive stones used in the construction bear  no chisel marks and were finely cut to interlock with the others. A lot of the stones were cut so precisely that the builders clearly had an extremely sophisticated knowledge of stone cutting, engineering, and geometry. The city also had a functioning irrigation system, waterproof sewage lines, and hydraulic mechanisms. With no record of its inhabitants or their methods, the technologies and processes used during Pumapunku's construction remain an enigma to experts.

4 Metal Cramps/Clamps

Continuing the mystery of Pumapunku, at this site as well as those of Koricancha, Ollantaytambo, Yuroc Rumi, and in ancient Egypt, metal clamps were used in their largest structures. Evidence of the grooves and holes in which they were used can still be observed. At first archaeologists believed that clamps were brought to these grooves to be placed, but recent scans have revealed that metal was poured into these indentations, which means the builders had portable smelters. It is said that the metals used could only be melted at very high temperatures, temperatures the ancients (to our knowledge) were not capable of. One has to wonder why this technology, as well as the incredible methods used to build these megalithic ruins, became lost in the immediate centuries afterward. A developed technology continues to fan out, but a less advanced civilization will lose the technology in time if they have not acquired the essentials.

3 The Baalbek Enigma

The archaeological site of Baalbek in Lebanon has some of the most well-preserved Roman ruins in the world. Called Heliopolis in ancient times, the temple ruins are truly amazing to behold. What makes this site mysterious though, is the massive megalithic ruin mound upon which the Romans built. Making their ruins pale in comparison, these monoliths that can weigh up to 1,200 tons each are the largest worked slabs of stone in the world. Some archaeologists believe that the history at the site goes back about 9,000 years, as excavations have revealed Middle Bronze Age (1900–1600 BC) and Early Bronze Age (2900–2300 BC) evidence on top of each other. Apart from the mystery as to how these stones were brought to the site from where they were quarried, given the site's location and the space available to maneuver, architects and engineers claim that we have no known lifting technologies available to us today that can lift and position these stones. They are simply beyond the construction capabilities of any accepted ancient or modern-day builders.

2 The Giza Plateau

Volumes have been written on the mysteries of ancient Egypt. We now know that the Great Pyramid's construction was so accurate and beyond

comprehension that it was probably never meant to house a king's remains. Furthermore, as it has been proven that the Sphinx's erosion came mainly from rainfall before the area became a desert, it is at least 7,000–9,000 years old, and some believe it could even be older than that. The sudden rise of the Egyptian civilization in the 3rd millennium BC has lead many experts to believe that theirs was a legacy of an earlier, forgotten civilization. Apart from the Sphinx, further predynastic construction is evident in Khafre's Mortuary and Valley Temples, and Menkaure's Mortuary Temple, as they were built from limestone blocks excavated during the Sphinx's construction and have the same evident erosion.

1 Gobleki Tepe

Dating back to the end of the last Ice Age (12,000 years ago), the recently discovered temple complex in southeastern Turkey has been called the most important archaeological discovery of modern times. Predating pottery, writing, the wheel, and metallurgy, its construction implies a level of sophistication and complexity thus far not associated with Paleolithic civilizations. With a construction date thousands of years earlier than Stone-henge, the site consists of 20 round structures (4 have been excavated so far) and elaborately carved pillars up to 18 feet tall and weighing up to 15 tons each. No one can say with any certainty who created the site or why, but one has to wonder how these supposed hunter-gatherers had advanced knowledge of masonry and stonework if they were the first civilization.

TOP 10 Mysterious Letters

by **Rob Grimminck**

10 Syracuse Anthrax Mystery

This is the least deadly entry on the list. The letters were sent from Syra-cuse in 1997, 1999, 2002, 2010, 2011, and 2012. Each letter contained white powder, which the writer claimed was anthrax. It later proved to be baby powder or laundry detergent. Five letters went to Bishop Ludden High School from 1997–2010; three went to Le Moyne College from 1999–2002; one went to Rep. Ann Marie Buerkle's office; one was sent to Gaylord Bros., a library supplies manufacturer in North Syracuse; and eleven more went to military and police associations, nonprofit groups, government officials, private businesses, and TV celebrities all across the East.

The FBI believes the letters were all written by one deranged man who is over the age of 35. He has probably been in the mental health system at some point. He is probably a loner who has problems functioning in society. He also has a fascination with H.P. Lovecraft, because he includes passages from the writer in his letters. The FBI is currently looking for tips on pos-sible suspects.

9 Amerithrax

After the 9/11 attacks, seven letters were mailed containing actual anthrax spores. Two sets of letters were sent out, the first to ABC, CBS, NBC, AMI, and the *New York Post*. The other set were sent to two Democratic sena-tors—Tom Daschle of South Dakota and Patrick Leahy of Vermont. Alto-gether, 4 people were killed and 17 were infected.

The notes seemed to indicate that the letters were sent by Muslim extremists because of the message "death to America and to Israel." Author-ities believe this was misdirection employed by the letter writer.

The FBI believes Bruce Edwards Ivins, a bio-weapons defense expert, was responsible for the attacks. When the FBI asked the National Academy of Sciences to review their work, they came to the conclusion that—with the information available—they would not be able to prove that Ivins created the anthrax. There have been many people, including senior microbiologists and other senators and congressional representatives who either believe Ivins is not responsible or he did not act alone. Ivins committed suicide in 2008.

8 Murder of Vindalee Smith

On October 20, 2012, 38-year-old mother of four Vindalee Smith was found dead in her Brooklyn home with a gaping wound in her neck. Smith was eight months pregnant and was going to get married the next day. Her fiancé was Anthony Jackman, who was already married. Under her body was a computer-printed note saying, "I will kill one pregnant woman a month starting now until Lee Boyd Malvo is set free!" The note was signed "the Apprentice" along with a smiley face.

Malvo and John Allen Muhammad were the D.C. snipers, who were responsible for the deaths of ten people. Police believe the note was used to throw investigators off. No one has been arrested in connection with the death.

7 Murder of Eva Kay Wenal

On May 1, 2008, shopping center magnate Harold "Hal" Wenal came home to find his wife of 20 years, Eva Kay, dead in a pool of blood. The 60-year-old former model was beaten and had her throat slit. She was apparently attacked as soon as she opened the door to her home. Despite the Wenal's wealth and home full of valuables, nothing was taken from the house.

In July 2008, a cut-and-pasted letter was delivered to the *Atlanta Journal Constitution*. The letter seemed to be an explanation of why Eva Kay was murdered, indicating she may have been having an extramarital affair. Authorities believe the letter is genuine and from the murderer.

6 Cindy James Case

The Cindy James case is an unusual crime that took place in Richmond, British Columbia. Forty-four-year-old nurse Cindy James was being stalked by a supposedly unknown assailant. Starting four months after her divorce, James was the victim of nearly 100 incidents of harassment. This included threatening phone calls and notes left on her front porch. When the police got involved, things escalated. James was found bound and gagged outside of her home. Another time she was stabbed through the hand with a paring knife. According to friends and family, the stalker wanted to scare her to death.

The police, on the other hand, believed that James was writing the notes herself and making up the phone calls. She was even committed to a psychiatric hospital.

On May 25, 1989, six years and seven months after the first threatening phone call, James went missing. Her car was found in a neighborhood parking lot. Her groceries were still in the car, her wallet was under the car, and there was blood on the door. Two weeks later on June 8, 1989, James's body was found in an abandoned house with her hands and feet tied behind her back and a black nylon stocking tied tightly around her neck. The cause of death was a drug overdose of morphine. Despite that James was found tied up, police concluded that she committed suicide. The author of the notes was never discovered.

5 Murder of JonBenét Ramsey

The bizarre case of JonBenét Ramsey started on December 25, 1996, when the six-year-old child beauty pageant queen was believed to have gone missing from her home in Boulder, Colorado. Sadly, her body was found in the wine cellar of the family home eight hours after she was reported missing. She was found under her favorite blanket with a nylon rope tied around her neck, her hands tied above her head, and duct tape on her mouth. There were also indications that she had been sexually assaulted. Her skull was fractured from being struck with a blunt object. A tweed cord combined with a paintbrush made a garrote that was used to strangle her.

JonBenét's mother found a two-and-a-half-page handwritten ransom note asking for $118,000, which was almost the exact amount of JonBenét's father's bonus from work. The letter is longer than a normal ransom note, and it seemed to indicate that it was from a group of foreigners. The letter contains many threats to the Ramseys telling them not to go to the authorities.

Authorities believe the author of the note is the murderer but have yet to find a match for the handwriting or a match for the DNA left on JonBenét's body, though some have speculated that the writing matches that of JonBenét's mother.

4 Circleville Letter Writer

Circleville is a small city in Ohio with a population of over 13,000. Its biggest event is the annual Circleville Pumpkin Show. It is also the home of the Circleville Letter Writer.

Starting in 1976 residents of Circleville began receiving mysterious, vindictive letters. Thousands of letters written in block letters were sent to city officials and even normal citizens. One recipient of the letters was school bus driver Mary Gillespie. She received letters accusing her of having an extramarital affair with a school official. On August 19, 1977, Mary's husband Ron Gillespie received a phone call seeming to indicate the identity of the writer. He left his house with his gun to confront the man. Gillespie was found dead a short distance from his house. His car was driven off the road and his gun had been fired once. He died as a result of the crash and it is unknown why he fired the gun. It is unclear if it was an accident or murder.

Later, while driving her bus, Mary saw signs along her route harassing her. She went to take one down and discovered a booby trap meant to fire a gun at her. The gun belonged to her former brother-in-law, Paul Freshour.

Freshour was convicted of attempted murder and was thought to be the Circleville Letter Writer. However, while he was incarcerated, the letters continued despite the fact that he was in solitary confinement without access to letter writing material and his mail was being monitored. He was denied parole because of the letters and received one himself after his parole was denied.

3 Murder of Ricky McCormick

The murder of Ricky McCormick is the top unsolved crime from the FBI's Cryptanalysis and Racketeering Records Unit (CRRU). McCormick's decomposing body was found in a cornfield in St. Charles County, Missouri, on June 30, 1999. McCormick was an unemployed high school dropout with a criminal record.

His body was found 15 miles from his home in a place with no public transportation. There was no official cause of death, but it was not ruled a homicide at the time because there was no reason for the police to believe he met with foul play.

Twelve years later, the FBI announced that McCormick's death was a homicide and asked for the public's help with two encrypted notes found on McCormick's body. Both the CRRU and American Cryptogram Association have been unable to solve the code. They believe the letter was written three days before his death. They have since set up a Web page dedicated to asking for help from the public.

2 Zodiac Killer

A serial murderer who enjoyed taunting the police and the public, the Zodiac Killer operated in California during the late 1960s and early '70s. He claimed five victims in total but injured two as well.

Like our number one entry, the Zodiac Killer created his own nickname in one of his letters, of which there were 18 in all. He also carved messages into a table at a library and a car door at a crime scene. He generally sent the letters to newspapers after the murders. The Zodiac complicated his letters with his use of cryptography. He wrote four coded messages, and to this day, only one has been partially solved. It was solved by amateur code crackers Donald and Bettye Harden, who read it in the newspaper.

The three other ciphers include the "340 Character Cipher," sent November 8, 1969, the letter sent April 20, 1970, and the June 26, 1970, cipher (the last two were sent to the *San Francisco Chronicle*).

Throughout the years, people have been trying to solve the other ciphers. Some have even claimed to have solved them but there is no confirmation that the codes were broken, and the crimes remain unsolved.

1 Jack the Ripper

The unknown infamous serial killer was active in and around the Whitechapel area of England in 1888. Altogether the Ripper claimed five victims—all prostitutes. There are three different letters that are thought to be written by the Ripper himself: the "Dear Boss" letter, the "Saucy Jacky" postcard, and the "From Hell" letter.

The "Dear Boss" letter was where the name Jack the Ripper came from; it was how the author of the letter signed off. In the letter, he taunted the police and explained the pleasure he got from the murders. He talked about how he would kill more women and how he planned to cut off his next victim's ear lobe. He even mocked the idea that the police thought he was a doctor. The letter was given credence when three days later two victims were found, one of them missing an ear lobe.

The second correspondence was the "Saucy Jacky" postcard, which referenced the "Dear Boss" letter before it was made public, as well as the double murder from the previous night. The postcard also appeared to be smeared in blood. These two letters were both sent to the Central News Agency.

The third letter was sent to George Lusk, who was the president of the Whitechapel Vigilance Committee, and it was written on a three-inch-square cardboard box. Along with the letter was a piece of kidney soaking in wine. One of the victims was missing their kidney, but it could not be determined whether the piece of kidney was actually from the victim. While the handwriting was similar to the first two letters, it was filled with blatant spelling mistakes unlike the first two. There have been many suspects in the case, but it remains one of history's great unsolved murder mysteries.

TOP 10 Strange Unsolved Mysteries

by **Nene Adams**

10 Hornsey Coal Poltergeist

On January 1, 1921, Mr. Frost bought a load of coal, which was delivered to his house at 8 Ferrestone Road, Hornsey, London. From the beginning, it was clear to Frost, his wife, and their three young children (or grandchildren; the family's relationships aren't consistent in newspaper accounts) that this was no ordinary coal. When burned in the fireplace grate, the coal exploded or, even more unsettling, jumped out of the grate, took a stroll across the floor, and vanished, only to reappear as showers of sparks in another room. Frost sought help from a police inspector, who experienced some of the frightening incidents firsthand.

The terrifying activity escalated in other homes in the Hornsey area. Objects like coal scuttles moved without being touched. A knife and a loaf of bread flew across the room. Knick-knacks fell off shelves. Events like these were witnessed by Rev. A. L. Gardiner, Vicar of St. Gabriel's, and Dr. Herbert Lemerle. Speculation abounded. The coal came from British mines, and it was supposed by some that disaffected miners had mixed dynamite with coal to cause explosions (the theory was later disproved). Others believed the poltergeist activity was caused by the spirits of angry mine workers, while skeptics blamed the Frost boys.

Frost's five-year old daughter, Muriel, died on April 1, purportedly frightened to death by the poltergeist activity in her family home. Her brother, Gordon, was hospitalized following a nervous breakdown after his sister's death.

9 Rain of Seeds

In February 1979, Roland Moody of Southampton, England, was startled to hear small, solid objects hitting the glass roof of the conservatory attached to his house. The objects turned out to be hundreds of seeds—small mustard seeds and cress seeds coated in a jellylike substance. More seeds continued to fall during the day, eventually covering his garden. One of his neighbors, Mrs. Stockley, told Moody she'd had a similar experience the previous year.

The following day, Moody's home was struck by corn, pea, and bean seeds that seemed to simply fall out of the sky. His neighbors on both sides were also pelted with peas and beans. Only those three houses in the neighborhood were targeted by the bizarre showers of seeds, and a police investigation was unable to pinpoint a source.

The phenomenon gradually decreased and went away. By that time, Moody and his neighbors had endured 25 separate barrages and collected ten pounds of beans from their gardens. Moody himself gathered eight buckets of cress seeds. He claimed the produce grown from the seeds was good quality. Both Moody and Stockley were interviewed for Arthur C. Clarke's *Mysterious World* television series in 1980. To date, no adequate explanation for the weird showers has been found.

8 Strange Death of Netta Fornario

Norah Emily Editha "Netta" Fornario, a writer, friend of Dion Fortune, and initiate of a branch of the Hermetic Order of the Golden Dawn called the Alpha et Omega Temple, believed herself to be a magical healer. In August or September 1929, Netta left London and traveled to Iona, an island off Scotland's west coast, where she met her death under mysterious circumstances. Explanations for her strange demise range from psychic murder, hostile spirits, or exposure to the elements and heart failure (listed as the official cause of death).

Arriving on Iona, Netta lodged in Traymore with a woman named Mrs. MacRae. By day, she explored the island. By night, she entered into trances and attempted to contact the island's spirits. She continued this routine for several weeks until Sunday, November 17, when her behavior inexplicably changed. She packed her bags, intending to return to London. She told Mrs. MacRae that she'd been telepathically disturbed and received messages from other worlds. The landlady noticed Netta's silver jewelry appeared to have turned black overnight. Later, Netta stated she'd changed her mind and would be remaining on Iona.

At some point the next day, Netta went missing. Her body was found on Tuesday on a "fairy mound" near Loch Staonaig. She was naked beneath a black cloak, and lay on a cross carved from the turf with a nearby knife. Her skin was marred by scratches. The soles of her feet were cut and had bled as if she'd run over rough ground. Was she killed by a psychic murderer? Lost her way and succumbed to hypothermia? Or died accidentally during a ritual? What caused her injuries? In the decades since the tragedy, the debate continues.

7 Odon Fire Poltergeist

At his farm near Odon, Indiana, one morning in April 1941, William Hackler finished having breakfast with his family and left the house. On his way to the barn, he smelled smoke. When he hurriedly returned to the house, he discovered a fire in the upstairs bedroom wall (note the house had no electricity). The local volunteer fire department was called in and the blaze was quickly extinguished. However, that was only the start of the Hackler family's day-long ordeal.

After the truck left, another fire broke out, this time in a mattress in an upstairs guest room. It seemed as though the fire had been set from inside the mattress! Throughout the day, more fires broke out all over the house, some under the gazes of astonished witnesses. By 2 p.m., more firefighters were called in, and by the end of the day, 28 seemingly spontaneous fires were extinguished, including one that started between the covers of a book.

The fires ended as mysteriously as they began. Hackler tore down the house and built a new one from the reclaimed lumber. Neither he nor his family experienced anything like the Odon fire poltergeist again.

6 The Third Eye Man

In November 1949, students from the University of South Carolina in Columbia were walking near the Longstreet Theater late one evening when they were stopped in their tracks by the appearance of a gray-faced man wearing a silver suit who removed a manhole cover and disappeared into the sewer. At the time, the strange man was dubbed "Sewer Man," but he would soon be given a much different name following another, more terrifying encounter in April 1950.

This time, a policeman discovered a man in silver near the remains of mutilated chickens. He shone his flashlight on the figure. To his horror, the strange man had a third eye in the center of his forehead. The policeman went to his squad car and radioed for help. By the time other officers arrived, the man was gone. Another encounter by students in the 60s in the steam tunnels under the university kept the memory of Third Eye Man alive.

Although the tunnels were thoroughly searched, no physical evidence of Third Eye Man's existence has ever been found. Is he a ghost? A creature? An alien? A prank? No one knows, but sightings continued into the early 1990s.

5 Connecticut Jabber

Beginning in February 1925, women in Bridgeport, Connecticut, were terrorized for months by a "phantom stabber" who used a sharp, pointed weapon to jab their buttocks or breasts before fleeing the scene. Witnesses gave a confusing variety of descriptions of the Connecticut Jabber, as he became known. One thing the statements had in common was whoever he was, the Jabber seemed unusually fast on his feet, disappearing while the victim screamed in shock and pain.

He had no particular victim profile and preferred no particular location or time of day. Every few months, another woman was attacked in the street or in a public place like a department store, a church, or a library entrance. Despite continuous police investigation that eventually garnered several suspects, the Jabber was never identified.

By June 1928, the Jabber's victims numbered 26. The attacks abruptly stopped and were never repeated in that city. While various explanations have been put forth over the years—mass hysteria whipped by media frenzy, a sadist indulging his whims, a ghost with a grudge against curvaceous women—no perpetrator was ever caught.

4 Angelique Cottin, the Electric Girl

In January 1846, a 14-year-old peasant girl from La Perrière in the Normandy region of France began distressing her friends with her strange powers. Angelique Cottin became known as the "Electric Girl" for the poltergeistlike effect she had on objects, such as making a weaving frame dance around the room or a heavy table float through the air. Chairs moved away when she tried to sit on them. Beds wouldn't stay still, either, and people received electric shocks when they came near her. Paper and pens flew off tables when she held out her left hand.

Angelique also suffered convulsions and injuries due to the frequently violent movements made by her body. Her parents believed she was possessed and took her to church, but a priest convinced them the girl's powers had a physical cause, not a spiritual one. The next step was examination by scientists in Paris, including famous physicist François Arago, who said the phenomena were genuine and the result of electromagnetism.

Against the scientists' advice, the Cottins decided to exhibit Angelique to paying customers. In April 1846—just a few short months after the ordeal began—the unexplained phenomena inexplicably stopped and she lost her electric powers for good.

3 Bladenboro Fire Poltergeist

In Bladenboro, North Carolina, in January 1932, Mrs. Charles Williamson—an ordinary housewife—was terrified when her cotton dress suddenly and inexplicably burst into flames. She hadn't been standing near a fireplace, stove, or other ignition source, and she hadn't been smoking or using flammable chemicals. Fortunately, her husband and teenage daughter acted quickly, ripping the flaming dress off her before she suffered any injuries. Curiously, neither Mr. Williamson nor the daughter, who'd put out the fire with their bare hands, were injured either.

The ordeal by fire continued the same day inside a closet when a pair of Mrs. Williamson's trousers burned until only ashes remained. The next day, in front of witnesses, a bed spontaneously began to burn, as did curtains in another room. For three more days, fires sprang out of nowhere, burning blue flames that couldn't be extinguished until they'd entirely consumed the household object in question. No one was injured by the flames, in any instances. The Williamsons had enough by the fourth day and left the house.

Police, electricians, and arson investigators searched the house but were unable to find a logical explanation for the fires. On the fifth day, the fires simply stopped. The Williamsons moved back home and weren't troubled by the apparent fire poltergeist again.

2 Margaret Foos, Blind Reader

Although there was nothing wrong with her vision, at age 15, Margaret Foos was skilled at "blind reading"—reading books through touch alone while tightly blindfolded. With her father's encouragement, she practiced and nurtured her talent. William Foos believed he'd discovered a way of teaching blind people to "see" through their skin in a form of extrasensory perception. As his first pupil, Margaret was to demonstrate this method.

In January 1960, Foos took his daughter to the Veterans Administration Center in Washington, D.C., to be subjected to scientific tests by psychiatrists. While wearing a "foolproof" blindfold supplied by the VA doctors, Margaret used her hands to read sections of the Bible, identify objects and colors, trace lines, and play checkers, among other tests. Her father was in the room, but he left occasionally, and did not appear to be giving her signals.

In the end, the VA psychiatrists admitted bafflement, but insisted that although Margaret had passed their tests, they couldn't explain how she'd done it, and therefore couldn't admit she could see without using her eyes. Was she fooling everyone, or did she have a genuine extrasensory power? Who knows, but the FBI thought enough of the idea of blind reading to investigate William Foos and his claims.

1 Ghost Sniper of New Jersey

An unidentified "ghost sniper" haunted the Garden State beginning in November 1927 in Camden, New Jersey. The car of Albert Woodruff and several other vehicles had their windshields shattered by bullets that weren't found on the scenes. A city bus on the Camden Bridge had its windshield broken too. Another bus on the Federal Street Bridge came under fire. More homes suffered attacks, and a store window was broken. In all cases, no one was injured except by flying glass, and the bullets vanished into thin air.

The mysterious sniper visited Collingswood and Lindenwood, New Jersey, and also briefly traveled to Philadelphia, Pennsylvania. His targets were mainly private automobiles, taxis, trolleys, buses, and residences, although he did fire on at least one policeman. Only a single witness testified to hearing the report of a shot. Another believed he'd heard a man's sinister laughter, but the other victims said they'd heard and seen nothing.

The attacks suddenly stopped in 1928. Despite police investigations and a few copycats whose missiles (like a blue marble and a screw) were discovered at the scenes, the ghost sniper and his phantom bullets were never found.

TOP 10 Mysterious Mass Animal Deaths

by **Simon Griffin**

10 Snapper Fish

In January 2011, hundreds of dead snapper fish washed up on the beaches of the Coromandel Peninsula in New Zealand. Fishermen that were out at sea described the water as carpeted with dead fish. What makes this example especially strange is that all of the fish were missing their eyes. While the Department of Conservation said the fish had starved, one witness said, "That's just completely untrue. This was something deliberate." While most people wouldn't be so quick to jump to the conclusion of fish genocide, the truth remains to be seen.

9 Jumbo Squid

In January 2005, thousands of jumbo squid beached themselves on California's shores. Very little is known about these squid, as they live at depths of up to 2,300 feet (700 meters), making it much harder for scientists to ascertain why they would suddenly engage in a mass suicide. Toxic poisoning is one theory, although if the water had been contaminated, more than squid alone should have been affected, and if it was something they ate, it is unlikely that so many would have been involved. A similar event occurred in San Diego in 2002, with toxins being the leading (but unconfirmed) suspect in that case too.

8 Whales

Hundreds of pilot whales died in Tasmanian waters in 2009. Over 400 died at sea with no explanation, and almost 200 beached themselves on King Island, along with a number of dolphins. Rescuers hurried to the animals' aid, but around 140 of the whales were dead by the time they arrived. The rest of the whales were saved, as were seven of the dolphins. A few months prior to this incident, 150 pilot whales died after beaching themselves on the west coast of Tasmania, and later, 48 sperm whales were found beached near Perkins Island. Disturbance in echolocation is the prevailing theory for why this occurs, but nothing has been confirmed.

7 Sheep

In 2005, a number of Turkish shepherds presumably lost their jobs when the 1,500 sheep they were looking after jumped off a cliff. It all started

when one sheep went over the edge, and as the old saying goes, was followed by the rest of them. The first 400 died as a result of the 50-foot fall, and the other 1,100 survived as they were lovingly cushioned by the bodies of their friends. This incident had an enormous impact on the local village, as many families depended on the sheep for their livelihood.

6 Cows

Sheep all running off a cliff together is one thing; they were all doing it at the same time. The cows and bulls in Lauterbrunnen, Switzerland, are a different story. Over the course of three days, 28 cows and bulls died after plunging off a much higher cliff than the Turkish sheep. The animals all fell off the same spot, which would be normal had they all gone together. But the fact that the incident was spread out over three days makes the whole thing more mysterious.

5 Shrimp

In March 2013, residents of the town of Coronel, Chile, woke up to find that their local beach was now red. The cause: millions of dead shrimp. Local fisherman have placed the blame on two coal-fired power stations located there, which they say has caused the temperature of the water to increase too much for the shrimp to bear. As this example is so recent, it will be a while before any definite explanation is given, if ever.

4 More Fish (and Seagulls)

In 2012, the aptly named Lake Erie in Ontario saw tens of thousands of dead fish, as well as seagulls, wash up on its shores. First reports said there was no indication of any pollution in the lake. One of the prevailing theories as to what caused so many fish to die is what is known as inversion, a natural phenomenon in which colder, less-oxygenated water rises to the surface and suffocates the fish. But researchers found no evidence of this, nor does this theory account for the dead seagulls.

3 Toads

In 2005, thousands of toads in Northern Germany and Denmark were mysteriously exploding. One minute, they could just be sitting there, and the next, they would explode with enough pressure to launch their insides over three feet away. Proposed explanations include an unknown virus or fungus that causes their bodies to bloat. Another theory is that the toads are having their livers picked out by crows and then puffing themselves up, which results in the explosion. Worse than the actual exploding is that the toads don't immediately die, and can be seen struggling for several minutes.

2 Dogs

The Overtoun Bridge in Milton, Scotland, has infamously become known as the "dog suicide bridge," and with good reason. As early as the 1950s, dogs have been leaping to their deaths off this 50-foot bridge. At least 50 dogs have done so since the first recorded incident, including 5 dogs within six months in 2005. In Celtic mythology, the bridge is said to be the place where heaven meets Earth, known as the Thin. Some people believe this supernatural presence to be the cause. Others believe the dogs smell the mink that are prevalent in the area and that they are jumping off in search of them.

1 Birds

Birds have been dropping dead worldwide in recent years, and this is a lot worse than finding your pet canary at the bottom of its cage. In Kentucky, hundreds of starlings and robins were found on one woman's property. In Chile, thousands of flamingos, 1,200 penguins, and 60 pelicans died over the course of two months. Mass bird deaths are happening with alarming frequency in recent years, but one place in particular stands out more than any other: Jatinga, India. Every year in this small village, birds will fly themselves into the ground. There are many mysteries surrounding this case: Why do they do this at all? Why does it affect different types of birds? Why do the birds only do this along a small stretch of the road? Why does it only happen in September? And why do the birds do this after sunset, when they are usually only active in daylight? Many people visit this spot every year to see the phenomenon occur for themselves.

TOP 10 Mysterious Prehistoric Sites from Around the World

by **Mark Thompson**

10 Carnac Stones

The Carnac stones are a dense collection of more than 3,000 standing stones around the French village of Carnac—the largest such collection in the world. The stones were erected between 4500 and 3300 BC.

There is a variety of theories as to the purpose of the stones. Some claim that the stones are aligned astronomically with the intention of creating an observatory or a calendar system. Others believe that they were actually used as primitive seismic instruments with the balanced stones acting as earthquake detectors. The Carnac site is also thought to support the controversial idea of the "megalithic yard," a theoretical common unit of measurement that was used to build most megalithic sites.

9 The Unfinished Obelisk of Aswan

In the ancient quarries near Aswan, Egypt, lies a gigantic piece of stone that was intended to be erected as an obelisk. The obelisk was never finished, likely due to cracks that formed in the stone during the quarrying (although some believe the builders may have been violently interrupted during their work).

The sheer size of this object is what makes it remarkable. It would have been a full one-third larger than any other ancient obelisk known to us. Standing 137 feet tall and weighing 1,200 tons, this single piece of rock would have been taller than a ten-story building. There are very few modern cranes that could move such a massive object—so how exactly did the ancient Egyptians plan on transporting and erecting it?

8 Antequera

The three most important *dolmens* (or passage mounds) in Spain—Cueva de Menga, Cueva de Viera, and the Tholos of El Romeral—are some of the largest in the world. The largest stones used in their construction weigh 180 tons and were transported from at least a mile away. The sites, which are located near the town of Antequera, are believed to have been established around 3700 BC, making them contemporaries of many famous megalithic sites such as Stonehenge.

Many of the walls feature anthropomorphic illustrations. Menga is aligned with the summer solstice, and El Romeral shares several traits and characteristics with the tholos *dolmens* discovered on Crete, which suggests contact with the Minoan civilization.

7 Ggantija

Ggantija is a complex of two megalithic temples on the Maltese island of Gozo. The stone temples were constructed around 3600 BC, making them the second-oldest religious structures ever found, just behind Gobekli Tepe in Turkey. For a little context, it's worth remembering that this was a time when metal tools were not available to the natives of the Maltese islands, and the wheel had not yet been invented.

It is believed that Ggantija may have been the site of a fertility cult, as figurines and statuettes associated with fertility have been discovered there. Small spherical stones have also been discovered, which archaeologists believe may have been used as ball bearings in the transport of the massive stone blocks that make up the temples. All that being said, we still don't know how or why the temples were built.

6 Stone Spheres

Ranging in size from a few centimeters to more than two meters in diameter, and weighing 15 tons, a collection of over 200 stone spheres has been found in Costa Rica. The spheres are believed to have been carved between 1500 and 500 BC by a civilization long since disappeared, although exact dating is impossible.

There are numerous myths and legends relating to the spheres, with some claiming that they are relics of Atlantis, and others claiming that the builders possessed a potion that softened rock. Although the stones have been weathered, damaged, and eroded over the centuries, some believe they were originally carved into perfect spheres. We still don't know what purpose was served by these stones.

5 The Olmec Heads

The Olmec heads are a collection of 17 colossal heads carved from stone, located in Mexico. The heads date from 1500–1000 BC and weigh between 6 and 50 tons. Each head is carved with a unique headdress, leading some to believe that they were meant to be representations of powerful Olmec rulers. Others claim that the face structure featured on the heads resembles that of an African male, suggesting that this might be evidence of an advanced African civilization visiting the Americas in prehistoric times.

4 Yonaguni Monument

In 1987, a group of strange formations was found underwater off the coast of Yonaguni Island, Japan. These formations feature flat parallel edges, right angles, sharp edges, pillars, and columns—leading many to believe that the site could be man-made.

The last time this area would have been dry land was 8,000–10,000 years ago, during the most recent Ice Age. This means that if Yonaguni really was constructed by humans, it would be one of the oldest structures on Earth, and would drastically change what we think we know of prehistory.

3 Gulf of Cambay

In 2001, evidence of a sunken city was found off the coast of India, in the Gulf of Cambay. Several man-made structures have been identified using sonar, including large buildings and canals. Artifacts such as pottery shards and hearth materials have been dredged up from the bottom.

The scale of the city is quite large, especially considering the fact that one piece of wood has been dated from as early as 9500 BC. If it really existed back then, the city would be thousands of years older than the previous oldest city found in India and would have existed thousands of years before humans were thought to be building cities of this size.

There are some people who scoff at the suggested date, saying that the carbon-dated wood proves nothing—but all the same, there is enough evidence to make this site one of the most intriguing in the world.

2 Moai

On Easter Island—one of the most remote inhabited islands on Earth—lies one of the world's most famous mysteries. The giant stone statues (Moai) of Easter Island are a favorite of tourists, but little is actually known about them. Although it was thought at first that the statues were merely heads, excavation has shown almost all of them to have bodies. Very few of the statues were ever actually erected; most were left in quarries, or abandoned during transport.

Archaeologists don't know why the statues were built, what they signified, how they were transported and erected, or why they were abandoned unfinished. There is a form of hieroglyphic writing on some of the statues, which no one has been able to translate. The people of Easter Island themselves are something of a mystery; it remains unclear where they originally came from.

One of the wildest theories about Easter Island is that the island is actually the peak of an underwater mountain—and all that remains of the lost civilization of Mu.

1 Gobekli Tepe

Gobekli Tepe in Turkey is generally considered to be the oldest religious structure ever found. Radiocarbon dating puts the site at between 10,000 and 9000 BC. To put this age in perspective, more time passed between the building of Gobekli Tepe and the building of Stonehenge than between the building of Stonehenge and present day.

The site contains stone structures and stone pillars that feature carvings of various predatory animals. The stone pillars—some of them reaching nearly 20 tons in weight—date to a time when humans were thought to be simple hunter-gatherers. Gobekli Tepe seems to have been built before the advent of agriculture, religion, written language, the wheel, pottery, the domestication of animals, and the use of anything other than simple stone tools.

How were these structures built at a time when humans were basically thought to have been cavemen? How did they quarry huge pieces of stone and cut them to size with no metal tools? What was the purpose of such a site, before religion was thought to have been established? The discovery and ongoing excavation of Gobekli Tepe could eventually change our conception of prehistory forever.

TOP 10 Entertainment Careers Cut Short by Unsolved Mysteries

by Robin Warder

10 Bobby Fuller

In 1966, 23-year-old Bobby Fuller and his band, the Bobby Fuller Four, were taking the music world by storm as their hit single, "I Fought the

Law," reached number nine on the national charts. However, it all came to an abrupt end when Fuller was found dead on July 18 inside his car, which was parked outside his Los Angeles apartment. The initial ruling was suicide, but no one could understand why a singer on the verge of stardom would take his own life.

Fuller had been doused with gasoline, and a gas can was found on the car's floorboard. However, a witness claimed he saw a detective throw the gas can in a dumpster instead of saving it for evidence. Authorities believed that Fuller had died from inhaling the gasoline fumes, but there were also bruises found on him and blood was on the car seat. His body was also in full rigor mortis, indicating that he had been dead for several hours. Yet his car had only been parked in front of his apartment for a short time before he was found, and one theory is that the perpetrator was in the midst of torching the evidence when they were forced to flee. There have been numerous conspiracy theories about what happened to Bobby Fuller—ranging from an accidental overdose to being murdered by the likes of the mob, his record company, and even Charles Manson—but his death remains clouded in suspicion.

9 Christa Helm

At the age of 17, Christa Helm left her Milwaukee home to pursue a career in modeling and acting in New York City. After garnering a lead role in a low-budget movie called *Let's Go for Broke*, Helm traveled to Hollywood to further her career and she managed to earn a few bit parts on television. She became a prominent figure in the gossip columns because of her rumored escapades with noted Hollywood celebrities. On February 12, 1977, the 27-year-old Helm was stabbed 22 times before being bludgeoned to death outside her agent's home in West Hollywood.

Helm was rumored to have kept a secret diary and recordings of her sexual escapades with her celebrity boyfriends. Since the diary and the recordings mysteriously vanished after her death, some people speculated that they may have been the reason for her murder. It was also theorized that Helm was killed by Lionel Ray Williams, who had murdered Sal Mineo in a similar fashion in the same neighborhood exactly one year before Helm's murder. However, there has always been a debate about whether Williams was in jail on the night Helm was killed. Thirty years later, a DNA sample found under one of Helm's preserved fingernails was determined to be from a female, and Helm was rumored to have been sexually involved with a female singer shortly before her death. In spite of all these leads, the identity of Christa Helm's murderer is still unknown.

8 David Bacon

In 1943, David Bacon was an aspiring 29-year-old actor who had just played his most prominent role after being cast as the title character in the film serial *The Masked Marvel*. However, Bacon's life came to an end on September 13 when he erratically drove his car off the road in Santa Monica, California. He stumbled out of the car wearing nothing but a swimsuit. After he collapsed and died, a small knife wound was discovered in his back.

The most crucial clue left behind was a camera inside Bacon's car. The film in the camera was developed to reveal one picture of Bacon nude and smiling on the beach, and it's been theorized that the photo was taken by his killer. Prior to his death, Bacon had told his wife—an Austrian cabaret singer named Greta Keller—that he was going for a swim. Shortly before the murder, Bacon was spotted driving around with another man in his car, and it was later discovered that Bacon had recently rented a house for a male friend whose identity was never established. Keller has always alleged that her husband was a closet homosexual and had an affair with Howard Hughes, the man who originally discovered him. However, none of these claims have ever been substantiated, and David Bacon's murder remains an unsolved mystery.

7 Tammy Lynn Leppert

Tammy Lynn Leppert was a model from Rockledge, Florida, who spent her childhood competing in over 300 beauty pageants, winning a large percentage of them. She was hoping to transition into an acting career and wound up securing bit parts in a couple of movies, including the 1983 gangster classic *Scarface*. However, one weekend in July 1982, Leppert attended a party where something seemed to happen that prompted her to start displaying patterns of erratic, paranoid, and violent behavior. During the shoot for *Scarface*, Leppert suffered a complete emotional breakdown in the midst of filming of a violent scene and became extremely frightened over the sight of fake blood.

After a violent outburst in June 1983, Leppert had a brief stay in a mental health center. On July 6, she left her family's home with a friend who dropped her off at Cocoa Beach after an argument. The 18-year-old Leppert has never been seen again. Police initially suspected that she ran away, but there have been numerous theories about her disappearance. One involves her being the victim of Christopher Wilder, a notorious Florida serial killer who was targeting young models around this time, and there's also been speculation that Leppert was murdered because of her knowledge of a drug and money-laundering operation. However, none of these theories has ever panned out, and Tammy Lynn Leppert remains missing 30 years later.

6 Barbara Colby

Barbara Colby was a 36-year-old actress who enjoyed reasonable success on Broadway and in Hollywood. After spending much of the 1970s working in television, her career received a major boost when she was offered a full-time role on the sitcom *Phyllis*. Colby had filmed three episodes of the series and was teaching an acting class in Venice, California, on the evening of July 24, 1975. While she and an acting colleague named James Kiernan walked to her parked car, they were both gunned down by two male assailants.

Colby was killed instantly, but Kiernan was able to describe the shooters before he passed away. There had been no attempt at robbery, and Kiernan claimed he did not recognize the two men, so no one could figure out the motive for these murders. Approximately 40 minutes before the shooting occurred, three armed men had murdered another woman named Gloria Witte in a robbery attempt in Santa Monica. At the same time, yet another robbery took place in the same vicinity when two other couples were ambushed by six armed men while returning to their homes. The perpetrators were all caught and charged for these crimes, but police could find no evidence that they might also be responsible for the Colby and Kiernan murders. It continues to be a baffling unsolved mystery nearly 40 years later.

5 Ylenia Carrisi

Ylenia Carrisi was the daughter of the popular Italian pop music duo Al Bano and Romina Power, and granddaughter of legendary Hollywood actor Tyrone Power. It seemed like Carrisi was destined to follow in their footsteps and have her own entertainment career, and she became a minor celebrity in Italy after earning a gig as the letter-turner on that country's version of *Wheel of Fortune*. After turning 23, she decided she wanted to do some traveling on her own, but after taking a trip to New Orleans, she mysteriously disappeared on January 6, 1994.

Most of Carrisi's belongings were left behind in the cheap hotel she was staying at. It was discovered she had been sharing a room with a 54-year-old street musician named Alexander Masakela, who had a history of drug use and sexual violence. He was evicted when he attempted to use Carrisi's passport and traveler's checks to pay for the room after her disappearance. Masakela was also arrested weeks later after an ex-girlfriend accused him of rape, but he was released for lack of evidence. A security guard also reported seeing a woman matching Carrisi's description jumping off a bridge the night she vanished, but no body was ever found to verify his story. There have been unconfirmed sightings of Carrisi in the years since her disappearance, but no conclusive evidence about what ultimately happened to her.

4 Peter Ivers

For years, Peter Ivers had a cult following as an alternative musician. He recorded numerous albums during the 1970s and was asked to write a memorable song called "In Heaven" for David Lynch's infamous cult classic *Eraserhead*. He was probably best known for being the host of a late-night television variety show called *New Wave Theatre*, which featured a unique lineup of punk and New Wave musical performers. However, the show came to an end after the 36-year-old Ivers was found dead inside his Los Angeles apartment on March 3, 1983. He had been bludgeoned to death in his bed with a hammer and there were no signs of struggle.

Ivers was very well liked and had numerous celebrity friends in Hollywood, many of whom showed up at his apartment once word spread about his death. Unfortunately, since police were completely overwhelmed by the large gathering of people, they neglected to seal off the crime scene. Since Ivers's friends were able to walk through his apartment, potential evidence might have been destroyed. The main theory behind Ivers's murder is that he was killed by an intruder during a robbery attempt, as the lock appeared to have been jimmied and some pieces of video equipment were missing. However, even after 30 years, authorities have never been able to find a solid suspect for the crime, so Peter Ivers's senseless murder is still unsolved.

3 Joe Pichler

Joe Pichler was a child actor who had prominent roles in such films as *The Fan*, *Varsity Blues,* and two direct-to-video *Beethoven* sequels. In 2003, he put his acting career on hold to return to his hometown of Bremerton, Washington, and finish high school. The 18-year-old Pichler had plans to go back to Los Angeles and resume his career when he mysteriously vanished during the early morning hours of January 5, 2006. After leaving a get-together and talking to one of his friends on his cell phone, no one heard from him again.

When his family went looking for him, the door to his apartment was discovered to be unlocked and the lights and television were left on. Four days later, Pichler's abandoned car was found with all his possessions inside, except for his wallet and car keys. There was speculation that

Pichler was suicidal, as he left behind some poetry that indicated he might be depressed, along with a note where he expressed his wish to be a "stronger brother" and to give his possessions to his younger sibling. Police theorized that Pichler may have taken his own life by jumping off a nearby bridge, but search dogs could not trace his scent there. Since there is no hard evidence that Joe Pichler committed suicide, his ultimate fate is still unknown.

2 Thelma Todd

In the late 1920s and early '30s, Thelma Todd was one of the most prominent actresses in Hollywood, appearing in nearly 120 films and acting alongside such comedy legends as the Marx Brothers and Laurel and Hardy. However, her life came to a sudden end on the morning of December 16, 1935, when the 29-year-old Todd was found dead inside her car of apparent carbon monoxide poisoning. Her vehicle was located inside a Pacific Palisades garage belonging to Jewel Carmen, the wife of director Roland West, with whom Todd was romantically involved.

The death was initially ruled an accident and later changed to suicide, but there was nothing to indicate that Todd was suicidal and there were a lot of suspicious elements to suggest foul play. She appeared to a have a broken nose and other injuries, and blood was also found on her face and dress, leading to the belief that she may have been knocked unconscious and placed in the car before it was started. Roland West was known to be very controlling and possessive of Todd and allegedly gave a deathbed confession implicating himself in her death, but this was never officially confirmed. Mobster Lucky Luciano and an abusive ex-boyfriend of Todd's were also looked at as possible suspects, but unfortunately, since Todd's body was cremated, a more thorough autopsy could not be performed. Her suspicious death remains one of Hollywood's biggest mysteries.

1 Jean Spangler

One of the greatest mysteries in Hollywood history occurred on the evening of October 7, 1949, when 26-year-old Jean Spangler disappeared. Spangler was a model and aspiring actress who had played bit parts in a handful of films. She left her daughter with her sister-in-law and claimed she was going to meet her ex-husband to talk about child support before going to work on a film shoot. However, there were no film shoots scheduled that night, and Spangler's ex-husband claimed he never saw her. Spangler's purse was found in Griffith Park two days later.

Things took a bizarre turn when a note was found in the purse that read: "Kirk, Can't wait any longer. Going to see Dr. Scott. It will work best this way while mother is away." Spangler had recently worked as an extra on a Kirk Douglas film, and some eyebrows were raised when Douglas contacted police to confirm he wasn't the "Kirk" in the note before they even considered questioning him. Police also heard rumors of a local man named "Scotty" who was known for performing illegal abortions, leading to speculation that Spangler was pregnant and that he was the aforementioned "Dr. Scott." Spangler was also rumored to be involved with an organized crime figure named David Ogul, and there was even a sighting of them together in Texas three months after she disappeared. In spite of all these theories, the Jean Spangler saga is still a mystery.

TOP 10 Secretly Connected Topics

by **Bryan Johnson**

10 Super Hornio Brothers and Nintendo

Nintendo is one of the largest consumer electronics companies in the world. In 1985, the company released the NES console, which helped set a standard for video game expansion. Nintendo's most popular character is Mario. To date, Mario has appeared in over 200 video games and is probably the most famous personality in the history of video games. Mario games have sold more than 210 million units, making the franchise the best-selling in history. Mario has inspired television shows, films, comics, and a line of licensed merchandise.

However, there are two films based on Mario that Nintendo doesn't want you to know about.

In 1993, two pornographic parodies of the Super Mario franchise were filmed called *Super Hornio Brothers* and *Super Hornio Brothers II*. The movies were made at the same time as the *Super Mario Bros.* film. The series tells the story of computer programmer Squeegie Hornio (Ron Jeremy) and his brother Ornio Hornio (T. T. Boy) who are teleported into a computer game after a freak power overload and forced to battle King Pooper (Buck Adams). Pooper has kidnapped Princess Perlina (Chelsea Lynx).

Initially, Sin City Entertainment funded the project, but dropped out, leaving Buck Adams to seek the help of Midnight Video. Before the movies were released to the public, Nintendo decided to halt their distribution. Ron Jeremy's official website notes that while he would love to make both films available alongside his massive library, Nintendo purchased the rights to stop the movies' distribution indefinitely. The evidence that the *Super Hornio Brothers* films are real wasn't confirmed until 2008. The movies are currently unavailable for viewing and considered by some to be the Holy Grail of parodies.

9 Tara Calico and the Polaroid Photo

One of the most bizarre human disappearances of the 20th century is Tara Calico. On September 20, 1988, Tara left her home in Belen, New Mexico, to go for a bike ride and never returned. After an extensive search, part of Tara's Sony Walkman and a Boston cassette tape were discovered along her normal bike route. Several people saw Tara riding her bicycle, but nobody witnessed her presumed abduction. The disappearance of Tara Calico received extensive media coverage in the United States and was featured on *Unsolved Mysteries*, *America's Most Wanted*, *The Oprah Winfrey Show*, and *48 Hours*.

The case went cold until June 15, 1989, when a Polaroid photo of an unidentified young girl and boy, both bound and gagged, was found in the parking lot of a convenience store in Port St. Joe, Florida. After the photo was released, it was immediately theorized that the girl was Tara. Her mother came forward and said that the photo was indeed of her daughter because of what appeared to be a scar on the girl's leg, similar to one Tara received in a car accident.

Scotland Yard analyzed the photo and concluded that the girl was Tara, but the Los Alamos National Laboratory and FBI tests were inconclusive. In the photo, the book next to the girl is the gothic horror novel *My Sweet Audrina* by V. C. Andrews, which was published in 1982. According to investigators, the picture was taken after May 1989 because the film used was not sold until that time. This means the picture was not taken until at least eight months after Tara's disappearance.

The boy in the picture was initially thought to be Michael Henley, also of New Mexico, who disappeared in April 1988, but after Henley's body was discovered in the Zuni Mountains where he was lost, the theory was dismissed. In the 1980s and '90s, there were several reported sightings of Tara, but her disappearance remains a mystery. Two other Polaroid photographs have surfaced over the years that might show Tara, but the pictures have not been released by the police.

8 Miasma Theory and Germs

Ignaz Semmelweis was a 19th-century Hungarian physician who was an early pioneer of antiseptic procedures. He has been described as the "savior of mothers" because in 1847 he postulated a theory that washing your hands in a hospital with chlorinated lime solutions would improve the high fatality rate of puerperal fever. Puerperal fever is a bacterial infection that can be contracted by women during childbirth or miscarriage. The infection can develop into puerperal sepsis, which is often fatal. The discovery eventually reduced childbed fever fatalities by 90 percent.

Despite the publication that washing your hands can greatly reduce puerperal fever, doctors did not wash their hands while working with pregnant women in hospitals until Louis Pasteur confirmed the germ theory, which stated that microorganisms are the cause of many diseases. The idea was highly controversial because people were convinced that diseases were caused by miasma. The miasma theory held that diseases such as cholera or the Black Death were caused by a noxious form of "bad air." The word *miasma* means "pollution."

Miasma was considered to be a poisonous vapor. It was said that the vapor was passed to people by way of contaminated water, foul air, and poor hygienic conditions. Miasma was identifiable by its bad smell, but the infection was not said to be passed between individuals. In the 1850s, miasma was used to explain the spread of cholera in London and Paris. Authorities told people that they needed to clean their bodies to prevent the disease, but in reality cholera was being spread through the water. The miasma theory was important to understanding the danger of poor sanitation, but it failed to recognize microbiology and germs.

7 Bob Lazar and Element 115

In 1982, a man named Bob Lazar made his first appearance in the media when an article was published in the *Los Alamos Monitor* that described a project in which he built a jet car with the help of a jet engine. In the article, Lazar is referred to as "a physicist at the Los Alamos Meson Physics Facility." Seven years later, in November 1989, Bob Lazar conducted an interview with investigative reporter George Knapp. The interview was broadcast on a Las Vegas TV station and included claims by Lazar that he worked at a top-secret facility named S-4, located near Groom Lake, Nevada, within Area 51.

According to Lazar, S-4 served as a hidden U.S. military location that was used to study the reverse engineering of extraterrestrial flying saucers. Lazar said that he saw nine separate flying discs and was given a briefing on the involvement between humans and extraterrestrial beings for the past 100,000 years. Lazar said that the beings originate from the Zeta Reticuli one and two star system and are therefore referred to as Zeta Reticulans, popularly called Greys. Bob Lazar claimed that S-4 contained nine aircraft hangars built into the side of a mountain, with doors constructed at an angle that matched the slope.

He described some specifics of the alien spaceships and provided details on their mode of propulsion. According to Lazar, atomic element 115 (ununpentium) served as a nuclear fuel for the aircraft. He said that the element provided an energy source that produced antigravity effects under proton bombardment. As the strong nuclear force field of element 115's nucleus was amplified, the gravitational effect would distort the surrounding space-time continuum and shorten the travel time to a destination. The description given by Lazar was extremely scientific and seemed probable.

However, after the interview made headlines, Bob Lazar was called a fraud. Government officials denied the existence of element 115 and said Lazar was lying. Lazar's educational history was put into question and his fellow scientists claimed to have no memory of meeting him. On February 2, 2004, Russian scientists and American scientists announced that they had completed the synthesis of ununpentium. The news was surprising and came 15 years after Bob Lazar said ununpentium was responsible for the propulsion of alien aircraft.

6 Operation Endgame and U.S. Immigration

In 2003, the U.S. Immigration and Customs Enforcement agency developed a ten-year plan called Operation Endgame. The objective of the program was to detain and deport all removable aliens and "suspected terrorists" living in the United States by 2012. In order to accomplish this goal, the U.S. passed a collection of laws that were aimed at getting rid of immigration. In 2007, the program Secure Communities was developed to identify criminal aliens, prioritize them on criminal activity, and remove them from the country.

The program identifies illegal immigrants with the help of modern technology, most notably biometric identification techniques, which rely on computer science. The Obama administration is a strong proponent of the Secure Communities program. From 2008–2011, the program arrested 140,396 criminal aliens and deported 72,445 of them. By 2013, Secure Communities was expected to be all over the U.S. with detention centers located in many cities.

On December 31, 2011, President Barack Obama signed an extremely important law called the National Defense Authorization Act (NDAA). The act authorized the spending of $662 billion "for the defense of the United States and its interests abroad." The act underwent a number of revisions before being accepted. Most notably, the federal court blocked a section of the bill that allowed government officials to detain American citizens that are suspected of being terrorists. Instead, the bill allows for the indefinite detention of illegal aliens and foreign travelers deemed terrorists.

On April 23, 2010, Arizona Governor Jan Brewer signed law SB 1070, which made it a state misdemeanor for an illegal immigrant to be in Arizona without carrying registration documents. In 2012, the U.S. Supreme Court ruled that most of the bill over-reached the state's power into federal jurisdiction. The three provisions of the bill that were removed included the rule that legal immigrants needed to carry registration documents at all times, that state police were allowed to arrest any individual for suspicion of being an illegal immigrant, and that it was a crime for an illegal immigrant to search for a job in the state.

All Supreme Court justices agreed to uphold the provision of the law that allows Arizona state police to investigate the immigration status of a person stopped if there is a reason to do so. Had the legislation passed, each individual state would have had the opportunity to hold vastly different immigration regulations. However, since the bill was deemed unconstitutional, some states, including Alabama, Georgia, South Carolina, Indiana, and Utah, will have to adjust their immigration laws to meet the new standards.

5 Cloud 9 and Cannibalism

Methylenedioxypyrovalerone (Cloud 9) is a psychoactive drug that was first developed in 1969. In 2004, Cloud 9 became a popular designer drug in the United States and stores began to sell the product as bath salts. Cloud 9 is easier to get than cigarettes and alcohol, so it has become a popular drug choice for teenagers. Very little is known about how Cloud 9 interacts with the brain, but a wide range of unpredictable symptoms have been reported, including violent outbursts and cannibalism. Starting in 2011, stories began to emerge about people who took Cloud 9 and then did some very strange things. The drug has also been connected with suicides and unexplained deaths.

The issue of bath salts and their impact on people reached a new level of exposure on May 26, 2012, when it was initially reported that Rudy Eugene was under the influence of Cloud 9 when he attacked and ate the face off Ronald Poppo on the MacArthur Causeway in Miami, Florida. During the shocking attack, Eugene chewed up most of Poppo's face, including his left eye. The event lasted for over 18 minutes until Eugene was shot to death by a police officer. Poppo survived the attack, but needed massive facial reconstruction surgery. After the event, police initially speculated that Rudy Eugene had been high on bath salts. However, toxicology reports ruled that only traces of marijuana were found in his system.

On June 2, 2012, a homeless man in Miami named Brandon DeLeon took Cloud 9 and began yelling obscenities at two North Miami police officers. He was arrested and he then tried to bite the hand off one of the police officers. On June 6, 2012, a man named Carl Jacquneaux, who was high on Cloud 9, attacked Todd Credeur at his home. Jacquneaux bit Credeur's face until he was subdued with wasp spray and forced to retreat.

At the end of May 2012, a man named Alexander Kinyua confessed to cannibalizing his roommate Kujoe Bonsafo Agyei-Kodie. In the same week, Wayne Carter stabbed himself repeatedly then threw his skin and intestines at police officers. In both cases, the men were said to be under the influence of Cloud 9. The current availability of Cloud 9 has been halted by many U.S. states and countries around the world. In the fall of 2012, Canada's drug policy started categorizing methylenedioxypyrovalerone (MDPV) as a schedule-1 substance under the Controlled Drugs and Substances Act, placing it in the same category as heroin and cocaine. Cloud 9 is a dangerous drug that can cause serious mental hallucinations and delusions.

4 Online Disinhibition Effect and Data Mining

"The online disinhibition effect" is a term used to describe the complete abandonment of social restrictions on the Internet. The behavior occurs because the Internet is an anonymous platform and doesn't involve face-to-face conversation. For this reason, people interact in a way that is opposite of their recognized personality. Some users will search the Internet in hopes of finding a person who they can get an emotional reaction from. These individuals will do whatever it takes to get someone to respond to their comments.

One has to remember that a mind will automatically assign characteristics and traits to a person on the Internet. In many cases, these assumptions are false, so the nature of the Internet throws off the basic hierarchical structure of society. You never know if you are talking with an old man, a police officer, a child, or a sexy 25-year-old woman who is looking for a date. People on the Internet behave badly because they don't fear reprisal.

Data mining is a growing field in computer science. The process is used by a large number of organizations to predict behavior. It involves the statistical analysis of data sets in order to organize trends and patters of information. Data mining is used by Internet companies to research behavioral output. It is also heavily used by government officials to monitor Internet activity and dangerous users.

One of the reasons that data mining is so effective is because of the online disinhibition effect. Google regularly tracks activity and uses a mathematical formula to identify certain keywords and threats. For this reason, anyone can be targeted if they write the wrong thing on Twitter or Facebook. Just ask Leigh Van Bryan and Emily Banting, UK citizens who were denied access to the United States because of things Bryan had posted on Twitter. The online disinhibition effect helps federal agencies and business organizations accurately track the true personal, political, social, and economic trends of the world.

3 Religion and Intelligence

A large number of studies have been carried out that examine the relationship between human intelligence and religious belief. The experiments have been done in order to determine if the overall IQ of atheists is different from people adhering to religion. In 2008, intelligence researcher Helmuth Nyborg conducted a study in which he compared religious belief and IQ in 137 countries. He found that a sample population of atheists scored 6 IQ points higher on IQ tests. Among the 137 countries, only 23 (17 percent) had more than 20 percent atheists. Of these 23 countries, they constituted "virtually all...higher IQ countries." The authors reported a correlation of 0.60 between atheism rates and intelligence, which was "highly significant."

As you would expect, many people have challenged the results of the study, saying that Nyborg did not examine a complex range of social, economic, and historical factors. A confounding variable is the fact that people from poor countries are generally more religious and uneducated. A correlation between highly educated people and religious belief has also been presented. In Australia, 23 percent of Christian church members have earned an undergraduate or postgraduate degree, whereas only 13 percent of the general population has earned a degree.

Gallup poll studies have shown that those with high IQs tend to not believe in God. A study in March 2010 published in *Social Psychology Quarterly* stated that "atheism correlates with higher intelligence." A study conducted at Harvard University found that participants who tended to think more reflectively were less likely to believe in God. Some have argued that a causal relationship between IQ and religious belief is impossible to determine. A 2004 study concluded that people who are extremely religious reported that they had higher intelligence than the average person, so the issue is really controversial.

2 Chilling Effect and Democracy

The chilling effect is a deterrent, usually in the form of a federal law or regulation, that is used to discourage the exercise of a constitutional right. It occurs when a government passes a law that causes people to hesitate to do something. Usually, free speech is the right that is suppressed. The chilling effect doesn't always prohibit speech, but instead imposes a collection of undue burdens. In some cases, the laws can cause outrage because they are deemed undemocratic.

In March 2012, Russian Prime Minister Vladimir Putin received 63.64 percent of the presidential vote and secured a record third term in the Kremlin. The event sparked a collection of protests in Russia because people felt it was unfair that Putin was allowed to run for a third term. People were upset at Putin and his government policies. The 2011 Democracy Index states, "Russia has been in a long process of regression culminated in a move from a hybrid to an authoritarian regime" under Putin. American diplomatic cables leaked by WikiLeaks alleged that Russia has become a "virtual Mafia state" due to Putin.

In response to the large-scale protests, Russia enacted a series of laws that had the intended chilling effect. Vladimir Putin set strict boundaries on protests and imposed heavy penalties for out-of-bounds action. He ordered government raids on protest organizers. A law was passed that imposed a $9,000 fine for individuals who participated in rallies that caused harm to people or property. The fine was devastating because the average annual salary in Russia is around $8,500. Putin basically said that if you want to protest, he would take all your money.

1 Abortion and Crime

Currently, approximately two-thirds of the female population lives in an area of the world where abortion is legal. The law varies by region, and China, North Korea, and Vietnam are the only countries that conduct mandatory abortions. The topic is controversial and has sparked a large number of court cases. Abortion wasn't made legal in every U.S. state until 1973.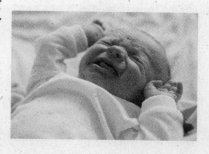
Since that time, millions of abortions have been carried out every year.

The number of abortions around the world has been increasing since the introduction of Mifepristone, which is a form of nonsurgical abortion. In the United States, the rate of abortion is much higher among minority women. In 2000, black women were three times more likely to have an abortion than white women. The most frequently listed reasons for abortions include: the mother wants to postpone childbearing, she cannot afford a baby, she has a relationship problem, she is too young, the baby will disrupt her education, or she doesn't want more children.

In 2001, a study conducted by John J. Donohue III of Yale University was published in the *Quarterly Journal of Economics*. In the paper, Donohue examines the connection between U.S. crime rates in the 1990s and the legalization of abortion in 1973. In the 1990s, the United States experienced a dramatic decrease in crime. On average, homicides and auto theft rates dropped 40 percent in cities across the country. Legalizing abortion produced the longest and deepest crime decline in the U.S. since World War II.

In the paper, Donahue argues: "We offer evidence that legalized abortion has contributed significantly to recent crime reductions. Crime began to fall roughly 18 years after the legalization of abortion. U.S. states that allowed abortion in 1970 experienced declines earlier than the rest of the nation." The theory argues that abortion is having an impact on future crime rates because unwanted children are more likely to become future criminals. Abortion is also more common among poor people. The paper has been challenged by a collection of economists, who call the theory pseudo-scientific and unproven.

Another interesting observation surrounding abortion is the Roe effect. The Roe effect is a hypothesis on the long-term impact of abortion on the world's political balance. The theory suggests that the practice of abortion will eventually become illegal because those who favor abortion are much more likely to get one than those who oppose it. Children follow their parents' political leanings, so the population of pro-choice people will gradually shrink until the pro-lifers become the dominant group. After generations, the impact will eventually cause the abolishment of the law. The process will then start over.

CHAPTER 2

CONSPIRACY THEORIES

1. Top 10 Creepy Pop Culture Conspiracy Theories
2. Top 10 Nefarious Conspiracies Proven True
3. Top 10 More Mysterious Conspiracy Theories
4. Top 10 Zombie Apocalypse Conspiracy Theories
5. Top 10 Plausible Conspiracy Theories
6. Top 10 Crazy Cinematic Conspiracy Theories
7. Top 10 Crazy Catholic Conspiracy Theories
8. Top 10 Laughable Conspiracy Theories
9. Top 10 Reasons the Moon Landings Could Be a Hoax

TOP 10 Creepy Pop Culture Conspiracy Theories

by **Mike Floorwalker**

10 Orson Welles

Prank Broadcast Was Psychological Warfare

The infamous Halloween Eve radio broadcast of *War of The Worlds* has long been part of pop culture folklore. That night in 1938, Orson Welles panicked the nation with a mock news broadcast depicting a deadly alien invasion, and the power of the media was revealed to the world. But, according to one conspiracy theory, the panic was no accident.

It is known that the Princeton University Radio Research Project, funded by the Rockefeller Foundation in order to study the effects of media on society, published a study on the broadcast. The conspiracy theory asserts that the foundation—and therefore, the Rockefellers, who figure prominently in a wide array of theories—actually hired Welles to produce the broadcast with the intent of studying how the populace would react in the event of a genuine invasion (alien or otherwise). Tellingly, the study found that fully 25 percent of the six million listeners thought a real invasion was taking place, although most believed the invaders to be not aliens, but Germans.

9 Deaths of Famous Actresses

Marilyn Monroe, Natalie Wood Murdered

While theories abound concerning any celebrity who dies young, two cases in particular have stuck in the public imagination in ways that few do: the deaths of Marilyn Monroe (in 1962) and Natalie Wood (in 1981). Monroe's death was a suicide, Wood's a tragic boating accident—but that's only if you believe the official line and Los Angeles coroner Thomas Noguchi.

While Marilyn's suicide was generally accepted by the public—she was troubled, getting old for an actress (at 36), and the story fit her tragic image—later revelations about her involvement with the Kennedy family cast a retroactively suspicious pall over her death. Theories about the exact nature of that involvement vary almost as widely as theories about John F. Kennedy's assassination, but the most prominent is that it was a Mafia hit at the behest of Robert Kennedy to keep her from revealing her affairs with Robert, John, and even Ted. As for Wood, theories around her death (while aboard a yacht with husband Robert Wagner and actor Christopher Walken) were not much more than idle rumors and innuendo. That is, until the yacht's captain, Dennis Davern, published a book in 2008 that suggested that the "accident" came close on the heels of a fight Wood had with Wagner. Speculation intensified when police reopened the case with little public comment in 2011, but so far, the theories remain just that.

Interestingly, the Los Angeles County coroner on Wood's case—so-called "coroner to the stars" Thomas Noguchi—was a deputy coroner on the scene when Monroe died almost 20 years earlier. But the case that made him and his team famous (as he told them it would) was the assassination of Robert Kennedy at the Ambassador Hotel in Los Angeles in 1968.

8 John Lennon's Death

Killer Was a Mind-Controlled CIA Assassin

The prototypical crazed stalker assassin, Mark Chapman shot John Lennon to death outside the Dakota apartment building on December 8, 1980. Beside the fact that he had just murdered one of the most famous and beloved figures in the world for no apparent reason, there were a few indicators that something was not quite right with Chapman: for one, the voice he claimed to hear in his head repeating "do it, do it." For another, the battered copy of *Catcher in the Rye* he was clutching as he sat waiting for the police, with one sentence scrawled on its inner front cover: "This is my statement."

Only three years earlier, there had been Senate hearings following the disclosure of the American CIA's project MKULTRA. One of the admitted goals of this project was brainwashing; specifically, it was alleged that one of the primary purposes of MKULTRA was to produce a "Manchurian Candidate," a mind-controlled assassin. One subjected to such treatment would display odd behavior indeed, and Chapman is not the only crazed shooter to display an odd fascination with *Catcher in the Rye*. But why would the powers-that-be want to kill Lennon?

Well, because he was a peace activist. Lennon was known to oppose the U.S. war in El Salvador, and it's even been suggested that his benefit concert for activist John Sinclair in 1971 had first gotten him on the wrong side of American intelligence agencies. It's easy to see why this theory has legs. For his part, Chapman says that he killed Lennon for the notoriety, telling his parole board that society is so celebrity-obsessed that he's surprised celebrities aren't killed by crazy people more often.

7 Gangster Rap
Conference Promotes Genre for Horrifying Reasons

In the late 1980s and early '90s, rap music was beginning to form pretty distinct subgenres; the two most popular, in direct opposition to each other, were "conscious rap" (from artists like Public Enemy and A Tribe Called Quest) and "gangsta rap" (like N.W.A. and the Geto Boys). But in a few short years, conscious rap had largely disappeared, while gangsta rap went on to dominate not just rap, but popular music in general. In April of 2012, a letter was posted to the blog *Hip Hop Is Read* positing a breathtakingly simple and perfectly chilling explanation for this.

The letter's anonymous author claimed to be a music industry "decision maker" who was present at an invite-only meeting of like types in 1991. The purpose of the meeting was to discuss the new direction of rap music at the behest of a small group of people—also present at the meeting—who represented the private prison industry. The general idea was to begin almost exclusively promoting music that glamorizes criminal behavior, with gangsta rap being an obvious choice, in order to keep underserved youth doing drugs and shooting each other—and to keep those prisons filled. It's also suggested that conscious or political rap was hurriedly phased out at this point since it would have been counterproductive to this goal.

Of course, due to the signing of a nondisclosure agreement (under heavily implied threats of violence), the letter's author can offer no verifiable details. The letter also fails to take into account the fact that gangsta rap's core audience consists of suburban white kids who relate to its images of violence and drug use in much the same way that they relate to similar images in action movies and video games (that is to say, as pure escapism). But to those who wondered just why violent, misogynistic rap suddenly took over in the mid-'90s (and continue to wonder why it dominates to this day), this theory offers a disturbingly plausible account of how it might have happened and why.

6 Predictive Programming
TV, Movies, Books Hint at Events to Come

One common theme in conspiracy theories has to do with behind-the-scenes puppet masters who are fond of dropping lots of clues about their master plans, usually in plain sight. These clues almost always have to do with significant symbols, numbers, or other identifiable references to the occult, Freemasonry (the Masons being a gigantic target for conspiracy theories of all sorts), or specific dates or imagery.

This can supposedly be done in many ways (in architecture, for instance, or artwork), the most modern of which is what is known as "predictive programming." For example, in a 1997 episode of *The Simpsons*, a New York City poster puts the number 9 right next to the image of the Twin Towers (which could be seen as an 11). There are far too many potential examples of this to list here, with some obviously reaching pretty far to make the connections, and others being downright creepy—like the plot of the 1998 pilot of the short-lived Fox series *The Lone Gunmen*, which had government operatives hijacking a plane and crashing it into the World Trade Center.

Beyond flaunting their nefarious plots, predictive programming is said to play a role in softening up the public for the traumatic events that they predict, in ways that are undetectable to those being affected.

5 Subliminal Messages

Tactic Is Used to Condition Consumers

It's no secret (at least, not anymore) that extremely brief or cleverly hidden words or images can be placed within another image or film in such a way that the observer, while not making a conscious connection, is subtly mentally influenced by the message. The efficacy of this tactic has long been open for debate and has never been proven—but of course, this doesn't stop corporations from doing things like hiding images within their logos to try to bolster positive association with their brands. It may not work, but it can't hurt, right?

But according to this conspiracy theory, not only does subliminal messaging work, it works far more efficiently than we've been led to believe—and it's everywhere. Supposedly, the practice is mostly used in advertising to induce consumers to buy, usually with references to sex. Certain Coke and Pepsi ads in the early '90s were famously found to contain hidden sexual references (which the companies both claimed were coincidences).

One would think that, if effective, the only message necessary in subliminal advertising would fall right along the lines of "buy this product, and lots of it." But the subliminal sexual references, odd as they may seem, are not limited to advertising. Whether coincidental or some animator's idea of a joke, it's also been established that hidden references to sex appear with alarming frequency in Disney cartoons. Which brings us to…

4 Walt Disney

The Disney Company Is an Evil Empire

This cannot be disputed: The Walt Disney Company is one of the United States' oldest and most successful entertainment conglomerates. It was founded in 1923 and consists of a huge number of subsidiaries. Disney has long owned the ABC network and all of its affiliated networks, including ESPN. The company made international headlines in 2009 when it acquired Marvel Entertainment for over $4 billion, and again in 2012 when it acquired Lucasfilm for over $4 billion more. The "House of Mouse" is probably the most influential and powerful of the tiny handful of huge corporations that control most of the media in the United States and, by extension, the world.

It also can't be disputed that, though a traditionally family-oriented business, Disney has allowed sexual images to make their way not only into completed cuts of their films, but also promotional and poster artwork. Many instances have been pointed out, from the overt (a couple of frames showing an image of a topless woman in *The Rescuers*) to the puzzling (a spire of the castle on the VHS cover of *The Little Mermaid* looks an awful lot like an erect penis) to the questionable (at one point in *Aladdin*, the Genie can be heard muttering off-screen something that sounds like "good teenagers, take off your clothes"). In each and every instance, changes were made to further releases and chalked-up to jokes by animators or simple misunderstandings. Why would Disney want to expose children (so to speak) to inappropriate sexual content, anyway?

Well, conspiracy theorists have their answer: Disney is all about sexualizing children. The Disney Company, they assert, wants to suck all of the money from the parents' wallets while rendering their children compliant, subservient consumers, and early exposure to these sexualized images is the first step in that process. Also, they say, because it's evil—mind-bogglingly, satanically evil. And here is where some of the theories begin to tie in with each other, and the rabbit hole begins to look pretty deep, so please stay with us.

3 Monarch Mind Control

Most Celebrities Are Mind-Controlled Puppets

When MKULTRA was exposed in the mid-1970s, the CIA claimed that the program, begun in 1950, had long since been scrapped and had produced no viable results. But some conspiracy theorists will take issue with both of those statements: They'll say that attempts by the "power elite" to perfect mind control predate the CIA to at least the 1930s. They also say that MKULTRA never stopped; it just changed its name to "Monarch" and not only has it been perfected, but practically all of the world's most famous celebrities have participated, especially those employed by Disney.

The programming supposedly consists of ritualized, regulated trauma and abuse designed to cause the subject to "dissociate" and undergo a break from reality. Then, the "handler" is able to wall off and create multiple personalities—blank slates that can be programmed for a variety of purposes, like singing and dancing. Or killing. Or sex. Or all of the above.

According to the theory, this programming usually begins in fairly early childhood, sometimes with the direct cooperation of the parent. The subjects are used throughout their childhood and teens as sex slaves for the rich and powerful, and their public images are carefully nurtured. These images are plotted on a trajectory from squeaky-clean child star, to subtly sexualized teen idol, to full-blown object of desire (like Lindsay Lohan or Britney Spears, both of whom were working for Disney as children). When such celebrities "melt down" (display bizarre public behavior), it's not simply the pressures of stardom, but broken mind-control programming. And they don't go off to rehab, but to be reprogrammed.

If it sounds like science fiction, consider the puzzling fact that Roseanne Barr once inexplicably blurted out—in the middle of an otherwise perfectly normal nationally televised live interview—that "MKULTRA mind control rules in Hollywood. If you don't know, Google that and look into it."

2 The Illuminati

Aliens Control Music, All Entertainment

For being little more than a Bavarian social club that disbanded in 1785, the Illuminati have taken a lot of flak over the years for supposedly orchestrating everything bad that's ever happened to any group of people at any point in time. And for such a shadowy organization, there certainly seems to be a wealth of information about their sinister agenda available to anyone with an Internet connection. In recent years, there have been rumblings that Lady Gaga is a tool of the Illuminati: Countless aspects of her stage shows, videos, and promotional photos, such as "all-seeing eye" symbolism, are said to reflect her status as an Illuminati puppet. But by no means is this limited to Gaga: Much of the same symbolism appears in videos by other female artists, like Katy Perry, Beyoncé, and Britney Spears. For that matter, it's not even limited to music. Illuminati/occult symbolism is said to be found all over popular culture, appearing in movies and books as well.

But why use mind-controlled sex slaves to sell sex to a sex-starved public while admitting the whole thing through a complex series of hidden symbols and imagery? Once again, conspiracy theorists are glad you asked.

1 Mass Media

Media Programs Our Thoughts

Consider the number ten entry on this list, which some will tell you was a psychological experiment conducted to see the potential impact that mass media could have on the psyche and behavior of the populace. If we accept this to be even partially true, then it stands to reason that a great deal was learned from that experiment, and that the gist of the conclusion may have been this: The public is far more susceptible to manipulation by mass media than anyone ever could have dreamed. It also stands to reason that this knowledge would be employed early and often by those seeking to manipulate public opinion—like politicians and advertisers.

We indisputably live in a society where social norms and behaviors are taught to us largely by the media from a very early age. We're taught to trust what we see and hear, and according to something of a Grand Unified Theory of pop culture conspiracies, that is no accident. We're very carefully conditioned from birth to consume, think, and behave in predictable ways. And while movies are great for conditioning social behavior, and music is great for instilling values and morals, it's network television that they say really plays a role in shaping your reality and your expectations of life, yourself, and others.

Which, of course, may all be a coincidence. And while we find it much more likely that social science is very weird, that those with a lot of money and power tend to behave badly in the service of getting more of those things, and that being famous tends to make people kind of crazy—what can we say? We love a good conspiracy theory.

TOP 10 Nefarious Conspiracies Proven True

by FlameHorse

10 Prohibition Alcohol

Theory: The FBI Poisoned Alcohol During Prohibition

Conspiracy theorists like to point out that the government (usually the U.S. government) is poisoning the national populace, which is blissfully unaware, via chemtrails and/or fluoridation. How laughable, most of us say, and yet, although there is no proof of either, the FBI did, in truth, poison liquor stores during Prohibition for the purpose of "dissuading" people from that demon hooch.

Prohibition lasted from 1920–1933 in the U.S., and was absolutely unenforceable. Every member of the public knew perfectly well that a drink now and then was not at all harmful and refused to accept alcohol's absence. Prohibition was impelled by the Temperance Movement, which promoted teetotalism, or utter abstinence from alcohol. Its most prominent activist was Carrie Nation, a six-foot, 180-pound, blue-haired battle-axe who stormed into bars and smashed kegs open with a hatchet. Amazingly, no drunks ever beat her up for this.

Once Prohibition went into effect, the FBI saw fit to enforce it as well as possible, since the law is the law, and, by adding potentially fatal impurities to it, endeavored to teach the public that it was going to lose with Mr. Booze. These poisons included methane, formaldehyde, ammonia, and even arsenic and kerosene. But the FBI's usual method, without informing the populace, of course, was to denature drinkable alcohol, which is called ethanol, by adding rubbing alcohol, which is made of water and propene. Propene is distilled from natural gas and oil; rubbing alcohol does a fine job cleaning wounds and preventing infection, but will destroy your intestines, kidneys, and liver if you drink it. The FBI also added acetone, which is paint thinner.

Not surprisingly, people started dying quite readily from what seemed like alcohol intoxication, and this only fueled the Temperance Movement's assertion that alcohol is the Devil.

9 Gulf of Tonkin

Theory: The Incident in the Gulf of Tonkin Is Only Half True

In history books, the Gulf of Tonkin incident is usually cited as the immediate instigation for war between the United States and North Vietnam. The general casus belli was to protect the democracy of South Vietnam from the North's Communist aggression. The straw that was seen in the West as breaking the camel's back occurred on August 2 and 4, 1964, in the waters between Vietnam and Hainan, China, when U.S. naval vessels were attacked by Vietnamese naval vessels and defended themselves, killing some Vietnamese sailors.

American public sentiment called for immediate retaliation, and congress resolved that Lyndon Johnson could defend any Southeast Asian nation from Communism. The war was on.

What the public was not told for a long time was that the incident on August 4 did not take place. The first incident was a legitimate naval battle, in which the USS *Maddox* fought off three Vietnamese torpedo boats and killed four Vietnamese sailors. But two days later, the Vietnamese were engaged in salvaging their vessels and no hostilities erupted. Nevertheless,

Johnson informed the public that the *Maddox* and the USS *Turner Joy* had been attacked in separate battles. The *Turner Joy* had not been attacked.

The CIA was for a time regarded as having deliberately spread this false information among the national public to sway favor toward a war against Communism. Dozens of senators and congressmen were calling for land invasions of North Vietnam, and then China, and then Russia if they dared retaliate, nuclear weapons be damned.

Today, we know that the misinformation was spread by the National Security Agency, and not for political reasons, but to cover up genuine mistakes they made during the second incident: Their radar showed what they thought were approaching enemy warships, but which were, in truth, tricks of light that confused their equipment.

8 Fascist Overthrow of the U.S. Government

Theory: The Fascist Plot to Overthrow the U.S. Government

In 1933, Franklin Roosevelt deemed it beneficial to the American economy to abandon the gold standard and operate on a pure American currency basis. This had proven very helpful in Great Britain in lowering the cost of products and boosting the citizens' buying power. However, many conservative businessmen of the time deemed the gold standard essential for a strong economy since gold does not devalue like a nominative currency.

Major General Smedley Butler testified before a senate subcommittee a year later that he had been approached by Gerald MacGuire and William Doyle of the American Legion veterans' organization. They asked Butler in confidence whether he would have any part in a military coup d'état to oust Roosevelt and set up a Fascist government with Butler as its head commander, secretary of general affairs. Their motive was money, of course, since they and their friends had their fingers in a lot of business pies.

Butler was pro-Communist in light of what he viewed as Roosevelt's very foolish ideas on the American economy, but Butler was not about to agree to the impossible. In his opinion, the United States government could not be successfully overthrown. To do so would entail a total military siege of every major city in the nation, especially Washington, D.C. So he ratted on the Fascist businessmen. His testimony earned a mixed reception from the subcommittee, which declared that there probably had been a conspiracy to stage a coup in favor of a Fascist system of government, but that it never left square one, and that most of the public figures Butler implicated, many of them retired generals and millionaire bankers, had nothing to do with it.

7 False Witness

Theory: The CIA Had Nayirah al-Sabah Bear False Witness

Nayirah al-Sabah was a woman in Kuwait who, in 1990, testified on the floor of the House of Representatives that she had personally witnessed Iraqi soldiers invade Kuwaiti hospitals and take newborn infants out of their incubators and throw them onto the cold floor to freeze to death. Nayirah was invited primarily by Tom Lantos, who had made no secret of his desire that the U.S. retaliate against Iraq for its offenses against Kuwait.

It was Nayirah's testimony that provided the largest part of the foundation for American public opinion in favor of military force against Iraq, and the CIA was responsible for organizing the funds and advertisements to disseminate Nayirah's testimony. They enlisted the help of Hill and Knowlton, a global public relations corporation that specializes in marketing, to reach the masses.

It was not until 1992 that John MacArthur of the *New York Times* discovered Nayirah was the daughter of the Kuwaiti ambassador for the U.S., and that her story had been utterly fabricated. Thus was it shown that the CIA assisted a few powers-that-were in America in waging war with Iraq for another purpose, and that purpose was oil. The Iraqis did invade Kuwait and should not have done so, but they did not throw babies out of incubators. The nurses and doctors who supposedly witnessed this with Nayirah had already fled, and most of them stated that she was lying. The CIA had paid her to lie, and even paid for her to attend acting classes to appear convincing. It worked.

6 Mockingbird

Theory: Operation Mockingbird

Mockingbird began the same year that the Office of Special Projects was founded by Frank Wisner. In 1951, the OSP, renamed Office of Policy Coordination, merged with the CIA and became the agency's covert paramilitary branch. Its first and principle assignment was to influence national media toward the hatred and fear of Soviet Communism. The CIA funded the operation with money from the Marshall Plan, and bribed journalists and newspaper editors who grew wise to their ulterior motive. Mockingbird led, directly and immediately, to Senator Joseph McCarthy's rise to power.

The operation became so widespread that the CIA started influencing international media and even international politics. It was due in large part to Mockingbird that Guatemala staged a coup d'état against Colonel Jacobo Guzman, whom the CIA deemed a Communist. Mockingbird was responsible for $300,000 of the funding of the 1954 *Animal Farm* animated film. They asked Walt Disney if he wanted to make the film, and he balked at the prospect. He was anti-Communist, but the novel does not end happily, and Disney wanted nothing to do with such a story.

Mockingbird also incited the 1953 Iranian coup d'état and the Bay of Pigs invasion. David Bruce, appointed by Dwight Eisenhower to investigate this covert propaganda, stated that Mockingbird was responsible for over 50 percent of international politics over the last half of the 20th century.

5 Asbestos

Theory: Asbestos Manufacturers Have Claimed It Was Perfectly Safe

Asbestos is a natural silicate mineral compound long used for sound-proofing and fire-retardation, among many other applications. It is extremely resistant to burning and was used for the majority of the 20th century as a protective suit for fire fighters, race car drivers, and many other people in high-risk occupations. Motorcyclist, stuntman, and actor Steve McQueen died from malignant mesothelioma, which is the cancer usually caused by inhaling asbestos fibers.

Asbestos has been in use for about 4,500 years, mined in the form of fibrous, hairlike material on and within rock ore, and the 20th century companies that mass-produced asbestos were beset from 1900–1981 by doctors, insurance companies, and occupational hazard organizations who investigated the adverse health effects of asbestos. It was well known in academic and medical circles since at least the turn of the century that asbestos was very dangerous to be around. Even the ancient Greeks described asbestos miners as suffering from lung ailments.

Yet the companies that mass-produced asbestos found it to be big business and did everything within their considerable power to cover up the truth about asbestosis, mesothelioma, and pulmonary fibrosis; these companies included Johns Manville Corp., Amatex, Carey Canada Inc., Celotex, Unarco, National Gypsum, and Eagle-Picher. Every one of these companies attempted to destroy the reputations of any independent medical authorities who sought to disclose the truth about asbestos. Physicians employed by the companies informed their superiors that asbestos does indeed cause severe health problems, but that as long as the workers are able to perform their duties, they should not be told of their medical conditions, since this would cause the companies financial woes.

Johns Manville was labeled "the greatest corporate mass-murderer in history." It was not until the 1990s that lawsuits, the first of which cropped up in 1929, finally took their toll on these companies, none of which ever admitted to any wrongdoing, and 25 of them filed for bankruptcy. Today, asbestos is still legally produced and used in the United States, and some of the companies still maintain that it causes their employees no medical problems. It is banned in Europe.

4 Civil Rights Activists

Theory: The FBI Sought to Neutralize Civil Rights Activists

The FBI referred to this as COINTELPRO, or Counter Intelligence Programs, specifically those targeted at activists of almost any organization from 1956–1971. During those years of turmoil, Martin Luther King, Jr., was the primary spokesperson for civil rights in America, and the FBI considered him and his movement equivalent to the Black Panthers, the American Indian Movement, the NAACP, the Congress for Racial Equality, and dozens of others of groups striving to attain equal rights for all races. COINTELPRO referred to all of these groups and movements as "black hate groups," even the American Indian Movement, and spent 85 percent of its money on attempts to subvert them; the remaining 15 percent it spent on the subversion of "white hate groups" like the Ku Klux Klan.

It is highly possible, albeit very unlikely, that the FBI in some way coerced James Earl Ray into killing Martin Luther King, or simply did the job themselves and pinned it on Ray. King's family concluded in 1998 that Ray had nothing at all to do with the assassination.

All these domestic political organizations and movements, as the FBI labeled them, were deemed threats to national security. In general, COINTELPRO targeted the entire left wing of political thought; anyone liberal was seen as a danger to American society and as a result they were slandered in print, sued, or threatened with imprisonment, imprisoned, or illegally wiretapped.

What may well be the FBI's most shocking atrocity occurred on December 4, 1969, when the home of Fred Hampton, a Black Panther Party officer, was invaded by the Chicago police, who used deadly force against him and Mark Clark. Clark was shot first, and Hampton was unable to wake to the sound of gunfire because FBI agent William O'Neal had infiltrated the Black Panther's organization and spiked Hampton's supper with barbiturates. The police shot him to death while he slept unarmed in bed.

3 Scientology

Theory: Scientologists Planned to Have Paulette Cooper Committed

This embarrassing moment in Scientology's history was called Operations Daniel, Dynamite, and Freakout, and the operation entailed having the church harass Cooper with unbelievable intensity. Scientologists are extremely easy to offend in this way, and they will undertake legitimate and illegal retaliation whenever they see fit.

Cooper published an article in a British newspaper in 1971 that the church sued to have withdrawn; Scientology won $8,000 from the newspaper. Cooper then promptly expanded this article into an entire book, *The Scandal of Scientology*. For the next six years, the church ran a covert mission to vilify, defame, ridicule, harass, threaten, and even assassinate Cooper, all with the intent to make her shut up about exposing Scientology's outlandish beliefs (namely, the story of Xenu). Their goal was either to cause Cooper to go insane from the constant stress or convince the authorities that she was insane, in either event leading to her committal or imprisonment. Over the years, as both sides threatened, pursued, and made good on civil legal actions, the church held meetings to discuss how they could kill Cooper and not get caught.

A member broke into Cooper's office in 1972 and stole a bundle of her stationery, then forged bomb threats on it to blackmail her. This worked to a small extent; Cooper was indicted and brought before a grand jury, but there was insufficient evidence to proceed. Operation Freakout consisted of a three-point plan to discredit Cooper in the public's eyes by having a professionally trained actress impersonate Cooper on the telephone to Arab consuls in New York. Then her stationery would be used for another bomb threat to be mailed to one of these consuls. A Scientologist would then impersonate Cooper in person in a New York laundromat, threatening to kill President Ford and Henry Kissinger.

Though Freakout was never implemented, Operations Daniel and Dynamite certainly were. The astounding truth of how far the Church of Scientology had gone, and was prepared to go, to protect its false image was revealed in 1977 by a full-scale FBI investigation. L. Ron Hubbard's third wife, Mary Sue, and a host of other officers in the church, were imprisoned for up to four years. They still did not stop slandering and libeling Cooper, filing suit against her 20 times through the 1970s and '80s. To Cooper's credit, she fought back the whole way, and the spectacle remained tooth-and-nail until 1985, when the church finally paid Cooper a tidy sum out of court.

2 Domestic Terrorism

Theory: The U.S. Joint Chiefs of Staff Plan to Terrorize the U.S. Populace

The Joint Chiefs are the five generals and admirals in charge of the five branches of the U.S. military. In 1962, those men were George Decker (army), David Shoup (marines), George Anderson, Jr. (navy), Curtis LeMay (air force), and Edwin Roland (coast guard), along with a few others, all chaired by Lyman Lemnitzer (army). The entire board of the Joint Chiefs of Staff proposed, drafted, and agreed on a plan to concoct a casus belli for war against Communist Cuba, under Fidel Castro. Their collective motive was to reduce the constant threat of Communist encroachment into the Western Hemisphere, as per the Monroe Doctrine.

This plan was named Operation Northwoods and entailed the most impossibly indifferent cruelty ever envisioned by a government against its own people. In order to sway public sentiment in favor of the war, the Joint Chiefs planned to bomb high-pedestrian-traffic areas in major American cities, including Miami, New York, Washington, D.C., and possibly Chicago and Los Angeles; to frame U.S. citizens for these bombings; to shoot innocent, unarmed civilians on the streets in full view of hundreds of witnesses; to napalm military and merchant vessels in port, while people were aboard; to sink vessels carrying Cuban refugees bound for Florida; and to hijack planes for ransom.

Not only did every single member of the Joint Chiefs sign his approval of this plan, they then sent it to Secretary of Defense Robert McNamara for his approval and then to President Kennedy. McNamara claimed years later never to have seen it, but insisted that he would have rejected it. Kennedy, however, did receive it, and promptly called a meeting of the Joint Chiefs, in which he threatened, with severe profanity, to court-martial and incarcerate every one of them. The president cannot actually do this, but he can order the Congress and military branches to do so, and in these circumstances, they most certainly would have. But Kennedy decided that it would cause irreparable disrespect around the world for the U.S. military. He did remove Lemnitzer from his position as chairman and assign him as supreme allied commander in Europe, which was not much of a demotion.

Theorists claim that the military may have had a hand in Kennedy's assassination because of his blistering rebuke of the Joint Chiefs. This, however, remains unproven.

1 Heart Attack Gun

Theory: The CIA Has a Heart Attack Gun

This weapon exists. The CIA actually invented it with taxpayer money in the late 1960s to early '70s. It was not disclosed until 1975, when Senator Frank Church displayed it to a subcommittee investigating the CIA's illegal activities. The CIA is specifically forbidden from directly killing anyone in the performance of espionage and intelligence gathering, so the gun was designed to be untraceable. It fires a bullet made of ice, about 0.11 inches wide, less than the diameter of a BB, which has been brushed with a minute amount of shellfish toxin. This toxin induces a myocardial infarction in any human, regardless of size or physical fitness. The bullet then melts, leaving no trace of any kind. Autopsies would discover the presence of shellfish toxin in the bloodstream, but if the victim has died of a legitimate heart attack, unnaturally induced or not, an autopsy is\unlikely. The entrance wound of the dart would appear about as minor as a mosquito bite.

There is no consensus on whom, if anyone, the CIA has assassinated with this gun, but it is most likely that they have used it. Theorists point to Andrew Breitbart, a conservative media mogul who published less than flattering stories and details about President Barack Obama. He had promised in the months prior to his death that he would publish proof that Obama's presidency was illegitimate. Breitbart collapsed on the sidewalk in a Brentwood neighborhood of Los Angeles on March 1, 2012, and was taken to a hospital where he died of a massive heart attack at the age of 43, despite being in relatively fine health. He was not seriously overweight, but the coroner report states that cardiomegaly (an enlarged heart) caused his heart to fail.

It is possible that the gun was used to assassinate Mark Pittman, the financial journalist who, in 2007, predicted the ongoing American economic recession, which was caused by subprime mortgaging. During the subsequent federal bailouts of major financial companies, Pittman famously sued the Federal Reserve for mishandling taxpayer money. The case is still on appeal. Pittman, however, died on November 25, 2009, in Yonkers, New York, in the very same circumstances as Breitbart. He was walking down the sidewalk and collapsed from a heart attack. He was 52. Possible victims notwithstanding, the heart attack gun does exist, and the CIA invented it. They could have had only one purpose in store for it. The conspiracy theorists got this one right.

TOP 10 More Mysterious Conspiracy Theories

by **FlameHorse**

10 Ararat Anomaly

Theories surrounding the Ararat Anomaly arose from a single black-and-white photograph taken in 1949 by a U.S. Air Force recon plane performing routine intelligence gathering of the Ararat massif, which was in an area of military interest at the time. This famous photo shows a shoulder of Mount Ararat only 1,300 feet from the summit, covered in snow, with an odd-looking object on the very precipice of a steep slope.

Conspiracy theorists, many of them Biblical literalists, claim that the odd-looking object is Noah's Ark, which the Bible states "came to rest on

the mountains of Ararat" after the Great Flood. Since the Bible plural-
izes "mountains," the question still stands, "Which mountain of the area?"
Mount Ararat is the tallest of the Armenian Plateau, but the whole area of
Eastern Turkey and Western Armenia is mountainous, and Mount Ararat
is actually two peaks, with the main peak a prominence for miles around.

The anomaly appears to be a very rounded elongation teetering on the
edge of a slope, buried under ice and snow, and it has so roused the curiosity of the U.S. government that planes and satellites have been used to take
numerous photographs of it, not all of which, the theory claims, have been
made public. The best public views of it can be found on the Internet for
free, and the anomaly does look very much like a big boat, approximately
1,000 feet long and 200–300 feet wide, which roughly matches the Bible's
description of the Ark.

A close-up of it appears to show two sets of three "prongs," one set on
each end, and this close-up does look very man-made. Why the U.S. government will not divulge anything further than what is available is not
universally established, but the theory claims that in order to do so, the
government would have to declassify top-secret spy satellites, which would
set a lot of unwanted media against them in terms of invasion of privacy.
The U.S. does have satellites that can photograph a postage stamp from
600 miles overhead, but there are no such photographs of the anomaly.

9 Suppression of the Cathars

Catharism is a branch of Christianity similar to Gnosticism. Its heyday
lasted from the 2nd–3rd century, and during that time, Cathars throughout Europe so irritated the Roman Catholic Church that the church first
tried to convert the Cathars without violence. When that didn't work, they
initiated a full-force crusade, the Albigensian Crusade, which brought 20
years of warfare against the Cathar movement. During that Crusade, the
fortress of Beziers was besieged throughout most of 1209, at the end of
which, the Catholic army won and slaughtered every single man, woman,
and child in the city—at least 7,000 people, possibly as many as 20,000. The
leader of the army stated, "Kill them all. The Lord will recognize His own."

In the end, the Cathars were very effectively suppressed. So why in
the world did the Catholic Church pursue this end so violently? Because,
according to the theory, the Cathars had copies of various texts sacred to
them and not Catholicism, including *The Book of the Two Principles* and
the *Gospel of the Secret Supper*. These and other texts depicted Jesus teaching that reincarnation is real, that heaven and hell do not exist, that the
God of the Old Testament was instead Satan, and that Almighty God is
either Jesus or his father in heaven, but not the Old Testament God. This is

a central tenet of Gnosticism also. The most earth-shattering point of this theory is that Jesus may have taught that reincarnation is real, leading theorists to speculate about who on Earth right now is Jesus and when he will make his presence known again. These apocryphal texts sacred only to Catharism are commercially available, most falling under the header of Gnosticism.

8 Nibiru Collision

This theory ties in with the 2012 Doomsday theories. It claims that there is a planet the size of Jupiter, called Nibiru or Planet X, that was on a collision course with Earth in 2012. The theory goes that the Infrared Astronomical Satellite (IRAS) launched in 1983 took a photograph of this object that was finally leaked to the Internet in 2009. The photograph was explained away by NASA as showing nine galaxies and some intergalactic cirrus, but no other objects.

The theory goes on to claim that the U.S. government funded the construction of a very powerful telescope at the South Pole to take pictures of Nibiru and track it. This telescope is claimed by NASA to be a radio telescope that cannot take pictures, but the theory ignores this and goes on to say that Nibiru could simply not be seen because it was behind the sun.

It is impossible to debunk this theory, not because it may or may not be true, but because conspiracy theories don't have to respect the authority of a government, especially that of the U.S. Any "debunking" of evidence in support of Nibiru was immediately denounced as a lie.

7 2005 London Bombings

At 8:50 a.m. on July 7, 2005, three suicide bombers, two of Pakistani descent and one Jamaican, blew themselves up onboard three separate subway trains in London, killing a total of 42 people, including the bombers. At 9:47, less than an hour later, the number 30 double-decker bus blew up because of a fourth bomber, killing 14 people, including himself. These are the facts as presented in news accounts in the days and weeks following.

The conspiracy theorists are not convinced. In fact, they are convinced of the opposite: The four bombers were not the culprits, not bombers, and merely innocent civilians along with all the other victims. The real killers, according to the theory, were members of the UK government's security, including MI5, and that Prime Minister Tony Blair, and even the queen, knew all about it.

So why cover it up? Al-Qaeda even took responsibility for it in a video appearing on Al Jazeera, but this video was proven by British authorities to have been edited after the attacks in order to include them and take credit for them. The bombers were officially dissociated with al-Qaeda, but the theory simply uses this video as one of many proofs that something fishy was going on.

Once the term "cover-up" enters a conspiracy theory, the theorists almost always diverge, because a government may have a great many things to hide: evidence of aliens on the subway trains and the number 30 bus; evidence of cooperation between the British government and al-Qaeda; the subtheory that the four "bombers" were really just tabloid photographers who had photographed Catherine, Duchess of Cambridge, the then-future-wife of Prince William, having sex with Queen Elizabeth's horses.

6 Operation Alsos

This theory centers on one man in particular, Samuel Abraham Goudsmit (1902–1978). Goudsmit was a nuclear physicist who headed Operation Alsos, a branch of the Manhattan Project. While America considered it vitally important to beat the Nazis at making the atomic bomb, they found it equally important to hinder the Germans as much as possible.

The Allied war effort saw to that magnificently by bombing Nazi ball bearing plants. Hardly any machinery in the world functioned without ball bearings, and while the Nazis attempted to research nuclear physics, Goudsmit organized a spy ring to report on how close the Germans were coming to the bomb. His published reports stated that they never got close, but the truth, according to this conspiracy theory, is much more insidious.

Goudsmit is said to have discovered that the Nazi nuclear physicists, led by Otto Hahn and Werner Heisenberg, actually built the bomb, or at least discovered all the technology involved in building one and were in the process of doing so, and that Hitler intended to use it on London. To counter this, Goudsmit informed the U.S. government, which found it more promising to buy off the Nazi scientists than to carpet bomb the areas where nuclear testing was occurring. Goudsmit had been unable to ascertain from the scientists where this testing was being done, and after the war, laboratories were discovered all over Germany, which means bombing would not have been feasible.

So Goudsmit was given millions of dollars to bribe the Nazi scientists into coming to America, with the bomb and all research and material, and those scientists partnered with Robert Oppenheimer, Enrico Fermi, and Edward Teller, and enabled the Americans to finish their fission research, then build bombs. The Trinity Test of July 16, 1945, is claimed by this theory to have been the original Nazi bomb.

5 Disclosure Project

This theory incorporates all known extraterrestrial conspiracies, then takes them one step further. Steven Greer claims to have been contacted by aliens with good news. He founded the Disclosure Project in 1992 as a convention for people who claim to have been contacted by aliens.

Meetings of the Project, which occur every year in various American cities, are not secret at all. They even boast some fairly authoritative government agents as members, all attempting to make the U.S. government "disclose" the truth about extraterrestrial existence.

The one step further is as follows: Greer claims the aliens' good news to him and others they have contacted is that they are on their way from distant planets (more than one), and that they come in peace to share scientific, medical, and cultural knowledge. Most importantly, they say that a specific aspect of their and our planets' histories is identical: that a certain member of each planet's most intelligent species was unjustly killed to remove the sins from all other members of that species.

4 President's Book of Secrets

This theory was used in the film *National Treasure 2: Book of Secrets* and claims that the presidents of the United States have passed down a book from Washington to Obama, to which some or all have added facts and histories earth-shattering in scope and implications, and that this book's location is only known to the president and the national librarian of Congress. Thus, if the president is assassinated, the librarian informs the next president of the book. After each president leaves office, the book's location is changed.

This book is rumored to contain the truth about the alien landings at Roswell, New Mexico, and the air bases near the Rendlesham Forest, UK, among many other UFO events; the truth about the JFK and RFK assassinations; the location of the Holy Grail; the fates of various high-ranking Nazis following WWII (and the facts concerning the U.S. government's assistance of them); and even the identity of the Antichrist. Assuming there is a book, and assuming it identifies the Antichrist, we are led to wonder if he and the president are on the same side, are one and the same, or whether the president fears for Earth's immediate future. Even more insidious, in terms of realism, is the claim that the book told of the attacks of September 11, 2001, before they took place, and also tells of the imminent coup d'état of Russia, followed by a Russo–North Korean invasion of South Korea, initiating World War III.

3 Osama bin Laden is Alive

Not many conspiracy theories spring to life as quickly as the theory that arose in the immediate aftermath of the Navy SEAL raid on bin Laden's hideout: that Osama bin Laden survived the raid or wasn't even present to begin with. The theory was bound to show up anyway, but it took off like wildfire when the White House refused to release official photos of bin Laden's dead body. Why not? Let's all see the justice that was done.

That was what conspiracy theorists shouted, but the pictures will likely never see the light of day. The official excuse, from the president himself, is that it would be kicking a man while he's down, and not in keeping with the appearance of fairness the U.S. government prefers to show the world; the sentiment in withholding these pictures was meant to be "We're better than this barbarian."

But without the photo, many are still crying "fake!" The photo was described by numerous politicians as "very gory" with the entire forehead blown off and brain matter exposed. These politicians, according to the theory, are just part of the cover-up. So if bin Laden is alive, where is he? Just claiming that he's still hiding in the Tora Bora mountains doesn't satisfy conspiracy theorists. They claim he is hiding in the last place anyone will ever look: the United States of America.

2 Cure for Everything

Theorists seem to have derived this one from a passage in Michael Crichton's novel *The Andromeda Strain*. In that book, one of the characters tells another about a top-secret U.S. government–funded medical research project that appears to have discovered a single drug that would not only inhibit the reproduction of a bacteria in the human body, but actively kill all biological and viral pathogens known to science without any serious repercussions to the body's health.

The fact that it may stem from a novel has not deterred conspiracy theorists from claiming that Crichton was stating facts but was afraid to admit to it, which is why he hid his facts in a work of fiction. In this passage, the drug is not named, but it is described as causing no more discomfort to the person than diarrhea, because it also kills the good bacteria in the intestines. It kills cancer within days and also kills AIDS, syphilis, herpes simplexes I and II, rabies encephalitis, and every single disease of any kind ever known.

The character who describes it remarks that it was about to be made commercially available until doctors took patients off the drug after several months and all of them promptly died within weeks from unknown diseases never before seen that caused bizarre and horrifying problems in the body: brains melted, cancer metastasized in every organ and tissue in the body within days, livers liquefied, and many others. The reason? While on the miracle drug, the human body had no need for its immune system, which stopped functioning. Then when the drug was discontinued, the only barrier the human body had between itself and all the weak bacteria and viruses humans never have problems with allowed germs to create unheard-of infections.

That's all courtesy of Crichton, but the conspiracy theory claims that this drug exists, was tried on people, and was taken off the market for a completely different reason: While the human immune system was not stopping (which is true; it will do its job unless suppressed by age and/or strong diseases), visits to doctors' offices were. And like all medical conspiracy theories, this one centers on the insidious motive of greed on the part of the American Medical Association, which would be put out of business completely and forever should the drug hit the open market.

1 Grand Grimoire

This one is based on the fact that the so-called *Grand Grimoire* exists. It is a book, also called *The Red Dragon* and the *Gospel of Satan*. The book is real because the Roman Catholic Church officially claims ownership of it but has never let the public glimpse it. It is fact that it was discovered in Jerusalem in 1750 in the tomb of Solomon, written in either Biblical Hebrew or Aramaic. The manuscript has not been dated to an earlier time than this, or else the church has not said as much, but the book itself is inscribed with the date of AD 1522. Theorists claims it was copied in that year from a manuscript written in the 13th century or earlier.

The earliest known proof of it comes from the writings of one Honorius of Thebes, whose existence has not been undeniably proven; he may have been Pope Honorius III (1148–1227). Honorius of Thebes is believed to have written something now referred to as the *Sworn Book of Honorius*, from which the *Grand Grimoire* was derived, or which is, in fact, the *Grand Grimoire* itself.

The theory claims that Honorius was either Satan himself or was possessed by Satan for the purpose of writing the book. It contains instructions on summoning Satan at any time, at any place on Earth, for various insidious intentions. The word *Grimoire* denotes a textbook of magic, any kind of magic, whether good or bad. A great deal of so-called copies are in circulation around the world, but none of these, the conspiracy theory claims, contains the true words of the actual *Grimoire*. It is very popular in the voodoo culture of Haiti, and practitioners there claim to use the book all the time, like a cookbook for spells and hexes.

Theorists claim the *Grand Grimoire* is itself supernatural in that it permanently resists burning and cannot be cut, pierced, penetrated, torn, or in any other way damaged or destroyed. It is the only book with the knowledge of how to summon Satan (all others being fakes that don't work), with a precise ritual to be performed, and it can also summon any number of named demons (Pazuzu, from *The Exorcist* among them). Being written by Satan, it details proofs of various supernatural miracles of the Bible, the precise locations of Biblical relics, and even contains Satan's personal sketches of the faces of Judas Iscariot and Jesus Christ. The theory goes on to claim that because it is in the Catholic Church's possession, every pope starts out a human and then becomes possessed by Satan once he is elected.

The 1989 film *Warlock*, starring Julian Sands as the prospective Antichrist, uses the *Grimoire* as a major plot device, and goes even further, claiming that the *Grimoire* contains the secret name of God, which, when uttered backward, will annihilate the universe. This last quality of the *Grimoire* was most likely invented by David Twohy, who wrote the story for the film. But conspiracy theorists have championed the idea ever since, claiming that everything in this entry is based on provable facts and that these facts are in the *Grand Grimoire* itself.

So where is the *Grimoire*? You guessed it—in the Vatican Secret Archives.

TOP 10 Zombie Apocalypse Conspiracy Theories

by FlameHorse

10 Nazi Medical Experiments

It is no secret that Nazis, with their "perverted science," as Churchill phrased it, feature prominently in conspiracy theory origins. It is also no secret that Josef Mengele devised some awesomely grotesque, despicable experiments carried out on Jewish guinea pigs. He repeatedly broke children's limbs in the same place to see how long it would take before the bone simply would not heal. He performed irradiation of victims, then vivisections without anesthesia to study organ damage. He also liked to harm identical twins to study whether one felt the other's pain.

Conspiracy theorists—taking into account these surgeries, as well as Hitler's and Himmler's fascination with the occult and the supernatural—have concluded that there was a cooperative intent on creating zombies out of the captured Jews, Gypsies, and other Nazi prisoners. The conspiracy theorists believe that the Nazis intended to kill their bodies and most of their minds, leaving only the base functions of the cerebellum intact. Such people would serve two purposes: obeying the Nazis' every order without hesitation and showing the world the apparent inferiority of all non-Aryans. What the Nazis didn't finish, it is understood the U.S. government will, by drawing on Nazi research.

9 Dulce Base, New Mexico

The Dulce Base is held by conspiracy theorists to be a secret underground medical research facility operated in part by aliens, whom the government allows to do what they want in exchange for advanced technology. Their research involves creating animal hybrids, like the minotaur and the centaur, by sewing dead animal carcasses together and then resurrecting them.

This subset of the theory contends that the aliens are also manufacturing human zombies, like Frankenstein's monster, and that the government is, unbeknownst to the aliens, researching methods for growing either bacteria or a virus that can infect ordinary living humans and turn them into "the walking dead," as it were. The infectious bacterial agent ties in with several other entries on this list.

8 The U.S. Air Force's "Gay Bomb"

This is no joke. In 1994, the air force, possibly in conjunction with the CIA, spent $100,000 of taxpayer money researching the feasibility of using homosexuality as a weapon. Their concept was to spray female sex pheromones over an enemy army, which might cause the soldiers to lose control of their libidos and have sex with each other. The U.S. military would then be able to overrun them more easily.

When this hit the Internet, the air force was ridiculed, but before you join in the banter, consider the principle behind this fact. Theorists are of the opinion that this "gay bomb" proposal was desperately idiotic, as in meant to distract the public from even more taxes funding some other top-secret research program. If the U.S. military is willing to investigate the psychoactive effects of human sex pheromones, it is no longer a giant leap to the investigation of infectious, psychoactive bacteria or viruses designed to kill every part of a person except their cerebellar functions. And if word of this investigation leaked, the air force could always act the part of the idiots they would once again appear to be.

7 Weaponized Rabies

In the same vein as number eight on this list, theorists strongly contend that rabies is the virus whose effects on the central nervous system most closely match the popular concept of the zombie. It has been all but eradicated in most countries with modern medicine. But the government has stockpiled every disease that has ever existed in varying amounts. This is defended as studying disease mutations to prepare for the worst.

But if we have rabies vaccine stockpiles, why do we bother keeping the disease? There is only one known strain of the rabies virus, and it kills by only one method, inflammation of the brain (encephalitis). It is 100 percent fatal without treatment, and causes the victim to go insane in the lead-up to death. Violent acts may or may not occur, but the person is no longer himself. He is something else.

If it were possible to keep such a person alive, his brain damage would be irreversible and almost total. Only the cerebellum would remain unscathed. If the cerebellum is inflamed, the person dies. Thus, theorists claim, the very existence of stockpiles of this virus proves the government's intent to weaponize it, and the result can only be the complete "zombification" of human beings.

6 Recall of Troops from Abroad

This is an auxiliary theory to the imminent outbreak of the zombie virus. The government's official explanation for the recall of all American military personnel from hostile countries is the de facto end of war on terrorism. "We got bin Laden," they say. "Why stay any longer? The war's over. We win."

However, splinter cell terrorism is global and al-Qaeda, for one, still has its leaders, primarily al-Zawahiri. With Hamas and Iran as open, growing threats to Israel, the U.S. strangely appears to be abandoning its ally. The real reason for the American military's sudden return to full strength at home is, of course, hush-hush. It has to do with the government's knowledge of an infectious agent capable of killing and then reviving humans as mindless cannibals. The troops are abandoning foreign terrorism and being brought back in anticipation of the zombie virus escaping into an urban environment.

5 Government Ammunition Purchases

Earlier this year, the Social Security Administration started a media firestorm when they were discovered to be buying well over 200,000 rounds of hollow-point and Hydra-Shok pistol ammunition in a single purchase. The SSA has its own, self-governed police force paid to protect the SSA offices and personnel. Millions of citizens, especially those over 65 years old and therefore qualifying for social security, demanded to know why. It appeared that the SSA was preparing for a major incident of self-defense, but their official explanation was that their police force required ammunition to practice at gun ranges, and that the order had nothing to do with anticipating any impending disaster.

The public didn't buy this answer, remarking that ammunition for target practice is almost always full metal jacket, which is much cheaper. Hollow-point ammunition is about $1 per round. Hydra-Shok rounds are hollow points with extra barbs inside and are extremely expensive, averaging about $80 for a box of 50. The two rounds are designed for extra stopping power and are wasted on paper targets.

Conspiracy theorists, of course, make the next giant leap, claiming that e-mails were leaked to the SSA from another department of the government concerning an imminent danger of civil unrest. This will be precipitated by the collapse of the nation's infrastructure due to a compromise in the security of a military research program on infectious diseases classified above top-secret. It is understood that many departments of the government are making such preparations and that the SSA is the only one that has been caught doing so.

4 Transmissible Spongiform Encephalopathy

The most well-known type of this viral disease is nicknamed "Mad Cow Disease." There are thousands of strains of encephalopathy, and many can be transmitted to humans. Humans are very rarely infected—about one in a million per year—but the disease is 100 percent fatal and there is no known cure, vaccine, or treatment. The conspiracy theorists' claim is that the military has long been hard at work researching methods by which to infect enemy soldiers with any of a number of these encephalopathies. They all operate in the same way, deteriorating the tissue of the brain by eating tiny holes  through it. The brain eventually looks like Swiss cheese, and the person's mental state consequently degenerates into dementia and quite frequently aggressive violence. If the infection eats through the centers of the brain that control ethics, the person no longer acts like himself, but like a monster. The last part of the brain to be invaded is invariably the cerebellum, thus maintaining life for as long as possible.

And what does human-to-human transmission require? Only a bite.

3 Stem Cell Research

In a nutshell, stem cells can divide into any specialized cells and can automatically propagate more cells. Thus, they could, in theory, be used to cure incurable diseases, such as Lou Gehrig's disease, cerebral palsy, maybe even HIV; and most famously, they can be used to regrow nerve tissue, enabling quadriplegics to walk again. The latter has been a reality since 2003, when a simple injection healed a Korean paraplegic; within three weeks, she was standing and walking for the first time in 19 years.

But conspiracy theorists are quick to argue that thanks to stem cells, the leap to the undead is just a baby step, given the medical establishment's official boast of immortality by the 2030s. Theorists claim that stem cells are the final step in realizing the horror fantasy of Mary Shelley's *Frankenstein*. In her novel, the only two details missing from the operation to resurrect a dead body are how to reconnect nerve tissue and how to counteract brain death. A defibrillator can only revive a person if the brain's cells are still alive. To this end, the conspiracy theory goes that the government is actively researching the value of stem cells in reanimating dead brains.

If stem cells are injected into a dead brain, they can assume the form and operations of neurons, most importantly those of the cerebellum, which controls all involuntary functions of the body. Only the centers for walking and balance would be revived, enabling brain life while providing only a single effective target, meaning such a resurrected corpse could be shot in the heart and keep attacking. And if stem cells can be used to cure incurable diseases, theorists maintain that they can just as easily be used to create infectious diseases.

2 Haitian Zombie Powder

Here is a true story of a zombie, Clairvius Narcisse. He was born in Haiti in 1922. Details of his death or current whereabouts are not widely known,

but on May 2, 1962, he was found unresponsive in his home and presumed dead. He was buried but then exhumed by unknown parties as punishment for breaking a Haitian code of honor.

He was given regular doses of jimson weed, which causes extreme hallucinations and a form of hypnosis, under which influence the user will obey any order. Narcisse was enslaved on a sugar plantation until the owner and the witchdoctor controlling Narcisse died, after which he was given no more doses of the poison. He eventually regained his health and reunited with his family.

This is all fact. But no one is certain whether there is any combination of drugs that can render someone dead in all aspects except brain death. The general opinion is that a minute amount of bufotoxin and tetrodotoxin, derived from the cane toad and the puffer fish, respectively, halted all Narcisse's bodily functions except consciousness in his cerebellum.

Conspiracy theorists take this a step further, claiming that the government thought that these toxins in combination with jimson weed would be a great idea for a weapon, went on to fully develop such a weapon, and stockpiled huge reserves of it for the purpose of biological warfare.

1 The Miami Face-Eating Attack

On May 26, 2012, Rudy Eugene, a 31-year-old high school graduate with entrepreneurial ambitions, attacked Ronald Edward Poppo, a 65-year-old homeless man, at random on an on-ramp of the MacArthur Causeway in Miami under an elevated train. Eugene was seen by hundreds of witnesses and security cameras crossing the bridge from west to east in his car; at the east end, the car broke down. He began walking back across the bridge around 12 p.m., taking two hours to walk the three-mile span. The attack began at just before 2 p.m.

Without provocation, Eugene, having stripped himself completely naked while walking the bridge, tossed away his Bible and assaulted Poppo, who was lying on the cement. Eugene gouged out both of Poppo's eyes and stripped off his pants, then choked him into unconsciousness. He then ate Poppo's face, from the beard to the hairline, including one eye and his nose. This assault lasted 18 minutes and was filmed via security camera from the Miami Herald Building and posted on the Internet. A summoned police officer shouted at Eugene to stop; he growled in response and resumed. The officer shot him once in the upper back with a .40 S&W hollow point, a very powerful pistol round. This had no effect, so the officer shot him four more times, killing him.

The official autopsy listed marijuana as the only drug in Eugene's bloodstream, but his actions are inconsistent with marijuana's effects. The popular term "bath salts" was taken up by media around the world as the culprit. "Bath salts" is slang for cathinones, psychoactive stimulants similar to methamphetamines. They are more powerful than LSD and can cause a person to become instantly insane and superhuman, albeit at the expense of destroying the mind and a large portion of the body with only one use.

But the autopsy found no such drugs in Eugene's system, and then the story rather quickly faded into obscurity. Conspiracy theorists argue that the government immediately covered it up because they have created a drug or virus that will cause violent, cannibalistic behavior in anyone, no matter how responsible and self-controlled. This is the singular event that has, for most conspiracy theorists, cinched the zombie apocalypse as entirely real and very near.

The fact that Eugene's friends and family all testified that he was thoroughly even-tempered and sociable is a central tenet of the theory. An infectious agent was either accidentally released into Eugene's body or deliberately tested on him. All evidence of it was either untraceable or erased from the autopsy. Although he was not "undead" and Poppo has not yet shown symptoms of infection, this was just the first stage of a drug or virus currently under development as a weapon to create zombies.

TOP 10 Plausible Conspiracy Theories

by **Morris M.**

10 Scott's Antarctic Suicide

Robert Falcon Scott's race to the South Pole in 1912 was one of exploration's biggest screwups. Not only did his team fail to claim the Pole for

the British, they were pinned down by a ten-day blizzard on the way back and froze to death. Crappy luck doesn't come much crappier than that.

Unless, that is, there was no blizzard. In 2001, science writer Susan Solomon caused a stir by claiming the ten-day storm was impossible. See, Antarctic weather follows some pretty neat patterns: When cold air builds up above the continent, it creates a sort of "reservoir" that overflows, causing storms. When this "reservoir" is empty, the storms let up. In decades of measurements, this has never taken ten days.

Even more damning, any superstorm that hit Scott should have by rights continued on to the coast. Except another team was taking measurements at the same time and recorded no indications of a storm raging inland. So what happened? According to the theory, Scott was so upset about losing the race that he and his teammates committed suicide, filling their diaries with stories of an impossible storm to hide the dismal truth.

9 The Moscow Bombings

In 1999, a series of explosions shook Russia. Gigantic bombs planted by Chechen terrorists leveled entire apartment blocks and killed nearly 300 people. In the aftermath, Russia launched the Second Chechen War, and the rest is history.

Except for the theory in which the FSB (the descendant of the KGB) deliberately bombed its own people. Now, theories like this emerge in the aftermath of any tragedy, but for once there's actually some evidence to back it up. First, the terrorists denied any involvement in the attacks—an unusual response given typical terrorist desire to claim responsibility.

Second, high-ranking ex-FSB defector Alexander Litvinenko claimed it was all a cover-up. That's the same defector poisoned in 2006 with polonium-210, a death so unlikely under any other circumstance they might as well have carved "the Kremlin was here" into his chest. Add to that the suspicious assassination of a journalist who investigated the claim, and it's easy to see why this particular theory is still around.

8 Iran's Lockerbie Connection

In 1988 Pan Am flight 103 exploded in the skies over Scotland, killing everyone onboard and raining deadly wreckage down on the village of Lockerbie. Thirteen years later, low-level Libyan intelligence officer Abdel Basset al-Megrahi was convicted of the bombing and imprisoned. And there the case would have ended, were it not for the enormous pile of evidence indicating that the attack was really carried out by Iran.

In 1988, Iran was still reeling from a tragedy of its own: Five months earlier, the U.S. Navy had shot down a civilian plane carrying 290 Iranian citizens, killing them all. In the immediate aftermath, the Ayatollah vowed retaliation, promising "the skies will rain with blood," so the motive was there—as was the means.

Weeks before the blast, a group of Palestinian terrorists was arrested with four devices identical to the Lockerbie bomb. Intelligence reports indicated that the group had strong Iran links, and that a fifth device was "missing." Then there's Libya's lack of motive, coupled with the unlikelihood of a single intelligence officer, in this case al-Megrahi, being able to carry out such a complex attack under his own steam. So why didn't we pin this on Iran decades ago? The short answer is: No one knows.

7 Harold Wilson, Spy

Harold Wilson was twice-elected prime minister of Great Britain and a mild social reformer. According to some sources, he was also an undercover KGB agent tasked with...well, no one's actually sure.

What's interesting about this theory is that almost everyone believed it—and this certainly had some bizarre consequences. When a high-ranking Soviet defector claimed the prime minister was a Russian stooge, MI5 immediately opened a file on him. By the time 1974 rolled around, the military was so sure Wilson was a traitor that they came within months of staging a coup d'état backed by the royal family. According to the BBC and the *Guardian*, army brass planned to seize Heathrow Airport, the BBC, and Buckingham Palace and force the queen to read a speech asking people to support the new military junta.

And all to remove a prime minister who resigned for health reasons a few weeks later anyway.

6 Richard Nixon, Traitor

Nixon is probably the most unpopular president in U.S. history. Aside from once nearly putting a hit out on a journalist, he was also at the epicenter of one of the few scandals in history where the conspiracy theorists were probably right. And I'm not talking about Watergate.

The 1968 presidential campaign was fought on a knife-edge. The Vietnam War had become an abattoir for America's youth and everyone wanted it over and done with. So when the two sides came to the negotiating table in the dying days of Johnson's presidency, it looked like a great boost for the Democrats. Then, on the eve of the election, the South Vietnamese pulled out of the talks. Bummer, huh? Well, not quite: According to a cache of recently released tapes, Johnson was certain Nixon was involved. As in, Nixon had deliberately sabotaged the peace process and then lied about it to give himself an electoral advantage.

If this were true (and there's a ton of evidence supporting it), that would mean Nixon committed treason, sentenced hundreds of thousands of kids (both American and Vietnamese) to violent death, and wrecked the lives of millions more—all so he could be king of the castle.

5 Shergar's Disappearance

In 1983, a group of armed men burst into the Ballymany Stud in County Kildare, Ireland, and kidnapped the prizewinning racehorse Shergar. After loading him into a trailer, they drove off into the morning mist, and the horse was never seen again. So what happened?

There are a number of theories, but only one likely one: that the IRA killed him in a botched ransom attempt. While nothing's been proven, there's quite a bit of testimony. IRA informer Sean O'Callaghan claimed Shergar was kidnapped to raise money for arms, while a *Sunday Telegraph* investigation in 2008 reported that the Army Council had the horse machine-gunned and buried when they realized he was worthless. However, insurance companies have never paid out against the horse's death, and to this day his disappearance officially remains a mystery.

4 Lost Cosmonauts

During the Cold War, Russia and the Allies weren't exactly BFFs. For 50 years, both sides tried to hide their failures from each other, creating a climate where you couldn't be sure what was real and what was propaganda. So when a Czech agent leaked information about a failed Russian spaceflight in December 1959, no one knew what to make of it. According to the story, Yuri Gagarin's successful 1961 trip into orbit was only one in a long line of Soviet space attempts—and merely the first one that didn't end in the pilot's gruesome death.

Worryingly, there may even be some evidence to this. In February 1961—two months before Gagarin's flight—a listening station in Italy apparently recorded two Russian voices broadcasting the words "Everything is satisfactory, we are orbiting the Earth" from space. A few days later, they picked up another garbled transmission that sounded like a scream of terror followed by empty silence.

Two later recordings were also made, including one of three sobbing people saying, "Conditions growing worse, why don't you answer?…We are going slower… The world will never know about us…" So what were they? Clever fakes? Evidence that Russia abandoned irrecoverable cosmonauts to a horrifying fate? We may never know.

3 Prisoner X

In 2010, an inmate at a maximum-security Israeli jail hanged himself, triggering a flash flood of accusations, revelations, and bizarre conspiracy theories. Articles linking "Prisoner X" to Mossad, Hezbollah, and Australian Intelligence surfaced, alongside accusations of Israeli foul play. At the time of this writing, all we really know is that he was an Australian-Israeli called Ben Zygier and probably had links to intelligence operations. But that didn't stop *Der Spiegel* from advancing a theory so lurid it may just be true.

This conspiracy theory has it that Zygier was a former Mossad field agent who had been demoted to a desk job. Bored with his new life, Zygier set up a rogue operation to crack Hezbollah and win over his superiors. What allegedly happened next is full-blown Hollywood. An agent Zygier recruited from Hezbollah turned double agent, reporting back to Lebanese Intelligence. This in turn led to the arrest of several high-level Israeli spies in Arab nations, and a rush to find the mole at Mossad. All told, Zygier was allegedly responsible for the biggest information leak in Mossad's history, leading to a prison sentence so harsh he saw only one way out. Could such a pulpy story possibly be true? You decide.

2 CIA Drug Trafficking

The CIA doesn't exactly have the most level-headed history, so when talking about CIA conspiracy theories, you have to bear in mind there are literally hundreds of them. And some, like Operation Midnight Climax, are so well documented they're no longer really theories, so much as "the truth." So it's nice to know that even in our jaded modern era, they're still capable of shocking stuff.

In the mid-'90s, a three-part newspaper series called "Dark Alliance" briefly made shock waves throughout the media. Basically, reporter Gary Webb more or less accused the CIA of having connections with Nicaraguan drug dealers operating in the United States. In the resulting furor, Webb was smeared in the media and his claims that the CIA was deliberately getting African Americans hooked on drugs were dragged through the mud. Only, Webb wasn't claiming that at all. All he was doing was saying that the CIA was working with some pretty bad dudes down south—including guys who were running drugs on American soil—and that he had the proof. So what happened? The media hounded him to suicide, and everyone completely forgot about his earth-shattering story.

1 Pearl Harbor

Did he or didn't he? It's one of the biggest conspiracy questions that will ever be asked: Did FDR know Pearl Harbor was about to be attacked? There's a good deal of (inconclusive) evidence that the British-sympathetic FDR may have known the Japanese were on the verge of launching an attack and allowed it to happen—triggering America's entry into WWII.

Think about it: If this is true, his decision changed the course of history. Without American firepower, the Western front would have reached a stalemate at best—leaving the Russians to knock down Hitler single-handedly. Without an advancing Allied army to keep them in check, the Soviets could have run riot across Europe, placing millions more people under Stalin's control. There would have been no atomic bomb, no Operation Paper Clip giving the U.S. an edge in the space race…in short, the world as we know it would be completely unrecognizable. Now there's a scary thought.

TOP 10 Crazy Cinematic Conspiracy Theories

by **Nolan Moore**

10 Randy Quaid and the Star Whackers

The Hollywood Star Whackers are dangerous killers at the center of Hollywood's most evil conspiracy—at least according to Randy Quaid. The Golden Globe–winning actor and his wife, Evi, claim there's an evil organization out to murder Hollywood stars. Quaid claims the Whackers have knocked off Michael Jackson, David Carradine, Heath Ledger, and Chris Penn. They framed Mel Gibson and Robert Blake, and they might be after Britney Spears and Lindsay Lohan. And the Quaids are next. Evidently, Hollywood producers are sick of paying their actors exorbitant sums of money, so they hired the Whackers to take out the A-listers. That way, they can use unknown talent and won't have to fork over millions of dollars.

The most noticeable hole in Quaid's conspiracy is that Randy has never been what you might call a "star." Additionally, Santa Barbara District Attorney Anthony Davis believes the whole thing is a bizarre excuse to avoid some serious legal charges. The Quaids have been arrested numerous times for breaking and entering, squatting, burglary, and damaging property. To avoid paying their dues (or to escape the Star Whackers, depending on what you believe), the Quaids took off for Canada. However, as of January 2013, Randy was having a hard time applying for permanent resident status, probably because Canada doesn't want to deal with his craziness. Or maybe they don't want to mess with the Star Whackers.

9 The Clark Gable Cover-Up

During the 1930s and '40s, Clark Gable was the king of Hollywood. As one of MGM's top leading men, Gable won an Oscar for his performance in *It Happened One Night* and achieved immortality in *Gone with the Wind*. However, despite his big-screen success, Gable was a heavy drinker. After an all-night bender in 1942, he found his car wrapped around a tree on Sunset Boulevard. Fortunately for Gable, MGM representatives showed up before the reporters did, and they were able to whisk him off to a hospital where he sobered up.

Hoping to save face, MGM told the press that Gable had been forced off the road by another car. No one really believed them, and people began whispering about what really happened that night. The craziest theory was that a drunken Gable had run over some unlucky woman. Obviously, MGM didn't want its big star going to prison for manslaughter, so the head of the studio, Louis B. Mayer, made a deal with a lower-level MGM executive. If the exec took the fall for the woman's death, he'd have a job at MGM for the rest of his life and get a very nice raise. According to the story, the exec served a year behind bars, and Gable continued acting.

8 Errol Flynn Was a Nazi Spy

Errol Flynn was Hollywood's favorite swashbuckler, famous for films like *The Adventures of Robin Hood* as well as his wild lifestyle. Born an Australian, Flynn became a naturalized American citizen on the eve of World War II, but when he tried to join the military, he was turned down because of his weak heart. So instead of fighting, anti-Fascist Flynn made World War II movies such as *Objective, Burma!* and *Desperate Journey*.

However, biographer Charles Higham questions Flynn's patriotism. In fact, he claims that Flynn was actually a Nazi agent. Higham points to Flynn's friendship with the Nazi doctor Hermann Erben as proof. He also unearthed a letter Flynn sent to Erben in which the actor used the phrase "slimy Jews." Higham went on to claim that Flynn had a secret meeting with Hitler, used his fame to spy on German Communists, and filmed his 1941 movie *Dive Bomber* on a Californian naval base so the Japanese could have a good look at American defenses.

This conspiracy has an interesting twist. A professor from the University of Ulster discovered a letter from Flynn to the OSS asking to be made a spy. Flynn offered to use his family connection with the Irish Republic to help the Allies. However, FDR turned him down because even the president had heard the Nazi rumors and didn't want to take a chance.

7 Snow White Is about Cocaine

The Walt Disney Company has been the center of countless conspiracy theories, most of them about sexualizing children. However, some claim Uncle Walt also wanted to teach the kids about doing blow, and that he intended *Snow White and the Seven Dwarfs* to be a timeless classic about cocaine. The biggest piece of "evidence" supporting this theory is the characters' names: Snow White is slang for cocaine, and the dwarfs' names supposedly represent the different stages of addiction. First, users are happy, and then they start sneezing. Eventually, they get sleepy, and then they'll feel depressed or bashful. Then users will act dopey, and eventually they'll need to see a doc.

Not surprisingly, there isn't any real proof to back these claims. No one who knew Walt Disney ever claimed that he or his animators used recreational drugs. Even so, *Snow White* was released in 1937, and the big drug of the '30s was alcohol, not cocaine. So perhaps *Dumbo* was part of a conspiracy to have kids grow up to be alcoholics.

6 Bruce and Brandon Lee Were Murdered

Bruce Lee died of a cerebral edema when he was 32. In a sad twist of fate, he passed away right before his movie *Enter the Dragon* became an international hit. Twenty years later, his son Brandon died while filming *The Crow*. During a key scene, he was accidentally shot and killed by a fragment of a dummy round that had been lodged in the barrel of a prop gun.

It's not surprising that the Lees' deaths are surrounded by controversy. It's a situation ripe for a conspiracy theory: They were related, they were young, and they died before the releases of their most popular films.

There are two main theories as to how the Lees died. The first is that the Chinese Mafia murdered Bruce for sharing martial arts secrets with the world. After Bruce's death, Brandon picked up his father's mantle and had to be eliminated as well.

The second major theory involves the Triads, a group of gangsters associated with the Chinese film industry. Supposedly, the Triads wanted Bruce to star in some of their films. When Bruce turned them down, they whacked him. And because gangsters hold grudges, they killed Brandon too.

5 The Dark Knight Rises Is Very Dark

The Dark Knight Rises will always be linked to the tragic movie theater shooting in Aurora, Colorado. However, some conspiracy theorists claim that Christopher Nolan's third and final Batman movie actually foreshadowed James Holmes's murderous rampage as well as the Sandy Hook school shooting.

Three days after Adam Lanza's shooting spree at the Connecticut elementary school, YouTube conspiracy theorist "Dahboo7" uploaded a video claiming that signs of a government conspiracy were hidden in *The Dark Knight Rises*. According to Dahboo7, there's a skyscraper in the film bearing a sign that reads "Aurora." Later on, Commissioner Gordon (Gary Oldman) is looking at a map of Gotham, and at the bottom-left corner of the map are the words "Sandy Hook." So what's going on here? According to Alex Jones's website *Infowars*, *The Dark Knight Rises* was meant to precondition audiences to these massacres, and the shootings themselves were actually ritual sacrifices.

All of this is pretty creepy, but if you pause Dahboo7's video and analyze the Aurora Tower, it's covered in Chinese characters, and no scene in *The Dark Knight Rises* takes place in China. However, as another conspiracy website points out, a tower bearing the "Aurora" sign does show up in the trailer for *Skyfall*, which actually has scenes in China. Was this YouTube video less than genuine? Or was Daniel Craig also in on the shootings?

4 The Patriot Is a Right-Wing Warning

Most cinematic conspiracy theories deal with hidden Illuminati messages or Satanic subtexts, but Uri Dowbenko, author of *Hoodwinked: Watching Movies with Eyes Wide Open*, has a very different interpretation of *The Patriot*. Instead of claiming that Roland Emmerich's 2000 war epic contains some sort of evil code, Dowbenko believes that it's actually a warning straight from Mel Gibson to Big Brother.

The Patriot revolves around Gibson's character Benjamin Martin, a peaceful man who finds himself drawn into the American Revolution after British troops murder his son. Armed with a musket and a hatchet, Martin launches a campaign of guerrilla warfare against the redcoats. According to Dowbenko, Martin's war against the British army depicts what will happen if the government ever tries to disarm the American people. He also claims that when British troops murder innocent Americans, it's symbolic of tragedies such as the Waco siege. Evidently, *The Patriot* is a warning shot, declaring that the American people won't sit by and let the Illuminati take over. As Mel Gibson said in some other movie, you can take away their lives, but you'll never take their freedom.

3 Labyrinth Is about Mind Control

It's well known that from 1953–1975 the American government experimented with mind control through its notorious MKULTRA project. So if they've done it once, they might do it again, right? Enter Monarch Programming. Named after the metamorphosis of a butterfly, Monarch Programming is supposedly used to create brainwashed slaves. By using extreme torture methods, secret agencies can create sleeper agents like Sirhan Sirhan, who assassinated RFK. But the torture isn't just physical. Conspiracy theorists claim that handlers use movies to mess with their slaves' minds—movies like *Labyrinth*.

Labyrinth follows a young girl named Sarah (Jennifer Connelly) who navigates through a dangerous labyrinth in order to rescue her baby brother from the clutches of Jareth the Goblin King (David Bowie). According to conspiracy theorists, Sarah's kidnapped brother represents her "core persona," which is controlled by her handler. Her quest through the labyrinth thus symbolizes her programming. Along the way, Sarah goes through traumatic episodes designed to break her will. She meets the Fire Gang, a band of monsters who want to rip her head off. This symbolizes a slave's "dissociation from reality." Later, she must go through the Bog of Eternal Stench, a smelly swamp that obviously represents the torture technique of dunking slaves in feces. Finally, after eating an enchanted peach (which represents drugs), she imagines herself in a masquerade (Illuminati) ball, which she can only escape after shattering a mirror, a symbol of her fractured personality.

After returning home with her brother, Sarah is sad she left her friends behind in the labyrinth. She decides she still needs them in her life, and then they magically appear in her room. Sarah and her friends dance the night away, signifying that Sarah has accepted Jareth's programming. She's now a monarch slave who's eventually going to assassinate someone.

2 Cannibal Holocaust Was a Snuff Film

Conspiracy theories rarely leave the realms of Internet chat rooms, YouTube videos, and late-night talk shows. But their theories sometimes end up having real-world repercussions, and the prosecution of Ruggero Deodato for his role in creating *Cannibal Holocaust* is a perfect example. *Holocaust* is one of the most controversial films of all time thanks to its depictions of torture, gang rape, and castration. The movie also shows the actual killings of animals, including a monkey, a pig, and a turtle. Obviously, it's a bad pick for family movie night.

The Italian government seized *Cannibal Holocaust* after its release and arrested Deodato on obscenity charges. However, Deodato was in trouble for a lot more than just making torture porn. *Holocaust* contains a scene in which a woman is impaled on a stake, and the special effects were so realistic that Deodato was suspected of murdering his cast members. The director was then forced to explain what really happened on set. Deodato convinced the government of his innocence by bringing one of his "murdered" actors to court and by explaining the impalement scene. The girl had been sitting on a bicycle seat that was fastened to a pole while holding a piece of wood in her mouth. The court was satisfied, and Deodato was free to go, but his film wasn't. *Cannibal Holocaust* was banned in nearly 40 countries, but it went on to influence directors like Quentin Tarantino and kick-start the found-footage horror genre.

1 The Shining Is about the Apollo 11 Moon Landings

Some folks say that Stanley Kubrick's *The Shining* is about a lot more than just a guy with bad parenting skills. Some claim it's really about the Holocaust, while others say that Jack Torrance (Jack Nicholson) is really a minotaur. However, the craziest theory comes from the mind of Jay Weidner. According to Mr. Weidner, *The Shining* is really about how Stanley Kubrick faked the Apollo moon landings. It's a conspiracy theory about a conspiracy theory!

The story goes that the American government asked Kubrick to fake the Apollo 11 moon landings in order to intimidate the Soviet Union. After filming Neil Armstrong moonwalk across a Hollywood set, Kubrick realized he'd become an expendable accessory and was now in danger. So to protect himself and his family, he filled *The Shining* with clues about the conspiracy. For example, Jack Torrance agrees to watch over the Overlook Hotel during the winter just like Kubrick agreed to help America during the Cold War.

Also, *The Shining* is based on a Stephen King novel. In King's book, the infamous haunted room is number 217. However, in the film, it's room 237. Why did Kubrick change the number? Because the distance from the Earth to the moon is 237,000 miles! (Actually, the distance is really 238,857, but we're rounding down here for some reason.)

Weidner also claims that the creepy guy in a bear suit (it's actually a dog) represents Soviet Russia, and he notes that Danny Torrance is wearing an Apollo 11 sweater. Finally, the phrase "All work and no play makes Jack a dull boy" is really a code. The word "all" is really "A11" which is short for Apollo 11. There's so much evidence here it points to just one thing: Jay Weidner has seen *The Shining* way too many times.

TOP 10 Crazy Catholic Conspiracy Theories

by Nolan Moore

10 Orchestrating Jonestown

Everyone knows about Jim Jones and the People's Temple. The mass suicide at Jonestown left a huge impact on our society and has inspired movies, books, and even the expression "drinking the Kool-Aid." However, conspiracy theorists claim that the Jonestown Massacre wasn't the work of a madman but was actually a sinister Catholic plot. Jim Jones was supposedly a Jesuit deacon (a priest on special assignment) and, of course, a warlock. The Vatican ordered Jones to set up a small fundamentalist cult and lead them to suicide in order to discredit all small Protestant churches.

For proof, conspiracy theorists often point to Jones's association with Father Divine, a charismatic preacher who claimed to be the second coming of Christ. Divine preached a message of heaven on Earth and borrowed ideas from various denominations such as Pentecostalism, Methodism, and—you guessed it—Catholicism. Conspiracy theorists also point to his meetings with ("Jesuit-trained") California Governor Jerry Brown and First Lady Rosalynn Carter, suggesting that these were ploys to raise his profile so that one day the media would have an excuse to focus on his cult's destruction. With evidence like this, you know these guys are drinking something way stronger than Kool-Aid.

9 Creating Islam

Several Catholic conspiracies are based on the testimony of Dr. Alberto Rivera, a conman who claimed to be an ex-Jesuit and one-time Catholic spy. Infamous evangelist Jack Chick believed Rivera's story (despite the doctor's history of fraud) and printed it in comic book form. According to the Rivera/Chick tract "The Prophet," the Catholic Church created Islam.

"The Prophet" makes the wild claim that Muhammad was a Catholic stooge. The greedy Vatican wanted to get its bejeweled hands on Jerusalem due to its religious significance and location in the Middle East. So the pope dreamed up the craziest real estate scheme in the history of mankind. He would unite the Arabic people behind a Messiah and sic them on Jerusalem. The Vatican ordered a wealthy nun named Khadijah to marry a suitable young man and help him to form one of the world's largest religions and take over the Middle East. She soon found and married Muhammad and trained him in the ways of Catholicism. She taught him to hate pretty much everyone who wasn't a Catholic, especially Jews. In addition to training Muhammad, the Jesuits also spread legends about how a prophet would arise to lead the Arabs to great victories. After Muhammad received his divine revelations, Rivera claimed, the groundwork was laid for the Arab people to flock to the new religion of Islam.

After the death of Muhammad, the pope made a deal with the Muslim armies, agreeing to supply them with wealth and weapons in exchange for conquering the Holy Lands. However, after the Muslims took over Jerusalem, they decided to keep the city for themselves. Enraged, the pope called on the forces of Europe to march into the Middle East. Hello, Crusades.

Don't bother looking for the proof of all this, because you'll never find it. According to Rivera, Muhammad wrote about his Catholic connections, but these dangerous texts are kept safely in the hands of the world's most powerful ayatollahs. We'll just have to take Dr. Rivera's word on this one.

8 Assassinating Lincoln

Abraham Lincoln's death was really the result of a conspiracy. While the actual involvement of some parties is debated, John Wilkes Booth and eight others were found guilty of a plot to kill Abraham Lincoln, as well as Vice President Andrew Johnson and Secretary of State William Seward. However, this explanation wasn't good enough for Charles Chiniquy. An ex-priest turned anti-Catholic, Chiniquy's autobiography *Fifty Years in the Church of Rome* supposedly revealed the real reason for Lincoln's death. In his desire to see justice done, Honest Abe had crossed the Jesuits.

Chiniquy claimed that Catholic authorities framed him for slander in order to silence him from speaking about abuses taking place within the church. Wanting to clear his name, Chiniquy asked a young Mr. Lincoln to come to his aid. As the story goes, Lincoln successfully defended Chiniquy, thus earning the hatred of the Jesuits. However, actual records show that Lincoln was court-appointed and simply had the case dropped. Chiniquy also claims that the Vatican backed the Confederacy in order to overthrow the Union and establish a papal dictatorship. However, Lincoln kept getting in the way of their plans, so the Jesuits assembled a team of assassins and had Lincoln murdered.

To prove the Vatican's involvement, conspiracy theorists point to Lincoln's anti-Catholic quotes as recorded by Chiniquy in their private meetings at the White House. For example, Lincoln allegedly said, "It is not against the Americans of the South, alone, I am fighting, it is more against the Pope of Rome, his perfidious Jesuits, and their blind and blood-thirsty slaves, than against the real American Protestants, that we have to defend ourselves." However, Chiniquy was the only witness to these statements, which is pretty convenient.

7 Sinking the Titanic

Everyone knows that the *Titanic* sank in the cold waters of the North Atlantic, but according to conspiracy theorists, that is only the tip of the iceberg. Groups such as the Pacific Institute claim the Jesuits intentionally sank the *Titanic* in order to create the Federal Reserve Bank.

As the story goes, in 1910, representatives of the Rockefellers, the Rothschilds, and J. P. Morgan (all rich, all powerful, all members of the Illuminati) met to discuss the creation of the Federal Reserve Bank. The Jesuits planned to use this central banking system to finance their evil schemes of world domination. However, the Vatican knew their plan would be opposed by John Astor, Benjamin Guggenheim, and Isador Strauss, three of the richest men in the world. So, logically, these men had to die, and they had to die in the craziest way possible so no one would ever suspect foul play. The Jesuits ordered J. P. Morgan, owner of White Star Lines, to build the *Titanic*. Astor, Guggenheim, and Strauss were all invited to sail on the unsinkable luxury liner, unaware the voyage would mean their deaths.

The whole plot hinged on the actions of Edward Smith, captain of the *Titanic*. As the story goes, Smith was actually a "Jesuit temporal coadjutor," someone who has sworn his life to the Jesuit order. His mission from God was to intentionally ram the *Titanic* into an iceberg and kill everyone aboard. It didn't matter that many of the passengers were Catholic immigrants. In fact, the Vatican intentionally filled the ship with church members in order to deflect suspicion from the Jesuits.

Finally, on April 15, 1912, Smith made his move. He steered the *Titanic* into an iceberg, sinking the ship and drowning Astor, Guggenheim, and Strauss. The church's enemies had been eliminated, and by December 1913, the Federal Reserve System was in place. The Jesuits would now be able to finance their dreams of taking over the world.

6 Creating Communism and the Nazis

Divided over issues like the pope's authority, clerical marriage, and the doctrine of the Trinity, the Eastern and Western Churches broke apart in 1054, dividing into the Roman Catholic and Eastern Orthodox Church. According to conspiracy theorists, the Vatican had been nursing a grudge against its eastern rival ever since the split, and as the 19th century gave way to the 20th, it was time for some papal payback.

The Jesuits planned to stage a Communist coup in order to murder the patriarch of the Russian Orthodox Church and depose his protector, Czar Nicholas II. Key Communists like Marx, Engels, and Lenin were supposedly controlled by the Jesuits, and the Bolsheviks were supported by the

Federal Reserve Bank. After Lenin's ascension to power, the czar and his family were imprisoned and eventually executed by the Jesuits themselves.

However, the whole plot backfired thanks to the patriarch, who had learned the location of the czar's secret treasure trove. When the Bolsheviks finally decided to kill him, the patriarch greeted them with a smile and a big pile of gold. They were so happy that they decided to let him live, and the pope's scheme was thwarted.

When Communism failed, Rome dreamed up another –ism to crush its Orthodox opponents: Nazism. The Jesuits took wannabe artist Adolf Hitler and turned him into a dictator. They wrote his autobiography, *Mein Kampf*, financed his government with loans from the Federal Reserve Bank, controlled the Gestapo, and supplied the Nazis with crucial information gained from Catholic confessionals. They also set Mussolini up in Italy and Franco in Spain in the hopes that these three would rule the world in the name of the pope.

In addition to wiping out the Orthodox Church, the Jesuits also planned to persecute the Jews, though conspiracy theorists differ on why. Some suspect it was to keep the Jews from controlling Israel, while others think it was to force the Jews to return to Palestine, where they would get involved in a long war with the Arabs. The pope would then visit the Holy Land, unite the two groups, and be hailed as a hero. But just in case the Axis Powers lost, the pope hid over 1,000 Jews to cover his tracks.

Another alleged goal of World War II was to punish Japan. During the 1500s, the Japanese government expelled the Jesuits from its shores. According to one theory, the Catholic Church responded in a Christlike manner by having atomic bombs dropped on Hiroshima and Nagasaki.

5 Starting the Vietnam War

The Vietnam War was one of the longest and most controversial wars in American history. It was also a Catholic plot to conquer Vietnam, at least according to conspiracy theorist Avro Manhattan. Manhattan claimed that the church, led by Pope Pius XII, wanted to Catholicize Vietnam through Ngo Dinh Diem, the puppet president of South Vietnam. While it is a fact that Diem was a Catholic dictator, Manhattan alleges that Pius was the real power behind the throne and that he ordered the American military to keep North Vietnam from crashing the party.

However, after Pius's death, his replacement, Pope John XXIII, wasn't so worried about the Communists. According to Manhattan, Pope John thought that siding with the North was a safer bet, so he started making secret deals with Ho Chi Minh while keeping up the church's relationship with the South. Basically, regardless of who won the war, the Vatican was going to come out on top.

Conspiracy theorist Eric Phelps has a different take on the situation. Phelps claims that the Vatican viewed the Vietnamese as "unconvertible." Since they wouldn't give up their Buddhist ways, the Jesuits initiated an Asian Inquisition. On top of that, the Catholic Church is supposedly involved in the global drug trade via the Mafia. If the papacy could conquer Vietnam, which was a major source of narcotics, they could then flood America with illegal substances.

4 Assassinating Kennedy

We all know who killed Kennedy: Lee Harvey Oswald. Or was it the military-industrial complex? Or perhaps it was Fidel Castro or the Mafia or the Cigarette-Smoking Man. It's the most famous conspiracy theory of all time, so it should come as no surprise that someone, somewhere, believes that the Jesuits had a hand in President Kennedy's demise.

There are multiple theories about why the Vatican felt Kennedy was a threat. One idea is that Kennedy wanted to deescalate the Vietnam War, which would have ruined Rome's chances of creating a Catholic base in Asia and halted the flow of their drug money. Another is that Kennedy wanted to close the Federal Reserve, which would have deprived the Jesuits of their global domination funds. Yet a third theory claims that Kennedy was tired of being the Vatican's puppet, and that he was planning to expose the Jesuits' influence on the American government. Conspiracy theorists point to a speech Kennedy gave on April 27, 1961 (known affectionately in conspiracy circles as the "Secret Societies Speech"), in which he spoke of how America was "opposed around the world by a monolithic and ruthless conspiracy that relies primarily on covert means for expanding its sphere of influence." Could he have been talking about Communism? Nope. That's too simple.

Whatever the reason, the Vatican decided it was time for Kennedy to go. It didn't matter whether Kennedy was a Catholic or not. He had betrayed the Church. So the Jesuits picked Lee Harvey Oswald, whom some claim was a Roman Catholic, to be the fall guy. Working with the CIA and various other agencies, the Jesuits had Kennedy assassinated in Dallas, Texas. However, conspiracy theorists are divided on whether or not Lyndon B. Johnson was involved. Some claim that he didn't know a massive conspiracy was underway, while others say he ducked seconds before the bullets started flying.

3 World Domination

Almost all Catholic conspiracy theories center on the shadowy organization known as the Society of Jesus, aka the Jesuits. According to history, the Jesuit order was established by St. Ignatius of Loyola, a soldier turned priest. Jesuits are known for their missionary work and for establishing schools across the world, but despite their good deeds, the Jesuits feature in practically every conspiracy known to man. Even notable figures such as John Adams and Samuel B. Morse suspected the order of foul intentions. Of course, their involvement in actual conspiracies such as the Gunpowder Plot didn't help their reputation, but some theories about the order are so insane they sound like Dan Brown novels in hyperdrive. According to conspiracy theorists, the Jesuits' goal is global domination. Their priests are trained in the ways of the Dark Side and are taught skills such as hypnosis, telepathy, and levitation. The Jesuits also act as an umbrella organization for conspiracy theory bogeymen such as the Illuminati, the Council on Foreign Relations, the Mafia, the Club of Rome, Opus Dei, the Freemasons, international bankers, and the New Age movement. They also oversee companies like Coca-Cola, McDonald's, Disney, and Home Depot.

In addition to controlling a number of secret societies, the Jesuits also run the Vatican itself. According to most conspiracy theorists, the pope (aka the "White Pope") is just a puppet leader, taking his orders from the infamous "Black Pope." The Black Pope, so named because of his dark clothing (and evil powers), is an actual church leader known as the Superior General of the Society of Jesus. In real life, the "Black Pope" is only in charge of the Jesuits and nothing more. But why should we let reality get in the way of a good conspiracy theory?

2 Ordering 9/11

As an event, 9/11 has attracted no shortage of conspiracy theories, but the Catholic conspiracy is the craziest, because it involves every single baddie in the conspiracy theory book.

Author Eric Phelps alleges that Peter-Hans Kolvenbach (the Black Pope) ordered 9/11 to instigate a modern crusade. The basic idea was to start a war between America and the Muslims in order to destroy the United States as well as the Dome of the Rock and the Al-Aqsa Mosque, Muslim holy sites located in Jerusalem. After destroying these buildings, the Shriners (who are really the remnants of the Knights

Templar, a group that is no stranger to conspiracy theories) would rebuild Solomon's Temple in their place.

In order to bring down the towers, the Jesuits employed members of "CIA/Nazi-trained, Masonic Zionist Mossad" in addition to their "CIA/Nazi-trained, Masonic Islamic Intelligence Agencies." These Islamic agents enrolled in flight schools so the Catholic-controlled media could claim that the 9/11 planes had been hijacked by Arab terrorists when they had really been remotely guided by the NSA.

Phelps says the Jesuits picked the World Trade Center and the Pentagon as targets because they were actually Catholic institutions—the World Trade Center supposedly housed Vatican gold in subterranean bunkers, though it was moved into the Federal Reserve Bank before the attack. Finally, the towers were destroyed not by the planes but by C5 charges.

In response to the attacks, President George W. Bush, who was secretly controlled by the Council on Foreign Relations, declared a war on terrorism. This enabled America to invade the Middle East and begin the pope's new crusade. Of course, over a decade later, the Dome of the Rock and the Al-Aqsa Mosque are still standing, as is America. However, conspiracy theorists claim that the Jesuits succeeded in destroying the Constitution by crafting the Patriot Act. The Vatican might have failed to win Jerusalem, but they've forced Americans to endure long lines and strip searches at airports.

1 Preparing for Alien Invasion

As a Jesuit, Pope Francis is at the center of several crackpot conspiracy theories, but none of them is quite as nutty as the idea proposed by Chris Putnam and Thomas Horn in their book *Exo-Vaticana*. According to these guys, Pope Francis is getting ready to reveal the existence of extraterrestrial life. He hopes to convince people that these visitors are fellow Christians, as there are probably alien versions of Jesus on other planets. When the UFOs show up, Pope Francis wants Catholics to welcome their Christian brothers with open arms.

However, as anyone who has seen *The Twilight Zone* can guess, these aliens don't have our best intentions at heart. In fact, they aren't even really aliens. These otherworldly beings are actually demons that have been to our planet before. These creatures (known as "Watchers") once landed on Mt. Hermon, located on the Syrian-Lebanese border, took human wives, and fathered a race of giants known as the Nephilim. Fortunately, the Genesis Flood wiped out these hybrids, but now the Watchers are coming back for a second helping. With Pope Francis as their spokesman, most people will blindly accept their message of peaceful co-existence, only to be enslaved.

However, the authors claim that a few humans are going to see through their disguise, perhaps with the help of special sunglasses, and this is going to lead to an interplanetary war between those who worship the demons and those who don't. So remember to keep watching the skies: According to Putnam and Horn, the end is coming soon.

TOP 10 Laughable Conspiracy Theories

by **Morris M.**

10 Saddam Hussein Owned a Stargate

Stargate was a 1994 action movie about explosions and dimension-hopping aliens. The Iraq War was a 2003 military action that killed hundreds of thousands of people, the effects of which drag on to this day. Most of us would accept that only one of them really happened. But conspiracy theorists aren't most of us.

According to some websites, the real reason we flattened a Middle Eastern country had nothing to do with oil or removing a despot from power, but to get our hands on a Stargate personally owned by Saddam Hussein. The story goes that Saddam was in contact with the Anunnaki on planet Nibiru and was about to use the device to trigger an alien conquest of Earth when the New World Order intervened.

9 Horny Palestinian Schoolgirls

The strained relationship between Israelis and Palestinians understandably fosters paranoia. So it's not surprising to learn that conspiracy theories about Israeli involvement in Gaza abound. What might be surprising, however, is the form some of these theories take—like the one about Israel feeding Viagra to Palestinian schoolgirls.

In 2009, a Palestinian man alerted the authorities when his teenage daughter started, how shall we put this, acting like an adolescent just discovering her sexuality. The authorities traced the source of the complaint to a stick of gum allegedly bought across the border and decided that Israel was attempting to corrupt the territory's youth with sex-drive-boosting sweets. In other words, it was paranoid claptrap on an epic scale, yet some still continue to believe that Israel spends thousands of dollars each year with no other objective than to make schoolgirls horny.

8 Sandy Hook Was an Israeli Attack

Late in 2012, Adam Lanza took a gun into Sandy Hook Elementary School and proceeded to commit one of the worst atrocities in U.S. history. All told, 26 people died, including 20 children. In the face of such a pointless tragedy, some people thought it must be a conspiracy.

Chief among these soulless idiots was former GOP gubernatorial candidate Michael Harris, who claimed the massacre had been carried out by Israel as part of a revenge attack. Rather than just being a lonely, stupid kid, Adam Lanza was a fall guy whose corpse was used to cover up the involvement of Israeli death squads, while Obama (obviously) knew about the whole thing. Despite the idea that Israel would murder American children for an unspecified reason being literally insane, the theory continues to make the rounds both online and in the official Iranian press. As a concept, it's idiotic. As a response to the murder of 20 children, it's downright offensive.

7 "Occupy Wall Street" Is a Cult

Despite all evidence to the contrary, most of us like to think of ourselves as rational. So when a large group of people chooses to support a cause completely antithetical to our beliefs, we tend to assume they've been somehow brainwashed. Case in point: Occupy Wall Street is a mostly left-wing protest movement that hates capitalism. But that's not all it is. According to the paranoid far right, it's also a cult.

The idea goes that Anonymous (and evidently therefore Occupy) is secretly being run by a Canadian non-governmental organization as a corporate cult, with the intention of plunging the U.S. into civil war. As a sort of add-on, the organization is pushing hard drugs at Occupy meetings and has been hiring rapists to stalk the protests, because this is a conspiracy theory and doesn't have to make any sense.

What's interesting about this theory is that it's pretty much identical to one the far left has about the Tea Party movement—only replace "evil Canadians" with "the Koch Brothers" and "civil war" with "corporate dominance." In both cases, it's kind of de facto assumed that the people involved in these movements must be brainwashed, as there's no way any nonmanipulated person could possibly support anarchism/free market principles. In other words, this is less a conspiracy theory than a demonstration of our collective idiocy.

6 The Muslim Brotherhood Runs America

The Muslim Brotherhood is a group of extremists, currently being murdered in Egypt by an entirely different group of extremists. According to Michelle Bachmann, they're also infiltrating the American government with the aim of bringing Sharia law to U.S. soil.

Only 0.8 percent of the U.S. population identifies as Muslim, which makes Sharia law an unlikely prospect in America. I've also covered how "Islamification" is basically just the media's way of selling more papers. But even so, this theory scales whole new heights of ridiculous. For starters, the Muslim Brotherhood is a legitimate political party—when they want to influence government, they field candidates like everyone else. Second, they're not even capable of holding onto power after winning an election in a Muslim majority country (Egypt). Finally, the highest-ranking member Bachmann could "identify" in Congress was Hilary Clinton's aide. And if you seriously think Hilary Clinton's coffee-fetcher is the person who secretly runs America, then you've officially failed at understanding politics.

5 The CIA Created HIV

HIV needs no introduction; it's one of the biggest killers on Earth, a disease so powerful we still haven't found a cure. And a ton of people think the CIA created it to kill black people and gays.

These aren't just wingnuts, either. Former South African president Thabo Mbeki has publicly agreed with this theory. A Nobel Prize winner once used her speech to signify support for it. Literally dozens of people who are otherwise completely respectable have brought this up at one time or another, so how can we be sure it really is as crazy as it seems?

Well, there's the sheer number of experts who say otherwise, for one thing. For another, Snopes.com has actually traced the origins of this rumor—to a Soviet propaganda campaign. In 1985, the Soviet newspaper *Literary Gazette* published the first-known reference to the U.S. government's involvement in the AIDS epidemic. The following year, a medical conference in Zimbabwe used the reference as a jumping-off point for a paper on the subject. After that, the rumor went supernova. To this day, "black-ops" types still insist the U.S. was responsible for one of the worst viruses in human history.

4 Vaccinations Control Your Mind

Vaccinations are one of the great medical advances in history. Without them, we'd all still be dropping dead from smallpox and anthrax. So it stands to reason that conspiracy theorists are certain they're a ploy to secretly control our minds.

The basic premise of this nonsense is that vaccinations are really a means of filling you with nanotechnology that can alter your DNA and turn you into an automaton. If you've ever even been in the same room as a science textbook, you know that last sentence makes absolutely no sense. But periodic attempts to scare people off vaccines are happening all the time. In the UK, a conspiracy theory linking the mumps, measles, and rubella (MMR) vaccine to autism caused hundreds of parents to excuse their kids 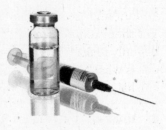 from getting the shot. The result? Repeated mass outbreaks of measles, a disease we'd nearly stomped out of existence beforehand.

3 The NESARA Law

Most of the theories on this list at least have some form of internal consistency. The NESARA conspiracy can't even boast that. At its most basic, the idea goes that Bill Clinton signed something called the National Economic Stabilization and Recovery Act into law just before he left office, only for the shadowy powers-that-be to hide it from the American people. So what was NESARA and what did it do? And why were the Illuminati (or whoever) so keen to suppress it?

Well, that's the beautiful part: NESARA is whatever anyone wants it to be. One website claims it wiped out all debt and guaranteed every American $100,000 a year for 11 years (have you seen your money yet?). Another website, on the other hand, claims it returned America to the gold standard and ordered the arrest of everyone from the president to all state governors and members of the judiciary. In other words, it's the pick 'n' mix of conspiracy theories—evidence that the government is stopping whatever you most want to happen from happening, all wrapped up in a handily meaningless acronym.

2 Hitler Is Still Alive

In the 1970s, there was a sudden flurry of "Hitler is still alive!" rumors that made the world sit up and pay attention. Nothing that looked even remotely like evidence was ever found, but it was technically plausible, at least compared to the other entries on this list. After all, the notorious death camp physician Josef Mengele lived in South America to a ripe old age, and it wasn't outside the realm of possibility that a geriatric Hitler might just be palling around with him down there. Unfortunately, this theory took hold to such an extent that some people continue to believe it to this very day.

Now, since modern-day Hitler would be literally the oldest person who had ever lived, this obviously poses some problems (the kind of problems that generally get solved with terms like "cyborg," "replicants," "New World Order," and "secret moonbase"). In other words, they don't get solved at all. Yet there remain websites out there that seriously link modern-day Hitler not only to 9/11, but to events such as the oil spill in the Gulf of Mexico. But guess what? Not only is this claptrap not the dumbest conspiracy theory on our list, it's not even the dumbest involving Hitler.

1 Jewish Leaders Deliberately Engineered the Holocaust

As anyone who has ever had to listen to one knows, racists aren't the most logical of people. So when a crazy anti-Semite comes out with a theory along the lines of "the Jews deliberately caused the Holocaust," sadly some people actually take notice.

The theory goes that an international cartel of evil Zionists planted Hitler in Germany with specific orders that he become a world-class douchebag and slaughter six million of their coreligionists. Just think about that for a minute. It's like an excerpt from the idiot's guide to casual racism: Take a group of people you hate, add a historical "bad thing," and try and claim the first group caused it. Only they've somehow missed the part where it needs to make any rational sense.

When you've gone this far down the conspiracy theory chain, there's really nothing you can say to change the minds of those who believe it. No matter how slowly and patiently you go over the historical evidence to suggest they're talking crap, they'll still insist that Jewish/Zionist bankers engineered the Holocaust, which didn't kill that many people anyway, simply to justify Israel's something-something-something anti-Semitism. That's it: If there's any conspiracy theory crazier than this one, I don't really want to hear about it.

TOP 10 Reasons the Moon Landings Could Be a Hoax

by **Josh Fox**

10 The Waving Flag

Conspiracy theorists have pointed out that when the first moon landing was shown on live television, viewers could clearly see the American flag waving and fluttering as Neil Armstrong and Buzz Aldrin planted it. Photos of the landing also seem to show it rippling in a breeze. The obvious problem here is that there's no air in the moon's atmosphere, and therefore no wind to cause the flag to blow.

Countless explanations have been put forward to disprove this phenomenon as anything unusual: NASA claimed that the flag was stored in a thin tube and the rippled effect was caused by it being unfurled before being planted. Other explanations claim the ripples were caused by the reaction force of the astronauts touching the aluminum pole, which is shown to shake in the video footage.

9 Lack of Impact Crater

The claim goes as follows: Had NASA really landed us on the moon, there would be a blast crater underneath the lunar module to mark its landing. On any video footage or photograph of the landings, no crater is visible, almost as though the module was simply placed there. The surface of the moon is covered in fine lunar dust, and even this doesn't seem to have been displaced in photographic evidence.

Much like the waving flag theory, however, the lack of an impact crater has a slew of potential explanations. NASA maintains that the module required significantly less thrust in the low-gravity conditions than it would have required on Earth. The surface of the moon itself is solid rock, so a blast crater probably wouldn't be feasible anyway, in the same way that an airplane doesn't leave a crater when it touches down on a concrete airstrip.

8 Multiple Light Sources

On the moon there is only one strong light source: the sun. So it's fair to suggest that all shadows should run parallel to one another. But this was not the case during the moon landing: Videos and photographs clearly show that shadows fall in different directions. Conspiracy theorists suggest that this must mean multiple light sources are present, implying that the landing photos were taken on a film set.

NASA has attempted to blame uneven landscape on the strange shadows, with subtle bumps and hills on the moon's surface causing the discrepancies. This explanation has been tossed out the window by some theorists; how could hills cause such large angular differences?

7 The Van Allen Radiation Belt

In order to reach the moon, astronauts had to pass through what is known as the Van Allen radiation belt. The belt is held in place by Earth's magnetic field and stays perpetually in the same place. The Apollo missions to the moon marked the first-ever attempts to transport living humans through the belt. Conspiracy theorists contend that the sheer levels of radiation would have cooked the astronauts en route to the moon despite the layers of aluminum coating on the interior and exterior of the spaceship.

NASA has countered this argument by emphasizing the short amount of time it took the astronauts to traverse the belt, meaning they received only very small doses of radiation.

6 The Unexplained Object

After photographs of the moon landings were released, theorists were quick to notice a mysterious object in the reflection of an astronaut's helmet from the Apollo 12 mission. The object appears to be hanging from a rope or wire and has no reason to be there at all, leading some to suggest it is an overhead spotlight typically found in film studios.

The resemblance is questionable, given the poor quality of the photograph, but the mystery remains as to why something is being suspended in midair (or rather, lack of air) on the moon. The lunar module in other photos appears to have no extension from it that matches the photo, so the object still remains totally unexplained.

5 Slow-Motion Walking and Hidden Cables

In order to support claims that the moon landings were shot in a studio, conspiracy theorists had to account for the apparent low-gravity conditions, which must have been mimicked by NASA. It has been suggested that if you take the moon landing footage and increase the speed of the film by 2.5, the astronauts appear to be moving in Earth's gravity. As for the astronaut's impressive jump height, which would be impossible to perform in Earth's gravity, hidden cables and wires have been suggested as giving the astronauts some extra help. In some screenshots, outlines of alleged hidden cables can be seen.

4 Lack of Stars

One compelling argument for the moon landing hoax is the total lack of stars in any of the photographic or video evidence. There are no clouds on

the moon, so stars are perpetually visible and significantly brighter than what we see through the filter of Earth's atmosphere.

The argument here is that NASA would have found it impossible to map out the exact locations of all stars for the hoax without being rumbled, and therefore left them out, intentionally falling back on an excuse that the quality of the photographs washes them out (a reason they did actually give).

Some photographs are high-quality, however, and yet still no stars are shown. Certainly eerie, considering you can take pictures of stars from Earth in much lower quality and still see them.

3 The "C" Rock

One of the most famous photos from the moon landings shows a rock in the foreground with what appears to be the letter "C" engraved into it. The letter appears to be almost perfectly symmetrical, meaning it is unlikely to be a natural occurrence. It has been suggested that the rock is simply a prop, with the "C" used as a marker by an alleged film crew. A set designer could have turned the rock the wrong way, accidentally exposing the marking to the camera.

NASA has given conflicting excuses for the letter, on the one hand blaming a photographic developer for adding the letter as a practical joke, while on the other hand saying that it may simply have been a stray hair which got tangled up somewhere in the developing process.

2 The Layered Crosshairs

The cameras used by astronauts during the moon landings had a multitude of crosshairs to aid with scaling and direction. These are imprinted over the top of all photographs. Some of the images, however, clearly show the crosshairs behind objects in the scene, implying that photographs may have been edited or doctored after being taken. Many objects are shown to be in front of the crosshairs, including the American flag in one picture and the lunar rover in another.

Conspiracy theorists have suggested NASA printed the man-made objects over a legitimate photograph of the moon to hoax the landings, although if they really planned on doing this, then why they used crosshairs in the first place is a mystery.

1 The Duplicate Backdrop

Two photos from the Apollo 15 mission clearly have identical backdrops, despite being officially listed by NASA as having been taken miles apart. One photo even shows the lunar module. When all photographs were taken, the module had already landed, so how can it possibly be there in one photo and disappear in another? Well, for hardcore conspiracy theorists, it may seem viable that NASA simply used the same backdrop when filming different scenes of their moon landing videos.

NASA has suggested that since the moon is much smaller than Earth, horizons can appear significantly closer to the human eye. Despite this, to say that the two hills visible in the photographs are miles apart is incontrovertibly false.

CHAPTER 3

CREEPY

1. Top 10 Most Morbidly Fascinating Places in the World

2. Top 10 Creepy Cave-Dwelling Cryptids

3. Top 10 Creepy Urban Legends from around the World

4. Top 10 Incredibly Spooky Things

5. Top 10 Lesser-Known Haunted Places

6. Top 10 Creepy Stories of Alleged Alien Encounters

7. Top 10 Terrifying Historic Medical Instruments

8. Top 10 Creepy Historical Vampires You've Never Heard Of

9. Top 10 Creepy Tales about Clowns

10. Top 10 Creepiest True Stories behind Movie Scenes

TOP 10 Most Morbidly Fascinating Places in the World

by **Caroline Coupe**

10 The Titanic's Cemeteries, Halifax, Nova Scotia

When the RMS *Titanic* struck an iceberg and sank on April 15, 1912, search-and-rescue teams from Halifax, Nova Scotia, were sent to assist with recovery. Many of the deceased (mainly crew members and third-class passengers) were laid to rest in Halifax following the sinking.

Fair Lawn Cemetery is the final resting place of 121 of the *Titanic*'s victims. Many of these names have become culturally significant, including a J. Dawson, whose name resembles a protagonist from James Cameron's film *Titanic*. But the most famous of these victims is the Unknown Child, a young boy whose identity was a mystery for 90 years. In 2007, DNA testing proved him to be 19-month-old Sidney Leslie Goodwin, a third-class passenger from England, whose entire family had also perished in the sinking.

Graves of *Titanic* victims can also be found in nearby Mount Olivet and Baron de Hirsh Jewish Cemetery. Halifax is also home to the Maritime Museum of the Atlantic, whose *Titanic* exhibit features items including the log of the ship's wireless messages, as well as one of the only surviving deck chairs from the doomed vessel.

9 Kehlsteinhaus (Hitler's Eagle's Nest), Berchtesgaden, Germany

Kehlsteinhaus was built on a mountain peak as a 50th birthday gift for Adolf Hilter on April 20, 1939. It was intended as a retreat and a place to entertain dignitaries. The chalet was incredibly opulent, and cost the modern-day equivalent of $115 million. It can be reached by a 400-foot elevator shaft drilled through the mountain itself, a tunnel that cost 12 workers their lives during its construction. Hitler is thought to have only visited Kehlsteinhaus 14 times over the years, preferring his nearby residence of Berghof.

In May 1945, less than a month after Hitler's death, Allied troops took the Eagle's Nest. The soldiers helped themselves to the contents of the wine cellar, and many chipped away pieces of the marble fireplace (a gift from Mussolini) as souvenirs.

The building is currently owned by a trust and used for charitable purposes. You can even go on tours of the lower rooms, where graffiti left by Allied soldiers can still be seen on the wood paneling.

8 Cele Kula (The Skull Tower), Nis, Serbia

The city of Nis in the south of Serbia was the site of the First Serbian Uprising against the Ottoman Empire. In 1809, the rebels were facing certain defeat when 36,000 Turkish soldiers invaded the city—but rather than submit, rebel leader Steven Sindelic fired his weapon into his own powder kegs, causing a powerful explosion and killing both his own soldiers and the invading forces.

In retaliation, furious Turkish commanders constructed Cele Kula, or "The Skull Tower." They desecrated the bodies and built 952 skulls into a 15-foot tower at the entrance to the city, with Sindelic's skull placed at the top. The skin from the skulls was stuffed and sent to Istanbul as proof of the victory.

Over the years, many of the skulls were removed by relatives for burial, and only 58 remain in the tower today. In 1892, a chapel was built around the site in order to preserve it. The tower did not prove to be as much of a deterrent as the Turks had hoped: The Serbs rebelled again in 1815 and gained independence 15 years later.

7 Atomic Bomb Museum, Nagasaki, Japan

The Atomic Bomb Museum is located right atop ground zero—the place where, on August 9, 1945, the second nuclear weapon ever used in war was detonated above a civilian population, instantly killing 74,000 people and injuring thousands more. It's a small but powerful building that highlights the effects this act had on the people of this Japanese city. Heart-wrenching photos of victims and videos of survivors' stories are the main exhibit. Among the other moving artifacts are eyeglasses with the lenses melted out, the rice from a child's lunch box fused into  a blackened ball, and a clock stopped at 11:02 a.m.—the precise moment of the explosion.

Many of the items are difficult to look at, and that's the point. From the museum, you can descend the outer stairs to the bomb's hypocenter, which is represented by a black stone pillar overlooked by a statue of an angel. Several other sculptures around the site, as well as thousands of colorful paper cranes made by the public, reinforce the theme of world peace.

6 Kaisergruft Imperial Crypt, Vienna, Austria

The Imperial Crypt beneath the Capuchin Church in Vienna is the resting place of most of the Hapsburg Royal family. It opened in 1633, and all but three of the Hapsburgs rest there, including 12 emperors and 19 empresses and queens. Many of the bronzed coffins are incredibly ornate, carved with angels, skulls, and crowns. The most opulent of these is the huge double sarcophagus of Empress Maria Theresa and her husband Franz Stefan, which sits under a sky-lit dome hand-painted with cherubs.

Perhaps the most famous remains belong to Emperor Franz Josef and his wife Elisabeth, known as Sisi, who were widely beloved by the Austrian people. Sisi was assassinated in Geneva, Switzerland, by an Italian anarchist in 1898. The site is looked after by Capuchin monks, and burials still take place in the crypt. The most recent additions were Otto von Hapsburg and his wife in 2011.

5 The Morbid Anatomy Library and Museum, Brooklyn, New York

Morbid Anatomy is a collection of macabre and bizarre curiosities "dedicated to the places where death and beauty intersect." Started in 2008 by fans of the unusual artist Joanna Ebenstein, the museum exhibits medical specimens, taxidermied animals, and a variety of creepy artifacts, books, and artworks. It also features photos of other morbid collections around the world (taken by Ebenstein herself) and classes in the arcane, the taxidermic, and the anatomical. In these classes you can create a shadowbox featuring a rhinoceros beetle in the scene of your choice, a stylish and wearable hat made from chicken parts, or even a diorama of stuffed mice in tiny costumes.

4 The Ruins of Pompeii, Naples, Italy

In Roman times, Pompeii was an elegant resort town, hosting distinguished citizens seeking sun and relaxation. But when Mount Vesuvius erupted

in AD 79, it rained ash for six straight hours, burying the town and killing everyone living there. The ash had the strange effect of preserving everything in Pompeii, leaving much of the city's history frozen in time.

Almost 2,000 years later, you can roam the streets of this once-vibrant city, enter its buildings, and study its artworks and artifacts. The most eerie sights here are the casts of some of Pompeii's estimated 2,000 citizens, which were made by pouring plaster into the hardened ash shaped by their bodies where they fell. Many of these victims have their arms outstretched in a desperate and futile attempt to save themselves from the debris. In the Garden of the Fugitives, you can find a row of these figures, including those of several children, huddled against a stone wall in a failed attempt to flee the destruction.

3 Truk Lagoon, Chuuk Islands, Micronesia

On August 17, 1944, Allied forces launched Operation Hailstorm, an attack on Japanese troops based in the waters of Micronesia. More than 50 ships and 240 aircraft were sent to the bottom of the sea, along with 3,000 people. Today, it is a spectacular and eerie underwater graveyard.

Most of the wreckage is still intact, and some sits only 15 feet below the water's surface, making the site incredibly popular with divers and even snorkelers. Tanks, railroad cars, motorcycles, radios, and a variety of weapons and munitions can all be found in the hold of the sunken cargo ships. Up on deck, gas masks and depth charges lay undisturbed, while down below there are even human remains.

2 Akodessewa Fetish Market, Lome, Togo

This Akodessewa Fetish Market in West Africa supplies everything you may need to practice voodoo—and it just might be the creepiest market on Earth. From crocodile heads to monkey paws, the items piled high on the tables here include animal parts of every description.

Followers of voodoo believe that these items can act as remedies to any problem, from infertility to a lack of athletic prowess. Medicine is made by crushing up animal skulls, mixing them with herbs, and reducing them to a black powder—which is then rubbed into three cuts made on the patient's back or chest. For many, it's a last resort when all else fails.

But if you're not into getting skull powder rubbed into your flesh, you can always pick up a nice, simple talisman for protection.

1 Body Farm, University of Tennessee, United States

While its official name is the University of Tennessee Anthropological Research Facility, it's far more commonly known as a body farm—and that alone puts this morbidly interesting location at the top of the list.

The Knoxville body farm sits on a 2.5-acre lot, which is strewn with up to 40 bodies at any given time. These corpses are left to the elements while the rate of decomposition and the effects of factors like weather and insect activity are carefully monitored. Bodies can be left aboveground, buried, underwater, or even in the trunk of a car in order to simulate various circumstances. The facility is also used as a training ground for crime scene investigation techniques. Surprisingly, the body farm is not short on volunteers, with over 1,300 people registering themselves for participation.

TOP 10 Creepy Cave-Dwelling Cryptids

by Andrew Handley

10 Tsuchinoko

Located deep in the mountainous regions of Western Japan, the Tsuchinoko is a creature straight out of Japanese folklore. Resembling a thick-bodied snake that grows to several feet in length, Tsuchinokos are believed to inhabit the watery caves of Shikoku and Honshu. They're usually seen in the rivers and streams that crisscross the mountains, but most sightings are only a glimpse before the creature darts back into the depths.

Descriptions vary, but most witnesses report many of the same features: large, platelike scales, a black tongue, small horns growing on the sides of its head, the ability to leap more than a meter at a time, and perhaps the most unusual feature of all—a variety of vocal noises that range from squeaking like a mouse to mimicking a human voice. To top it all off, Tsuchinokos are supposed to have fangs capable of shooting venom at their attackers.

The town of Mitaka claims to have captured one, but they also haven't taken any steps to verify its authenticity, so it remains a cryptid for the time being.

9 Cherufe

According to legend, the Cherufe is a beast made of fire and rock that lives in the volcanoes of Chile. Twelve feet tall and shaped like a vaguely reptilian human, the Cherufe of myth is believed to be an actual creature—one that has evolved to withstand the normally lethal temperatures of a volcano, much like the tube worms that cluster around volcanic vents on the sea floor, basking in temperatures surpassing 750°F.

Other people believe that while the Cherufe cryptid doesn't actually live inside volcanoes, it does live around volcanic regions, which led to the connection to the mythological beast. In the Mapuche myths, the Cherufe was responsible for volcanic eruptions and could be placated with a virgin sacrifice.

8 Grootslang

In the Northern Cape province of South Africa is an arid, mountainous wasteland called the Richtersveld. Somewhere in this vast desert is what the locals refer to as the Bottomless Pit—a massive cave system that has never been fully explored. At night, a cryptid known as the Grootslang is supposed to emerge from the cave and lure prey back into its lair. Shaped like a monstrous elephant with the tail of a snake, the Grootslang feeds on trespassers and fiercely guards a stash of thousands of diamonds and gemstones.

The most popular story about the Grootslang comes from the escapades of British explorer Peter Grayson. In 1917, lured by the stories of diamonds in the Bottomless Pit, Grayson took a small team of men to find the cave. On the journey to the cave, tragedy struck: Two of his men were killed by a lion, one was bitten by a venomous snake, and another became sick. The final two team members carried the sick man back to the nearest town, leaving Grayson alone to continue the quest. He was never heard from again, and locals came to believe he had been killed by the Grootslang.

Modern sightings of the beast suggest that it may be a massive python— eyewitnesses claim that they have seen an animal resembling a snake, but 50 feet long. Another witness claims to have found mysterious footprints a meter wide that eventually disappeared at the edge of a river.

7 J'ba Fofi

Stories of giant spiders come from all over the world, but the most famous one is the J'ba Fofi, a massive arachnid that's believed to live deep in the African Congo. The largest-known spider is the Goliath spider, with a legspan of 14 inches. That's long enough to make most grown men shiver. But the J'ba Fofi is supposed to be several times that size, with a four-foot legspan in most cases, and eight feet according to at least one report.

According to a tribe of pygmy people indigenous to the region, the giant spiders will spin large, circular webs at ground level and crouch in the middle of them, eating birds, rodents, even forest antelope. Other stories say the spiders dig holes in the ground with a hinged trapdoor, like Ctenizidae spiders. And the stories aren't centralized in one region—similar stories have come from tribes in Uganda to the east and the Central African Republic to the north.

Tales of giant spider cryptids aren't specific to Africa either. In 2011, a filmmaker named Richard Terry was told of giant four-foot-wide spiders living in deep holes in the Amazon jungle.

6 Reptilians

If David Icke is to be believed, Reptilians are shape-shifting, humanoid lizards from space that have infiltrated the top levels of government and are even now impersonating our world leaders. Dick Cheney has been called a Reptilian, as have George W. Bush and Barack Obama.

While Reptilians are able to change their shape to resemble humans, conspiracy theorists also believe that they have a vast underground civilization. One eyewitness reports a subterranean encounter in 1995 with a group of cavers in Missouri: "This 'creature,' because it was not a man, stood about 7 foot and had brown scaly skin. The face and head were shaped like a human with a flat nose but there were no ears or hair... It also had a massive 4–5 foot tail that tampered (sic) to a point. It was dressed in a gold metallic outfit with long pants and shoes."

Other people have since claimed to have run across strange, Reptilian creatures in caves. One person supposedly managed to take a picture of the creature.

5 Melon Heads

In the northern United States, specifically rural areas throughout Ohio and Michigan, small creatures with elongated heads called Melon Heads have been reported attacking people in the woods. According to the stories (which are all eerily similar), the Melon Heads were once orphans with hydrocephalus, a condition in which fluid builds up in the skull, who lived in an insane asylum.

Through various circumstances—escaping from the asylum, murdering their doctor, becoming cannibals after the asylum burned down—the children turned feral and took to living in a system of underground caverns deep in the woods. What's interesting is that reports have come from vastly different geographic regions across state borders, and the legend in each state begins some version of the asylum story. There are dozens of reports from people who claim to have been attacked by bands of small, misshapen creatures with bulbous heads.

4 Minhocão

The Minhocão is a giant earthworm that's rumored to live in the Amazon jungle. While the word "earthworm" may not exactly be nightmare fuel, "giant" in this case truly means giant—the Minhocão is supposed to be somewhere close to 75 feet long, much larger than the deadly carnivorous worms from the Tremors film trilogy. And much like those movie monsters, the Minhocão burrows through the earth and attacks from below, leaving giant tunnels in its wake. Reports of collapsed houses have been blamed on the Minhocão, along with the mysterious disappearances of cattle.

According to Karl Shuker, a cryptozoologist, the Minhocão (if it exists) is more likely a caecilian than an earthworm. Caecilians are amphibians that resemble overgrown worms, except for the fact that they have eyes— and teeth. People who claim to have seen the Minhocão say that it has massive teeth, black skin covered in scales, and two tentacles protruding from its head. There haven't been any Minhocão sightings for over 100 years, so if there was an enormous underground worm lurking under the Amazon at some point, it's probably dead by now.

3 Olitiau

Often described as a "cave demon," the Olitiau is an elusive giant bat with a wingspan of 12 feet, a black body, blood-red wings, and two-inch serrated teeth. There are stories of these bats from the local tribes in the forests of Cameroon, in West Africa, but the first story to reach the Western world came from the biologist Ivan T. Sanderson in 1932. Sanderson was studying hammer-headed fruit bats, another large bat species, when he was attacked by the largest bat he had ever seen, with wings more than four times as large as a hammer-headed bat's.

When Sanderson reported his encounter to the native guides he was with, they became excited and attributed it to what they called the Olitiau, which is a combination of the words *ole* and *ntya*, and which they named after a type of ceremonial mask that was carved in the shape of a demon. According to them, the Olitiau lived in nearby caves and came out at night to feed. There have been no other reported sightings.

2 Ahool

While we're on the topic of giant batlike cryptids, we have to mention the Ahool, which has been spotted several times in the Java rainforests of Indonesia. Like the Olitiau, the Ahool is massive—reported to have a ten-foot wingspan with giant claws at the ends of its forearms. The Ahool was first documented in 1925 by a naturalist named Dr. Ernest Bartels, who watched the giant bat emerge from behind a waterfall near dusk. He named it based on its distinctive cry, a long "ahooool" as it flew overhead.

Two years later, Bartels heard the creature again. He pulled together a search party and rushed out into the jungle to find it. It's been suggested that the Ahool is really a large owl, but everyone who saw it claimed that it was definitely a batlike creature, not a bird. Other theories are that it is a flying primate, and even a living pterosaur that managed to remain secluded from the world deep in the nearly impenetrable Indonesian rainforest.

1 Tatzelwurm

The Tatzelwurm is one of the most famous European cryptids—a lizardlike animal that looks something like a dragon but with a row of spiked ridges running down its back and a cat-shaped head. The first sighting of the Tatzelwurm was in 1779, when a man claimed that the creature jumped out in front of him, scaring him so badly that he had a fatal heart attack (how he reported the story after dying is anyone's guess).

More and more people began seeing the Tatzelwurm throughout the 19th and early 20th centuries, providing similar reports in most cases: The animal was about seven feet long, with razor teeth, a short neck, and a short, blunt tail. Some people even said the Tatzelwurm bit them. In Germany, the cryptid is named the *Stollenwurm*, which means "worm that lives in holes" because it's believed to hibernate in mountain caves during the winter.

The most recent sighting was in 2009, when a research assistant near the border of Switzerland and Italy claimed that she saw it running by on two legs, like a "prehistoric velociraptor." Is it real? What do you think?

TOP 10 Creepy Urban Legends from around the World

by **Theodoros II**

10 The Choking Doberman

This urban legend comes from Sydney, Australia, and features a bizarre story involving a choking Doberman dog. One night, a couple who had been out for a few too many drinks came home to find their dog choking in the living room. The man panicked and fainted, but the woman decided to call a vet and arranged to drop the dog off at the vet clinic.

After dropping off the dog, she decided to go home and get her husband into bed. It took her a while to do this, and in the meantime, the phone rang. The vet screamed hysterically that they needed to get out of the house immediately. So without any clue as to what was going on, the couple left the house as quickly as possible.

As they came down the stairs, several policemen ran up to meet them. When the woman asked what the problem was, a policeman gently told her that the dog was choking on a man's finger. A burglar must still be present in their home. Soon enough, the former owner of the finger was found unconscious in the bedroom.

9 The Suicidal Boyfriend

This story, also known as "The Boyfriend's Death," has many variations and has been interpreted as a more generalized warning not to stray too far from the safety of home. This version takes us to Paris in the 1960s. A girl and her boyfriend—both of them college students—were making out in his car. They were parked near the Forest of Rambouillet so that they wouldn't be seen by anyone. After a while, the boy got out to smoke a cigarette, and the girl waited for him in the safety of the car.

After waiting for five minutes, the girl got out of the car to look for her boyfriend. Suddenly, she saw a man in the shadows. Frightened, she got back into the car to drive away—but as she did this, she heard a very faint squeak, followed by more squeaks.

This continued for a few seconds, until the girl decided that she had no choice but to drive off. She hit the gas as hard as possible, but couldn't go anywhere; someone had tied a rope from the bumper of the car to a nearby tree.

Finally, the girl slammed on the gas again and then heard a loud scream. She got out of the car and realized that her boyfriend was hanging from the tree. It turned out that the squeaky noises were made by his shoes, scraping across the top of the car.

8 The Slit-Mouthed Woman

There is a legend in Japan and China about a girl called Kuchisake-Onna, also known as the slit-mouthed woman. Some say that she was a samurai's wife. One day, she cheated on her husband with a younger and better-looking man. When the husband returned, he discovered her betrayal; enraged and furious, he took his sword and slit her mouth from ear to ear.

Some say that the woman was cursed to never die and still wanders the world so that people can see the horrible scar on her face and pity her. Others claim to have actually seen a very beautiful young lady, who asked them, "Am I pretty?" And once they replied positively, she ripped off a surgical mask, and showed them her horrible wound. She then asked the same question—and anyone who no longer found her pretty was met by tragic death at her hands.

There are two morals to this story: A compliment won't cost you a thing, and honesty isn't necessarily the best policy.

7 Crybaby Bridge

According to this legend, a couple was driving home from church with their baby, arguing about something. The rain was falling in torrents, and they soon found themselves having to drive over a flooded bridge. As they started across, the water was deeper than they first thought, so they got stuck and decided to find help. The woman stayed behind, but left the car for reasons we can only guess at.

While her back was turned to the car, she heard her baby crying out loudly. She returned to the vehicle, only to find that her baby had been carried away by the water. According to the same legend, if you go to that same bridge, you can still hear the baby crying (the bridge's location is conveniently unknown).

6 Zanfretta's Alien Abduction

Fortunato Zanfretta's abduction story has become one of the most famous urban legends in Italy over the last few decades.

According to his own accounts (originally made while under hypnosis), Zanfretta was abducted by aliens called Dragos from the planet Teetonia and experienced repeated abductions by the same group over a period of several years (1978–1981). As frightening or creepy as this case might sound, it seems like we can paint a more optimistic picture of the intentions of these visitors when we consider the words of Zanfretta during one hypnosis section:

> "I know you are trying to come more frequently…no, you can't come to Earth, people get scared if they look at you. You can't make friendship. Please go."

Zanfretta has probably given more details about his alien abduction than any other person in history; his detailed accounts may give even the most vehement skeptic pause. To this day, the Zanfretta case remains one of the most curious and fascinating "X-files" around the world.

5 The White Death

This is a story about a little girl in Scotland who hated life so much that she wanted to destroy every last trace of herself. She finally decided to commit suicide, and shortly afterward, her family found out what she'd done.

In a horrible twist, every member of her family died only a few days later too, their limbs torn apart. The legend says that when you learn about the White Death, the girl's ghost might come and find you and knock repeatedly on your door. Each knock gets louder until you open the door and she kills you for fear that you'll tell someone else of her existence; her main goal is to prevent anyone from knowing about her.

Like most urban legends, the story is probably nothing more than the wild imagination of a modern Aesop—but all the same, it's always good practice to find out who's standing behind the door before you answer it.

4 The Black Volga

A black Volga automobile was supposedly spotted frequently in the streets of Warsaw back in the 1960s, packed with kidnappers who were bent on snatching children. According to the legend (and helped along by propaganda, no doubt) high-ranking Soviet officials drove the black Volga in Moscow during the mid-1930s, kidnapping young, pretty girls for the sexual pleasure of the highest-ranking Soviet comrades. Another version of this legend tells us that vampires, mysterious priests, Satanists, body venders—and even Satan himself—drove the black Volga car.

According to different versions, children were kidnapped with the intention of using their blood as a cure for wealthy leukemia sufferers around the world. Of course, none of these versions were ever found to be true.

3 The Greek Soldier

This lesser-known legend tells us of a Greek soldier who, after WWII, was returning home to marry his fiancée. Unfortunately for him, he was captured by fellow Greeks who had hostile political beliefs, tortured for five weeks, and eventually murdered. In the early 1950s—mainly in north and central Greece—there were stories about a very attractive Greek soldier in uniform who appeared and disappeared overnight, seducing beautiful widows and virgin girls with the sole purpose of impregnating them.

Five weeks after the babies were born, the man would disappear for good—leaving a letter on the table explaining that he had returned from the dead merely to spread his seed, so that his sons might avenge his murder.

2 Elisa Day

In medieval Europe, there apparently lived a young woman named Elisa Day, whose beauty was like that of the wild roses that grew down the river. One day, a young man came into town and instantly fell in love with Elisa. They dated for three days. On the first day, he visited her at her house. On the second, he brought her a single red rose and asked her to meet him where the wild roses grow. On the third day, he took her down to the river—where he killed her.

The horrible man supposedly waited till her back was turned, then took a rock in his fist, whispering, "All beauty must die"—and with one swift blow, he killed her instantly. He placed a rose between her teeth, and slid her body into the river. Some people claim to have seen her ghost wandering the riverside, blood running down the side of her head, a single rose in her hand.

1 The Well to Hell

Sometime in 1989, Russian scientists in Siberia drilled a borehole some 14.5 kilometers deep into the Earth's crust. The drill broke through into a cavity, and the scientists lowered some equipment to see what was down there. The temperature was more than 1,8000°F—but the real shocker was the sound recorded by their instruments.

They only captured about 17 horrifying seconds of audio before the microphone melted. Convinced that they'd heard the screams of the damned in hell, many of the scientists quit the job immediately—or so at least the story goes. Those who stayed were in for an even bigger shock later that night. A plume of luminous gas burst out of the borehole, the shape of a gigantic winged demon unfolded, and the words "I have conquered" in Russian were seared into the flames. Even though today it is considered to be a hoax, there are many who believe that this incident really happened; the "Well to Hell" urban legend remains alive to this day.

TOP 10 Incredibly Spooky Things

by **Gareth May**

10 The Ghost Cane

Would you pay $65,000 for a metal walking cane? Especially a haunted one? The "Ghost Cane" was put on eBay by Mary Anderson, a woman from Indiana who hoped the sale would ease the fears of her six-year-old son who had come to believe that his grandfather's ghost roamed the family home. The cane reached 132 bids on eBay and was only accepted on the online bidding site, which usually rejects "intangible items such as spirits or souls" because Miss Anderson made it clear she was only selling the cane so that her son would no longer freak out.

However, she also asked the winning bidder to write a letter to her son telling him that the cane and the ghost were doing just fine. The Ghost Cane's new home is the Golden Palace Casino in Antigua, where it will take a place of pride alongside a grilled cheese sandwich. But not just any grilled cheese sandwich; this sandwich bears the face of the Virgin Mary and was bought on eBay for a cool $28,000.

9 The Conjure Chest

In the mid-19th century, Jacob Cooley ordered his African American slave Hosea to build a chest for his first child. Hosea set to work, crafting a wooden chest of some remark. For some unknown reason, his master was displeased with his efforts and beat Hosea to a pulp, killing him. Cooley's other slaves vowed to avenge the death of their friend and sprinkled the dried blood of an owl in the chest and had a "conjure man" curse it. As if by magic, Cooley's first born died in infancy, and over the following years, a total of 17 deaths were attributed to the chest. Eventually the curse was lifted by a "conjure woman." The chest can be found in the Kentucky History Museum in Frankfort.

8 Valentino's Ring

Rudolph Valentino (1895–1926) was considered one of Hollywood's greatest silent movie stars. Valentino died of a perforated ulcer at the age of only 31. Some blame his early demise on a ring he purchased from a jeweler in 1920. The ring had a gem called the tiger's eye embedded in it.

The legend goes that Valentino showed the ring to a close friend immediately after he bought it, and his friend said he saw a vision of a pale and deathly Valentino. Regardless of what his friend did or did not see, Valentino's next few major pictures flopped at the box office and he died within six years. But Valentino wasn't the ring's only victim: His lover Pola Negri became gravely ill after wearing the ring, so much so that her career had to be put on the back burner for years and it never fully recovered; Russ Colombo, the actor hired to play Valentino in the biopic of his life, wore the ring and was killed in a shooting accident some days later; and the gangster Joe Casino bought the ring and refused to wear it until the curse had faded. After several years he finally put the ring on—and was dead within a week due to a car accident. The list goes on, but since the 1960s the ring's whereabouts have remained unknown. Perhaps it's on your finger, dear reader?

7 The Cursed Painting

"The Crying Boy" is a mass-produced print of a Bruno Amadio painting that proved popular throughout the 1950s and beyond, particularly in the British Isles. However, the painting attracted some media attention in the 1980s when UK tabloid the *Sun* ran a story saying that a Yorkshire firefighter claimed to have been at the scene of several house fires where the painting had been the only household item left unscathed. He also said that no firefighter would dare to have the painting in their home for fear of inciting a house fire.

The tabloids went wild with the story, interviewing several people who had owned the painting and suffered fires. Within six months, the *Sun* had started a cursed painting campaign, telling its readers to pass the painting to someone else, hang the boy painting next to a girl painting, or send the print to the newspaper, which would then perform a mass bonfire burning—all of which would lift the dreaded curse. After a BBC investigation into the paintings, it was revealed that they were covered in a fire-repellent varnish. Was this the reason for their unblemished record with fires, or were there more sinister forces at work?

6 The Possessed Bunk Beds

The case of the Haunted Bunk Beds was so famous that the tale found its way on to the hit TV show *Unsolved Mysteries*. In February 1987, in Horicon, Wisconsin, Alan and Debby Tallman brought home a bunk bed from a second-hand store and put it in the basement. That May, the couple moved the beds upstairs—and nine months of hell ensued. From the very first night the bunks were in their new room, things quickly escalated from wacky to just plain creepy.

First, the children of the house became ill, then a radio would jump from station to station without anyone touching it, and to cap things off, the first two children to sleep in the bed said they saw a witch. The Tallmans brought a pastor in and things cooled for a while. But when Alan Tallman returned home a few weeks after Christmas in 1988, he heard a voice telling him to "come here." He followed it to the garage, where he witnessed a blazing fire. Rushing to grab an extinguisher, Alan returned to the scene only to see the fire had vanished. A few more creepy circumstances later and the Tallmans had had enough—they burned the bunk beds. And would you believe it, just like that, the paranormal activity ended.

5 Screaming Skull of Burton Agnes Hall

By all accounts, the mystery of the screaming skull is one that seems to belong to the British Isles alone. There are several accounts of skulls being removed from homes, resulting in a series of unexplained events such as poltergeist activity and ear-piercing screams. One of the most famous screaming skulls is the one from Burton Agnes Hall in Driffield, East Yorkshire. The hall was

built during the reign of Queen Elizabeth I by Sir Henry Griffiths and his sisters. During construction, one of Sir Henry's sisters, Anne, was stabbed and killed by an unknown assailant. Before she passed away, she insisted that her other sisters promise that her head would be removed from her body and kept in the hall—a bizarre last request if ever there was one.

The sisters, putting the request down to near-death delirium, never made good on their promise, and instead buried her body in a grave, intact. Shortly after the burial, groaning could be heard throughout Burton Agnes Hall. A little freaked out, the sisters visited the family vault and found their sister's head had decayed to a skull and was, remarkably, detached from the body. The sisters took the skull and placed it in the hall where upon the groaning and moaning ceased. Sir Henry and the sisters eventually died and their descendants and new occupants of the hall attempted to remove the skull, but each time the skull was removed the building would tremble and portraits would fall from the walls. Finally, one of Sir Henry's descendants agreed to keep the skull in the house but only if it was bricked up behind a wall, where it remains today.

4 The Chair of Death

Baleroy Mansion in Pennsylvania was built in 1911. Since its construction, the building has accrued many artifacts of not only considerable monetary value but historical importance as well. The mansion houses items that once belonged to the Founding Father Thomas Jefferson, for instance. But alongside its palatial and opulent merits, Baleroy Mansion also has some paranormal prestige.

The mansion's last inhabitant, George Meade Easby (a descendant of seven signers of the Declaration of Independence), died in 2005. Before his death he claimed to have seen many ghostly goings-on all around the house, most notably the ghost of his brother, Steven, who died suddenly as a young child, his mother, and none other than the ghost of Thomas Jefferson himself. However, the most unsettling tales come from the infamous Blue Room and the "Chair of Death" that can be found there. The chair is a 200-year-old blue upholstered wing chair, which some say once belonged to Napoleon Bonaparte.

But this isn't the kind of chair you'd want to show off to your neighbors, and it's certainly not the kind of chair you'd want them to sit in either. Several paranormal investigators believe a female ghost haunts the chair, and George's nickname for the spirit found in this particular room would back that claim up: Spectral Amelia. It is said that whenever Amelia is present, a blue mist descends upon the room and that anyone who is brave enough to sit in the chair when the spirit is in attendance will die suddenly. To this day, four people have ignored the claim and brazenly sat in the chair. Those very same people perished.

3 The Haunted Wedding Dress

As the daughter of Elias Baker, the rich iron magnate of Blair County, Pennsylvania, in the 1800s, Anna Baker wanted for nothing. Her father lavished her with jewels and all that money could buy. But as a typical teenager, Anna wanted that which could not be bought—true love, something her father would have been happy for her to experience, as long as it was with a man of equal social standing. In true star-crossed-lover fashion, however, Anna fell for a handsome, low-paid iron worker at her father's blast furnace.

The loving father turned to archetypal angry dad in a heartbeat. Legend has it that his screams of rage could be heard from miles around. Elias simply didn't want his little girl running off with someone who wasn't good enough for her, in his eyes at least. And being the man of the house—and a very opulent house it was—Elias had the final say. But being as stubborn as her father, Anna decided that if she was not to marry the man she most wanted to, she would not marry a man at all. She lived a spinster and died a spinster. And she never got to wear the flamboyant wedding dress she'd picked out with her mother. Not in this life at least.

Until recently, that very wedding dress was on display at the Blair County Historical Society's museum in the Baker Mansion, in Anna's old bedroom no less, in front of a mirror. It was kept in a glass box, where it was said to sway from side to side. Some believe loose floorboards were to blame, others drafts, but for those of a paranormal disposition, the answer is simple—Anna, the bride from beyond, dressed for her wedding day for eternity, was adoringly admiring herself in a mirror.

2 Annabelle the Possessed Doll

Famous investigators Ed and Lorraine Warren took on the case of Annabelle the Haunted Doll in the early 1970s. The antique doll had been bought as a present by a mother for her daughter, Donna, in 1970. Donna was a student at the time, training to be a nurse. She lived in a small apartment with her friend, Angie. The doll took a place of pride on her bed. And then—you guessed it—weird stuff started happening. The doll seemingly had the ability to move about on its own. Sometimes the girls would come home to find the doll in a different room from where they had left her, even finding her sitting crossed-legged on the couch with her arms folded.

Some time after this, the girls would come home to find hand-written notes written in a crude child's writing. The message read, "Help us."

Who was writing the notes? And where was the old-looking parchment the messages were written on coming from? But the girls couldn't analyze for too long, because within a few days, more strange occurrences happened, namely blood started to appear on the doll from nowhere. The girls called for a séance, where they were acquainted with a spirit girl called Annabelle Higgins—a seven-year-old girl who had been found murdered on the plot of land the apartment the girls lived in was built on.

Annabelle "moved" into the doll so she could have some female company and once they heard Annabelle's story, the girls agreed that that spirit could stay in the doll and in the apartment. It was a bad decision—for one of their close friends, at least, Lou. Lou had told the girls over and over again to ditch the doll, and the dislike was clearly a two-way street. One evening when Lou was in Angie's bedroom, he was attacked by an unseen force. The attack left him with seven claw marks on his chest. Enter paranormal investigators Ed and Lorraine Warren.

After looking into the case, the Warrens concluded that the doll was not possessed by a spirit girl but by a malevolent spirit who wanted to eventually possess a human host. According to the Warrens, the "demonic spirit" had manipulated and preyed on the girls' emotional weaknesses, currying favor with them and lying in wait until eventually it would have tried to possess them. The Warrens removed Annabelle from the apartment and to this day it remains in the Warren Occult Museum in Moodus, Connecticut. Annabelle still moves around on the odd occasion and, it is said, even growls at visitors.

1 The Haunted Mirror

Myrtles Plantation can be found on the outskirts of Baton Rouge, Louisiana. Through the years this 200-year-old, ten-acre plantation has served as a family home, but these days it's run as a bed and breakfast—and is a hotspot for paranormal-seeking tourists. Every night at 3 a.m., a total of 15 ghosts comes out to play. Four of these ghosts come from one tragic tale—that of the Woodruff family and a young slave named Chloe.

In 1817, Sara Mathilda inherited the plantation from her father. She moved in with her husband, Clark Woodruff, and their three children. Clark decided to bring one of his slaves, Chloe, with him from his own home. One evening, when Clark caught Chloe eavesdropping on one of his private conversations, he cut off her ear. From that day on, Chloe wore a green turban to cover up her mutilation. To win back the trust of her owner so she would not be sent to toil in the fields, Chloe hatched a plan. She made a birthday cake for the Woodruffs' eldest daughter but spiked it with oleander leaves—a poisonous plant found on the plantation.

The family would become sick and Chloe, knowing the antidote, would be on hand to nurse them back to health and in doing so get back in her master's good graces—or that was the plan, at least. In actual fact, Chloe got her dosage wrong and Clark's wife and two of his children died of poisoning. Distraught by her actions, Chloe confessed to the other slaves, who panicked, believing they'd be blamed for hiding the culprit. They hanged Chloe and threw her lifeless body in the Mississippi River. Creepy already, right? It's about to get a whole lot creepier.

According to fable, there's an old Southern tradition stating that when a family member dies, all the mirrors in the home must be covered up so that the soul of the deceased will pass on to the next world and not become trapped in a reflection of this world. As was the norm, on the night of the tragic poisonings, all the mirrors in the house were covered up—except one. Aside from witnessing a "dark-skinned" ghost with a "turban" on her head wandering the plantation, visitors to the bed and breakfast are also shown an ornate mirror inside the home where the souls of the mother and children are said to be trapped.

Some claim to see handprints, others the faces of children, but one thing's for sure, it's not the mirror you'd want to regularly do your hair in. On a side note, when Clark learned of the fate of his family, he surrounded the house with crepe myrtle trees, hence the plantation's name.

TOP 10 Lesser-Known Haunted Places

by **Nene Adams**

10 Bucksport, Maine

Between Bangor and Belfast on Maine's coast lies the small town of Bucksport, whose most famous 18th century citizen was Colonel Jonathan Buck. Buck's grave in the local cemetery is marked by a large granite monument. The stone bears a curious stain or inclusion in the shape of a partial human leg and foot, supposedly due to a curse placed on Buck by a woman accused of witchcraft and later executed by hanging. After Buck's death, the foot shape formed on the monument and numerous attempts to clean it off were unsuccessful. Is the "Cursed Tomb" real? We'll never know. Over many decades, details have changed, but the legend's core remains the same: Buck wronged a woman and his memorial stone was marked by the vengeful spirit. The poet Robert Peter Coffin romanticized the legend of Colonel Buck and the witch in his poem "The Foot of Tucksport."

9 Cherry Hill, New York City

Cherry Hill was a neighborhood in the old Fourth Ward of the Lower East Side of Manhattan, which became infamous for having the worst tenement slum in the city, Gotham Court. However, in 1900, a three-room flat on Cherry Street gained brief notoriety for being haunted. According to reports, for 19 years, even in overcrowded New York, no tenant had been able to remain in the apartment longer than a few hours before terrifying disturbances began: Pictures turned upside down on the walls, furniture moved, and residents were physically assaulted. The poltergeist activity was believed to be due to the spirit of an old French woman, a widow who committed suicide by hanging herself following her husband's death. This location shouldn't be confused with the Cherry Hill estate in Albany, which is also supposed to be haunted.

8 Bristol, England

In 1852, the newly built vessel *Good Times* was launched from Bristol. In the beginning, superstitious sailors pegged the *Good Times* as a lucky ship: No one was hurt during construction, she launched ahead of schedule, saved eight days on her maiden voyage, and on the same trip made an $18,000 profit. But soon, always between midnight and 4 a.m., the men aboard began hearing a muffled voice crying, "Oh, my," beneath the main hatch. A comprehensive search of the ship revealed no stowaways, but the voice continued to be heard every night. The unnerved sailors threatened mutiny. After several months of the phenomenon repeating, the ship was sold, and *Good Times*' reputation as haunted was sealed.

7 St. Mary's Episcopal Church, Kansas City, Missouri

Henry David Jardine was rector of St. Mary's Episcopal Church in Kansas City from 1879 until his death in 1886. During his time at the church, a newspaper printed unsubstantiated accusations alleging Jardine had committed a number of crimes, including sexual misconduct with young girls. Jardine sued for libel and lost. His "priesthood" was revoked. His body was found in St. Louis, where he'd traveled to contest the church's decision. He held a rag soaked in chloroform, and some believed he'd committed suicide. The murky circumstances surrounding his death led to his burial in unconsecrated ground. Years later, his body was exhumed and cremated, and his ashes rest in St. Mary's, where mysterious footsteps have been heard. People have also claimed the priest's ghost makes an appearance.

6 LeBaron Hotel, San Jose, California

In 1982, California newspapers reported on the LeBaron Hotel (now the Wyndham San Jose Hotel and Resort)—specifically room 538, which was said by employees and visitors to be haunted. The story began with housekeeper Lupe Moncivais, who claimed she first came across the spirit haunting the room in 1979 or 1980 after the death of a young woman from a drug overdose in that same room in November of that year. She heard a voice whispering her name and her hair was pulled, but she was alone at the time. Following the report, the hotel was deluged with requests to reserve the haunted room for the night. Guests reported other phenomena such as the elevators stopping on the fifth floor by themselves, faucets in Room 538 turning on and off, and a "woman in white" was seen entering the unoccupied room.

5 Burrville Cider Mill, Watertown, New York

The Burrville Cider Mill (formerly Burr's Mill), located just outside Watertown, was built in 1801 and remains in operation today pressing apples into cider. The mill is believed to be haunted by the ghosts of former owners—Captain John Birr (rumored to have pirated on Lake Ontario) and Homer Rebb. Strange phenomena are said to have occurred, including the disappearance of a 25-pound bag of sugar from a locked room. The current owners and employees as well as visitors have seen apparitions and heard unaccountable noises such as heavy objects dropping, balls bouncing across the floor, the wheels of the old cider press turning, and have smelled cigar smoke. Equipment tends to malfunction, but an appeal to Homer Rebb takes care of it.

4 Villa Paula, Miami, Florida

The former Cuban consulate, Villa Paula, is located in the Little Haiti district of Miami. Built in 1925, the building ceased to be an official residence a few years later, after the death of its namesake, Paula Milord—wife of consul Domingo Milord—following complications during a leg amputation. Villa Paula fell into private hands and gained a reputation as Miami's most haunted location. The ghost of a one-legged, black-haired woman was seen floating down the hall. Witnesses smelled coffee and roses and heard ghostly piano music. Dishes were thrown on the floor. Three cats of a former owner were killed. A visiting Satanist entered and began choking. During a séance, a psychic claimed five separate spirits haunted the premises. The current owner has stated the property is peaceful now.

3 Valence-en-Brie, France

In late June 1896, the house of M. Lebégue at Valence-en-Brie near Paris was suddenly beset by strange, ghostly manifestations. Witnesses heard raps, furniture was overturned, and windows were broken. But the strangest and most frightening phenomenon to residents, servants, and visitors was a mysterious voice, described as "the hoarse voice of the giant at the fair" that issued from various places in the house, including the cellar, the kitchen, the invalid Madame Lebégue's bedside, the chimneys, under the plates on the dining room table, and elsewhere. The voice insulted policemen and doctors and occasionally seemed pleased with itself when something destructive occurred. Many people heard the voice, including reporters. Although it was theorized that a servant girl might be responsible for the physical phenomena, the auditory occurences couldn't be explained.

2 Big Bull Tunnel, Virginia

Newspapers reported in August 1905 and 1906 that the Big Bull Tunnel in Virginia, part of the Norfolk and Western Railway line, had been the site of paranormal manifestations as reported by a train crew. Local citizens were also disturbed by the phenomena, which included ghastly sounds such as a man groaning in pain. A voice made declarations like, "They are drinking my blood." According to witnesses—respectable railway employees—the tunnel was examined and no evidence of trickery could be found. It was believed at least three men lost their lives in the tunnel. Possible sources of the haunting? We found a report about the tunnel from 1901 indicating Robert Lemon, engineer, had his skull crushed and wasn't expected to live, and in 1904, a flagman was knocked off a train and fatally injured.

1 Flaherty, Indiana

Flaherty, near Laporte, Indiana, was the location of sightings of a ghost believed to haunt the station on the Lake Erie Railway in 1904 and 1905. According to reports, the apparition was seen after sundown, terrifying the townspeople—the manifestation was of a headless man standing near the station platform close to the water tank. The man held a dinner pail and waved his arms. Just before disappearing, the ghost let out hair-raising shrieks. Locals identified the spirit as Columbus Cole, a popular resident of the town who had been decapitated very near that same spot during a train accident when a boiler exploded. The visitations began shortly after Cole's death. Many eyewitnesses in the neighborhood and surrounding areas claimed to have seen the ghost. The general theory was that Cole died with some unfinished business.

TOP 10 Creepy Stories of Alleged Alien Encounters

by Gregory Myers

10 Betty and Barney Hill

One night, Betty and Barney Hill were driving home from their vacation in Canada. They saw what they first assumed was a shooting star, until it moved upward. The two of them got out of the car, curiosity overtaking their sense of reason for a moment. While they were looking at the UFO, it suddenly veered right at them.

Naturally, the two rushed back to their car and took off, but this wasn't the end of their experience—they claimed to have lost two hours they cannot account for. They recalled "repressed memories" of an abduction while they were hypnotized, and both claimed that their watches stopped after the incident.

9 Russian Politician Abducted

Russian politician Kirsan Ilyumzhinov claimed he was abducted in the 1990s by aliens wearing yellow spacesuits. He was allegedly taken aboard a long, transparent spaceship and was unable to understand the aliens' speech. Despite this, they had some sort of exchange of ideas—more of a mutual understanding than actual communication, it would seem.

8 Abducted in Kentucky

Three women were driving near Stanford, Kentucky, when they were allegedly abducted by aliens. Afterward, all three women were given hypnosis sessions, and all of them had the same story. They even took a lie detector test and passed with flying colors. At the very least, they all believe it happened. Stranger still, many people in the area reported a UFO sighting around the same time the women were abducted.

7 Lights in Texas

One man in Texas claims to have escaped from the aliens that abducted him. To support his claims, he supplied pictures that he believes prove the incident happened. While these pictures may be proof enough for some, many people will need much better pictures to believe in UFOs.

Supposedly, a large UFO was seen near the Dyess Air Force Base in Texas, and some witnesses say that it has shown up many times in the surrounding area. Others claim to have seen multiple "pulsating orbs" near the Georgetown area of Texas. These UFOs were all lined up in two rows, then they vanished. I just wish these UFO-watchers would start buying decent cameras.

6 Aliens Invade Sleeping Man's Living Room

Peter Khoury was asleep on his couch when he woke to find two strange women in his house. One had blonde hair, the other appeared to be Asian, and the blonde was clearly in charge. The blonde woman pushed his head into her breast several times, which disoriented him, so he bit down on her nipple. The woman didn't appear to react or bleed from the injury. Then the women left.

Khoury later found a blonde hair that was constricting his foreskin. I should note that Khoury had recently suffered a serious head injury, but the hair makes the story harder to explain.

5 Woman Captures Abduction on Camera

A woman named Sonia believed that she had been abducted, and days later, she saw a helicopter that was piloted by a strange man in black. That same night, her daughter complained about something "pulling at her leg." After this, her husband put CCTVs in the house to record any further happenings. Some who saw the video believed Sonia's story, but others may not be so easily convinced. The video shows her "disappearing," which isn't hard to fake in a video.

4 Sergeant Moody

Sergeant Moody was stationed in New Mexico when he witnessed a meteor shower. As he was watching, a UFO landed right in front of his car. When Moody tried to run, he couldn't get the car's starter to turn over, and he passed out. Before everything went black, he thought he saw a humanoid shape inside the craft. There was a large chunk of time he couldn't recall, and he later went under hypnosis in an attempt to uncover these repressed memories. According to his "memories," when the aliens tried to abduct him, he slammed one of them with his car door and punched another. They still managed to subdue him and performed several experiments, but at least he (allegedly) went down fighting

3 Buff Ledge

Two teenagers claim they were abducted while working at their summer camp, Buff Ledge. They saw a UFO at the docks and could see aliens inside. Then they were hit by a beam of light and didn't remember anything else. They believe they were taken aboard an alien craft and had various samples taken from their bodies.

The aliens didn't have ears or lips and only had slits for noses and webbed fingers. One of the teenagers also recounted them wanting world peace for our planet (which they claimed they had already achieved). Independent investigations found that some people who were unaware of their story reported strange lights at the camp on the same night, and others at the camp have reported being abducted.

2 Twin Abduction

Two twin sisters reported regularly encountering aliens since they were as young as five years old. They claimed they would see a light and then aliens wearing capes would enter their room and take them aboard their ship. The girls had their own nickname for the aliens: the bald men. One of the twins claimed that during an abduction, the entire spaceship became transparent on the inside and she could look down at the planet below.

1 Dr. Hopkins and the Man in Black

In 1978, a man named Dr. Hopkins had been studying a UFO case when he received a mysterious phone call from a man who claimed to represent a UFO organization—which later proved to be false. When Hopkins agreed to talk, the man was at the door immediately. The man was completely bald—even his eyebrows—and he didn't actually have lips, but he tried to hide it by wearing red lipstick.

He spoke in a monotone voice and made a coin disappear. Then he told the doctor to cease all research and destroy his evidence. The man behaved as if he were running out of power near the end of the encounter and vanished into a light outside.

Hopkins had another encounter with the same man, but a similarly odd woman accompanied him. This time, the man made sexually inappropriate comments in addition to behaving in the same strange robotic manner and disappearing mysteriously. Luckily for Dr. Hopkins, this was his last encounter.

TOP 10 Terrifying Historic Medical Instruments

by **Nene Adams**

10 Osteotome

While technically a type of chain saw, this medical instrument, invented by Bernard Heine around 1830, wasn't used to cut down trees. The osteotome was initially used in trepanning, or cutting circular sections of bone from the skull. The sharp spike was driven into the patient's skull to hold the instrument in place, then the doctor cranked the handle to turn the saw-toothed blade. The osteotome was considered superior to a reciprocating saw or hammer and chisel when it came to getting through human bone without splintering or damaging nearby tissue. Later variations made the tool useful in arm and leg amputations and dental surgeries.

9 Stricture Divulsor

When a male patient's urethra became too narrow to permit proper urine flow, doctors used a stricture divulsor. Basically, the instrument was inserted into the urethra via the tip of the penis and navigated to the required place. Then a screw in the handle was turned to separate the blades and dilate the urethra as far as possible. The majority of doctors believed tearing a tight stricture was better than stretching it too little, and seeing blood flow afterward was actually considered a good sign. Horrifyingly, it seems some patients preferred to turn the screw themselves, taking up to a half hour to complete the operation to the doctor's satisfaction.

8 Dental Phantom

A "phantom" or model was used to let doctors learn and practice techniques. This particularly nightmarish, articulated dental phantom looks like something designed by H. R. Giger for the Alien movie franchise and likely dates from the 1930s. Judging from the design, the aluminum model was probably covered by a rubber head, now lost. Older versions were simpler, lacking the "silently screaming soul damned to an eternity in hell" quality of later pieces. Dental phantoms often used human teeth extracted from corpses, and modern dental students still use similar models.

7 Louse Cages

A cheat, perhaps, as this item isn't a medical instrument, these devices were used to help create a vaccine that saved many lives. In the history of warfare, far more soldiers died from illnesses than from injuries sustained on the battlefield. Typhus epidemics swept through armies—not to mention poverty-stricken areas of cities, where people lived in close quarters without access to proper sanitation. The disease was carried by human lice and had no cure until the 1920s, when Professor Rudolph Weigl discovered a somewhat distasteful method for producing an effective vaccine. Lice were bred, hatched, and fed human blood, thanks to men and women called "feeders" who strapped the cages to their thighs or calves. Once grown, the lice were infected with the disease, dissected, and the vaccine was created.

6 Tonsil Guillotine

Any infection, no matter how small, had life-threatening potential in a time before antibiotics. To treat tonsillitis and its related complication, peritonsillar abscess, commonly known as quinsy, the tonsil guillotine was developed.  The instrument permitted a doctor to reach into a patient's throat, pierce the tonsil with a fork as if spearing a cocktail wiener at a Super Bowl party, and sever the tissue with the guillotine's blade. By the late 19th century, a mild anesthetic in the form of a cocaine solution was injected before the guillotine's use. The instrument was a boon to doctors, who had previously risked being bitten while sticking their fingers into a patient's mouth.

5 Hemorrhoid Forceps

Lacking modern comforts like Preparation H and squeezable, soft toilet tissue, patients with bothersome hemorrhoids usually learned to live with them unless a serious problem arose. If it did, ligation or amputation was the preferred treatment. Once he had the patient bent over a table, the doctor reached for the hemorrhoid forceps. This instrument worked by tightly grasping and crushing an external hemorrhoid to restrict the blood supply. The damaged tissue would eventually die and wither off. Internal hemorrhoids were first coaxed out using hooks (enticing, right?) and cauterized or snipped off with scissors.

4 Lithotome Caché

A bladder stone, or vesical calculus, was a common problem when many people, particularly those without much money, ate low-protein diets. Doctors typically "cut for the stone" by making an incision in the perineal raphe, exposing the bulb of the urethra. That's when the lithotome caché came in.

The instrument contained two adjustable hidden blades that would spring out and cut and dilate the neck of the bladder (hopefully in a controlled way). The surgeon would then begin probing with forceps for the calculus felt earlier through the wall of the rectum. Because doctors didn't want to prolong their patient's suffering in the days before anesthetics, such operations took around five minutes or so.

3 Écraseur

For the removal of hemorrhoids and other growths, tumors, polyps, and cysts in the esophagus, larynx, uterus, or ovaries, an *écraseur* (French for "crusher") was the instrument of choice. The loop on the end of the instrument could be a saw-toothed chain or a simple wire and was employed to strangle and crush the growth, preventing hemorrhage by restricting blood supply like a tourniquet. After lassoing the base of the growth, the doctor turned a screw to apply pressure. Variations of the écraseur continued to refine the design. Similar instruments were used in veterinary medicine to castrate cattle.

2 Dental Key

Back in the day, with dental hygiene primitive at best, the causes of cavities and gum diseases unknown, and teeth-damaging impurities in bread and other staple foods, most people were forced to seek a doctor—or sometimes the local barber—to relieve their suffering at some point. Before the invention of the tooth key, or dental key, in the early 18th century, extracting teeth was done by brute force. If the tooth broke during the operation, the doctor had to chip out bits from the gum using a bone chisel. The dental key allowed the doctor to clamp the patient's tooth with the claw at the end of the instrument. By rocking or rotating the key, the tooth was levered out of the gum, roots and all—without anesthetic. It's no wonder people held off treatment for as long as possible.

1 Fetal Destructors and Extractors

At a time when performing a Cesarean section was certain to kill a woman in labor, and attitudes toward infant mortality were somewhat different from today, doctors facing a life-or-death situation while attending a delivery often chose to sacrifice the unborn child instead. Without getting into too many details, if the doctor determined the fetus was already dead, he would use an instrument to decapitate the corpse in situ, then extract the body by means of a hook or crochet. If the fetus were alive, a perforator delivered a killing blow before extraction. This was considered an act of compassion.

TOP 10 Creepy Historical Vampires You've Never Heard Of

by **Aaron Short**

10 Peter Plogojowitz

Peter Plogojowitz was a man from 1700s Serbia who died. Except—according to some—he didn't really stay dead. Within ten weeks of his death, nine people died suddenly from a mysterious illness, and prior to their deaths they all accused Peter Plogojowitz of throttling them in their dreams. Peter's own son reported seeing him in the kitchen three days after his death, demanding food—before he also died mysteriously. Peter's wife fled town after she alleged he'd shown up late one night to demand a pair of shoes.

The army was called in, and Peter's body was exhumed. It was reported that he was breathing and that his open eyes were moving. A stake was put through his heart, resulting in a Tarantino-esque gushing of blood, and his was body burned. The deaths and dreams all ended abruptly.

9 The Alnwick Castle Vampire

The Alnwick Castle vampire actually predates the term "vampire." The events were recorded by an English chronicler named William of Newburgh. He reported the story of a man who returned from the dead after he died while spying on his cheating wife—he was crouched on the roof and fell. He then returned as a revenant—a walking, rotting corpse—spreading plague in his wake.

Eventually, a priest gathered some of his parishioners and found the vampire's grave. They opened it and stabbed the corpse with a shovel. Warm blood ran from the body and confirmed their suspicions that it had been drinking the blood of the living (remember this was almost 800 years before Bram Stoker's *Dracula*). They burned the body, and the attacks ceased.

8 Highgate Vampire

In 1969, dead animals—completely drained of blood and sporting neck wounds—began to appear in Highgate Cemetery in London. Then witnesses reported a tall, dark figure that emitted an evil aura and had a hypnotic stare. One man reported that he became confused and totally lost when trying to leave the cemetery. Suddenly, he found himself facing the

Highgate vampire—which transfixed him, gluing him to the spot. After a while, it disappeared.

Reports in the press led to the graveyard being trampled by an army of self-proclaimed vampire hunters. They dug up several graves, leading conservationists to lobby for the graveyard to be closed at night. Eventually, sightings and reports of the vampire decreased.

7 Sava Savanovic

The only thing scarier than vampires is ghosts. But imagine something scarier still: a ghost vampire. Say hello to Sava Savanovic. Sava was a Serbian vampire who lived in an old mill and fed on unwary travelers and millers who approached the mill after dark.

Savanovic wasn't killed or driven off like most of the other bloodsuckers on this list. According to locals, he simply stopped attacking villagers. Meanwhile, the mill where he lived was passed down from generation to generation, each new owner too scared to repair the building until it eventually collapsed. Now locals report that he's awoken from his long slumber and roams the Serbian countryside—looking for a new home. And it's not just superstitious locals making these claims. The actual council themselves are the ones who put out the warning. Of course it's probably a publicity stunt by the area's tourist board—we hope.

6 The Vampire of Croglin Grange

This event began in the 1800s, when the Cranwell Family took up residence in Groglin Range in Cumbria, England. Lady Cranwell noticed strange lights in the garden below, but thought nothing of it until she woke to find the lights at her window—but they weren't lights. They were eyes.

Lady Cranwell was frozen in terror as she saw the thing outside her window remove the panes one by one before reaching a rotten hand through and opening the latch. Her brothers heard her screaming and ran in to help her, arriving just in time to see her bleeding profusely from the neck as a catlike figure darted out into the darkness.

The brothers decided to slay the vampire. Some time later, they returned to the estate and set a trap. Lady Cranwell pretended to sleep in the same room the original attack happened in. When the vampire tried to come through the window again, the brothers jumped out with pistols and shot at it. It screamed and ran off into the night. The next day, the brothers gathered an angry mob and searched the graveyard until they found an open crypt. Inside were gnawed bones and an open coffin containing a rotten corpse with a recent bullet wound. Needless to say, they burned it.

5 Jure Grando

Jure Grando was a peasant from Istria, Croatia, who died in 1656. He allegedly terrorized villagers in the area for 16 years after his death. Official documents from that time name him a *strigon*, the local name for "vampire."

Jure Grando's case is important in vampire folklore, as it was the first time in history that the word "vampire" was officially applied to a person. According to locals, he would wander the village by night and knock on people's doors. Whoever's door he knocked on would die. When he wasn't doing that, he was bothering his widow for sex. Eventually, people got tired of being terrorized by an undead monster, so a local priest took a stand and went out to face him. Grando was no match for the priest, who warded him off with a cross. The priest and some of the villagers chased him back to his grave, dug him up, and decapitated his corpse.

4 The Hunderprest of Melrose Abbey

The "Hunderprest" was a nickname given to an 11th-century priest of Melrose Abbey in the Scottish Borders region of Scotland. He was given the nickname because of his favorite pastime: hunting on horseback with a pack of hunting dogs (*hunderprest* means "dog priest").

The story of the vampire of Melrose Abbey is based sometime around the year 1138. In life, the Hunderprest was a bit of a bad man, so when he died, he returned as a revenant. He was forced to drink the blood of innocents and change into a bat. It's said that the monks of the abbey, displaying some impressive turn-the-other-cheekery, were content to let him run around being undead—until he began to bother his mistress for sex.

Eventually, the frightened monks and priests banded together in order to bring him down. They set up a lookout at the Hunderprest's grave where he rose at nightfall. The monks, showing a rather un-monkish capacity for kicking butt, took him down with a well-timed blow to the head from an axe. They cremated the vampire's body and spread his ashes, ending his reign of terror. But some legends say that he still haunts the area.

3 The Vampires of New England

There weren't many tales of vampires in America until the dark discovery of a grave in Griswold, Connecticut, in 1990. The grave contained the bodies of farmers from the 1700s. All were normal except for one. One body had been beheaded, and its skeleton was rearranged into the shape of a Jolly Roger.

It was decided that this wasn't just a simple grave robbery, as it had been done ten years after death and no valuables were removed. It mirrored a case in neighboring Jewett City where, around the same time, 29 bodies were exhumed postmortem and burned. This was something of a vampire epidemic. The most famous case from this time is that of Mercy Brown, a girl who died from tuberculosis. Some time later, the rest of her family started to fall ill and die one by one until Mercy's body was dug up, found to be remarkably un-corpsefied, and burned.

2 The Gorbals Vampire

This tale started with the rumor that a vampire with iron teeth was at Gorbals graveyard in Glasgow, Scotland, in the 1950s. The vampire had apparently taken two children. Within a few hours, the graveyard was full of children with makeshift weapons like sticks and knives, hunting for the vampire.

Authorities blamed the occurrence on hysteria and the influence of American comics like *Tales from the Crypt*. But it's since been pointed out that there were no comics from this period featuring vampires with iron teeth. Was there some truth to the iron-toothed vampire prowling the graveyard at night and feeding on children? Was the vampire imaginary? Or had it just been scared off by the sight of dozens of armed Glaswegians excited by the prospect of beating and stabbing it back to hell?

1 Elizabeth Bathory: The Blood Countess

Elizabeth Bathory is perhaps the most famous vampire in history after Vlad the Impaler. But while Vlad wasn't really a blood-sucking vampire—merely the inspiration for one—Elizabeth Bathory may have actually fed on and bathed in blood. She was a Romanian countess in the 16th century who found joy in torturing peasants. The torture ranged from simple beatings and stabbings to piercing fingers and lips with iron nails or dousing them in freezing cold water and letting them die in the snow.

Rumors that Elizabeth was a vampire began when it was alleged that she bathed in the blood of young maidens. It's reported that she began this to reduce the effects of aging, though some historians refute this claim as being added to the story after the fact. Eventually Bathory was walled inside her castle alive, with only enough space for her to receive air and food until she died years later.

TOP 10 Creepy Tales about Clowns

by Lui B.

10 The Union Screaming House

In May 2001, Steven LaChance and his three children decided to move from a small apartment to a larger antique house in Union, Missouri. The house had a basement that also included an old butcher's shower area and fruit cellar. With almost all its features in perfect condition, the house was exactly what they wanted—or so they thought.

During the following weeks, Steve and his children were haunted by mysterious entities and unexplained phenomena. For instance, a dark, misty figure of a man was seen lurking in different corners of the house. Steve's younger son, on the other hand, witnessed something more terrifying: a demonic clown ghost walking in the hallway. As it turned out, his son had a crippling fear of clowns, and the ghost was clever enough to prey on his weakness. They eventually decided to leave the house, but Steve made sure to warn every family that would later move in. His horrifying experience was later featured in Discovery Channel's *A Haunting* and in a book written by Steve himself.

9 Zozzaby's Stinky Ghost

Frederick Zozzaby was a Czechoslovakian clown who moved to Liverpool during the Edwardian era. He tragically committed suicide, but his ghost remained behind to haunt unsuspecting children.

In December 2002, 13-year-old Thomas and his younger brother, Aaron, were awakened in their bunk beds by what sounded like an echoing laughter. They soon opened their eyes to see a hair-raising apparition standing in their doorway. Dressed in a one-piece maroon suit, the ghostly clown had one hand on its belly and the other pointing directly toward the terrified children, as if taunting them. His face was even more bizarre: A long, crooked nose, hollow eyes like that of a skull, and heavy makeup made the clown completely unrecognizable. Witnesses also tell of a sickly sweet smell that accompanies Zozzaby's ghost anywhere it goes—a repulsive odor thought to be embalming fluid.

8 Klutzo the Christian Clown

Amon Paul Carlock, Jr., was a popular Christian clown from Springfield, Illinois. Using the stage name Klutzo the Clown, he entertained countless Sunday school kids and even orphans from countries like Mexico and the Philippines. The fact that the entertainer was a former minister, magician, police officer, and youth counselor made people believe that he was in the business for all the right reasons. But as it turned out, Carlock was just another wolf in a clown's clothing.

In June 2007, Carlock arrived at the San Francisco International Airport after working as a clown at an orphanage in the Philippines. Because he just came from a country known to be high-risk for sex trafficking, Carlock was stopped by immigration authorities. Nude photos of young boys, some of whom were not aware that they were being photographed, were found on his laptop and digital camera. A search warrant was then issued and at least 21 child pornographic movies were recovered from Carlock's home.  Three boys from The House of Joy orphanage also came forward, revealing that Carlock had molested them. Klutzo the Clown gave his alibis, of course, but nothing saved him from multiple child porn charges—unless you count death. Carlock died after being tasered by a security officer.

7 West Palm Beach Murder

In May 1990, Marlene Warren opened the door of her Wellington, Florida, residence to receive an unexpected visitor: a clown holding a bouquet of flowers and two silver balloons. But before she could even say "thank you," Marlene was shot and killed with a .38-caliber revolver.

Initial investigations came up with two possible suspects: Michael Warren, the dead woman's husband, and 27-year-old Sheila Keen, who was rumored to be romantically involved with the former. Both denied the allegations. Sheila claimed that she and Michael were just business partners. Michael, on the other hand, claimed that he was en route to Calder Race Course with some of his friends on the day of the murder. Despite evidence pointing toward them both being guilty, there wasn't enough for a conviction, and the identity of the killer clown remains a mystery.

6 Clown Kidnappers

From the 1980s to the early '90s, child abductors dressed up as clowns terrorized a number of towns in the U.S. One notable incident happened in

May 1981, when police officers from Brookline, Massachusetts, released a bulletin regarding a mysterious van lurking near the local elementary school. A clown or group of clowns hiding inside the vehicle allegedly used candies to lure young victims toward the van.

The most recent sighting took place in Chicago, where a community alert was subsequently issued in late 2008. The similarities were striking: An unidentified man was spotted wearing clown makeup and offering balloons to lure children into his white van.

5 Camanche Road Mystery

In September 2004, Eric Dau and his wife, Sherrise, were driving into a mobile home court in Camanche, Iowa. Everything was going smoothly until they saw a startling sight ahead of them: Lined up in the middle of the road were dozens of spooky Ronald McDonald dolls.

The incident happened at approximately 12:30 a.m., yet a volunteer firefighter in the area claimed that he had driven on the same road two hours earlier and saw nothing unusual. Eric's wife suspected that it was a scheme used by assailants to lure women out of their cars. Strangely, all the clown dolls disappeared without a trace the following morning.

4 Vincent Hitchcock

Named after the two legends of the horror genre (Vincent Price and Alfred Hitchcock), this clown doll is a toy and ghost rolled into one. Renee, a real estate agent from Oregon, first saw the doll in an online auction and, as a lover of all things creepy, she purchased the item for $500.

Shortly after putting Vincent in a designated corner in her house, she began experiencing bizarre occurrences. There were several instances when the clown doll suddenly vanished from where it was left, only to reappear in unexpected places. In fact, Renee said that she once found the doll with both arms mysteriously raised in the air. Later, a tape recorder left near the doll captured a deep voice of a man uttering the words "wake up!" while no one was in the room. Although it is believed that Vincent Hitchcock is possessed by a spirit of a child, the identity of the ghost remains a mystery.

3 The Clown Statue

This creepy story was first popularized by a chain of e-mails several years ago. Legend has it that a teenage girl was hired as a babysitter by a rich couple somewhere in California. The parents went out for a late dinner date and gave the babysitter freedom to watch TV.

The girl did as she was told, but found the life-size clown statue displayed in the room with the television too disturbing, so she called the owners and asked if she could cover the statue with a blanket for the evening. Surprised, the couple immediately asked her to call the authorities, because they didn't have a clown statue.

Different versions of this story have slightly different details, but the moral is always the same: Be terrified of clown statues.

2 The Harlequin

The Harlequin is often described as an androgynous creature with wide-open, dark eyes, long limbs, and an extremely white complexion. In most cases, Harlequins only appear to children as young as five or six years old—and according to author Brad Steiger, they are real.

Dan Mitchell, who was only five during his first Harlequin encounter, described the creature as very thin and exuding a "damp, fresh smell like summer rain." It also gives a sinister laugh and chills to anyone who hears it. Karen Davis, on the other hand, says that she woke up one night only to see a Harlequin sitting on the foot of her bed. In both incidents, the Harlequin appeared to be harmless.

1 Pogo's Other Victims

We all know John Wayne Gacy as the guy who gave party clowns a bad name. A prolific serial killer, Gacy was convicted for the murder and sexual assault of 33 young men—all of these while offering his services as "Pogo the Clown" at children's parties. Sadly, the mystery of the "Killer Clown" didn't end when he was executed in 1994: Private detective Bill Borsch believes Gacy's victims didn't stop at number 33.

Raffle Tovar, a Des Plaines detective, claimed that he once asked Gacy about the whereabouts of his other victims. "That's for you guys to find out," was Gacy's only sarcastic reply. Another detective also discovered that Gacy traveled to 15–20 states in the 1970s. These data open up the possibility that there might be other bodies buried somewhere else—but to this day, none have been found.

TOP 10 Creepiest True Stories behind Movie Scenes

by **Dustin Koski**

10 Dau

Dau was, as of 2011, a project that had broken down in a sense, though that's not to say filming stopped. What happened instead was director Ilya Khrzhanovsky turned this intended film tribute to Nobel Prize–winner Lev Landau into an insanely overimmersive act of "method" cultism. The cast and crew were required to dress in mid-20th-century Russian clothing to match the time period of the film; they weren't allowed to have cell phones or anything else so modern. Food had to be in cans from the era and all documents and passes typewritten. Anyone who so much as mentioned aspects of the modern world or left the set without permission was fined. That one person should exert that much power for something so clearly unnecessary is, as the director himself said, "pure delirium." And this was under circumstances in which people had to do the same torturously repetitive tasks until they were fired—some of them described it as being akin to a "prison experiment."

9 Eraserhead

Eraserhead is well known for being enigmatic and creepy. It's a story of a loser everyman, Henry Spencer (Jack Nance), in a bizarre setting who experiences strange visions while fathering an even stranger child who doesn't look remotely human. But it's what you might expect from David Lynch if you've heard anything about him and much milder than you'd expect after you hear the sorts of things he was up to behind the scenes.

For example, he refused to talk about how the effect of the baby was done decades afterward (nor did he allow others to talk about it). Given the appearance of the object, the budget, the skin textures, and the fact it's so articulated that its eyes will close vertically, the leading theory is that it's a preserved calf fetus.

The idea that Lynch wired a corpse to bring it to life is well supported by something he did for fun that he put in an ultimately deleted scene. He asked a vet to provide him with a dead cat (on the promise it wouldn't be recognizable on film) then cut it open and found the colors quite vivid. Then he put the cat in a pit of tar and left it there for a year until he could have a scene in which Henry's shoe catches on a cord connected to the cat. It's enough to make you think Lynch started making movies to justify all the eccentric stuff he'd be doing anyway.

8 Noah

Celebrity stalkers are nothing new. But one that went after Emma Watson during the shoot for *Noah* was more aggressive than most. During the shoot, Emma Watson decided to go off in the woods near the location of the shoot. While she was there, a stalker that she recognized from outside her home appeared. Members of the crew intervened, and while Watson was uninjured and did not press charges, those involved with the shoot described how it put a pall over everything. The decision not to press charges is somewhat questionable in light of the encouragement this might provide other stalkers.

7 Skippy

A 1931 Best Picture nominee, this film features a scene in which child star Jackie Cooper was required to cry. Director Norman Taurog came to the conclusion that genuine emotion was required for the scene. He had a stagehand take Cooper's pet dog out behind the studio and pretend to shoot it. Even though it was revealed after they got the take that the dog was okay (and Cooper's performance was nominated for Best Actor), the event made such an impact on Cooper that he entitled his autobiography *Please Don't Shoot My Dog*.

6 Alien

Everyone's heard by now about the infamous chest-bursting scene in this 1979 horror classic, when some of the cast members were completely surprised by the scene. Much creepier (and less well known) is a story from Dan O'Bannon about artist H. R. Giger. To design the xenomorph's head, Giger purchased real human skulls from India and cut them apart. O'Bannon was suspicious, but he didn't really do anything about it until the mid-1980s when he wrote the idea into the comedy *Return of the Living Dead*. Subsequently, a news story came out that India had shut down the companies supplying skeletons, making it quite possible something unsavory was going on. And O'Bannon ends on a particularly chilling note: The teeth of the skulls he saw Giger working with were very much like those of children.

5 Aguirre, the Wrath of God

The most famous story from this 1972 film by Werner Herzog is that Herzog threatened star Klaus Kinski at gunpoint to keep him from leaving the movie. This is quite silly, because Kinski admitted in his autobiography he was the only one with a gun. And he didn't just threaten to shoot people with it. Kinski fired shots into a cabin the crew was staying in because of how loud they were being. Even though the room was crowded, the shot only took off the tip of someone's finger. Kinski had another close call when he almost killed an extra by bashing him in the head with his sword during a shot. The blow was hard enough to cut the man's head open, and doubtless would have killed him if he hadn't been wearing a helmet. Is it any wonder that Herzog later seriously attempted to murder Kinski?

Also, one of the dead bodies in the film is real. Herzog said that his brother had to fly it in from Europe to bring it to the set. To keep it safe from unreliable luggage handling, his brother took it on the plane with him and sat next to it for the flight.

4 Neon Genesis Evangelion: The End of Evangelion

This 1997 feature is one of those anime films from the '90s that solidified the stereotype that they're all full of violence and impenetrable symbolism. But almost none of them can match the bizarre happenings that are sprinkled throughout this movie, which details a prophecy in which science and monstrous energy beings are used to end the world. For example, in his final hours, the male lead has hallucinations full of random images such as letters and children's drawings.

Well, it happens those drawings came from children who were victims of real abuse, so some very real events of extreme private pain were being immortalized there. And those letters? Among them are death threats that were sent to director Hideaki Anno because fans were discontent with the previous installment of a television show, which was meant to connect the events of the series to the movie. And worst of all, one of the leading voice actresses actually strangled another actress during recording because that was what was happening in the scene. It was bad enough that she had difficulty continuing the recording.

3 Come and See

Come and See was a 1985 film from the Soviet Union that told the story of shell-shocked victims of the Third Reich's invasion of the USSR. While filming it, director Elem Klimov might have been a bit too realistic. Actual bullets were fired at cast members. Even though no one was actually trying to shoot anyone, lead actor Aleksey Kravchenko described how bullets came within inches of his head during a take. As reviewers have noted, the feeling of this danger does somewhat manage to come across to the viewer, but was it really worth it?

2 Last House on the Left

This 1972 movie was Wes Craven's breakout film, and it's one where he feels he went too far on the content. According to him and actors David Hess and Marc Sheffler, things got too serious behind the scenes as well. For example, to get a properly scared reaction out of his costar Sandra Cassel, Marc Sheffler grabbed her, held her over a drop, and threatened to throw her off if she didn't get the take in the next shot. Later, during a rape scene, David Hess threatened to really assault the actress to get a better performance. Hess suffered some real and completely reckless fear later when the actor playing the father of Hess's character threatened him with a chain saw, which was live, fully functional, and being used without any safety precautions. And this was after filming scenes in which the actors were really punching each other.

1 Men Behind the Sun

It's understandable that the director of this 1988 film felt justified in doing so many disturbing things. T. F. Mou was making a film about the systematic torture and human experimentation that occurred in Unit 731 during World War II, and to communicate the horror of that, he probably felt there should be few boundaries between the audience and the real atrocities he was simulating. To that end, there's a scene in the film in which a collection of rats are set on fire, which was done for real. But far worse is the scene in which a child who died from exposure is put on an autopsy table. This was a real person who had died just before the shoot. It's no wonder the film is often described as one of the most disturbing people have ever seen.

CHAPTER 4

WEIRD WORLD

1. Top 10 Weird Things That Have Happened at Walmart
2. Top 10 Bizarre Medieval Medical Practices
3. Top 10 Ways Our Ancestors Made Murder Fun
4. Top 10 Bizarre Uses for Human Skin
5. Top 10 Bizarre Murder Weapons
6. Top 10 Bizarre Aspects of Japanese Culture
7. Top 10 Bizarre Theories about the Earth That People Believe
8. Top 10 Bizarre Toilet Tales from around the World
9. Top 10 Insane Beauty Treatments
10. Top 10 Silliest Lawsuits Ever Heard in Court

TOP 10 Weird Things That Have Happened at Walmart

by Sophia Rienne

10 Walmart Wedding

People have very different ideas about what they want their wedding to be like. A lot of couples decide to go the romantic route and get married where they first met. Usually that means getting married on a cruise, in a specific city, or at a restaurant where the couple had their first date. For a North Carolina couple, that location happened to be a Walmart.

Wayne Brandenburg was a Walmart customer who became interested in a cashier working at the store. Eventually, he asked her out to a Chinese buffet. She agreed and they started dating. When they got engaged, they ultimately decided on Walmart as the ideal location for their wedding. The store agreed to let them get married there, and even the wedding cake was from the store's bakery.

9 Milk Thief

In 2011, at a Walmart in Virginia, an 18-year-old man decided to walk (or rather crawl) into a Walmart and steal 26 gallons of milk. Apparently the staff didn't notice him on all fours, carrying many gallons of milk and wearing a cow suit. The weirdest part is that, upon leaving the store, he started to casually hand out the milk to people passing by. All that stealing must have really worked up his appetite, since he was later found sans costume at a McDonald's, where he was identified by the police.

8 Naked Shoplifting

Most of us have desperately needed socks at one point or another. They're easy to misplace and develop holes from constant use and washing. Verdon Lamont Taylor, a 32-year-old man in Philadelphia, was in that situation one day. He did what a lot of us would do and headed to a local Walmart in hopes of solving his sock dilemma. However, instead of walking in and purchasing the item on his list, he decided first to get naked in the parking lot, then steal his new socks. Police had to use a stun gun to neutralize him after he spat in an officer's face and remained uncooperative.

7 Sex

The main appeal of Walmart is that you can find practically anything you're looking for at a cheap price. Customers at a local Kansas store probably didn't realize they would find a couple having sex inside the store in broad daylight, entirely for free. Justin Call and Tina Gianakon found themselves at Walmart one day and decided to steal a bottle of lubricant. After stealing the lubricant, they presumably thought it would be wise to test it before they left the store. The test eventually led the couple to full-on intercourse in front of the store's many customers.

Of course, the police showed up and arrested them. The most surprising part of the story is that they were both completely sober.

6 Human Teeth

Shopping for a new wallet at Walmart sounds simple enough. Unfortunately for one shopper at a Massachusetts store, he bit off more than he could chew when he found ten human teeth inside a brand-new wallet. He informed Walmart employees, who contacted the police. Officers were baffled, confirming that they were human teeth but unable to find out whose teeth they were or how they had gotten there.

5 Kidnapping Mix-Up

When you go to a supermarket or any large retail chain, it's filled with mothers and fathers with their children. Most people don't think twice about seeing a parent with their offspring. At a Virginia Walmart, however, a customer was concerned about seeing three girls with their father. Normally, when someone is concerned in a situation like that, it's because the parent is being physically or verbally abusive. In this case, the concerned customer didn't see any signs of abuse or foul play—they simply believed that the children had been kidnapped since the man was white and the little girls were mixed race.

The white father, Joseph, had gone to Walmart with his three daughters to cash a check. After he went home, Joseph and his wife Keana received a visit from a police officer. The police officer told them he was there to ensure that the children were theirs. Evidently the concerned customer had alerted Walmart security, who had then contacted the police. The officer asked one of the kids to verify that Joseph and Keana were her real parents.

According to Walmart, the customer was the one who decided to involve the police. The customer had told store employees that she didn't think the man and his children "fit together."

4 Giving Birth

The movie *Where the Heart Is* stars Natalie Portman as a young woman who gives birth at a Walmart after the store has closed for the day. Over the years, there have been various stories of this happening in real life. Nevertheless, it's surprising to find out how common it actually is.

In July 2013, a 16-year-old girl was at Walmart with her mother when she gave birth to a baby boy in the bathroom. When the baby was born it wasn't breathing, so a Walmart employee successfully gave the baby CPR. The girl and her child were then taken to a hospital to be checked out. She claimed that she'd had no idea she was even pregnant until she went into labor.

3 Cooking Meth

When we think of Walmart, we don't usually think of methamphetamine. And while Walmart isn't exactly a hotbed of methamphetamine usage, it's had more than its fair share of involvement with that particular narcotic.

A Walmart in Kentucky had to be evacuated after a man went into the bathroom with a backpack. The man was in the bathroom for long enough that employees became suspicious and checked up on him. When they found him, he was unconscious. The police arrived only to find that the backpack contained a mobile meth lab, and the man was arrested on multiple drug charges.

Another of the many famous meth cases at Walmart involves a woman in Missouri. Jennifer Vaughn-Culp was caught shoplifting at Walmart and kept in a holding area. When the police arrived, they realized that in addition to theft, the woman was also cooking meth in a soda bottle in her purse. As in the previous case, the store had to be evacuated for several hours. Vaugn-Culp did not learn her lesson, nor was she very loyal to Walmart. A few weeks later she was arrested for the same thing outside a gas station.

2 Semen Stalker

At a Walmart in Delaware, a 22-year-old man stalked a woman and threw semen at her. Frank J. Short, Jr., decided to go to Walmart to "kill time" and noticed a woman whom he thought was attractive. He followed her around the store before walking past her and throwing semen on her legs and buttocks. The woman was mortified and at first assumed it was just spit. After examining the fluid, she realized it looked more like semen. The woman went to the store's security and Short was arrested.

Short told the police that he had a cold and the fluid in question was just a result of him sneezing. Later he said it was saliva. However, the police were able to determine that it was, in fact, semen. The weirdest part is that this was not an isolated incident. Not only had Short done this before at Walmart, he'd also done it at Kmart. According to the police, he's a loner and this is something that he does to women to whom he feels sexually attracted. Whatever happened to simply complimenting a woman and asking her out for coffee?

1 Murder

During the holidays, customers at a South Carolina Walmart witnessed a heinous crime when a man stabbed his wife to death. Lilia Blandin was an employee at the bank located in the Walmart. She got into an intense altercation with her husband, who proceeded to stab her repeatedly. Several customers heard and saw the incident. The man was initially able to escape before being apprehended by the authorities. Unfortunately, Lilia Blandin succumbed to her injuries and was pronounced dead at a local hospital.

As if this story weren't repulsive enough, Walmart decided to remain open after the incident. The police were able to make the crime scene inaccessible to the public, but shoppers were allowed to continue their browsing as if nothing had happened. Understandably, many of them were disgusted that the store hadn't closed.

TOP 10 Bizarre Medieval Medical Practices

by **Gareth May**

10 Boar Bile Enemas

Enemas in medieval times were performed by devices called clysters. A clyster was a long metal tube with a cup on the end. The tube would be inserted into the anus and a medicinal fluid poured into the cup. The fluid would then be introduced into the colon by a series of pumping actions. Although warm soapy water is used for enemas today, things were a little earthier back then: One of the most common fluids finding its way into a clyster was a concoction of boar's bile.

Even kings were high up on the clyster. King Louis XIV of France is said to have had over 2,000 enemas during his reign—some even administered while he sat on his throne.

9 Urine Was Used as an Antiseptic

Though it may not have been common, there is evidence to suggest that urine was occasionally used as an antiseptic in the medieval era. Henry VIII's surgeon, Thomas Vicary, recommended that all battle wounds be washed in urine. In 1666, the physician George Thomson recommended urine to be used on the plague. And there was even a bottled version: Essence of Urine.

This isn't quite as insane as it seems: Urine is sterile when it leaves the body and may have been a healthier alternative than most water, which came with no such guarantee of cleanliness.

8 Eye Surgery (with a Needle)

During the Middle Ages, cataract surgery was performed with a thick needle. The procedure involved pushing the cornea to the back of the eye.

Eye surgery changed rapidly once Islamic medicine began to influence European practices. Rather than a needle, a metal hypodermic syringe was inserted through the sclera (the white part of the eye) and then used to extract cataracts via suction.

7 Hot Iron for Hemorrhoids

It was once believed that if a person did not pray to St. Fiacre (the "protector against hemorrhoids"), they would suffer from, you guessed it, hemorrhoids. If you were one of those unlucky fellows, you'd be sent off to the monks—who would put a red-hot iron up your anus. Nasty, but the less painful alternative was equally less effective: They'd send you to go and sit on St. Fiacre's famous rock, the spot where the 7th-century Irish monk was miraculously cured of his hemorrhoids. It was for this reason that throughout the Middle Ages, hemorrhoids were called "Saint Fiacre's illness."

By the 12th century, things had changed. Jewish physician Moses Maimonides wrote a seven-chapter treatise on hemorrhoids calling into question the contemporary state of treatment. He prescribed a far simpler method: a good soak in a bath.

6 Deadly Surgery

Despite what blockbuster movies may have taught you, going under the knife without any anesthetic wasn't as common in the medieval period as some people claim. In fact, medicine throughout this time was quite progressive. As the world expanded and travelers came from far afield, doctors from two different cultures would often share notes, and new practices were constantly being put to use.

However, even if the will for better medical care was there, the knowledge of chemicals certainly wasn't. Although anesthetic was administered, analgesics, antibiotics, and disinfectants were a far cry from what they are today. As a result, many people died from infected wounds.

5 Poisonous Anesthetics

As stated above, anesthetics were far from the established science they are today. In fact, general anesthesia is only about 150 years old. Before these advances, a rather crude brew of herbs mixed with wine was used to sedate the patient instead. The most common of these herbal anesthetics was known as dwale.

There were numerous ingredients in dwale—from the innocuous, such as lettuce and vinegar, to the deadly, such hemlock and opium. Much like modern knockout drugs, mixing these ingredients incorrectly could result in the patient's death.

4 Trepanning

Trepanning involved boring a small hole into the skull to expose the dura mater, the outer membrane of the brain. The practice was believed to alleviate pressure and treat health problems localized within the head, though it was also thought to cure epilepsy, migraines, and mental disorders and was a common "fix" for more physical problems such as skull fractures. Needless to say, such exposure of the brain to airborne germs would often be fatal.

Trepanning as a practice has not been completely abandoned: It was performed as recently as 2000, when two men in the U.S. used it to treat a woman suffering from chronic fatigue syndrome and depression.

3 Surgery on the Battlefield

In medieval times, battlefield medicine was about as grisly as it gets, and arrows were one of the main culprits. Arrowheads were commonly attached

to the shaft with wax for one single purpose: so that when the arrow was pulled out, the tip would break off inside the victim's body. "Arrow removers"—designed to pinch the tip and pull it from the body—were used to heal wounded soldiers. The wound was then cauterized with a red-hot iron to stop the bleeding and prevent infections.

While much has been forgotten about the medical capabilities of this era, research has shown that it may have been more effective than you might think. A set of bones from AD 500–700 discovered in Italy in 2011 shows that soldiers of that era could survive massive blows to the head. One of the remains even shows evidence that the individual had survived after suffering a two-inch hole to the head.

2 Medical Astrology

Back in medieval times, astrologers were so revered that many thought they were real-life magicians. The truth is, they were respected scholars who advised on increasing crop yield, predicted the weather, and informed a family-to-be what sort of personality their child would have. The latter would often have consequences for the child's medical care.

Doctors would refer to special calendars that contained star charts in order to aid with diagnosis. By the 1500s, the physicians of Europe were legally required to assess a patient's horoscope before embarking on any medical interference.

Astrology suggests that each body part is influenced by the sun, moon, and planets, and that each star sign presides over different parts of the body. Aries, for example, pertains to the head, face, brain, and eyes; whereas Scorpio represents the reproductive system, sexual organs, bowels, and excretory system. After the patient's star chart was examined and the current position of the stars was taken into account, a person's ailment could be predicted and a diagnosis would be made.

1 Bloodletting

Doctors of the medieval period believed in things called "humors." The word "humors" referred to certain fluids found in the body: blood, yellow bile,

black bile, and phlegm. "Humorism" was developed from the musings of Greek and Roman physicians who believed an excess or deficiency of any of the four humors would strongly influence a person's health.

For some reason, in the Middle Ages, blood—and excess blood in particular—was often seen as the cause of multiple ailments. Therefore, doctors would remove large quantities of blood from a person's veins in the hope that it would cure them. The two main ways of doing this were leeching and venesection.

In leeching, a leech was placed on the part of the body that was a concern and the "blood worm" would suck blood (and, in theory, the illness) from the patient. Venesection was a little bit more direct: A doctor would literally open up a vein using a knife called a "fleam" and allow blood to drain from the body.

Bloodletting was so common that some people drained their blood regularly just because they believed it would keep them healthy. Surely a half-hour jog is a better way to stay fit?

TOP 10 Ways Our Ancestors Made Murder Fun

by Nene Adams

10 Broadsheets and Pamphlets

Writers of broadsheets often employed doggerel verse in these poorly printed, highly imaginative accounts of murders, which were sold in poorer neighborhoods. Several editions focusing on the same murder might hit the streets within hours. Broadsheet sellers made sure to keep abreast of the latest developments in the investigation, arrest, trial, and eventual execution, often making up details about the crime or the killer's contrite confessions on the gallows to satisfy their audience. Pamphlets could be equally fictitious in relating the details, but were generally a bit better written and printed. It wasn't uncommon for a group of people to pool their money to buy a broadsheet or pamphlet to share.

9 Ballads

Songs about murders have been around for a very long time. In the 19th century, song writers continued to take advantage of the public's morbid fascination with murder by writing catchy topical tunes about killers and their victims. The music sheets were sold in shops and by vendors on street corners. Dance saloons played popular ballads for their customers. Individuals who could read music but had no access to an instrument sang the songs on the street to rapt audiences. The practice of writing and performing this kind of ballad hasn't changed much in modern times. Ever heard "Tom Dooley"? That's an enduring murder ballad. Joan Baez sang a few too, including "Banks of the Ohio."

8 Theatrical Productions

Whether for the penny gaffs—a rough, cheap form of theater for poorer folk—or the more upscale playhouses frequented by middle and upper class patrons, murder meant "butts on seats" for playwrights and actors. Of course, as in today's television melodramas, the details were tweaked to make them more exciting. One incredibly popular play, *The Colleen Bawn* (1860), was based on the murder of Ellen Scanlan by Stephen Sullivan in

Ireland around 1819. The story was not only turned into a play, but a novel, an opera, and three films. The true tale of the crime is rather mundane, but writers spiced it up.

7 Marionette Plays

We think of marionettes as solely children's entertainment, but in 19th century fairgrounds, these puppets on strings played out famous murders on their toy stages, delighting lower class children and adults alike. The effects were more sophisticated than you might expect, sometimes including pyrotechnics or spurting blood (actually an explosion of red ribbons from the puppet's body). A perennial favorite was "Maria Marten, or the Murder in the Red Barn." According to legend, the son of the unfortunate victim, Maria Marten, went to see a marionette performance of the drama and didn't show any emotion.

6 Souvenirs and Memorabilia

In the days before licensing agreements, anything belonging to or having a connection with a murderer or victim was fair game. For example, a structure in which a notorious murder took place might be torn apart (not necessarily with the owner's consent) by an ambitious entrepreneur, who sold the pieces as memorabilia. Wood from a crime scene might be turned into matchboxes or snuffboxes and put up for sale. Even pottery companies got in on the act by producing figures of the major players and the scenes. In fact, bits of the murderer's own body might be turned into keepsakes such as a cigar case or a pair of shoes. And handkerchiefs dipped in an executed murderer's blood have always been collectible.

5 Murder Tours

Before forensic science or autopsies were common, a murder victim's body was often left in situ so the scene could be examined by the jury of a coroner's inquest. While the police were supposed to guard the location, it often transpired that a member of the victim's household (family, friend, or servant) would permit paying members of the public to enter and gape at the blood, the terrible wounds, the gore-clotted murder weapon, footprints, and anything else that may or may not have relevance. These tourists might help themselves to whatever struck their fancy at the scene, such as door handles, drawer pulls, and textiles. Even after the body was removed, gawkers would continue to come and take a look.

4 Murder in Miniature

The Raree Show

If one couldn't make it to the murder scene in person, the next best thing was viewing a model at a fair or from a street entertainer. The customer paid the fee, put his eye to a hole in the side of a wooden box, and was able to view a re-creation of the crime scene in miniature. The luridly painted backdrops (complete with the victim writhing in his or her gore) could be changed while the operator recited the story of the crime, which might also include the murderer's hanging. At night, the scenes were dramatically lit with candles. For some reason, 19th century newspapers sometimes called these exhibitions "camera obscura." They remained popular until the invention of the mechanical peep show.

3 Storytelling

If broadsides, pamphlets, and ballads were too middle of the road, one only had to wait for the patterers (or storytellers) to come around one's neighborhood. These men carried signs painted with exaggerated pictures of the victim, the killer, the crime scene, the courtroom, the prison, and/or the gallows. Patterers exhibited the signs to draw in people eager to hear the details. After collecting a large enough crowd and passing the hat for his fee, a patterer would tell the story of the murder in an entertaining way. From the police's initial investigation to the killer's last dance at the end of a rope, material for a good storyteller never ran out.

2 Public Spectacle

The execution of a murderer could bring thousands of people flocking to the gallows to see the hanging (until 1868, when a law was enacted to place all executions behind prison walls). Owners of buildings with a good view of the proceedings sold seats to gawkers. Vendors of broadsheets, souvenirs, and food worked the crowd, as did pickpockets. If the hangman was inept or sloppy, the condemned man or woman might suffer slow strangulation (which could take up to 15 minutes) instead of a quick neck snap, or might be decapitated, spewing blood everywhere. Afterward, there might be an auction of the dead person's personal effects, and the rope would be sold by the inch. The body might be displayed for several days or given to the scientific community, which leads me to...

1 Scientific Experiments

Apart from serving as fodder for medical dissection, some murderers' bodies were experimented on, and sometimes the experiments were put on public view. Take William Corder, for instance, the killer of Maria Marten (mentioned in number seven in this list). Following his hanging, his body was placed on a cart and driven to the Shire Hall. His guts were removed by a doctor, and a plaster cast taken of his head to be studied by phrenologists. In addition, a battery was brought from Cambridge for the express purpose of performing "galvanic experiments" on Corder's body. All these proceedings were witnessed by a fascinated public, some of whom walked 30 miles into town to see the execution and its aftermath.

TOP 10 Bizarre Uses for Human Skin

by **Nene Adams**

10 Drum

A 15th-century undefeated Hussite military commander, Jan Ziska—real name Jan z Trocnova—wouldn't let a little thing like dying bring an end to his Protestant uprising against the Catholic Church. He'd already led his forces into battle to whip the Holy Roman Emperor's armies, invaded Austria and Moravia, and participated in a civil war even after losing both his eyes! According to legend, when he lay dying from the plague while on the march to Bohemia, Ziska ordered that after his death, his body should be flayed, and his skin cured and stretched over a drum to continue terrifying the enemy on the battlefield with his sheer badassery.

9 Waistcoat

During the Reign of Terror in an 18th-century France torn apart by revolution, Saint-Just rose to become a political leader, military commander, and close friend of Robespierre, as well as a member of the Committee of Public Safety, which condemned quite a few people to the guillotine. In a story attributed to de la Meuse's *Anecdotes*, Saint-Just's romantic advances toward a tall, young, beautiful woman were spurned. In a hell-hath-no-fury moment of madness, he had her arrested, executed, her skin removed by a surgeon, cured by a tanner, and made into a fashionable waistcoat he wore every day. Another version of the story is that the woman was a thieving maid who got her just desserts.

8 Cigar Case

Henri Pranzini, the late-19th-century French conman-turned-murderer—nicknamed the "Splendid Darling"—made a splash in more ways than one.

His trial caused a worldwide sensation, and he ended his days with a visit to the guillotine. As a grotesque, unconfirmed, but entirely possible coda, it's said that bits of his body were sold to collectors hungry for a piece of the infamous killer, including one of his teeth that was knocked out for a woman who had it set into a ring. The report goes that a member of the *Sûreté* (secret police) got hold of some of Pranzini's skin as a souvenir *du jour* and had a cigar case made from the leather.

7 Book

This is one of the more famous items on this list. Today held in the collection of the Boston Athenaeum library, the book has the title *Hic Liber Waltonis Cute Compactus Est* (This Book Is Bound in Walton's Skin). James Allen—real name George Walton—was a notorious 19th-century highwayman who died of tuberculosis while incarcerated in 1837. Before he died, he requested that his skin be removed and used to bind a volume of his autobiography to be presented to John Fenno, a former robbery victim who'd bravely stood up to him after being shot. The book remained in the Fenno family until it was donated to the library.

6 Calling Card Case

The 19th-century body snatchers and murderers William Burke and his partner, William Hare, killed 17 people in Edinburgh, Scotland, and sold their bodies to a doctor for dissection. Burke was convicted and hanged, but didn't go peacefully to his grave. His body was dissected—his skeleton and death mask are in the Anatomical Museum, University of Edinburgh—and other parts of his corpse made into useful items such as the binding of a pocketbook, and a very elegant calling card case made from the skin of his left hand, now on display at the Police Information Centre on Edinburgh's Royal Mile.

5 Wallet

In Morristown, New Jersey, in 1833, French immigrant Antoine LeBlanc battered three people to death, stuffed a pillowcase full of their valuables, and fled the blood-splattered scene. He was caught, convicted, and sentenced to hang. The judge also ordered that the infamous killer's body be dissected after death. According to reports, LeBlanc was flayed, his skin tanned, and some made into wallets and change purses. Other strips of the skin signed by Sheriff Ludlow (the man who had caught LeBlanc) were sold as mementos to curiosity-seekers. Long-considered mere rumor, the stories were proved plausible in 1979 when LeBlanc's death mask and what appeared to be a human leather wallet were discovered in the house of the town's unofficial historian and collector of 19th-century artifacts.

4 Boot

In this case, the skins' unwitting donors are unknown. In 1876, Mr. Mahrenholz of H&A Mahrenholz in New York, a shoemaker who enjoyed experimenting on various types of leather, including catfish and anaconda, procured the stomach, back, and buttock skins of a pair of unidentified elderly men who'd died and been previously dissected. After tanning the pieces of skin in dog manure and water—yes, there was a roaring trade in dog poop gathered and sold to tanneries, it was called "pure"—he made a handsome display boot and sent it to the Smithsonian Institute in Washington, D.C., where it remains in their collection.

3 Slippers

Around 1633, the French king Louis XIII founded the Cabinet du Roi, a private museum or cabinet of curiosities at the Palace of Versailles containing some interesting oddities. In the late-18th-century, it was reported by Valmont De Bomare in his *Dictionnaire* that a Paris surgeon, Pierre Sue, donated a pair of slippers made of human skin to the Cabinet du Roi, which already contained a human leather belt (nipple still visible). Eugène Sue, a descendant of Pierre, continued the family tradition by having an 1854 volume of *Le Mystères de Paris* bound in *peau de femme*—the skin of a woman who loved him.

2 High-Heeled Shoes

A noted Dutch physician and botanist in Leyden in the late-17th and early-18th centuries, Hermann Boerhaave is said to have owned a private collection of curiosities, including what's been reported as a pair of ladies' high-heeled shoes made from leather obtained from the skin of an anonymous, executed male criminal. The contributor's nipples were neatly centered on the uppers to form a grisly accent. How Boerhaave acquired this fashionable footwear is not known, but in *Notes and Queries Volume II, Series II* (1856), Henry Stephens wrote about seeing the shoes himself in 1818.

1 For the People, of the People

During the French Revolution, as the story goes, someone noticed that a potentially valuable resource was being wasted—the corpses of people executed by the guillotine. Accordingly, the Committee of Public Safety gave permission to use the castle of Muedon outside Paris as a tannery to process leather from human skin. Quite a number of gentlemen allegedly wore breeches and boots made from the product, which is said to have been supple and high quality. In fact, if you believe the author Montgaillard, men's skins were preferred for fashion, having the texture of chamois. Women's skins were too soft to be very useful.

Over the centuries, a few of the deceased have taken on new life by contributing body parts to dentures, fertilizer, fashion, the decorative arts, and other pursuits. Does the thought make you shudder? You're in good company. The living will probably always have a morbid fascination for objects made from the dead, perhaps a reminder of our own mortality.

TOP 10 Bizarre Murder Weapons

by S. Grant

10 Breasts

The next time you have an urge to go face-first into an ample bosom, you may want to consider the case of Donna Lange.

In January 2013, police were called to a trailer park in Snohomish County, Washington, after residents heard fighting from a neighbor's home. When police arrived, they found 192-pound Lange apparently passed out on her 175-pound boyfriend—with her chest completely smothering his face. Although some might consider death by breasts the best way to go, it seems the boyfriend did not enjoy his final moments, as witnesses heard him screaming for Lange to get off, and investigators discovered clumps of her hair in his dead hands.

Lange was charged with second-degree murder.

9 Guitar

Friends and family of Derrick Birdow said he was "out of his head" in the days before he drove a car into a Baptist church and then beat a pastor to death with an electric guitar he had picked up in the church's music room. Birdow's widow told authorities he was paranoid that someone had injected him with drugs, and he had tried in vain to get help from a medical center. While he was never professionally diagnosed, she believed he was mentally ill.

Of course, no one will ever know for sure what was going through Birdow's mind when he assaulted a beloved member of the community with a stringed instrument, since he died at the scene while in a patrol car. Officers used a stun gun to restrain him before placing him in the car, but when they went to check on him ten minutes later, they discovered he had no pulse.

As it turns out, someone (probably the deceased himself) had injected him with drugs, as toxicology reports from February 2013 showed Birdow was high on PCP on the day of the incident. PCP is a hallucinogen known to cause mood disorders, paranoia, hostility, and feelings of physical strength and invulnerability.

8 Corkscrew

When 55-year-old Murat St. Hilaire didn't show up for work and missed his daily telephone call to Carline Renelique, the mother of his children, Renelique became worried and took her three children with her to Hilaire's Prospect Heights, New York, apartment. Once there, the 11-year-old daughter found Hilaire in his bedroom, lying face up with a corkscrew stabbed in the side of his head.

Reportedly, the young girl ran out in shock saying, "Daddy's dead! Daddy's dead! Somebody stabbed him!"

This incident happened in 2008, and it appears no arrests have been made. Still, there are a couple things we can learn from this tragedy: If you want to play it safe, only drink wine from bottles with screw caps, and don't have young, impressionable children hunt for missing persons.

7 Xbox 360

In April 2013, police in Fort Lauderdale, Florida (a state with no shortage of weird crimes), discovered the dead body of Monica Gooden alongside a "broken and bloody Xbox 360," undoubtedly giving a new meaning to Xbox's infamous "red ring of death." The Xbox-wielding murderer was her boyfriend, Darrius Johnson, and, as it turns out, the peculiar choice of weapon isn't the strangest thing about this story.

Evidently, Johnson said he had to sacrifice her because she was somehow controlling him against his will, and killing someone born under the Taurus astrological sign was the only way to set his soul free. Incidentally, Gooden wasn't even a Taurus, so there's no telling who has control of Johnson's soul now. He also told police that she "would not die" and he "fought her like he was fighting a dragon."

Not only did Johnson beat his girlfriend with the Xbox, he also stabbed her repeatedly with a knife in some kind of postmortem ritual. I think it's safe to say the guy was completely crazy.

6 Crucifix

If you're going to kill someone with a crucifix (on Christmas, no less), you have to be really confident in your stance as a non-Christian or be willing to risk a few lightning strikes. We're not sure which side Karen Walsh of Ireland was on, but the woman was definitely willing to press her luck with the law when she used that religious ornament to mortally bludgeon her 81-year-old neighbor, Maire Rankin. Adding insult to injury, the soccer-mom-looking murderess sexually assaulted the granny in an effort to throw off police.

The body was discovered by Rankin's family, who went to check on the elderly woman when they could not reach her by the phone. She was discovered lying naked, bruised, and bloodied on her bedroom floor with imprints of the crucifix's thorns on her chin.

Walsh was convicted of murder in 2011 after the prosecution argued she'd killed Rankin in a drunken rage when the older neighbor admonished Walsh to quit drinking and go take care of her two-year-old son. Walsh continues to assert her innocence and says she only consumed a small amount of vodka that day and merely went to visit Rankin to wish her Merry Christmas.

5 Prosthetic Leg

In 2011, Debra Hewitt, a homeless Louisiana woman, was convicted of killing her boyfriend with her own prosthetic leg. Although she'd been accused of killing twice before (acquitted both times) and looked far from heavenly, Hewitt had picked up the nickname "Angel" somewhere along the line. The prosecution immediately twisted it into the more appropriate "Angel of Death," which the press pounced on as well.

According to reports, the "Angel of Death" stomped on her boyfriend, Dwayne Ball, then took off her prosthetic leg and used it to beat him to death—all while balancing on one good leg. After the pounding, she left Ball for dead in Lafayette Parish. The body was found six weeks later.

Hewitt was given a mandatory life sentence, so the formerly homeless killer is now getting three square meals a day, free health care, and a roof over her head. That'll teach her.

4 Poisoned Vagina

While no one actually died in this case, even attempting to murder someone via poison-laced lady parts is too weird not to mention.

Here's how it went down: After a Brazilian woman's husband refused to grant her a divorce, she apparently figured the next best option was to get rid of him permanently. There are any number of murder weapons she could have chosen and many methods of poisoning (if that was her preferred technique), but astoundingly, she figured the best plan was to stuff a toxic concoction up her cha-cha and invite her husband to perform oral sex.

The plan failed, however, because when the husband started the deed he became concerned about the strange odor coming from his wife's privates and immediately took her to the hospital. Ironically, his quick action likely saved his would-be killer, since the wife could have just as easily died from the poison.

3 Fat

Günther Kaufmann, an actor of some fame in Germany, claimed to have fallen on a friend and accidentally suffocated him with his hefty 265-pound body. "I simply fell on him—I didn't mean to kill him," Kaufmann said. "All of a sudden he was no longer moving."

That assertion alone is fishy enough, yet the tale gets even more suspicious when you find out the dead friend wasn't just a "friend," but also an accountant who had loaned Kaufmann money—which he had not repaid. Furthermore, the accountant suffocated from having his face pinned down into the carpet and wasn't killed instantaneously by crushing (as Kaufmann alluded). Medical examiners said the process would have taken around five minutes, which, even if it was accidental, seems long enough for Kaufmann to notice he was squashing the life out of his buddy.

Surprisingly, a Munich court didn't find the fat actor guilty of murder, but they did give him 15 years in jail for grievous robbery and blackmail with fatal consequences. In an unexpected twist to the tale, Kaufmann was released from prison in 2005 when police uncovered new evidence that suggested the actor's late wife was the perpetrator. Authorities believed Kaufmann confessed to the crime of burglary to protect his wife.

2 Stiletto

Breasts, vaginas, and now stilettos—it seems some women are walking killing machines. Unfortunately, Alf Stefan Andersson, a professor from the University of Houston, crossed one of these lethal sirens and ended up with more than ten holes in his head via a remarkably sharp stiletto shoe.

Some of the holes were one-and-a-half inches deep and all were allegedly delivered by Ana Lilia Trujillo, who was found at the crime scene covered in blood.

Trujillo, a former massage therapist, alleged Andersson attacked her while they were together in his apartment and that she acted in self-defense. She claimed he became jealous after another man bought her a drink at a club earlier that night, which started an argument. They continued fighting once they reached his apartment and neighbors called the police after hearing sounds of a struggle. Of course, the damage was already done by the time the police arrived.

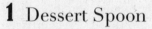

According to a motel manager where Trujillo lived, she had said in the past that her shoe was for protection and she'd use it to get anyone who "messed" with her. Apparently, she wasn't kidding. Trujillo was arrested in June 2013 and is being held on a $100,000 bond.

1 Dessert Spoon

In case you needed any more convincing that you can be offed by just about anything, let us introduce you to Timothy Magee—a man who was taken out by a mere dessert spoon.

On the day of this particular incident, a man named Richard Clare escaped out a window in a drug rehabilitation center in Hertfordshire, England, to collect money the disabled Magee supposedly owed him. When he couldn't get any cash off the man, Clare took Magee's cell phone as part of a heroin deal. It was when Magee went to get his phone back that Clare hit him on the back of the head with the deadly spoon, which ruptured an artery and caused fatal bleeding between Magee's brain and skull (talk about bad luck).

The courts deemed Clare innocent of murder (believing his assertions of self-defense) yet gave him a whopping seven days in jail for stealing the phone. Seven years later, in 2010, Clare was convicted of a different homicide and given no fewer than 27 years in prison. In the second killing, Clare opted for an axe instead of a spoon and went so far as to bury his victim in a metal box in their garden.

TOP 10 Bizarre Aspects of Japanese Culture

by **Mike Devlin**

10 Hikikomori

Although Earth's population is rising at an exponential rate, the Japanese are slowly dying off behind an aging infrastructure. Compounding this is a growing problem: the shut-in *hikikomori*. To be sure, every society is home to a small number of people who could be described as "reclusive"—though most of these recluses tend to be older individuals, marked with mental illnesses such as depression and agoraphobia.

Japan's *hikikomori* hermits, on the other hand, are decidedly young. They're mostly disaffected teenagers and twenty-somethings, withdrawn almost completely from society. There is no precise explanation to account for the rise in *hikikomori*, though there are several known contributing factors, including the rise of the Internet, intense academic pressures, and parents willing to shelter their children well into adulthood. Psychiatrists (many of whom are forced to make house calls to visit their patients), have only recently set upon the task of helping the group dubbed by some as "the missing million."

9 Crime

Although legends of the Yakuza are prevalent, crime rates are particularly low in Japan. It is illegal to own a handgun, and even ceremonial swords must be registered with the police. The country enjoys the second-lowest homicide rate in the world, behind only Monaco (a country about half the size of New York's Central Park). If you ever have the misfortune of standing trial in Japan, however, you can be almost certain that you're going to jail. Indeed, the conviction rate is said to exceed 99 percent (the career of a judge can suffer greatly for handing out acquittals).

Capital punishment is exercised in Japan, and around two or three inmates are executed every year. Unlike most other countries, death row inmates are only informed hours beforehand when their time is up. The family is not informed until the condemned parent, sibling, or child is already dead. Although Japan has a history of rather gruesome and unconventional methods of execution, prisoners are generally executed by hanging today.

8 Food

The Japanese have a predilection for novelty foods and beverages; indeed, the range of flavors they utilize often seems repellent to Western palates.

Due to a coincidence of language, the KitKat chocolate bar is enormously popular in Japan. "KitKat" is remarkably similar to the Japanese phrase *kitto katsu* (literally, "you shall surely win"), which is used as a sentiment of good luck. Students are often given the candy before an exam as a good luck charm. Unlike the rest of the world, which features only a milk chocolate version, Japan maintains dozens of exotic flavors, such as grilled corn, miso, Camembert cheese, baked potato, and soy sauce.

7 Job Performance

Although the Japanese are known for their industrious work ethic, the stereotype of the boozy businessman warbling "Margaritaville" in a karaoke bar is not that far from the truth. Marathon drinking sessions are often seen as a cornerstone of the Japanese business model; corporate relationships are forged over gallons of sake, with younger businessmen struggling in vain to keep up with their seasoned bosses.

That said, it's also relatively easy to nurse a hangover. The Japanese business culture values an employee who naps on the job. *Inemuri*, as it is known, is a quick catnap meant to recharge the batteries. It is seen as a sign of hard work and commitment.

6 Kodokushi

Nothing appears to be more tragic than dying alone—but it happens in Japan all the time. One of the unfortunate side effects of maintaining such an elderly population (one in five Japanese are over the age of 65, many of them well into their 80s and 90s) is that people tend to die at home. These people often go undiscovered, sometimes for months or even years—a phenomenon known as *kodokushi*, the lonely deaths. Thousands of cases occur in Japan each year, especially among men who have few social ties. Sometimes the bodies are left for so long that they self-mummify.

There are even companies that specialize in cleaning out the apartments of people who have succumbed to such a fate—even dealing with the grisly "*kodokushi* stains" left behind by a rotting body. It is estimated that in another 20 years, one in three Japanese will be senior citizens—an estimation that does not bode well for a halt in lonely deaths.

5 Porn

Japan has always been something of a restrictive society, and that prudishness extends all the way to its pornography. Although hardcore sex acts are allowed to be filmed, the genitalia is required to be blurred out in order to uphold moral laws. This has steered Japanese porn-makers toward a trend called *bukkake*—the prominent display of "resultant fluids"—as proof that the actors are really engaging in sex.

Curiously enough, a huge number of Japanese youths have reported that they have very little interest in sex. This is especially true for many males, who are often referred to as *soshoku danshi*, or "herbivore men."

4 Pachinko

Pachinko is a kind of cross between pinball and slot machines; it involves an upright machine, in which players shoot balls that descend through a series of pins. If the balls land in the right spot, more balls will be produced. Although gambling is technically illegal in Japan, winners are provided with a token based on their score that can be redeemed elsewhere for cash (a little bit like turning in your tickets at Chuck E. Cheese for a prize).

There is currently a push to legalize *pachinko* in Japan, with industry insiders estimating a potential gambling revenue that would approach $10 billion a year—nearly double that of Las Vegas.

3 Yaeba

Anyone who has suffered through the stigma of wearing braces (or any parent who has shelled out thousands for orthodontia) understands the importance of straight, even teeth. In Japan, however, there is a growing trend among young women for *yaeba* (literally, "double tooth") caps on the canines, which lends their smile a kind of crowded appearance. As bizarre beauty trends go, this one is somewhat costly to implement—but at least it's reversible.

2 Suicides

Although homicides in Japan are almost nonexistent, the country has one of the highest suicide rates in the world—in some cases more than twice that of other developed countries. Although attitudes are changing, suicide was for a long time accepted by the culture as a noble act—a way of protecting honor, and defending the reputation of the family.

One of the most startling suicide trends involves leaping in front of commuter trains. This has become such an issue that rail companies usually fine surviving family members for the inconvenience. Japan is also home to the chilling Aokigahara Forest. Located near Mount Fuji, Aokigahara is well known as a hotspot for suicides.

1 Kentucky Fried Chicken

The typical Japanese diet is quite healthy; daily staples like rice, tofu, and fresh vegetables make Japanese citizens some of the longest-lived people on earth. But many Japanese people also have a weakness for American comfort food—most notably, fried chicken. In major cities, there is often a KFC to be found every few blocks, with each restaurant hosting a life-size statue of Colonel Sanders standing out front.

Although only a small handful of Japanese are Christian, they have adopted KFC as a Christmas Eve tradition. On December 24, every KFC in Japan has lines out the door. Many people make reservations months in advance.

The KFC legend is not confined only to the holiday season. In 1985, when the Hanshin Tigers baseball team won the Japan Series, revelers spilled into the streets. Amid the chaos, a statue of Colonel Sanders was thrown into a canal in Osaka. In the subsequent years, the Tigers have continually failed to win another championship— as a result of the "Curse of the Colonel." In 2009, most of the statue was recovered from the river. The glasses and the left hand are still missing, however, and some locals believe that the curse will not lift until the Colonel is whole.

TOP 10 Bizarre Theories about the Earth That People Believe

by **Jeff Kelly**

10 Lemuria and Atlantis

We're going to focus mainly on Lemuria here, but it would be foolish not to mention both of the so-called "missing continents" that people have theorized for years simply must have existed. Just like Atlantis, Lemuria was said to have been a giant landmass located in the Indian and Pacific Oceans, and in both cases one of the primary reasons for the creation of the theory of these lost continents was to explain how similar species could exist on two landmasses so far from one another.

In the case of Lemuria, it basically all comes down to a man named Philip Sclater, who found himself puzzled as to why he was finding lemur fossils on the island of Madagascar and India, but not Africa or the Middle East. According to Sclater, the only possible explanation was that there simply must have been a giant landmass connecting the two nations, and he decided to name it after the glorious lemur itself. Over the years, people have pretty much dismissed the notion that Lemuria ever existed, but the myth has continued thanks largely to some pretty batty writers, such as Helena Blavatsky, who wrote about the occult, so you know she's a trustworthy source.

9 Geoterrapinism Theory

Don't look now, but according to some, we are living on the back of a giant turtle. We might also be living on the back of an elephant or a serpent, but let's stick with turtles for now, because the Cosmic Turtle is the most widely recognized "belief" in this particular category.

The Great Turtle myth was first brought to the public's attention in the 17th century, after a man named Jasper Danckaerts learned of it from several tribes of Native Americans he encountered. The Native Americans, however, are not the only ones who believed that the world rested on the shell of a giant turtle, as the myth is also prevalent in Chinese and Indian culture.

8 Tectonic Strain Theory

Unlike other theories on this list, which are meant to explain the Earth itself and the various events that have taken place over the millennia, Tectonic Strain Theory sets out to explain something otherworldly: UFO sightings throughout history. Not only UFOs, mind you, but also ghosts, spontaneous combustion, and basically anything else thought of as an otherwise inexplicable event.

Tectonic Strain was theorized by Professor Michael Persinger in 1975, and suggests that every UFO sighting and basically unexplained phenomena people claim to have seen can be explained away by electromagnetic fields that occur when the Earth's crust strains near seismic faults. According to Persinger, these electromagnetic fields create hallucinations, which are based on images from popular culture.

7 Contracting Earth Theory

Contracting Earth Theory, or geophysical global cooling if you want to get all scientific about it, was a theory before the idea of plate tectonics ever came about that said the Earth is actually getting smaller over time, and the shrinking Earth is what causes natural disasters as well as the natural wonders of nature, such as mountain ranges.

The idea is that the Earth consists of molten rock, and as the Earth's interior cools and contracts, so too does the surface, leading to mountains springing up left and right, often turning into volcanoes when the planet needs to vomit up whatever it can't keep down in its own planetary version of a stomach. The theory has in fact been used in real, bona fide scientific research, notably by a man named Professor Edward Suess in order to explain an earthquake.

6 The Expanding Earth Theory

On the flip side of the Contracting Earth Theory is the Expanding Earth Theory, which is exactly what it sounds like. It was believed by some that the Earth is ever-expanding, just like the universe it occupies, and fortunately since people started to realize that plate tectonics are a thing that happen, they've more or less rejected either of these two theories.

Of course, I hesitate to really scoff too much at the people who have theorized that the Expanding Earth Theory wasn't actually stupid and nonsensical, largely because one of the most noteworthy minds who put the theory to work was Charles Darwin himself, but thankfully he quickly realized that would make no sense and went back to doing what he did best: irritating the hell out of Creationists.

5 Fixed Earth Theory

Also known as the geocentric model, the Fixed Earth Theory states that the Earth is, despite all evidence to the contrary, located at the very center of the universe, and the rest of the cosmos revolve around our very own planet. Though this theory was challenged by the likes of Copernicus and Kepler and has been generally accepted as being nonsense, some people have still refused to let go of the idea that anything but humans could be at the center of the universe.

Fixed Earth Theory was most notably argued by Ptolemy, and his geocentric model was used for astrological charts for 1500 years. It wasn't until those guys Copernicus and Kepler, along with Galileo, came along that people started to realize that maybe, just maybe, it's actually the Earth doing the rotating, and the sun that's located at the center of our universe. By the way, believe it or not, people still believe in the Fixed Earth Theory.

4 Time Cube Theory

Gene Ray is a little bit of a strange guy. Even as recently as 1997, he decided to ignore all facets of science and concoct his own theory called Time Cube,

 which states that what we think of as the rules of physics are completely wrong, and that each day is actually four different days all happening at the same time.

Basically, what Ray is suggesting is that the Earth consists of four equidistant "time points," because we have such things as midday, midnight, sunup, and sundown. Clearly, according to Ray, the only logical explanation is that these are actually four days taking place at the same time, and have nothing to do with the Earth's natural rotation and the fact that the sun hits different parts of the globe at different times. So adamant about his theory is Ray that he went to MIT and actually bet the professors there $10,000 that they could not disprove it. None took him up on the wager, either because he wasn't worth their time, or because they don't want us to realize the terrifying truth.

3 John Symmes's Hollow Earth Theory

When you look up into the stars at night, you can pretty much be sure of a couple things. You're looking up, you're looking out, and you're looking at a whole lot of empty space. However, in the 19th century, there arose an infamous theory that continues to thrive today despite being utterly insane, and that's that what you're looking at is actually located in the center of the Earth.

That theory was brought about in large part thanks to John Symmes, a former captain in the U.S. Army in the War of 1812 who believed that the Earth had a shell 800 miles thick, with openings at each magnetic pole and several inner shells that made up a series of concentric spheres upon each of which people and animals lived. We're not quite sure why this was called Hollow Earth Theory and not Russian Nesting Doll Theory.

2 Cyrus Teed's Cellular Cosmology Theory

An extension of Hollow Earth Theory popularized by Cyrus Teed, Cellular Cosmology proposes that, rather than the universe existing all around us, we live in an inside-out universe that occupies a "hollow cell" of rock that is 8,000 miles in diameter. And at the center of this hollow cell inside a giant rock is the sun, only in this case Teed believed the sun to be an electromagnetic battery.

Teed was a certified crackpot and alchemist who believed everything in the universe was made of the same substance. He was told that the entire universe that existed within the Earth was delivered to him by "The Divine Motherhood" and that he was a new Messiah. So we should probably take his ideas with a grain of salt.

1 Flat Earth Theory

The most famous wacky theory about the Earth is also one that at this point is pretty much universally known to be completely, unequivocally untrue, yet believe it or not, there are some folks who have perpetuated the idea with the Modern Flat Earth Theory. These people make up the Flat Earth Society, which came about in 1956 and still exists.

These are the people who believe that, despite all scientific evidence to the contrary, the Earth is, in fact, flat. In 1980, a member of the Flat Earth Society named Charles Johnson actually managed to get an article published in *Science Digest*, in which he claimed that the Earth must be flat, because otherwise there would be curvature on bodies of water like Lake Tahoe, and to the best of his knowledge, there was no evidence that the water was anything other than flat. Never mind photographic evidence from space showing the Earth to be spherical, a flat surface on a lake is enough evidence for us!

TOP 10 Bizarre Toilet Tales from around the World

by **Mike Devlin**

10 Makeshift Electric Chair

Found guilty of sexual assault and murder, 28-year-old Michael Anderson Godwin was sentenced to death in South Carolina. An appeal rescued him from the electric chair, but destiny apparently wasn't done with him. In March of 1989, Godwin was perched on a steel prison toilet, attempting to fix a pair of headphones attached to his television set. He bit into the wire, and was electrocuted.

9 Singapore Flush Fine

The city-state of Singapore is well known for its bizarre, often draconian laws. The sale of chewing gum is prohibited, as are pornography and the possession of durian fruits on mass transit. Punishment can range from extreme fines to prison terms, as well as corporal punishment and the death penalty. One of the stranger rules involves toilets. If you use a toilet in public and neglect to flush, police (who check randomly), can arrest you. You can be subject to a $500 fine and even a public caning for leaving behind a present for the next unsuspecting patron.

8 The Beaver

It is believed that the first toilet shown on television was featured in a 1957 episode of the sitcom *Leave It to Beaver*. In the episode, Beaver and his big brother, Wally, order a pet alligator named Captain Jack from a comic book ad. Hoping to hide their pet from their parents, the boys stash Jack in the toilet tank. It is interesting to note that network censors so feared a public backlash that they only showed the tank, not the complete toilet.

7 Carson and the Toilet Paper Shortage

In 1973, perhaps having no more pressing concerns, a Wisconsin congressman named Harold Froelich voiced a concern that the United States faced an impending paper shortage in the coming year. The story made very minor headlines, and would have ended there if the staff of *The Tonight Show Starring Johnny Carson* hadn't happened across the article. Like today's late-show hosts, Johnny Carson was well known for riffing on the headlines, but on December 19, 1973, viewers took him quite seriously when he warned of a nationwide shortage in toilet paper. The next day, shoppers went wild, buying every roll off store shelves and hoarding it. Some stores took advantage, price-gouging customers on this suddenly scarce  commodity. Although Carson took to the air the following night to assure his viewers the warning had been meant in a purely tongue-in-cheek fashion, the damage had been done.

6 The Permanent Throne

In February of 2008, authorities were summoned to the home of Kory McFarren in Ness City, Kansas. McFarren reported that there was "something wrong" with his girlfriend. What was wrong was that 35-year-old Pam Babcock had been sitting on his toilet for some two years, so long that her skin had grown around the seat. Paramedics were forced to remove the seat, where it was surgically removed at the hospital. It has since been revealed that Babcock suffered from some mental disorder; when McFar-ren asked her to leave the bathroom, she would reply, "Maybe tomorrow."

Although there was some debate as to whether or not the boyfriend would face charges, McFarren was eventually convicted of misdemeanor treatment of a dependent adult for waiting so long to seek help. He was sentenced to six months probation. Strangely enough, this is not the only case of a woman holding long-time residence of the toilet; a Chinese woman in Singapore also held a two-and-a-half year vigil on the bowl beginning in March of 2009. She claimed that she "felt a force holding me down."

5 Before Toilet Paper

Toilet paper as we know it is actually a very recent innovation, only about 150 years old. Before commercial T.P., almost anything at hand was used: leaves, corncobs, and shells, among other items. In some Asian nations, it was customary to use the left hand and a pitcher of water. This goes to explain some of the prejudice exercised toward left-handed people; through-out India and the Middle East, the left hand is considered unclean, and using it to pass someone an item is considered an insult. The use of actual paper came with the rise of department stores, who distributed catalogs to their customers. Indeed, there was a terrible backlash when the Sears & Roebuck catalog began using glossy, nonabsorbent paper to publish photos.

4 Air Toilets

The modern bathroom is far from a universal convenience; billions world-wide have little or no access to sanitary facilities. In many Third World nations, people are lucky to have a hole in the ground. In many places, especially heavily populated slums, even that luxury is often denied. In the harshest sections of Nairobi, the capital of Kenya, the most commonly used method of waste disposal is the "flying toilet." Euphemisms are rarely gen-tler; a flying toilet is little more than a plastic bag that is defecated in, then hurled away as far as possible. The streets are covered with mountains of such filth, a hazard that allows diseases such as malaria and typhoid fever to thrive. The rainy season is especially treacherous, with floodwaters washing the waste through people's homes and into their drinking water. Some entrepreneurs have begun installing public toilets and charging the public a small fee to use them, but progress toward improvement is very slow.

3 German Toilets

In Germany and Austria, it is common to encounter "washout toilets," which feature an inspection shelf to catch your deposit. Upon rising, you are able to inspect your leavings for health reasons (mostly to check for the presence of worms or other parasites). While this construction eliminates the possibility of the dreaded "splash back," it is reported that a near immediate mercy flush is required to alleviate the odor. For this reason, many Germans find it quite important to employ a good plumber in the case of emergencies.

2 Attacks

There are few more vulnerable moments than those spent sitting on the toilet. Indeed, visiting the bathroom is not without its perils from the local wildlife. Modern plumbing has greatly minimized human contact with the deadly black widow spider, who love to dwell in outhouses, dark areas teeming with edible insects. However, all of our innovations fail to save us from rats, who have been known to swim up through pipes and enter homes through toilets, even attacking those unfortunate enough to be sitting there at the time.

1 High-Tech Toilets

The design of toilets has not changed much in generations; in the Western world, most toilets are of a simple flush design. However, there is a growing trend for computerized "smart toilets"; the Japanese in particular are well known for their high-tech commodes. With some varieties priced well over $5,000, Japanese toilets sport an array of options more advanced than those found in most cars. High-end models have automatic lids, temperature-controlled bidets, heated seats, driers, deodorizers, music, and even medical sensors with options for measuring the pulse, blood sugar, and body fat of the user. In addition to more practical developments, the Japanese have also developed bathroom video games such as Sega's *Toylet*, a urinal game controlled by the stream of the player.

TOP 10 Insane Beauty Treatments
by **Mike Devlin**

10 Thai Face Slapping

While many of the procedures on this list are quite risky, the face slapping technique is in good fun. Offered by Bangkok masseuse Tata in her San Francisco massage parlor, the treatment consists of pinching and manipulating the skin and delivering light slaps that are said to cure wrinkles and shrink pores. Whether this is at all helpful in restoring a youthful appearance is highly debatable, but it doesn't come cheap. A single 15-minute session will set you back $350.

9 Stem Cell Cosmetics

The use of stem cells in medical treatments remains highly controversial, with detractors claiming their use is "playing God." Very basically, stem cells can "transform" into any other cell, and are used by the body to make repairs. The only stem cell treatment approved by the U.S. Food and Drug Administration is a bone marrow transplant in the instance of leukemia, but that hasn't stopped many patients from seeking cutting-edge plastic surgeries, wherein the cells are drawn from the body via liposuction and then re-injected into the face to repair wrinkles. Unfortunately, the procedure is in its infancy, and there is no way to predict exactly how the cells will behave. In at least one horrifying instance, a woman grew bones in her eyelid.

8 Fish Pedicure

Native to the rivers and springs of the Middle East, the doctor fish is a toothless creature around the size of a guppy. Like a lot of fish, these guys are not particularly picky eaters. In fact, they have been used for some years to perform pedicures, gnawing the dead and callused skin away from the feet. The creepy procedure is apparently quite effective, and those who have had it done claim it is painless. However, in much of the world, just as these pedicures began  taking off, they were banned, as letting fish in communal baths chew on toes of multiple customers is not in the least bit sterile. Seized fish have been shown to carry a wide array of bacteria, including that which causes cholera and streptococcal infections.

7 Bird Poop Geisha Facial

The idea of the geisha is quite foreign to Western sensibilities. Her role often varied; she could be anything from servant to concubine to entertainer, and everything in between. Perhaps the best-known aspect of the geisha is her white pancake makeup, which was once lead-based and ravaged the skin. To restore their appearance, the geisha used a cream made from the droppings of nightingales, which contained revitalizing enzymes. Or so the staff at Shizuka New York, a swanky Japanese spa in Manhattan, would lead you to believe. For just $180, they will paint your face with bird poo, carefully sanitized under ultraviolet light and mixed with some other ingredients to hide the rather disagreeable smell. While the claims seem dubious, some customers have reported a "glow" on their face after the treatment.

6 DC-CIK Cancer Therapy

DC-CIK treatment is another controversial procedure that involves drawing blood from a patient suffering from cancer. The blood is then turned over to a lab, where it is concentrated, then injected back into the body after chemotherapy or surgery. It is said to promote healing. However, some dubious clinics in Hong Kong have begun offering the treatment to give patients a more youthful appearance. At least one death from septic shock has been reported, and several other people have been sent to the hospital, infected by mycobacterium abscessus, a nasty bacteria known to cause lung disease and wound infections.

5 Urine

Most of us have a relationship of absolute necessity with our urine; one quick flush and it's gone. There is, however, a small but dedicated community that extols the supposedly restorative properties of urine. These people claim drinking urine can cure (or at least relieve the symptoms of) a vast number of diseases, ranging from lupus to multiple sclerosis, and even cancer. Urine is also used for beauty treatments; advocates claim that, when applied topically, urine is excellent for the skin, clearing up psoriasis, eczema, and acne. The best urine is apparently taken midstream, first thing in the morning, when beneficial hormones have been able to build up overnight. Perhaps not surprisingly, the legitimate medical community has not recognized any benefits of the consumption of urine.

4 Toe-Besity

Although many bodily modifications made in the name of beauty could be described as frivolous, toe narrowing is among the most foolish. A growing number of people, unsatisfied with "fat" toes, have been turning to podiatrists for help. The procedure, which is somewhat gruesome, involves splitting the toe open and grinding down the bone and fat inside. While not a terribly risky procedure, it still carries the dangers inherent in any surgery. There is also usually a long recovery time.

3 Micro-Needle Therapy

The micro-needle roller resembles some kind of medieval torture device; sporting hundreds of tiny spikes, it is designed to puncture the skin at the microscopic level, both inducing it to heal itself and allowing for the penetration of creams. Many celebrities are said to use micro-needle treatment, and it is particularly popular in China. While the effectiveness of the treatment itself is debatable, the danger is not: There is no way to truly sterilize the equipment, and using it on multiple people provides a vector for infections, including blood-borne pathogens like HIV and hepatitis.

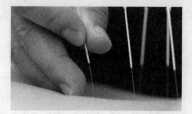

2 Bee Venom Mask

Advertised as a "safer" version of Botox (itself a tamed version of the botulinum toxin, one of the deadliest known substances), bee venom wrinkle cream has become all the rage, the beauty secret of the UK's duchess of Cambridge and duchess of Cornwall. Quite expensive, the cream apparently induces a reaction in the skin that causes the body to believe it has been stung or damaged, increasing blood flow and collagen and repairing the area. The venom itself is harvested in a process wherein a "harmless" mild electric current is run through a pane of glass, inducing the bees to sting. There has been a larger movement for some years to use bee venom to cure all sorts of maladies, from multiple sclerosis to arthritis, but tests have shown it to be largely ineffective. Obviously, the use of venom carries with it serious risks; those who find themselves allergic can easily succumb to anaphylactic shock.

1 Tittooing

This one takes masochism to extremes rarely imagined. A few decades ago, the vast majority of those sporting tattoos were bikers and sailors, outlaws of a sort. Today, sorority girls the world over are inked. Cosmetic tattooing is not a terribly new phenomenon, with many women getting their eyebrows or lips done. But a strange new craze has begun sweeping the UK: women getting their nipples darkened and defined. Over a dozen salons offer the treatment, and word continues to spread. Local anesthesia is administered and a color complementary to the patient's skin tone is added. Every year to year and a half, a follow-up appointment is scheduled to maintain the appearance.

TOP 10 Silliest Lawsuits
Ever Heard in Court

by **Andrew Handley**

10 Batman vs. Batman

You may not know this, but there's a city in Turkey called Batman, located beside the Batman River in the Batman Province. What you do probably know is that Batman is a superhero and titular hero of the Dark Knight trilogy, directed by Christopher Nolan. In 2008, the city of Batman sued Christopher Nolan and Warner Bros.—the production studio behind the films—for using their town's name without getting permission first.

The mayor of Batman, Huseyin Kalkan, who either has the best sense of humor or a complete lack of one, stated, "There is only one Batman in the world," in his defense of the lawsuit. He claims that not only should the city receive royalties for the use of the Batman name, but that they should be compensated for the "psychological impact" on residents, as well as for an inexplicably high suicide rate among females in Batman—all apparently caused by the Dark Knight films.

9 Disabled vs. Disney

A few years ago, Disney banned the use of Segways— those two-wheeled scooters that you stand up on—in its parks for safety reasons. Since then, they've faced a barrage of criticism from the disabled community, culminating in a lawsuit by a couple from Illinois and a woman who lives in Iowa, who claimed that not allowing its visitors to use Segways was a violation of the Americans with Disabilities Act.

The kicker is, there's no ban on seated scooters or motorized wheelchairs, and Disney has started providing its own version of standing scooter that is slower and easier to maneuver, reducing the chance of accidentally running over children. They charge a fee to use the scooters, but they also agreed that they could waive the fee if the guest brought their own Segways.

So with all of that in mind, the only grounds for suing is that it would be inconvenient for someone to learn to operate a scooter that they're not used to. The lawsuit was dismissed almost immediately, but the three plaintiffs tried again, and managed to win $4,000 each (with Disney picking up the $185,000 court tab). And at the end of it all, Segways are still banned in the parks, and the plaintiffs used their $4,000 settlements for a week at Disney World. Justice at last.

8 Andrew Burnett vs. Dog Owner

In the year 2000, Andrew Burnett got into a fight over a fender bender on a highway in San Jose, California. The situation became heated, words were exchanged, and Andrew Burnett grabbed the lady's dog and hurled it into traffic. The dog was killed, and Burnett went to jail for three years. Everybody got what they wanted, sort of.

Then in 2003, Burnett filed a $1 million lawsuit against the dog's owner, claiming that she had defaced his image and caused him mental anguish, along with lost wages from the time he had to spend in prison. Thankfully, the judge decided not to compensate the dog tosser, and threw the case out of court.

7 Wanita Young vs. Free Cookies

Cookies will brighten up anybody's day—especially if they're being given away for free. At least, that's what two teenage girls thought when they surprised their neighbor with a plate of homemade cookies. But they were in for a surprise.

The two girls, Lindsey Zellitti and Taylor Ostergaard, wanted to do something nice for their neighbors. So they went around their neighborhood, knocking on doors and leaving a small package of cookies in front of every door. When they got to 49-year-old Wanita Young's house, the sound of the girls knocking on the door apparently drove her into an anxiety attack, causing her to call the police who eventually took her to the hospital.

After the girls apologized, and after they offered to pay her hospital bills, Young still decided to take them to court and sue them for $900—and she actually won the case.

6 Homeless Man vs. His Parents

In February 2013, a homeless man named Bernard Bey filed a (currently pending) lawsuit against his parents on the grounds that his current situation—homelessness—was caused by their emotional neglect. He's asking them to pay $200,000 for emotional damages, stating that he feels "unloved and abandoned." And that's actually the normal part of the lawsuit. Bernard ran away from home at the age of 12 and claims he was abused by his father as a child; since then he has lived in and out of poverty—and jail—for nearly 20 years. That's terrible parenting at best.

But Bernard Bey's lawsuit doesn't stop at $200,000—and this is where it begins to get a little odd. In addition to the money, the lawsuit asks his parents to mortgage their home and purchase two Domino's Pizza franchises, through which they might then employ the entire family. He's suing them to give them a career. And with a final heartbreaking twist, Bernard said that he's willing to drop the lawsuit completely if his family will just sit down and talk with him over dinner.

5 William Baxter vs. His Wife's Cat

In 2011, William Baxter was watching over a friend's cat when the animal "viciously" attacked him and bit his finger. So Baxter took the only reason-able option left open to him: He sued the cat's owner for $100,000. He demanded $50,000 for scratches on his arm, and then another $50,000 for the bite to his finger. The finger in question was his ring finger, a subtle irony because the owner of the cat, Christine Bobak, might actually be his wife—the newspaper that originally reported the lawsuit, the *Southtown Star*, did some digging into the case and found that the two were listed as married on Facebook.

Either way, the lawsuit claims that not only is Baxter suffering now, but he will "in the future continue to suffer," which is probably a reference to the procedure of tearing off his Band-Aid.

4 John Coomer vs. The Kansas City Royals

In 2009, John Coomer was watching a baseball game when a hot dog crash-landed in his eye. The culprit: Sluggerrr, the mascot of the Kansas City Royals, who had been tossing hot dogs into the crowd between innings. Blinded by fury and mustard, Coomer filed a lawsuit against the team and took them to court.

He claimed that the hot dog caused a detached retina in his left eye, which resulted in surgery, and that the act of chucking hot dogs was a danger to the crowd. After some deliberation, the jury ruled that the incident was 100 percent Coomer's fault, and that airborne foodstuffs are inherent risks involved in watching a baseball game. They also agreed that, since Coomer had been to 175 Royals games and witnessed the "Hotdog

Launch" dozens of times, he was definitely aware of the sausage-shaped danger.

But Coomer and his attorney appealed to a higher court and somehow got the verdict reversed. The judge ruled that—and I quote—"...the risk of being hit in the face by a hot dog is not a well-known incidental risk of attending a baseball game," which is a sentence we can only hope to hear in real life.

3 Karl Kemp vs. New York's Homeless

Karl Kemp Antiques is a high-end antique shop located on Madison Avenue in New York City, owned by Karl Kemp. After putting up with homeless people living outside his shop for more than two years, Kemp decided to take action: He filed a lawsuit against four of them for $1 million, and sought a court order to keep them 100 feet away from the door of the shop.

Ignoring the obvious fact that if any of them had a million dollars they probably wouldn't choose to sleep on his sidewalk, Kemp's lawsuit has been deemed "mean-spirited" by the policy director of the Coalition for the Homeless. Even Kemp's lawyer admitted that the homeless people weren't really breaking any laws, and that they only put $1 million on the lawsuit because they "had to name a figure."

2 Sentry Insurance vs. Keipper

On February 4, 2004, a worker for a local meal-delivery company slipped and fell on a patch of ice while walking across the driveway of Anne Keipper, a then-78-year-old woman living in Milwaukee. An ambulance came, the delivery woman left, and nothing more was heard about the incident.

Nothing, that is, until 2007—three years after the fall occurred—when Sentry Insurance contacted Anne Keipper to inform her that they were suing her to pay for the medical expenses of the worker who fell on her driveway (Sentry was the injured worker's insurance provider). The worker herself, Dolores Tanel, was named an involuntary plaintiff, which is someone who refuses to join a case as a plaintiff.

That means that Sentry Insurance—a company with an estimated $2.3 billion in total revenue—was suing Keipper—an 81-year-old woman who happened to have a driveway at the wrong place and time—of their own volition, simply to cover a compensation claim they paid out to their own client, which is the reason they're in business in the first place.

1 Pearson vs. Chung: The Pants Lawsuit

In 2005, Judge Roy L. Pearson brought a pair of pants to a Washington, D.C., dry cleaner called Custom Cleaners. The cleaners happened to misplace the pants, and Judge Pearson then smacked them with a lawsuit so ridiculous it should have been thrown out immediately. Instead, it took three months and two further appeals (including another lawsuit against the city of D.C. itself) before it was finally laid to rest. Pearson originally asked for $67 million, then dropped his claim to a more reasonable $54 million—that's $1,000 for the pants, and $53,999,000 for court fees and mental distress.

And apparently it was indeed very distressing: On the first day of court, Pearson broke down in tears as he described how frustrated he was on the day his pants went missing. The court ruled in favor of the dry cleaners, but Pearson came back just weeks later, asking the court to reexamine the case. They refused, and the appropriately embarrassed D.C. court also decided to terminate Pearson's contract with them (remember, he was a federal judge).

So Pearson did the only thing that made sense to him: He sued Washington, D.C. And the worst part of it all? The dry cleaners apparently found his pants two days after they lost them, but Pearson refused to take them back. He claimed to be "crusading for the people."

CHAPTER 5

FACTS AND MISCONCEPTIONS

1. Top 10 Weird Facts about Cereal

2. Top 10 Common Misconceptions about the Ancient Greeks

3. Top 10 Common Myths about Famous Landmarks

4. Top 10 Myths Involving the Nazis

5. Top 10 Fantastic Facts about Beer

6. Top 10 Weird Facts about Cats

7. Top 10 Weird Facts about Dogs

8. Top 10 Lesser-Known Facts about the Titanic

TOP 10 Weird Facts about Cereal

by **Mike Devlin**

10 Pink Poop

In 1971, General Mills debuted two monster-themed cereals: the sickeningly sweet Count Chocula and its strawberry equivalent, Franken Berry. Later cereals in this vein would include Boo Berry, Fruit Brute, and the unfortunately named Fruity Yummy Mummy. The line would prove extremely profitable, but in 1972, General Mills faced a public relations disaster. The dye they used to make Franken Berry pink often was not absorbed by the digestive system. Terrified parents found their children's poop stained a garish pink and rushed them to the emergency room, fearing internal bleeding. The condition, called "Franken Berry Stool," was thankfully quite benign. The offending dye has long since been discontinued. Today, Franken Berry, Count Chocula, and Boo Berry are only available for a few months around Halloween time.

9 Extinct Cereals

More than any other product, cereal relies upon the whim of children. Kids, most of whom would live on chicken nuggets if they were allowed to, hardly possess the palates of cultured food critics. The recipe for success is quite simple—make it sweet and team it up with something popular. This formula has led to a plethora of forgettable cereals, including Mr. T Cereal (capitalizing on the success of Mr. T's roles in *Rocky III* and *The A-Team*). Even *Family Matters* über-nerd Steve Urkel had a brand.

Perhaps not surprisingly, many of these rare vintage cereal boxes have become collector's items, trading on websites like eBay for many hundreds of dollars. Among the most valuable are those portraying athletes like Michael Jordan and Mickey Mantle.

8 Cap'n Crunch

A word on the Cap'n: His full name is Horatio Magellan Crunch, and he was born on Crunch Island in the Sea of Milk. In 2013, a food blogger noticed a scandalous disparity on Cap's uniform. His sleeves only sported three yellow stripes instead of four, making him technically a commander in the Navy, a position one rung below a captain. When the disgrace was revealed, Cap'n Crunch immediately headed to Twitter to defend his position, claiming, "All hearsay and misunderstandings! I captain the S.S. *Guppy* with my crew—which makes an official Cap'n in any book!" and "Of course I'm a Cap'n! It's the Crunch—not the clothes—that make a man."

7 Vegan

Cereal would seem like a perfect food for vegans (provided it isn't served with milk), but there are actually a large number of cereals that use animal-based ingredients. Vitamin D3, found in many cereals, is generally derived from the lanolin of sheep. Many cereals that contain marshmallows, like Lucky Charms, use gelatin. The gelatin comes from the bone, cartilage, tendons, and skin of pigs. Many cereals also include dairy ingredients, and vegans consider the description "natural flavoring" to be quite dubious.

6 John Harvey Kellogg

The rise of the Kellogg empire could easily comprise a list of its own. The short version begins with John Harvey Kellogg, who was trained as a doctor and promoted a vegetarian lifestyle in accordance with his Seventh Day Adventist beliefs. But Kellogg took the restrictive Victorian conventions of the day and threw them out the window.

Among other weird practices, Kellogg espoused the constant administration of enemas. After your enema, you'd be treated to a pint of yogurt. The patient was allowed to eat half of the yogurt, but the other half would go straight up the patient's rectum, ostensibly to replenish the bacterial levels of the digestive tract.

Of course, J. H. Kellogg's greatest contribution to society is the corn flakes he distributed with his brother William. Some years after founding the Sanitas Food Company, the two brothers would butt heads on the issue of whether to add sugar to the cereal. William would go on to found the company that would later become Kellogg. Sugar has since been an integral ingredient of the company's success in the peddling of such products as Frosted Flakes and Pop Tarts. A highly fictionalized account of John Harvey Kellogg's life can be found in T. C. Boyle's novel *The Road to Wellville*.

5 Mascots

Cereal mascots generally fall into one of two categories. The first is the traditional salesman touting the quality of the product. Examples would include Cap'n Crunch, Sugar Bear, and Tony the Tiger (voiced for five decades by Thurl Ravenscroft, who sang "You're a Mean One, Mr. Grinch" in the animated Dr. Seuss Christmas classic).

The second group is infinitely more pathetic: those with some kind of deep-seated pathological addiction to a cereal that is always held just beyond their grasp. Examples of this sorry group include Barney Rubble (constantly trying to pilfer neighbor Fred Flintstone's Fruity Pebbles), Sonny the Cuckoo Bird, and of course, the Trix Rabbit.

The Trix Rabbit is perhaps the world's most profound cereal junkie. His schemes to obtain Trix were baroque and desperate, invariably ending in failure. Sociopathic children would inform him in his defeat that "Trix are for kids." Mail-in "Let the Rabbit Eat Trix" campaigns held in 1976 and 1980 redeemed the world's youth when they voted in a landslide to give the rabbit some Trix.

4 Yukon Territory

In the 1950s, CBS's hit show *Sergeant Preston of the Yukon* was sponsored by Quaker Oats. Bruce Baker, a Chicago ad executive, was charged with creating a promotion that would link the two together. Rather than dumping a toy Mountie into a box of cereal, Baker had a truly novel idea. Quaker would give a deed for one square inch of Yukon Territory in exchange for a box top from their cereal. The promotion was far more successful than anyone could have anticipated, and Quaker flew through 21 million deeds in just weeks.

The deeds said:

> Witnesseth that the Grantor for good and valuable consideration now paid by the Grantee to the Grantor (the receipt whereof is hereby by it acknowledged) doth grant, bargain, sell, alien, enfeoff, release, remise, convey and confirm unto the Grantee, his heirs and assigns forever and estate in fee simple.

They featured a corporate seal and a line for the new landowner to sign his name. Although people continue to write in to the company to check on their land, the territory Quaker purchased was reverted back to the Canadian government in 1965. The leftover deeds are readily available; you can purchase one on eBay for around $25.

3 Atomic Bomb Ring

In 1947, Kix cereal capitalized on the newfound recognition of atomic technology. Where other cereals were distributing lame toys like whistles and tops, Kix released a silver bullet Lone Ranger ring. Available for 15 cents plus a box top, the ring contained trace amounts of radioactive polonium, which would glow when it struck a screen made of zinc sulfide. Although this might sound dubious, the instructions indicated the ring was completely safe. They said: "PERFECTLY SAFE—We guarantee you can wear the KIX Atomic 'Bomb' Ring with complete safety. The atomic materials inside the ring are harmless."

Unfortunately, the polonium inside the rings had a short life and none of them work today. Like the Yukon deeds, these are easily available for purchase online.

2 Crunch Berry Lawsuit

Nature has provided us with a marvelous array of berries, including bananas, pumpkins, watermelons, and tomatoes. (Read that sentence again, slowly. Yeah, it's true.) Crunch Berries are not one of them. In 2009, a California woman named Janine Sugawara filed a class-action lawsuit against PepsiCo, the parent company of Quaker, which makes Cap'n Crunch's Crunch Berries. Sugawara claimed she had been duped into buying the product for four years due to misleading advertising claims that the Crunch Berries were real fruit. Sacramento judge Morrison England quickly dismissed the frivolous suit, writing, "As far as this court has been made aware, there is no such fruit (Crunch Berries) growing in the wild or occurring naturally in any part of the world."

1 Phreaking

The son of an air force engineer, John Draper enlisted in the USAF in 1964 and promptly put his technical skills to work by hacking into a telephone switchboard and allowing his friends to make free phone calls. Perhaps best defined as "eccentric," Draper spent the next few years operating a pirate radio station from his van. His greatest claim to fame would come when he learned that the whistle given away in a box of Cap'n Crunch would make a tone that would give him operator's control over phone lines. Blind friends of his had learned that by taping the hole of the whistle shut, they could duplicate the tone AT&T ran on.

After being featured in a 1971 *Esquire* article, the "phone phreaker" (nicknamed "Cap'n Crunch") was arrested and sentenced to probation. He has since served time in jail for manipulating phone systems (he once claimed that his skills allowed him to call President Nixon directly) and even worked briefly with Steve Jobs and Steve Wozniak developing software during the early days of Apple. Today, Draper continues to do programming work and even runs his own website.

TOP 10 Common Misconceptions about the Ancient Greeks

by Gregory Myers

10 The Trojan War

The Greeks' war with the Trojans is still one of the most famous stories in the world, and the expression "Trojan Horse" has become well known for meaning a sneak attack disguised as a gift. The legend of Achilles also stems from this war, and created the term "Achilles' heel"—but the thing is, there is no reason to believe that the Trojan War ever happened.

After much research, historians have found remnants of what they believe might have once been Troy and believe that the city could have been attacked and possibly pillaged at some point—but there is no evidence to support all of the popular mythology in regards to the war story. All historians can say for certain is that there might have been a siege laid on a city called Troy.

9 The Battle of Thermopylae

The Battle of Thermopylae has been made popular by movies such as *300*, but historically, the movie is not really all that accurate. Many people believe that the Spartans defending the pass saved Greece, but that's not exactly true.

Even though Xerxes's men were somewhat delayed, they still managed to do great damage to Greece and only retreated after a failed naval battle. Furthermore, the movie depicts only 300 brave Spartans standing up to the entire Persian army, which is also inaccurate. When the battle started, the Spartan force actually had 7,000 people backing them up. On the last day of the battle, they were still 1,400 strong—300 of them were Spartans, sure, but there were also 400 Thebans, 700 Thespians, and 80 Mycenaeans.

This is not to say that the Spartans did not show bravery—just that their significance was greatly distorted.

8 Spartan Warriors

The modern idea of a Spartan soldier is one who does absolutely nothing else but train to fight and kill people. Many people get the idea that young Spartan warriors spent all their time training and never really had any exposure to women while young, but this is not true.

Young Spartans, while engaged in their military education, still spent much time in activities around girls their age while growing up. The truth is also that Spartan warriors did not just fight and train; they also sang, danced, and performed in plays. Spartan men also educated young Spartans when they got too old to fight themselves. Their lives weren't merely an endless fight until they died.

7 Spartan Women

Many people think of women in the ancient world as being subservient to men, but nowhere was this less true than in Sparta. Spartan women had to do pretty much everything while the men were off fighting, and they were incredibly respected and powerful in Spartan society. Aristotle even wrote mockingly in regards to the high place women had in Spartan society, and their ability to own land.

Spartan women were expected to do most of the child raising, were encouraged to be intellectual and to learn about the arts, and, in fact, they owned a very large portion of the land in Sparta. It is the stuff of legend that an Athenian woman once asked a Spartan queen why Spartan women were the only women allowed to rule men. The Spartan queen responded, "Because we are the only women who give birth to men."

6 Homosexuality

The Greeks—especially the Athenians—were well known for being "boy lovers," or at least that's what many seem to think. It's become a common trope to equate pedophilia with the men of ancient Athens. But the issue is quite a complicated one, certainly much less simple than saying that they either "did" or "didn't" make love to young boys.

Some believe that pederasty—the relationship between an experienced man and a young one—may have been more of an intellectual mentor relationship, whereby the elder male helped a younger one find his place in society.

5 Ancient Greek Theater

Many people have misconceptions about ancient Greek theater, which often entertained very large groups of people, usually during important festivals. A lot of people misunderstand what the ancient dramas were actually like. The truth is that the theater productions in ancient Greece were very symbolic; to understand a play, you had to have some knowledge of the symbolic significance and mythical background underlying nearly every part of the dialogue. The plays actually included audience participation—much like modern stand-up comedy—and were originally part of religious rites in honor of the gods.

4 The Olympic Games

The ancient Olympic Games were so popular that they are still held (in a slightly different form, it must be said) around the world today. But there are some common beliefs about these games that are inaccurate. For starters, many people think of them as existing only in very ancient times, but they were still played even during Roman rule for many years, until Theodosius did away with them in an effort to ensure that Christianity would triumph as the religion of the Roman Empire.

Also, women were actually not allowed to watch the Olympic Games at all. The Olympians usually competed while completely nude, and would cover themselves in olive oil to improve the quality of their skin and to make themselves more visually appealing.

3 Greek Statues

Many of the Greek statues were actually taken from Greece and put in the British Museum in the 1800s, and many of the rest have been damaged either by violence or simple wear and tear, making them hard to recognize. The common conception of Greek statues—and architecture, for that matter—is that they appeared unpainted, and that civic squares would flash in the sunlight with brilliant white marble.

But it turns out that the statues and temples are only white because the paint faded from them over time; originally, they were incredibly bright and vibrant. Many of these statues also had bronze attachments and black stone inlaid in white to make eyes stand out more.

2 Technology

While we all know that the ancient Greeks were skilled at art, mathematics, philosophy, and many other pursuits, many of us don't realize how technologically advanced they were.

In the early 1900s, a diver exploring near the island of Antikythera found several old green lumps of stone that had once been part of a mechanical device. Scientists studied the device, which they have dubbed the "Antikythera Mechanism," and discovered that it was capable of quite a few interesting feats.

The device could predict solar eclipses and was capable of keeping track of the Olympiad calendar cycle. It seems to have had complicated dials and to have kept in sync with both the moon and the sun, making it the first computer. Recent findings suggest that it may have been built by Archimedes, who is well known for having been a mathematical genius.

1 Athenian Democracy

Many people have the mistaken notion that Greeks invented modern democracy, and this belief has become incredibly pervasive. But Athenian democracy was very different from any democratic institution today. It was actually one of the few examples of direct democracy in history, in which nearly all matters of policy were voted on (in theory, at least) by all Athenian citizens.

If that sounds reasonable, bear in mind that the citizenship excluded women and slaves, and that foreign-born citizens were also ineligible for the vote. Many among the poor were also unable to take the time away from work necessary to get involved. This effectively meant that only free, adult, and relatively well-off males born in Athens were able to participate—which isn't exactly representative of the whole population's interests. Athenian democracy did have its good points, though, especially when you consider the tyrannous political systems that existed in other parts of Greece at the time. It was an important political innovation that those who voted did not have to be particularly rich or aristocratic to take part in the most important decision making.

TOP 10 Common Myths about Famous Landmarks

by **Adam Wears**

10 The Architects of Saint Basil's Cathedral Were Blinded

Situated inside Moscow's Red Square, Saint Basil's Cathedral has tall towers and multicolored spirals that wouldn't look out of place in a Disney cartoon. It has been designated a world heritage site by UNESCO. The cathedral was built from 1555–1561 under orders from Ivan the Terrible, and apparently the architects did a pretty good job—legend has it that Ivan the Terrible blinded them afterward so that they could never design anything better.

However, records show that a quarter of a century later and four years after Ivan's death they were employed again to add an extension to the cathedral. This is an unlikely feat for blind architects, unless they had some particularly clever seeing-eye dogs. Maybe this Ivan guy wasn't so terrible after all.

9 Buckingham Palace Is the Official Residence of the Queen of England

Maybe you're wondering how your old pal the queen is doing, and feel like popping in for some tea and a crumpet. Of course you won't need to look up her residence, because everybody knows it—Buckingham Palace, right?

Sort of. Sure, Her Royal Highness may technically live at Buckingham Palace, but she's clearly slightly embarrassed by this fact as she continues to call St. James's Palace her official place of residence, as it has been for British sovereigns for over 400 years.

It was built by Henry VIII between 1531 and 1536, and was where British royalty lived until 1837. When Queen Victoria took the throne she made her home in Buckingham Palace—a trend that has apparently stuck, though not on paper.

8 A Penny Dropped from the Empire State Building Will Kill Someone

Do you have an insatiable thirst for murder? Popular wisdom on the Internet would say that all you need to do is lure your target to the front of the Empire State Building and drop a penny on them from the top floor. By the time it reaches them, it will have reached speeds capable of killing them instantly. Hey, who are the police going to arrest? Isaac Newton?

Fortunately for residents of New York City, the Internet has got it wrong again. The small, flat shape of a penny means that when it falls it will be subjected to massive amounts of wind resistance. Unless you know of a way to suck all the air out of New York City and drop the penny into a vacuum, the penny will quickly reach terminal velocity—a constant speed at which the penny cannot accelerate any more. At this speed, a dropped penny may hurt a little but is totally unable to pierce a human skull.

7 Big Ben Is the Name of a Clock Tower

England: home to the queen and rain. You'll also find Big Ben, a huge clock tower that looks over the capital. If you've ever seen a movie or TV show set in London, there's a good chance you saw it in an establishing shot.

However, that isn't actually the name of the clock tower. That's a myth repeated so much by tourists that if you repeat it in front of a policeman, they're legally entitled to shoot you. "Big Ben" is actually the name of the bell inside the tower—the tower itself is called "Elizabeth Tower."

6 The White House Was Painted White after the British Set Fire to It

Legend has it that when the White House was built between 1792 and 1800 it was gray, and the white came later. In 1814, while the War of 1812 was still raging, British forces did something totally out of character and set fire to the White House. When the fires had been put out and the building repaired, it was repainted white, henceforth to be known as the White House.

Part of this story is true: The British did burn down part of the White House in 1814. However, the "white" part of the White House predates the fire by a good 16 years. It got its iconic paint job as early as 1798, when it was given a coat of whitewash to protect it from the winter weather. More damningly, it was already known as the White House to the British in 1811, years before the fire.

5 Nothing Can Be Taller Than the Capitol Dome

It's always strange to hear when someone says that Washington, D.C., has no skyscrapers. After all, it's the capital city of one of the most powerful countries in the world. If you're wondering, that's because local laws prevent anything being built taller than the dome of the United States Capitol, because nothing can be bigger than politics in this town.

Lies. The reason that buildings in Washington, D.C., are so short isn't because politicians have an inferiority complex over the size of their dome, it's because the Height of Buildings Act of 1910 limits building heights to no more than the width of the street plus 20 feet. Why? Blame Thomas Jefferson. He wanted Washington, D.C., to be "low and convenient," a vision that made it into law.

4 Galileo Dropped Cannonballs from the Leaning Tower of Pisa

Galileo was an Italian physicist, mathematician, astronomer, and philosopher responsible for dozens of experiments. His most famous, of course, is when he dropped two cannonballs from the Leaning Tower of Pisa to demonstrate that two similar falling bodies of different mass will fall at the same speed.

However, it is doubtful it ever actually happened. Historians think that the whole story was made up in order to make Galileo seem like some sort of science god or that he did it as a "thought experiment," a hypothetical experiment not involving actually doing anything.

3 Stonehenge Was Built by Druids

If you were to ask anyone on the street who built Stonehenge, there's a very good chance they'll reply with "druids." After all, just look at it! There's no way that some sort of mystical ritual didn't take place in there.

Well, sorry to ruin this for you, but Spinal Tap lied to us. The link between druids and Stonehenge was made in 1640 by archaeologist John Aubrey using the age-old scientific method of "pulling it out of his butt."

In fact, modern archaeologists seem to think that Stonehenge was built by everyone *but* the druids, with current theories arguing that Stonehenge construction was not at any one time, but added to over the course of hundreds of years. Recent radiocarbon dating of Stonehenge has identified the first stones as being raised between 2400 and 2200 BC, while most recent evidence of construction in the area dates to 1600 BC—well before druids occupied the region.

2 Hoover Dam Is Full of Bodies

For those of you who didn't pay attention in school, the Hoover Dam is one of the world's largest dams. Its construction between 1931 and 1936 was a mammoth task, resulting in over 96 deaths. According to popular belief, many of these workers were buried inside the concrete of the dam, a resting place they occupy to this day.

While it's true that at least 96 men died during construction, none of them is entombed inside the dam. The dam was built from thousands of interlocking concrete blocks. These blocks were poured individually over time, and it's virtually impossible that anyone could have been buried inside with no chance of recovery.

Another interesting fact about the dam is that the first man to die in its preparation, J. G. Tierney, was the father of the last man to die in its construction, Patrick W. Tierney...13 years to the day later.

1 The Great Wall of China Is the Only Man-Made Structure Visible from Space

The Great Wall of China represents one of the biggest construction projects in history. It seems entirely plausible that the whole thing can be easily seen from space—it is the world's longest wall, after all.

Or so you would think. It turns out that the wall isn't visible from space, a point that was clarified in 2003 by Yang Liwei, one of China's own astronauts and a man who would definitely know where to look. The Chinese government has now vowed to remove that myth from every student textbook in the country.

Former NASA astronaut Jeffrey Hoffman says that although he couldn't see the Great Wall of China from space, he could make out runways, desert roads, and irrigation ditches, simply because they contrasted with their surroundings.

TOP 10 Myths Involving the Nazis

by Hestie Barnard Gerber

10 The Ark of the Covenant

Bearing the stone tablets on which the Ten Commandments were inscribed, the Ark was said to be lined with gold inside and out. Four men were needed to carry it; they used gold-plated poles, as it was considered too dangerous to go within a hand's-breadth of it. Charged with divine energy, the Ark could level mountains, knock down the walls of cities, and strike Israel's enemies with cancerous tumors and fiery bolts. The Ark disappeared sometime between 597 and 586 BC. The myth claims that the Nazis wanted to acquire and harvest the Ark's powers—as it would have been the ultimate weapon in World War II. Be that as it may, no known records exist to prove that the Nazis necessarily made any effort to locate or recover the Ark at any time.

9 The Cross

The cross is a near-universal symbol of the center of things, the heart of man, the Earth as center of the universe, and the cycle of seasons. The Nazi swastika (however abnormal and depraved) was meant to resemble the cross within a circle by means of its shorter secondary arms. Shown with a crescent, as it was in Babylon, the cross represented lunar gods or the moonboat, a female receptive symbol. When Hitler was placed in charge of propaganda, he decided on a dramatic symbol that

would stand out and attract the masses. In his eyes, the swastika stood for racial purity.

8 Hollow Earth

In the Nazi period there was an idea, derived from ancient underworld myths, that various things might be buried deep within the Earth, such as kingdoms, planets, phantom universes, super humans, or aliens. Some of Hitler's top advisors—and possibly the man himself—believed that the Earth was hollow. The military launched various expeditions in an attempt to confirm the notion and to acquire the strategic advantage this knowledge would entail. There are further theories surrounding the annual expeditions to Tibet between 1926 and 1943, claiming that the German mission was to find and maintain contact with their Aryan forefathers in Shambhala and Agharti, cities which supposedly existed beneath the Himalayas.

7 Jews and Anti-Semitism

Jews have been scattered and enslaved for most of their history. In northern Europe, their scholastic talents bloomed, but since they were forbidden from marrying Gentiles (non-Jews) by Jewish law, the separatism that followed led to a surge in fantastic myths. Some of these purported that the Antichrist would be a Jew, that Jews slaughtered Christian children to drink their blood, that Jews poisoned wells, and that Jews were responsible for the Black Death (1348–1350).

The expected slaughter began in the 12th century. Thousands of Jews were killed in France, Spain, and England. The Protocols of the Elders of Zion—the most well-known conspiracy about Jewish plans to take over the world—appeared in Russia in 1903. It later formed a dominant part of Hitler's "Final Solution." Today the protocols are still in circulation, even though they have long since been dismissed as a total forgery.

6 New World Order

Conspiracy theorists regularly identify Nazi Germany's ideologies, with their mass appeal and fierce nationalism, as the forerunner or harbinger of the New World Order. Hitler's attempts to establish forms of national Socialism through the whole of Europe saw their propaganda that used the term *Neuordnung* often poorly translated as "New Order." It actually referred to the restructuring of all European borders and the resulting dominion of greater Germany. Taking everything into consideration, one could still suggest that Hitler and the Nazi movement did try to create a New World Order—with a totalitarian world government at its head.

5 The Holy Grail

Otto Rahn, one of the most mysterious young men in Himmler's Secret Service, was said to have been a Mason, an agent of the Thule Gesellschaft, a Rosicrucian, a Luciferian, an initiated Cathar, and even the leader of a mythical international secret society. He firmly believed that the Cathars knew of the Holy Grail's location.

Hitler presumed the Grail would confer immortality on all Aryans, and he gave credence to the idea that the Christians had stolen the artifact from the ancient pagans. He maintained that the Grail should be restored to its rightful place in Germany. Himmler designated Rahn to search for the object. He traveled through Europe, the Middle East, and Iran, but by the end of the war, the artifact still eluded him, and he was forced to commit suicide.

4 Aryan Controversy

Hitler and the Nazis claimed that they belonged to the Aryan master race: blonde, blue-eyed, and fair skinned, congenitally a cut above the rest—especially those with darker skin. But just who were the Aryans? *Arya* is a Sanskrit term used to describe the invading tribes and horse tamers of 1700 BC who believed themselves superior to those that they defeated. After a few generations, people started applying it to the social or ethical condition of being superior. Furthermore, the Medes were once known as Arii, and Persians who replaced them were called Aria, hence Iran, the modern name for Persia. In the 19th century, Max Muller modernized the term when he tried to describe the "Indo-Germanic" race, though ironically he later claimed there was no evidence that such a race ever existed.

3 The Spear of Destiny

The Holy Lance, or Spear of Destiny, is said to be the lance that pierced Jesus's side as he hung on the cross. Hitler reportedly first saw the lance in 1908, and from that moment on did everything he could to get his hands on it. Once owned by Roman Emperor Constantine the Great and more than 40 other great men, emperors and leaders managed to possess it at one point or another, including Frederick the Great. In 1938, as Hitler oversaw the annexation of Austria, he transferred the lance to Nuremberg.

With the lance safely in Germany—so the myth goes—Hitler began the war in earnest. A few hours after the Allied Forces took possession of the lance in 1945, Hitler committed suicide in his bunker. Coincidence? Or does this lend some truth to the stories of Hitler's obsession?

2 Nostradamus and Hans Hörbiger

The Nazis claimed that Hitler's rise to power had been predicted by Nostradamus. Seen as "destiny" by many Germans, the movement under Adolf Hitler kept gaining momentum. Hitler also reportedly believed in the mystical cosmology of Hans Hörbiger. Hörbiger claimed that various moons and other stellar bodies once circled our world, gradually falling and dying as time went on. The last moon that fell caused the great flood and the ruin of Atlantis, the supposed homeland of the Aryans. Today it is commonly believed that both Hitler and Himmler favored the theory only to counterbalance the perceived Jewish influence on the sciences, in a similar way to the Deutshe Physik movement.

1 Hitler

The Führer cult saw Hitler as something of a demigod figure. He was vested with the power to shape his people, pave the way for the Aryan super race, and act as their protector. The propaganda of the day was wrought with these ideals, and such myths were an extremely potent tool in creating unity and loyalty among the German people. Hitler was seen as strong: He presented the national interest before anything else, restored order with an iron fist, and meted out fanatical justice to perceived enemies of the people.

The myth was widely believed and trusted; if any proof was needed, one could simply point to the fact that Hitler had restored the German economy to life in a span of what seemed like months. Most of the Nazi Party members felt that they would either win or die alongside him—he had people completely under his spell. To his ecstatic devotees, he embodied all the true Germanic properties. In the end though, the Nazis denied both reason and humanity, instead substituting it with an apocalyptic belief based on grandiose racial self-assertion and superiority.

TOP 10 Fantastic Facts about Beer

by Pauli Poisuo

10 Beer and Facial Hair

Facial hair can make drinking beer rather difficult. However, it can also produce drinkable beer. A brewmaster in Oregon has actually discovered a way to make beer from yeast collected from his own beard.

Although this may sound rather disgusting, it is actually a valid way to collect yeast. Most of the fermenting yeast in the world is harvested from rotten bits of nature, so snagging some from someone's beard is just a logical (if slightly disturbing) extension of the normal process.

9 The Foam

Many drinkers disapprove of the foam on top of a beer glass: It makes drinking difficult and looks unappetizing to some. However, the foam is a very important part of the beer. The foamy "head," as it is called, is formed by a complex carbon-dioxide reaction and can say a lot about the quality of the beer. Many stout beers, Guinness in particular, are characterized by their gloriously foamy head. The lack of head, on the other hand, can mean that your beer is probably flat and bland tasting.

The so-called Holy Grail of foam is called Brussels Lace. It is the perfect foam that refuses to go away and forms a lacelike residue pattern once the glass is empty. This can only be achieved with a high-quality beer. Interestingly, Brussels Lace will never form on a dirty glass, so it also tells the drinker that their glass has been properly cleaned.

8 Marijuana and Beer

Not many people are aware that marijuana and beer are actually quite close relatives. The flavoring agent in beer, hops, is a member of the Cannabaceae family, which (as you might deduce from the name) also includes *Cannabis sativa*, the marijuana plant.

Although the plants are of the same family and share many genetic similarities, you can't just replace one with the other. Still, they are similar enough that enterprising souls have attempted to graft hops into marijuana and brew marijuana beer. Details of these projects are hard to find, which presumably means the results have been less than pleasant.

7 Dead Animal Beer

Taxidermy is definitely one of the few things that doesn't go well with beer. At least, that's what most people think. The UK brewery BrewDog politely disagreed with the release of their new product (which also happened to be the world's strongest beer at an alcohol volume of 55 percent) in 2011.

The beverage, fittingly titled "The End of History," came from inside a real, dead animal. The poor creature—your choice of either a weasel or a squirrel—had been stuffed with a bottle, with the neck and cork sticking out of its mouth.

6 World's Oldest Drinkable Beer

Although there is plenty of information on beer drinkers throughout recorded history, actual recipes for ancient beer are difficult to find.

In 2010, an early-19th-century shipwreck near Finland was found to have carried a hidden treasure: the oldest drinkable beer in the world. Preserved in its bottles by the cold abyss, the beer was found to taste very old (unsurprisingly), with some burnt notes and an acidic aftertaste. The last part was attributed to fermenting, and the actual taste is presumed to be much more pleasant.

The Finns take their beer seriously, so the five preserved bottles are currently being researched, and Finnish scientists are trying to determine their exact recipe. They will then start manufacturing this ancient beer and selling it under the brand name "Shipwreck Beer."

5 Michael Jackson and Beer

When discussing Michael Jackson, most beer enthusiasts are not referring to the King of Pop. They are talking about the British Michael Jackson (1942–2007), beer scholar and foremost authority in anything related to the beverage. Nicknamed "the Beer Hunter," Jackson was a writer and journalist who single-handedly rescued beer from obscurity in the late 1970s, a time when beer was considered a loathsome, poor man's drink.

Jackson always thought beer was an important component of culture, which is why he always described the beers he wrote about in their cultural context. He also popularized the idea of categorizing beers by their style. Without him, the world of beer would be extremely different and probably much less exciting. Beer aficionados throughout the world recognize this and have showered him with praise and numerous awards.

4 Water and Beer

Although water is generally quite tasteless, it is actually a very important factor in the taste of a beer. The vast majority of beer is water, after all—no amount of skill or fine ingredients will save a beer if the water is low-quality.

Throughout history, many breweries chose their location exclusively because there was quality water nearby. Purity is obviously a factor: Many home brewers get unfortunate surprises because they have been using chlorinated tap water. Also, water reservoirs in different areas vary in taste and beer-making quality.

Many think that some of the best beer-making waters in the world come from Ireland's mountains. This water is used to make Guinness. Take that as you will.

3 Pyramids and Beer

In ancient Egypt, the Nile's bacteria content was so high the locals often drank beer instead of water. It could still get you drunk, of course—it was essentially nourishing soup with alcohol in it. This came in handy during the Egyptians' massive construction projects.

When the pyramids of Giza were built, workers were partially paid with beer. They were kept in a nice alcohol buzz throughout the project, with beer given to them at three meals a day. They considered it both a source of refreshment and a reward for their hard work and would probably have rebelled if they'd run out. In fact, the workforce was so adamant about getting their beer fix that the pyramids might not have been built at all if beer had not been around.

2 Peruvian Spit Beer

Chicha is a traditional Peruvian corn beer that is said to date back to Incan times. Its secret ingredient is extremely strange: spit.

The human mouth hosts many strange bacteria and enzymes. Some of them can actually replace the malting process used to make beer. This means that the fermentation process of the corn can be activated by chewing on it, moistening it in your mouth, and then putting it in the beer mix. Just chomp it up and spit it out, soaked in saliva.

Corn *chicha* tastes like sour beer, and it is a popular refreshment in Peru even today. Most people replace the spit fermentation with malted barley nowadays, but some are said to still make it the old way.

1 The Best Beer in the World

Beers are extremely difficult to rank. One's superiority to another is largely a matter of taste. However, when it comes to naming the absolute best beer in the whole world, beer lovers are in complete agreement. This honorable drink is called Westvleteren 12. It is a 10.2 percent alcohol by volume Trappist beer that has been in production since 1940.

Westvleteren 12 is a dark beer with a refined, chocolatelike taste that is said to be unrivaled by any other beer. It is instantly recognizable by its distinct yellow cap and complete lack of any labels. Usually, it is only available by driving to the monastery that makes it (located deep in the countryside of Belgium) and buying it straight from the monks, which often involves waiting patiently in a line of cars that can extend for miles. However, the monks are fully aware of the superiority of their product and are willing to use its reputation to their benefit on occasion. When their monastery needed a new roof in 2012, they briefly exported Westvleteren 12 to various countries with prices ranging between $75 and $85 for a six-pack and two tasting glasses.

It sold out in minutes.

TOP 10 Weird Facts about Cats

by **Mike Devlin**

10 Mousers

Cats were first domesticated for their appetite for mice and rats. Today, the average pet owner is content to have kitty do little more than nap, but the

cat still possesses a fierce hunting instinct. Those who allow their cats to roam outside will often attest to receiving "gifts" on the welcome mat, the corpses of birds and rodents their pet has hunted down. Even today, cats are employed to kill off rats and mice at such places as Disneyland and the State Hermitage Museum in St. Petersburg, Russia.

Although history has likely graced us with even more voracious hunters, *The Guinness Book of World Records* recognizes Towser, of Scotland's Glenturret distillery, as the world mousing champion. A female long-haired tortoiseshell, Towser, who lived nearly to her 24th birthday, was stationed in a distillery in Crieff, Scotland, the home of Famous Grouse Whisky. During her reign, she killed some 28,899 mice (per Guinness record). Towser's successor at Glenturret was a cat named Amber, who, despite a nearly 20-year life of her own, was not known to have caught a single mouse.

9 Mating

Anyone who has ever owned a female cat that wasn't fixed can probably attest to the absolute misery of her heat cycles. She will yowl and constantly attempt to escape the house to meet up with suitors. Male cats who can sense her eagerness will gather around, waiting for their opportunity. The actual mating process is a lurid exchange, as far removed from romance as imaginable. The female looses dreadful screams during the encounter, and for good reason: A male cat's penis is less an instrument of pleasure than an object of medieval torture. It sports backward-facing barbs like fish hooks made of keratin that rake the inside of the female's vaginal canal. This agonizing part of the courtship is thought to bring on ovulation.

8 Roadkill

It is probably inevitable that at some point in your life, you will run over an animal while driving. For most, it is a sickening feeling, and we will pull over to do anything we can to help, especially if the animal is obviously a pet. Unfortunately, there are a shocking number of people who will continue on their way even after hitting people, let alone a pet. In the UK, it is illegal not to report a car accident involving a dog, or even a farm animal, but strangely enough, there is no legal obligation to stop if one strikes a cat.

7 Milk

Although your average cat will lap up a saucer of milk like it's sweet ambrosia, the fact is, they are lactose-intolerant. Like some humans, as they grow, cats stop making the enzyme lactase, which breaks down their mother's milk. What your friend leaves behind in the litter box after this treat will likely convince you to never give it to her again. Strangely enough, your cat (and his mortal nemesis, the rat), has kidneys efficient enough to allow it to drink seawater to rehydrate, unlike most species.

6 Heroes

Dogs are well known for tales of lifesaving heroism, but most people think cats seem generally too self-involved for valor. In practice, this is hardly the case. In 2012, a cat that had only been rescued from the Humane Society hours before managed to save its new owner's life when she had a diabetic seizure. The cat leaped onto the woman's chest as she lost consciousness, nudging and biting at her face until she awoke. The cat then darted into the woman's son's room and pestered him until he woke up to call for help.

An even more unbelievable story emerged from Argentina in 2008, when a one-year-old boy was found by police in the city of Misiones, being kept alive by a band of feral cats. The boy, who'd been separated from his homeless father, would likely have died without the intervention of the cats. They snuggled up to him at night to keep him warm and brought him scraps of food. When police approached, the baby's guardians hissed and spat ferociously at them.

5 Savannah Cat

The tradition of mating domestic cats with their wild ancestors goes back over 100 years, when the first Bengal cats (domestic felines crossed with Asian leopard cats) were produced. However, despite their exotic appearance, Bengals are for the most part many generations removed from the jungles of their forebears, and possess a devoted, genial nature.

The serval is a small, leopard-spotted African cat that weighs between 20 and 40 pounds and is perhaps best known for its extremely long legs. Unlike many wild cats, servals can make good pets. In 1986, the first domestic cat was crossed with a serval, producing the Savannah cat. Since becoming available to the public in the '90s, the Savannah has enjoyed a growing popularity.

Owners claim that Savannah cats have a temperament akin to dogs; they tend to follow their masters and can even be taught to walk on a leash and play fetch. They have incredible leaping ability and many seem to love water. Depending on your location, it may be illegal to keep one of these cats. Australia in particular, which already has a terrible problem with feral cats decimating native fauna, has banned the importation of Savannah cats. And even if regulations allow you to have one of these beautiful exotic pets, you'd better have deep pockets if you want one—depending on the amount of serval in the bloodline, they can sell for well over $10,000 each.

4 The Godfather

The Godfather is recognized as one of the greatest films in history, ranked at number two behind *Citizen Kane* by the American Film Institute. The winner of three Academy Awards, including Best Picture, Best Actor, and Best Adapted Screenplay, the movie and ever aspect of it have been exhaustively studied, especially the marble-mouthed patriarch, Vito Corleone (Marlon Brando). When we are introduced to the ruthless mob boss, he is decked out in a tuxedo, celebrating his daughter's wedding, absently stroking his cat. It is a powerful moment, the dichotomy of the Don's ruthless power and his tenderness toward his pet. It was, however, entirely accidental. The cat did not feature in the screenplay at all—it was a stray that had wandered onto the set. Marlon Brando picked it up to play with it, and the rest is cinematic history.

3 The Black Death

Gregory IX was the pope from 1227 until his death in 1241, his reign characterized by provoking crusades and brutal inquisitions against those deemed heretical. He also seemed to be convinced that the people were worshipping black cats as manifestations of the devil. His influence led to large-scale massacres of cats throughout Europe, a campaign that would go on to have horrible, unforeseen consequences 100 years later. In the late 1340s, when rats infected with the Black Plague swept out of Asia, they found Europe to be a veritable utopia, unprotected by the cats that would have thinned their ranks (and likely saved millions of lives). Thankfully, recent popes have been more tolerant of cats. Pope Benedict was known to have a particular affinity for felines, who would follow him around the Vatican grounds.

2 Declawing

Like the cropping of ears and the docking of tails in dogs, declawing cats is a hot-button issue in the pet community. While many owners who have come home to find a shredded couch might believe that declawing is a reasonable solution to their problem, the surgery required to remove the claws is quite brutal. Because the nail grows out of the bone, the veterinarian is required to cut off the end of the cat's toe, something akin to snipping your fingers off at the first knuckle. Declawing is a relatively common process in the U.S., with only a few localized areas outlawing it (such as the city of San Francisco), but it is seen as animal cruelty and is illegal in several countries throughout the world, including most of Europe, Israel, Brazil, and Japan.

1 Nine Lives

The phrase "cats have nine lives" has become such a common part of the vernacular that few pause to consider its implications. The cat, with its speed and uncanny agility, would seem to defy death at every turn. The animal's greatest accomplishment would seem to be its ability to regularly survive falls from any height. Human beings, for want of comparison, are terrible at falling. Although there are cases of people surviving insane tumbles (in 1972, flight attendant Vesna Vulovic lived after falling over 30,000 feet from a damaged plane), a human is generally in big trouble after about three stories.

A falling cat has several mechanisms for survival. Perhaps most importantly, its sense of balance acts as a sort of internal gyroscope called aerial righting reflex. After dropping a few feet, it is all but guaranteed to land on all fours. The cat's loose, muscular legs act as springs upon landing, distributing the sudden impact. Being relatively lightweight, the cat has a much lower terminal velocity (the maximum speed at which it can fall) than a human: Cats reach about 60 mph, while humans easily double that.

This is more than mere conjecture; there are dozens of reports of cats falling from enormous heights and walking away with little more than bruises. In 2011, an elderly cat named Gloucester fell 20 stories from an Upper West Side, Manhattan, apartment with minor injuries. The following year, a cat in Boston named Sugar tumbled 19 floors. In 2009, another Manhattan cat fell an astonishing 26 floors, this time with photo evidence taken by nearby window washers. This fortunate feline's name? Lucky.

TOP 10 Weird Facts about Dogs

by **Mike Devlin**

10 Baboons Keep Pet Dogs

For many years, it has been asserted that the only animals that keep pets are human beings, but a troop of hamadryas baboons near Ta'if, Saudi Arabia, seems to have debunked that theory. Although some remain skeptical, claiming that the animals merely coexist rather than share any bond, it is believed that the baboons kidnap the dogs as puppies and enjoy a symbiotic relationship with them much in the way that humans do. In exchange for food and companionship, the dogs protect the troop, particularly the vulnerable babies, against other dogs. There has been very little research on the phenomenon, but the footage captured by a French film crew seems to be very compelling evidence.

9 Turnspit Dogs

Throughout history, dogs have been called on to perform dozens of tasks, from guiding the blind to fighting our enemies on the battlefield. But few realize that centuries ago, dogs also served in the kitchen. The so-called turnspit dog was a sturdy, long-bodied, short-legged canine called upon to operate a wheel (something like a hamster wheel), which would turn a roast on a spit, thus cooking the meat evenly. Turnspits were also used for powering treadmills that would pump water or churn butter, among other things. The harsh treatment of turnspit dogs at least partially inspired Henry Bergh to start the American Society for the Prevention of Cruelty to Animals. Although now extinct, it is believed that the turnspit dog is probably related to the modern-day Glen of Imaal Terrier, listed by some sources as the world's rarest domestic dog breed, likely to go extinct itself within the next decade or so.

8 Detection Dogs

Detection dogs, trained to sniff out a wide variety of things from bombs to drugs to cadavers, are an invaluable part of any law enforcement team. But there has been a growing outcry against K-9 units, particularly drug dogs, who have been shown in many cases to give "false positive" readings, or react as though they smelled drugs although none are present as often as 80 percent of the time. This is an extraordinary risk to the civil liberties of innocent people. In the United States, during a traffic stop, a police officer has no right to search your vehicle without probable cause that a crime is being committed (e.g., possession of narcotics). However, probable cause is automatic the second the dog alerts. There is also some concern that some disreputable officers can give their dogs cues (consciously or not) to alert even when there is nothing to detect. The problem is by no means confined to the United States, with Australian politicians calling for reform in how drug detection dogs are used.

7 Seeing Eye Dogs Poop Too

A guide dog is one of the best trained animals on earth, but given the handicap of its owner, you might think that the dog has carte blanche to poop wherever he wants (some communities allow this, but most do not). This would be a small price to pay given the service the animal provides. But these dogs are actually trained to eliminate on command. After giving the signal, the handler reaches down and runs his hand over the dog's back. If it is straight, the dog is peeing (male guide dogs are trained to squat like females). If it is rounded, the dog is going *numero dos*. By following the spine down to the tail, the handler can find the mess and pick it up with a plastic bag like any other pet owner.

6 Sylvester Stallone

Any fan of Sylvester Stallone's Rocky franchise would recognize Butkus, the slobbery 145-pound bullmastiff that stars as Rocky's pet. What some might not realize is that Butkus actually belonged to the actor, and in many ways, the rags-to-riches tale of boxer Rocky Balboa mirrored Stallone's own life story. Before selling the script for the movie, Stallone was desperately poor. He had no car, a pregnant wife, and $100 in the bank. Unable to afford his giant dog, he wound up selling Butkus to a little person named Little Jimmy for $50. After selling the script, he returned to Little Jimmy, desperate to get his pet back. According to Stallone, Jimmy was loathe to return the dog. Stallone said, "He wanted to fight me and said he was gonna kill me—he was a crazy little person. I couldn't fight him— they'd arrest me—so I offered to pay double. Anyway, $3,000 and several threats later..." In the end, Stallone was reunited with Butkus, and Little Jimmy got a bit part in *Rocky*. The rest is history.

5 Titanium Teeth

The Navy SEALs are among the most elite commando units on the planet. The SEALs' most high-profile mission was Operation Neptune Spear, an attack on a compound in Pakistan in the dawn hours of May 2, 2011, which resulted in the death of al-Qaeda leader Osama bin Laden. One of the integral members of the team during this raid was Cairo, a Belgian Malinois dog. The Malinois resembles a smaller German shepherd in appearance. It is often chosen for police and military work because its slighter build allows it to be carried by its handler, but with a high drive and 65 pounds of muscle to back up its opinion, it is quite capable of stopping a grown man cold. One of the strangest rumors regarding these dogs is that the military actually removes their teeth and replaces them with titanium fangs, chosen for their apparent "armor piercing" capability. In truth, these dogs cost many thousands of dollars and man-hours to train, and should one lose a natural tooth, it is replaced with a metal implant, although this is not standard procedure. Implants are actually less effective and are more likely to come out during combat.

4 Google Is a Dog Company

Like many Internet companies, Google is a fairly unorthodox workplace. Along with free gourmet meals, daily summer barbecues, pool tables, and slides, another perk is that employees are actually encouraged to bring their dogs with them to work. Of course, the pups are required to be fairly well-behaved and housebroken; overly vocal or otherwise ill-tempered dogs are asked to stay at home. From Google's own codes of conduct: "Google's affection for our canine friends is an integral facet of our corporate culture. We like cats, but we're a dog company, so as a general rule, we feel cats visiting our offices would be fairly stressed out."

3 Lifespan

For a long time, it was assumed that one human year was equal to seven dog years; thus a dog of nine or ten years would be considered a senior citizen. However, this algorithm doesn't exactly match up. Like humans, dogs age rapidly from puppyhood to sexual maturity, then things slow down a bit in adulthood. Longevity is largely dependent on size: Small dogs like miniature poodles and Yorkies can make it to 15, while massive breeds like mastiffs and Great Danes rarely exceed 7 or 8. Mutts of similar size generally hang on a year or so longer than their pedigreed cousins, mostly because they come from a deeper gene pool. In a few cases, dogs have survived to 20. It is difficult to investigate many claims of extreme longevity, because owners often lack proof of birth date. The oldest verifiable dog ever was named Max, who died on May 18, 2013, just 83 days shy of reaching 30. Max was a terrier mix from Louisiana, purchased from a sugar cane farmer in 1983.

2 Dirty Mouth

One of the most pervasive old wives' tales regarding the dog is that, despite some rather execrable habits, its mouth is cleaner than any human's. Bad news for those who enjoy smooching with their mutt: This is most definitely a myth, probably rooted in several common observations, such as the dog's habit of licking its wounds, and the fact that a bite from a human is much more likely to get infected than a bite from a dog. A dog's saliva certainly doesn't have any overtly medicinal properties; when he licks an injured area, he is likely removing dead tissue from the area, which would speed up healing. And the reason dog bites have a lower risk of infection than human bites is because bacteria is often species specific. Bacteria that  might be potentially deadly to another dog can be harmless to a human and vice versa.

1 Moscow Strays

The life of a stray dog is particularly short and grim. In Moscow, the situation is more dire still. There, any given dog is forced to compete for resources with some 35,000 other strays. Over generations, these intuitive canines have learned to adjust to their urban surroundings. Their strategies are impressive: Muscovite strays have been witnessed obeying traffic lights to avoid being hit by cars. Their antics in getting handouts from humans are equally remarkable. Packs are known to send out adorable little puppies to beg for treats while the more frightening members wait in the wings. But easily the most extraordinary feat exhibited by these dogs is their ability to navigate the elaborate Moscow subway system. Showing uncanny timing and sense of direction, some strays use the trains to travel all throughout the city. Moreover, the typically surly and snappish feral dogs completely alter their behavior when riding the train, acting friendly toward human commuters, lest they be kicked off.

TOP 10 Lesser-Known Facts about the Titanic

by Gareth May

10 Profit

Fact: Silent Screen Star Survives and Makes a Profit Off the Tragedy

Dorothy Gibson was a pretty big deal in her time. A star of the silent screen alongside such luminaries as Buster Keaton and Charlie Chaplin, the first-class passenger was a household name by the time she stepped on the *Titanic*. She had become popular as a comedienne in *Miss Masquerader* (1911) and *Love Finds a Way* (1912). But out of the 1,502 people to perish on the vessel, Gibson survived to tell the tale. Well, not just tell it, to star in it as well. *Saved from the Titanic*, began filming just five days after the *Titanic* sank. It was a hugely successful silent movie and the first of many hit *Titanic* films (although all reels of the movie were destroyed in a fire in 1914). Gibson even wore the same clothes she was wearing on the ship on the day of the tragedy in the movie—a dress, sweater, gloves, and black pumps.

Eventually, however, another shadow of the 20th century would be cast over Gibson. After a relatively short film career she moved to Europe. Although she was at first a Nazi sympathizer, by 1944 she had denounced her involvement with the Third Reich. Her subsequent arrest by the Nazis and brief imprisonment at San Vittore would lead to her death two years later at the age of 56, after a cardiac arrest.

9 Wrong Captain for the Job

Fact: The Captain Was Used to Sail Ships Not Steam Powered

At the point of setting sail, Captain Edward John Smith was a 37-year veteran making what he planned to be his final crossing of the Atlantic. He'd served with the White Star Line for 28 years, but the truth is Smith was probably not the best man to have at the helm. Smith had spent the majority of his sailing life manning sail ships, and the odd steamer here and there. At the age of 62, the old sea dog wasn't up for learning new tricks, and his lack of experience showed when he commanded the crew to stay at 22 knots (full speed) when entering an area notorious for icebergs... and we all know how that ended up. In fairness to the man, he did go down with his ship, but his final hours onboard remain shrouded in mystery. Many eyewitness accounts record the "millionaire's captain," as he was known to some, going to pieces, losing confidence, and being rather bewildered by the whole ordeal.

8 Dogs

Fact: Women and Children...and Dogs First

It is well recorded that not only were there not enough lifeboats on the *Titanic* to save every passenger but that they were not as full as they should have been when they disembarked from the ship (Lifeboat 1 was by far the worst, only carrying 7 crew and 5 passengers, a total of 12 people, despite having the capacity to carry up to 40). However, what isn't known is that among the 713 survivors there were also three dogs—two Pomeranians and a Pekinese to be exact. Twelve dogs were recorded as passengers but only three made it off—in lifeboats.

7 Mystery Ships

Fact: Mystery Ships Could Have Saved Hundreds of Passengers

As the *Titanic* sank the usual distress calls were sent out. But no one answered until it was too late. What few people know is that someone could have answered. Namely the captain of the SS *Californian*. Only 8–15 miles away when the *Titanic* struck the iceberg, the *Californian* did not react to mysterious lights in the night sky (what were in actual fact SOS flares of the larger ship). The crew woke up the captain, but he went back to bed stating that the wireless operator had already turned in for the night—the reason the *Titanic*'s distress calls were not heard over the radio.

Another ship, the *Samson*, a 250-plus-ton schooner of Norwegian registry, was apparently even closer—only five to eight miles. However, some theorists believe the *Samson* wouldn't have answered any calls—distressful or not—for the simple fact that they were partaking in illegal seal hunting. Both ships were closer than the *Carpathia*, the ship that would eventually rescue all the survivors of the *Titanic*.

6 Bad Conditions

Fact: Conditions on the Boat Were Far from Palatial

Despite being surrounded by water, it seems that on the actual ship there really wasn't that much to go around. Long before the days of power showers, people had to rely on the good old bath tub. And although sharing them was common practice back in the day, third-class passengers on the *Titanic* had to share two baths, one for men and one for women, among 700 people. That's right: 700 people. That's an awfully long wait for a scrub in the tub.

5 Real Hero

Fact: Leonardo DiCaprio Wasn't the Real Hero—Second Officer Lightoller Was

Second Officer Charles Herbert Lightoller was the most senior officer to survive the *Titanic*. Taking charge of an overturned lifeboat, Lightoller then suppressed panic and took control of all 30 survivors on the boat, ensuring their safe passage onboard rescue vessel RMS *Carpathia*. Lightoller wasn't just a hero on the *Titanic* either. He served with the British Navy in World War I and World War II, helping soldiers evacuate Dunkirk at the latter.

Conversely, Douglas Spedden was just six years old when his nurse got him off the *Titanic* and on to a lifeboat. Although the young boy survived, tragically he was killed just three years later. He was struck by a car in what was one of the first ever recorded automobile accidents in the state of Maine.

4 Posthumous Bill

Fact: "Sorry to Hear about the Tragic Death of Your Son. Here's the Bill"

As the legend goes, the eight members of the all-male *Titanic* orchestra went down with the ship, still playing their instruments. Only three bodies were ever recovered, including that of John Hume Law. Shockingly, just two short weeks after the tragic events, Law's father would receive a bill from C. W. and F. N. Black, the employment firm from Liverpool, England, who had employed the orchestra. The bill was for five shillings and four pennies, the cost of Law's son's uniform. In stark contrast, at the Apollo Club in Brooklyn, New York, a month after the sinking, a concert was performed in memory of the ship's orchestra. All proceeds went to the mourning families.

3 Not a Big Deal

Fact: *Titanic* Might Be a Big Deal Now, But It Wasn't Back Then

Regardless of what you see in the movies, the White Star Line never made any claims that the *Titanic* was "unsinkable." In fact, it appears that no one really cared about the *Titanic*'s maiden voyage at all. The *Olympic*—*Titanic*'s sister ship—was the one in the limelight when it journeyed from Southampton to New York in 1911. The truth is there wasn't even any footage of the *Titanic* leaving British shores, and when the news wires realized they didn't have anything to show in the picture houses once the tragedy struck, they used images of the *Olympic* instead, with any clear *Titanic* markings scratched off the reels.

2 Publicity Stunt

Fact: The *Titanic* Was Used as a Nazi Publicity Stunt

Some 30 odd years after the sinking of the *Titanic*, the publicity wing of the Nazi Party released *Nazi Titanic*, commissioned by none other than propaganda minister Joseph Goebbels. In an odd interpretation of the facts, *Nazi Titanic* tells the tale of a vessel attempting to cross the Atlantic in record time in order to boast the White Star Line share price. Whereas in real life the lookouts—Fredrick Fleet and Reginald Lee, both Englishmen—spotted the iceberg, in *Nazi Titanic*, the man who could have saved the ship from disaster was, of course, the German First Officer, whose warning was ignored.

Furthermore, in real life, J. Bruce Ismay, the English chairman and managing director of the White Star Line, was vilified by the international press for stealing a lifeboat all for himself. In Goebbels's retelling, he even managed to exaggerate this, depicting Ismay as a Jewish businessman who bullies the captain—again, a German—into plowing through the iceberg and killing pretty much everyone onboard (an act that James Cameron also has Ismay perform in his 1997 epic film).

Ismay's story is perhaps the most butchered in any and all fictional accounts of the sinking. The true Ismay was anything but the selfish man he was painted as. During the British Inquiry Report of 1912, its leader, Lord Mersey, concluded that Ismay had in fact helped other passengers off the ship before he himself departed in the last lifeboat. Perhaps the stigma allotted to Ismay was the fact that he was the highest-ranking White Star official of all the 713 survivors.

1 Missing Key

Fact: One Key Could Have Saved Thousands of Lives

What does the lookout in the crow's nest need most? Not just a good pair of eyes but a good pair of binoculars as well. And that's exactly what lookouts Fredrick Fleet and Reginald Lee were suppose to have. When Second Officer David Blair was removed from the crew list mere days before the ship left the dock, he forgot to give his replacement, the more experienced Henry Wilde, a senior officer from sister ship the *Olympic*, the key to the lookout's locker—the locker that housed the binoculars.

To add insult to injury, when Fleet, who survived the sinking, gave his testimony at the official inquiry he stated that if the lookouts had had binoculars, they would have seen the iceberg much sooner and probably have saved the ship from its watery fate.

CHAPTER 6

POP CULTURE

TOP 10 Creepy Video Game Urban Legends

by **Jonathan Kaulay**

10 Killswitch

Killswitch is a game that was supposedly created by Soviet gaming company Karvina Corporation in 1989. Only limited copies of the game were produced (between 5,000 and 10,000 copies) and it was very popular among Soviet gamers. The game itself was a pioneer in the survival horror genre. You had to choose between two characters, a girl or an invisible demon. The goal of the game was to navigate through an abandoned coal mine while battling demons and coal monsters. As it was hard to navigate the game with an invisible character, people typically chose to complete the game with the girl character. Unfortunately, no one ever completed the game with the demon, because upon beating the game all trace of it would be erased from your hard drive.

In 2005, an unopened copy of the self-deleting game surfaced on eBay where it was promptly bought for $733,000 by a man from Japan named Yamamoto Ryuichi. Ryuichi had planned to document his play-through of the game on YouTube. The only video Ryuichi posted was of him staring at his computer screen and crying.

9 Squall Is Dead

Final Fantasy VII and *VIII* are the two primary reasons twenty-somethings will never be able to play a *Final Fantasy* game without being disappointed, because nothing can compare to them. Those two games were ahead of their time and featured a handful of memorable characters, including Squall. He is the main character in *Final Fantasy VIII*, and much like the "Paul is dead" conspiracy theory about the Beatles, there are many who believe that Squall is dead as well.

At the end of disc one, Squall is impaled by an ice shard while fighting one of the game's main bosses, Edea. Squall awakens at the beginning of disc two with no wounds at all from the battle, and no one ever brings up that Squall was killed. It is also at this point when the game goes from being a fairly realistic game to being an over-the-top fantasy where all realism goes out the window. I mean, a good portion of the plot takes place in outer space. It is believed that Squall actually dies from the wounds that he suffers during his fight with Edea and the rest of the game is simply a dream Squall is having as he passes away. This would explain why the game has such a surrealist tone after that first disc. It would also explain the collage of images shown at the end of the game as Squall's life flashes before his eyes. Among those is a shot of Squall without a face, which just adds icing to the creepy cake.

8 Lavender Town Syndrome

Back in 1996, the *Pokemon Red* and *Green* video games delighted Gameboy owners all over the world. Well, except for in one part of the world.

The game was first released in Japan and it supposedly correlated with a huge spike in suicides and illnesses in children ranging in age from 7 to 12. The children did not fall ill or commit suicide until reaching Lavender Town in the popular game. The game's musical score was said to be the source of the sinister ailments. The piercing tones of the music caused headaches, nausea, and eventually suicidal tendencies in young children. The music in the level was changed before the game was shipped overseas.

7 Fallout 3 Predicts the Future

Fallout 3 is a vast, open-world role-playing game. Therefore, it would not be surprising to find that there are things within the game that many people have yet to discover. However, it is claimed by some that they have found something in the game that may predict the future.

The story goes that the postapocalyptic game predicts the future, in the real world, using Morse code and hidden messages within the game's radio stations. There are stations that broadcast Morse code in the game, and some claim that you can hear a DJ on the station rambling off such cryptic phrases as, "The Queen has died today. The world mourns, as on days like these we are all Brits," and, "I can't believe Britney's actually won an Oscar!" These phrases are followed by a series of numbers in Morse code that can be interpreted as dates. Whether or not the queen will die on March 19, 2014 remains to be seen. Bethesda, the company that designed the game, denies that these cryptic radio stations exist.

6 Earthbound's Final Boss Is an Abortion

The title of this listing is not a cheeky critique of the final boss battle in the game *Earthbound*, but is meant to be taken literally. In the game, the cute characters essentially perform an abortion in order to kill the final boss, an alien that wants to destroy the world.

In order to defeat the powerful alien Giygas, the main characters travel back in time where Giygas will be "weaker." What is creepy is that when they travel back in time to fight the weaker Giyga, he looks remarkably like a fetus.

The game's creator has all but come out and said the final boss battle is an abortion. He has also, however, admitted that the ending of *Earthbound* was inspired by a movie he accidentally saw and was traumatized by as a child called *The Military Policeman and the Dismembered Beauty*.

5 Herobrine

Minecraft is a game that is brilliant in its simplicity. You mine for different materials in a large open world and use said materials to build structures, monuments, or whatever your creative mind can conceive. However, some claim that something sinister is happening in their games.

Some players say they have found mysterious structures appearing on their maps. Others even claim to have seen the source of the structures, a mysterious, white-eyed version of the game's protagonist. Theories regarding the existence of "Herobrine" range from the logical—that he is a glitch—to the extraordinary, that Herobrine is the ghostly manifestation of the game creator's deceased brother. Mojang, the team behind *Minecraft*, do not do much to discredit the legend of Herobrine, as in many of the game's updates they list that one of the improvements made is the removal of Herobrine.

4 Haunted Majora's Mask

The legend of the haunted *Majora's Mask* game was born on the popular web community 4Chan. A user posted a story about how he obtained a blank Nintendo 64 cartridge with "Majora's Mask" written across it in black magic marker. He posted photos and videos along with the story that showed a twisted and sinister version of one of the most beloved games of all time.

Upon starting the game, the user noticed that there was already a game saved on the cartridge simply titled "Ben." He ignored the saved file and started a new game and noticed that all the NPCs (non-playable characters) would refer to him as Ben. He deleted the "Ben" file and tried to start a new game. The game became more erratic. The music would play backward and his character began to be followed by a statue of the game's main character with a creepy smile on its face. Eventually, the "Ben" file returned to the game. Along with it was another new file simply titled "drowned." Every time the user played after the two files appeared, his character would simply die and creepy messages would sprawl across the screen:

"You've met with a terrible fate, haven't you?"

3 Morrowind Mod jvk1166z.esp

The Elders Scrolls 3: Morrowind is an expansive RPG, and to this day is considered to be the best game in the *Elder Scrolls* series by a lot of fans. It has a huge online community where users modify, or "mod," the game to add custom quests, characters, weapons, and armor. Legend has it that there exists a very creepy and sinister mod to *Morrowind* that could potentially drive a player insane.

The mod first popped up on the Internet a couple of years ago and was originally thought to be a virus because when you loaded the game with the mod, your game would freeze on the title screen and corrupt all the saved files, essentially ruining the game. However, it was soon discovered that if you ran the game in DOSbox, software that allows gamers to play older PC games on their modern computers, the game would work. When the player starts the game with the mod, all the main characters in the game are already dead. Also, if you stay in one spot for too long, your health slowly begins to deplete. If you die from standing still too long, a new character will reveal himself. Players took to calling him "the assassin." He appeared to be a man, except his legs and arms were long and bent like a spider's. Players began to notice that if you paid close attention, you could see the assassin around corners or scurrying up the walls, but only for brief moments. Another creepy element added to the game was that all the characters left living would come outside at night and just stand there. When a player would attempt to interact with one of the characters they would simply say, "Watch the sky."

Inside the dungeon was what players called the "hall of portraits." The hall was lined with picture frames, and inside the frames were photos from the player's computer's "My Pictures" folder. At the end of the hall was a locked door. No one has ever posted proof that they figured out how to open the door, but there are some unbelievable stories of players obsessed with trying to open it, playing the modified game for days straight with very little sleep. Some claim that after long hours of playing they began to hallucinate, seeing the assassin in real life quickly crawling on their bedroom ceilings or down their hallways as they took a bathroom break from the game. As fantastic as this story sounds, the creepiest part is that this mod does in fact seem to exist, but download it at your own risk.

2 Berzerk

Berzerk is considered to be one of the greatest games of the arcade-era of gaming. In the game you battle an onslaught of robots. It also has one of gaming's most iconic boss battles in Evil Otto, which was a simple smiley face. *Berzerk* also holds the macabre honor of being the first video game linked to the death of a person. The game would then go on to kill again a year later.

Jeff Dailey was the first person to die after playing *Berzerk* in 1981. Then again in 1982, a healthy 18-year-old named Peter Burkowski was playing *Berzerk*. Within 15 minutes, he was typing his initials into the game for getting a high score. Burkowski took a few steps away from the game and then collapsed dead. The causes of death in both cases were ruled as heart attacks.

1 Polybius

The legend of *Polybius* is likely the oldest gaming myth and had the honor of guest starring in an episode of *The Simpsons*.

Polybius was an arcade game that mysteriously appeared in an arcade in Portland, Oregon, in the early 1980s. The game unit was completely black except for the green joysticks and the logo at the top of the machine. The game combined elements of classic shooters like *Tempest*, mazes like in *Pac-Man*, and spatial puzzles. When played, it supposedly caused all sorts of health problems, including amnesia, blackouts, nausea, seizures, headaches, night terrors, and, in some cases, players were reported to commit suicide not long after playing. It is also said that men dressed in all black would often be seen messing with the game, leading some to speculate that the device was not a video game but a government experiment. Whether or not this insidious arcade game ever actually existed is not known.

TOP 10 Internet Hoaxes and Pranks
by G Dragline

10 Helicopter Shark

This is the original: the first true Internet hoax. In 2001, this image appeared on the Internet and captivated the masses of naive new Internet users. It was passed around via e-mail, along with the claim that it was *National Geographic*'s "Photo of the Year."

It is a composite of two separate images—one of a helicopter performing a training maneuver in front of the Golden Gate Bridge and an image of a great white shark taken in South Africa. Once the myth was debunked, it was featured in multiple psychology and marketing texts and even *National Geographic* itself.

9 Reddit Serial Killer

A young girl who thought her uncle was a serial killer created a blog that detailed the evidence. The blog included photographs taken by "the girl" showing her uncle's newspaper clippings, bloodstained clothes, and other incriminating evidence.

A quick Google search linked the evidence directly to multiple Wikipedia pages about past murders and suspicions were aroused. The blog, the young girl, the evidence, and even the historical murders all turned out to be fake. It wasn't until the young girl's blog began making rounds on Reddit that the myth was debunked—it only lasted 26 minutes. But what was so interesting about this hoax was who was behind it; the whole thing had been staged by students of George Mason University as part of a course.

Many people called for any George Mason University IP addresses to be banned from Wikipedia on account of "Internet vandalism." That suggestion was discarded even after the professor of the course, T. Mills Kelly, vowed to strike again.

8 Mets Get Rickrolled

The Internet prank known as "Rickrolling" involves posting a link or video that seems too good to be true, but that redirects the user to the music video for Rick Astley's "Never Gonna Give You Up."

A week before opening day in 2008, the New York Mets Web page asked fans to choose a new sing-along song to be played every night to pump up the crowd. In true Internet fashion, "Never Gonna Give You Up" was the clear winner and the new official Mets song. A week later, it was played on game night to a chorus of boos.

Mets staff were puzzled at first and couldn't understand how an '80s British pop song could beat out songs like Bon Jovi's "Living on a Prayer." After it was explained, the Mets were a bit ticked but still played the song once every six games.

7 Exiling Pitbull

A promotional Facebook campaign offered to send hip-hop artist Pitbull to the Walmart store that received the most "likes." They likely assumed he'd be going to New York or Los Angeles—or at the worst, Omaha. What they didn't anticipate was David Thorpe and Jon Hendren of SomethingAwful. com getting involved.

By enlisting the help of eager Internet pranksters, Thorpe and Hendren were able to seize control of Pitbull's fate. Soon, "#exilepitbull" was trending on Twitter, and the Facebook page of a humble Walmart on the frozen island of Kodiak, Alaska—Walmart's most remote location—had received more "likes" then the entire population of Kodiak.

When the Alaskan Walmart won the competition, Pitbull said he wasn't disappointed and traveled to perform in Kodiak. He even invited Thorpe and Hendren to join him, which they took him up on.

6 Death Star Petition

In early 2013, an online petition on the White House's official Web page for the U.S. government to begin construction on a Death Star gained some attention. According to the website, if a petition garners 25,000 signatures, it will be reviewed and responded to by the current administration. This one in particular received nearly 35,000 signatures.

The official response from the administration was that the $850 quadrillion projected cost was simply too high, and the current administration doesn't support blowing up planets. The also posed their own question: "Why would we spend countless taxpayer dollars on a Death Star with a fundamental flaw that can be exploited by a one-man starship?"

5 Save Toby

Toby was the pet rabbit of James and Brian, creators of SaveToby.com. They made their website in early 2005, promising to kill and eat Toby if they didn't receive $50,000 dollars by June 30. The website included pictures and videos of Toby, as well as information about how they planned to cook him.

Later, James and Brian published a book called *Only You Have the Power to Save Toby*, a collection of recipes for cooking rabbit. They claimed that if the book didn't sell 100,000 copies, they would follow through with their promise.

Animal rights activists claimed it was animal cruelty and attempted to shut down the website. While they were able to shut down the PayPal link provided for donations, GoDaddy.com refused to remove the site. Their official statement was: "It is perfectly legal to eat a rabbit."

The site was eventually revealed as a hoax when it was purchased by Bored.com. However, the creators claimed they had collected more than $20,000 in donations.

4 Dub the Dew

Internet crowd-sourcing campaigns always seem like a good idea until you realize how little the average Internet user cares about any form of decency.

In this case, Mountain Dew was launching a new green apple flavor, and they wanted the Internet to suggest and vote on the name. As it turns out, almost no one took the contest seriously. The top suggestions were things such as "Gushing Granny," "Sierra Mist," and "Diabettus." Mountain Dew finally shut down the promotional website when "Hitler Did Nothing Wrong" topped the voting charts.

3 Bald for Bieber and Cutting for Bieber

A Photoshopped image of *Entertainment Tonight*'s Twitter feed began making rounds on the Internet in fall 2012. The image showed apparent confirmation that Justin Bieber had been diagnosed with cancer, along with the hashtag "#baldforbieber." The hashtag soon appeared with images of fans who had shaved their heads in support.

Another similar story appeared in January 2013. After recent reports of Justin Bieber's drug use, many fans appeared to be participating in self-harm protests to discourage their idol from continuing down his path. Photos, tweets, and the hashtag "#cuttingforbieber" began circulating on Twitter. The photos and tweets suggested that thousands of fans were following the lead of the pranksters who suggested the protest.

2 Taylor Swift School for the Deaf

In 2012, *VH1 Storytellers*, Papa John's, and Chegg launched a competition that promised Taylor Swift would perform at the school that received the most votes. Reddit and 4Chan jumped at the opportunity to prank another celebrity, and it soon looked like the Horace Mann School for the Deaf and Hard of Hearing would be hosting a private Swift concert.

However, after the overwhelming victory, Taylor Swift and her sponsors disqualified the school. The school's headmaster was displeased, and when he claimed that hearing-impaired people could still enjoy the music, Taylor Swift donated $10,000 to call it even.

1 LonelyGirl15

In June 2006, a 16-year-old girl began posting video blogs about her everyday life under the YouTube username "lonelygirl15." But as it began to gain some followers, the video blog took a darker turn. The girl, Bree Avery, began to hint that her family was participating in strange cult practices and that the cult members were imprisoning her in her house. The videos began to gain more and more of a following as Bree's parents went missing and she was pressured to take part in secret cult ceremonies.

The videos captured the minds of concerned viewers until it was outed as fictional four months after it began. Some viewers were already skeptical, but the hoax was so elaborate that it took a sting operation to uncover the actress behind lonelygirl15.

The show continued to thrive and branched off into several spin-off shows with dozens of characters until its official end in 2008.

TOP 10 Logos That Mean Way More Than You Think

by **Scott Hillard**

10 FedEx Logo Subliminally Tells Us They Are Fast

The FedEx logo is basically just the company's name: "Fed" in bold purple writing and "Ex" in bold orange. There's nothing particularly clever about that. So why has such an unassuming logo won dozens of awards? For its use of negative space. In the FedEx logo, the "e" and the "x" are positioned in such a way that an arrow is formed in the space between them. A lot went into the creation of this logo, including months of work and the creation of an entirely new letterform. But what is represented in the logo is apparently very effective on a subliminal level. Many people don't specifically notice the arrow but still process it on an unconscious level, associating it with the sense of speed and proficiency that the company certainly hopes to be linked to.

9 The Golden Arches Are Boobs

One would be forgiven for thinking that the McDonald's logo is nothing but a large yellow representation of the first letter in the company's name. And it technically is, but there's more to it. To some, the rounded "m" subconsciously represents our mother's breasts. In the 1960s, McDonald's was retooling its image, which included discussing a possible new logo. Louis

Cheskin, a psychologist and design consultant hired by McDonald's, urged them to keep the current logo, claiming that the golden arches had a Freudian effect that made customers imagine a pair of nourishing breasts, which then made them hungry. Some find this hard to believe, but one thing's for sure—you won't look at the big "m" the same way again.

8 Museum of London Logo Shows History

The Museum of London is dedicated to recounting the history of London through all eras, from medieval times to today. In 2010, the museum needed a revamp, hoping to update their image and appeal to a younger audience. The new logo they presented was certainly capable of that due to its vibrant color, but on top of that you can learn about the history of London just by looking at it. The logo features several colored layers, each representing a different geographical shape London has taken in its evolution through time. This reflects the history and change that the museum displays as well as documents displayed inside, and it is almost impossible to miss due to its color.

7 Adidas Logo Makes You Work Harder

Adidas manufactures sports clothing and accessories, but it's probably most known for the shoes. The name "Adidas" originated as a combination of the first and last name of the company's creator, Adolf Dassler. Even at the very beginning, Adidas put heavy interest into marketing, with "the brand with the three stripes" almost becoming their motto. Throughout time, the company's logo has changed, but has always incorporated the three stripes. The current logo features three slanted stripes in a triangle shape, but referencing the logo of times past isn't all that's represented here. This new logo symbolizes a mountain, a metaphor for the challenges and perceivable goals that all athletes must meet and overcome.

6 Mitsubishi Logo Shows Company Lineage

Mitsubishi was first established as a shipping firm in the 1800s and involved the merging of two groups to become one company. The logo represents this by combining two "crests"—the three-leaf crest of the Tosa Clan and the Iwasaki family crest, which showed three diamonds stacked on top of each other. The three diamonds are said to signify reliability, integrity, and success, and are colored red because red denotes confidence and attracts customers to the brand.

5 Google Logo Is a Rebel

The Google logo appears to be made of fairly humble, simple colors with no flashy font or symbols, but even simple colors can have a deep relation to company image. During the creation of the Google logo, designers wanted a way to display a sense of playfulness without bulky objects or symbols in the logo limiting what they could do. This was initially achieved by skewing some of the letters, but this idea was scrapped and instead focus was directed toward color. The current logo features a pattern of primary colors being broken with a single letter shown in the secondary color of green. The broken pattern represents playfulness and the idea that Google isn't a company that plays by the rules.

4 Animal Planet Logo Is Feral

The Animal Planet logo used to be an elephant reaching out to a miniature Earth. An animal and a planet—that's simple enough. The channel relaunched in 2008 with the intention of appealing to a wider audience, and the elephant-globe logo was replaced. With its relaunch, Animal Planet sought to rid itself of the slow and boring pace associated with documentaries and replace it with more primal and exciting programming, and they attempted to present a new logo to match. The new logo is said to represent instinct, with the shades of green bringing to mind images of a jungle and feelings of primal urges, emotion, and "animalistic boldness." That's a lot of feeling to be had from what is essentially the name of the channel with one letter turned sideways.

3 NBC Logo Makes Us Buy Stuff

Most people know that the NBC logo is a peacock; that part isn't a secret. But many fail to ask why the peacock is there in the first place. It was all a marketing trick to make people buy color televisions. At the time of the logo's development, NBC was owned by the electronics company Radio Corporation of America (RCA). Color televisions were just beginning to emerge, and RCA wanted a way to show the public that the relatively high price of the units was worth the enhanced experience of viewing in color. They needed a logo that required color to be fully appreciated, reminding viewers with black-and-white units that they were missing out. Rainbows were rejected as too obvious, butterflies were too tame and eventually the peacock was selected, bringing with it the connotation that NBC was proud of its new color programming because of the then-common phrase "proud as a peacock."

2 The Amazon Logo Represents Diversity and Smiles

The Amazon logo looks fairly simple at first glance. The company's name, Amazon.com, in bold black lettering with a simple yellow line curving underneath. But what does that arrow represent? It's intended to be two things. It represents the smile customers should find on their faces after a great Amazon experience. The position of the yellow line forms a visible smile with each "a" in the word acting as the eyes.

The yellow line is also an arrow, beginning at the first "a" and spanning over to "z." This signifies the diversity among Amazon's products—"everything from 'a' to 'z'"—as well as denoting a link to the diversity in the Amazon forest itself. At one point this logo was animated with the yellow arrow beginning at the "A" and slowly growing out toward the "z," but it was later changed for being too phallic.

1 The Pepsi Logo Represents Everything

The Pepsi logo is a simple circle. The top half is red, the bottom half is blue, and a wavy white line runs through the center. The colors intentionally represent the American flag, but that's just scratching the surface of this simple globe. Pepsi spent hundreds of millions on their current logo, which is very similar to their previous ones, but tweaked in a way that it (apparently) means a lot more.

When submitting the new logo, the branding agency hired by Pepsi presented a 27-page document explaining the many, many connotations their design represented. According to this document the new logo represents the Earth's magnetic field, feng shui, Pythagoras, geodynamics, the theory of relativity, and plenty more. Makes you wonder if the logo is working as intended or if the branding company lied their way into a big fat check.

TOP 10 Insane Facts about Marvel Comics

by **Gareth May**

10 They Banned Werewolves

The Comics Code Authority was an organization established in 1954 to make comics more kid-friendly, but in addition to cutting down on violence and gore, they also decided to enact an outright ban on werewolves in an attempt to discourage the horror genre. Marvel eventually got around this rather bizarre artistic barricade by developing slightly skewed takes on the wolf-something combo. The best example of this was Sauron, a were-pterodactyl from the Savage Land who debuted in *X-Men* No. 60 in 1969.

In 1971 the code was—thankfully, for all your lycanthrope lovers—revised, and werewolves were allowed to be included in comic book stories as long as they related to the "classic" tradition of the Gothic literature of authors like Edgar Allan Poe and Sir Arthur Conan Doyle. Of course, after the repeal came a flurry of werewolf titles and characters, such as the popular Werewolf by Night of the 1970s and the awful "Man and Wolf" storyline running in *Captain America* in the early 1990s, which saw the shield-wielding superhero turned into Cap-wolf.

9. One of Their Most Influential Artists Was Also a Magician

Jim Steranko was a revered artist on *Nick Fury, Agent of S.H.I.E.L.D* in the 1960s, but his artwork wasn't the only notable thing about him. Before he became a comic book artist, Steranko was an amateur Houdini enthusiast, putting on shows of escapology involving live burials and the like. He was also in a rock band that once opened for Bill Haley and His Comets. He stole guns and motor vehicles, and in 1956 he was arrested for the theft of 25 cars and two trucks. And he was a fire-eater. Stranger than fiction or what?

On a side note, Michael Chabon's Pulitzer Prize–winning novel *The Amazing Adventures of Kavalier and Clay* has an escape artist lead character named Joe Kavalier, who was based on Jim Steranko.

8 Marvel's Founder Narrowly Escaped Death in the Hindenberg

If a man named Martin Goodman had stuck to his original travel plans in 1937, Marvel Comics would have never existed.

That year, Goodman was on his honeymoon in Europe with his wife. For their return leg to the U.S., Goodman had planned to ride the exciting new *Hindenburg* airship, but he was late to buy tickets and couldn't secure two seats next to each other, so they took a plane instead. Of course, the *Hindenburg* famously crashed, killing 35 of the 97 people onboard.

Martin Goodman, however, made it back from his honeymoon and went on to found Timely Comics later that year, which became Atlas Comics in 1951 and, finally, Marvel Comics in 1961.

7 Marvel Helped Create the Transformers Universe

Marvel isn't just responsible for your love of Spider-Man and Wolverine—they also developed the Transformer names Optimus Prime and Megatron.

Toy manufacturer Hasbro approached then Marvel editor-in-chief Jim Shooter and writers Denny O'Neil and Bob Budiansky in the 1980s. Hasbro had bought the robots that disguised themselves as cars and planes from Japanese company Takara and needed to repackage them. O'Neil came up with Optimus Prime and Budiansky created Megatron, while Jim Shooter developed an eight-page treatment that chartered the relationship between the Decepticons and the Autobots, explained their backstory, and gave a brief breakdown of several robots' personality traits and moral alignments.

6 One of Their Most Famous Artists Later Turned to Porn

Troubled but seminal Marvel artist Wally Wood may be revered for his design of Daredevil's signature red costume, but by many he's also known as Dirty Wally Wood. In his twilight years, under the name Wallace Wood, Woody turned his hand to pornographic cartoons such as explicit versions of Disney's *Snow White and the Seven Dwarfs* and a *Disneyland Orgy*. He also did a randy version of Flash Gordon, brilliantly titled *Flasher Gordon*, and a comic book called *Gang Bang*. In 2012, Disney bought Marvel, presumably forgetting about their former artist's penchant for playing around with their princesses.

5 "Sex" Easter Eggs

Comic collectors, stop reading this and go grab your copy of *New X-Men* No. 118. Back? Cool. Now see how many times you can see the word "sex" in the issue. Quick warning: It won't be easy to spot. The word "sex" is concealed within the illustrations at least 18 times. That's pretty much one on every page. Some of the places to look include hair strands, bottles of whiskey, a hedge, a puddle, tree branches, and protest signs.

Artist Ethan Van Sciver said he included the lewd mentions in the book because Marvel was working him overtime at the time, and he decided to have a bit of a laugh.

4 They Once Owned the Word "Zombie"

As with many creative industries, comic publishers rely heavily on trademarks and the ability to allow licensing of these trademarks, through movies and merchandise for example, to generate income. The term "superhero" therefore is trademarked by DC and Marvel jointly. But what about the term "zombie"?

After publishing *Tale of the Zombie* in 1973, Marvel applied for the publishing trademark of the term "zombie" for use in their comic books, and two years later "zombie" was officially trademarked to Marvel. By this time however, *Tale of the Zombie* was ready for the chopping block.

But Marvel held the trademark until 1996 when, due to the overwhelming popularity of the archetype, they realized the trademark was almost impossible to enforce. Marvel then went on to trademark "Marvel Zombies" with the registration document stating, "No claim is made to the exclusive right to use 'zombies.'"

3 They (Accidentally?) Published an Artist's Resignation Letter

Dave Cockrum. Marvel artist. Resigned from Marvel in 1979. But whereas a resignation letter is usually a private correspondence, in this case the letter was printed in a comic.

In *Iron Man* No. 127. Tony Stark's butler, Jarvis, resigns after being abused by an inebriated and angry Stark. The letter says, "I am leaving because this is no longer the team-spirited 'one big happy family' I once loved working for." The letter went on to say that the disintegration of morals at Marvel and the "unfair, malicious, or vindictive treatment" of some individuals has lead to Cockrum not wanting to wait "around to see what's next."

The only change in the letter was the replacement of the word "Marvel" with "Avengers." Three issues later in *Iron Man* No. 130, then-writer David Michelinie explained to readers that the mistaken mix-up of the letters had happened "due to a production error." But to this day, no one knows for sure.

2 Steve Ditko Carved Up Art History

Steve Ditko is considered by many to be the greatest comic book artist of all time. However, Ditko left Marvel after a dispute over who owned the original artwork of Spider-Man, a character Ditko was the first to pencil. After years of legal wrangling, Marvel relented and accepted that all original artwork belonged to the artists and gave that artwork back. But only as a gift, not in any form of copyright or royalties.

But Ditko didn't take the gesture—whether it was genuine or mocking—lightly. Instead, he put the famous artwork to good use: When comic historian Greg Theakston visited Ditko, he couldn't believe the amount of slashed-up original comic panels spread throughout Ditko's studio. In an act of defiance, Ditko refused to display or preserve the famous boards, instead using them as, among other things, cutting boards. Some of the world's most famous artwork was destroyed all because of a greed-fueled feud.

1 They Killed Nixon

Barack Obama famously appeared on the cover of *The Amazing Spider-Man* No. 583, but he wasn't the first president featured in the Marvel Universe. While George W. Bush and Jimmy Carter have also shown up in the comics, the most shocking appearance has to be Richard Nixon in *Captain America* No. 175, published a month before Nixon resigned over the Watergate scandal. In the storyline, Cap is trying to smoke out a corrupt top government official who's hatching an evil plan to enslave the entire country.

The story arc, written by Steve Englehart, came to a head in 1975 when Cap tracks the mastermind down inside the White House. The baddie, cornered and isolated, decides to take his own life. Although we never see Nixon's face on the panels, Englehart later said, "Cap followed a criminal conspiracy into the White House and saw the president commit suicide." He goes on to say, "People often ask if Marvel hassled me for the political vibe in this series and others, and the honest answer is that they almost never did. It was a wonderful place to be creative. Here, I intended to say the president was Nixon, but wasn't sure if Marvel would allow it and so censored myself—probably unnecessarily."

TOP 10 Ways Magic Tricks Your Brain
by **Scott Hillard**

10 Focus

Multitasking is a myth. The human brain simply wasn't designed to focus on two things at once, and magicians take full advantage of this. Our attention is pulled to one thing in particular due to the "moving-spotlight" theory. In short, the theory says that our attention is like a spotlight, highlighting one thing while leaving what surrounds it in the dark. When an item or action is within the spotlight, the parts of the brain involved in processing it  work more efficiently, but anything beyond the spotlight is barely processed at all, at least not by our conscious mind. This allows magicians to pull a sleight of hand right under our noses; as long as something else is drawing our spotlight to what happens beyond it, to our brain isn't processing the trick at all.

9 Made-Up Memories

The "misinformation effect" occurs when information we are given after an event alters our memory of it. For example, a magician asks you to choose a card from the left side of the deck and return it without telling him. Before the razzle-dazzle where he guesses your card, he may say something like "Now you chose any card you wanted, correct?" and in the heat of the moment you will say you did. The truth is you were only given the option of the left side of the deck, but the ambiguous comments from the magician alter how you remember the trick, leaving you with a false memory, making the trick seem perhaps more incredible than it was.

8 Predicted Wrong Future

When you see a ball get thrown in the air, it comes back down. You've seen it a million times. You know that what comes up must come down and so does your brain. In fact, because of something called the "memory-prediction framework," our brain sometimes remembers certain actions so well that it stops paying close attention because it predicts how they will end. When a ball gets thrown in the air our brain instantaneously recalls memories of similar events and produces an idea of what's going to happen next, but sometimes it's wrong. When a magician puts a ball in a cup only to have it disappear when the cup is lifted, we are shocked because what our brain predicted didn't come true. Our brains often feed us a prediction and convince us we saw it happen, which leaves us even more shocked when the predicted action didn't happen at all.

7 Free Will

When we "pick a card, any card" we are very rarely picking at random, no matter what it seems. It is usually the magician choosing for us, only

without our knowledge. In many card tricks, the card we apparently choose is "forced," meaning the magician did something, mental or physical, to make us choose exactly what they wanted us to. But our brain will often overlook or deny this as an option in favor of free choice. Our brain simply does not want to believe it was forced and will often omit facts that may indicate that it was, instead jumping fully into the false idea that all choices were all our own.

6 Filling in the Blanks

The "woman sawed in half" trick is old enough that most people know the secret. The head we see in one end of the box doesn't belong to the legs we see at the other. But our brain insists and assumes it does—why? Because our brain is a sucker for continuity. When it sees a head in rough alignment with a set of legs, it uses past experience to fill in the blank and tell us that obviously a torso exists between those two body parts. In many magic tricks, an object is partially covered and our brain uses what it *can* see to continue the image and fill in the blank, which of course is exactly what the magician wants.

5 Change

Quick, look out the window. What did you see? Now look again, has anything changed? If the first time all you saw was your backyard and the second time there was a tiger, you're probably going to notice. But what if that bird perched in the tree moved slightly? What if a plant had moved in the wind? Our brains are susceptible to something called "change blindness," basically meaning that it's actually quite bad at immediately detecting small changes. It's not necessarily that we don't see them, but more that our brains have trained themselves not to worry about changes that won't greatly affect us, and as a result, if we aren't very specifically focusing on something, we'll rarely register it consciously. Obviously magicians can utilize this to the extreme, as we never notice small changes in what's going on until the magician directs our focus to it.

4 Our Brain Has an Ego

Our brain insists we have free will, and it also insists that it's always right. Due to something called "cognitive dissonance," our brain will make up excuses to rationalize events, even if it means you are going against what you thought or felt only minutes earlier. Our brain will force us to justify events if they don't go how we expected. Magicians present a reality that doesn't obey the idea of reality your brain is used to seeing. This creates a cognitive dissonance, and a point is eventually reached where, no matter how hard it tries, your brain cannot rationalize the events it's just seen. Our brain is used to 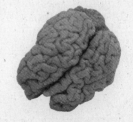 rationalizing events after they occur, and magic creates a situation that can't exist, which leads to the unique sense of astonishment we feel.

3 Seeing and Feeling Too Long

You've probably seen any number of Internet illusions where you stare at a black image then stare at a white wall to find the image still exists in your vision. That's called an "after image," and it's really your brain seeing something for a short time after its gone. A magician can use this when switching an item from hand to hand; to your brain, a coin may appear to be in one hand slightly longer than it was due to an after image, which gives the magician a fraction of a second longer to make the switch. A magician might even use an after image to remove your watch. Squeezing your wrist can leave an after image feeling, leading your brain to believe your watch is still there even after it has been expertly removed.

2 Your Brain Loves New Things

Simply speaking, when your brain sees something new, fast, and exciting, it is helpless not to take notice. Due to "exogenous attentional capture," your brain will always be drawn to something new that it has trouble predicting. A dove erratically flying from a hat will have your attention almost immediately as your brain takes at least a few seconds to process the event and assess its importance. Even a fast, curving hand movement will draw more attention than a slow straight one, and magicians know this and will use exciting actions that your brain can't help but look at.

1 Your Brain Falls for Charm

Many magicians use humor in their acts in an attempt to charm their audience into submission. But this charm and charisma is actually having a chemical affect on your brain. It's possible that the simple act of laughing with (or at) the magician's terrible puns releases oxytocin, the bonding hormone, which makes acts of cooperation and social interaction feel good. Oxytocin release means you are less likely to be critical of the tricks you're watching and even more likely to miss sleights of hand as your attention will be drawn to the magician's face. So everything, even the terrible puns, are part of the trick.

TOP 10 Real-World Technologies Inspired by Video Games

by **Nathan Blumenthal**

10 Medpac

Anyone who's ever played a first-person-shooter game knows that when you're injured, you'll need a Medpac to heal yourself. Although we haven't quite gotten to the "just walk over it" part, scientists have been hard at work inventing gels that can instantly stop bleeding and heal wounds: A college student named Joe Landolina has invented a gel that can stop bleeding instantly just by squirting it into a wound. The gel apparently binds cells together while triggering the body's natural clotting mechanism.

The Defense Advanced Research Projects Agency (DARPA, a branch of the U.S. Department of Defense) has gotten into the Medpac business too, inventing a foam meant to stabilize internal bleeding. While it doesn't heal the wound, it does buy time to rush an injured soldier to a hospital. Apparently, the foam can be removed quickly as well, which is good because the last thing a surgeon wants is to perform a delicate operation on a body filled with Styrofoam packing peanuts.

9 Auto-Aim

Do you like shooting, but suck at it? If you have a spare $17,000 and think the worst part of hunting is the actual hunting, you could buy the XS1, a Linux-powered rifle developed by TrackingPoint. Yes, that's "Linux" the operating system. The XS1 has a tracking button that, when pressed, marks the target and will even follow it as it moves. From there all you have to do is hold the trigger and line up your dot with the tracking target. The gun automatically fires when the two targets are aligned and accounts for wind speed, elevation, etc.

Like a good video game, the gun even incorporates smack talk. If you choose, the gun will post your kill online so you can brag to your friends about what a great shot your bank account is. If you really want one of these guns, you'll have to wait: There's a huge backlog of orders.

8 Programmable Grenades

It used to be that if you found yourself in a battle and your enemy used the time-honored cheat of ducking behind a wall, that was that, you couldn't hit him—but then some government scientist spent a weekend playing *Gears of War* and got the idea for a smart grenade. Thus, the XM-25 was invented. It's a rocket launcher with programmable grenades that can be set to detonate at a specific point in space, such as when it's directly over your enemy's head, and spray shrapnel straight down. The XM-25 is currently being used by some U.S. special forces, and the army is considering a larger rollout.

7 Gimmicky Ammunition

Default weapons are all well and good, but to really dominate, you need to use the fancy stuff: bullet-mounted cameras, proximity mines, and other fancy devices. In video games, anyway—that's not how real life works, right?

Nope! Check out the M32 multiple-grenade launcher. It's capable of shooting six rounds in less than six seconds and comes with a variety of ammo, including HUNTIR rounds, which are basically miniature video cameras that float to the ground via parachute to provide battlefield surveillance, and HELLHOUND rounds, which are extremely powerful projectiles that cause massive damage.

6 Heads-Up Displays

When you're in the middle of an Xbox shootout, you need to be able to see three things: where your friends are, a map of the area, and an inventory list. That's where the heads-up display (HUD) comes in handy. You've no doubt heard of Google's Project Glass, which aims to bring the Internet to your glasses, but there are several other companies working hard to bring a heads-up display to life.

Engineers at Ulsan National Institute of Science and Technology in South Korea have invented a soft contact lens with all the benefits of Project Glass and none of the side effects of looking like you lost the bottom half of your eyeglasses. It's different from previous electronic contact lenses in that the creators use an off-the-shelf contact and mount it with a light-emitting diode. Researchers at the University of Washington have been working on something similar, and have so far managed an 8 x 8-pixel array. It's only a matter of time before you can easily keep track of your ammo and health bar while walking down to the corner drugstore.

5 Ammo Counter

People who fire guns a lot occasionally run out of ammunition, and not just when they're flying through the air in slow motion with a gun in each hand, firing at the Russian terrorists who've kidnapped their daughter. Which is why someone invented an actual ammo counter to help them out.

The counter is basically a tiny computer running on AAA batteries that attaches to your gun. It uses an accelerometer to measure the recoil of each shot and displays how many shots you've taken. It's significantly more accurate than the person actually shooting the gun because it's a computer and won't get distracted.

4 Vehicle Armor

In the *Battlefield* series of video games, your tank can easily take a few direct hits from a rocket launcher—but try that in real life and you'll discover that tanks aren't magic. DARPA took their disappointment and used it to crush reality by inventing a vehicle armor system called the Iron Curtain. It uses multiple metal plates to create an electric field and a range of sensors to identify potential projectiles. These two things work in tandem to detonate any explosives right before they can make contact with the vehicle—saving both repair costs and lives, but not paint.

3 Power-Ups

Anyone who's played *Bioshock* is familiar with "Plasmids," those awesome power-ups that give you psychokinesis or telekinesis. While we may not have exactly those powers, new drugs can expand your mental powers—although there may be some side effects.

We've already heard about drugs like Adderall and Ritalin used to supposedly enhance concentration, but the newest drug that everyone's talking about is Modafinil. Originally designed to assist people with narcolepsy or those who are working night shifts, its use has been appropriated by people looking to get a leg up on their competition. Supposedly, Modafinil enables people to stay awake for 40 hours without any reduced mental capacity, and it's been studied by the U.S. Air Force as an effective drug for fighter pilots who routinely need to stay airborne and alert for long stretches of time.

2 Controlling a Character

The one thing common to just about every video game is the fact that you, the player, are controlling another character. But for those for whom controlling a digital person has never quite been enough, take heart: Scientists are quickly discovering that they can do the same with animals.

North Carolina State University's iBionics Lab has wired up the brains of several cockroaches to create the world's most disgusting cyborgs. Scientists are then able to steer the cockroaches via computer with amazing precision. The head of the lab claims they can be used as first responders to reach impassable places during a disaster.

Not to be outdone, scientists at the State University of New York have created robo-rats. The benefit of using live animals, as opposed to machines, is that you don't need to manufacture complicated parts. All you have to do is wire directly into the rat's brain and then train it to respond to certain stimuli. It sounds expensive, but the researchers claim each rat can be controlled for less than $40!

1 Extra Lives

If you've ever been frustrated that Sonic the Hedgehog gets a new life for every 100 rings he collects while you're stuck with only one life no matter how much stuff you steal, take solace: In the not-too-distant future that might not be the case. Mark Stephen Meadows is one of many people who think it would be possible to create an artificial body you could control from the comfort of your own home or specially designed facility. The ability to transfer data rapidly and turn physical and mental controls into output via some sort of interface are technologies we already have available. It's only a matter of time before they become more advanced, cheaper to build, and easier to use. One Russian billionaire has unveiled plans to create a fully holographic body by the year 2045 and you can sign up to follow his progress.

Someday, second chances will be available at the push of a button.

TOP 10 Amazing but Overlooked Innovations by Walt Disney

by **Ross Yaylaian**

10 Switchback/Interactive Lines

Disney often displayed his innovations at the annual New York World's Fair. His attractions drew record crowds that spilled out from the waiting areas inside the pavilions and onto the fairgrounds. The implementation of switchback lines (lines that fold in on themselves instead of remaining straight) allowed more people to be condensed into a smaller area in an efficient and organized fashion. Switchback lines today can be seen in banks, airports, and of course, Disney theme parks. Disney later took the "waiting in line" concept to an entirely new level with the introduction of interactive lines. These are lines that actually become part of the ride itself. For example, Disney attractions like the Haunted Mansion, Tower of Terror, and Midway Mania all feature unique interactive lines.

9 Shopping Malls

Disney was responsible for many hugely influential innovations in his lifetime, some of them even unintentionally. Main Street USA in Disneyland is widely recognized as the world's first indoor shopping mall. Shops on either side of the street have openings which allow you to walk from one shop to the next, all under cover, from one end of the street to the other. The design may not have been done with malls in mind, but businesses have certainly taken the idea and run with it.

8 Transportation/Monorails

Moving large groups of people quickly and efficiently was one of the main tenets of EPCOT (back in the days when EPCOT was going to be a model city of the future). Disney pioneered the use of the all-electric PeopleMover system, which was planned to shuttle residents around EPCOT. Also on the drawing board was the use of monorails for mass transportation of residents to and from the urban section of the city. Both systems are still in use today. The PeopleMover is located in the Magic Kingdom and actually passes through Space Mountain where a portion of the model of EPCOT can be seen. The monorail is located in and around both the Magic Kingdom and EPCOT. Disney's monorail was America's first daily-operating monorail system.

7 Merchandise

Disney was a trailblazer in merchandising. He understood early on that the right merchandise could become an effective tool to promote Disney movies and TV shows. As soon as Mickey Mouse became popular, Disney manufacturers flooded Walt with ideas to cash in on the phenomenon. Disney only wanted the best products to bear Mickey's name and image, however. The studio negotiated a 2.5–5 percent royalty on all items, and at the height of the Great Depression, consumers bought hundreds of thousands of items from toys and ice cream cones to the famous Mickey Mouse watches. In the early 1950s, the Disney television program aired the show *Davy Crockett*. A trade embargo with China led to surpluses of raccoon skins and inspired Disney to negotiate a deal for coonskin hats like the one worn by Crockett on the show. Demand exceeded expectations and the hats sold by the millions. Composer George Burns put together a song titled "The Ballad of Davy Crockett" for the show. The track quickly became a hit, selling ten million copies and spending a month at number one. Even though we take merchandising for granted these days, in Disney's time these fresh innovations helped change American entertainment.

6 Television

Long before a television sat in every living room, Disney understood their power. During the early stages of planning Disneyland, Walt and his  brother Roy knew they needed money to help fund such an ambitious project. Roy traveled to New York to meet with network executives to discuss TV's ability to finance and promote the park. ABC agreed to a weekly Disney series. The series debuted in 1954 with major success. The studio used the series to hype the theme park and promote Disney films. Walt insisted on filming as many segments as possible in color, even though most televisions still used black and white, because he believed color would become the new standard. A few years later, he moved his show to NBC, where the entire program was broadcast in color and retitled *Walt Disney's Wonderful World of Color*. With this 1961 television series, Disney Studios became the first ever to provide regular color programming for television. Disney clearly saw the value of the then-infantile medium of television. He was aware of the power of promotion through TV and he used it to connect with the public in an entirely new way.

5 Fully Enclosed Attractions

The 1965 New York World's Fair saw Disney successfully introduce a number of never-before-seen ride innovations. Traditionally, theme park attractions included outdoor rides and perhaps a fun house or haunted house walk-through. Disney radically changed this model, creating the standard for what we now consider "theme park rides." When Disney was working on the "It's a Small World" attraction, it was planned to be a walk-through attraction. Disney realized however, that he couldn't handle enough people using a walk-through format. So the attraction became a boat ride, where flat-bottomed boats were gently pushed along by underwater jets. The ride system was so successful that the Pirates of the Caribbean ride, originally meant to be a walk-through, was changed to a more realistic boat ride. Rides like the Matterhorn, the world's first enclosed steel roller coaster, and Soarin' in EPCOT also fall into the parameters of "fitting into the theme of the show." The omni-mover ride system, where ride vehicles glide along on a continuously moving track, was developed for the World's Fair and was used on the Ford Magic Skyway attraction. Rides like the Haunted Mansion in the Magic Kingdom (the fabled doom buggies) and Spaceship Earth in EPCOT still employ the system.

4 Family Theme Parks

Walt Disney dreamed of creating the first entertainment enterprise where children and parents could have fun together. While we may take such a concept for granted today, the idea was truly novel in the mid-20th century. Traditionally, amusement parks only catered to children, leaving tag-along parents with nothing to do. Walt envisioned a place where parents and children could share fun experiences with each other. Disneyland, which opened on July 17, 1955, was that place. Disney also surrounded his innovative park with an earthen barrier to insulate his guests from the intrusions of the outside world and place them in a reassuring atmosphere. Disney emphasized that the parks were about reassurance, that the world could be OK, that you could talk to a stranger in a public place, and that a public place could be clean.

3 Audio-Animatronics

Hastened by Disney's participation in the World's Fair, audio-animatronics became one of the most significant breakthroughs in the history of theme park entertainment. Attractions like The Carousel of Progress, Ford's Magic Skyway, and Great Moments with Mr. Lincoln all featured Disney's never-before-seen robots. The audio-animatronic figures moved and talked, grunted and gesticulated like real, live beings. It was a new toy for Disney's creative staff, and a new way to tell stories in a three-dimensional fashion. While the Carousel of Progress and the Magic Skyway featured rather anonymous characters, the Lincoln figure recreated the famed U.S. president in jaw-dropping fashion. It turned out, in hindsight, to be a radical machine, the first time the world was ever going to see a really believable animated figure. The latest and most sophisticated audio-animatronic figures continue to play prominent roles throughout the Disney entertainment world.

2 Animation and Film

It is hard to imagine any aspect of animation that was not influenced by Walt Disney. He created the first cartoon to successfully synchronize sound and picture (*Steamboat Willie*, 1928). He was responsible for the first feature-length animated film (*Snow White and the Seven Dwarfs*, 1937). He pioneered the use of the Circle Vision–filming technique, which allowed him to shoot and present movies in 360 degrees, surrounding the audience. He was even the first to develop an optical printer that could combine live-action and animation together (*The Three Caballeros*, 1945). And as if this weren't enough, perhaps his largest contribution to the world of animation was his invention of the multiplane camera, a special motion-picture camera that allowed Disney to transform flat, one-dimensional animation into layered shots with depth and movement. Various parts of the artwork layers are left transparent, to allow other layers to be seen behind them. The movements are calculated and photographed frame-by-frame, with the result being an illusion of depth by having several layers of artwork moving at different speeds. It transformed animation in much the same way that computer graphics did years later.

1 City of the Future

EPCOT stands for "Experimental Prototype Community of Tomorrow." No one can say just when the idea of creating a model city of the future occurred to Walt Disney, but as early as 1964, operating in secrecy, Disney began planning a true city of the future: a development combining the latest technologies and materials with time-tested concepts about livable communities. EPCOT's radial design surrounded a high-density urban core with low-density neighborhoods; at its center was a 50-acre downtown area housing hotels, apartments, convention centers, and offices, along with shopping and entertainment venues. Towering above was the spire of a cosmopolitan 30-story hotel, providing guests with a panoramic view of Disney's sleek metropolis.

Transportation was important to Walt's EPCOT; the layout of the city was designed to discourage car use. Facilities could be accessed via People-Mover, or, for those who did drive, an intricate system of roads that allowed motorists to travel around the city without gridlock or even stoplights. An enclosed downtown Transportation Lobby enabled transfers between the city's PeopleMover system and monorails linking to other parts of the planned Disney World development. Walt said EPCOT would constantly be updated to project a vision of "optimum patterns of urban living" 25 years in the future, and was designed to be a dynamic environment that would "always be introducing and testing and demonstrating new materials and new systems." Sadly, Walt Disney died in 1966, before EPCOT could be realized. Walt's brother Roy decided to suspend master planning in favor of focusing all efforts on finishing the Magic Kingdom. The vision of EPCOT still lives on today, however, as one of four theme parks in Walt Disney World.

TOP 10 Classic Toys and Games That Are Older Than You Think

by **Adam Wears**

10 The Yo-Yo

The yo-yo is undoubtedly one of the 20th century's most iconic toys—a fact you can thank Pedro Flores for. While working as a bellhop in a Santa Barbara hotel, he was inspired to adapt the yo-yo (a traditional toy from his homeland, the Philippines) for the mass toy market. After opening the imagina- 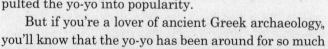 tively named Yo-Yo Manufacturing Company in 1928, he then went on to produce over 100,000 yo-yos before selling his company to the larger toy manufacturer Donald Duncan Yo-Yo Company, which then cata-pulted the yo-yo into popularity.

But if you're a lover of ancient Greek archaeology, you'll know that the yo-yo has been around for so much longer. In dig sites across the Mediterranean, archaeologists found exam-ples of Greek yo-yos made from materials such as bronze and terracotta. Indeed, one example held by the Metropolitan Museum of Art is made from terracotta and dates to between 460 and 450 BC. In addition, several ancient vases—including one that dates to 440 BC—depict children and adults playing with yo-yos.

9 Roller Skates

To many, roller skates are synonymous with the 1970s. After all, this was the age of roller disco, a curious sport that attempted to combine the high-stakes world of disco with the unpredictability that comes from wearing shoes attached to wheels.

Actually, the first roller skates were invented in the 1770s by a Belgian named John Joseph Merlin. He was so impressed by his invention that he felt confident enough to unveil it in the most flamboyant way imaginable: at a high-society ball, while simultaneously skating around the room and playing a violin. While no evidence remains as to the precise design of his skates, we do know that they were designed without brakes, since this demonstration ended with him skating (at a reportedly high speed) into a mirror.

8 Pen-and-Paper RPGs

If we asked you to name the first role-playing game that utilized a scaled gaming board, a gamemaster, and a complex set of rules that governed how players moved and attacked foes, there's no doubt that you'd say Dungeons and Dragons (created in 1974 by Gary Gygax and Dave Arneson).

You'd be wrong, though: enter Kriegsspeil (or Instructions for the Representation of Tactical Maneuvers under the Guise of a Wargame). Invented in 1812, it was used by the Prussian army to teach military tactics to officers in training. Players were pitted against each other on a D&D-esque gridded gaming board, which itself was lined with dozens of removable modular tiles that simulated landscapes such as rivers and hills in order to allow the creation of a near-unlimited number of practice battlefields. Game pieces were used that represented not individual soldiers, but entire military formations (such as companies and divisions). Meanwhile, a gamemaster oversaw the process and enforced the game's litany of rules, and also ensured that (since each game was based on an actual real-life battle) the player stuck to these scenarios throughout.

7 Remote-Control Toys

It's generally assumed the first remote-control toys were produced in the 1960s, after the Italian toy company Elettronica Giocattoli produced the first remote-control car (a 1:12 scale model of a Ferrari 250LM) in 1966.

However, the first remote-control toy was actually invented in the late 1890s by—and this might not come as a huge shock to some people—famed inventor Nikola Tesla. At the 1898 Electrical Exhibition in Madison Square Garden, Tesla unveiled a remote-control boat outfitted with functioning lights, rudders, and a propeller.

6 The Sims

The Sims (2000) is the classic video game where your only task is guiding your personalized character through a life fraught with love, career changes, infinite amounts of decorating, inexplicable house fires, and mysteriously disappearing pool ladders.

With the exception of the latter two, those were also the objectives of the 1985 video game *Little Computer People*. Like *The Sims*, players had the ability to customize their houses and command their characters to perform actions (like watching TV, reading, playing poker, etc). You also had the ability to communicate with your character directly; for instance, you could order them to play a specific song on the piano, play a board game with you, or send you messages.

5 Paintball

The game of paintball that we know and love was invented in the 1970s by two friends, Charles Gaines and Bill Gurnsey, who found an alternative (and painful) use for the paint-pellet guns that until then had only been used by farm workers to mark livestock.

But, if you'd lived in the early 1900s, you might have played an earlier form of paintball known as wax dueling: a sport in which men would partake in duels using pistols that fired wax bullets. Competitors were required to wear specialist armor to (ideally) protect them from any serious injury. Indeed, an issue of the *Pittsburgh Press* dated August 1908 describes how one player had "the soft piece of flesh connecting the thumb and forefinger" of his right hand shot out, and also warned that spectators risked being blinded by ricocheting rounds. Nevertheless, this sport soon became so popular that it even made an appearance at the 1908 Olympic Games in London.

4 Snakes and Ladders

The only way someone wouldn't know about Snakes and Ladders would be because they're more familiar with it as Chutes and Ladders.

But we're betting that you didn't know that the game has existed in some form since the 16th century. Originating in India, the objective for players back then was still the same—reach the end of the board by climbing ladders and avoiding snakes—but in this version, the ladders symbol-ized the virtues of faith, reliability, generosity, knowledge, and asceticism. Meanwhile, the snakes symbolized vices such as vanity, theft, rage, greed, pride, murder, and lust. The game aimed to teach players that in order to reach salvation (the end of the board), they must perform virtuous acts throughout their lives, as opposed to indulging in the aforementioned vices. For this reason, there are more snakes/sins on the board than ladders/virtues. The makers wanted to reinforce the idea that a virtuous life was harder to attain—and therefore more worthwhile—than a life of vice.

3 Cap Guns

You might think that cap guns are a relic of the 1940 and '50s. After all, that was the great age of the cowboy movie, when children clamored to relive the adventures of onscreen cowboys such as Roy Rogers, the Lone Ranger, and Hopalong Cassidy.

Actually, cap guns have a history that predates the American Civil War. In 1859, the J & E Stevens Company—a toy manu-facturer that specialized in the production of cast-iron toys—released a fire-cracker pistol similar in design to the modern-day cap gun. Several years later, and after achieving great success with this product, Stevens began producing novelty cap guns in the 1890s, including a model shaped like a sea serpent (which, on pulling the trigger, detonated a cap placed on its jaw) and another shaped like a monkey, which would trigger the cap by slamming a coconut-shaped hammer into it.

2 Monopoly

Monopoly, for those of you who have actively avoided all forms of popu-lar culture, is the fun, hyper-capitalistic game that's been tearing families apart since 1934.

However, Monopoly was itself inspired by a 1904 board game called The Landlord's Game. Created by Elizabeth Magie, The Landlord's Game was intended to teach people about how property owners at the time made vast fortunes at the expense of tenants like themselves, many of whom were already a paycheck away from poverty. Magie hoped that any children who played the game would recognize the inherent unfairness of this sys-tem and be able to protect themselves against it in later life.

Magie later sold the patent to the company Parkers Brothers in 1934, who obviously abandoned her initial goals. The major company had recently acquired the rights to produce Monopoly and wished to gain ownership of any patents that could prove problematic in the future.

1 Duck Hunt

Duck Hunt is regarded by many as being one of the greatest games ever. Released in 1984, it pits players against an army of (admittedly harmless) ducks to shoot—as well as a dog that will taunt you into your grave. Luckily, players were armed with a lightgun: a gun-shaped controller that mimics any real-life movements onscreen and allows wannabe hunters to blast any wayward ducks.

Incredibly, this wasn't the first time that people had the opportunity to shoot fictional ducks with imitation firearms for the purposes of entertainment; that honor instead goes to 1936's Ray-O-Lite Rifle. Created as an arcade game, it offered punters a lightbeam-firing rifle and tasked them with shooting as many wooden ducks as they could within a given time. To add an extra element of difficulty to the proceedings, the ducks were also able to move around the shooting gallery courtesy of a hidden conveyor belt. The makers also created several other varieties of this game, where targets included bears, chickens, and—in an edition made in 1942—even Adolf Hitler.

TOP 10 Interesting Histories of Iconic Products

by **Mike Floorwalker**

10 Dr Pepper

It's somewhat of a misconception that Dr Pepper was created by a doctor (we can't imagine why), but it's not too far from the truth. The inventor of the world's oldest soft drink, created in 1885, was Charles Alderton, a pharmacist at Morrison's Old Corner Drug Store in Waco, Texas. It's also somewhat commonly believed that it was created as a medicine, but that's untrue: Alderton just enjoyed mixing up flavorful, fizzy stuff. He enjoyed the smell of all the fruity syrups from the soda fountain mingled together, and set out to create a drink that tasted like that smell.

Owner Wade Morrison loved the new drink, and supposedly named it after a friend, a Dr. Charles

Pepper. As demand grew, Alderton and Morrison found it easiest to simply sell the syrup to merchants around town, who could mix it with carbonated water themselves—thus becoming the first manufacturers of soda concentrate.

Eventually, Alderton grew tired of fizzy mixings and sold his side of the business to Morrison, who promptly partnered up with Robert Lazenby, owner of a moderately successful ginger ale company. The pair introduced their concoction to the public at large at the 1904 World's Fair Expo in St. Louis—the very same world fair that introduced the hamburger, the hot dog, and the ice cream cone—and Dr Pepper has been one of the top soft drinks in the U.S. ever since.

9 Olay

Olay is a multibillion dollar skin care line from the venerable Proctor & Gamble company that, until 1999, was known as Oil of Olay in the U.S. and many other countries. Today, most of us are familiar with the company and the white, creamy stuff in the plastic bottle. But neither of those things applied at the product's inception, and its developers relied on some pretty unusual testing and marketing techniques.

Graham Wulff, a chemist from South Africa, developed the product in 1949 and called it Olay as a variation of lanolin, the main active ingredient. It began as a pink fluid in a heavy glass bottle, and Wulff—along with partner Jack Lowe, a copywriter and ad man—initially tested the product on their wives, because what's the worst that could happen?

Fortunately, nothing bad did, and in fact the product proved effective in softening wrinkles and contributing to healthy-looking skin. Early advertisements simply promised to share the "secret of a younger you," and didn't refer to the product as a moisturizer, or…anything else. Similarly, nowhere on the bottle did it say what the product was for—it relied largely on mystery, curiosity, and word of mouth. Obviously, it worked; the product known in various countries as Oil of Ulay, Ulan, or Olaz has become quite entrenched in the beauty industry.

8 Listerine

Listerine was developed by Dr. Joseph Lawrence, based on pioneering work done by Joseph Lister, whom he named it after. It wasn't intended for oral use however—it was simply an antiseptic, and the first one. Before Lister's discovery that carbolic acid killed germs, far more people died from infections incurred during surgery than from the injuries themselves (illustrated by a saying from the time: "The operation was a success, but the patient died.")

Consider: Since no one knew how to stop infections before Lister, amputations were the most common major surgery of the time to keep the infections from spreading, and the death rate from this procedure was around 40 percent. By the time Listerine had been in use for about 25 years, in 1910, the death rate from amputations had dropped to a measly 3 percent. One shudders to think how many more who were injured in World War I (still one of the deadliest wars of all time) would have died if not for Listerine.

Because carbolic acid is hard on the skin, surgeons eventually began using boric acid in its place. But Listerine's use had been growing as an oral antiseptic, and eventually that use eclipsed any other. The mouthwash market was originated by Listerine, the only product (with the possible exception of the condom) to both save millions of lives and make date night more awesome.

7 Play-Doh

Noah McVicker and his nephew, Joseph, are the inventors of Play-Doh, the nontoxic modeling clay that smells weird yet really makes you wonder what it tastes like. The story goes that Joseph McVicker had a conversation with a teacher friend about what a pain regular modeling clay—the kind his students used in class—was to work with and clean up, and a light bulb went off over Joe's head.

The McVickers were the owners of Kutol Chemicals, a reasonably successful company that sold a claylike substance that bore the company's name as a wallpaper-cleaning compound. He shipped off a box to his teacher friend, and the kids loved it—even though the only color available was a dull off-white and the packaging was a little less fun than what we've come to associate with the product.

The word started getting around, and before long the McVickers decided that the wallpaper-cleaning game was for suckers. They started a new company, Rainbow Crafts, and began marketing their clay under the familiar name and in a variety of colors. The company was bought by General Mills in 1965 and merged with Kenner in 1971; some two billion cans of the stuff later, it's hard to believe Play-Doh was ever anything but a fun way to sculpt stuff.

6 Bayer Aspirin

We doubt there are many people over the age of five in the world who haven't taken a Bayer aspirin. Bottles of Bayer grow spontaneously inside empty medicine cabinets. It seems like it's been around since the Middle Ages, but it actually got its start in the 19th century.

German professor Johann Buchner isolated salicin from willow bark in 1828, and within years, an Italian chemist by the name of Raffaele Piria had converted the compound into salicylic acid, the active ingredient in aspirin. No one knew what to do with it, for its beneficial pain-blocking properties were mitigated by the fact that it tended to tear stomach lining. The game of musical chemists continued as Frenchman Charles Frederic Gerhardt was able to buffer the compound—creating a new one, acetylsalicylic acid, which neutralized the problem, but he simply lost interest and discontinued his work on it.

German chemist and Bayer employee Felix Hoffmann rediscovered this work in the late 1800s, successfully using the compound to treat his father's arthritis, and aspirin was patented by Bayer in 1900. Bayer, however, had to give up that patent as a condition of the Treaty of Versailles after losing World War I, along with its patent on another wonder drug: heroin.

5 WD-40

The inventor of WD-40 was Norm Larsen, who started his company Rocket Chemical with two other employees in 1953. As a chemist, Larsen was self-taught—his only education was high school, but he loved reading books about chemistry and really, really wanted to invent something helpful and useful.

This was early in the U.S. space program, and a major monkey wrench in the Atlas rocket program was corrosion caused by moisture. Larsen and his employees figured this was not a problem that a little chemistry couldn't solve, and went about attempting to create a formula capable of displacing water and preventing corrosion. After many failed attempts—39, to be exact—they hit upon the successful formula on attempt number 40, and Water Displacement formula 40 was born.

Larsen sold the company and the product in the mid-'50s for $20,000—a flat price, no royalties or any other considerations, as he felt he could always go and invent something better. WD-40 was put into aerosol cans and released for consumer use in 1958, and by 1993 it was estimated that you could find a can of the stuff in 80 percent of American households.

4 Jack Daniel's

Jack Daniel was a master distiller of whiskey in Lynchburg, Tennessee, in the mid-1800s. Since the ingredients for making spirits were abundant in that region, he had plenty of competition; as such, he decided that the thing to do would be to make his whiskey better than everyone else's. It so happened that he had a spring with remarkably clean water on his property, and he was also very picky about the grains used in his product. Also, he developed a method of filtering his booze through ten feet of charcoal to produce a nice, smooth belt.

Demand began to seriously take off in the mid-20th century, with Jack fueling the artistic output of luminaries like William Faulkner and Frank Sinatra (who referred to Jack as "the nectar of the gods"). Jack is one of the most recognizable brands of spirits in the world, but the origin of it recipe was murky—until recently.

In 2012, Welsh businessman Mark Evans was researching family history when he happened upon a book written by his great-great grandmother—an herbalist who wrote down a recipe in 1853 that may very well be the original formula for Jack Daniel's. The company's website states that its founder is from Wales, and Evans uncovered the fact that his great-great uncle split for America later that decade. His name? John "Jack the Lad" Daniel.

3 ChapStick

Virginia physician Charles Fleet invented lip balm in the mid-1800s, selling the first version of his product as little waxy-looking tubes wrapped in tinfoil. The product was successful, but decades of wrapping little waxy tubes in tinfoil must do something to a man, because by the early 1900s Dr. Fleet was eager to sell off his idea.

The endeavor had begun to lose money, so in 1912 Fleet sold his recipe to John Morton for the whopping sum of five bucks. Morton began mixing up batches of the stuff in his bathtub, while his wife would melt it down, cool it, and chop it into pieces in their kitchen. Apparently their heart was in the lip balm business to a greater degree than Dr. Fleet's, as they were able to use their profits to fund the startup of Morton Manufacturing and begin pumping out ChapStick in earnest.

In the 1930s, the company commissioned artist Frank Wright, Jr., to produce the iconic ChapStick logo, which of course is still used today. Wright's fee? Fifteen bucks, which you'll notice is three times the amount paid for the recipe. If there has ever been a more shrewd 20 dollars spent, we'd love to hear about it.

2 Turtle Wax

Benjamin Hirsch loved chemistry and cars. Shiny cars, and the shinier the better. He invented a product he called Plastone (mixed up in batches in the bathtub), an auto polish, and took streetcars around town to all the gas stations, giving demonstrations and hoping to sell a case or two.

Hirsch was struck by inspiration passing by Turtle Creek while out on sales calls in Wisconsin—as a turtle's hard shell keeps out harmful stuff (and is shiny), so does his wax for your car! The rechristened Turtle Wax became his life's work. He traveled all over the country giving demonstrations, even going so far as to stealth-wax people's cars in the hope of making a sale when they came back.

Ben's tenacity grew the brand quite effectively, and Turtle Wax is notable for another reason as well: While Hirsch himself died in 1966, his company is to this day owned by his family and employs mostly family members and friends, with the average employee having been there for 10 or 12 years. Turtle Wax, started by a determined guy with $500, now posts annual sales exceeding $100 million.

1 Cheerios

When cereal was first conceived of as a breakfast food, most people were just fine with bacon and eggs and such. No one was talking about heart-healthy anything in the 1930s and '40s, and cereal required cooking then as well. The first cold cereal, called Cherrioats, was created by General Mills in 1940. It was the first ready-to-eat cold cereal that one could just pour milk on and chow down. It was marketed as "the breakfast food you've always wanted," and rightfully so. It was an  instant hit, shipping a couple of million cases in its first year.

This must have made Lester Borchardt feel vindicated—he was the General Mills employee who decided to tinker with puffing oats, basically firing little dough balls out of an air cannon. While that sounds like a lot of fun, Lester's boss told him to quit screwing around and come up with something they could sell. Lester, of course, didn't listen, and spent a full two months in defiance of his boss's orders continuing to develop the machine.

Another problem was another (poorly) competing product that was already using the name. After five years of steadily growing sales, this company decided it wanted a piece of the action—so General Mills promptly changed the name. Dozens of "O's" have been spawned in the decades since, and at about the same time, the company began marketing the cereal almost exclusively to children through advertisements on the *Lone Ranger* and *Mickey Mouse Club* shows—a business strategy that would not only be copied to a ridiculous degree, but which made Cheerios the most popular cereal ever within a short time.

TOP 10 Totally Ridiculous PR Disasters

by **Jeff Kelly**

10 Abercrombie & Fitch Finds Itself in a Bad Situation

Abercrombie & Fitch made the mistake of insulting their market when they attacked a *Jersey Shore* star.

If you've ever walked past an Abercrombie & Fitch store, you can probably guess who shops there. Frat boys, party girls—basically, the MTV generation. But that isn't the market Abercrombie wants, so they begged *Jersey Shore* star "The Situation" to stop wearing their clothes.

The brand thought that insulting one of the most famous icons of their biggest fan base was a good idea. It was not. It turned out to be a PR disaster. Abercrombie's stock fell 15 percent in the wake of this PR nightmare, proving that biting the teenage hands that feed you is never wise.

9 Philip Morris Says Smoking Deaths Equal Financial Boons

Philip Morris Tobacco suggested that smoking is great for a country because it kills sick people.

Most of us know that smoking is bad for you. But tobacco giant Philip Morris seems to think that death-by-smokes can be good. In 2000, the company studied the cost of smoking deaths in the Czech Republic. They ended up saying that those deaths helped the economy.

They claimed that early death—and money made through cigarette taxes—made more sense to the country than the cost to treat sick smokers. This did not go down well with antismoking groups. Or anyone who didn't work for Philip Morris.

8 Susan Boyle's Unfortunate Hashtag

Susan Boyle's PR company made an embarrassing Twitter blunder when they created her new hashtag: #susanalbumparty.

Twitter is an advertiser's dream. It lets people cheaply promote their products to a huge audience. But when Twitter promotions fail, they fail on an epic scale. During a Twitter campaign for British singing superstar Susan Boyle, no one in her PR company noticed that the hashtag "#susanalbumparty" had a somewhat racier meaning than intended.

Boyle's PR team soon found that their catchy hashtag had gone horribly wrong. They rushed to change it to "#SusanBoylesAlbumParty." But the damage was done. The horrifying mental image had already been burned into the minds of millions of Twitter users.

7 Always Remember to Sign Out of Your Personal Twitter

Be careful what you tweet when you're using your office computer—you might be tweeting as your boss.

It's easy to forget which Twitter account you've most recently signed into and send out the wrong tweet. Most times, it's a harmless tweet that will be deleted so fast no one will notice. But that was not the case with KitchenAid. One staffer, still logged in to the company's Twitter account, sent out a nasty tweet about Barack Obama's grandmother who had died just before Obama became president.

KitchenAid quickly deleted the tweet in question and issued an apology. But the damage had already been done.

6 Blackberry Maker Offers Plenty of RIM Jobs

Looking for a job? How about a Rimjob? Research in Motion is right up your alley.

Twitter can be great, but as Blackberry maker Research in Motion learned, it isn't always. You would think that a company that prides itself on tech research would know its way around the Internet. That was not the case: They chose to tweet about their job openings with the hashtag "#rimjobs." It was an innocent mistake, since the company's initials are RIM. But it seems that they're either very sloppy, very funny, or very innocent.

5 American Apparel Makes Money from Hurricane Sandy

Step 1: Take Advantage of a Disaster. Step 2: Lose customers and money.

Hurricane Sandy thrashed the northeastern United States: People were killed, homes were lost, and thousands were left without power. Surely no one would try to take advantage of such a disaster—right?

Wrong. American Apparel did. The clothing company thought this was the perfect time to launch a sale. They didn't even hide their greedy motive, and used the hashtag "#sandysale." Then they sent out an e-mail to customers that said, "In case you're bored during the storm."

4 Kenneth Cole Doesn't Understand Trending Topics

Kenneth Cole himself tweeted an insult to the people in the Cairo Riots.

Clothing company Kenneth Cole thought that the riots and protests in Egypt were the best time to promote its new line. It wasn't just some staffer at fault, either. Kenneth Cole himself wrote the tweet. He tweeted that the folks in "uproar in #Cairo" must have been rioting because "they heard our new spring collection is available online."

What's even worse is that right after, someone at the Kenneth Cole store in San Francisco stuck the tweet on a glass case for all to see. Well, Kenneth, at least one person thought your joke was funny.

3 Celeb Boutique Doesn't Watch the News

What does Kim Kardashian have in common with a mass shooting? Nothing, but the folks at UK shop Celeb Boutique didn't think so.

While the last two companies on the list made the most of bad times, at least they knew what was going on in the world before their dumb moves. The same cannot be said for Celeb Boutique. After the mass shooting at a showing of *The Dark Knight Rises* in Aurora, Colorado, "#Aurora" became a trending topic on Twitter. The guy running the Twitter account for Celeb Boutique only saw that Aurora was trending but did not ask why.

He sent out a tweet saying that Aurora must be trending because of a Kim Kardashian dress called Aurora. The tweet stayed on their Twitter page for an hour before someone finally read the news.

2 Department of Defense Has a Very Short Memory

The Department of Defense foolishly flew a plane near ground level at Ground Zero for a photo op.

In 2009, New Yorkers saw a terrible sight when a large plane flew low in the airspace near Ground Zero. People instantly thought of the September 11 attacks. Even Mayor Michael Bloomberg thought they were facing another attack. But then someone decided to let him and the rest of the city know that it was just a Department of Defense photo op.

The plane was Air Force One, though the president was not on board. The Department of Defense said it had warned authorities that the flyover was going to take place. But it seems that they didn't bother to clear it with the right people. Even Barack Obama was "furious" when he heard of the stunt.

1 Cartoon Network's Accidental Terror Scare

A publicity campaign, confused for a bomb scare, caused emergency services to freak out.

On January 31, 2007, there was a huge bomb scare in Boston, when strange LED placards popped up around the city. Police took the threat seriously, and it made national news in the U.S. as the Boston Police and Fire Department tried to make sense of what they were dealing with. As it turns out, they were dealing with a promotion for a cartoon aimed at stoners.

The LED placards were meant to look like characters from the show *Aqua Teen Hunger Force*, which was then on its way to the big screen. It's easy to see why police might have confused the placards for bombs: They had exposed wiring and electrical tape. Except for the weird animated characters on each of them, that is.

Boston police were mocked after this farce, making it one of the only cases in which the people staging the stunt *and* the people reacting to it suffered a public relations disaster.

CHAPTER 7

MOVIES AND TV

1. Top 10 Weird Facts about Game Shows

2. Top 10 Odd and Fascinating Facts about The *Wizard of Oz*

3. Top 10 Hollywood Myths People Still Believe

4. Top 10 Fascinating Facts about Sesame Street

5. Top 10 Weird Ways Iconic Movie Costumes Were Created

6. Top 10 Movie In-Jokes and Traditions

7. Top 10 Crazy Movie Plots That Happened in Real Life

8. Top 10 Bizarre TV Incidents

9. Top 10 Behind-the-Scenes Stories of Simpsons Guest Stars

10. Top 10 Shocking Documentaries

TOP 10 Weird Facts about Game Shows

by **Mike Devlin**

10 The Intercept

Grand Theft Auto is one of the most popular video game franchises in the world, but one can immediately see serious logistical problems in adapt-

ing it to a game show setting. Leave it to the Russians to put this concept on wheels. *The Intercept* was a game show in which contestants were instructed to steal a car.

Once they were on the road, they had to evade the show's police force for 35 minutes. If they could escape, they were given the car as a prize. Of course, winning was nearly impossible—the cars were outfitted with tracking devices, making staying ahead of the police a true miracle.

9 Man vs. Beast

In 2003, Fox aired *Man vs. Beast*, a show that consisted of people competing (and largely losing) against animals in different events, including an eating contest between former Nathan's Hot Dog champion Takeru Kobayashi and a half-ton Kodiak bear. The most distasteful competition occurred between 44 little people and an Asian elephant in an airplane-pulling race.

The only event clearly dominated by man was an obstacle course race between a U.S. Navy SEAL and a chimpanzee. The SEAL, Scott Helvenston, wouldn't have long to celebrate his victory though. The following year, he started as a contractor for the private security firm Blackwater and became the victim of one of the most savage acts of violence in the Iraq War. His team was ambushed by insurgents, torched, butchered, and dragged through the streets.

8 The Price Is Right

Each episode of *The Price Is Right* concludes with two finalists guessing the price of a showcase, an assembly of big-ticket items like cars, furniture, and vacations. The contestant who guesses close enough to the actual price (without going over) wins.

For the most part, it's an inexact science. But on September 22, 2008, contestant Terry Kneiss blew everyone away when he buzzed in with the exact amount of his showcase ($23,743), which consisted of a billiards table, a karaoke machine, and a 17-foot camper. Host Drew Carey's reaction was noticeably deadpan, as he feared yet another game show scandal might have been in the works.

However, Kneiss hadn't cheated; a longtime viewer of the show, he merely noticed that many of the items were repeatedly featured. He memorized the prices of many items, and fortunately, those appeared in his showcase. And the $743? That was a fluke. Kneiss randomly used his PIN.

7 Jeopardy!

Quiz show *Jeopardy!* is perhaps best known for the 2004 reign of Ken Jennings, a Mormon genius featured on 75 episodes of the show, until losing on the Final Jeopardy answer "Most of this firm's 70,000 seasonal white-collar employees work only four months a year." Jennings responded "What is FedEx?" but the correct question was "What is H&R Block?"

In response to the kind of advertising that money couldn't buy, H&R Block granted Jennings free tax preparations and financial advice for life. He would go on to appear in several more *Jeopardy!* tournaments, including one against IBM "artificial intelligence" supercomputer Watson (who beat him soundly).

However, winning *Jeopardy!* is only a matter of having the most money of three contestants. While Jennings often triumphed by tens of thousands of dollars, in 1993, Air Force Lieutenant Colonel Darryl Scott won a game with a score of $1. In case you're wondering, the maximum amount one can win in a single game, provided you answer every question correctly, land on the Daily Double questions last in each round, and bet the maximum amount in Final Jeopardy is $566,400.

6 Wheel of Fortune

Wheel of Fortune tends to aim at a less academic audience than *Jeopardy!* does, with contestant auditions that rely less on intelligence than personality. Amiable host Pat Sajak runs the show while statuesque cougar (she's in her late 50s!) Vanna White manipulates the electronic letter board.

Today, players can win hundreds of thousands of dollars, cars, and exotic vacations, but back in the 1980s, the show was "boring" according to Sajak. Instead of competing to win cash, players won symbolic funds that could be used to buy lame prizes like appliances. In 2012, Sajak admitted that the format took so long to film that he and Vanna used to sneak off for margarita-fueled dinners at a nearby restaurant. He claimed he and Vanna would have "two or three or six" margaritas before returning to the set, where they would "have trouble recognizing the alphabet."

5 Family Feud

Family Feud premiered in 1976 and was hosted by Richard Dawson, a charming Englishman known for kissing the female contestants. Dawson was succeeded by Ray Combs, a somewhat forgettable figure who hosted the show for six years. He was infamous for walking off the set after the final episode without even saying good-bye to anyone. In 1994, he was in a car accident that left him with permanent, painful spinal damage.

His career stalled, he suffered financial setbacks (including the foreclosure of his home), and he and his wife filed for divorce. Combs became psychotic, spending time in the hospital after a suicide attempt. Upon his release, he proceeded to destroy the inside of his home and smash his head into the walls. Police were summoned and took him to the Glendale Adventist Medical Center in Glendale, California, to be evaluated. The next day, he hanged himself in the closet of his hospital room with his bedsheets. He was just 40 years old.

4 Press Your Luck

Press Your Luck was a mid-1980s game show that was part quiz show and part "dumb luck." Contestants played against an illuminated game board that lit up prizes in different patterns, and they could stop it at any time to win the cash or prizes it landed on.

If they stopped the board on a "Whammy" (a caricature of a villain), they would lose everything. It all seemed entirely random until 1984—when unemployed ice cream truck driver Michael Larson appeared on the show and begun to run the board, playing 45 rounds in a row before striking out. His turn went on so long that it had to be incorporated into two episodes of the show.

Larson won an improbable fortune of $110,237. An investigation by CBS found that he had been using the stop-motion function on his VCR to painstakingly review episodes of the show. He realized that the random illumination of the game board actually worked in a predictable sequence. They determined this was not cheating and gave Michael Larson the prize money, but they made sure to reprogram the game board so that no one could duplicate the stunt.

3 Amaan Ramazan

Amaan Ramazan is a Pakistani game show in which guests are presented with prizes like laptops, smartphones, and land deeds for correctly answering questions about Islam.

Hosted by the lively Aamir Liaquat Hussain, one of the most famous television personalities in the country, the show has been criticized by opponents for doing wild stunts in the name of ratings. But during the 2013 holy month of Ramadan (which ran from July 9 to August 7), a time when shows in the Islamic world fight for ratings, Hussain unveiled his most audacious stunt yet: He gave away orphaned babies.

Although it appeared on the show that the babies were given away as prizes, the families were approved and fully vetted beforehand. Although this may seem like a controversial move, *Amaan Ramazan* may have actually saved these children's lives. Babies are abandoned in Pakistan frequently, especially girls, who are seen by many as less desirable.

2 Cash Cab

Cash Cab is a quiz show in which a cab driver lobs increasingly difficult trivia questions at taxi passengers while driving them to their destination. It has a three-strikes rule that dumps you on the sidewalk if you rack up three wrong answers during your ride.

The Canadian version of the show endured an ugly scandal in 2011, when the Cash Cab struck and killed a 61-year-old pedestrian in Vancouver, British Columbia. Fortunately for the fate of the show, the accident did not occur during filming, but later in the day when one of the show's producers was bringing the cab back to a garage for the night.

There have been more than two dozen international versions of the program throughout the world. The American version went off the air in 2012.

1 Who Wants to Be a Millionaire?

Who Wants to Be a Millionaire is notable for its "lifelines," which contestants can use to seek help with a particularly tricky question. Although the lifelines have evolved somewhat throughout the run of the series, two of the common choices were "phone a friend" and "ask the audience." Objectively, the best "phone a friend" moment occurred on November 19, 1999, when John Carpenter called his father while answering the million-dollar question. Carpenter didn't need help—he just wanted to tell his dad he was going to win. And he did, becoming the first million-dollar winner in the U.S. version of the show.

In "ask the audience," the audience is prompted to provide their answer to the question, usually leaving the contestant with a clear majority choice. In the American version of the show, this is typically the correct answer. However, audiences in international renditions of the show can be quite fickle, instead choosing to troll the contestant and provide the wrong answer intentionally. This has been observed in the French version, and especially in the Russian version.

TOP 10 Odd and Fascinating Facts about *The Wizard of Oz*

by **Mike Devlin**

10 Glinda the Good Witch

Glinda is the Good Witch of the North in the film, and she appears in a beautiful pink dress with flowing auburn hair, a woman of great beauty. She was portrayed by veteran actress Billie Burke, who shockingly enough, was 54 years old at the time—18 years older than her counterpart Margaret Hamilton, who played the Wicked Witch of the West.

9 Marriage

Early versions of the script had insinuated that Dorothy and the Scarecrow's Kansas equivalent had some romantic feelings for each other. But it was to the Tin Man that she would eventually have a connection. Judy Garland's (Dorothy) daughter Liza Minnelli married Jack Haley's (Tin Man) son Jack Jr. in 1974. It was a rocky relationship and they divorced just five years later.

8 Tin Man

Jack Haley was not the producers' original choice for the Tin Man. The role belonged to Buddy Ebsen (best known for playing Jed Clampett on *The Beverly Hillbillies*). Ebsen attended ten days of filming before the aluminum powder makeup artists slathered him accumulated in his lungs and made him deathly ill. He was brought to the hospital, where he required an iron lung to recover. When Haley took over, his makeup was switched to an aluminum paste, which was applied over greasepaint.

7 Suicidal Munchkin

One of the strangest and most pervasive legends (as discussed in Chapter 1) surrounding the film is that during the scene when Dorothy first meets the Tin Woodsman, a munchkin can be seen hanging himself in the background. Fortunately, the aberration was not the result of a suicidal little person. The Los Angeles Zoo lent several birds to the film to give the background a more natural look. What appears to be a lovelorn munchkin taking his life is really just a big bird spreading its wings.

6 Box Office Flop

The Wizard of Oz was released in 1939 in the midst of the Great Depression, when going to the movies would have been an unimaginable luxury for many households. It was initially unsuccessful, barely recouping its $2.8 million budget. Only upon theatrical rerelease did it begin to generate any real profit. Since 1956, when it was first shown on television, the film has become enormously popular, and is shown on TV multiple times a year.

5 Nazi Director

The Wizard of Oz director Victor Fleming had a banner year in 1939. Shortly before production wrapped on *Wizard*, he was brought on to direct another incredibly famous film, *Gone with the Wind*. According to James Curtis, author of *Spencer Tracy: A Biography*, Fleming was pro-Nazi and had been opposed to America entering World War II. He hoped that the Reich would sack England after the fall of France.

4 Witch Is Burned

The Wicked Witch of the West has terrified millions of children over the years, so it may come as a bit of a surprise that actress Margaret Hamilton's initial career was that of a kindergarten teacher. While filming a scene wherein the witch vanishes into a cloud of smoke, Hamilton was badly burned, the green makeup on her face and hands igniting. She recuperated, but refused to do any more scenes involving fire. Hamilton reprised her role as the witch to appear in both *Sesame Street* and *Mister Rogers' Neighborhood*.

3 Toto

Cairn terrier Toto was actually a female dog named Terry. Like many of the other actors, Toto was hurt during filming when one of the witch's guards accidentally stepped on her and broke her foot. Judy Garland became enamored of the dog while shooting and begged Terry's trainer Carl Spitz to let her keep the dog as a pet, but Spitz refused. Terry had a long career and was featured in 15 different movies.

2 Auntie Em

Actress Clara Blandick appeared in 118 films, but she will always be best remembered for her role as Auntie Em. After returning from church on April 15, 1962, Clara put on her best dress and fixed her hair, scattered articles and photographs from her career around the room, then took an overdose of sleeping pills and lay down on the couch. Her final act was to pull a plastic bag over her head. She'd been in terrible pain from arthritis and was becoming progressively blind. Her suicide note read, "I am now about to make the great adventure. I cannot endure this agonizing pain any longer. It is all over my body. Neither can I face the impending blindness. I pray the Lord my soul to take. Amen." Seven years later, Judy Garland also died of a drug overdose.

1 Professor Marvel

The Wizard's real-life counterpart was itinerant showman Professor Marvel. Marvel's look was supposed to be shabby chic. To that end, the film's wardrobe department needed to find a tattered coat for him to wear. They purchased several at a secondhand store and chose their favorite. Actor Frank Morgan was wearing it one day when he reached into the pocket and was astonished to see a name inscribed: The coat had belonged to L. Frank Baum, the author of the Oz books. Although some have since refuted the amazing coincidence, the tailor who made the coat and Baum's own widow swore it was true. She was presented with the coat after filming was completed.

TOP 10 Hollywood Myths People Still Believe

by Amanda Mannen

10 Marilyn Monroe Was a Size 16

Whenever someone wants to remind our weight-obsessed culture that curves can be beautiful, they often mention that the most revered sex symbol of the Western Hemisphere, Marilyn Monroe, wore a U.S. size 16. Either way, she was as wide as several of today's starlets standing side by side.

It couldn't be less true. Several of Monroe's famous costumes were recently auctioned off, including the white dress from *The Seven Year Itch* and the red sequined number from *Gentlemen Prefer Blondes*, and spectators were shocked to see the teeny, tiny mannequins on which they were displayed. Monroe actually didn't fit any standard size, because her waist was disproportionately smaller than her bust and hips. Her dresses averaged 22-inch waists and 34-inch busts, so she was somewhere around a 2 or 4 in today's U.S. standard dress sizes—about the same as most modern actresses.

9 The Ghost Boy in *Three Men and a Baby*

In the years following the 1987 release of *Three Men and a Baby*, thousands of viewers reported spooky sightings of what appeared to be the ghost of a little boy in the background of one scene. Unsurprisingly, they quickly started making stuff up to explain it, and rumors circulated that the son of the couple whose New York apartment was rented for the filming had been killed there, and it was his image that appeared in the film. They even insisted the parents had appeared on *60 Minutes* or *20/20* to tell the tale.

First of all, the movie wasn't even filmed in a New York apartment; it was a Toronto soundstage. More importantly, the filmmakers swiftly provided an explanation for the startling sight—it was a cardboard cutout of star Ted Danson that someone had misplaced. Poor attention to detail, yes, but nothing supernatural. Even though it was quickly debunked, the rumor persists.

8 *Back to the Future* Predicts the Future

When the Miami Marlins won the World Series in 1997, rumors circulated that their triumph was predicted in *Back to the Future Part II*. People claimed that Biff perused a sports almanac and quipped, "Florida wins the 1997 World Series, yeah right." Alternately, people claimed this was a broadcast displayed on a holographic billboard shown in the future.

Biff never makes any such remark. What the billboard actually said was that the Chicago Cubs would defeat an unspecified Miami team represented by an alligator, which you might recognize as the furthest possible thing from a marlin.

This defeat would've taken place the same year as the movie, 2015, which hasn't actually happened yet as of this writing. The year in which the film takes place seems to be an ongoing point of contention, despite being clearly stated in the film, and altered images of the dashboard of the DeLorean keep popping up, claiming that we've reached the date that it reads. For the record, it's October 21, 2015. We've got a little while left to go.

7 A Famous Actor Was the Gerber Baby

Since the adoption of the mascot in 1931, people have been speculating about the identity of the iconic Gerber Baby, which was kept secret by the company for over 40 years. The name that seems to come up the most often (inexplicably) is Humphrey Bogart. A poll conducted by the company found that many people still believed that either Bogart, Elizabeth Taylor, or Senator Bob Dole were the Gerber Baby, even though it was revealed to be mystery novelist Ann Turner Cook in 1978.

6 Steven Spielberg Got His Start after Sneaking into Universal Studios

Over the years, Spielberg has told the story of how, as a young unknown, he snuck into Universal Studios and moved into an empty office. He fit right in with his suit and briefcase, casually chatting with employees as if he had every right to be there, so nobody thought to check whether he actually did. The bluff was so successful that they started actually giving him work, and the rest is history.

Except, according to other people working at Universal during that time, it never happened. His career at Universal began when he was legitimately hired as an unpaid intern by family friend and editor Chuck Silvers. Silvers's officemate, purchasing agent Julie Raymond, said that Spielberg is lying. It's true that he had to sneak onto movie sets to talk to people and make connections, but Spielberg was authorized to work in Silvers's office. Spielberg's version of events has changed a lot over the years. For instance, he's claimed to be anywhere from 17–21 years old when it happened, with Silvers claiming he was hired at 16—so even Spielberg isn't sure what the story is.

5 Richard Gere and the Gerbil

Poor Richard Gere has been plagued by rumors since the early '90s that claim he had sexual relations with a gerbil. According to the story, the *LA Times* ran a report claiming that Gere checked into the Cedars-Sinai hospital to have a furry friend removed from his cavity, but nobody seems able to track down such a report. According to Sylvester Stallone, Gere blames him for starting the rumor after a falling out, but Gere denies it.

4 The Goldfinger Death

In a rumor about 1964's *Goldfinger*, the actress who played the woman killed by being covered in gold paint really did die the same way. As Bond explains, covering the skin entirely in the paint will cause suffocation—because people breathe through their skin.

Obviously, that's not how it works. Sometimes people refer to letting their skin "breathe," but no, all real breathing is done with the lungs. Blocking your pores like that still isn't a great idea, and you can be slowly poisoned if the paint contains toxic elements, but it won't cause instant death. The actress in the film, Shirley Eaton, is alive and well.

3 Brandon Lee's Final Moments Captured on Film

The promising career of Bruce Lee's son came to an abrupt and tragic end in 1993 while shooting *The Crow*. In an opening scene in which his character is murdered, a series of events led to a stunt gun being loaded with real bullets, and Lee was really shot and killed. Fans claimed this gruesome moment stayed in the film for all to see, but it's not true. The scene was reshot with a double, and it was decided that the character would be murdered by knife—presumably by filmmakers not wanting to tempt fate a second time.

2 The Haunting of the Amityville Horror Really Happened

The fact that it was a true story was a huge selling point for the book—and later, the movie—about the terrifying events that plagued the Lutz family after they bought a haunted house in Amityville, New York. But when the movie was released, the lawyer defending the original murderer, William Weber, was livid.

The Lutz family originally agreed to write the book with him, and according to him, they made up the entire story together. The Lutzes eventually ditched him for a better deal; apparently they hadn't fled the house in terror so much as an inability to pay for it. A long paper trail of lawsuits and backroom deals is on his side, as well as the sequel, which was based on the book he was writing with the Lutzes.

1 Jayne Mansfield Was Decapitated

The beheading of *The Girl Can't Help It* star is one of the most notorious pop culture references. Everyone knows she died in a car accident, and some even claim that it was her signature scarf that pulled her head off when it got stuck in the accident. It's all a big misunderstanding though—

Mansfield was wearing a wig when the accident happened. It flew off and was mistaken by witnesses for her head. An employee of the funeral home informs us, rather creepily, that her head was very much attached when he...attended to her.

TOP 10 Fascinating Facts about Sesame Street

by **Mike Devlin**

10 Bert and Ernie

In recent years, as many around the world have begun pushing in earnest for gay marriage to become legal, a grassroots Internet campaign has surfaced urging longtime *Sesame Street* characters Bert and Ernie to finally acknowledge their homosexuality and tie the knot. Although the show has been renowned for preaching a message of tolerance, they carefully backpedaled away from these claims, stating, "Bert and Ernie are best friends. They were created to teach preschoolers that people can be good friends with those who are very different from themselves. Even though they are identified as male characters and possess many human traits and characteristics (as most *Sesame Street* Muppets do), they remain puppets, and do not have a sexual orientation."

9 Torture

Although blasting loud music to psychologically torture people is not an entirely new concept, its use has really come to the forefront since the opening of the U.S.'s Guantanamo Bay detention camp in Cuba. The purpose of the camp was to detain and interrogate subjects captured in the "War on Terror," which began following the events of 9/11. A great deal of controversy has arisen as pictures and stories have leaked to the public, and President Obama has made promises to close the camp that have yet to materialize. Among far more sinister and humiliating tactics, the soldiers at Guantanamo have been known to inundate al-Qaeda operatives with blaring, repetitive songs, including hard rock music and the *Sesame Street* theme that are known to break down mental resistance. Amnesty International has condemned this ploy, while the Pentagon has called it a mere "disincentive."

8 Death

One of the original human characters on the show, Mr. Hooper, ran a general store that served as a focal point and offered such fare as birdseed milkshakes. When actor Will Lee died of a heart attack in 1982, there was some debate by the show's producers as to how to handle the situation. Some leaned toward having the character retire, but eventually it was decided the best course of action was to deal with the issue. A child psychologist was consulted and the situation was handled gently, but head-on, with Big Bird unable to understand that his friend wasn't coming back. When Big Bird expresses concern that it "won't be the same" without Mr. Hooper, another of the adults tells him, "You're right, Big Bird. It'll never be the same without him. But you know something? We can all be very happy that we had a chance to be with him and to know him and to love him a lot when he was here."

The episode aired on Thanksgiving Day, 1983, to ensure that the children who saw it would be around family who could help them with their feelings when they saw it. In retrospect, Mr. Hooper's passing has been honored by many as one of the most important moments in television history.

7 Location

The main focus of *Sesame Street* is a three-apartment brownstone building (Bert and Ernie live in the basement). The show is filmed in Astoria, Queens, but the actual location of *Sesame Street* has been under debate for years. It is intended to be a neighborhood in Manhattan, though which exactly is up for debate, even among staffers of the show. Some suggest the Upper West Side, and others claim that it is modeled after the Alphabet City area of the Lower East Side. Some detail-oriented investigators have tried to pin down the location based on clues from the show itself, including zip codes printed on envelopes and background shots of characters walking around.

6 The Count

Despite the terror they invoke, vampires are really terribly vulnerable creatures with a laundry list of weaknesses: sunlight, garlic, and religious symbols, among others, depending on which franchise you are considering. But folklore speaks of one of the more rarely considered chinks in the vampire's armor: arithmomania, an aspect of obsessive-compulsive disorder that results in an uncontrollable urge to quantify and count things. Should one find himself confronted by a ravenous, undead ghoul, he could merely throw a handful of rice on the ground. The vampire would be helpless but to fall on his knees and count every single grain. This vulnerability has been rolled into the popular *Sesame Street* character "Count von Count," the world's least intimidating vampire, who teaches children basic concepts of arithmetic.

5 Elmo

A bright red puppet known for his falsetto voice and habit of talking about himself in the third person, Elmo is one of the most popular denizens of *Sesame Street*. Elmo has been around for years, but he was relegated to the background for some time, until he was picked up in 1984 by young puppeteer Kevin Clash. Clash breathed life into Elmo, and over the next decade, his star rose exponentially. Elmo hit his stride in the mid- to late-'90s, with the release of the "Tickle Me Elmo" toy and the film *The Adventures of Elmo in Grouchland*. And then in 2012, 22-year-old Sheldon Stephens emerged, claiming that he and Clash had inappropriate sexual relations when Stephens was underage. Clash acknowledged the two had shared a relationship, but that it had been between two consenting adults. Stephens later recanted his statement, but other men came forward, claiming that Clash had also slept with them when they were teenagers. Clash quickly resigned from *Sesame Street*. When he left the show, he made the statement that "Personal matters have diverted attention away from the important work *Sesame Street* is doing and I cannot allow it to go on any longer. I am deeply sorry to be leaving and am looking forward to resolving these personal matters privately." Since leaving, additional allegations have been levied against Clash. He came back into the spotlight when he was nominated for four Emmy Awards, despite the scandal.

4 Snuffleupagus

Aloysius Snuffleupagus is a woolly mammoth Muppet who spent 14 years as Big Bird's "imaginary" friend. Whenever adults would appear, Snuffy would vanish by way of coincidence, and the grownups would disbelieve Big Bird that he ever existed. Snuffy was revealed to the entire cast in 1985. According to Martin P. Robison, who plays the character, the producers decided that due to stories of abuse of children, they did not want to portray a situation between adults and a child character who wasn't believed despite being honest. They were afraid they were giving kids the message that their parents might not listen to them in case they had an "unbelievable" story to tell, such as being sexually abused by a relative.

3 HIV/AIDS

AIDS has devastated sub-Saharan Africa like no place in the world; hundreds of thousands of children are born with the disease each year. Most of them die before the age of five. A staggering percentage of the children in the area have been orphaned by the virus. First appearing on 2002's *Takalani Sesame* in South Africa, five-year-old Kami is an upbeat yellow "monster" Muppet like Grover. She is portrayed with a perpetual case of the sniffles as a nod to her condition, which has also claimed the lives of her parents. Kami contracted HIV from a blood transfusion. Along with educating the children of South Africa and Nigeria about the disease, Kami helps them to deal with the societal stigma attached to HIV/AIDS and the inherent sense of loss and fear. Kami has since been appointed a representative of UNICEF projects throughout the world.

2 International

Africa is not the only place to host its own version of *Sesame Street*. There are varieties throughout the world in Europe, Asia, Australia, and the Middle East. The earliest international adaptation was Brazil's *Vila Sésamo*. Many other versions exist, each tailored to the specific language, environment, and social circumstances of the area in which it is aired. While many of the characters carried over, others were added or replaced. In the Canadian version, the main character was a giant polar bear named Basil who learned French from his bilingual friend. In the version from the Philippines, the Big Bird character is a giant pink turtle named Pong Pagong; in Israel it is a hedgehog named Kippi Kippod, and in Kuwait it is a camel named No'Man. According to Joan Ganz Cooney, one of the creators of the Sesame Workshop, she was stunned at the international interest in the show: "To be frank, I was really surprised, because we thought we were creating the quintessential American show. We thought the Muppets were quintessentially American, and it turns out they're the most international characters ever created."

1 Mourning

In 1990, Jim Henson, the creator of *Sesame Street*'s Muppets, died suddenly of bacterial pneumonia. In the wake of his passing, two memorial services, one in New York and one in London, were staged wherein characters from both Henson's *The Muppet Show* and *Sesame Street* performed, which included a heartrending version of "Being Green" by Big Bird. Henson's only request was that no one wear black. Although the services were open to the public, they were not televised, and only certain recorded segments exist. Along with Muppet performances and eulogies from friends and collaborators, excerpts from Henson's correspondence to his children were read, including this passage: "Please watch out for each other and love and forgive everybody. It's a good life, enjoy it."

TOP 10 Weird Ways Iconic Movie Costumes Were Created

by **Josh Winning**

10 Lord of the Rings

In Peter Jackson's epic adaptation of JRR Tolkien's trilogy, Aragorn is a wanderer who probably never sees the inside of a shower. Which is exactly why the actor who played him—Viggo Mortensen—decided it was up to him to give his costume that vital lived-in appearance.

Mortensen took his outfit home, then lived, breathed, and sweat in it until it looked as beaten and battered as possible. He even repaired the costume whenever it needed it—something that Aragorn himself would have done on the road. "That's the best you can hope for in making costumes," says costume designer Ngila Dickson. "That the actors will participate and make them their own, a part of their character."

The actor's efforts definitely paid off. While Mortensen delivered a stand-out performance, he also looks 100 percent the part.

9 Halloween (1978)

Michael Myers is a horror institution. The knife-wielding antagonist of the Halloween slasher series, he's the thing of nightmares—an emotionless, white-faced murder machine who starts out stalking babysitters and goes on to rack up one heck of a body count. Funny thing is, his infamous mask actually began as something entirely innocent.

Discovered by *Halloween*'s editor, Tommy Lee Wallace, in a Hollywood Boulevard store called Burt Wheeler's Magic Shop, Myers's iconic visor was originally a Captain Kirk Star Trek mask.

In order to fulfill the script's notation of Myers possessing the pale features of a human face, Wallace customized the mask by making the eye holes larger and giving the entire thing a blue-white spray-paint job. The end result didn't look like Shatner at all. "Which is probably for the best," director John Carpenter has noted.

Myers wasn't the only one given the thrifty treatment; scream queen Jamie Lee Curtis also had to buy her own wardrobe for the film. She ended up spending just $100 at J.C. Penny.

8 Batman Returns (1992)

Comic book prowler Catwoman has appeared on-screen numerous times (most recently in 2012's *The Dark Knight Rises*), but arguably her finest hour came in Tim Burton's *Batman Returns*, which had Michelle Pfeiffer slipping into PVC.

Costume designer Mary Vogt came up with an unusual way of giving Catwoman that glossy sheen. When Pfeiffer put on her cat costume, the costume department used big sponge brushes to lather her in thick silicone.

It was a messy process—"she [was] dripping all over the place," Vogt has said—but the final look was perfect, and the costume department was particularly pleased with how the costume shone during night-time scenes—fluid, elegant, and just the right side of raunchy.

7 Alien (1979)

Swiss surrealist H. R. Giger infused his sinewy designs for the monsters in *Alien* with an unsettling sexuality. Fitting, then, that condoms were used to bring his creations to physical life.

As well as using plasticine, parts from a Rolls-Royce, and vertebrae from dead snakes, the costume designers on Ridley Scott's genre-defining sci-fi picture also turned to K-Y jelly and condoms to get the right texture for the alien xenomorph.

The K-Y jelly was used for the alien's gloopy saliva, while shredded condoms created the tendons in the creature's jaw. No wonder Sigourney Weaver was so desperate to get away from it.

6 Tron: Legacy (2010)

This belated sequel to the 1982 cult classic was all about going hi-tech. When it came to those iconic light-up suits, though, costume designer Christine Clark found that an old-school approach worked best.

Researching special effects houses in Los Angeles, Clark discovered that Quantum Creation FX had developed a special material for Japanese security vests. A thin, flexible material, it was ideal for the *Tron: Legacy* costumes.

As for the way the suits lit up, that was accomplished by hot-wiring the costumes. Lithium batteries were fitted into the disks on the actors' backs, which gave the suits roughly 12 minutes of light. On the more hi-tech end of things, the production also had a remote control station on set that would monitor the suits and alert them whenever a battery was almost out of power.

"Normally on a set, you hear them say, 'Sound speeding, camera speeding, action!'" says Clark. "We also had: 'Light 'em up.'"

5 Coraline (2009)

When it comes to stop-motion animation, the devil's definitely in the details. As if creating a 90-minute movie by posing tiny figurines one frame at a time wasn't painstaking enough, *Coraline*'s miniature costumes were also completely hand-stitched.

That eye-catching, star-spangled blue sweater that Coraline wears? It was knitted by Althea Crome, who was hired to create every piece of clothing that would be worn in the film—including underwear. It took Crome between six weeks and six months to knit the sweaters for the film, depending on the intricacy of the design.

"I think knitters are often fascinated with the fact that I use such tiny needles," she says. "Some of the needles are almost the dimension of a human hair."

4 The Wizard of Oz (1939)

This one's the thing of movie legend. When Buddy Ebsen accepted the role of the Tin Man in *The Wizard of Oz*—after initially landing the role of Scarecrow—he was subjected to numerous costume tests in order to attain the right look for the character.

Eventually, he wore white face paint that was coated in aluminum dust. But nine days into shooting the film, Ebsen complained of shortness of breath, cramping, and eventually the inability to breathe and was rushed to hospital in an oxygen tent, where he remained for two weeks. After some tests were completed it turned out he was having an allergic reaction to the aluminum dust in his makeup.

Ebsen was swiftly replaced by Jake Haley and the costume was changed (the aluminum was blended into the white paint, rather than speckled on top). In a much happier development, during scenes in which Haley was squirted with oil, the crew actually used chocolate sauce as it looked better on camera.

3 Grease (1978)

It's one of the most famous scenes in movie history: innocent wallflower Sandy (Olivia Newton-John) breezes into a fairground to show off her transformation into a black-wearing babe.

In reality, that iconic costume was a nightmare for the actress, whose skin-tight pants were so tight that she had to be sewn into them.

Not only that, but Newton-John wasn't allowed to go to the bathroom during the day because it would mean putting the crew on hold while she was unstitched and then re-stitched up again. Talk about commitment.

2 Edward Scissorhands (1990)

Tight, creaky leather. A big fright wig. Oh, and the scissors of course. Johnny Depp was almost unrecognizable in Tim Burton's '60s-set fairy tale, which puts him front and center as a tragic Frankenstein's monster–style creation who changes the lives of little suburbanites.

Though Depp's costume looks restrictive and uncomfortable, every effort was made to minimize his discomfort for those long shooting days. That meant installing Depp's outfit with a special cool suit that would stop him from overheating in the baking Florida sun. Despite these efforts, the actor would still have to rush over to special fans after finishing a scene in order to cool down further still.

Other than latex and leather, parts of the costume were also made from bits of an old sofa from Tim Burton's first apartment. Clearly he knew there's no art without suffering.

1 Saturday Night Fever (1977)

John Travolta became a (brief) style icon in the late '70s thanks to his figure-hugging wardrobe in *Saturday Night Fever*.

Hard to believe, though, is that as the film went into production, disco was dying such a sudden death that Travolta strug-  gled to find suitable clothes to play foot-tapping dance floor–hogger Tony Manero.

Tasked with sourcing his own costumes, he was forced to root through boxes in the back of Green- wich Village stores in order to find the platform shoes and bell-bottom trousers the role demanded. The iconic white three-piece suit everyone pictures when thinking of John Travolta in this film was bought very cheaply from a men's clothing store in Brooklyn.

TOP 10 Movie In-Jokes and Traditions

by **Andrew Jones**

10 555 Telephone Number

You may have noticed that in films where a telephone number is spoken or somehow visible, it almost always starts with "555." This dates back to the 1960s, when some telephone companies in America set up a range of fictional telephone numbers for use in movies and TV shows. This was to avoid customers being harassed by coincidentally having the same telephone number that might appear in a film. For the most part, films abide by this guideline, but watch out if you live outside North America, because the 555 prefix is only protected in that region and may be a valid phone number in other countries.

9 Hello, Sally!

Sally Menke was a film editor who had a long-time association with Quentin Tarantino, working on all his films up until *Inglorious Bastards* before she passed away in 2010. Editing a film involves many hours sitting in front of a screen, assembling raw footage into sequence and trimming any fat until the film looks and feels as intended. The raw footage, apart from the obviously intended performances, often includes actors and crew in and around the set before and after the scene, for example, the director calling "action" and "cut."

As a thoughtful gesture for Sally, slaving away on the rough cut in the editing suite, cast and crew would often wave at the camera at the start and finish of the take, and say "Hello, Sally!" sometimes adding a message of their own to keep her amused during her work.

8 The Cameo Appearance

Often included as a nod to a small section of the audience, to be overlooked by the rest, cameo appearances involve someone of significance making a brief and unexpected appearance in a film, often without saying a single line. Some directors are particularly known for this, Alfred Hitchcock probably more than anyone, who had walk-on parts in most of his own films. Quentin Tarantino also likes to appear in his own films, though he often plays a more significant, albeit supporting, role.

7 Pixar Self-References

Pixar, a studio that specializes in animated films, has developed a tradition of referencing their own movies, characters, and employees throughout their work. This started back when it was producing short animations, and has continued on through all their output. Here's a quick list: John Ratzenberger, everybody's favorite bar fly from *Cheers*, has had a role in every Pixar film since he voiced the grumpy Hamm *in Toy Story*; the books on the shelf in Andy's room in *Toy Story* bear the names of Pixar short films; a Buzz Lightyear toy is visible in the dentist's office in *Finding Nemo*; a Pizza Planet truck (again from *Toy Story*) shows up in most other Pixar films; and the Luxo bouncy ball (from one of Pixar's shorts) often appears in the background somewhere.

Maybe the easiest self-reference to spot is the text "A113." It's a reference to the animation class that John Lasseter and Brad Bird attended, and it appears in all Pixar movies and some other work directed by Brad Bird. You can see it on license plates, serial numbers of objects, train numbers, room numbers, and even in the spoken words of some characters.

6 See You Next Wednesday

Featured in most films by John Landis is a reference to a nonexistent film called *See You Next Wednesday*: It first appeared in the film *Schlock* in 1973, and then in *Blues Brothers*, *Trading Places*, *Twilight Zone* (a movie partially credited as an Alan Smithee; see number two), and *An American Werewolf in London*, to name a few.

5 Die-Cast

Some actors, whether intentionally or otherwise, become so identified with a type of character that they find it hard to break away and become known for anything else. A list of examples might include William Shatner as Captain Kirk, Hugh Grant as the bumbling English romantic, or Samuel L. Jackson as the cool badass. However, there are a few actors who—though not exclusively—seem determined for their character to die in as many films as possible.

Gary Oldman, Michael Biehn, Leonardo DiCaprio, Robert De Niro, Steve Buscemi (who always seems to get the grisly deaths), and Gary Busey have all made a habit of dying before the credits roll. But I can't think of any actor who has popped his clogs on screen more than Sean Bean, who has around 20 film deaths to his name. These include (spoilers alert!) *Golden Eye*, *Patriot Games*, *The Lord of the Rings*, *The Island*, *Equilibrium*, *Out-*

law, Essex Boys, Far North, Don't Say a Word, and *The Field*—the last of which sees him killed by a cow.

4 Wilhelm Scream

To make the process of adding sound effects a little less tedious, there are collections of stock sound effects that film makers use to fill particular requirements. An example might be the sound of a rusty gate opening, a distant explosion, thunder, or a faceless villain's death rattle.

Something called the "Wilhelm Scream" has become a frequently used audio sample for whenever the evil henchman/soldier/unlucky bystander happens to meet his maker. It was named after the character Private Wilhelm from the 1953 Western *The Charge at Feather River,* though it was actually first used two years previously in a film called *Distant Drums.*

The Wilhelm Scream was popularized by sound engineer Ben Burtt, who used it initially (and repeatedly) in *Star Wars* and many other George Lucas and Steven Spielberg films. Several other film makers started using it in their work and it has now spread to most action films, and even TV and video games. Once you know what it sounds like, you'll start hearing it everywhere.

3 Orange and Blue Contrast

Ever since this was pointed out to me, I haven't been able to miss it. Films seem to have an obsession with using orange and blue images, shades, and backgrounds on posters and artwork. According to Johann Wolfgang von Goethe's color wheel, blue and orange are complementary to each other. As are red and green, and yellow and violet.

When used together, complementary colors are naturally aesthetically pleasing, which is important for attracting people's attention to a movie through its poster or DVD cover. There are many interpretations of exactly what emotions orange and blue are meant to evoke, but some say orange makes us imagine excitement and vitality, whereas blue has a calming and cool mood. Whatever their meaning, movie promoters seem to believe that they have the desired effect, and if you look through the covers of your film collection, you may find a pattern emerging.

2 Alan Smithee

When creative control of a movie has been taken away from a director, he or she could ask to be credited as "Alan Smithee." This first happened with the 1969 film *Death of a Gunfighter,* which was initially under the direction of Robert Totten, before being taken over by Don Siegel after Totten was fired midway through production.

Neither director wanted to take credit for the film, and argued that the lead actor Richard Widmark had been the de facto director throughout the whole production. To solve the problem, the movie's direction was instead credited to Alan Smithee. Despite not being a real person, he allowed everybody to save face without attracting attention, the name being both unique, yet ordinary.

Directors Guild of America rules also stated that directors receiving the protection of an Alan Smithee credit were not allowed to discuss their motivations for removing their identity from a movie in the press. As a consequence, Alan Smithee was, for a time, believed to be an actual director, although word eventually got around regarding the pseudonym and its real purpose.

1 More Money in Sequels

Extending the profitability of a story by making sequels is nothing new; novels were doing it long before film. The first movie sequel was *Fall of a Nation* in 1916, the follow up to the technically brilliant but incredibly racist *Birth of a Nation*. There's nothing necessarily wrong with the idea of sequels: Some have been excellent, including *Godfather II*, *Aliens*, *Toy Story 2*, and *The Dark Knight*.

Sometimes, however, sequel-making comes across as little more than a cynical business endeavor (how dare movie studios want to make money?!). I'm not sure we really needed a *Rocky V*, *Jaws: The Revenge*, or *Oceans 13*. The same goes for prequels: *Hannibal Rising* and *The Thing* didn't really do anything to elevate their respective series. Increasingly, there is also a habit of spacing out a movie series, with some sequels having more than one part (Harry Potter, Twilight), or being stretched into a trilogy (The Hobbit), or each character being given their own introduction movie (The Avengers).

TOP 10 Crazy Movie Plots That Happened in Real Life

by **Mohammed Shariff**

10 The Truman Show

The Truman Show is about Jim Carrey's character realizing that his whole life is a lie. Everything is staged by a TV crew and his entire life is followed by an audience. In the end, he breaks out and finds his way to the real world. Sounds crazy, right? Well, in real life there was this Japanese game show called *Nasubi*. Get ready for some depressing stuff.

They took a man who had merely signed up for a reality show (he wasn't told which one), stripped him naked, and locked him in an apartment for about eight months. He had no clothes, food, or water. His only belongings were given to him if he won a sweepstakes. Because some of the audience felt bad for him, the producers let him wear one piece of clothing— unhappily enough, it was pink women's underwear. Finally, they told him that he'd passed and took him to what he thought was a celebration. It was another apartment. He went through this for 15 months.

9 Wanted

Now, this one isn't necessarily the real life version of a movie plot, but it is pretty badass in its own way. In the opening scenes of *Wanted*, a sniper shoots a guy in a suit from an impossible distance a few miles away. As though more spice needed to be added to the craziness, his bullet navigates a city and multiple buildings. Real life can't match that, right?

Well, once upon a time in Iraq, SSG James Gilliland was with his patrol when an enemy sniper took out one of his men from a hospital half a mile away. That shot's impressive, but what happens next is better. Gilliland, a sniper himself, immediately figured out where the shot came from and shot back, killing the sniper. This was a three-quarter-mile shot through buildings into the exact hospital window. For those of you non-gun nuts, it's currently the seventh-best recorded army sniper shot ever.

8 Book of Eli

In this movie, Denzel Washington's character fights a group of 15 men with a sword, kills them all, and doesn't even get touched. He says he is protected by God, and that's why he's so good.

In real life, Alvin C. York was one badass fighter. A soldier in WWI, he was once surrounded by more than 100 Germans. What seems like insane odds was just a walk in the park for York. He took out a semiautomatic and a pistol and shot them all down, not missing one shot. Even through all the machine gun fire, he didn't get hit once. To add to the similarity, even Alvin didn't think his aim was normal. He believed he was protected by God.

7 The Hills Have Eyes; Breakdown; Vacancy

Movies like *The Hills Have Eyes* are the reason many Americans are afraid of hillbillies. In those movies, hill people kidnap or lure innocent people into their "cozy" homes. They then proceed to murder, rob, and rape their victims (and if you're very lucky, in that order). But come on. If that were real, the police would be all over it, right?

Turns out, no. Hill people are very real. A few years ago, a bunch of hicks lured people into their abodes with the promise of work—and then killed them. This isn't the only movielike incident, either. Back in 1846, a group of settlers got lost in the mountains. After running out of supplies, they resorted to killing and eating other people in their caravan.

6 The Three Musketeers

I'll be damned if you don't know who the three musketeers are. The three fictional musket-toting Frenchmen were massively popular, famous not only for the classic book that created the legend, but also for the sweet, sweet candy bar that took their name.

What you probably don't know is that all the characters actually existed. Arthos, Parthos, and Aramis were all real Frenchmen who were active between 1615 and 1620, and went by the name "the Three Brothers." Don't believe us? We'll even throw in that d'Artagnan and Cardinal Richelieu were real, for good measure. Alexander Dumas basically ripped off their lives and didn't credit them.

5 Goodfellas

Goodfellas is one of the staples of the gangster movie genre. Not only did it launch the careers of everyone involved and embolden the veterans already there, but it helped set several of the gangster tropes that we continue to see in movies today. More than anything, the movie just seems so realistic. It's like when you watch *The Dark Knight* and realize that a man could actually dress as a bat and protect a city. Well, as it turns out, the realism is there for a reason. The whole thing is based off a book called *Wiseguy*. Everything from the movie's opening line to its grand finale heist at JFK Airport was completely, utterly real.

4 Footloose

The movie about forbidden dancing is actually reflected in Elmore City, Oklahoma. In that city, public dancing is outright banned. Also, there are no movie theaters and only one bar. It seriously reads like the movie where kids sneak out to barns to dance in secret. And the whole town is one huge anti-teen-sex PSA. Everyone from pastors to school administrators thinks that "sexual arousal" is of the devil and that dancing teens are against the Bible.

3 Accepted

Accepted is a wacky movie about a group of kids with assorted intelligence who decide they hate the popular university that everyone goes to because it's arrogant and rich. They decide to make their own college with a former professor and it becomes wildly successful and even gets accreditation.

In real life, a group of students in Germany decided in 1948 that they hated the popular Nazi Humbolt University. The students—along with some old professors—decided to break off and make their own. With funds from the U.S., they made their own university and called it the Free University of Berlin. Today, it is ranked number nine in the nation.

2 Up

National Geographic decided to build a house, not of straw or wood or bricks, but topped off with helium-filled balloons. The goal was to create one that could imitate the house featured in Pixar's hit movie *Up*. They succeeded: The house actually took off. Unfortunately for our vivid imaginations, no one actually lived in the house and it was just a project. But for the first time ever, *National Geographic* proved that the world really can be as awesome as a cartoon, if you throw enough money at it. As for real life imitating the other half of the movie, in 2007, a man attached some helium balloons to his lawn chair and sailed for nine hours from Oregon to Idaho.

1 The Great Escape

The Great Escape is a classic film for its portrayal of pure American bravery in the face of danger. The film stars a number of men who break out of their respective prisons in an attempt to return to Allied territory using ingenious escape techniques.

In real life, Captain Richard Carr was captured and thrown into a German prison during World War II. He tried several times to escape. Just like in the movie, each attempt was more elaborate than the previous one. He first attempted to escape by digging a secret tunnel. He and 13 compatriots dug and dug for six days. As the first one out, Captain Carr bolted to make sure the coast was clear and hid in a nearby barn. Unfortunately, he was recaptured.

Next, he snuck out during prison relocation and boarded a train. When the Gestapo came for him, he literally jumped off the train after what I can only imagine was a Bond-esque chase. Again, he was recaptured. But this still didn't deter the man: He tried sneaking out for a third time, dressed as a French worker—to no avail.

TOP 10 Bizarre TV Incidents

by Gregory Arden

10 The Tommy Westphall Universe Hypothesis

On May 25, 1988, the final episode of the show *St. Elsewhere* aired on NBC. At the end of the episode (spoiler alert!), it is revealed that the events of the entire show were all in the mind of the character Tommy Westphall, as played by Chad Allen, an autistic actor.

Many characters from *St. Elsewhere* appeared in other shows, such as *Law & Order, The X-Files, Homicide: Life on the Street, Law & Order: Special Victims Unit*, and *Law & Order: Criminal Intent*. Therefore, many people theorized that each of these shows was contained within the imagination of Tommy Westphall. Furthermore, anytime any of the characters from those shows appeared in other shows, those shows also became a part of Tommy's admittedly impressive imagination. The process could continue, almost indefinitely, spanning much of the television universe. Thus, the "Tommy Westphall Universe Hypothesis" was born.

However, there are some who remain skeptical of this hypothesis. Brian Weatherson, a professor of philosophy at Cornell University, theorized that the entire series was not the result of a complex imagination, but rather, a dream. When we dream of places like, say, Beaufort, North Carolina, it is not as if the real Beaufort ceases to exist.

Therefore, Professor Weatherson concluded that the Tommy Westphall Universe Hypothesis is nonsense. However, this does not stop fans from believing in it.

9 Tomorrow's Pioneers

What do you get when you cross a show for kids, a cheap Mickey Mouse rip-off, anti-Semitism, a giant bumblebee, and "Resistance Jihad"?

You get *Tomorrow's Pioneers*, which is probably the most bizarre—and sickest—kids' show ever made. First airing on a Palestinian network

(Al-Aqsa TV) on April 13, 2007, *Pioneers* is about Farfour (the Mickey Mouse knock-off) and Nahoul (the giant bee), and the host, Saraa Barhoum, as they deal with Israeli interrogators (in fact, Farfour gets killed by one, believe it or not), Western ideologies, and capitalism. Kids could even call in to the show—some of the children who called in were as young as three years old.

The show aired until October 2009, but only after killing off the character Nahoul via illness. Later, they would depict Hamas as Simba from *The Lion King*; they would also introduce the character, Assoud, which was a Bugs Bunny rip-off. Assoud would get killed off on the show, due to injuries suffered from an Israeli attack (Assoud only dies after threatening to "finish off the Jews and eat them," of course).

Despite the, shall we say, "unpopular" beliefs contained in *Tomorrow's Pioneers*, the show did at least preach the importance of drinking milk. Oh, and—believe it or not—Disney never sued the show's makers.

8 The Puppy Channel

After the despondency and seriousness of the previous entry, only puppies can cure the situation. A channel showing nothing but puppies all day should do the trick.

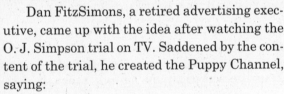

Dan FitzSimons, a retired advertising executive, came up with the idea after watching the O. J. Simpson trial on TV. Saddened by the content of the trial, he created the Puppy Channel, saying:

There's a need for a parking place on television. If you don't want to watch something that is there, you could have the TV set on, and it'd be playing something that didn't bother you, and would hold the place until your favorite show [is on]… [I conceived a channel that would be] 24 hours a day, seven days a week, footage of puppies fooling around…acting the natural comedians…that they are, with no people, no talk, accompanied only by…instrumental music."

The bizarre channel went off the air in 2001, but their website is still active. Despite the unusual nature of the channel, 37–41 percent of people in focus groups said that they'd prefer watching the Puppy Channel to TBS or CNBC.

7 The Mull of Kintyre Test

For years now, people have been dying to see nudity on television. Despite the presence of the Erotic Networks, however, nudity is still uncommon on network television. A few attempts have been made in the United States (Dennis Franz's nudity in *NYPD Blue* is perhaps the most well-known case), but most of them were purely accidental (like Janet Jackson's accidental nudity during the Super Bowl halftime show). However, the UK found a measure by which nudity—male frontal nudity, to be precise—can be shown.

According to Wikipedia, the British Board of Film Classification (BBFC) "would not permit the general release of a film or video if it depicted a phallus (penis) erect to the point that the angle it made from the vertical (the 'angle of the dangle,' as it was often known) was larger than that of the Mull of Kintyre, Argyll, and Bute, on maps of Scotland." This unnecessarily complex rule was devised in 1992 by John Hoyles, a professor from the University of Hull, for the BBFC. Basically, the test was designed to ensure that no erect penises were shown on film, in print, or on television.

By the year 2000, the BBFC officially denied the existence of the Mull of Kintyre Test; by 2002, the test was mostly abandoned. The rule was officially broken for the first time in the UK in 2003, in an episode of the show *Under the Knife with Miss Evans.*

6 Guy Goma

Every person on the planet has probably encountered a case of mistaken identity, as either a mistaken identifier or a mistaken "identifiee." The vast majority of us are fortunate, however, in that the mistake is not broadcast on national television.

But BBC News 24 and a man named Guy Goma were not so lucky. On May 8, 2006, the news channel intended to interview Guy Kewney, a British technology expert, about the then-ongoing conflict between Apple and Apple Corps, the Beatles' record label. Instead, Guy Goma was guided to the makeup room and interviewed on national television.

A college graduate specializing in business from Brazzaville, Republic of Congo, Guy Goma arrived at the BBC for a job interview. BBC News 24 was looking for a data support cleanser in the company's IT department.

The producer of the show, who had been mistakenly told that Mr. Kewney was waiting in the main reception area, mistook Mr. Goma for Mr. Kewney, and sent the other Guy to get his makeup applied for the broadcast. The televised interview began shortly thereafter, with Mr. Goma trying his best to be (or at least appear to be) knowledgeable. He was polite and played along. At the time, he may have thought it was just part of the job interview.

Ultimately, BBC News 24 made up for the error. Despite not getting the IT job, Guy Goma cashed in on his new-found celebrity with appearances on *Friday Night with Jonathan Ross* and *The Big Fat Quiz of the Year*, among others.

5 Australia's Naughtiest Home Videos

When *America's Funniest Home Videos* was at the height of its popularity, other networks wanted to capitalize on its success. Thus, *Australia's Funniest Home Video Show* was born and ran on the Australian channel, Nine Network. Much like its American counterparts, it was quite funny.

However, the Australian show had collected an awful lot of risqué, yet humorous, home movies. Instead of destroying them, they kept them (since the show promised viewers that movies would never be returned to their senders). Eventually, they had collected so many naughty movies that the producers decided to create a one-time-only special aimed at a more mature audience. And so *Australia's Naughtiest Home Videos* was born.

Many of the videos shown involved animal genitalia, graphic (yet humorous) depictions of animal sex, graphic (yet humorous) depictions of human sex, and various collections of filmed gross-out humor, most notably a child touching a kangaroo's scrotum and testicles. The episode premiered on September 4, 1992.

Eventually, Kerry Packer, the owner of Nine Network, saw the show, and called the studio. He yelled at them to "get that shit off the air!" Mere minutes later, the show was yanked off television. When the show was to return from its commercial break, a notice citing "technical difficulties" informed viewers that an old rerun of *Cheers* would be shown instead.

This "change up" bewildered and perplexed the viewing audience. Surprisingly, despite Mr. Packer's objections to the content of the show, 65 percent of all calls received by the studio were to complain about the program's withdrawal.

On August 28, 2008, the complete episode was finally shown on the Nine Network. While it was largely unedited, all humorous references to childhood obesity were removed. The message that was shown during the inaugural viewing, referring to the so-called technical difficulties, remained intact.

4 Alternative 3

In the UK in the late 1970s, many people believed that intelligence levels were dropping across the nation. In June of 1977, a belated April Fools' Day prank sought to explain it all.

The show, called *Alternative 3*, was created by the crew of another British show, *Science Report*. The show claimed that scientists throughout the nation were being abducted by Americans and Soviets in an attempt to colonize Mars and the moon. *Alternative 3* said this secret plan was initiated in the event of a cataclysmic environmental event on Earth. The show also talked about these incidents as though they were going to happen at any moment.

While it sounds silly now, at the time it quickly became the British version of the *War of the Worlds* broadcast. *Alternative 3* was shot with the same film—and the same seriousness—of *Science Report*. This led to widespread panic, and hundreds of phone calls flooded the telephone lines. Ultimately, however, it was finally revealed to be what it had always been: an elaborate hoax.

Despite the fact that it was a hoax, it has gained notoriety. In October 2007, *Alternative 3* was made available on DVD in its entirety.

3 The Southern Television Broadcast Interruption

On November 26, 1977, an alien named either "Asteron," "Gillon," or "Vrillon" (no one is sure which) broadcast a long message on the Independent Broadcasting Authority, which is excerpted here:

> This is the voice of [Vrillon/Asteron/Gillon,] a representative of the Ashtar Galactic Command, speaking to you. For many years you have seen us as lights in the skies. We speak to you now in peace and wisdom as we have done to your brothers and sisters all over...planet Earth.
>
> We come to warn you of the destiny of your race...so that you may communicate to your fellow beings the course you must take to avoid the disaster which threatens your world and the beings on our worlds around you...All your weapons of evil must be removed...
>
> We of the Ashtar Galactic Command thank you for your attention. We are now leaving the plane of your existence. May you be blessed by the supreme love and truth of the cosmos.

Wow. If you watched the whole broadcast, you could be forgiven for assuming that aliens would be more likely to get to the point quickly. In any case, the entire "message" was a hoax, from an as-of-yet unknown, entirely human, intruder.

2 The Flemish Secession Hoax

Following President Obama's 2012 re-election, many citizens signed petitions for their state to secede from the U.S. These petitions were quickly shot down and faded from the public's memory. What if, however, a news report claimed that the attempts to secede were successful? Well, that's what happened in the Flemish Secession Hoax!

On December 13, 2006, a news bulletin interrupted the broadcast of the Belgian show *La Une*. The report indicated that Flemish parliament had officially declared independence from Belgium. The report showed the royal family being evacuated from their home, and also featured interviews from well-known Belgian politicians.

The problem? It was all a hoax. Belgian journalist Philippe Dutilleul—with the help of some Belgian politicians—created and executed the idea, code-named "Bye Bye Belgium." Half an hour into the hoax, the French media minister, Fadila Laanan, notified the public of the story's fictional nature.

Prominent Belgian and Luxembourgian politicians blasted the hoax, dubbing it an "issue you [don't] play around with."

1 The Max Headroom Broadcast Signal Intrusions

When someone appears on our televisions at random, our inclination is to assume that it is some sort of emergency news bulletin. The last thing we'd expect to see would be a man getting spanked with a flyswatter.

But that's exactly what happened on November 22, 1987, in Chicago, Illinois. During the sports segment of *The Nine O'Clock News* on WGN-TV, the first broadcast signal intrusion occurred. It featured a man wearing a suit and Max Headroom mask, standing in front a wall of corrugated metal, which simulated the background commonly seen in the *Max Headroom* show. There was no standard audio, just a buzzing noise. The engineers at WGN had stopped the first intrusion by switching the frequency to their studio link. This first intrusion lasted for only about 30 seconds.

The second—and more well-known—intrusion occurred on a local Chicago-area PBS station (WTTW) during an episode of *Doctor Who*. The same man, in the same costume, had about 90 seconds to intrude this time.

At 11:15 p.m., the man began ranting about everything from Chuck Swirsky (calling him a "freakin' liberal") to New Coke (their slogan, "Catch the Wave," was mentioned in the intrusion). At one point, he even hums the *Clutch Cargo* theme and gives the audience the finger—although it was cut off due to the close-up nature of the shot—and mocks WGN. Other topics, such as the dirtiness of his prosthetic glove (and the fact that his brother had the other glove) continued the energetic chaos of the Max Headroom Broadcast Signal Intrusion Part Two. The second intrusion concluded with a shot of the man getting spanked by another man with a flyswatter; following that, the engineers at WTTW managed to shut it down. The engineers admitted publicly to being a few steps behind the hackers.

To this day, the identity of the intruders is unknown. Some on YouTube have speculated that one of the hijackers was a man with autism who built his own video sender and low-power microwave signal generator. Others believe that they were disgruntled ex-employees of both WGN and WTTW. Still more believe that there are more Max Headroom Broadcast Signal Intrusions to come.

TOP 10 Behind-the-Scenes Stories of Simpsons Guest Stars

by **Alex Gunn**

10 Jose Canseco Acts Like a Douche

With so many off-field dramas, including his own steroid use and the controversial tell-all book *Juiced*, in which he ratted out fellow baseball players for steroids, Jose Canseco is well known for being an unsavory character. But when *The Simpsons* episode "Homer at the Bat" first aired, starring Canseco and eight other Major League Baseball stars, he was one of the most popular power hitters in the game.

Unlike his costars, Canseco was extremely uncooperative and intimidated the cast. The famous scene in which he misses the game after rescuing a woman's possessions from a burning house came as a result of numerous forced rewrites, which were designed to make him as heroic as possible, as he disliked his original scenes. He also disliked his animation, but stated that the voice-acting was very easy.

9 Lawrence Tierney Intimidates Cast

Tough-guy actor Lawrence Tierney was famous for his portrayals of gangsters and hardened criminals in film, but his off-screen troubles made him legendary. He was frequently arrested for brawling and was a self-professed alcoholic. His indiscretions led to him being imprisoned, and at least once he was stabbed.

True to form, his character in *The Simpsons* episode "Marge Be Not Proud" was just as intimidating: a towering, chain-smoking security guard. During production, Tierney abused employees of the show and refused to perform lines when he didn't get the jokes. Thankfully, the writers refused his request to change his character's voice to an over-the-top Southern accent, and his performance remains one of the best and most subtle guest appearances on the show.

8 Barney Beats Up Joe Frazier

Smokin' Joe Frazier is often considered to be one of the greatest boxers of all time. The former World Heavyweight Champion is known in the boxing world for his legendary fights with Muhammad Ali and George Foreman, and by *Simpsons* fans for his hilarious third-season guest spot.

You might remember the great scene in which he was provoked by Barney Gumble ("Hey, Frazier, shut up!") leading to a street fight outside. Originally, the joke was that Barney would knock Frazier out. However, Frazier's son, not content with winning every "my-dad-could-beat-up-your-dad" debate in history, opposed this scene and the roles were reversed—Frazier took the much-loved Barney outside and left him a bloody mess in a trash can.

7 Albert Brooks Improvises Classic Scenes

Albert Brooks is a semiregular guest star, appearing in six episodes and *The Simpsons Movie*, and his role as criminal mastermind Hank Scorpio is often regarded as one of the greatest guest star performances in *Simpsons* history. Huge chunks of Brooks's dialogue were improvised, including the entire "hammock" speech. Brooks was so well regarded for his improvisation that the writers barely bothered to work on his character's dialogue, knowing that Brooks would say new lines in their place anyway.

6 Elizabeth Taylor and Maggie's Sexy First Word

Legendary Golden Age actress Elizabeth Taylor was part of a significant fourth-season *Simpsons* milestone: providing the voice for Maggie's first (and only) word. However, problems arose when Matt Groening and the producers found Taylor's voice "too sexual" for a baby. After 24 takes, Taylor allegedly said "fuck you" to Groening and stormed out, although there are conflicting accounts of this. Whatever the case, she and the staff seemed to patch things up, and she returned later in the season for a second guest spot. After her death in 2011, the *Simpsons* dedicated an episode to her.

5 Justin Timberlake Punk'd by Writers

Episode "New Kids on the Blecch," starring boy band 'N Sync now seems like an early indication of the show's future direction and its frustrating tendency to cast storytelling aside in favor of transparent cameos from trending celebrities. Fortunately, the band did a decent job as far as these things go, and the episode is a good one.

The boys of 'N Sync were enthusiastic about appearing on the show, although Justin Timberlake had some reservations about saying "word," as he thought it was misrepresentative of how he actually talked. In response, the staff replayed the one take where Timberlake actually said the phrase after almost every 'N Sync line.

4 Tony Blair Makes Staff Jump through Hoops

Season 15 marked the first time a head of government appeared on *The Simpsons*. After being denied an appearance by every U.S. president from Gerald Ford onward, *The Simpsons* gave Great Britain a try and were rewarded with Prime Minister Tony Blair after much perseverance.

After eight months of negotiations and requested script changes, Blair finally agreed, giving showrunner Al Jean 15 minutes to record the part on one day's notice.

3 Julian Assange Records Lines under House Arrest

There's not much to say about Julian Assange that hasn't already been said—he is dually seen as both a champion for democracy and a traitor of it. Everything the man says or does is taken ultraseriously, but somehow between leaking classified military documents and hopping between countries, he found the time to appear as himself in *The Simpsons* 500th episode.

Assange was under house arrest in England at the time, pending extradition to Sweden. Al Jean managed to acquire a phone number to call, but no information on Assange's whereabouts. As a result, Assange's lines were recorded over the phone and his voice sounds muffled. His performance isn't really that great, but the magnitude and controversy of the WikiLeaks phenomenon makes his guest spot instantly memorable.

2 Stephen Hawking Makes Technician Work 36-Hour Shift

Stephen Hawking, one of the world's greatest minds, suffers from amyotrophic lateral sclerosis, a disease which has left him almost completely paralyzed. As a result, he speaks through a speech synthesizer. In spite of this disease, he has produced some of the most significant works in the history of physics and has admirably maintained the ability to make fun of himself, appearing in several *Simpsons* episodes.

The crazy thing about Hawking's first appearance was his utter determination to take part: His wheelchair broke down days before he was due to record in Los Angeles, and he made his assistant and a technician work a 36-hour shift to get it repaired in time. When he arrived, he told the staff, "Sorry for being late."

1 Sonic Youth Won't Star with Courtney Love

The episode "Homerpalooza" from *The Simpsons*'s seventh season is one of the show's greatest episodes, and starred a myriad of '90s music icons, evidence that despite criticism of the show, huge rosters of guest stars don't necessarily make for a bad episode. Those featured are pioneering rap group Cypress Hill, alt-rock icons Sonic Youth and Smashing Pumpkins, and singer-songwriter Peter Frampton.

Originally, the Courtney Love–fronted band Hole was wanted for the episode, but one of the bands (later revealed to be Sonic Youth) stated that if Love appeared in the episode, they would not. It is unclear exactly what the disagreement was over, but the band was friendly with Love's late husband, Kurt Cobain.

TOP 10 Shocking Documentaries

by Eva Fauen

10 High on Crack Street: Lost Lives in Lowell (1995)

Following the struggle of three crack addicts, *High on Crack Street* digs deep into the complex daily lives of individuals striving to obtain their next fix. From prostitution to pregnancies to STDs, we see the true dark side of drugs they don't show you in school. There's something quite shocking about just how badly crack ruins lives. Unfortunately, there is no happy ending to this story—six months after filming, featured character Boo Boo was still hooked on a $200-a-day habit, Dicky was imprisoned, and, sadly, Brenda died. A remarkable film about a horrific plague, *High on Crack Street* is unwavering in its portrayal of crack addiction.

9 Aokigahara: Suicide Forest (2012)

Lying at the base of Mount Fuji, Aokigahara Forest has a rather unsettling reputation as a suicide hotspot. This documentary follows a geologist as he performs a walk-through of the forest looking for both those who have, and may soon, succumb to depression. After spotting an abandoned car in the parking lot on the way in, passing signs dissuading suicide, and taking an ill-trodden path into the bewildering forest, it isn't long before the geologists shows us our first images of forsaken souls—all of whom hang from Aokigahara's thick trees. From this point onward, it only gets worse. I encourage all with a strong heart to watch this bleak, but brief, portrayal of the utter desperation in full.

8 The Iceman Tapes: Conversations with a Killer (1992)

"Vicious," "ruthless," "remorseless," "brutal," "fearless," "violent," "disturbed," and "callous" are just some of the words that can be used to describe serial contract killer Richard "The Iceman" Kuklinski. *The Iceman Tapes* attempts to take the viewer into the broken mind of a cold-blooded, paranoid psycho-sociopath through a series of interviews conducted by psychiatrist Michael Baden. Watching Kuklinski describe his atrocities in detail with little to no emotion from his upbringing to his reasons for killing, is a truly unsettling, yet compelling, experience. In his own words: "I am what you call...a person's nightmare."

7 Nuit et Brouillard (1955)

Drawing the viewer in with an almost poetic charm, few films portray the intricacies of the Holocaust better than this 1955 French film, *Nuit et Brouillard*, or—to give it its English title—*Night and Fog*. Featuring the camps at Auschwitz and Majdanek, it takes viewers on an uncompromising and unforgiving journey through the encampments' history and the fate of their occupants. From construction to destruction, the history portrayed in *Nuit et Brouillard* etches horrific images onto the minds of its viewers that will seldom leave their memories.

6 Atomic Wounds (2006)

For all the propaganda and scaremongering that occurred during the Cold War, it is difficult for us to imagine the human effects of nuclear weapons— besides the massive loss of life, of course. We tend to imagine nukes as pulverizing all who stand in their way, but a nuclear weapon doesn't simply destroy: It poisons, it burns, it corrupts. Those unlucky enough not to be obliterated are left to suffer horrific and painful deaths—often over months, years, or even decades, rather than minutes or seconds. *Atomic Wounds* takes us on an up-close-and-personal trip  to visit the victims of Nagasaki and Hiroshima, documenting the terrifying effects of atomic warfare on those who were not struck down in the initial cataclysm. It is difficult to watch this film without asking, "How could we ever do this to our fellow man?" We often forget that the victims of Nagasaki and Hiroshima were living and breathing humans. We see a statistic. This film ensures that we remember there is only misery under those numbers.

5 Conspiracy of Silence

Conspiracy of Silence has never been released, and numerous parties have been attempting to prevent this documentary, which exposes the perversion and abuse of power that occurs at the highest levels in society. A representation of how influence and wealth can be used for personal gain and the suppression of criminal acts, *Conspiracy of Silence* takes us into the world we all know exists and yet hope does not.

4 The Killing of America (1981)

A warning up front, *The Killing of America* consistently provides the viewer with very real and very graphic footage of criminal activity. From showing riots to outright murder, this documentary is far from shy about presenting the truth as is, with no sugar coating. "What truth?" you ask? Well, the fact that the United States was the most violent first-world nation on earth. *The Killing of America* attempts to understand why this was the case, and although it may seem outdated, one should remember that the U.S. is still one of the most violent first-world nations on earth, despite the fact that violent crime has fallen considerably each year since its peak in the early 1990s. This documentary thus gives us an uncompromising look at America's dark past, and perhaps also provides us with one piece of the puzzle that persists today.

3 Interview with a Cannibal (2012)

What drives a man to kill and cannibalize an innocent woman? Well, why not ask such a man…in his own living room? *Interview with a Cannibal* does just that, with the infamous case of Issei Sagawa. Propelled to fame through his crimes, he was deemed insane by the courts and thus released without charge. A fascinating insight into the life of a man lost in his own fantasies, this documentary challenges perceptions about what humans are truly capable of, as well as allowing us to understand the path one must take to sit where Sagawa now does.

2 Bulgaria's Abandoned Children (2007)

Words simply cannot explain what is expressed in this BBC documentary. Put simply, Bulgaria has a serious problem with child abandonment, particularly of the disabled. Worse yet, the government is apparently unable to care for them sufficiently. Recording numerous children over a nine-month period, the film offers a unique insight into the appalling inner workings of a Bulgarian orphanage. With many of the children's poor lives consisting mainly of sitting in a room rocking back and forth by themselves, these children have little hope for the future: no education, no therapy, no help. The plight of an otherwise intelligent young lady known as Didi starkly highlights the failing of the Bulgarian system: She is classified as "untreatable" and thrown among the disabled, despite being quite the opposite—a maddening position if you ask me, and her behavior soon reflects this fact as she eventually succumbs to self-harm to burn away her days.

One may be happy to know that after the film was broadcast in the UK, there was a public outcry that brought servitude for most of the children featured, the majority of whom are now recovering in more suitable care. Didi attended a special boarding school and excelled in her classes. She now enjoys a relatively normal life, frequently visiting museums and art galleries. Aside from this, other EU nations have also put pressure on the Bulgarian government to reform the system and help these outcasts.

1 Child of Rage (1992)

Child of Rage documents the horrific effects of sexual abuse upon a young child named Beth. Consisting primarily of short clips of Beth being interviewed by a clinical psychiatrist, we learn—from both Beth herself, and the additional research done by the TV crew—that she was sexually violated and neglected at a young age by her birth father. This has resulted in the immersion of reactive attachment disorder, a psychiatric condition that, in this case, can in many ways be compared to sociopathy, although their causes are radically different. Beth simply does not feel empathy, and she lacks the ability to connect with others—a product of her mind's attempts to shut out and detach herself from her past abuse.

Within this film, the young girl admits to engaging in highly sadistic, cruel, and often sexual acts upon her brother and animals, as well as just generally displaying a blatant disregard for the rights of others, as well as social norms, including the right to life. There is a certain poignancy in hearing a young child's wishes to murder her parents, as well as her attempts to kill her brother. Demonstrating how abuse can turn innocent young individuals into brutal, remorseless killers, *Child of Rage* ultimately expresses hope that, if caught at a young enough age, reactive attachment disorder can be treated with rigorous therapy and the damage can be reversed—thus bringing a conscience back to a child who would otherwise go through life without one. Beth's final interview, in which she breaks down in remorse for her past self, is truly a tearjerker.

CHAPTER 8

MUSIC

1. Top 10 Wild Rock and Roll Urban Legends People Believe

2. Top 10 Fascinating and Unusual Music Techniques

3. Top 10 Music Recordings for the Insanely Determined

4. Top 10 Beatles Innovations That Changed Music

5. Top 10 True Rock Music Stories

6. Top 10 Famous Songs with Unknown Originals

7. Top 10 Major Stars Who Sang Backup on Hits by Not-So-Major Artists

8. Top 10 Rock Concerts That Were Just Messed Up

9. Top 10 Unpleasant Facts about John Lennon

TOP 10 Wild Rock and Roll Urban Legends People Believe

by R. Kurosawa

10 White Stripes a Big Happy Family?

Myth: Jack White and Meg White are brother and sister.

Fact: This one was actually started by Jack White, who originally claimed that he and Meg White were siblings during the early days of The White Stripes. The reality is that Jack White and Meg White are not related at all.

They were married for a while, but divorced many years and albums ago. Jack, born Jack Gillis, took Meg's last name during the marriage and decided to keep it following their split. So next time you hear Meg telling an interviewer, "I love Jack White like a little brother," don't fall for it. At this point they just love playing with the media and fans.

9 Music Group 311 and their "Racist" Passwords

Myth: 311's name stands for the KKK because "K" is the eleventh letter of the alphabet.

Fact: This rumor has followed the band since the '90s. It's not completely out of the ordinary for hate groups to use numerology or initials as code — 88 is a popular number in the Neo-Nazi community, standing for HH, or "Heil Hitler." But that's not the case for 311. The band is not related to hate or racism at all, and 311 is generally known as an alternative rock band.

The band's name originates from the police code for indecent exposure in Omaha, Nebraska, after the original guitarist for the band was arrested for streaking. The vocalist and guitarist of the group, Nick Hexum, has of course denied any connection with this rumor of hidden racism, which he finds ridiculous and unworthy of discussion.

8 Is Gene Simmons Part Animal?

Myth: KISS vocalist and bassist Gene Simmons, famous for wagging his tongue as part of his onstage antics, had a cow's tongue surgically attached to his own.

Fact: Rumors said that Simmons had a cow's tongue surgically attached onto his own tongue to help him create the character of the "Demon" that he portrayed onstage. Teenagers from the 1970s were convinced that no human could have a tongue that long without surgical enhancement and, while Simmons does have indeed an abnormally long tongue, there is no truth at all to this myth.

The fact is that '70s medical technology didn't extend to successfully attaching animal parts to humans, and a cow's tongue looks nothing like Simmons's or any other human's. This is just another rock 'n' roll myth birthed from the effects of drugs and alcohol.

7 Lady Gaga: Male or Female?

Myth: Lady Gaga is a hermaphrodite.

Fact: Every famous person has, at some point, been the subject of rumors and outright hoaxes. The more mysterious their personal life is to the public, the wilder the rumors. When Lady Gaga burst onto the music scene with "Just Dance" in 2008, her unique style and fascinating persona made her the source of a number of urban legends. One of them suggested that Lady Gaga was born a hermaphrodite or even a man.

This rumor is actually an adaptation of a much older tale. The young Jamie Lee Curtis was the subject of widespread speculation that she had been born intersex. It was suggested that her androgynous name was to allow her to choose a gender herself. After a photograph of Lady Gaga seemed to reveal a possible bulge, the rumor switched to the pop sensation.

Her love of gay culture and outrageous public persona add more fuel to the fire. Despite false reports of her issuing a statement confirming she was intersex, the truth emerged. Lady Gaga demonstrated definitively to the press that she was born female. However, the rumor persists.

6 Michael Jackson Didn't Have Many Plastic Surgeries.

Myth: Michael Jackson had only two plastic surgeries during his lifetime.

Fact: The funniest (or saddest) part of this myth is that Jackson's dedicated  fans believe this. Actually, they believed anything their idol said. Michael Jackson told Oprah in 1992 and Martin Bashir in 2003 that he only had two plastic surgeries on his nose and a constructive plastic surgery on his scalp after he got burned. Jackson may have told a few fibs in his day, but it feels like he underestimated our intelligence a little too much with this one.

If you pay attention to Michael's nose during his debut album *Off the Wall* and then check on it again in the *Thriller* album and so on until his 2001 studio album, *Invincible*, you will notice that he has a different nose for every single one, which means that he probably kept having surgeries. Also add to the mix his obviously different cheekbones, chin, eyebrows, lips, and eye shape and you easily find out that Jackson probably forgot to add a zero after the "two" surgeries he claimed to have had.

5 Marilyn Manson Likes "Extreme" Sports.

Myth: Marilyn Manson removed a pair of ribs to be able to perform self-fellatio.

Fact: It might be true that when you mention Marilyn Manson, most people think of the disgusting (yet so legendary!) fictional surgery he supposedly underwent to have the lower half of his ribs removed so he could give himself auto-fellatio.

Of course, all this is nothing more than a dirty rumor, a myth that some of the rocker's filthy haters started. In Manson's defense, the man had a really sexy wife during the time these rumors arose and he didn't really need to practice such habits. And according to most plastic surgeons, removing your lower ribs does not allow you to do that type of act; it only helps you to make your waist appear thinner.

4 The Real Paul McCartney Has Been Dead for Years.

Myth: McCartney died in an auto accident in 1966 and was replaced by an impersonator.

Fact: The McCartney myth started with (apparently) legitimate wire service reports being fed to radio stations. It all began on October 12, 1969, when Russ Gibb, a DJ for Detroit's underground station WKNR-FM, received a phone call from a man named "Tom," who claimed that some Beatles records contained hidden clues suggesting that Paul McCartney had actually died. The fact that it took McCartney a while to deny the rumor added even more fuel to it.

The rumors became so noisy that Paul McCartney himself had to reassure his fans that he was still alive. In an exclusive 1969 interview with *Life* magazine, he stated, paraphrasing Mark Twain, "Rumors of my death have been greatly exaggerated. However, if I was dead, I'm sure I'd be the last to know." He also offered a number of explanations for the mysterious clues.

3 Elvis Presley Was a Racist.

Myth: Elvis stated that "The only thing Negroes can do for me is buy my records and shine my shoes."

Fact: According to some people, this one sentence that was never verified or witnessed by any credible or existing person confirms the belief that

Elvis was a cynical racist who "stole" everything he knew from black men. There's no doubt (and Elvis never denied) that he was heavily influenced by black music and black musicians, but was he a racist? There's no evidence proving such a thing. If anything, all the evidence points to Elvis's love for black music.

Of course, this ridiculous urban legend should be nothing but comedy material nowadays: If Elvis were racist for being influenced by other artists, then every artist is a thieving racist. Elvis was envied by some for good reason: He did what he did really well and he had the looks and charisma to go with it. Elvis was the one who influenced almost every artist of his generation, and black and white artists alike copied his style and attitude.

And, as the great Little Richard said, "Elvis was an integrator. Elvis was a blessing. They wouldn't let black music through. Elvis didn't steal but he opened the door for black music."

2 Jim Morrison Is Still Alive.

Myth: Jim Morrison is alive and someone else's body is in his grave.

Fact: In spite of extensive and largely irrefutable evidence to the contrary, there are still those who believe that Jim Morrison is alive and is periodically spotted in convenience stores, restaurants, and trailer parks all over the world.

Some won't even believe that Morrison's body is the one buried in his grave in a Paris cemetery. The official cause of Morrison's death was listed as a heart attack—believed by many to have been drug related—in 1971.

One conspiracy theorist has even produced a video, and he claims that Morrison lives the life of a cowboy in the Pacific Northwest. People who have seen the video say the man in it bears no resemblance to Morrison and, other than the fact that many of his song lyrics had mystical themes, there is no evidence to suggest that his death was faked. Truth is, there are a few unanswered questions and many coincidences regarding his sudden death that don't make much sense. However, the legend that is Jim Morrison will live on forever. Some things are just too good to be forgotten.

1 Courtney Love is behind Kurt's Cobain's Death.

Myth: Courtney Love murdered Kurt Cobain.

Fact: No matter how the strongly the hardcore fans disagree, the sad reality is that Kurt Cobain probably killed himself. He struggled his entire life with bipolar disorder and drug addiction, and he had tried to kill himself several times before.

There are many unanswered questions regarding his death, however, that feed the minds of the people who invent such theories and conspiracies. California private investigator Tom Grant maintains that Cobain's body tested for three times a lethal amount of heroin, suggesting a self-inflected gunshot wound would be impossible. Grant also believes Courtney Love was involved in the murder, yet there is no evidence to support his claim.

Also, recent accusations from Love and Cobain's daughter that Love is an unstable mother figure who killed her pets, constantly pops pills, and starts fires by smoking in bed, only served to rekindle all the rumors about her murdering Cobain.

TOP 10 Fascinating and Unusual Music Techniques

by **Andy Martin**

10 Drumming on a Frozen Lake

Lake Baikal is the world's biggest lake by volume of water; it's so big, in fact, that it contains one-fifth of the world's unfrozen surface freshwater. It's also the world's deepest lake (just over a mile in depth), and is perhaps the world's oldest as well. Baikal is home to a number of fascinating animals, including one of the only freshwater seal species, as well as an extremely fatty, scaleless, translucent fish called a golomyanka.

But what's this got to do with music? Well, a Russian percussion group known as ETHNOBEAT—from Irkutsk Technical University—sojourned to Lake Baikal in March of 2012 to drum on the lake's frozen surface. The group's members braved the -4°F (-20°C) weather to produce a beautiful array of percussive sounds using only their hands and the different types of ice at their disposal. The group owes the project to a piece of clumsiness—Tatiana, the wife of one of the drummers, had previously fallen on her bottom on the ice, producing an intriguing musical sound when she hit the surface. From there, a singular concert arose, turning frozen water into a symphony.

9 Eephing

Eephing (sometimes spelled "eefing") can probably best be understood as a type of "hillbilly beatboxing"—although it predates beatboxing by nearly 100 years. It's a fast-paced Appalachian singing technique that can be crudely broken down as one-third saying "eef" (or another vowel + F), one-third mouth farting, and one-third gasping. Jennifer Sharpe, who profiled legendary eepher Jimmie Riddle on NPR, described it as "a kind of hiccupping, rhythmic wheeze." It originated in rural farming communities in Tennessee where eephers would imitate the sounds of their pigs and turkeys.

Eephing has never seen much in the way of mainstream success, but got its 15 minutes of fame in 1963 when Riddle was featured on Joe Perkins's single "Little Eefin' Annie." The song reached number 76 on the Billboard charts and exposed a generation of listeners to the unique sounds of eephing.

8 Konnakol

Konnakol—sometimes colorfully referred to as "Indian scat singing" or "Indian beatboxing"—is the South Indian art of vocal percussion. It is a component of "solkattu," the language of drum syllables, along with "tala" (or "taal"), the percussive part done with the hand on a "mridangam" drum. With tala, the meter is kept with waves, claps, and finger counts, while the musician simultaneously vocalizes the konnakol.

Performers of konnakol learn very complex, systematic, almost grammatical rules and techniques to produce rapid-fire vocal percussion. As with any advanced musical system, it must be seen and heard to be fully appreciated. John McLaughlin, a British musician and guitar virtuoso who studied konnakol and other Indian techniques and styles, said of konnakol, "If you can understand konnakol—the most superior system of learning rhythm in the world—you can understand any rhythm from any country on the planet."

7 Through-Composed Music

"Through-composed music" refers to a piece of music that does not repeat any part of itself, or does so rarely. Nearly all compositions have musical elements that occur again and again, especially pop music, which has a fairly rigidly set structure that sees relatively few deviations.

Truly through-composed music is fairly rare, but there are a few well-known examples. Schubert wrote a number of *lieds* (romantic German poems set to music), in which he wrote different music for every line. Haydn's "Farewell Symphony" is also through-composed. In popular music, most so-called through-composed pieces do, in fact, have some amount of repeating elements, but are still largely considered to be a part of the genre. Perhaps the best-known example in rock is Queen's "Bohemian Rhapsody"; the 1975 classic doesn't have a chorus and is divided into distinct sections that include elements of folk, rock, hard rock, opera, and ballad. The Beatles have a number of tunes (including "Happiness Is a Warm Gun" and "A Day in the Life"), which are hybridlike songs comprising two very distinct parts.

6 Hollerin'

Hollerin' is an ancient singing tradition whose origins can be traced back as far as the early days of language. It served a practical purpose—to communicate information over long distances. In the 1700s in North Carolina, loggers hollered to communicate important instructions to one another; it survived for many years in various forms. There are many different purposes to a holler, including distress (danger), communicative (usually a basic greeting), functional (day-to-day farming calls), and expressive (the pure pleasure of hollerin'). Though hollerin' has been functionally dead for some time, a revival has been underway since 1969 in the form of the National Hollerin' Contest in Spivey's Corner, North Carolina. Held on the third Saturday every June, the contest seeks to revive the extinct art and keep its legacy alive.

Field hollering, an African-American cousin to hollerin', is a type of singing that can be considered a close relative of the "work song." Believed to be a potential forerunner to the blues, field hollering doesn't show up on any recordings until the mid-1930s but is known to have much older roots. It involves falsetto, portamento (sliding from one pitch to another), and sudden pitch changes.

5 Tuvan Throat Singing

Tuvan throat singers accomplish something pretty amazing: They are able to sing multiple pitches simultaneously. These singers from the Siberian region of Tuva are using a vocal technique that's a type of "overtone singing," a style of singing that exists all over the world. Overtone singing likely originated in Mongolia in the regions now known as Khovd and Govi-Altai. Traditionally, these *xöömei* have been men, but more and more women are beginning to learn the practice.

When you listen to a piece of throat singing music for the first time, it's fairly breathtaking, and probably unlike anything you've ever heard. The singer begins with a deep, low, guttural droning sound, and then over time he breaks it up into its component tones, amplifying each one separately so it can be heard as a distinct note. It's a tremendously difficult technique to master, as it involves several different components—throat singers must breathe circularly (number two in this list) to allow the voice to be continuous and unbroken, then control various parts of their throat and mouth (lips, tongue, jaw, velum, and larynx) to create echo chambers in their vocal folds. From there they manipulate the sound to create distinct, multifaceted, unique music.

4 Keening

That wailing, unsettling sound that a banshee makes? That's called "keening"—a type of musical, vocal lamentation usually associated with Ireland, though it exists in various forms in many other cultures. To keen is "to make a loud and long cry of sorrow; to lament with a keen." Though it's not commonly heard in Ireland nowadays (most keening ceased in the early 1900s), it used to be standard practice at funerals, either by a single woman or a group of women. Once upon a time, keeners (*mná caointe*) performed these *caoineadh* at wakes and funerals as a way of joining the community together in a display of grief and mourning. Keeners would praise the dead, but would also wail curses at those who had done the deceased wrong. More than simple mourners, *mná caointe* helped communities manage death, holding spiritual duties as well, including assisting the deceased in their journey to the afterlife.

The practice may date all the way back to the Israelites (and perhaps even further), who passed the custom along through Eastern civilizations, then through the Greeks and Romans. In the Irish language, the word was written *cine*, very similar to the Hebrew word *cina*, meaning "lamentation or weeping with clapping of hands."

3 Hannes Coetzee and His Spoon Guitar

Hannes Coetzee lives in the small South African town of Herbertsdale, where he makes a living extracting aloe from succulents in the desert. He's known around the world, however, for his unique style of playing guitar—he bills himself as a "teaspoon slide guitarist." With a spoon in his mouth serving as a type of slide, Coetzee coaxes a distinct, twangy music from his steel-string guitar. The technique is called *optel an knyp*, which means "pick up and pinch," and it's a style of playing that, as far as anyone knows, was invented by Coetzee himself.

Coetzee's story received some broader recognition in a 2003 documentary called *Karoo Kitaar Blues*. The film chronicles South African musician David Kramer's 2001 efforts to put on a concert featuring some of the country's best unknown musicians.

2 Circular Breathing

Circular breathing is a fairly tricky technique that effectively allows a person to sustain a musical note (or succession of notes) indefinitely. On the surface, it isn't overly complicated—when you perform this technique, you're essentially breathing normally, while storing a small amount of extra air in your cheeks so that when you run out of breath in your lungs, you can breathe quickly through your nose while you use that cheek reserve to keep playing. The mechanics are not complex to grasp, but actually doing it takes a lot of practice. Certain instruments, perhaps most famously the didgeridoo, require this type of breathing to properly play; while the origins of circular breathing are not known, it is possible that Australian Aborigines developed the technique specifically for the didgeridoo.

While many musicians have made a name for themselves (at least in part) through their use of circular breathing—including Mexican trumpeter Rafael Mendéz, British saxophonist Andy Sheppard, and American bandleader Irvin Mayfield—it's none other than Kenny G who set a world record. In 1997, the adult contemporary smooth jazzist played an E-flat on his soprano saxophone for 45 minutes and 47 seconds, managing to hold the note by using the circular breathing technique.

1 Talking Guitars

The most well-known talking-guitar musician is likely Peter Frampton, who famously sang into his "talk box" on the hit singles "Do You Feel Like We Do" and "Show Me the Way." The talk box is an effects unit that allows the user to connect their voice to an instrument; Frampton has his own line of talk boxes and owes at least some of his success to the distinctive sound of his voice spoken through his electric guitar.

Frampton, however, was hardly the first musician to experiment with talking guitars. Alvino Rey, an American swing-era musician often credited with inventing the pedal steel guitar, pioneered a carbon throat microphone that was wired to affect the tone of his electric guitar. Rey placed the microphone on the throat of his sister, who mouthed words, producing what Rey called the "singing guitar." Many of Rey's tunes featured a small guitar puppet named "Stringy," who acted as a sort of singing, guitar-voiced ventriloquist dummy.

In 1964, music pioneer Pete Drake released *Forever*, an album whose single of the same name was a huge hit. The "singing guitar" style was resurrected, and the song reached number 22 on the Billboard charts. Drake's mastery of the guitar, both "talking" and otherwise, led to him being featured on dozens of hits in the 1960s, including "Lay Lady Lay" and (most likely) "Stand by Your Man."

TOP 10 Music Recordings for the Insanely Determined

by **Mike Floorwalker**

10 Tom Waits's Super-Limited Edition 78 RPM Record

The New Orleans Preservation Hall has been defending the legacy of Big Easy jazz for over 50 years. Their house band is held in high regard, and for a benefit recording in 2010, they enlisted Tom Waits to sit in on two tracks. The songs, "Tootie Ma Was a Big Fine Thing" and "Corrine Died on the Battlefield" were made available in one format only: 78 RPM vinyl. An interesting decision to use such an archaic format, but I suppose that was the point—it is called the Preservation Hall, after all.

These were a pretty limited edition, so getting your hands on one won't be easy. At the time, a small number of custom-made 78 RPM turntables could be bought along with the record. Today it would be hard enough finding the record, let alone the turntable.

9 The Residents' $100,000 Ultimate Box Set

A band that apparently consists of sentient eyeballs, the Residents released the Ultimate Box Set of their work. It is a $100,000 monstrosity that contains over a hundred records, CDs, and DVDs. Why so costly? It comes in a refrigerator and is collectible art. Specifically, it includes 563 songs, 40 vinyl LPs, 50 CDs, and dozens of singles, EPs, DVDs, and CD-ROMs.

In addition to the downright unwieldy amount of material, you'd have a tough time thinking of less convenient packaging. Was it all they had? Does the music need to be refrigerated for some reason?

8 Indie Rock Band's Eight-Track-Only Album

Dallas, Texas, band RTB2 released their grammatically challenged album *We Are a Strange Man* exclusively on a format that's been dead for about 30 years. Why? For the hell of it, apparently. The band has released plenty of music the "normal" way, but for this release went as retro as they could and released it on eight-track tapes only.

Of course, eight-track decks haven't been manufactured by anyone for decades. Your best bet for checking out *We Are a Strange Man* involves spending lots of time at questionable garage sales.

7 Gescom, Minidisc

In 1998, English electronic dance band Gescom released an 88-track album called *Minidisc*. You may remember that a minidisc was once a format for recorded music, a defining feature of which was its seamless shuffle mode. True to its name, this album was released only in the minidisc format and was meant to be played on shuffle.

While it got a CD pressing in 2006, to listen to it as intended you'll need to hunt down a minidisc player. They can get expensive, as they are no longer made.

6 Brian Wilson, Sweet Insanity

Sweet Insanity was supposed to have been Brian Wilson's second solo album, planned for release in 1991. It went unreleased and exists only on a handful of promotional cassette tapes. While a bootleg or two have shown up, none seem to be complete, and some are even re-recorded versions of the original songs.

The album is a sort of rare recording holy grail, but this may not be a bad thing as it has been described as "unlistenable." With Brian Wilson attempting to rap at one point and Weird Al Yankovic on accordion, I'm not surprised.

5 Ynys Enlli, "Ygam"

A Welsh mathematician and composer of electronic music, Enlli only released 33 copies of a track called "Ygam" on…wax cylinder. Presumably because he has the names and numbers of all 33 people in the world that own a wax cylinder player in his Rolodex.

Listening to this track would involve tracking down one of the 33 people who own one of the recordings, because they're sold out. Then, somehow get your hands on a wax cylinder player. You may need to build it yourself, because they haven't been commercially mass-produced since 1929. You'll then need to connect it to your stereo using magic.

4 Flaming Lips, Zaireeka

This truly strange 1997 release is a portmanteau of "Zaire" and "eureka," a "mess with a purpose," as described in the album booklet. *Zaireeka* was released in four discs and intended to be played on four stereos simultaneously. Most listeners, not having four stereos lying around, listened to them separately. Listening to it in its intended form would take three friends, perfect timing, and a great deal of dedication.

To prove there is no end to their weirdness, the Flaming Lips revisited the idea in 2011, releasing a digital track in 12 parts through YouTube entitled "Two Blobs F--king." It is intended to be played simultaneously on 12 mobile phones.

3 The Unreleased Works of Prince

Most people with an interest in music know that The Artist Previously Known as The Artist Formerly Known as Prince (or TAPKATAFKAP) has a lot of unreleased material. What they may not know is just how much. By some accounts, he has written and recorded roughly a song a day for over 30 years. Even a conservative estimate gives dozens of albums worth of material, and TAPKATAFKAP has let it be known that he has no plans to release any of it.

So if you ever want to hear this amazing stash of incredible unreleased music, you'll need to break into Prince's vault, which I would advise against. It's guarded by purple-laser-shooting robots and exotic attack tigers, and you really don't stand a chance.

2 Hardcore Band's One-Inch Record

Californian hardcore power-violence band Spazz released a record in a format that ensures only the most determined fans will ever hear it—a One-inch record entitled *Funky Ass Li'l Platter*. Only 14 copies are known to exist, with side A played at 78 RPM and side B played at 33 RPM. Of course, you may want to dig deep for this one—you know you're dying to hear Spazz's "Hemorrhoidal Dance of Death" (side A).

Assuming you can find someone who owns this record, you're still not going to get them to give it to you. Play it for you, perhaps. But tracking them down, befriending them, and buying them a beer seems like a lot of trouble to go to for what is less than a minute of power-violence.

1 The Shout Out Louds, "Blue Ice"

Indie band the Shout Out Louds released their ice-themed tune "Blue Ice" on an ice record. Literally, a record made of ice—sold as a mold and a bottle of water capable of producing a seven-inch playable record.

So to listen to the song, first you must secure one of the only ten sets that were made. Next, pour water into the mold and put it in the freezer. While you're waiting, find a turntable you really don't care about. Place the ice record on the turntable, drop the needle, stand back and wait for it to… melt and ruin your player? Electrocute you? Who knows what will happen.

TOP 10 Beatles Innovations That Changed Music

by **Tom Daniel**

10 Music Video

Although early jazz artists created short music-film performances of their songs, and Elvis filmed his songs as parts of movies, the Beatles were the pioneers of marrying the two ideas into the concept we now know as the music video—a short, stand-alone film of a musical act presenting a current song that may or not be a live performance. The idea came to the Beatles as a way to ease their ridiculously tight schedule. Instead of the band having to make tons of public appearances on TV shows around the world, they could send a video of themselves instead. The first dedicated music video was for the single "Paperback Writer/Rain" in 1966.

9 Concept Album

Prior to 1966, popular musical acts went into the recording studio in order to create a stack of singles. These singles were first released individually by the record company, and then again in a few months as part of a long-playing album. Typically, the band had no input as to which songs went on the album, the order in which they were presented, or what was used as the cover art; these were all decisions made independent of the band by the record company. However, with the invaluable guidance of their producer, George Martin, the Beatles released the industry's first concept album, *Sgt. Pepper's Lonely Hearts Club Band*. The idea behind *Sgt. Pepper* was that the Beatles were playing the part of another band giving a concert in the park, and all of the songs on the album were part of that outdoor affair. None of the songs on that album were initially released as a singles; the first time the public heard any part of *Sgt. Pepper* was when the entire album was released in June 1967.

8 Stadium Concert Venues

Although the Beatles were highly successful in selling out their early concerts in 1963, 1964, and 1965, they were only playing shows booked in auditoriums, theaters, and amphitheaters that seated anywhere between 1,000 and 10,000 ticket holders. When manager Brian Epstein initially booked the Beatles to play a concert in New York's Shea Stadium in August 1965, the idea was considered almost too absurd to consider. However, the tickets sold out within hours (priced between $4.50 and $5.75), and over 55,000 berserk, screaming fans (mostly teenage girls) packed Shea Stadium for the first-ever stadium rock concert. The Beatles only played for 30 minutes, the fans were not allowed onto the infield where the stage was located, and the stadium's sound system was atrocious for a musical concert, but the night's gross was over $300,000, which stood as an industry record for many years.

7 Self-Contained Record Label

This was one of those magnificent ideas where everyone learned more from Beatle mistakes than Beatle successes. In 1966, the Beatles' recording contract with EMI Records expired, and they re-entered into a nine-year contract with EMI in 1967. The next year, the Beatles decided to form their own record company, Apple Records, and discovered that EMI was not willing to release them. In a complicated series of confusing maneuvers, the Beatles remained with EMI, but signed a separate agreement between EMI's American subsidiary, Capitol Records, and Apple. The result was that American releases contained the Apple label while British releases did not (at first). In addition to this mess, the Beatles legally hired two different business managers (American Allen Klein and Paul's new father-in-law Lee Eastman) at Apple, and all contracts between Apple, EMI, and Capitol were revised. Hilarity and lawsuits soon followed, and the Beatles painfully set the standard for what NOT to do when forming your own record company.

6 Live Global Television Broadcast

Although the Beatles did not invent satellite television, they were the highlighted subject of the first-ever live global satellite television broadcast in June, 1967. The TV program was called "Our World," and it featured the contributions of artists and citizens of 19 different nations. Using four different orbiting satellites, the program was able to be broadcast live to anyone interested in receiving the signal anywhere in the world, and the Beatles performed an in-studio live version of "All You Need Is Love," which was specially written by John for the broadcast, to close out the program.

5 Chart Success

Although many different musical acts hold variously scattered chart-topping marketing successes, no specific artist has ever come close to the nearly inexplicable global phenomenon the Beatles enjoyed in the spring of 1964. On March 21, the Beatles held numbers 1, 2, and 3 on Billboard's Hot 100 (for a total of seven songs in that week's poll). On March 28, they held numbers 1, 2, 3, and 4 (ten songs in all) on that week's Billboard Hot 100.

On April 4, they staggeringly held numbers 1, 2, 3, 4, and 5 (for a total of 12 songs). On April 11, the Beatles added two more songs to the Billboard Hot 100 (14 in all). During this same time frame, they were also snagging most of the album and singles top-ten lists in the UK, Canada, and Australia.

4 Studio Techniques

This item could almost be a separate list in and of itself. The Beatles (and their recording engineers) either pioneered or popularized Artificial Double Tracking (ADT), back masking, tuned feedback, spliced audio loops, distortion, equalization, stereo effects, multitracking (overdubbing), compression, phase shifting, and innovative "microphoning." Although the Beatles are not credited with the invention of most of these studio tricks, they were responsible for directly inspiring countless musical acts that were desperate to copy their unique sounds.

3 Lyrics Printed on the Album

The first pop album to feature actual printed lyrics with the album was the Beatles' 1967 epic release *Sgt. Pepper's Lonely Hearts Club Band*. Soon, it would be considered non-standard to not do so.

2 No Touring

The typical music industry standard recording contract of the 1960s required a band to record and release enough singles for a company to release at least one album per year, and the Beatles went way above and beyond the call of duty (they released two albums per year in every year with EMI Records except 1966). Another aspect of the standard recording contract required a band to give a prescribed number of public concerts as a highly effective means to promote and sell the band's singles and albums. However, in August 1966, at Candlestick Park in San Francisco, the Beatles played their last public concert after over six years of extended touring. The decision for the Beatles (or any band, for that matter) to end touring was a breathtakingly landmark decision, and theirs was based on multiple factors, such as exhaustion, inability to perform their newest songs in a live format, inability to hear themselves onstage, wandering musical focus, safety concerns following death threats and boycotts, and boredom. The Beatles would only make one more public musical appearance, and it would come in January, 1969, in the form of an impromptu semiprivate concert on the rooftop of their London studios.

1 American FM Radio

By 1968, the American radio dial preferred to have music on AM and talk radio on FM, and most AM stations played music in a three-minute single format. This meant that any singles significantly longer or shorter than three minutes were ignored by AM stations because it would wreck their repetitive hourly format to play it. When the Beatles released "Hey Jude" as a single in August 1968, it was nearly seven-and-a-half minutes long, and AM stations simply chopped off the song at the three-minute mark. At KSAN-FM in San Francisco, radio pioneer Tom Donahue used the promise of a whole "Hey Jude" single coupled with other innovative ideas (commercial-free blocks of music, playing whole album sides at a time, etc.) as a means to lure listeners away from local AM stations to his uniquely programmed FM station, and the idea eventually snowballed across the country. Within ten years, American radio stations had almost completely switched places, and put music on FM and talk radio on AM.

TOP 10 True Rock Music Stories

by **Bryan Johnson**

10 Dylan, the Beatles, and a Joint

In late August of 1964, the Beatles started their first official U.S. tour. The group began at the Cow Palace in San Francisco and finished at the  Paramount Theatre in New York. On August 28 and 29, the Beatles played at Forest Hills Stadium in New York and were befriended by Bob Dylan. The two parties were introduced by the writer Al Aronowitz at New York's Delmonico Hotel.

After a brief chat with the Beatles, Bob Dylan asked John, Paul, Ringo, George, and Brian Epstein if they wanted to smoke a joint. Epstein looked apprehensive and said that the band hadn't tried marijuana for years. Dylan was immediately surprised because he had been under the impression that they smoked weed because of the song "I Want to Hold Your Hand." He mistook the lyrics "I can't hide" for "I get high."

The Beatles were never ones to back down from a new experience and agreed. Lennon took the joint and passed it to Ringo whom he called his "royal taster." Ringo smoked the entire thing, not knowing the tradition of sharing the joint between people. In response, Dylan rolled a joint for each of the Beatles and they smoked. During the event it was reported that Epstein said, "I'm so high I'm on the ceiling. I'm up on the ceiling." McCartney got more philosophical and asked their road manager Mal Evans to write down everything he was saying.

9 Ozzy Osbourne Snorts Ants

Ozzy Osbourne is one of the most controversial figures in the history of music. He has sold over 100 million albums and helped popularize the

genre of heavy metal. Osbourne has been addicted to drugs for most of his life and has experimented with a wide variety of substances. During his career, Osbourne has been involved with two separate incidents in which he bit the head of an animal. In 1981, after signing his first solo record deal, Osbourne bit the head off a dove. In 1982, he bit the head off a bat that he thought was plastic while performing in Des Moines, Iowa. After decapitating the bat, Ozzy had to be treated for rabies.

In 1982, Ozzy Osbourne got drunk and urinated on a cenotaph erected in honor of those who died at the Alamo in Texas. He was arrested for the act and banned from the city of San Antonio for a decade. In 1984, Ozzy joined Mötley Crüe on the road and the tour has been called one of the "craziest drug- and alcohol-fueled tours in the history of rock and roll." During their time in hotel rooms, Ozzy and Nikki Sixx of Mötley Crüe underwent a competition to see who could be the most extreme. After Sixx set himself on fire, Osbourne responded by snorting a line of ants off the pavement. After he snorted them up, some of the ants came out his mouth. The event was highlighted in a book written by Ozzy's wife, Sharon Osbourne. Many accounts say that the ants were fire ants, but this is not confirmed.

8 Bowie and Jagger in Bed

David Bowie is an innovative English musician who has sold over 140 million albums. He is an extremely popular singer and has done a lot of work to help fight important world issues. In 1972, Bowie became one of the first popular singers to reveal to the public that he was bisexual. Bowie gave an interview that was broadcast around the world. Since that time he has bounced back and forth on the issue and remains married to Somali model Iman.

In 1970, David Bowie was married to a woman named Angela and the couple divorced in 1980. In 1990, after a ten-year gag order ended, Angela

Bowie appeared on *The Joan Rivers Show* and gave some controversial details about her time with David. She is quoted as saying, "I caught him in bed with men several times. In fact, the best time I caught him in bed was with Mick Jagger." At this point, Howard Stern, who was involved with the interview, asked Angela if Jagger and Bowie had their clothes off. She said, "They certainly did." The accusation became international news and Jagger released a statement that dismissed the claim.

A week after the interview, Angela Bowie went on television and said that although she had seen Mick Jagger and Bowie naked, it didn't necessarily mean they weren't sleeping. She clarified, "I certainly didn't catch anyone in the act." Some people have linked the event to the 1973 Rolling Stones hit song "Angie." However, David Bowie said it best: "About 15 or 16 years ago, I really got pretty tired of fending off questions about what I used to do with my penis in the early '70s. My suggestion for people with a prurient interest is to go through the 30 or 40 bios on me and pick out the rumor of their choice."

7 Keith Richards Snorts His Dad

Keith Richards is one of the most talented guitarists in history. In 1962, he helped form the Rolling Stones, and since that time the band has sold over 200 million records. Interestingly, Keith Richards regards the acoustic guitar as the basis for his playing, once saying that he felt the electric guitar would cause him to "lose that touch." Richards is also a talented lyricist. The songwriting partnership of Jagger and Richards has been responsible for the majority of the Rolling Stones' catalog.

In the 1970s, music journalist Nick Kent described Keith Richards's personality as "mad, bad, and dangerous to know." In 1994, Keith said that his image was "like a long shadow," implying that people don't know much about the real man, but instead focus on the things written in articles. Richards has a long history of drug abuse and has been tried for drug-related charges five times.

In April of 2006, Keith Richards made headlines when he fell out of a tree in Fiji and suffered a bad head injury. The event caused a delay in the Rolling Stones tour, but Richards made a full recovery. The following year, Keith made international headlines after he was asked by a journalist what the strangest thing he ever snorted was. Keith responded: "My father. I snorted my father. He was cremated and I couldn't resist grinding him up with a little bit of blow. My dad wouldn't have cared. It went down pretty well, and I'm still alive."

The comment shocked the journalist and the story instantly became a media sensation. Keith's manager responded with the statement that the anecdote had been a joke, but many feel the story is true. In the same interview, Keith was asked about his most life-threatening drug experience and mentioned an event in which, "Someone put strychnine in my dope. It was in Switzerland. I was totally comatose, but I was totally awake. I could listen to everyone, and they were like, he's dead, he's dead, waving their fingers and pushing me about. I was thinking I'm not dead." Richards remembers, "I was number one on the Who's list of people who were likely to die for 10 years. I mean, I was really disappointed when I fell off the list."

6 Kickstart My Heart

One of the most notorious party animals of the 1980s was Mötley Crüe's bassist Nikki Sixx. In 1981, Sixx founded Mötley Crüe with drummer Tommy Lee. To date, Mötley Crüe has sold over 80 million records. In the 1980s, the band gained a reputation for drugs, loud music, sex, and wild parties. They were known for backstage antics, groupies, outrageous clothing, extreme high-heeled boots, and heavily applied makeup. All the members of Mötley Crüe suffered from alcoholism and long addictions to drugs, but Sixx was the only one who abused heroin. Nikki Sixx has estimated that he overdosed on heroin "about half a dozen times."

In 1986, Nikki Sixx overdosed on heroin at a drug dealer's house in London. The dealer reportedly tried to beat the life back into Sixx with a bat

but was unsuccessful, so he dumped the body in a nearby dumpster. Sixx eventually woke up in the trash. The event was the inspiration behind the lyric "Valentine's in London, found me in the trash" from the Mötley Crüe song "Dancing on Glass."

In 1987, Mötley Crüe was part of the Guns N' Roses Appetite for Destruction Tour. During the tour, Guns N' Roses was the opening act for a number of poplar bands, including Mötley Crüe. On the night of December 23, 1987, Nikki Sixx was doing heroin in guitarist Slash's hotel room when he suffered a drug overdose. Slash was not in the room at the time, but his girlfriend called the authorities. When the paramedics arrived, Sixx was hardly breathing.

During the ride to the hospital Sixx stopped breathing and was declared dead for two minutes. The paramedics continued to apply care until he was eventually revived. Sixx claims to have had an out-of-body experience during the event. When he woke up in the hospital, Sixx ripped the tubes out of his nose and escaped into the parking lot. He hitched a ride to his house wearing just a pair of leather pants. He then continued to shoot up heroin and was found sleeping with the syringe still in his arm. Soon after the story made international news, Mötley Crüe entered rehab. In 1989, the band released the hit single "Kickstart My Heart," which was inspired by the infamous overdose.

5 Frank Zappa Attacked

Frank Zappa was an American musician who had a large impact on musical freedom. His father was Francesco Vincente Zappa, an extremely intelligent chemist and mathematician who worked with the United States defense program. Zappa grew up near the Aberdeen Proving Ground and was regularly sick as child. He suffered from extreme asthma, earaches, and sinus problems caused by mustard gas exposure. Zappa's upbringing gave him a negative stance on the use of chemical weapons. He often wrote references to germs, germ warfare, and the U.S. defense industry in his lyrics.

Frank Zappa was a great performer and his musical message was important but deemed bizarre and strange by the media. His band's debut album featured a song that asked "Who Are the Brain Police?" and in 1968 Zappa satirized the hippie culture as a motivation for money and profit. He was a charismatic personality and his music was extremely popular in some European countries. He was also highly monitored by the U.S. government.

On December 4, 1971, Frank Zappa and the Mothers of Invention were performing a concert at the Montreux Casino in Switzerland when a member of the audience decided to fire a flare gun into the rattan-covered ceiling. The casino quickly caught fire and burned to the ground. All of Zappa's equipment was lost, but he survived the fire. The event was the inspiration for the song "Smoke on the Water" by English rock band Deep Purple.

A week after the casino fire, Frank Zappa and the Mothers played at the Rainbow Theatre in London with rented gear. During the show's encore, an audience member rushed the stage and pushed Zappa into the concrete-floored orchestra pit. It was a long fall, and Zappa was nearly killed. He suffered serious fractures, head trauma, and injuries to his back, legs, and neck. He crushed his larynx, which caused his voice to drop a third after healing. Zappa was lucky to survive the event and was forced to use a wheelchair for an extended period. The assailant was a man named Trevor Howell, who told reporters that he believed Zappa was eyeing his girlfriend.

The two events had an emotional impact on Frank Zappa and he was concerned that someone was trying to murder him. After making a recovery, Zappa went on to have a successful career, but was regularly bashed by the U.S. media for his edgy lyrics. Frank Zappa is quoted as saying, "What do you make of a society that is so primitive that it clings to the belief that certain words in its language are so powerful that they could corrupt you the moment you hear them?"

In 1990, Frank Zappa was diagnosed with terminal prostate cancer and the disease killed him in 1993. For some reason, he was buried in an unmarked grave in Los Angeles. Many people have wondered why Zappa was not given a gravestone for identification. Some theories suggest a family request or evidence of mustard gas exposure Zappa experienced as a child.

4 Metallic K.O.

Iggy Pop is one of the most flamboyant performers in the history of music. He has an incredible stage presence and has given credit to Jim Morrison for introducing him to a free attitude and wild stage antics. Iggy Pop is credited with being the first performer to do a stage dive. Some of his more descriptive exploits include rolling around in broken glass, exposing himself to the crowd, and vomiting on stage. He has been known to spark riots and has the ability to whip the crowd into a frenzy.

On February 9, 1974, Pop's band the Stooges performed at Detroit's Michigan Palace. It was the band's last show together before they broke up for three decades. Before the 1974 concert, Pop gave a radio interview in which he challenged a Detroit motorbike gang, the Scorpions, to a fight. He called them all a bunch of cats. In response, the gang attended the show and pelted the band with broken glass, beer jugs, urine, eggs, ice, jelly beans, and shovels. Despite the hostility, Pop continued to taunt the crowd, saying, "You pricks can throw everything in the world…your girlfriend will still love me."

The Stooges fed off the crowd's anger and continued to perform. During the show, Pop finally told the bikers, "All right, you assholes, want to hear 'Louie, Louie,' we'll give it to you." The Stooges continued to play a 45-minute version of "Louie, Louie," which included improvised lyrics by Pop. During the song he continued to yell and verbally assault the gang.

The concert finally ended after Iggy Pop focused his attention on one particular heckler and said, "Listen, asshole, you heckle me one more time and I'm gonna come down there and kick your ass." The biker told Pop to come over, so he jumped off the stage and confronted the man. The biker beat the crap out of Pop, which ended the event. Luckily, the concert was captured on a reel-to-reel tape machine and recorded live. In 1976, the Stooges released the recording in an album titled *Metallic K.O.* It is the only rock album on which you can hear beer bottles breaking against guitar strings. The album remains a favorite among Iggy Pop fans.

3 Jim Morrison in Concert

Jim Morrison was one of the most charismatic singers in the history of rock music. He was a smart man and had a genius-level IQ of 149. Morrison was a great poet and was known for using spoken-word poetry passages during his live performances. Morrison would sing and then talk with the crowd. He was a social rebel who suffered from severe drug and alcohol abuse. Morrison had the ability to spark riots and shifted the behavior of a crowd with his intense emotional sound. For this reason, he became a target for music censorship and was closely monitored by the U.S. government. He was accompanied by police on stage at many venues.

Morrison was also known for making wild and outrageous remarks during shows. One of the most infamous cases occurred on December 9, 1967, while the Doors performed at the New Haven Arena in Connecticut. During the concert, Morrison was arrested by local police and became the first rock star to be taken off stage during a live performance. On the day in question, Morrison was discovered kissing a fan in the shower before the concert. A police officer found the couple and told them to separate, so Morrison responded, "Eat it." The policeman warned Morrison with mace saying, "Last chance," to which Morrison replied, "Last chance to eat it." In response, the officer sprayed Jim Morrison in the face with the mace.

The New Haven concert was delayed for an hour so Jim could recover, but the event made him extremely angry. During the Doors' first set, Morrison suddenly broke into an obscenity-laced tirade to the audience and explained what had happened backstage. He verbally abused the New Haven police, so they arrested him. After Morrison was taken off stage, the crowd began to riot. The violence spilled from the gates of the New Haven Arena into the streets.

Over the next couple years, Morrison's behavior became more erratic and unpredictable. On March 1, 1969, the Doors gave their most controversial performance at the Dinner Key Auditorium in Miami. During the show, Morrison began to preach messages of peace and hate. He taunted the crowd by screaming, "You're all a bunch of idiots. What are you gonna do about it?" Then he said, "Let's see a little skin, let's get naked." In response, people began to take off their clothing, including Morrison. He was later convicted of indecent exposure. He turned down a plea bargain from the Miami police, who agreed to drop the charges if the Doors performed a free concert.

The Doors gave their last public performance with Jim Morrison at the Warehouse in New Orleans on December 12, 1970. During the show, Morrison experienced a breakdown on stage and slammed the microphone numerous times into the floor until the platform beneath was destroyed. He then sat down on the ground and refused to perform for the remainder of the show. The event caused the Doors to end their live acts, citing their mutual agreement that Morrison was ready to retire from performing.

2 Keith Moon Blew Stuff Up

When Keith Moon was 17 years old, he joined the Who and replaced drummer Doug Sandom. He immediately impacted the band's sound and became known for his innovative drumming style. Along with Roger Daltrey, Pete Townshend, and John Entwistle, Moon would help the Who become one of the most popular bands of the 1960s and '70s. The group was known for explosive concerts and destructive behavior. The first such performance occurred in 1964 at the Railway Tavern in Harrow and Wealdstone, London, when Townshend accidentally broke the head of his guitar through the ceiling, so he continued to smash it on stage and the crowd loved it. More people came back the next night wanting the band to smash and break something again.

Keith Moon had no problem fitting in with the rock star lifestyle. He had an erratic personality and gained the nickname "Moon the Loon." In one famous performance, Moon filled his clear acrylic drums with water and goldfish, and dressed like a cat. He was a jokester, and his ability to make his bandmates laugh around the vocal microphone led to him being banished from the studio when albums were being recorded. In response, Moon would sneak into the studio and join in the singing. He can be heard on several tracks, including "Bell Boy," "Bucket T," and "Barbara Ann." He is the high backing vocals on "Pictures of Lily."

Keith Moon was known to demolish hotel rooms and was incredibly destructive. He would often throw furniture from high buildings and set objects on fire. However, his favorite hobby was blowing up toilets with explosives. The blasts would destroy the toilet and oftentimes disrupt plumbing to the hotel. It has been estimated that Moon's destruction of toilets and plumbing ran as high as US$500,000 (UK£300,000). He was banned from several hotel chains, including all Holiday Inn, Sheraton, and Hilton Hotels, and the Waldorf Astoria.

According to Tony Fletcher's biography, Moon was quoted as saying, "All that porcelain flying through the air was quite unforgettable." Fletcher wrote, "No toilet in a hotel or changing room was safe" until Moon had detonated his supply of explosives. In one case, hotel management asked Moon to turn down his cassette player. In response, he asked the manager up to his room and blew up the toilet right in front of him. Moon then turned the cassette player back up and said, "This is the Who."

In 1967, Keith Moon allegedly drove a Cadillac or Lincoln Continental into a Holiday Inn pool. In 1973, the Who were performing at the Cow Palace in San Francisco, and Moon passed out during the show. Townshend noticed that he was sleeping and asked the audience, "Can anyone play the drums? I mean somebody good." An audience member named Scot Halpin stepped up and finished the concert for Moon.

Ringo Starr once told Keith Moon that his lifestyle would eventually kill him. Moon simply replied, "Yeah, I know." Keith Moon died on September 7, 1978 at age 32 after he ingested 32 tablets of clomethiazole (Heminevrin). The digestion of six pills was sufficient to cause his death. The other 26 were found undissolved in his stomach. This caused some to speculate that Moon's death might have been on purpose. Officially it was ruled a drug overdose.

1 Mudshark Incident

The Edgewater is a hotel in Seattle, Washington, that is located on a pier over Elliott Bay. It is currently the only hotel in Seattle that sits over the water. In the 1960s, the Edgewater became a popular destination for famous rock stars. Some of the bands to visit the hotel include the Beatles in 1964, and the Rolling Stones, Frank Zappa, and Led Zeppelin. The Edgewater is unique because in the past it allowed customers to fish from their rooms on the north elevation.

On July 27, 1969, Led Zeppelin performed at the Seattle Pop Festival and stayed at the Edgewater. The band was known to have wild parties and was often joined by groupies. According to Zeppelin's road manager Richard Cole, during one incident, things between a fish and a sexy redhead got a bit intimate. On the day in question, Cole was in his room fishing with drummer John Bonham when they were joined by some women. Cole and Bonham had caught a large collection of sharks, at least two dozen, stuck coat hangers through the gills and then left them in the closet. The hotel room was also scattered with various types of smaller fish.

As parties go, one thing led to another and people began to lose their clothing. One particular woman in the crowd with red hair found herself with Cole. She made a unique request, so he decided to reach for a fish and the shark episode was born. Cole was later quoted as saying, "Let's see how your red snapper likes this red snapper." It was the nose of the fish and the girl liked it. There was nothing malicious or harmful, and Mark Stein of Vanilla Fudge filmed the whole thing. After the story was published by the media, a large collection of rumors began to circulate, but many were exaggerated. The band received bad press, so they stopped talking about the event.

In 1973, Led Zeppelin returned to the Edgewater and the band was officially banned from the hotel after it was discovered that they had caught some 30 mudsharks and left them under beds and in closets, elevators, hallways, bathtubs, and all over their rooms. They threw stuff out the windows into Elliott Bay, including beds, TVs, mattresses, lamps, drapes, and glassware. Since that time, Robert Plant has been welcomed back to the Edgewater. The mudshark incident remains one of the most popular rock stories from the 1960s.

TOP 10 Famous Songs with Unknown Originals

by Saint Cad

10 "Video Killed the Radio Star," Bruce Woolley & the Camera Club

This song is best (only?) known as being the first video aired on MTV. An argument can be made that this and the version by the Buggles are the same exact song since Bruce Woolley wrote it with Trevor Horn and Geoff Downes, who would later form the Buggles. However, since this was released first and has Thomas Dolby on keyboards, I'm crediting it as the original.

9 "Susie-Q," Dale Hawkins

A moderate hit for Hawkins and released just as what would eventually become Creedence Clearwater Revival was in its infancy, this became the first hit for CCR 11 years later as their first single off their first album. CCR reworked the song specifically for airplay on KMPX, an alternative radio station in San Francisco.

8 "Moon of Alabama," Lotte Lenya

I've always thought that the Doors' song "Alabama Song (Whiskey Bar)" didn't sound like their regular work, and I've found out why. The song was written in 1925 by Bertolt Brecht and set to music in 1927 by Kurt Weill, who was probably not on drugs when it was written. The song was written in English for the German operetta *Mahagonny* and was sung by Weill's wife, Lotte Lenya (who sounds a lot like Lili von Schtupp). The song was later used in the full opera *Rise and Fall of the City of Mahagonny*, being the only non-German song.

7 "The Crying Game," Dave Berry

An absolutely perfect song for its circumstances. Named for the movie that it appeared in, it could not be sung by anyone else other than Boy George. The plaintive singing sets up perfectly the mood of the film as key plot points play out. At least, this is what a lot of people think. But the song was around for almost 30 years before the movie was named after it, rather than the other way around. I'm sure you'll agree that while emotional in its own way, it has a very different feel than the more well-known 1992 version.

6 "Piece of My Heart," Emma Franklin

Let's be perfectly honest here. In the 1950s and '60s, there were many little-known R & B songs that were quickly redone in another style by a different singer that became more mainstream. You can attribute that to American society and racial views at that time, or you can use it to show the influence R & B has had on American music development. Either way, "Piece of My Heart" was fairly popular on the R & B charts but became a classic when Janis Joplin sang it a year later with her band Big Brother and the Holding Company.

5 "Twist and Shout," Top Notes

With many of these songs, the unknown original and the famous cover sound very similar and are easily identifiable as the same song. However, the original "Twist and Shout" by Top Notes sounds nothing like the cover done by the Beatles. The interesting thing is that many people think the original version, which sounds a lot like the Beatles' rendition, was by the Isley Brothers, but no: That was a reworking of the Top Notes' song as produced by Phil Spector in one of his first assignments as a record producer. The songwriter, Burt Berns, hated what Spector did with the song and gave it to the Isley Brothers to redo.

4 "Hound Dog," Big Mama Thornton

We all know that Elvis did not write his own music and that also in the 1950s, a lot of singers would sing the same songs, so it should be no surprise that he was not the first to sing "Hound Dog." The song was originally done by Big Mama Thornton and reached number one on the R & B charts, with Elvis's version coming out four years later. It would be natural to think that Elvis did a cover of Thornton's song, but that's not exactly true. Notice how some of the lyrics are different between Thornton's and Elvis's, and that some of the more famous lines seem to be missing from Thornton's version? That's because Elvis did a cover of the Freddie Bell version done in Las Vegas, in which Bell changed a few of the lyrics.

3 "Killing Me Softly with His Song," Lori Lieberman

One argument about music that everyone can take a side on is whether or not Lauryn Hill's cover of "Killing Me Softly" was better than the original version from Roberta Flack. Flack's song reached number one on the charts and took home three Grammy Awards—two for Flack and one for the song itself. This version of the song was later inducted into the Grammy Hall of Fame. Lauryn Hill's cover won a Grammy for her group the Fugees and helped the album *The Score* win a Grammy as well. It reached number two in the U.S. and number one in the UK.

But this is not the only controversy associated with the song. Lori Lieberman claims to have inspired the song based on a poem she wrote about Don McLean, but lyricist Norman Gimbel and music writer Charles Fox disagree and say that Lori talked about the song and Don McLean after they had written it.

Wait! Who?

Lori Lieberman, a Jennifer Aniston lookalike, sang the original version of the song a year before Roberta Flack catapulted it into the national consciousness. While Flack's version is soul, Lieberman's is pure early '70s folk music.

2 "Kiss," Mazarati

Besides being a music polymath, Prince is probably best known for forming bands and making pancakes. Besides his more famous girl bands, Prince (well OK, really his bassist) formed the R & B boy band Mazarati. If you're one of the four people who has ever heard of them, then you are familiar with their one hit, "100 MPH." There was another song that they wrote based on a short demo Prince gave them. They expanded the lyrics and wrote the music, and it was such a great song that Prince decided he wanted to do the song himself, so he took the song and songwriting credit. As a result, Mazarati did not release the number one and Grammy Award–winning song "Kiss" on their album. However, to be fair, the Grammy was for Prince's performance and not the song itself.

1 "Lion Sleeps Tonight," Solomon Linda & the Evening Birds

Originally done under the original title "Mbube," with the famous style of singing that was actually named for this song, it was recorded in 1939 in Johannesburg, South Africa. Starting with Pete Seeger, the song was repeatedly covered and redone. The value of the royalties alone were around $15 million. The song wasn't copyrighted because back then (unlike today) you had to actively copyright your work; but it wasn't in the public domain either, and to make things worse, Gallo Records was not interested in protecting Solomon Linda's interests. Pete Campbell—an alias for a team of producers associated with Pete Seeger and the Weavers, but not Seeger himself, who always supported Linda's rights—was in the business of claiming the copyright for older songs as his own. He did the same with the now renamed "Wimoweh," and the publishers made a mint while Linda made a pittance (even counting the ten shillings he sold the song for to Gallo), dying broke in 1962. However, under British law, all of the ownership rights went back to Linda's estate in 1987, in time to cash in (after a lawsuit of course) on its use in *The Lion King*.

TOP 10 Major Stars Who Sang Backup on Hits by Not-So-Major Artists

by **Mike Floorwalker**

10 Stevie Nicks in "Gold" by John Stewart

A former member of the Kingston Trio and author of such songs as "Daydream Believer" (among many others), Stewart was a music industry veteran who released a ton of albums and wrote many songs for artists like Anne Murray and Joan Baez. As a solo recording artist, he met with only limited success. His only top-ten hit featured a huge assist from a couple members of Fleetwood Mac (one of the biggest bands in the world at the time), including Stevie Nicks's distinctive harmony vocals.

"Gold" peaked at number five in 1979.

9 Elton John in "Bad Blood" by Neil Sedaka

John shows up on Sedaka's decidedly un-Sedaka-like 1975 hit. Known for such saccharine gems as "Breaking Up Is Hard to Do" and "Calendar Girl,"

Sedaka's career took a nosedive in the mid-'60s with the advent of the Beatles and the British Invasion. After over a decade of consistent commercial failure, he enlisted buddy Elton John to provide killer counterpoint and harmony vocals to a surprisingly cool song about a really terrible girlfriend.

With a slinky, almost funky groove and lyrics like "the bitch is in her smile," "Bad Blood" was about as radical a departure as anyone could reasonably expect Neil Sedaka to muster, and it went straight to number one in 1975.

8 Tom Petty in "Girls" by Dwight Twilley

In 1974, the Dwight Twilley Band signed their first contract with Shelter Records. By 1984, Twilley had been a professional recording artist for ten years and had scored exactly one top-20 single, "I'm On Fire" in 1975—and considering his luck, the song may have been written while Twilley was actually on fire. See, one of the only other bands signed to Shelter was fellow unknowns Tom Petty and the Heartbreakers, who would go on to have a teensy bit more success than the Twilley Band, who cashed it in after only two albums.

But Twilley pressed on as a solo artist with zero success. During the recording of his 1984 album *Jungle*, longtime friend Petty decided it was time for Dwight to get a little recognition and lent his superdistinctive croon to the chorus of what would become the record's first single, "Girls." In addition, two versions of the high-school locker room–themed video were shot, both featuring Petty—one for MTV and an R-rated version for cable channels like HBO and Playboy. The strategy worked: "Girls" reached number 16 on the Billboard Hot 100, and *Jungle* even cracked the top 40.

7 The Eagles in "Fire Lake" by Bob Seger

"Fire Lake" is a song that had a hard time coming into existence. Seger began writing it in 1971 but didn't finish until 1975. Then he planned to record it for his album *Beautiful Loser* but didn't finish that recording until 1980. When "Fire Lake" finally got to us, it was notable only for a couple reasons: It didn't sound remotely like anything else Seger had done before (he called it "an R & B meets country kind of thing"), and three of the Eagles (Don Henley, Glenn Frey, and Timothy B. Schmidt)—at the time an insanely popular band—lent their distinctive harmony vocals to the track.

6 Daryl Hall in "Original Sin" by INXS

Although little-known in the U.S., INXS's fourth album *The Swing* was very successful in their native Australia and remained on the charts for two years. The album was produced by Chic guitarist and all-around badass

Nile Rodgers, who had just produced a single called "Adult Education" for American rock/soul duo Hall and Oates. Rodgers called ace vocalist Hall out of the blue to sing backup on the chorus of the lead single off *The Swing*, "Original Sin." While Hall and Oates were cleaning up in the U.S., the guest spot did little to help sell INXS, and it wasn't until their next album, *Listen Like Thieves,* that they began to take off stateside.

5 Mick Jagger in "Glamour Boys" by Living Colour

While many hard rock fans are familiar with Living Colour, few knew then (or recall now) that Mick Jagger produced two tracks on their breakthrough album *Vivid*. Similarly, while debut single "Cult of Personality" is an enduring classic, third single "Glamour Boys"—on which Jagger sang backup is not. Which is kind of too bad, because it's a cool song with a catchy little melody, and you can barely hear the Jagger at all.

4 Michael Jackson in "Somebody's Watching Me" by Rockwell

The son of legendary Motown Records founder Berry Gordy, Rockwell still only managed one top-ten hit—and that's only because the guy singing backup had released the biggest album in the history of music just the year before. With both of those advantages, it's safe to say that he could have had a top-ten hit, but Rockwell went on to do so little that he may have actually undone some of his successes with his lack of activity. MJ also sang backup on follow-up (and top-40) single "Obscene Phone Caller"—which literally no one remembers, despite the fact that Michael Jackson sang on it in 1983.

3 Bryan Adams in "Don't Forget Me When I'm Gone" by Glass Tiger

Glass Tiger was a Canadian pop band in the early '80s whose debut album was produced by Jim Vallance, who wrote some songs with Bryan Adams. So obviously, Vallance enlisted Adams to sing a counterpoint vocal on the lead single, "Don't Forget Me When I'm Gone"—not a great name for your first single. It was a huge success and got the band some Juno Awards, which is the Canadian equivalent of a Grammy. The band went on to record a few more albums to a response of deafening silence, then disappeared. Which is to say they're gone, and despite their plea nobody remembers them.

2 Phil Collins in "I Know There's Something Going On" by Frida

Following the breakup of Swedish pop megaband Abba, female vocalist Anni-Frid Lyngstad (who goes by Frida) was divorcing from another of that group's members. So, this being 1982, she was listening to Phil Collins's "In The Air Tonight" on repeat while crying for about a year. When it came time for her to record a solo record, she enlisted Collins to assist with the production, and he sang backup on the single (and only hit) "I Know There's Something Going On." While the song was a monster worldwide smash, Frida would soon fade into relative obscurity until Abba's more recent Broadway musical-based revival, *Mama Mia*, while Collins would go on to utterly dominate the '80s as a solo artist and with band Genesis.

1 Michael McDonald in "Ride Like the Wind" by Christopher Cross

Adult contemporary vocalist Christopher Cross crossed over to the pop charts several times in the early '80s and is perhaps known best for "Arthur's Theme (Best That You Can Do)" from the Dudley Moore comedy *Arthur*. For his debut single from his debut album, Cross had a little assist from one of the most distinctive voices in all of music: hugely successful R & B singer (and then lead singer of the Doobie Brothers) Michael McDonald. Cross's debut album won a smattering of Grammys, but he never again flirted with mainstream success. McDonald rode out the '80s with a string of hits and is still a legend, particularly for his soulful, uplifting "Eyes Of A Child" from the *South Park: Bigger, Longer, and Uncut* soundtracks.

TOP 10 Rock Concerts That Were Just Messed Up

by **Ryan Thomas**

10 Vanishing Act

Pink Floyd Pig Disappears During Concert, Safely Returns

Starting off the list rather light, this concert was surely messed up (at least for one man). During Coachella 2008, Roger Waters of Pink Floyd unveiled his floating, politically charged, Obama-endorsing pig during a rendition of the Floyd song "Pigs," from the antigreed album *Animals*. Soon thereafter, the pig floated away into the night with Waters telling the crowd, "That's my pig." It obviously meant a lot to Waters, as the owners of two driveways to which the pig found its way and ultimately landed were offered a $10,000 reward. The irony of the matter is, who else could afford to offer such a large sum of money but someone directly benefited by a capitalist society? To be fair, it is a pretty great-looking pig.

9 Bird Poop

Kings of Leon Cancel Show Due to Inclement Bird Droppings

On July 23, 2010, at the Verizon Amphitheater in St. Louis, Missouri, the

Kings of Leon had to cancel their show due to an intolerable torrential downpour—not of rain, but of bird poop. And try as they did to trudge on, bassist Jared Followill threw in the towel after he claims some droppings found their way into his mouth. He said, "I was hit by pigeons on each of the first three songs. We had 20 songs on the set list. By the end of the show, I would have been covered from head to toe." While concert-goers were reimbursed, it seems this kind of unforeseeable circumstance was rather unprecedented.

8 Stage Collapse

Big Valley Jamboree Stage Collapses

In August 2009, during a Canadian country music festival called Big Valley Jamboree, a gust of wind blew down the main stage, like the Big Bad Wolf were merely blowing down a house of sticks. The result was one death by a falling speaker and upward of 60 injuries, as well as a handful of lawsuits against contractors who failed to ensure a proper level of safety. What's most surprising is how few people were actually killed given how dramatic and terrifying the whole scene was, at least according to the video footage. Concert-goers were fast to flee at the first signs of collapse only to rush back in to assist any possible victims.

7 Hells Angels

Hells Angels Do Security Detail for Rolling Stones, Goes Awry for Some Reason

The date is December 6, 1968. The place, Altamont Speedway Free Festival, which featured, along with the Rolling Stones, some Woodstock notables. However, the show turned nasty in the middle of the Stones' performance of "Under My Thumb." Hired as a form of rudimentary security and paid with $500 worth of beer, the Hells Angels got into a scuffle with one individual who attempted to rush the stage. The Angels saw to it, through the use of violence, that he didn't get very far, and when the man—while high on meth at the time—went to pull out a revolver, they stabbed and stomped him to death. Other incidental deaths and property damage took place, but nothing was quite as gruesome as this scene. Meanwhile, on stage, the Stones finished up their set as if nothing had happened. The Grateful Dead, however, scheduled to perform right after them, decided to pull out.

6 Murder Onstage

"Dimebag" Darryl Murdered Onstage by Deranged Concert-Goer

"Dimebag" Darryl Abbott, cofounding guitarist of the now-split-up heavy metal band Pantera, was performing with his new band Damageplan on December 8, 2004, in Columbus, Ohio. During the show, a member of the audience leapt onstage, gun in hand, and shot Abbott three times in the head, the third immediately fatal. This individual, who from written accounts appeared to believe from their lyrics that the members of Pantera could read his mind and were laughing at him, continued firing, killing three more people (including the band's head of security, who had leapt on the assailant) and wounding seven more, as he had brought an ample supply of ammunition for the occasion. Ultimately, he was subdued by a shotgun blast to the face after cops rushed in.

5 Brain-Dead

Korn Concert Attendee Beaten Brain-Dead

On the Atlanta, Georgia, date of Korn's 2006 Family Values Tour, a man asked some excessively drunk moshers to be careful around his pregnant girlfriend (as a well as a mentally impaired child who was with them), only to be slammed headfirst onto concrete and left unconscious and bloody. While declared dead (being effectively brain-dead and on life support to preserve organs for donation), police launched a full-on homicide investigation, as they deemed the incident a proper murder.

4 Sexual Assault

Death, Destruction, and Sexual Assault at Woodstock '99

The return of Woodstock led countless baby boomers to believe their day had come once more, as they had flashbacks deep in their spinal cords to the days of peace, love, and understanding...and being trampled to death? Out were the love-promoting sounds of Jefferson Airplane and the Mamas and the Papas, in was the fear and hatred of Nine Inch Nails, Limp Bizkit, Korn, and Bush. Especially during Limp Bizkit's set, utter chaos ensued. During the song "Break Stuff," people did just that, and it was reported that a bodysurfing woman had been gang-raped. Aside from myriad counts of sexual assault and rapists running free, bonfires, unrestrained carnage, and humans being trampled to death ensued, as if the stage for the apocalypse had a distinct grunge and nu-metal tinge.

3 Crushed to Death

Pearl Jam Concert-Goers Crushed to Death

On June 30, 2000, at the Roskilde rock and dance festival in Denmark, several fans slipped on the muddy earth only to be steamrolled by an overzealous mob. About 8 or 9 died, while 26 more were injured by the human avalanche. Upon hearing of this, Pearl Jam stopped their set abruptly and the Cure, scheduled to follow, canceled as well.

2 Crushed Again

Who Fans Crushed, Unable to See Show

In December of 1979, the Who played the Riverfront Coliseum in Cincinnati, Ohio, to fans who were way too eager to get in the door. While general admission seating was on a first-come, first-serve basis, several fans rushed the doors (which were closed to prevent concert stowaways) as they mistook a sound check for the beginning of the show. As layers of humans compressed before the hermetically sealed entrances, so did the lungs of those who were trampled beneath the impending stampede. Eleven fans were literally dying to see the show; many others were injured.

1 Misfire

Great White Pyrotechnics Misfire, Fans Suffer

Great White is a prototypical '80s trash rock band, with the hair and stage theatrics to match. Unfortunately on one night back in 2003, their insistence upon flashy visuals ended in panic and horror at Station Nightclub in West Warwick, Rhode Island. A fire was caused by some unruly—not to mention indoor—pyrotechnics that ignited the highly flammable sound insulation that enveloped the place. With blocked exits, thick smoke, and a veritable hellfire, 100 people died, while 230 more were injured. In spite of one of Great White's comeback venues becoming a literal deathtrap, the band presses on, releasing albums and touring as if it never happened.

TOP 10 Unpleasant Facts about John Lennon

by **Edward Benjamin**

10 Wife-Beater

There's simply no way of disputing this: The revered icon of peace and love had a serious problem with violence against women. This has been documented all the way back to Lennon's Liverpool days, and he eventually admitted it himself later in life. His first wife, Cynthia, and his second, Yoko Ono, were both victims of Lennon's brutality at one point or another, and given that most men who beat their spouses or girlfriends regularly are not particularly discriminating about the object of their violence, it's frankly impossible that they were the only ones. It seems clear in hindsight that the gentle icon the hippies worship was actually a man with very serious psychological problems who often flew into uncontrollable fits of rage that he took out on the women in his life.

9 Emotionally Abused His Son

Without question, the greatest victim of Lennon's character failings was his oldest son, Julian. Lennon clearly resented the young boy, whose conception had forced Lennon into a marriage he didn't want and trapped him in a domestic routine he was too immature and narcissistic to sustain. Both Julian and his mother, Cynthia, have publicly stated that Lennon was alternately absent, indifferent, drug-addled, and generally unpleasant to be around during Julian's early childhood. After he divorced Cynthia, Lennon took off with Yoko Ono and dropped out of his son's life for years. After they reconnected, Lennon severely emotionally abused his son on several occasions, berating and screaming at him until the boy was reduced to tears. Once, Julian giggled and Lennon shouted back, "I hate the way you fucking laugh!" Julian was not yet a teenager at the time. In perhaps the saddest statement ever made about Lennon, Julian later stated that Paul McCartney was more of a father to him than his real father was.

8 Pathological Liar

Put simply, John Lennon made up his own life—exaggerating, embellishing, and outright lying when it suited him. Usually, he did so out of pure egomania, a desire to make himself appear better than he actually was. Everyone does this to some extent, but in Lennon's case, he rewrote almost every major event in his life to suit his tastes. He claimed he had been a working class lad from Liverpool before the Beatles; he was actually raised in a comfortable middle-class home. He denied being married during his early years of stardom. He claimed to have met Yoko Ono at an art show and that their love blossomed spontaneously; in fact, Ono had stalked him for months before he gave in to her advances. He claimed to have lost interest in the Beatles due to Paul McCartney's tendencies toward pop music and his dominant role in the group, as well as Lennon's desire to do his more avant-garde work outside the band; in fact, he had all but left the band in its last two years as the result of a serious addiction to heroin. When Lennon emerged back into the public eye shortly before his death, he claimed that he had been spending time baking bread and being a stay-at-home dad; in fact, he had been living in a drug-induced haze most of the time. The truth in all of these cases was embarrassing, but no more than the kind of behavior many rock stars acknowledged engaging in during the 1960s and '70s; Lennon compulsively lied about it anyway.

7 Broke Up the Beatles

Contrary to later tales of a spontaneous break and/or the decision by Paul McCartney to leave the band, it was John Lennon who destroyed the Beatles. Certainly, all was not well with the band during the final years of the 1960s, but it was Lennon and Lennon alone who brought down the axe, announcing at an otherwise routine meeting that he was leaving the group. It was kept under wraps for some time, but no one was under any illusions about the ability of the group to go on without him. Essentially, Lennon's departure made the death of the Beatles inevitable; it just took a year or so for the obituary to be written.

6 Politically Clueless

People tend to see Lennon as some sort of divine guru of peace and love because of his political activities in the early 1970s. The truth is that most of Lennon's reputation as a political activist is based on photos of him with various '60s radicals and his own press statements. He never actually did anything whatsoever of note in the political realm, and most of the radicals he cultivated thought he was an ignorant poseur. The few things he did actually do, like giving money and publicity to violent groups like the Black Panthers, are nothing to be proud of.

5 Talentless

This is probably the most controversial item on this list, and it must be admitted that it is an inherently subjective issue, but a very good case can be made that even as a musician and a songwriter, Lennon was remarkably undertalented. First, he was at best an average guitar player, mostly confined to basic rhythm parts, and his piano playing wasn't much better. As for his songwriting, yes he did write a handful of truly inspired songs, but as time passes and the nostalgic hype surrounding the Beatles begins to fade, a lot of his work comes off as silly and dated. Try reading the lyrics to "Strawberry Fields Forever" or "Come Together" sometime. They're pure hippie psychedelic babbling, the kind of thing that passed for profundity in the drug-induced haze of the late 1960s. The only thing that makes them work is the terrific production, for which credit easily goes to producer George Martin and the other Beatles as much as to Lennon himself.

In fact, looking back on the Beatles' legacy, one can make a pretty good case that both Paul McCartney and George Harrison (on the later albums, at least) were superior talents to Lennon in the songwriting department. The truth is, after about 1965, Lennon more or less dropped out of the Beatles. He had almost nothing to do with the *Sgt. Pepper* album, and most of what came after was—by everyone's admission—largely at the behest of Paul McCartney. By the end, as you can see in the film *Let It Be*, McCartney was desperately trying to motivate a Lennon who simply didn't want to be there. As for Lennon's solo career, there are five or six memorable songs and the rest...well, can you name a single track from *Sometime in New York City*?

4 Follower Not a Leader

This is true of pretty much all the Beatles, but with Lennon it's particularly obvious. In the beginning he was following the American rhythm and blues tradition with a smattering of Roy Orbison–style pop ballads. Later he's obviously trying to channel Bob Dylan. Then he's aping the psychedelic stylings of the California drug bands. After that, he gloms on to avant-garde, John Cage–influenced modern art music. Truth be told, there wasn't much Lennon did that hadn't been done before by more original and talented artists.

3 Mindless Conformist

Despite his reputation as a freethinker following his own path, Lennon was an obvious case of someone desperate to fit in. Yes, he was trying to fit in with groups that were considered nonconformist, but conformism is conformism. Right from the beginning, Lennon was posing. Back in the day, the teddy-boy look was the in thing, so he showed up in leather jackets and a pompadour. Then it was the cute pop look. Then the psychedelic hippie thing. Then the angry avant-garde hipster. It never ends. Everything about

Lennon, from his music and politics to the way he dressed, was an attempt to fit in with sub- or countercultures that already existed.

2 Desperate for Money and Fame

As much he liked to pretend to be a misunderstood artist following his own uncompromising vision, the truth is that Lennon pursued fame and fortune from the beginning. Even in the early days when the Beatles were a struggling bar band, he used to extol them by saying they would go "to the topper most of the popper most." He happily went along with the Beatles' haircuts, suits, and calculated image, as well as the band's innumerable media appearances, only denouncing it all as shallow and empty later in life when he was cultivating an avant-garde reputation. His relentless antics with Yoko Ono in the early '70s now seem to be such a blatant plea for attention that one wonders how anyone took them seriously back then. And of course, he never turned down any of the fat paychecks that came his way as a result of his fame and success.

1 Hypocrite

This is the toughest one and the hardest to say in public, mainly because Lennon's murderer cited it as his primary motive, but that doesn't make it any less true: Lennon was a perfect example of someone who lived by the hypocritical dictum of "do as I say, not as I do." As his critics sometimes point out, all you have to do is go straight to his songs. The man who sang "imagine no possessions" lived a millionaire's life in a posh New York hotel. The man who sang "imagine no religion" was obsessed with every spiritual and New Age fad that came his way, including Hindu meditation, the I-Ching, and astrology of all kinds. The man who sang "all you need is love" was a bitter, violent, and angry man who abused his family and friends. The man who praised having "nothing to kill or die for" helped finance and publicize radical groups who extolled the use of violence. Quite literally, everything his fans see personified in the icon of John Lennon are ideals the man himself either couldn't or wouldn't live up to.

CHAPTER 9

CULTURE

TOP 10 Books That Prove the Victorians Were Kinky

by **Nene Adams**

1 The Pearl, William Lazenby, 1879–1880

This first entry is a slight cheat: *The Pearl* was not actually a book, but a magazine published briefly in 18 volumes and two Christmas annuals until the publishers were threatened with prosecution for distributing obscene literature.

The Pearl contained pornographic stories. Many were serialized and included such classics as "Lady Pokingham or They All Do It" and "Sub-Umbra or Sport Among the She-Noodles"—plus dirty jokes, limericks, and humorous song and poem parodies. The magazine's primary focus was humor; the stories were often satirical in nature, though still very explicit.

9 The Romance of Lust, Anonymous, 1873–1876

This verbose, first-person narrative follows the fictional Charlie Roberts from his young sexual awakening all through his maturation and development. *The Romance of Lust* is noted for the perversity of the acts it portrays, which include orgies and incest.

8 The Sins of the Cities of the Plain, 1881

Also known as *The Recollections of a Maryanne*, *The Sins of the Cities of the Plain* is a pioneering work of gay erotic fiction chronicling the experiences of a rent-boy—a "Maryanne" (19th-century slang for a homosexual). Some of the characters are drawn from actual people, such as the transvestites Ernest Boulton and Frederick Park. The author's name, Jack Saul, is certainly a pseudonym, and while the author is unknown, it has been suggested to be the work of Simeon Solomon and James Campbell Reddie. Intimate encounters include cross-dressing and orgies.

This book gives a fascinating glimpse into the hidden world of upper- and lower-class gay Victorians.

7 The Nunnery Tales, Anonymous, 1866

This book is also known as *Cruising Under False Colors, A Tale of Love and Lust*. It features plenty of sacrilege-flavored action, with bawdy nuns and salacious priests among the fictional characters. It also includes raunchy humor, possibly exaggerated explicit intimacy, and lesbian encounters (no surprise, as the story takes place in a convent), erotic flagellation and spankings, group encounters, incest, and a little cross-dressing.

Interestingly, it may have been adapted from a much older 17th-century French work and has been reprinted often.

6 Venus in Furs, Ritter von Leopold Sacher-Masoch, 1870

This famous erotic and somewhat autobiographical work is actually the origin of the term "masochism" (for those who wonder, we can thank the Marquis de Sade for "sadism"). The protagonist, Severin, is infatuated with a beautiful woman and offers himself as her slave. Obsessed with his total submission to her, he urges the woman, Wanda, to humiliate and degrade him more and more cruelly as the story goes on. The book is focused on fetish and S&M, and remains very popular.

It's more of a literary drama than the usual explicit offering. Roman Polanski adopted *Venus in Furs* for the silver screen in 2012.

5 The Autobiography of a Flea, Anonymous, 1887 or 1888

This is a work of social satire with a wafer-thin plot containing many erotic scenes as witnessed by a flea (hitching a ride on a young woman) traveling from home to home and peeping at the sexual activ-ities of the residents. What does the flea see? Quite a lot, including explicit intimacy, group encounters, lusty priests, seduction of the innocent, deflowering, incest, corporal punishment, and bukkake. Many of the characters are caricature types that would have been recognized by 19th-century readers.

4 The Lustful Turk, Anonymous, 1828

Another slight cheat since this one's pre-Victorian, but the popular and notorious novel remained in print even into the 20th century. Given the 19th-century appetite for exotic places and cultures (and more than a touch of xenophobia), *The Lustful Turk* satisfied readers on several levels. An English lady writes letters to her friends back home about her capture by Turks and forcible ravishment, after which she wholeheartedly embraces a variety of explicit, erotic encounters with men and women in the Sultan's harem. The book is so popular it was even made into a sexploitation film in 1968.

3 The Mysteries of Verbena House, Etonensius, 1881

Also know as *Miss Bellasis Birched for Thieving*, this book is one of the classics of Victorian erotica, showcasing the 19th-century fascination with discipline. It was first published in two volumes with illustrations. When naughtiness, like theft, ensues at a fashionable girls' boarding school, the wishy-washy headmistress calls in a stern male disciplinarian to oversee the lovingly described chastisements and intimate encounters of students and staff. Applications of punishment effect positive changes to everyone's morality and character. The authorship of *Verbena House* has been in dispute for over a century.

2 The Whippingham Papers, St. George Stock, 1887

The most notable detail of this book is the flagellation-themed poetry of Algernon Charles Swinbure. All the stories and other poems in the volume deal with the so-called "English vice." A small sample of Swinburne's unsigned work is included here:

- How those great big red ridges must smart as they swell!
- How the Master does like to flog Algernon well!
- How each cut makes the blood come in thin little streaks
- From that broad blushing round pair of naked red cheeks.

Possibly due to the prevalence of harsh corporal punishment at school and at home, many Victorian gentlemen enjoyed reading about the birch and the cane (and paying for similar treatment in popular flagellation brothels).

1 Gynecocracy, attributed to "Viscount Ladywood," 1893

This is a fine example of the so-called "petticoat governance books." While Englishmen may have been lords and masters of their homes and families, it's clear from the popularity of this type of novel that many had secret submissive longings. This particular example features lots of incidents in which a young man is forced to wear women's clothes, including a corset, and serve very dominant females' whims as a young woman. The narrative includes explicit encounters with women and men, humiliation, bondage, discipline, a drag king, and some imaginative corporal punishments.

TOP 10 Fascinating Typographical Origins

by **Andy Martin**

10 The Pilcrow — ¶

The pilcrow, also less elegantly called the "paragraph mark," serves a number of purposes, most of which involve denoting the presence or location of a paragraph in one way or another. Most commonly, it's used in word processing programs to indicate a "carriage return" "control character"; that is to say, a non-permanent mark showing where a paragraph ends. There is disagreement over the origin of the name; *The Oxford English Dictionary*, for one, likes to think it comes from a string of corruptions of the word "paragraph." *The Oxford Universal Dictionary*, on the other hand, suggests that the sign itself looks a lot like a featherless crow—a "pulled crow." The symbol itself derives from the letter "c," which stood for the Latin *capitulum*, or "chapter." The two lines that ended up vertically crossing the C were a sort of editorial note from the writer.

The pilcrow was used in the Middle Ages, in an earlier form, as a way of marking a new train of thought before the paragraph became the standard way of accomplishing this. Now, its myriad uses include academic writing (when citing from an HTML page), legal texts (when citing a specific paragraph), and in proofreading (an indication that a paragraph should be split in two).

9 The Ampersand — &

The ampersand is a logogram used to mean "and." The symbol itself is based on a shorthand version of the Latin word for "and"—*et*—and in certain fonts, you can still clearly see an "e" and a "t" linked together (Adobe Caslon, for instance). The word "ampersand" has a somewhat unusual origin—it's a corruption of the hard-to-parse, multilingual (English and Latin) phrase "& per se and," which means "&" by itself is "and." Confused? Don't worry—that's only natural. All it means is, the symbol &, all by its little self, simply means and. And where did this phrase come from? Well, in the early 1800s, & was considered the 27th letter of the English alphabet, and since saying "x, y, z, and" would be confusing, "and per se and" was said instead. It doesn't take a major stretch of the imagination to fathom how this could quickly turn into "ampersand," which it did by around 1837.

Because people like to make up urban legends based on everything, including stodgy old typographical marks, there's a vicious rumor floating around that French physicist and mathematician André-Marie Ampère used the mark so much that it eventually got called "Ampere's and." Don't believe it for a second. In the end, we're left with a pretty little symbol that has more than a few variants.

8 Interrobang — !?, ?!, or ‽

What?! You've never heard of the interrobang!? Really? Well, now you have, so all is forgiven. An interrobang is described as a "nonstandard punctuation mark" (it's part of the punctuation counterculture), used to end sentences where you really want both the exclamation point and the question mark. While the use of both marks side by side had been prevalent for some time, it wasn't until 1962 when an advertising executive named Martin K. Speckter decided that enough was enough—no longer would he withstand the tyranny of two separate punctuation marks when one would suffice. He asked readers to suggest names, rejecting such fine ideas as "rhet," "exclarotive," and "exclamaquest," and ultimately settled upon "interrobang," a combination of the Latin root *interro* (think "interrogate"), and "bang," which is printer's slang for the exclamation mark. The word is used to describe both the two side by side (!? or ?!) or the combined symbol (‽).

7 At Sign — @

What we know as @ has a lot of different monikers—including "at sign," "at symbol," "ampersat," and "apetail"—but it is unusual in that it doesn't have a widely accepted name in English. In Spanish, it is known as an *arroba*, and in French the *arobase*. The symbol @ has two primary usages—its original one, used in commerce to mean "at the rate of," and more recently, "directed at" (primarily in e-mail and in social media like Twitter). It has been claimed by Italian professor Giorgio Stabile that the symbol is actually over 500 years old, to represent an "amphora"—a unit of capacity used in commerce. It first made its way onto a typewriter as early as 1885 and has since found its way into our hearts.

A couple of fun facts:
- The Spanish *arroba* was a unit of weight equivalent to 25 pounds.
- The names for @ in other languages often derive from the idea that it looks like an animal. To wit: *apenstaartje* (Dutch for "monkey's tail"); *papacy* (Greek for "little duck"); *dalphaengi* (Korean for "snail"); *sobachka* (Russian for "little dog").

6 Guillemets — « »

Guillemets are what the French use instead of quotation marks. In addition to the physical differences, the usage differs as well—generally, guillemets open and close entire conversations or exchanges rather than individual utterances. Amusingly, the guillemet is named after a French printer named Guillaume Le Bé from the 16th century; "Guillemet" is a diminutive of "Guillaume."

5 Obelus — ÷

The obelus, more commonly known as "the division sign," comes from an ancient Greek word for a sharpened stick or other similar pointy object. It shares its roots with the word "obelisk." The obelus was once used to denote sections of writing that were considered incorrect or suspicious; in other words, it would have been perfect for Wikipedia editors. It was first used to mean "division" in 1659 by Swiss mathematician Johann Rahn. While still used frequently in the U.S. and in Britain, it is not commonly used to mean division in most of the rest of the world.

4 Inverted ? and ! — ¿ and ¡

In Spanish, when a sentence ends with a question mark or an exclamation point, it also starts with an inverted one. *¿Porque?* In 1754, the Spanish Royal Academy decided that the Spanish language had a dire problem: When you start reading a sentence, you often have no way of telling if it's a question or not until you get to the very end.

Consider the sentence *Vas a ir a la tienda?* (Are you going to go to the store?). Up until you get to the question mark, you are totally in the dark— is it a question, or simply a declarative sentence stating, "You are going to go to the store"? In English, we have ways of indicating that a question is coming, so that proper inflection can be used, as well as to help with comprehension. In Spanish, you used to need contextual clues to help you out before the Royal Academy had its way. They also decided that the exclamation point would be lonely, so they advocated for its inverted use as well.

Though the language was slow to adopt this new convention, it is now a fully integrated part of the language. A few interesting usage notes:

- Short, unambiguous questions are often written without the inverted mark—*Quien eres?*
- In digital communication (e-mails, instant messages, text messages), the inverted mark is frequently left off.
- Some authors refuse to use inverted marks.
- Writers can get playful with the marks, including starting a sentence with a ¡ and ending it with a ?
- ¿ can be used in the middle of a sentence if the whole sentence is not a question, but rather the final clause.

- Note that ¿ and ¡ are positioned differently from ? and !; they hang below the line.

3 Ditto Mark—"

Ditto marks are those quotation-looking guys you use to save your tired wrist from a few more seconds of writing, indicating that what's directly above should be repeated. Though one might suspect that the word "ditto" may have been related to the Latin root *di* (meaning "two," as in when you say "ditto" you mean "me too!"), it in fact derives from an early (c. 1620) form of the Italian word for "to say." Originally, it was used to avoid needless repetition when writing a series of dates in the same month.

A "ditto mark" is a type of "iteration mark." Other languages have their own, notably Chinese, Japanese, and ancient Egyptian.

2 Percent Sign—%

Take a look at the percent sign. Look at each of the three individual marks—a circle, a line, a circle. Remind you of anything? Does it, perhaps, remind you of a certain number, with the digits rearranged and realigned? A very important number? Maybe...the number 100?

The % sign, of course, means that the preceding number should be understood as being divided by 100—"per cent." The slash mark used to be straight across, with zeroes above and beneath, but it gradually became slanted—leading to what D. E. Smith, in 1925, called the "solidus form" of the percent sign. The solidus, aka slash, virgule, fraction bar, and other names, is this sign: /.

Because there is disagreement about everything, there is disagreement over whether there should be a space between the number and the % sign, over whether it should be "per cent" or "percent," and when you should use the % symbol and when you should instead write out the word.

1 Upper Case and Lower Case Letters

In the early days of printing, when each letter was set individually, the letters were kept in cases. The capital letters were kept in—you guessed it—the "upper case," less convenient to the printer because of how relatively few capital letters are used, while the lower case letters were kept in the more accessible—wait for it—"lower case." It's as simple as that, really. This usage of the terms dates back to 1588.

Fun facts about cases:
- The use of two cases in a written language is called "bicameral script." Languages with only one case are called "unicase."

- So what were lower-case letters called before they used cases at all? Well, we have other words to describe them. Upper-case letters are called majuscules (and, of course, capitals), and lower-case letters are called minuscule. Note the spelling difference with the word "miniscule."

TOP 10 Everyday Words with Unexpected Origins

by **Andrew Handley**

10 Blatant

What it means now: Completely lacking in subtlety; very obvious.
What it used to mean: A thousand-tongued beast from hell.
In the 1600s, the British began using the word "blatant" as a way to describe people who were vulgar and noisy. Granted, that's not a major change from the present day definition, but before 1596, "blatant" wasn't even a word; it was invented by Edmund Spenser in his fantasy story *The Faerie Queen* to describe a monster from hell, a giant beast with a thousand tongues—the Blatant Beast.

The Faerie Queen was essentially a long, drawn-out allegory for 16th-century English religion, and each character symbolized either a person or ideal in the real world. The Faerie Queen, for example, was Queen Elizabeth I. The Blatant Beast represented slander and wickedness, and as the story became popular, people began using the idea of the Blatant Beast as an insult to people who were too loud. It would be like calling a person who's obnoxiously silly today a "Spongebob." Eventually, "blatant" lost the negative connotations of "vulgarity" and just became a synonym for "obvious."

9 Geek

What it means now: An unfashionable or socially inept person, or someone with an eccentric devotion to a particular interest (like a computer geek).
What it used to mean: A circus sideshow freak.
We all know what a geek is nowadays; the Internet's covered in them. Aside from the whole socially inept stereotype, geeks are also usually seen as pretty smart, even if that intelligence manifests as an encyclopedic knowledge of which enhancement gems give more agility to a Feral Druid in *World of Warcraft*, or something like that.

But originally, the word meant something completely different: a circus sideshow freak. As recent as the early 1900s, traveling circuses would display what they called "geek shows," featuring either performers with some utterly bizarre ability or feature (the Bearded Lady, Pretzel Man, etc.), or a performance in which something bizarre happened. Usually, that meant a person eating something disgusting, like biting the heads off live chickens.

And as a further departure from the intelligent geeks of today, it's believed that the word "geek" in those shows came from the old German word *geck*, which was basically a stupid person.

8 Hazard

What it means now: A danger or risk.
What it used to mean: A gambling game played with dice.

In the 14th century, Geoffrey Chaucer wrote *The Canterbury Tales*, one part of which describes young men playing a dice game called Hazard. This was a fairly popular game of chance in France at that time, in which one person rolls a die while onlookers place bets on how a series of rolls will turn out. The rules were complicated to say the least. Try to make sense of this:

> The caster begins by throwing the dice to determine the Main Point. This must be a score between 5 and 9. Now the caster throws the dice again. If the score is the same as the Main Point, this is known as a nick and the caster wins. If a 2 or 3 was rolled, that's an out and the caster loses. 11 and 12 are also outs, except in certain cases: a roll of 11 after a Main Point of 7 is a nick, and so is a roll of 12 after a Main Point of 6 or 8."

Over time, the negative image of gambling led to the name of that particular game, Hazard, being used to describe any type of chance game, such as, "He's off playing hazards again." Over about 200 years, the word further evolved to mean any kind of risk. Interestingly, the game stuck around in a sense—Craps is a simplified version of Hazard.

7 Ostracize

What it means now: To exclude someone from a society or group.
What it used to mean: A government procedure to literally ban someone from Athens for ten years.

The Athenian Democracy was incredibly influential from 550 BC to around 320 BC. They practically created the model by which many other Greek city-states built their own democratic governments. Nevertheless, they had a few customs that might seem strange to us today. One of those was the ostracism. Every year, Athenian citizens were given the chance to vote for any person to be banned from the city-state for a decade. There was no specific list of people they could choose from; they could vote to ostracize a criminal just as easily as they could vote to get rid of their brother (although usually a political figure was chosen).

As long as at least 6,000 people voted, whoever received the most votes was given ten days to leave. If they returned before the ten-year period was over, they were put to death. But they wouldn't return penniless—their possessions and status would all be restored. It would be like they never left.

Archaeologists have discovered something close to 12,000 *ostraka*, the pottery shards used for writing the votes. Out of those, nearly 5,000 are votes for a man named Megacles. Talk about unpopular.

6 Toxic

What it means now: Poisonous.
What it used to mean: Greek archery.
In ancient Greek, the word *toxon* means "bow," as well as "the arrows shot from the bow," and really just archery in general. The Greeks later added to that, creating the word *toxicus*, which means "poison for use on arrows." *Toxicus* made its way through Latin, then French, and finally English, ending up as the word we use today, "toxic." The unusual combination of poison and bows, however, started with Hercules.

In the story of Hercules, the mythical hero had to face 12 Labors, or challenges. The second challenge he faced was the Hydra, a serpent with nine heads and poisonous blood. The Hydra was seemingly invincible—chopping off one of its heads only caused it to grow two more heads in that spot. Hercules eventually defeated it by cauterizing each neck with a torch after slicing off a head. Then, after removing the Hydra's final head, Hercules dipped his arrow tips in the blood—he "made his *toxons* poisonous."

5 Villain

What it means now: A person guilty or capable of a crime or wickedness.
What it used to mean: A farm worker.
Everyone is familiar with villains. Thanks to over half a century of movies, we all know that the villain is the bad guy. Back in the 14th century though, villains were the backbone of agriculture. That is to say, they were the guys who worked on farms. The word "villain" is actually an old French word that pulls its roots from the word *villa*, Latin for "country house."

Over time, the meaning of the word gradually changed: Farm workers were poor, practically peasants. Peasants, being poor, are untrustworthy. Untrustworthy people commit crimes. And eventually we ended up with the modern-day definition of "villain," which is a rich person who gets killed by James Bond.

4 Poop

What it means now: Well, you know.
What it used to mean: An abrupt sound from a wind instrument.
The word "poop" means quite a few things, all of them completely different. In nautical terms, the poop is the stern deck of a ship, a phrase that came about in the 1700s. As a verb, the word "poop" was originally used in the 1500s to describe a short blast of sound from a wind instrument, such as a horn. By the 1700s, the sound of a "short blast of wind" had already begun to be associated with something else that involved gas moving through pipes.

From there, it was only a matter of time until it reached its modern-day definition. At first it was a term used by children, then "poop" slowly seeped into modern culture, and by the turn of the 20th century, it was a household word—about the same time indoor plumbing became commonplace, as a matter of fact.

3 Quarrel

What it means now: An angry argument or disagreement.
What it used to mean: A square-headed crossbow bolt.
Technically, no one really uses the word "quarrel" on a day-to-day basis. "Argument" works just as well. That said, it's still a universally known word in the English language. "Quarrel" usually means something like a verbal shouting match, but it can also mean a long-standing dispute between two people, such as an old quarrel between families that goes back for generations. That definition was widely used during the 15th century.

Go back to the 13th century, though, and "quarrel" is a special type of arrowhead on a crossbow bolt; it is four sided, and the name stems from the Latin word *quadrus*. "Quarrel" also became the word used for a square pane of glass, again coming from the Latin root for "four." There's no indication of how "quarrel" went from describing a crossbow bolt to becoming the word for an argument, but we'd like to think it's because arguments were resolved with crossbow fights during the Middle Ages.

2 Swastika

What it means now: The symbol of the Nazi Party and the Third Reich.
What it used to mean: Well-being and good luck.
Well before Hitler plastered a swastika on every flag and military uniform in Germany in the 1930s, the symbol had already been around for nearly 3,000 years. The oldest known record of the use of the swastika comes from pieces of pottery dated to ancient Troy circa 1000 BC. The word itself comes from the word *svastika* in the Sanskrit language, which translates to "being fortunate." As Sanskrit originated in the Indo-Aryan region, especially around India, it's no surprise that swastikas appear heavily in Buddhist and Hindu symbolism. To Buddhists, the swastika represents eternity; Hindus use a swastika to represent the god Ganesha.

When Hitler commandeered the swastika for his own purposes, he was attracted to its Indo-Aryan significance, claiming that it represented the "mission of the struggle for the victory of the Aryan race."

1 Sabotage

What it means now: To deliberately destroy, damage, or obstruct.
What it used to mean: To walk noisily wearing wooden shoes.
In 13th-century France, wooden shoes were unfashionable. These wooden shoes, called *sabots*, were worn by lower-class citizens because they were

cheaper than leather shoes. Now, if you've ever tried to walk more than a few steps in a wooden shoe, you know it's difficult, clumsy, and noisy. The French noticed that fact as well, and came up with a word to describe it: *saboter*, meaning "to walk noisily wearing *sabots*."

Eventually, *saboter* changed to "sabotage" and the meaning we know today, but the jump from "noisy walking" to "deliberate destruction" comes with a fun story: When French workers went on strike, they would angrily hurl their wooden shoes into the factory machinery, damaging them beyond repair. Thus wooden shoes became a symbol of destruction.

Unfortunately, that story hasn't been verified, and most etymologists think that the modern meaning came about through a comparatively boring story: Wooden shoes make you clumsy, and so *saboter* became known as any sort of bungle, like getting the words wrong in a speech and completely bungling the whole thing. By 1910, *saboter* had further progressed to malicious bungling, and the word was changed to "sabotage."

TOP 10 Mind-Blowing Stage and Circus Acts

by **Nene Adams**

10 Mazeppa

In 1864, Adah Isaacs Menken—an indifferent actress—rode into fame playing the title role in *Mazeppa and the Wild Horses of Tartary*, one of the equestrian plays popular at the time. While the plot is a fairly standard romance, the horseback exploits of Menken's heroine sold out box offices around the globe.

Actually, the flesh-colored, full-body stocking she wore to simulate nudity while being bound to the back of her horse caused a sensation, which drew in gaping crowds all over Europe and America. Among her fans were Mark Twain, Charles Dickens, and Bret Harte. I doubt it was her talent they admired.

9 Scott, the Celebrated Diver

When Samuel Gilbert Scott made a spectacular headfirst dive from a cliff near Niagara Falls, his reputation as a daredevil performer was secure. He dove from bridges, ships' masts, and other structures, delighting the crowds who flocked to see him. In 1841, he issued a challenge to the public, saying he would run from a Drury Lane pub to Waterloo Bridge, dive 40 feet into the Thames, and return to the pub in one hour. The audience couldn't wait.

On the appointed day, Scott reached the bridge in good time and climbed the previously erected scaffold. Putting a rope around his neck, he dangled in mid-air as usual, performing acrobatic stunts to warm up. Suddenly, the rope slipped. He hung there for several minutes before audience members realized he was in trouble—too late—and cut down his body.

8 Alar, the Human Arrow

Pansy Zedora (aka Alar the Human Arrow) and her sister thrilled audiences on both sides of the Atlantic. After arranging herself on a gigantic crossbow high above the audience, Pansy was shot into the air. She flew through a paper target to be caught on the other side by her sister, who swung from a trapeze. The American public loved the sisters when they toured with circuses in the 1890s.

7 LaRoche

An Austrian acrobat and contortionist, LaRoche (real name Leon Rauche) depended on precise physical effort and balance in his mystifying act. A perilously steep, 24–30-foot-high spiral track was set up, and at the bottom was placed a metal ball about 2 feet in diameter. To the late-19th-century audience's amazement, the ball began to ascend the track, apparently under its own power. At the top, a pair of hands holding flags shot out of holes in the ball—proof that LaRoche, a full-sized man, was inside. The ball descended just as smoothly, and LaRoche emerged to much applause. *La Sphere Mystérieuse* was a hit. No one knows exactly how he did it, but speculation continues to this day.

6 Signora Josephine Giradelli, the Fireproof Female

First performing in 1816 and causing much comment, Italian-born Josephine Giradelli was a famous "fire queen." Her act consisted of holding boiling lead in her mouth, running a red-hot iron bar over her head and bare arms, walking barefoot on a red-hot metal plate, dripping melted sealing wax on her tongue, and cooking an egg in hot oil held in her hands, among other feats. Part illusion, part hard-earned skill, part dedication to her craft, her acts were unusual for a woman of the time and drew in crowds to attend sell-out shows. Later fire resisters would add poison-eating to their acts.

5 El Niño Farini and Mademoiselle Lulu

Samuel Wasgate, an orphan adopted by wire-walker Guillermo Farini, became famous in 1866 at the age of ten for a death-defying stunt called *Le Tambour Aerial* by El Niño Farini. He balanced on his neck on a trapeze bar high in the air while playing a drum. Sam would also balance on Farini's shoulders when he crossed the high wire. Beginning in 1870, as part of the act, he began impersonating a female acrobat and aerialist billed as "Mlle. Lulu" and "the Circassian Catapultist." Imagine how much consternation was caused in 1878 when "Lulu" suffered an injury on stage and his true sex was revealed to his admirers. Afterward, he cut his hair and continued performing, this time, as a man.

4 Richard Sands, the Human Fly

Apart from his phenomenal success as a circus owner, Richard Sands was a highly skilled acrobat in his own right. One of his claims to fame was being a "ceiling walker" or "antipodean pedestrian," as the press of the day termed it. His act consisted of literally walking upside down across a ceiling while hanging by his feet from rings. In 1853, he expanded his act to "air walking" by taking a stroll across a Drury Lane theater's ceiling while wearing special rubber suction cups on his feet. In 1861, he was killed during a performance when a plaster ceiling gave way and he fell and broke his neck.

3 Hadji-Ali, the Amazing Regurgitator

While the ability to vomit is inherent in all humans, some take it to the next level. And then there's the famous Egyptian called Hadji-Ali, who could (and did) regurgitate objects and liquids at will. His skill as a "water spouter" brought him considerable fame in the early 20th century, including a cameo in a Laurel and Hardy film. The pinnacle of his act was consuming a gallon of water followed by a pint of kerosene. Due to his outstanding control over his stomach muscles, he would first bring up the kerosene and light a model castle on fire, followed by the water to put out the flames. He died of heart failure in 1937.

2 Aloys Peters, the Man with the Iron Neck

In the 1930s, the Great Peters, as he was billed, thrilled and terrified audiences with his dangerous "hangman's act," during which he climbed 75 feet to a rigging suspended in the air, put an elasticized rope with a noose around his neck, and swan-dived to the ground.

Like a modern bungee, the rope would snap back before he struck, sending him flying upward, and he'd make a controlled descent. He died at the age of 45 in 1943 when something went wrong during the stunt and his neck broke. His body dangled high in the air for 20 minutes in front of a crowd of 5,500 horrified spectators while the St. Louis fire department struggled to reach him and cut him down.

1 Mademoiselle Octavie LaTour

Also billed as Mlle. Mauricia De Tiers, this daredevil stunt driver performed in Ringling Bros. and Barnum & Bailey Circus in 1905, when the automobile was still relatively new technology. The act, called *L'Auto-Bolide* or the Dip of Death, featured the attractive lady driving a small car at breakneck speed down a long ramp that doubled over at the end. The car turned upside down and hurtled off the end of the track into a back flip over a 20-foot gap, and landed on the receiving track. Out stepped Mademoiselle LaTour, looking unruffled and fashionably feminine in her long Edwardian dress and beautifully trimmed hat. *Voilà!*

TOP 10 Sinister Origins of Nursery Rhymes

by Marsebil

10 Lucy Locket

Lucy Locket lost her pocket
And Kitty Fisher found it.
Not a penny was there in it,
Only a ribbon around it.

Both Lucy and Kitty were real people back in the 18th century. Lucy Locket was a barmaid and some-time prostitute. When one of her wealthy lovers (the "pocket") lost all his money, she dropped him like a hot potato, only to learn afterward that her rival, Kitty Fisher, had taken up with him despite his poverty ("not a penny"). The spat between the two ladies was well-known at the time, as Kitty taunted Lucy for dropping her lover. Kitty claimed she had found a ribbon around him—a serious jibe at Lucy, as prostitutes at that time kept their money tied around the thigh with a ribbon.

So not such a nice theme for the kiddies. Luckily, the passing of time has been enough to hide the truth: that this rhyme records a spat between two prostitutes!

9 Georgie Porgie

Georgie Porgy pudding and pie
Kissed all the girls and made them cry.
When the boys came out to play
Georgie Porgie ran away.

Georgie Porgie could be one of two men: either George Villiers (16th–17th century) or Prince Regent George (late-18th century).

The first was an upstart who wormed—or earned—his way into the court of King James I. George Villiers was likely a bisexual who had an intense and fairly well-documented attachment to the king. King James was extremely fond of George and gave him money and titles. While there is no sure, definitive proof of a homosexual relationship between the two, King James's affection was without doubt. Either way, George still loved the ladies and was rumored to be fond of seducing noblemen's wives, sometimes without the consent of the ladies in question. This fact, together with well-known (and probably very necessary) ability to avoid confrontation, makes him a good fit for the nursery rhyme.

As much as George Villiers may seem like the perfect candidate, my money is actually on Prince Regent George. He was enormously fat and notoriously gluttonous. He couldn't fit in regular clothes, but he certainly fits the rhyme. He wasn't the sharpest tool in the shed, but he definitely loved the ladies. The last couplet might refer to an incident when George attended a bare-knuckle boxing match that left one contestant dead. He ran away and hid himself, afraid of a potential scandal.

So Georgie Porgie is really a coward, a cad, and a glutton. Not the best moral for your children, perhaps.

8 Oranges and Lemons

Oranges and lemons
Say the bells of St. Clemens,
You owe me five farthings
Say the bells of St. Martins,
When will you pay me?
Say the bells of Old Bailey,
When I grow rich
Say the bells of Shoreditch,
When will that be?
Say the bells of Stepney,
I do not know
Says the great bell of Bow,
Here comes a candle to light you to bed
And here comes a chopper
To chop off your head!
Chip, chop, chip, chop
The last one is dead!

The second part of this rhyme is a clue to the purpose of the first part—the poor guy ends up dead! The bells belong to famous churches in London; it's possible that these were the churches a condemned man would pass on his way to his execution.

St. Clemens, the first church, is likely that in Eastcheap. The Eastcheap docks saw the unloading of cargo from the Mediterranean, often including oranges and lemons. But not only fruit was unloaded at Eastcheap; it was also the dock at which condemned men would disembark to begin their final journey.

7 Pop Goes the Weasel

Half a pound of tuppenny rice
Half a pound of treacle
That's the way the money goes,
Pop goes the weasel.
Up and down the City Road
In and out of the Eagle
That's the way the money goes,
Pop goes the weasel.
Every night when I go out
The monkey's on the table
Take a stick and knock it off,
Pop goes the weasel.
A penny for a ball of thread
Another for a needle
That's the way the money goes,
Pop goes the weasel.

"Pop Goes the Weasel" seems at first glance to be a nonsense rhyme, one without any purpose behind it at all, but really it's an account of poverty, pawnbroking, minimum wage, and a serious night out on the town.

The "weasel" in the rhyme is a winter coat, which has to be pawned—or "popped"—in exchange for various things. The first verse describes the cheapest food available; the narrator of the poem has no money, so "pop" goes the weasel. The second verse describes a night out at a music hall called the Eagle Tavern, which was located on the City Road. But music halls—and drinks—cost money. Pop goes the weasel. The third verse is a bit more obscure than the first two; "a monkey" is slang for a tankard, while "knocking off a stick" was slang for drinking. The last verse probably refers to the narrator's day job.

So this little nonsensical ditty is actually about struggling to make ends meet. It's still an upbeat tune, letting the reader see that a night on the town is well worth the week of terrible food, wages, and general living conditions.

6 Rub a Dub Dub

Rub a dub dub,
Three men in a tub,
And how do you think they got there?
The butcher, the baker, and the candlestick maker
It was enough to make a man stare.

At first it's a bit homoerotic, but then we read the original, or at least the oldest-known, version:

Rub a dub dub,
Three maids in a tub,
And how do you think they got there?
The butcher, the baker, and the candlestick,maker
And all of them gone to the fair.

Well, it sounds like a peep show might be in town. Peep shows were a popular form of entertainment in the 14th century, and it appears that our friends have gone to catch a glimpse of the maids in the tub. Rub a dub dub…

5 Mary Mary Quite Contrary

Mary, Mary, quite contrary
How does your garden grow?
With silver bells and cockleshells
And pretty maids all in a row.

This one has a bit of a sad, nostalgic ring to it that only increases when you realize that in some versions, "garden" is replaced with "graveyard." The Mary here is probably Mary I, daughter of Henry VIII and sister to Elizabeth I.

Henry VIII was initially married to Catherine of Aragon, and the couple had one child, Mary. But Henry wanted a son, and always true to the notion of killing two birds with stone, he decided to do this by getting into the pants of Anne Boleyn, one of his wife's ladies-in-waiting. To make a long story short, Henry was refused a divorce by the pope, so he created the Anglican Church with himself at the head, thereby isolating himself from Catholic Europe. After divorcing Catherine and marrying Anne, he had one child with the latter—Elizabeth. Needless to say, that marriage didn't work out either. Henry had Anne executed, and went through another couple of wives in an attempt to find a son.

After his death, the throne went to Mary, who promptly tried to make England Catholic again. So Mary went "quite contrary" to England's wishes; by this time, a lot of people were happily Protestant. In the rhyme, "garden" sounds a lot like "Gardiner," the name of Mary's only religious supporter. It could also be a dig at Mary's own infertility, or if "garden" is replaced by "graveyard," a reference to the growing pile of dead Protestants.

Given that "silver bells," "cockleshells," and "maids" are also terms for torture devices of the age, it no longer seems such a pretty little rhyme.

4 Baa Baa Black Sheep

Baa baa black sheep,
Have you any wool?
Yes sir, yes sir,
Three bags full.
One for the Master,
One for the Dame,
And one for the little boy
Who lives down the lane.

And with the original ending...
And none for the little boy
Who cries down the lane.

The song is definitely not about black sheep, or even little boys—it's about taxes! Back in the 13th century, King Edward I realized that he could make some decent cash by taxing the sheep farmers. As a result of the new taxes, one-third of the price of a sack of wool went to the king, one third to the church, and the last third to the farmer. Nothing was left for the shepherd boy, crying down the lane. As it happens, black sheep are also bad luck: The fleece can't be dyed, and so it's worth less to the sheep farmer. "Baa Baa Black Sheep" is a tale of misery and woe.

3 Humpty Dumpty

Humpty Dumpty sat on the wall,
Humpty Dumpty had a great fall,
All the King's horses and all the King's men
Couldn't put Humpty together again!

Humpty Dumpty wasn't a real person, nor was he an odd, fragile egg-shaped thing. It turns out that Humpty Dumpty was a cannon. Owned by the supporters of King Charles I, Humpty Dumpty was used to gain control over the city of Colchester during the English Civil War. Once in Colchester, the cannon sat on church tower until a barrage of cannonballs destroyed the tower and sent Humpty into the marshland below. Although retrieved, the cannon was beyond repair. Humpty the cannon was a feared and effective weapon, as the full rhyme demonstrates:

In sixteen hundred and forty-eight,
When England suffered pains of state,
The Roundheads laid siege to Colchester town
Where the King's men still fought for the crown.
There one-eyed Thompson stood on the wall,
A gunner with the deadliest aim of all,
From St. Mary's tower the cannon he fired
Humpty Dumpty was his name.
Humpty Dumpty sat on the wall,
Humpty Dumpty had a great fall,
All the King's horses and all the King's men
Couldn't put Humpty Dumpty together again!

And you thought it was all about an egg? A 19th-century illustration in Lewis Carroll's *Through the Looking-Glass* created this myth. When Alice talks to Humpty Dumpty on the wall, the illustrator—apparently on a whim—made him egg shaped. Given the popularity of the book, a generation of kids grew up thinking that Humpty Dumpty was a nonsense rhyme about an egg rather than a fearsome killing machine.

2 Ladybird Ladybird

Ladybird, ladybird, fly away home,
Your house is on fire and your children are gone.
All except one called Anne
For she has crept under the frying pan.

This poor little ladybird is really a Catholic in 16th-century Protestant England. "Ladybird" is a word that comes from the Catholic term for "Our Lady." It was illegal for Catholics to practice their religion, and nonattendance at Protestant services meant hefty fines for absentees. Catholics were forced to say Mass and attend services in secret, often outdoors and in outbuildings. The fire may refer to the Catholic priests who were burned at the stake for their beliefs.

1 Ring a Ring of Roses

Ring a ring a roses,
A pocket full of posies,
A-tish-oo, a-tish-oo,
We all fall down.

This is one nursery rhyme origin we think we already know to be sinister. But it has nothing at all to do with the Black Death. The first known reference to the rhyme is in 1881, more than 500 years after the plague swept across Europe. By all accounts, it seems to be a nonsense rhyme, and in its 1881 form, there isn't even any sneezing. Here's a version from the mid-20th century:

> Ring a ring a roses,
> A pocket full of posies,
> One, two, three, four,
> We all fall down.

The sneezing was added sometime in the last 50 years or so. So this one really is just a nice little rhyme—no ulterior meanings at all!

TOP 10 Unusual Little-Known Fairy Tales

by **Melita Linaker**

10 "Verde Prato" by Giambattista Basile

A stunningly beautiful young princess named Nella is having a secret affair with a handsome prince who lives many miles away. The two lovers build a glass tunnel that runs underground from the prince's castle into the princess's bedroom. Every night, the prince runs through the tunnel naked at top speed to "spend time" with his young princess.

Nella's two sisters, who are ugly and evil, learn of the affair and smash the glass tunnel. That night, the prince is running so fast to reach his young lover that he doesn't see the broken glass, and because he is naked, the skin all over his body is sliced to ribbons. Because the glass that cut him was enchanted, his wounds will not heal. The prince's father vows that the woman who can find a remedy for the enchanted wounds will be the prince's wife.

Nella is heartbroken upon hearing of her wounded prince and goes out into the wild to find a remedy that will heal him. Luckily, she overhears two ogres telling each other that the only thing in the whole world that will heal the prince is to smear the fat from their own bodies all over the prince. Nella, pretending to be lost in the woods, begs the ogres to let her into their house. The ogre husband, fancying a bit of human flesh, lets her in eagerly, but sadly he drinks so much alcohol that he passes out before he gets to eat her.

Nella quickly gets to work and slaughters him, then collects all the fat from his body in a bucket. She then rubs dirt all over her face to disguise herself and makes her way to the prince's castle. She smears the fat into the prince's wounds and he is healed as if by magic, then she reveals her identity and the marriage is swiftly arranged. And her sisters? They are burned alive, of course.

9 "The Flea" by Giambattista Basile

A king feeds a flea on his own blood until it is the size of a sheep, then he slaughters it, skins it, and promises his daughter to the man who can guess what animal the skin came from. Suitors come from far and wide, but none can guess the origins of the pelt. Then a hideously ugly old ogre decides to try his luck—he sniffs the pelt and identifies it immediately as that of a flea.

The king, true to his word, hands over his daughter. She begs and pleads with him, but he sends her away, calling her names like "breath of my arse" and threatening that he will "leave her not a whole bone in her body" if she refuses to marry the ogre.

The princess is horrified to find that her new home is made from human skeletons, and more horrified still when her new hubby prepares her a feast made from human carcasses. She begins to vomit repeatedly and the ogre promises to catch her some pigs to eat until she can stomach human flesh. While the ogre is hunting, an old woman hears the maiden wailing and sends her seven sons (who are all endowed with magical powers) to rescue the princess. They eventually defeat the ogre by shooting out his eyeball and beheading him, and the princess returns home to her father who is (surprisingly) overjoyed to see her home safe.

8 "The Wonderful Birch" by Andrew Lang

While searching for her stray black sheep in the woods, a woman comes across the path of a witch who turns the woman into a sheep. The witch  then disguises herself as the woman and returns to the house where woman's husband and daughter live. The witch convinces the husband to slaughter the sheep to prevent it from wandering again. Their daughter weeps, but her mother (still a sheep) tells her not to eat of her flesh once she is slaughtered and to bury her bones at the edge of the field. The father slaughters the sheep and the witch makes soup from the meat and bones. The daughter buries what's left of her mother in the field and a birch tree grows from the bones.

The witch hates her new stepdaughter, but eventually she and the husband have a daughter of their own. One day, a king declares that a festival is to be held for three days. The stepmother sets the stepdaughter an impossible task, threatening to devour her if she is unable to complete it before the witch, the father, and their daughter return from the night's festivities. The girl weeps over the birch tree, and the spirit of her dead mother completes her task for her and sends her off to the feast in beautiful garments. When she arrives, the prince falls instantly in love with the maiden.

As they dine, the witch's daughter gnaws bones under the table and the prince, thinking she is a dog, boots her so hard he breaks her arm. The beautiful sister flees before her family can return home to find her missing, but her ring is stuck on the palace door handle, which the prince has spread with tar. The next two nights go the same way, with the prince breaking the witch's daughter's leg on the second night and dislodging her eyeball the third night.

The beautiful girl loses her bracelet, then her golden shoe in the tar the prince spreads to trap her. The prince wishes to marry the woman who will fit the lost items, and the witch forces her ugly daughter into them. However, when the prince discovers who the real bride is, they throw the ugly sister across a river to act as a bridge so they can escape the clutches of the witch.

7 "Faithful Johannes" by the Brothers Grimm

A young king falls madly in love with the princess of the golden palace after laying eyes on a portrait depicting her likeness and devises a plot to kidnap her. The young king and his faithful servant Johannes travel to the golden kingdom, trick the princess into coming onto their boat, and then set sail when she is below deck. Initially she is terrified, but when her kidnapper reveals he is a king, all is forgiven and she agrees to marry him.

As they are sailing, faithful Johannes overhears three ravens conversing with each other. They predict three misfortunes that will befall the king: a fox-red horse, a poisoned shirt, and the death of his wife. The only way to save the king is if someone shoots the horse in the head, burns the poisoned shirt, and takes three drops of blood from the right breast of the new queen.

However, the savior must not utter a word of his tasks or he shall turn to stone. When they arrive ashore, the king leaps onto the back of a fox-red horse, which faithful Johannes promptly shoots in the head. When they arrive at the palace, the king finds a shirt that looks to be made of gold, but faithful Johannes throws the shirt in the fire. At the wedding dance, the queen falls down as if dead on the palace floor, but faithful Johannes quickly takes three drops of blood from her right breast, saving her life.

The king, angered at the sight of his servant fondling the new queen's breast, sentence's Johannes to hang. Johannes reveals the plot but turns to stone. The king and queen eventually have two children and one day the statue of Johannes tells the king that if he will slaughter his own children, his trusty servant will be brought back to life. The king eagerly takes his sword and lops off his own children's heads. He smears his children's blood onto the stone and Johannes comes back to life.

As a reward for the king's willingness to execute his own children, faithful Johannes places the children's heads back onto their corpses and brings them back to life; they continue to run around as if nothing had happened.

6 "The Dog and the Sparrow," the Brothers Grimm

A starving dog runs away from its cruel master and meets a sparrow. The two become great friends. The sparrow steals meat and bread for the dog, and when the dog has eaten his fill he goes to sleep on the road. A wagon drives by, and the sparrow flutters about the driver's head, telling him to watch out for the dog, but the driver pays no heed and runs the dog over, killing it. The sparrow swears vengeance, saying "Thou hast killed my brother dog, it shall cost thee thy cart and horses!"

The sparrow then pecks out the eyes of one of the horses. The driver swings his axe at the sparrow, but chops open his horse's head instead. The sparrow pecks out the eyes of the other two horses, and the unfortunate beasts also get their heads chopped open as their master swings his axe at the sparrow. The sparrow then sings, "It shall cost thee thy home" and flies to the driver's house.

The sparrow flutters from room to room as the driver, blind with rage, smashes up his entire house in his attempts to kill the bird. Then the driver sits amongst the rubble and says, "What an unfortunate man I am!" "Not unfortunate enough," says the sparrow. "It shall cost thee thy life!" The driver catches the sparrow in his hand, and wanting it to suffer a fate worse than death, he swallows it whole—but the bird begins to flutter about his body and pokes its head out of the driver's mouth. The driver tells his wife to kill the sparrow with the axe as the bird sits in his mouth, but as the wife swings the sparrow flutters away and the wife chops open the driver's head instead, killing him.

5 "The She-Bear" by Giambattista Basile

After his wife dies, a king decides that the only woman in the world who matches his dead wife's beauty is his own daughter Preziosa; therefore, Preziosa must now marry her deranged father. He tells her that if she will not marry him that very evening, then "When I am finished with you, there will be nothing left but your ears."

An old woman then gives the terrified girl an enchanted piece of wood that will turn her into a bear when she puts it in her mouth. Preziosa—now a bear—flees into the forest and resolves never again to reveal her true form lest her father learn of her whereabouts. A prince discovers the wonderfully friendly she-bear in the woods and takes her home to be his pet.

One day when she believes she is alone, Preziosa takes the bit of wood out of her mouth to brush her hair. The prince looks out his window, spies a gorgeous maiden in his garden, and rushes out to find her, but she hears him coming and quickly puts the wood back into her mouth. The prince searches throughout the garden but he cannot find the maiden anywhere—in her place is only his pet she-bear.

The prince becomes sick with lust for the girl and begins to waste away. On request from her son, the prince's mother sends for the she-bear, who is now to reside in the prince's bedroom, cook his meals, and make his bed for him. The prince becomes overcome with lust for the bear, and begs his mother to let him kiss the animal.

While the mother watches and encourages them enthusiastically, man and bear lock lips. They are kissing so passionately that the bit of wood slips from Preziosa's mouth and the prince finds that he now holds a stunningly beautiful maiden in his arms. Rejoicing, they get married, and presumably everyone lives happily ever after.

4 "The Red Shoes" by Hans Christian Andersen

Karen is a very poor girl who goes barefoot until an old lady adopts her and buys her a beautiful pair of red shoes. When Karen is old enough to be confirmed, she chooses to wear her beautiful red shoes to church. During the church service, Karen can think only of her red shoes. After the service, the old lady scolds Karen, telling her now that she is a grown-up Christian, she must never wear red shoes to church again.

The next Sunday, Karen chooses to wear her red shoes to communion and again can focus only on how pretty she looks for the entire service. As they are leaving the church, her shoes start to dance on their own, and when Karen climbs into the carriage, she kicks the old woman violently before the coachman removes the shoes from Karen's feet. The old lady falls ill and it is Karen's job to care for her, but Karen is invited to a ball and decides to wear her red shoes to the dance rather than care for the sick old woman.

When Karen begins to dance, the shoes take on a life of their own. They dance Karen away into the dark woods. Terrified, she tries to tear the shoes off but they have become one with her feet. She continues to dance through field and meadow, rain and shine, for many days. While dancing through a graveyard, she sees an angel who tells her she shall dance until she is cold and dead, and will continue to dance even when she is nothing but bones.

Karen dances unceasingly over hills and plains, and over thorns and branches until her skin is torn and bleeding. She eventually comes to the house of an executioner and begs him to chop off her feet, so that she can finally rest. The executioner does as Karen wishes and the shoes dance away with her little feet still in them. She kisses the hand that wielded the axe and he fashions her little wooden feet and a pair of crutches.

Karen now wishes to go to church to repent, but the red shoes, with her feet still in them, dance in front of the church doors so that Karen cannot enter. Karen weeps bitter tears in her narrow bare room and eventually the angel returns to her: He transforms her room into a church and as the organ plays, Karen becomes so full of peace and joy that her heart breaks and she dies.

3 "Sweetheart Roland" by the Brothers Grimm

A witch's ugly daughter grows jealous of her stepsister's beautiful apron, so mother and daughter plot to kill the stepdaughter. When the girls go to bed, the witch's daughter is to lie near the wall, and the mother will chop off the stepdaughter's head as she sleeps. The stepdaughter overhears this conversation, so when her stepsister falls asleep, the beautiful sister pushes the ugly one to the edge of the bed, and lies by the wall.

In creeps the witch and chops off her own child's head; then she goes to bed. The stepdaughter then takes her sister's dismembered head and drips the blood around the house, one drop of blood by the stove, one on the stairs, and one by the bed. She then steals the witch's wand and flees with her lover, Roland.

In the morning the witch calls for her daughter and the first blood drop sings from the kitchen "I am here warming myself." The second blood drop calls, "I am on the stairs." And the third calls out, "I am here by the bed." Then the witch finds her own daughter's beheaded body lying in a pool of blood. In a rage, the witch catches up to the lovers, but her stepdaughter turns her lover into a lake and herself into a duck.

The witch cannot entice the duck from the water, so she returns home. The next day the girl turns herself into a flower in the middle of a bramble hedge and her lover turns into a fiddler. The witch comes by hunting for the lovers and spies the beautiful flower, which she recognizes as her step-daughter. As the witch reaches into the hedge to pick the flower, Roland begins playing the fiddle. The music is enchanted and the witch begins to dance around the bramble bush as the thorns tear at her clothes until she is naked. She continues to dance wildly around and around as her skin is shredded to ribbons and eventually she falls down dead.

2 "The Maiden with the Rose on Her Forehead" by Consiglieri Pedroso

This twisted little tale begins with a prince and princess who are brother and sister. The brother has to go away to war and entrusts his beloved rose

garden to his sister, who must tend to it day and night. The princess pines away among her brother's roses, then quite mysteriously she gives birth to a baby girl. The princess is deeply ashamed of the baby girl, who was born with a rose on her forehead. As the little girl grows, the princess swears to her daughter every day that she will kill her if the girl should reveal her identity.

After five years, the prince returns, and the princess swears to her daughter repeatedly that if she should reveal who she is to the prince, her mother will kill her. The prince visits the little girl's school but she refuses to eat the cherries he offers her. The other girls in her class eagerly eat the cherries, but become so excited that they begin to throw the fruit around and a cherry becomes lodged in the daughter's hair. The next day, the princess finds the cherry stuck in her daughter's locks.

The princess, assuming the girl has removed her hood and revealed herself in the prince's presence, stabs her comb violently into her little girls head, killing her. She then puts the girl into an iron chest and locks the chest in a room in the palace. The princess grows ill with guilt and eventually dies, entrusting the key to her brother and beseeching him never to open the door. Once his sister is dead, the prince becomes lonely and takes a wife.

One day the prince goes away on a hunt and leaves the key with his wife, telling her not to open the locked door. His wife's mother convinces her to open the door and they find the iron chest, which they open to discover a beautiful young woman sitting inside happily sewing. Thinking the prince is keeping her in the chest for his own enjoyment, the mother and daughter pull the fair maiden out and burn the skin all over her face and body with a heated iron. When the prince comes home they tell him she is their new slave.

The prince eventually overhears the young slave telling her sorrowful story to a talisman, and realizing she is his niece (and possibly his daughter) he releases her and asks her how his wife should be punished. Mother and daughter are both burned all over with hot irons, then buried alive inside a wall to die slowly and miserably. The prince and his niece/daughter remain alone together in the castle and the prince never remarries because presumably she is all the company he needs.

1 "The Marsh King's Daughter" by Hans Christian Andersen

An Egyptian princess dons the garb of a wild swan and flies to a distant marsh to find a flower that will heal the king of Egypt. The princess removes her plumage and climbs naked into the marsh to gather the healing flowers, but the Marsh King pulls her down into the murky black depths beneath the water and rapes her. Many months pass, and eventually a water lily opens on the surface of the water. Inside the flower is a baby girl. A stork carries the baby to the wife of a Viking lord, who names the little girl Helga.

As Helga grows, she becomes ever more beautiful, but she is evil and black of heart. She likes to splash about in the blood of animals and bite the heads off roosters. However, by night she turns into a hideous dwarf-sized frog that has a kind soul but can only croak mournfully.

When Helga is 16, the Viking lord captures a Christian priest. Helga begs that savage dogs be let loose upon the priest, but the Viking lord insists the priest is to be sacrificed upon the death stone, according to tradition. Helga gleefully stabs her knife into a dog, just to make sure the blade is sharp enough.

When night comes, the gentle frog Helga rescues the priest and they ride away together on Helga's horse. In the morning, however, the beautiful Helga tries to stab the priest but he enchants her with a symbol of the cross he makes out of two sticks and she becomes dumb and silent until they are confronted by a band of robbers. In the hopes of getting their hands on Helga, the robbers slice the horse's neck with an axe and blood spurts out, then they smash the priest's head open with an iron hammer and his blood and brains are spattered around. The group of men then seize Helga, but luckily for her the sun is setting and she turns back into a monstrously ugly frog. The terrified men flee.

Helga eventually makes the sign of the cross and her frog skin falls away as if by magic, never to return. She falls asleep and when she wakes she finds the ghosts of the dead priest and his dead horse standing before her. They ride away together to the marsh where Helga was conceived and the priest lifts Helga's birth mother from the water. Then the phantoms of priest and horse vanish and Helga and her birth mother are left alone beside the marsh.

They return to Egypt where Helga is eventually married to an Arabian prince, but on the night of the wedding, the spirit of the priest comes to Helga to show her what heaven looks like. After three minutes have passed in heaven she returns to Earth but finds that hundreds of years have gone by. Helga's body turns to dust and all that is left of her is a faded water lily.

TOP 10 Curious Facts about Your Favorite Childhood Authors

by **George Ryan**

10 From Chickens to Oz

Fact: L. Frank Baum's first book was all about raising chickens.
Called *The Book of the Hamburgs: A Brief Treatise upon the Mating, Rearing, and Management of the Different Varieties of Hamburgs*, this book with an insanely long title was all about chickens—scintillating. It came out in 1886 and was written by none other than L. Frank Baum, the famed author of *The Wonderful Wizard of Oz*. Baum was 30 years old, and at the time, raising fancy poultry was all the rage.

Hamburgs—the focus of Baum's book—were rare and valuable. Baum was a self-styled expert on the breed, and he loved his chickens. Before writing this book, he was running a monthly trade journal about all things poultry. Oz, the work that would bring him lasting fame and fortune, would not appear until 1900.

While Baum managed to refrain from including chickens in Oz, his passion could not be restrained forever: In its sequel, *Ozma of Oz* he featured the character of Billina the chicken, who ends up settling in the Emerald City wearing a pearl necklace given to her by the King of Ev.

9 From Humor to Horror

Fact: Before he was scary, R. L. Stine was funny.

Stine was a true comedian before his name became synonymous with youth horror in the form of his Goosebumps books. He was Jovial Bob Stine, literary clown and purveyor of jokes for kids. He wrote silly stories, joke books, and even created a humor magazine. Stine's early foray into comedy is probably the reason for his success with horror books for kids: His ability to mix the creepy with the funny is probably the reason he has sold nearly half a billion books.

It seems to be particularly difficult to find any of Stine's jokes online, but reading the reviews of some of his comedy books at Amazon.com strongly implies that he was not as good at humor as he was at horror.

8 Lazy Days

Fact: E. B. White didn't want to go to the office.

E. B. White was content with sending manuscripts to *The New Yorker*, but the magazine wanted him on the staff. It took the magazine's editors months to persuade him to pay them a visit. Then it took a few more weeks to talk him into working for them. When at last he agreed, he made it known that he didn't want to go to the office. But in the end the editors won—White agreed to go in once a week.

This arrangement defined White's entire association with the *New Yorker*. He wrote his articles, showed up every Thursday, and fled for the fire escape every time a stranger appeared at the office. In between writing for magazines, he wrote stories for children. *Stuart Little*—his first book for children—appeared in 1945.

7 Truth in Journalism

Fact: Neil Gaiman gave up journalism because he didn't like the fact that newspapers were making things up (and getting away with it).

The British press has been known—on more than one occasion—to lie, cheat, and steal. It has even gone so far as to invent stories. Gaiman had his feet squarely planted on journalism early in his career. He did interviews and wrote reviews and articles for a number of publications. He wasn't very happy, however, with the way newspapers were making things up. So he left journalism altogether, and decided to make things up himself by writing comic books such as *The Sandman*.

6 Daredevil

Fact: Roald Dahl was a spy and a World War II flying ace.

He may not have looked the part, but Roald Dahl was actually a first-rate, real-life action hero. The fun-loving author of *Charlie and the Chocolate Factory* once fought six enemy planes while flying solo. In another battle, he helped reduce 22 German planes into useless hunks of smoking metal. He was a wing commander and a verified flying ace by the time he left the Royal Air Force.

His military career didn't end there, though. He was sent to the U.S., along with a crack team of operatives, to combat isolationism among distinguished, influential Americans. Britain wanted the U.S. in the war, and Dahl and his compatriots made sure those who thought otherwise got the message. In other words, forget Pearl Harbor: The Americans entered the war because the creator of the Oompa-Loompas made them.

5 Pseudonym

Fact: Carolyn Keene is not a real person.

Carolyn Keene's name may appear in every book featuring Nancy Drew, but many authors are actually involved in the writing of these hugely popular mystery stories. Carolyn Keene is really nothing more than a pseudonym (and a necessary marketing ploy to keep the byline uncomplicated). Every author who had worked on the series was bound by his contract to hand over all rights to the work to the Stratemeyer Syndicate, the company behind the Nancy Drew books. In the early days of the series, every Nancy Drew book earned its writer a whopping $125.

4 Hatred over Mary Poppins

Fact: P. L. Travers and Walt Disney were not exactly the best of friends.

P. L. Travers didn't like a lot of things in Disney's adaptation of her book *Mary Poppins*. She didn't like the music and she hated the film's weak depiction of the main character. Finally, she didn't see the point of using animated sequences in the film. She was very vocal about her objections but no one listened.

Travers wasn't invited to the film's premiere, either. She had to beg Walt Disney to let her in. After watching the movie, she proceeded to give Disney a piece of her mind. Disney just walked out on her, reminding her that the time for any change had passed. Travers never allowed Disney to use any of her work again.

3 C. S. Lewis and His Buddy's Mom

Fact: C. S. Lewis had a thing going on with his dead friend's mother.

It all started with a pact: Lewis and his buddy, Paddy Moore, vowed to take care of the other's families if anything happened to them. World War I was underway, and both men were preparing for the worst, which did happen. Paddy died in combat, and Lewis stuck to their agreement.

There was much speculation that Lewis did more than the pact asked of him. He was particularly close to Paddy's mother, Jane King Moore. Moore was 26 years older than Lewis, but that didn't discourage him from cozying up to her. While the two never admitted to anything, those who knew them saw something else altogether.

2 Real-Life Peter Pan

Fact: J. M. Barrie used to impersonate his dead brother.

J. M. Barrie was six years old when his brother, David, died in an ice-skating accident. The death left their mother distraught. David was her favorite son, and he died two days short of his 14th birthday. To help his mother cope, young Barrie decided to stand in for his brother. He wore David's clothes. He walked in his manner. He even taught himself how to whistle like him.

Barrie's mother eventually overcame her depression, but not because of Barrie's odd actions. She consoled herself with the belief that David would remain with her forever—a boy who would never grow up. Sound familiar? Barrie liked the idea so much that he went on to create his own boy who would never grow up: Peter Pan.

1 Fairy Tales

Fact: Hans Christian Andersen swung both ways.

The lusty but otherwise luckless Andersen never shot it straight. He loved women with a passion, but he also worshipped men with surprising ardor. He may be renowned for his straightforward fairy tales, but in real life he actually played the part of both the knight and the damsel in distress. It is believed that his Little Mermaid—horribly butchered by Disney—was actually a gay love letter.

The list of women he loved is long. The list of men he loved is no shorter. Andersen, however, did not see much love come his way. His gangling, awkward ways didn't endear him to women. The men, on the other hand, were simply unable to respond to his advances. He may have had an intimate relationship with a young, handsome dancer whom he met when he was in his fifties, but whatever their relationship, it did not last long.

He took to his grave an old letter from a girl whom he had loved in his youth. Sadly, this man who gave us so many happy endings never had one of his own.

TOP 10 Deleted Chapters That Transformed Famous Books

by **Evan V. Symon**

10 Dracula by Bram Stoker

Bram Stoker's iconic novel is by far the most influential horror book. But what many don't know is that the final chapter was taken out by Stoker at the last minute. In the deleted chapter, Dracula's castle falls apart as he dies, to hide the fact that vampires were ever there. But, either wanting to possibly write a sequel or being mindful that it would echo the ending of Edgar Allan Poe's "Fall of the House of Usher," he dropped it. So, rather than becoming known as "that guy who copied Poe," Stoker has gone down in the annals of history for having penned one of the greatest works of horror literature.

9 The Picture of Dorian Gray by Oscar Wilde

When Oscar Wilde showed this book to his editors in 1890, it caused a big stir, particularly due to the many homoerotic passages that were not socially acceptable in Victorian England.

The editors told Wilde to add seven new chapters to dilute its effeminacy. He was also told to take out all parts alluding to "grubbing muckheaps," Victorian for "man-on-man action." While the final book was selling like crazy, Wilde was sent to jail for his sexual tastes.

The Picture of Dorian Gray may have been the first popular book to address homosexuality if it were not so harshly edited. It was so widely read and loved that it could have paved the way for tolerance and acceptance of homosexuality earlier in history.

8 Great Expectations by Charles Dickens

Great Expectations—one of Dickens's most notable works—tells the story of an English boy named Pip as he grows in age and maturity. In time he helps criminals, finds love, and watches old widows burn to death. He doesn't ultimately see his great expectations come to fruition. In the end, Pip meets his old love. They embrace and depart as friends.

Dickens originally had a slightly different ending envisioned: A bitter Pip meets his severely stressed-out and depressed old love. Her husband has recently died and Pip has just lost all his money. Pip says he never could have had her and he sees they both have dark hearts. In this version they part ways on very unfriendly terms.

When Dickens showed this version to friends, they found it too sad and depressing, so he switched it out. His friends obviously felt that reading about an old lady burning to death while still wearing the wedding gown she wore the day she was left standing at the altar was not so depressing.

7 Harry Potter and the Deathly Hallows by J. K. Rowling

Rowling considered two possible endings for the final Harry Potter book. In the end she chose the version we all know: Voldemort dies and Harry saves everyone. The alternative ending was not so happy. Instead, it is implied that Voldemort may have lived on as a statue in the grounds of Hogwarts.

Furthermore, Harry, now the headmaster of Hogwarts and an old man, wipes everyone's memories of Voldemort and it is suggested that Harry's own great-grandson is to be the next great dark wizard. Rowling never intended for this to become public knowledge, but a friend (the only one who knew about it) leaked it to the Internet.

6 The Time Machine by H. G. Wells

The Time Machine was one of the first science fiction novels. In the book, a Victorian Englishman invents a time machine and travels 800,000 years into the future. He discovers that man has become two distinct species: the small, pinkish Eloi (ruling class) and Morelocks (hairy underdogs). After much adventure, he travels back to the present day (around 1894).

During the editing stage of the book, wanting more of "the ultimate degeneracy [of man]," Wells's editor ordered an extra chapter to be written. Wells was compelled to write a new plot in which the traveler visits the distant future of the Eloi and Morelocks. He discovers an evolved form of the Eloi, which he kills because he doesn't recognize it.

Wells was not happy with the addition and after much argument it became a deleted chapter. For the curious, the cut text is available in print as *The Grey Man*. If undeleted, the public could have hated the book, spelling doom for the whole genre.

5 Through the Looking-Glass by Lewis Carroll

In this sequel to *Alice in Wonderland*, Lewis Carroll decided to outdo Alice and write an even better book than the first. This second book was based around the game of chess, which helped make that popular. It also inspired *Alice in Wonderland* imagery that isn't found in the first book. But there was one chapter that had to be cut.

Carroll's illustrator was used to styling weird imagery for him, but one drawing was too much: a wasp in a wig. Try as he might, there was no way he could draw it. As a result, Carroll dropped it and wrote around the character. Many of the characters ultimately influenced popular songs, such as "I Am the Walrus" by the Beatles.

4 The Autobiography of Malcolm X

The Autobiography of Malcolm X has been described as one of the most important books of the 20th century. It is curious, then, that three of the chapters were removed and that those chapters have been called "the most impactful." They were written during the last months of Malcolm X's life and they show his disillusionment with the struggle for civil rights, as well as his personal struggle with depression. He is also shown to be wary of his own death.

The chapters were removed to give the book a more optimistic ending so that, despite the threats against his life, his message would prevail. It is bittersweet noting that he died shortly after this, but had the missing chapters remained in the book, his cause may not have had such an enduring impact on American society.

3 Picnic at Hanging Rock by Joan Lindsay

Picnic at Hanging Rock is one of Australia's greatest novels. In the book, a group of school girls disappears while climbing Hanging Rock. One girl mysteriously returns with no memory of what happened. Soon, the whole town suffers from mysterious events, deaths, and fires. In the end, the mystery is not revealed and the book simply describes the events and demise of the town.

Joan Lindsay, the writer, wrote an ending that explained the fate of the girls, but the editor told her to drop it. By climbing the rock, the children go into a trance and discover a hole in time. Three of the girls enter and are turned into crabs—yes, really—while the fourth girl (the one who returns) is stopped by a falling rock. It was all meant as an allusion for white and Aboriginal tension.

Picnic at Hanging Rock was seen as a true story—the *Blair Witch Project* of its time—with many readers and filmgoers believing the whole thing to be real. The deleted chapter would have revealed its fictional nature, destroying its power and allure.

2 Charlie and the Chocolate Factory by Roald Dahl

Charlie and the Chocolate Factory is Dahl's most famous work, spawning a sequel and two movies. The story has five competition winners going on a tour of Willy Wonka's chocolate factory, with four meeting ironic punishments and the virtuous one winning out. But the original version had several more children in it, and after reading the cut chapter devoted to the last deleted character, you have to wonder why Dahl was not sent to an insane asylum.

The chapter entitled "Spotty Powder" introduces Miranda Piker— daughter of a principal—who is devoted to her studies. Both she and her parents are enraged after learning that Wonka has made a machine to create "Spotty Powder," a cereal mix-in that causes a child to get red dots on their face for an hour, letting them skip school. So furious are they that they rush in to sabotage the machine. That's when the screaming begins.

Wonka tells Piker's mother that they are to be ground up into Spotty Powder themselves. He then—in his characteristic way—tells her he is joking and the Oompa-Loompas escort them out. But barely any time passes before the Oompa-Loompas start singing about how Miranda's friends at school will like how she tastes.

1 The Bible

The Bible comes in many variations with some books omitted or added. But, in general, the versions tell the same tale. In the past, however, a large number of books were excluded that would have completely altered its meaning. These were the Gnostic Gospels, and they turned out to be excluded for good reasons.

Take the Gospel of Mary. It calls women to a more active role in the church and is the only book to call Mary Magdelene a prostitute—truly. The Gospel of Thomas bad mouths Saint Peter and says Saint Thomas was Jesus's go-to guy.

Other deleted gospels go on to dispel most beliefs of Christianity. The early church, at the Council of Nicaea in AD 325, took one look at these and said a resounding "No!" and tossed them. Since the Bible has influenced pretty much everything, it can be safely said that these books would have changed history as we know it.

TOP 10 Stupidly Banned Children's Books

by Her Ladyness

10 Winnie-the-Pooh by A. A. Milne

Winnie-the-Pooh has been introduced to generation after generation as a model of a child's best friend. If you ask most people who their favorite silly old bear is, they'll probably tell you it's Pooh. However, not everyone has found Pooh's "rumbly tumbly" and honey obsession so endearing. According to *Banned Books Awareness* (bannedbook.world.edu), this classic has been banned in a variety of countries at one point or another, including Russia, China, Turkey, and even its home turf, England. In fact, even some places in the United States have banned this book!

So why would anyone ever want to keep children from the joy of Milne's classic? In the case of Russia, *Winnie-the-Pooh* was banned in 2009 because of alleged Nazi ties. In truth, the entire ban was based on the fact that a single person known for supporting the Nazi party, was found to own a picture of a swastika-adorned Pooh. Apparently, this isolated case was enough for Russia to decide that *Winnie-the-Pooh* is pro-Nazi, and therefore anti-Russia. In fact, if you investigate any of the claims or reasons schools or governments give for banning this *Pooh*, you'll find them to be silly and utterly absurd. As Pooh might say, "Oh, bother."

9 The Wonderful Wizard of Oz by Frank L. Baum

MGM's classic adaptation from the 1930s is still one of the most beloved films of all time, and the book isn't anything to snub either. Originally published in the year 1900, *The Wonderful Wizard of Oz* is one of the foundations of the fairy tale genre. It doesn't matter if you've never read an Oz book in your life—and believe me, there are plenty to be read—somewhere, at some place or time, you've heard or used an Oz reference. Who, then, would seek to ban a book that has become so important to the American experience?

America, that's who. It might surprise you to know that this timeless classic has been contested for many years and for a variety of reasons. According to an article called "Book's Alive" by Vincent Starret, the Detroit Library banned *The Wonderful Wizard of Oz* in 1957 for allegedly having no value for children. It was also said that the book perpetuated cowardly behavior, despite the fact that the character afflicted by cowardice was, in fact, never cowardly to begin with. The Land of Oz has also come under fire from religious communities, who claim that it presents children with a positive image of magic and sorcery. Clearly, whatever the reason, people who would seek to ban this classic are living somewhere on the wrong side of the rainbow.

8 A Wrinkle in Time by Madeleine L'Engle

This classic takes children into the realms of both science and magic. While *A Wrinkle in Time* may have been inspired by quantum physics theories, surprisingly it resonates very well with young children. This is the sort of story that teaches readers to look beyond the world they know and into the something spectacular, and it has often been praised for its imagination and vision. However, not everyone has been cheering for L'Engle's work.

Interestingly enough, while L'Engle has religious imagery in her books—a little like fellow author C. S. Lewis—*A Wrinkle in Time*'s chief naysayers come from religious communities. According to *Banned Books Awareness*, many religious individuals felt that L'Engle was too passive in her inclusion of Christian imagery. A foundation in Iowa even claimed that book had Satanic themes. In fact, some of the claims against this book are so absurd that a L'Engle fan might suspect that the book's nefarious villain, the Black Thing, is behind them.

7 Charlotte's Web by E. B. White

White's heartfelt tale of the relationship between two unexpected creatures, a spider and a pig, has been drawing children in for over half a century. Published in 1952, this classic has been readily available on most library shelves for children to read. However, some people would much rather that it never see the light of day.

In one extreme case, a school in England banned *Charlotte's Web* for fear that the pig Wilbur might be offensive to Muslim students. Fortunately, the Muslim Council of Britain saw the folly of this ban: The book, and all other pig books, were quickly restored to their rightful place on the shelves.

6 Bridge to Terabithia by Katherine Paterson

This classic title is number nine on the American Library Association's list of most commonly banned books of the 1990s. The complaints have been many, though perhaps the most commonly contested aspect is the book's portrayal of death. While some people applaud Paterson for crafting a story full of both fantasy and realism, others find the very real depiction of the death of a child to be too much for children to handle. Aside from the alleged morbid elements of this tale, *Bridge to Terabithia* has also been accused of promoting a variety of religious philosophies, including Satanism, Occultism, and New Age practices.

5 Alice in Wonderland by Lewis Carroll

Everyone has heard of Lewis Carroll's *Alice in Wonderland*. If they have not read the book, then they have at least seen one of the many adaptations, the most famous of which is Disney's animated classic. Terms like "vorpal sword," "chortle," and "galumph" were born from Carroll's work.

Alice in Wonderland has inspired several nonsensical complaints. While some reasons are similar to those levied against the sentient animals in *Charlotte's Web* and *Winnie-the-Pooh*, some of the more outrageous claims made against this book include alleged references to sexual acts and the encouragement of child abuse and drug abuse. Though most of these claims have been answered with explanations and rebuttals, there are still people today who find this book inappropriate for the intended audience. However, with well over 50 films, novels, and comics that have been either inspired by or directly based on Carroll's classic work, it's unlikely that *Alice in Wonderland* will be thrown down a rabbit hole anytime soon.

4 Green Eggs and Ham By Dr. Seuss

American author Dr. Seuss has become a household name, and you'd be hard-pressed to find a library or bookstore that does not carry at least one of his 46 children's books. *Green Eggs and Ham* is a book about trying new things and going against the status quo. Evidently, however, China did not wish to expand its citizens' palates. In 1965, the People's Republic of China banned this poetic classic, claiming that it promoted Marxist and homosexual ideas. Apparently, the Chinese government feared that the ham in *Green Eggs and Ham* represented some sort of sexual imagery and that Sam was a minion of temptation. The ban in China was only lifted after Dr. Seuss's death, and as far as anyone knows, it can now be read freely by Chinese schoolchildren who seek it out. Whether said schoolchildren read the book in a box or with a fox, is yet to be determined.

3 Where the Wild Things Are by Maurice Sendak

This classic, published in 1963, was adapted into a trippy, live-action film in 2009. Though it's been around for over 50 years, this book hasn't always been readily available in libraries and bookstores. After its release, *Where the Wild Things Are* was banned in libraries all across the U.S. for its dark tone and unruly lead character. Some parents were apparently uneasy about the fact that Max, the story's protagonist, acted far too much like a regular little boy—he was loud, chaotic, prone to tantrums, and full of mischief. Nowadays, you'll find far fewer libraries that still hold this ban, though some censors have stuck to their guns. Said censors have clearly lacked the desire to become kings or queens of their Wild Things.

2 Charlie and the Chocolate Factory by Roald Dahl

The chief complaint filed against this classic is the depiction of Mr. Wonka's Oompa-Loompas. While those of us only exposed to the 1971 film adaptation (as well as subsequent revisions of the book) might find this hard to believe, book-savvy folks—as well as Tim Burton fans—might be able to identify some problems. In the original text, Oompa-Loompas are depicted as dark-skinned pygmy people who work for cocoa beans rather than money. While Dahl claims that he never intended to work racist themes into his book, people were offended all the same. The book was banned for a short while in some parts of the U.S., though *Charlie and the Chocolate Factory* didn't spend too long stuck in the chocolate pump.

1 Watership Down by Richard Adams

Watership Down is sort of like a rabbity version of *Lord of the Rings*. The epic plot is filled with trials and tribulations, and it features a large party  of rabbits with different skills and attributes. These rabbits seek a new home, and they have to fight to get there every step of the way. In fact, the conflict and brutal realism of *Watership Down* is one of the factors that has caused this classic to be banned time and time again. Though never banned nationally to my knowledge, select schools in the U.S. have been known to ban this book. New York is one state that is home to schools enforcing such a ban, though the phenomenon doesn't appear to be too widespread. Whatever the case, the epic tale seems to either terrify or inspire people—so what's the outlook for this timeless classic? If you asked Fiver, the oracular rabbit of the party, I think he'd say that *Watership Down* will be around for a very long time, indeed.

TOP 10 Horribly
Disturbing Fairy Tales

by **Melita Linaker**

10 "Biancabella and the Snake" by Giambattista Basile, from Il Pentamerone (Entertainment for the Young), 1634

Features: Bestiality, unnatural pregnancy, dismemberment/bodily mutilation, death by being burned alive

While a woman sleeps in the garden, a snake crawls under her skirts and makes its way "into her body," where it comes to rest in her womb. The woman becomes pregnant, and when the baby (Biancabella) is born, she has a tiny snake coiled around her neck. The snake quickly slithers away into the garden.

When Biancabella is ten, she discovers the snake in the garden. The snake reveals itself to be her own sister and gifts her with great beauty. With her new beauty, she is quickly married off to a king.

The king's evil stepmother hatches a plan to be rid of Biancabella, and when the king is away at war, she pays a group of men to take the new queen into the forest and kill her. The men are unable to go through with the murder, so instead they cut off Biancabella's hands and tear out her eyes, which they give to the stepmother as proof of the queen's demise. The stepmother then places her own hideously ugly and deformed daughter in Biancabella's bed, and when the king returns home, she tells him that his precious Biancabella miscarried a child and has become hideous with grief.

Meanwhile, Biancabella decides to kill herself, but as soon as she attempts to do so, her sister appears in human form and magically heals Biancabella's horrible wounds. They return to the kingdom where the false queen now reigns. The evil plot is revealed, and the stepmother and her two daughters are burned alive in a furnace.

9 "The Myrtle Tree" by Giambattista Basile, from Il Pentamerone (Entertainment for the Young), 1634

Features: Unnatural birth, murder, dismemberment, death by angry prostitutes, execution by being buried alive in the sewer

A peasant woman gives birth to a stick of myrtle, which a prince then purchases for a great price. It turns out that a stunningly beautiful fairy lives within the myrtle stick and she soon begins sneaking into the prince's bed in the dark to "play at mute sparrow" with him. The prince takes her for his secret lover after she confesses that she is a slave to his every whim and desire.

Sadly, because the prince is entirely satisfied by the fairy, seven of his former prostitutes now find themselves out of work. So when the prince is away on business, they sneak into his bedchambers and discover his fairy lover. The enraged prostitutes smash the fairy's head open and break her body into pieces. They all take a piece of her corpse, except the youngest, who takes only a single lock of golden hair. All that is left of the unfortunate fairy are her teeth, hands, blood, and some bones. A servant, who was entrusted to water the myrtle, finds the grisly mess and buries it in the pot under the myrtle tree.

The fairy manages to grow a new body from the buried flesh and bones, and she reveals to the prince her murderers' identities. The prostitutes are all buried alive in the public sewer, except the youngest, who is married to the servant.

8 "The Little Mermaid" by Hans Christian Anderson, from Fairy Tales, 1839

Features: Mutilation, long-term suffering, suicide
A young, beautiful mermaid falls in love with a dashingly handsome human prince after saving him from drowning. In the hope of winning the prince's heart, she asks the sea witch for a pair of human legs. The witch agrees to give the mermaid the most beautiful pair of legs known to man. But there's a catch: Every step the mermaid takes will feel like it was taken on razorblades and her feet will bleed ceaselessly. And even worse, her greatest possession, a beautiful mermaid voice, will forever be silenced. But the mermaid is in love with the prince and agrees to the deal.

The next morning, the prince finds the mermaid washed up on the shore, naked, with her beautiful new human legs. Long story short, he marries another woman. The mermaid, after toying with the idea of killing the prince, eventually throws herself into the ocean and dies.

7 "Doralice" by Giovanni Francesco Straparola, from The Facetious Nights of Straparola, circa 1550

Features: Incest, infanticide, extremely cruel and unusual punishment/torture, death by being quartered
Evil Prince Tebaldo vows to kill his only daughter, Doralice, after she refuses to marry him. The terrified Doralice, having learned of her inces-

tuous father's intentions, hides inside a wooden chest that Prince Tebaldo sells to a merchant. She remains in the chest for months but is kept alive by a magical elixir given to her by her kindly old nurse. The chest ends up being sold to a king, who catches Doralice sneaking out of it and—rather spontaneously—makes her his wife.

Prince Tebaldo manages to track Doralice down. His disguise is so good that she doesn't recognize her evil father and lets him sleep in the nursery with her newborn infant twins. Tebaldo slaughters the twin babies and pins the crime on Queen Doralice herself. Her enraged husband has the unfortunate queen buried up to her neck in the ground. She is to be fed and watered to prevent her dying of starvation so her body can be slowly eaten alive by worms. Eventually, Tebaldo's crime is revealed: Doralice is removed from the ground, more dead than alive, and Tebaldo is tortured, quartered, and fed to the dogs.

6 "Sun, Moon, and Talia" by Giambattista Basile, from Il Pentamerone (Entertainment for the Young), 1634

Features: Coma sex/rape, attempted infanticide/forced cannibalism, death by being burned alive

This is the earliest written version of "Sleeping Beauty." It is prophesied at Talia's birth that she will one day face great danger from a chip of flax. Her father therefore orders that all flax be removed from the kingdom. When she is grown, Talia manages to find the only piece of flax in the entire kingdom, gets a splinter of it stuck beneath her fingernail, and falls into a deathlike sleep. Her father, beside himself with grief, orders the palace and surrounding countryside be abandoned so he can put the event out of his mind.

Eventually, another king stumbles upon the abandoned kingdom and finds Talia sleeping alone. Unable to wake her, he decides to rape the sleeping girl. He then returns home to his wife.

Talia becomes pregnant and, without waking, eventually gives birth to twins. While the babies try to find her breasts to suckle, one starts sucking on her finger and the flax splinter is loosened. Talia wakes up, and is overjoyed to find herself the mother of twins, whom she names Sun and Moon.

The king decides to return for a little more action, but instead of finding a comatose girl, he finds Talia awake and the mother of his children. A relationship soon develops between them. The king's wife learns of the affair and, pretending to be the king, sends for Sun and Moon. She gives them to the cook and tells him to slaughter and roast them and serve them to the king. The cook, unable to kill the babies, hides the twins and serves up two baby lambs instead. The queen watches gleefully as the king devours the meal. She then sends for Talia and demands she be burned alive. The King hears Talia screaming, and rescues her just in time. The awful queen is thrown in the fire instead and roasts to death. The cook then produces the twins, alive and well, and they all live happily ever after.

5 "The Old Woman Who Was Skinned Alive" by Giambattista Basile, from Il Pentamerone (Entertainment for the Young), 1634

Features: Old-lady sex, death by being skinned alive

This one may be rather long, but believe me: It's a story worth reading. A king mistakenly believes that two hideous, smelly, deformed old women are actually the most delicate, beautiful, and scrumptious of tender young maidens.

As you might expect, he has never actually laid eyes on them, since (fortunately for them) they're hidden behind a large wall. But he becomes so passionately aroused after kissing one of the old women's fingers through the keyhole in the gate, that he begs to be able to spend the night with her. She agrees to bed him, but only if he will take her in the dark, since, according to herself, she is "far too modest to expose her nakedness to him." The king rushes home to wait in anticipation for night to fall and his love to come to him.

In an attempt to make herself feel more youthful to the king's touch, the old woman takes all her loose, sagging skin and ties it behind her back with string. She then covers herself with a long shroud and limps in the dark to the king's chambers.

After he has finished "the deed" and she's fallen asleep, the king discovers the secret his "tender maiden" has hidden behind her back, and after lighting a candle he finds that his bedmate is actually a disgusting old hag. He freaks out and throws her out the window.

Luckily, the old woman has so much loose, sagging skin that she gets caught in the branches of a nearby tree and is left hanging there. Some fairies fly by and find the sight of the old woman so funny that they endow her with gifts of wondrous beauty, intelligence, and youth as a reward; she now has the body and face of a 15 year old! The king looks out his bedroom window in the morning, discovers a stunningly beautiful girl sitting in his tree, and immediately takes her for his wife.

The new queen, not wanting to reveal her beauty secret to her sister, tells the old hag that she has had herself skinned alive. The remaining old woman—presumably not wanting to be left out—quickly takes herself to the nearest barber shop, and requests that she also be skinned alive. When the barber has removed her skin down to her navel, the old woman dies of blood loss and pain, and her sister and the king live happily ever after.

4 "The Robber Bridegroom" by the Brothers Grimm, from Children's and Household Tales, 1812

Features: Murder, dismemberment, cannibalism

A miller marries his only daughter to a man who seems to be very respectable and well-off. The young woman visits her groom for supper but finds his house empty. Empty, that is, save for a bird that keeps telling her to leave and an old woman who tells her that her bridegroom is actually a murderous cannibal who eats his young brides and any other maiden he can get his hands on. The old lady then quickly hides the young woman behind a barrel. From her hiding place, the bride-to-be watches as her bridegroom and a group of men return home drunk, dragging a beautiful young maiden with them who is screaming and crying. Ignoring her pleas, they force the maiden to drink three different colored wines, after which her heart "bursts in two." The group of men then strip her naked and begin to dismember her body, sprinkling her flesh with salt in preparation to cook and eat it.

One of the unfortunate victim's fingers, adorned with a golden ring, rolls behind the barrel where the bride-to-be is hiding. She puts the severed digit in her pocket, then witnesses the entire macabre feast. When the men all fall into a drunken stupor, she creeps out over their prone bodies and runs all the way home.

The bridegroom is exposed for the monster he is when the bride-to-be produces the dead girl's finger at their wedding. He and his gang of murderers are all swiftly executed.

3 "The Rose-Elf" by Hans Christian Andersen, from Fairy Tales, 1839

Features: Murder, beheading, quite-possibly-incestuous domestic abuse, "mild" necrophilia, death by flowers

A young woman's lover is stabbed to death, beheaded, and buried by her wicked and possessive brother. After committing the murder, the brother is described as "entering the beautiful, blooming girl's bedroom as she lies dreaming of her lover, and bending over her, laughing hideously as only a fiend can laugh as he does so." This could mean he just stands at the foot of her bed and laughs, but it could also represent something a lot more sinister.

As the brother was burying the corpse, a dry leaf settled in his hair. A tiny elf, who witnessed the brutal act, hid under this leaf, which then settled on the girl's bed as her brother "bent over her." The elf climbs into the girl's ear, tells her of her lover's murder, and informs her where the body lies. The girl wakes up, brokenhearted, and goes into the woods to dig up her lover's head. She shakes the earth out of his hair, kisses his cold, dead lips, and carries the severed head home with her. She puts the head in a large flower pot, covers it in earth, and plants a twig of jasmine over it.

She weeps over the pot day and night, and the jasmine twig begins to grow beautiful flowers. Seeing his sister constantly kissing these flowers, the brother is furious, thinking she is going mad.

The girl eventually dies a quiet death. The elf hides in her ear and whispers sweet stories about her lover to comfort the girl as she dies. The brother carries the flower pot into his bedroom, and as he sleeps, tiny spirits come out of the flowers and kill him with spears to avenge the dead lovers. The murdered man's skull is later discovered in the flower pot and the evil deed is uncovered.

2 "The Tale of the Grandmother" by Anonymous

Features: Cannibalism, disturbing sexual content/pedophilia

Thought you knew "Little Red Riding Hood"? In this version, the Big Bad Wolf rushes to Grandmother's house after a little girl tells him she is delivering some milk and bread to the old woman. The wolf devours Grandmother, and after putting some of her flesh in the pantry and some of her blood into a bottle, he climbs into Grandmother's bed. When the little girl arrives, the wolf calls from the bed, "Eat some of the meat in the pantry my dear, and drink some of the wine in the bottle," and the girl proceeds to devour the grisly meal. As the girl eats, a little cat sings, "It is a slut that eats and drinks of her own grandmother's flesh and blood!"

The wolf then forces the little girl to burn all of her clothes and climb into bed naked with him. After feeling his hairy body and his big shoulders, and noticing his large teeth, she realizes it is not her grandmother she is in bed with at all, and tells the wolf she needs to go outside quickly to pee. He ties a bit if woolen yarn around her ankle so she cannot escape, but she ties the yarn around a tree and runs home naked. The wolf, growing impatient, calls out, "Are you taking a dump, child?" Not hearing any answer, he leaps out of bed and runs after the girl, but his plans are foiled when she makes it home before he catches her. No little girl for this big bad wolf tonight.

1 "The Juniper Tree" by the Brothers Grimm, from Children's and Household Tales, 1812

Features: Filicide (parent/child murder), dismemberment, parent/child cannibalism

An evil woman hates her stepson so much that she hatches a plan to get rid of him and thereby secure her husband's inheritance for their young daughter alone.

Feigning kindness to the little boy, the stepmother tells him to reach into a chest to get an apple. As he reaches in, she slams the lid of the chest down on his neck and his head is chopped off.

She then props the child's body up in a chair and places the head back on his corpse, covering the wound with a handkerchief. His little sister, Marlene, arrives, and the mother tells the girl that if her big brother won't answer her, she should cuff him around the ears. Unable to get an answer from her big brother, Marlene smacks him in the face and his head falls off.

Marlene becomes hysterical, believing she has killed her brother. Her mother comforts her, saying that they will hide the dead boy in a stew and no one will be any wiser. So they proceed to chop up the little boy's body and put the pieces into a pot—skin, bones, and all. Marlene cries so much during the horrific act that the stew does not need salt, for her tears have seasoned the meal beautifully.

When the father returns home, his wife explains that the boy has gone on holiday to the countryside, and she dishes up the macabre feast for him. The father greedily devours his own child, proclaiming that this is the best food he has ever eaten; he noisily sucks the meat off the bones, which he then throws under the table. Marlene cries ceaselessly as she watches her father eat her brother. When the father has finished eating, the little girl gathers up her brother's bones from under the table and places them beneath the juniper tree where the boy's dead mother is buried. A beautiful bird flies out of the tree and begins to fly around the countryside singing, "My mother killed me! My father ate me!"

This bird eventually kills the stepmother, and from the woman's burning remains the little boy appears, alive again. The father, brother, and sister walk hand in hand into the house and sit down at the table together to eat lunch.

CHAPTER 10

HISTORY

1. Top 10 Strange Fates of People Connected to Abraham Lincoln's Assassination

2. Top 10 Notorious Witches and Warlocks

3. Top 10 Terrifying Historic Villains

4. Top 10 Weird Historical Coincidences

5. Top 10 Brutal Atrocities People Continue to Defend

6. Top 10 Badass Gangs from History

7. Top 10 Horrible Historic Homicides

8. Top 10 Mad and Murderous Victorians

9. Top 10 Weird Stories about Famous People

10. Top 10 Historically Significant Sites Destroyed for Awful Reasons

11. Top 10 Dirty, Secret CIA Operations

12. Top 10 Greatest Impostors of the 20th Century

TOP 10 Strange Fates of People Connected to Abraham Lincoln's Assassination

by **Mike Devlin**

10 Mary Todd Lincoln

Many historians argue that Mary Lincoln suffered from bipolar disorder, or possibly narcissistic personality disorder, and a head injury sustained in a carriage accident caused her to suffer frequent migraines. Her carelessness with money was an issue when Abe was alive, but after his death, her spending spiraled out of control. She became known for buying strange multiples of items, like ten pairs of gloves at a time. She made bizarre spiritualist claims and told her son Robert that someone had tried to poison her.

In 1875, Robert had his mother committed to an asylum. Mary wrote letters to friends and the press that pressured her son into releasing her, but as soon as she was free she tried to order a suicidal overdose of laudanum. The pharmacist, realizing what she was about to do, gave her a placebo. She spent her final years with her sister Elizabeth, crippled by cataracts and spinal injuries, and died at 63. She was buried beside her husband.

9 Tad Lincoln

Thomas "Tad" Lincoln had it tough from the start—he was born with a cleft lip and palate. The result was a terrible speech impediment that only his father and those closest to him were able to understand. Perhaps because of his own rough childhood, Lincoln was very lenient toward his kids, and Tad and his brother Willie were described by insiders as "notorious hellions" given to rampaging about the White House, interrupting meetings, and turning their father's offices upside down.

In February of 1862, Tad and Willie both contracted typhoid fever. Tad survived, but Willie didn't make it. Afterward, his parents tended to let him get away with anything. He was so wild that he didn't attend school, and tutors couldn't handle him.

When Lincoln was shot, Tad was attending a play for children at nearby Grover's Theatre. The manager made an announcement about the tragedy to the crowd. Tad was traumatized and ran screaming from the room. Later, he spent time in Europe and Chicago with his mother. He died at only 18 years old from a mysterious ailment that has alternately been described as pneumonia, tuberculosis, pleurisy, or a heart attack.

8 Lewis Powell

Lincoln's murder was only a part of Booth's plot; he intended to take out the entire federal leadership. Former Confederate soldier Lewis Powell was designated to assassinate Secretary of State William H. Seward. He would be accompanied by co-conspirator David Herold (who was probably a little simple-minded). Powell was allowed into Seward's house after claiming that he was delivering medicine to the secretary, who had suffered serious injuries in a carriage accident. Powell attacked Seward with a knife, but a splint he was wearing protected him from having his throat slit. Other members of the household joined in the scuffle, and Powell injured several while making his escape. He was captured when he attempted to return to the house of the Surratts, where the conspirators were headquartered. Powell was known for his gentlemanly manner, and when the hangman slid the noose over his head, he told the young man, "I hope you die quick." He didn't. Powell was the last to die, thrashing for more than five minutes before finally going limp. His cohort, Herold, was also hanged.

7 George Atzerodt

Co-conspirator George Atzerodt was charged with assassinating Vice President Andrew Johnson. Atzerodt took a room in the hotel Johnson was staying in, but ended up losing his nerve and just getting drunk at the hotel bar. The next day, the bartender reported Atzerodt's suspicious behavior, which included repeatedly asking about Johnson's whereabouts. His room was searched, and evidence was found linking him to John Wilkes Booth, along with a knife and a loaded revolver. Atzerodt was found guilty. When he was hanged, his body jerked at the end of the rope for several minutes before he died.

6 Mary Surratt

Mary Surratt's role in the conspiracy to assassinate the president has long been debated. She owned the boarding house where the conspirators met, and was the mother of John Surratt, with whom John Wilkes Booth had once considered kidnapping Lincoln. It is likely that her only crime was trying to cover up for her son during the investigation. While George Atzerodt condemned her, Lewis Powell maintained that she was innocent. Pleas for Surratt's clemency fell on deaf ears, and she was executed alongside the men. Her death appeared to occur almost instantly. Her last words were

"Please don't let me fall." After she died, people began looting souvenirs from her boarding house until the police forced them to stop. Today, the building houses a restaurant. Mary Surratt was the first woman ever executed by the U.S. federal government.

5 John Wilkes Booth

The majority of would-be presidential assassins have tended to be deeply mentally unstable outcasts. John Wilkes Booth was cut from a different cloth. Part of a celebrated acting family, he was a dashing leading man: wealthy, smart, and devastatingly handsome. A strong sympathizer of the Confederacy, Booth had originally planned to kidnap Lincoln and then ransom him for the release of Confederate prisoners. But when he learned that Robert E. Lee had surrendered and all was lost, it became obvious that Lincoln had to die.

We all know what happened next. Six days after Lee surrendered at Appomattox, Lincoln was murdered. After shooting the president, Booth escaped on horseback into the wilds of Virginia. Cornered in a tobacco barn with accomplice David Herold, Booth refused to surrender. Herold turned himself over and the barn was set ablaze. Union soldier Thomas "Boston" Corbett shot Booth as he staggered about in the fire.

Booth did not die easily. Mortally wounded, he was dragged to the porch of the neighboring farmhouse. The bullet had smashed into his vertebrae and paralyzed him. He languished in agony for some three hours. His last words were "Useless, useless."

4 Boston Corbett

The killer of John Wilkes Booth may well have been the most disturbed individual on this entire list. Thomas "Boston" Corbett was a Union soldier and former hatter—a profession historically linked with lunacy due to mercury usage. He became devoutly Christian in his mid-twenties, growing his hair long in an imitation of Jesus and using scissors to castrate himself so he would not be tempted to enjoy the company of prostitutes.

Corbett was a part of the 16th New York Cavalry Regiment, assigned to capture John Wilkes Booth. They had been ordered to take Booth alive, but after a standoff in a tobacco barn in Virginia, Corbett shot Booth in the head, almost in the same spot Lincoln had been shot. Witnesses contradicted Corbett's report that Booth had been going for his weapon, but he was nonetheless widely praised for his action. Afterward, he returned to work as a hatter, but devolved into lunacy. After at least two incidents of threatening people with his revolver, he was remanded to the Topeka

Asylum for the Insane. Corbett eventually escaped, and after staying with a friend, claimed he was going to Mexico. He was never seen again.

It is widely believed Corbett actually built a cabin near Hinckley, Minnesota, and died in a massive wildfire on September 1, 1894. However, this is merely speculation, and Corbett's fate will likely never be known.

3 Major Henry Rathbone

When the Lincolns went to Ford's Theatre to watch *Our American Cousin*, they took along Major Henry Rathbone and Clara Harris. Rathbone was a promising young soldier in the Union Army, and Harris was his fiancée (and stepsister—but that's another story). When Booth shot Lincoln, Rathbone confronted him, but the assassin drew a dagger and stabbed the major in the arm. Rathbone himself nearly died from blood loss.

The couple soon married, but over the years Rathbone was haunted by the tragedy and descended into madness. On Christmas Eve in 1883, while staying in Germany, he shot Clara to death and attacked her corpse with a knife. Distraught, he turned the knife on himself, stabbing himself six times. He spent the rest of his life in an asylum for the criminally insane.

2 Clara Harris

We know the terrible fate that awaited Clara Harris that Christmas, but there was more to her story. During the scuffle at Ford's Theatre, Clara was covered in Lincoln's blood, which splattered all over her face and dress. She kept vigil with Mary Lincoln for hours afterward and the dress was never cleaned. Clara kept the bloodied garment in a closet in the family's Albany home, claiming that it brought on visions of Lincoln's ghost. The sightings were chalked up to bad dreams until other people began seeing the apparition. Eventually, the Rathbones had the closet bricked up, entombing the dress. In 1910, their son smashed the brick wall and burned the bloody dress, claiming that it had cursed the family.

1 Lincoln's Ghost

Some would say that not even death could release Abraham Lincoln from his earthly obligations. His is the spirit most frequently observed in the White House. A great number of very prominent people have been known to witness the ghost, including First Lady Grace Coolidge, President Theodore Roosevelt, and Queen Wilhelmina of the Netherlands. He seems to have been particularly active during Franklin Delano Roosevelt's tense wartime presidency, appearing to multiple staffers. FDR's wife, Eleanor, said she never saw Lincoln, but felt his presence many times.

Doubtless, the most amusing tale of confronting Lincoln came from Winston Churchill. While staying in the White House, Churchill took a hot bath. Upon returning to his room stark naked, he found Lincoln leaning on the fireplace mantle. They made eye contact, and Churchill claims to have told him, "Good evening, Mr. President. You seem to have me at a disadvantage." Lincoln smiled and vanished.

TOP 10 Notorious Witches and Warlocks

by **Pauli Poisuo**

1 Moll Dyer

Moll Dyer lived in the 17th century in St. Mary's County, Maryland. Many things about her are shrouded in mystery, but she was known to be a strange woman. An herbal healer and outcast who survived mostly through the generosity of others, she was eventually accused of witchcraft and burned out of her hut during a freezing-cold night. She fled into the woods and was not seen for several days until a local boy found her body. Moll Dyer was frozen to a large rock, in a kneeling position, with one hand raised to curse the men who had attacked her. Her knees had left permanent impressions on the stone. The villagers quickly found out they had been harassing the wrong woman (or, since they had accused her of witchcraft, the right woman). Moll Dyer's curse fell upon the area for centuries, causing cold winters and epidemics.

Her ghost, often accompanied by various strange spectral animals, has been seen many times and is still said to haunt the area. Her eerie reputation eventually served as inspiration for the movie *The Blair Witch Project*. Although Moll Dyer is an influential folk figure in American witchcraft, reliable historical evidence of her existence is scarce.

9 Laurie Cabot

Laurie Cabot has been one of the instrumental forces in popularizing witchcraft in the United States. A California girl with a storied history as a dancer, her keen interest in the magical arts led her to New England. After years of studying the craft, she set up shop in Salem, Massachusetts, a historical epicenter of witch hunts. Initially she was wary of declaring herself as a witch. But when her pet—a black cat—was stuck up a tree for days and the fire brigade refused to rescue it, she was forced to say she needed the cat in her rituals. The year was 1970 and the word "witch" still carried weight in Salem. The cat was immediately rescued by the firefighters.

Now officially out of the broom closet, Cabot became a national celebrity. She set up a coven and a witchcraft shop, both of which were instant hits. The shop, which has since moved online, became a tourist destination.

Cabot rapidly became one of the most high-profile witches in the world. Even the local government got in on the action—the governor of Massachusetts, Michael Dukakis, declared her the official "Witch of Salem" thanks to her influence and good work in the community.

Cabot maintains that any curse by a witch will come back to haunt her and never performs evil magic. According to her, witchcraft is magic, astrology, and environmentalism combined in a scientific manner. She is the author of many books and a major influence on the Wiccan religion, which partially formed around her beliefs and approach to witchcraft. Although she is hailed as the High Priestess of Wicca, she says she does not actually practice the religion because she was already doing it long before Gerald Gardner introduced Wicca to the world.

8 George Pickingill

George Pickingill sounds as though he walked straight out of a horror story. A tall, frightening 19th-century man with a hostile demeanor and long, sharp fingernails, he was a famously cunning practitioner of folk magic. Old George, as he was commonly known, was a farm worker who claimed to be a hereditary witch. According to him, his magical ancestry could be traced all the way back to the 11th century and the witch Julia Pickingill, who was a sort of magical assistant to a local lord.

Pickingill was a vile, unlikeable man who often terrorized the other villagers for money and beer. However, he was respected as well as feared. He was said to be a skilled healer and occasionally settled disputes between villagers.

In occult circles, Pickingill was a superstar—essentially the Aleister Crowley of his time. He was recognized as an acolyte of an ancient horned god, a frequent ally of Satanists, and the foremost authority on magical arts. As such, his counsel was widely sought by other witches. However, this authority was somewhat spoiled by the fact that Pickingill was a bit of a bigot (he would only endorse a coven if its members could prove they were of pure witch lineage) and something of a sexist (all the work in his covens was done by women, who also had to submit to some fairly unsavory practices).

7 Angela de la Barthe

Angela de la Barthe was a noblewoman and a notorious witch who lived in the 13th century. She was burned at the stake for a number of atrocious deeds she'd committed, according to the Inquisition. Her many crimes included, but were not limited to, nightly sexual relations with an incubus, giving birth to a wolf-snake demon that was blamed for the disappearances of children in the area, and generally being an unpleasant person.

In reality, of course, Angela was nothing but an eccentric or perhaps mentally ill woman whose only crime was supporting Gnostic Christianity, a religious sect frowned upon by the Catholic Church. Her uncommon behavior led to accusations of witchcraft, which in turn led to a horrifying death. In those times, such a fate was all too common.

6 Abramelin the Mage

The true identity of the 15th-century man known as Abramelin the Mage has been lost to history. However, his legacy lives on in the form of thousands of followers and imitators. Abramelin was a powerful warlock described by Abraham of Würzburg, a magical scholar who convinced Abramelin to teach him his secrets.

Abraham produced painstaking manuscripts of Abramelin's magical system, which was a complex process of commanding good and evil spirits to do his work. The system was based on magical symbols that could only be activated at certain times and using certain rituals. In 1900, the manuscript was printed as a book called *The Book of the Sacred Magic of Abramelin*. It was an instant hit in the occult community, and acted as a direct influence on many notorious practitioners, including big-name players such as Aleister Crowley.

5 Alice Kyteler

For a long time, Ireland was more relaxed about witchcraft than mainland Europe. However, witch hunts eventually arrived there too. One of the first and most notorious victims of these changing attitudes was Dame Alice Kyteler, a wealthy moneylender whose husbands had a nasty habit of dying and leaving everything to her. When husband number four started to feel sickly and his fingernails began to drop off, his children smelled a rat—especially when they found out he was just about to sign a will that would leave everything to Kyteler.

In 1324, church officials put Dame Alice on trial for heading a secret society of heretical sorcerers. She was not only the first witch to be accused on Irish soil, but also the first who had been directly accused of relations with an incubus. Authorities attempted to charge and imprison her multiple times. However, Dame Alice had many allies and always managed to escape.

Kyteler eventually disappeared, leaving her servant and her son to be charged in her stead. She is said to have fled to England, where she lived in luxury for the rest of her days. Whether she actually dabbled in the dark arts or not, she is remembered to this day as the first witch in Ireland.

4 Tamsin Blight

A famous figure in 19th-century Cornwall, England, Tamsin Blight was an esteemed healer and hedge witch. Hedge witches were named for the hedges that surrounded villages, which acted as a symbol for the boundary between this world and others.

Blight was said to be especially good at removing spells and curses, and was also a crafty healer. She could enter a trancelike state and tell the future. However, she had an arsenal of bad juju too, and her reputation was somewhat tarnished by her husband, a fellow magician called James Thomas. Although a respected conjurer, Thomas was a drunken bully and widely disliked for his antics. Tamsin eventually parted ways with him, but they got back together toward the end of her life.

Tamsin Blight's curses were effective, in part because of her reputation and the esteem in which she was held. Once she cursed a cobbler who wouldn't mend her shoes—she hadn't been paying her bills—and said he'd soon be out of a job. When word got out, no one did business with the man anymore, and he was eventually forced to leave the area.

3 Eliphas Levi

Alphonse Louis Constant was known better under the name Eliphas Levi, which he claimed was his birth name translated into Hebrew. He was the man largely responsible for the mystical arts as they are known today. During the 19th century, Eliphas Levi distilled a number of belief systems—from Christianity and Judaism to fringe beliefs such as Tarot and the writings of historical alchemists—into a strange hybrid that became known as Occultism.

A trained theologist who almost became a priest, Levi was always more of a scholar than a practicing magician. Still, he was extremely charismatic and had vast knowledge in many areas of magic. He authored many books of ritual magic.

Levi was particularly known for his work with Baphomet, the gargoyle-like entity allegedly worshipped by the Knights Templar. He considered this figure a representation of "the absolute." He drew the famous picture of Baphomet as a winged, goat-headed female figure—often the first picture anyone thinks of when the occult is mentioned.

2 Raymond Buckland

Raymond Buckland, "The Father of American Wicca," was deeply impressed by modern Gardnerian Wicca. He took Gerald Gardner's teachings to the New World and eventually refined them into his own variation called Seax-Wicca.

A veteran of witchcraft, Buckland has been involved in covens since the 1960s, usually as a leader. He is a Wiccan priest and a revered expert in all things neo-pagan. Until his retirement from active witchcraft in 1992, he spent decades as the most recognizable spokesman and the foremost expert of the craft. These days, he lives in rural Ohio, where he writes books about magic and continues to practice a solitary version of the craft.

1 Agnes Waterhouse

Agnes Waterhouse, commonly known as Mother Waterhouse, was one of the most famous witches England has ever known. The crimes she was accused of were pretty heinous—Mother Waterhouse and two other witches stood trial for dallying with the devil, cursing people, and even causing bodily harm and multiple deaths through their black magic. The strange thing about the case was that the church had nothing to do with accusing Agnes. She was the first English witch sentenced to death by a secular court.

In her testimony, Agnes freely admitted to practicing the dark arts and devil worship. She owned a cat she called Satan, which she claimed to have sent to kill her enemies' livestock and, on occasion, the enemies themselves. She was unrepentant, stating that Satan had told her she would die by hanging or burning and there was not a lot she could do about it.

Mother Waterhouse was indeed sentenced to hang for her crimes, despite the fact that the two other witches facing similar charges were let off lightly (one was found not guilty, the other sentenced to a year in prison, although later charges led to her death). Her Satanic bravado didn't last for long after sentencing. On her way to the gallows, Waterhouse made one last confession—she had once failed to kill a man because his strong belief in God had prevented Satan from touching him. She went to her death praying for God's forgiveness.

TOP 10 Terrifying
Historic Villains

by **Pauli Poisuo**

10 Pietro Caruso

When Fascist Italy aligned itself with the Nazis, few embraced the alliance more than Pietro Caruso. He was the police chief of Rome and responsible for upholding law and order. However, he ended up doing the exact opposite.

Caruso was a loyal bloodhound of Mussolini. Together with Herbert Kappler, the Gestapo commander of Rome, he participated in many horrors and gleefully pursued Mussolini's enemies. His greatest atrocity was the Fosse Ardeatine mass execution in 1944: In just one day, he gathered over 300 people in front of Nazi rifles. Caruso was especially famous for his sadism, a notable achievement during a time when bloodthirsty Nazis freely roamed the country.

After the war, Caruso was put on trial for his crimes. He was found guilty and sentenced to death by firing squad. But he almost didn't make it to his own execution: The furious Romans stormed his guard before the shooting and attempted to drown him in the Tiber River.

9 Hiroko Nagata

Western people often think of Japan as a restrained, misogynistic culture with little room for extremists—let alone female extremists. While this may be true to a certain extent, Hiroko Nagata managed to break the mold way back in 1972. Unfortunately, she broke it by forming a terrorist faction and killing a lot of people.

Nagata was the leader of United Red Army, a militant leftist group that wanted a Communist revolution in Japan. Her group was notorious for its extreme brutality, and before long, she got in trouble for conspiring to kill two people who tried to leave the group. But mere conspiring wasn't enough for her. In a single year, she led a number of horrifyingly violent group killings. The 12 victims were brutally beaten, tortured, and stabbed. These people weren't even her enemies—they were fellow members of her faction that she said weren't "revolutionary enough."

She was eventually arrested in an incident that involved hostages and the deaths of two police officers and one civilian. In the end, she died a lonely death, perishing on death row after a brain tumor operation and a long illness. She was 65.

8 Goran Jelisic

When a person is commonly known as "Serb Adolf," you know he's probably not a particularly nice person. Goran Jelisic certainly lived up to his nickname. Originally a humble farm-machinery mechanic, Jelisic's talent for murder and cruelty became apparent during the Bosnian War.

Fighting for the Bosnian Serb forces, who were responsible for 90 percent of the war crimes during the conflict, Jelisic rose in the ranks until he was placed in charge of a detention camp. His camp held hundreds of Muslims and Croats, who were all tortured, murdered (often by Jelisic himself), and buried in hidden graves during the Serbs' ethnic cleansing campaign in 1992.

Jelisic, who was only 23 at the time of his crimes, was arrested in 1998. He pleaded guilty to charges of war crimes and crimes against humanity. However, he was acquitted on the charges of genocide because the prosecution could not prove them conclusively. He was sentenced to 40 years in prison and is currently serving his sentence in Italy.

7 Kenji Doihara

Kenji Doihara was a Japanese general during World War II. He was in charge of operations during the Japanese invasion of Manchuria, which earned him the nickname "Lawrence of Manchuria." But this was merely because he was able to dress and act like the Chinese natives—not because he was heroic.

Unlike his *Lawrence of Arabia* counterpart, Doihara wasn't out to help people. He was in it for personal gain and didn't care how many people he hurt to get there. Despite his high rank, Doihara was a rampant opium user and a thoroughly corrupt soul. He was heavily involved in Japan's conquest of massive areas of China, which broke traditional Chinese societal structures and plunged the country into deep confusion.

Doihara seized the opportunity to become the mastermind behind all Manchurian crime. He controlled the drug trade and was the kingpin behind almost every criminal faction. Luckily, his near-total control of the underworld didn't last. After numerous terrifying deeds, he was caught, prosecuted for a long list of war crimes, and hanged in December 1948.

6 Laszlo Baky

Laszlo Baky had two passions: politics and violence. His brutal, counter-revolutionary work in Hungary earned him a high-ranking place in the Gendarmerie (a military faction acting as a police force). Baky became a prominent figure in the Hungarian Nazi party and eventually rose to the rank of state secretary.

In 1944, Nazi Germany invaded Hungary, and Baky was the happiest man on earth. Teaming up with SS leader Adolf Eichmann and a fellow Hungarian Nazi named Andor Jaross, Baky became responsible for gathering Hungary's Jews and sending them to concentration camps. Baky loved his job and was horrifyingly good at it. In a terrifying display of efficient logistics, Baky and his companions shipped hundreds of thousands of Hungarian Jews to their deaths.

Luckily, Baky was removed from power before the end of 1944. He fled the country but was caught a year later and sentenced to hang.

5 Pedro the Cruel

Tall, muscular, and well educated, Pedro of Castile seemed like the perfect king for Castile, a part of Spain. However, he soon proved the opposite. A petty and angry man with little talent as a leader, Pedro reacted to most situations with violence. He was an immoral and unfaithful husband and thought little of killing his wives and lovers if they became a burden.

Pedro was originally a decent ruler, but the combination of bad political decisions, a controlling mother, and a close call with the Black Death changed him. Pedro started to brutally murder anyone and everyone in Castile whom he perceived as a threat. A series of awful deaths followed, and it seemed that no one in Castile was safe from Pedro's cruel madness. Ironically, he was kind of right about his paranoia: In the end, he was assassinated by his own brother.

4 Ion Antonescu

Ion Victor Antonescu was one of the lesser-known despots of World War II. He was a career officer who seized power in Romania by forcing the king into exile. Antonescu sympathized with the Nazis in their mission to "purge" the world.

Antonescu was a cruel man who had no problem with killing hundreds of thousands of people in vain. During his rule, 300,000 Jews and up to 100,000 members of other "impure" ethnicities were murdered. His powerful army also provided more military support to the Nazis than all other Axis powers combined.

Because he wanted to keep Romania strong, he allowed most Jews within his "Old Romania" borders to live and continue working. He even refused Hitler's requests to deport them to Nazi death camps. Still, a death toll of up to 400,000 people and a close alliance with Hitler were more than enough to earn Antonescu a death sentence when the war was over.

3 Ieng Sary

Ieng Sary was a rather strange villain. By his own admission, he only ever killed one person (whom he seemed to think didn't count). He consistently claimed to be a nice, innocent man. As the foreign minister of Cambodia, he was the smiling face of their government. He used his charisma and diplomatic skills to negotiate support for his government and direct hatred toward Cambodia's enemy, Vietnam.

However, behind his flawless facade he hid unspeakable deeds. In reality, Ieng Sary was Brother Number 3 in the dreaded Khmer Rouge. He was close friends with their leader, Pol Pot, and was well aware of (and actively participating in) their terrifying, genocidal rule. Ieng Sary's task was to mask the horrors of the Khmer Rouge and gather support from their only ally, China. Sary's propaganda was a lethal weapon in itself; he presented Pol Pot's Cambodia as a utopia of pure Communism, where all possessions, family, and religion were truly and successfully thrown away. With such talk, he lured thousands of Cambodian students and intellectuals back to their home country. As soon as they arrived, they were thrown in jail as spies, tortured, and killed.

Ieng Sary was too slick and well-connected to suffer the fate of many other historical monsters. When the Khmer Rouge fell to Vietnam in 1979, he escaped to Thailand, where the Chinese embassy provided him with new clothes and a ticket to Beijing. There, he kept the Khmer Rouge movement going for two more decades, using his contacts to get filthy rich in the process. Although he was finally arrested in 2007, he was able to stall the process until his death in 2013.

2 Bleda the Hun

Attila the Hun was the ruler and creator of the Hunnic Empire. His sheer, over-the-top supervillain antics earned him the nickname "Scourge of God." Bleda the Hun was Attila's meaner older brother.

For years, Attila and Bleda ruled the Huns as equals. They fought wars, razed their enemies, and conquered everyone else's lands together. Attila, the guy who's now remembered as a fearsome, powerful warrior king, was actually the small, brainy kid brother of the duumvirate. Bleda was the physically imposing barbarian chieftain type.

Bleda was not only an imposing figure and a dangerous conqueror, but a true supervillain in all senses of the word: He even got himself a Moorish dwarf that he kept around as a cruel combination of "pet," jester, and (during battles) an Austin Powers–style, armor-clad Mini-Me.

The reason Bleda isn't better known is that he was unlucky enough to cross the only person more dangerous than himself: Attila. The younger Hun started getting fed up with Bleda, particularly with his dwarf fixations. The brothers' relationship spiraled into a power struggle. Soon enough, Bleda mysteriously perished in either a genuine hunting accident or—more likely—an "accident" orchestrated by his brother.

1 Lavrentiy Beria

Lavrentiy Beria was, on the surface, the silver-tongued lackey of Joseph Stalin. However, his meek appearance was deceiving: Beria was one of the few men who could frighten even Stalin.

During the 1920s and '30s, Beria rose through the Communist ranks like a rocket. He specialized in the intelligence and counterintelligence operations of Cheka (the secret police) and its many successors, ultimately becoming the leader of the People's Commissariat for Internal Affairs (NKVD). According to legend, he personally strangled the man who held the job before him.

Beria was a skilled political player. What's more, he was a remorseless killer who didn't hesitate to terminate anyone in his way. As head of NKVD, he would do anything to get a confession. Wherever he went, people went missing. Beria personally oversaw many of Stalin's political purges and used this as an opportunity to satisfy his desire for mass murder. The infamous gulag work camps all operated under his supervision.

And then there was his main job: Beria's NKVD charged and convicted hundreds of thousands of Russians for high treason, often under false or absurd accusations. Beria also created an effective worldwide spy system and dabbled in assassinations. By February 1941, Beria became the deputy prime minister. Along with his other duties, he oversaw strategic raw materials production for the war effort, naturally using the people he sent to the gulag camps as slave labor.

If he wasn't despicable enough already, Beria was also a sexual deviant of the highest order. He routinely raped and abused women who had often been taken from the street for that purpose. Those who resisted were murdered. His depravity was well known, and Stalin himself was said to be terrified when he heard his daughter was alone with Beria.

TOP 10 Weird Historical Coincidences

by **Dylan Angeles**

10 The "My Way" Killings

People in the Philippines love karaoke. The country is full of karaoke bars, and singing is a large part of their culture. For the most part, karaoke is a playful activity, but some people have taken it very seriously. On more than one occasion, people in the Philippines have been murdered while performing Frank Sinatra's 1969 song "My Way." The deaths have been called a coincidence by some because it is a popular karaoke tune, but many Filipino karaoke bars have banned the song.

In some places, the term "videoke rage" has been used to describe the deaths. In one case, 29-year-old Romy Baligula was shot to death by a security guard after he wouldn't stop singing the song. The song has been known to spawn riots and many people refuse to sing it because of the trouble it might cause.

9 July 11, 1991

On July 11, 1991, a wave of unexplained UFO sightings occurred over Mexico City. The events were witnessed by thousands of people and investigated by the Mexican government. Coincidentally, the UFOs were seen during a total solar eclipse.

During the eclipse, people in Mexico City reported a large metallic disk in the sky. The object was videotaped by multiple people and broadcast on the news. The event was one of the first widely reported UFO sightings in Mexico City, and since that time, the area has become a hotbed of unexplained activity.

The connections between the solar eclipse and the UFOs have caused some to speculate that the aircraft were predicted by the Dresden Codex of the Mayan calendar. The calendar identifies the July 11 eclipse as the Sixth Sun of Quetzalcoatl and says it will bring about changes and cosmic awareness. In 2010, a story appeared on the Internet that suggested the United States was keeping the events of July 11, 1991 hidden from the public. It also suggested that the U.S. government was fighting a secret war against aliens near the continent of Antarctica.

8 Chris Benoit and Wikipedia

In June of 2007, professional wrestler Chris Benoit murdered his family and committed suicide. Benoit was a popular member of World Wrestling Entertainment, and the news of his death shocked people all over the world. Over a three-day period, Benoit strangled his wife and suffocated his seven-year-old son. He then used a weight machine to hang himself. In the wake of the tragedy, it was revealed that Benoit had previously been accused of abusing his wife and was prone to fits of rage. Some felt he might have experienced a case of "roid rage," been a severe alcoholic, or had brain damage.

In a strange coincidence, 14 hours before the police discovered the bodies of Benoit and his family, his English Wikipedia page reported his wife's death. It said, "Chris Benoit was replaced by Johnny Nitro for the ECW World Championship match at Vengeance, as Benoit was not there due to personal issues, stemming from the death of his wife Nancy." The event has been called an "unbelievable hindrance" by the police, who seized the computer of the man who posted the information.

Chris Benoit did not leave a suicide note, but sent out a series of texts before killing himself that said: "My physical address is 130 Green Meadow Lane, Fayetteville, Georgia 30215." The circumstances surrounding his death may have been bizarre, but the evidence points to Benoit murdering his family, despite what some might think.

7 Windshield Pitting and Operation Castle

Starting in April of 1954, people in Bellingham and Seattle, Washington, started to report unusual holes, pits, and dings in their car windshields. The reports quickly spread to different areas of the state and thousands of people were affected. At first, it was thought to be the work of vandals, but after parking garages and secluded neighborhoods were targeted, the reports began to spread.

By April 15, 1954, close to 3,000 windshields were damaged, and police released a statement indicating that 95 percent of the cases were caused by public hysteria. Others put forth the theory that the damage was being caused by the infestation of flea eggs, cosmic rays, or nuclear fallout.

On March 1, 1954, the United States started Operation Castle, a series of high-yield nuclear tests carried out at Bikini Atoll, a group of islands located in the Pacific Ocean about 4,800 miles from Seattle. The initial test of Operation Castle was named Castle Bravo, and it was the first dry-fuel thermonuclear hydrogen bomb detonated by the U.S.

After Castle Bravo was set off, it became clear that the U.S. government had misjudged its power. It was approximately 1,000 times more powerful than each of the atomic bombs used during World War II, and the nuclear fallout surrounded the island and spread quickly. The event was the most significant case of accidental radiological contamination in U.S. history.

Five more nuclear tests were carried out in the area after Castle Bravo. The amount of nuclear fallout released into the atmosphere was difficult to measure because the data was skewed by previous explosions. By coincidence, the timeline for Operation Castle falls directly in line with the 1954 Windshield Pitting Epidemic. The city of Seattle is located in a region where it is possible that nuclear fallout from Bikini Atoll could have hit.

6 Sirente Crater and Triumph of the Church

During the reign of Emperor Constantine, Christianity became the dominant religion of the Roman Empire. It remains unclear what caused Constantine to favor Christianity, and the event has become known as the Triumph of the Church. During his childhood, Constantine was exposed to a form of Christianity by his mother, Helena, but wasn't baptized until shortly before his death. Officially, Constantine and Licinius legalized Christian worship in AD 313.

The Sirente Crater is a seasonal lake located in central Italy. It's pretty much in the middle of nowhere. In the late 1990s, the area was studied by Swedish geologist Jens Ormö, who suggested that ridges near the site indicated the crater was formed by a bolide collision (a collision between a relatively large asteroid and the Earth). A study performed by the Sirente Crater Group concluded that the lake was created by the impact of a meteor with the force of a small nuclear bomb.

However, other scientists have pointed to a lack of evidence for a collision and hypothesized that the lake was formed by human excavation. The area is littered with small pieces of exploded bombs and grenades, which has caused some to wonder if explosives might have played a factor.

The existence of the Sirente Crater has caused people to re-examine why Constantine converted to Christianity. Jens Ormö has noted that Constantine and his army were once camped only 60 miles from the Sirente Crater before the Battle of the Milvian Bridge. The coincidence between the two events is speculative, but still interesting.

5 Violet Jessop

Violet Jessop was an ocean liner stewardess who survived three separate disasters on Olympic-class ships, including the sinking of the RMS *Titanic*. The three ships were the largest and most luxurious boats of the early

20th century, but coincidentally, they experienced horrible accidents early in their careers.

Jessop was an Irish emigrant who worked her first job as a stewardess with the Royal Mail Line on the *Orinoco*. On June 14, 1911, Jessop was on the RMS *Olympic* when the boat crashed with the cruiser HMS *Hawke*. At the time of the accident, the *Olympic* was the largest civilian liner in the world. It took heavy damage and flooding in the crash, but was able to make it back to Southampton.

On April 10, 1912, Violet boarded the *Titanic* on the ship's maiden voyage. Four days later, the boat hit an iceberg and sank in the North Atlantic. During the sinking, Violet was asked to set an example for the people who did not speak English and were having a hard time following directions. She was able to board the sixteenth lifeboat and was given a baby to look after.

After the outbreak of World War I, Jessop worked as a stewardess for the British Red Cross. On November 21, 1916, she was onboard the HMHS *Britannic* when the ship hit a mine and sank in the Aegean Sea. The *Britannic* was the largest ship to be lost during World War I, and 30 people died in the tragedy. As the ship went under, Jessop was forced to jump off her lifeboat and was pulled under the water. She hit her head on the ship's keel, but was able to surface and be rescued. Before the *Britannic* was lost, Jessop made sure to grab her toothbrush because it was the one item she most missed in the aftermath of her *Titanic* experience.

4 Eleanor Rigby

"Eleanor Rigby" was released by the Beatles on August 5, 1966, a week before the band's last commercial tour. In 1966, McCartney gave an interview about how he came up with the lyrics for the song. He said that he originally came up with the idea of "Father McCartney" but figured it was inappropriate to use his dad's name, so looked in the phone book and found "McKenzie." Ultimately, the name "Father McKenzie" was used in the song's lyrics.

McCartney came up with the name "Eleanor" from actress Eleanor Bron and "Rigby" from a store in Bristol called Rigby & Evens Ltd, Wine & Spirit Shippers. In 1984, Paul was quoted as saying, "I just liked the name. I was looking for a name that sounded natural." In the 1980s, a grave was discovered in St. Peter's Parish Church in Woolton, Liverpool, with the name Eleanor Rigby on it. Even more coincidentally, a few yards from Eleanor's grave is another tombstone with the last name McKenzie on it.

The cemetery is located near the spot where Lennon and McCartney first met, and the two spent a lot of time in the cemetery sunbathing as teenagers. In response to the news that there was a gravestone with the name Eleanor Rigby, McCartney said that he might have been subconsciously influenced by the name on the gravestone. The coincidence is one of the most famous in rock history and gave momentum to the "Paul is dead" conspiracy.

3 Death of Ahmad Shah Massoud and 9/11

Ahmad Shah Massoud was a military leader in Afghanistan who was assassinated on September 9, 2001—two days before 9/11. At the time of his death, Massoud was the head of the United Islamic Front (Northern Alliance) and strongly opposed the Taliban. He was a central figure in the resistance against the Soviet Union in the 1980s and became a hero in Afghanistan after the war.

On September 9, 2001, two men posing as journalists killed Ahmad Shah Massoud in a suicide bombing. The culprits placed a bomb in a camera and blew it up while meeting with the military leader. One of the assassins died in the explosion, and the other was reportedly shot and killed while trying to flee the scene. Despite an attempt by the Northern Alliance to keep the news quiet, Massoud's death was almost immediately reported by the BBC and North American news outlets.

Several months before 9/11, Ahmad Shah Massoud gave a speech to the European Parliament that warned against a major terrorist attack in the United States. It is thought that he was murdered by al-Qaeda to help protect Osama bin Laden and the Taliban in the wake of 9/11; bin Laden likely felt he could take control of the Northern Alliance with Massoud out of the picture. al-Qaeda has never taken responsibility for the assassination.

2 Peshtigo and Great Chicago Fires

On October 8, 1871, the Midwestern United States experienced an enormous firestorm that burned 62,300 square miles of land around Peshtigo, Wisconsin. The event is the deadliest fire in U.S. history and killed 1,500–2,500 people. The firestorm was caused by strong winds and forest fires. After gaining enough energy, the blaze quickly developed into a massive wall of fire that reached a speed of 100 miles per hour and produced tornado-style winds. The fire was so hot that sandy beaches were turned to glass and people were incinerated. The fire jumped over the waters of Green Bay and destroyed 12 separate communities in the area. It tossed rail cars and houses into the air and left thousands of people with nothing.

Some 250 miles south of Peshtigo, Wisconsin, the city of Chicago also experienced one of its largest fires in history on October 8, 1871. The Great Michigan Fire also started on October 8 and burned a large number of cities in the area. When looking over the destruction, some have come to wonder what triggered the fires.

The coincidence has caught the attention of a group of researchers who have proposed that the fires were all started when Comet Biela broke up over the Midwest. Meteorites are not known to start or spread fires, as they are cold to the touch when reaching the ground. However, it has been suggested that the methane in comets could potentially ignite if the object is large enough and hits a dry patch of land that has experienced forest fires. Others have suggested that an airburst over a forest fire–riddled area could cause a massive firestorm. On October 8, 1871, people all over Wisconsin reported seeing a series of spontaneous ignitions, balls of fire, blue flames, and a lack of smoke usually representative of a firestorm.

1 Chelyabinsk Meteor and 2012 DA14

On February 15, 2013, an asteroid entered the Earth's atmosphere over the southern Ural region of Russia and exploded. The event was witnessed by

thousands of people and became the largest known airburst since the 1908 Tunguska event. The blast produced a light brighter than the sun, and the shock wave was felt by people all over the area. The energy of the explosion was equivalent to 20–30 of the atomic bombs used at Hiroshima.

The asteroid was not detected by the authorities before the airburst, and the event surprised many people. It wounded 1,500 and damaged over 7,000 buildings. The meteor was caught on tape by multiple sources, which show a giant fireball in the sky followed by an enormous explosion of light. It was reported that the meteor made the ground hot, and the city smelled like gunpowder after the explosion. The event was an extremely rare occurrence and the only time in history that a meteor has been known to cause human injury.

Approximately 16 hours after the Chelyabinsk Meteor hit Russia, another asteroid named 2012 DA14 came within 17,200 miles of the Earth's surface. The asteroid gained a new record for the closest passage to Earth for an object of its size (98 feet).

Despite the incredible rarity of the Chelyabinsk Meteor and close approach of DA14, it has been determined that the asteroids were in no way related because they had significantly different orbits. The coincidence is just crazy because the two events are so rare.

TOP 10 Brutal Atrocities People Continue to Defend

by **Morris M.**

10 Pinochet's Regime

Augusto Pinochet was one bad dude. After overthrowing Chile's elected government in a coup, he proceeded to set up one of the most feared regimes in Latin American history. Over the course of 15 years, his secret police engaged in an open campaign of mass rape, torture, and disappearances. Special camps were set up deep in the Atacama Desert where inmates were electrocuted, beaten with chains, and sexually assaulted. Thousands were executed, their remains ground down and buried in the sand. Nearly a quarter of a century later, their relatives are still looking for these fragments of bone. In short, Pinochet was a monster—and the people of the radical right are utterly enthralled by him.

See, Pinochet's regime managed the double whammy of ousting a Socialist government and introducing sweeping free-market reform. Since a violent coup and the horrific torture of 40,000 people apparently doesn't compare to cheap point scoring, plenty of U.S. academics and journalists continue to defend his rule as a necessary step on the road to democracy. As the Argentine writer Ariel Dorfman pointed out, "saying Pinochet brought democracy to Chile is like saying Thatcher brought Socialism to Britain."

9 Rwanda

Everyone accepts that the Rwanda genocide was one of the worst atrocities of the late-20th century. So it's no surprise that the man who brought an end to the ethnic strife—President Paul Kagame—is celebrated as a hero. Unfortunately, this hero worship extends to ignoring his own human rights abuses.

Last year, the *Guardian* reported on the authoritarian streak Kagame was developing and reached some worrying conclusions. Alongside the intimidation of opposition parties and attacks on journalists, they found evidence of civilians being detained without trial and tortured with beatings, suffocation, and electrocution. Even more worrisome, they found reports of state-sponsored death squads carrying out revenge attacks on everyone from ordinary people to politicians—including the near-decapitation of an opposition party deputy. Basically, Kagame seems to be shaping up to become the next Robert Mugabe; yet people from Tony Blair to Bill

Clinton continue to praise his rule, even as it drags Rwanda back toward a very dark place.

8 Castro's Cuba

Castro is the far left's version of Pinochet: a violent lunatic who remains unfathomably popular despite his track record of murder. And while it's kind of fun to watch from the outside as Cuba thumbs its nose at U.S. imperialism, the reality on the inside is a whole lot more depressing.

For starters, there's the prevalence of prison camps that look worryingly like gulags, including one specially designed to house children. Then there's the detention and torture of up to 100,000 people over the last 40 years. Finally, there's the brutal oppression of gay people. Into the 1970s, Cuba imprisoned gay men in concentration camps without trial or appeal. Often they were forced to undergo a process of "re-education"—a code word that more or less translates to an attempt to torture them straight. In other words, it was a bad time to be openly gay; it wasn't until 2010 that the victims received so much as an apology.

7 Indonesia's Hidden Genocide

In 1965, Indonesian paramilitaries embarked on one of the bloodiest peacetime genocides in history. Over the course of a year, 500,000 suspected Communists were rounded up and murdered—beaten to death, strangled with wire, or knifed and dumped by the roadside. Although the killings were theoretically political, in practice they were a smokescreen for the slaughter of emigrant Chinese families. Entire villages were burned down; children were forced to watch as their parents were strangled, and girls as young as 14 were brutally gang-raped. So, with that in mind, how do you think these killers are currently seen in their home country?

They're regarded as heroes. Across the whole of Indonesian society, the rebranded death squads attract tens of thousands to their Fascist marches; they have members in high levels of government and are publicly lauded for finding "humane" ways of exterminating Communists. Almost no one challenges this official version of events, and mass murderers walk around freely, respected for their role in the genocide—a state of events that may well be contributing to yet another round of ethnic cleansing currently being undertaken.

6 Stalin

Living in the West, it seems laughable that even the most staunch Communist would defend Stalin. After all, the man killed more people than Hitler, set up the most vicious secret police the world has ever known, and opened the door to other psychopaths like Ceausescu and Lukashenko. He also engineered the famine that left three million Ukrainians dead—so it can come as a surprise to learn that his most vigorous defenders are Ukrainian natives.

In 2010, the Ukrainian city of Zaporizhia commissioned a new statue of Stalin for their town square. Read that again and let the true extent of its madness sink in. The people of a nation that Stalin expressly set out to eliminate honored his memory not by burning effigies of him, but by erecting statues. But Ukraine's love affair with Stalin goes beyond statues to even using him to advertise utility companies. It sounds crazy, and that's because it totally is.

5 The Firebombing of Germany

By any sane measure, the firebombing of Germany was deeply immoral. For three years, the Allies rained incendiary death down on civilian targets, killing nearly six times as many people as the Hiroshima and Nagasaki bombings combined.

Take the bombing of Dresden: Aside from one or two industrial areas, the city contained almost no military targets. What it did contain was hundreds of thousands of refugees, thousands of whom suffocated in the attack. At Hamburg, 50,000 people were wiped out in one night, while other towns of no strategic value were completely annihilated. And you better believe it was brutal. Survivors reported climbing over mountains of corpses, bodies melting into the tarmac roads by the intense heat, and seeing shell-shocked mothers carrying the remains of their dead children in suitcases. In short, the human cost of the campaign was so high that even Winston Churchill was disgusted by it—yet there are people out there who still claim the attacks were justified as just a part of winning the war.

4 The Armenian Genocide

In 1915, the Turkish army systematically rounded up and exterminated 1.5 million Armenians using methods that would later find fame in the corridors of Auschwitz. Women and children were sent on long death marches into the Syrian Desert without food, water, or shelter. Others were taken to camps and worked to death, while even more were executed and dumped in mass graves. Most horrific of all, though, was the Turkish penchant for using smoke-filled caves as a primitive form of a gas chamber. The effect of these policies was instantaneous and depressing: From two million in 1914, the Armenian population dropped to just 400,000 by 1922.

It was, by any imaginable definition, genocide, but despite all this, the federal government has never explicitly recognized it as such. The Turkish government, meanwhile, claims it was an unfortunate side effect of World War I—a bit like if Germany claimed the Holocaust was a "misunderstanding." And if there's one thing we should never willingly allow our leaders to do, it's downplay a tragedy of this scale.

3 The Palestinian Massacre

In 1982, the Israeli army opened the gates of a Palestinian refugee camp and quietly allowed Lebanese paramilitaries inside. What followed was a massacre. The Lebanese troops went from house to house armed with axes and raped and dismembered at least 800 women and children while Israeli flares shot overhead, flushing the Palestinians out of their hiding places. Like so much on this list, it was a hideous atrocity, a preventable bit of psychosis that was found to be the responsibility of one man: Ariel Sharon.

As defense minister, he allowed the paramilitaries into the compound. At the time, he was quoted as saying "terrorists" needed "mopping up," and telling the American envoy, "If you don't want the Lebanese to kill them, we will kill them." All of this is well-documented historical fact. Yet there are people who continue to airbrush this part of Sharon's legacy—despite the Israeli Kahan Commission finding him responsible, and despite Sharon himself privately admitting he could be prosecuted for genocide.

2 The British Empire

As the leading superpower of the Victorian age, the British Empire had some incredible accomplishments. Technology, science, literature, and engineering, for example, as well as genocide, bloodthirsty repression, and murder.

Take the Irish famine. What started out as an ordinary disaster soon transformed into slaughter as the British implemented brutal free-market reforms that resulted in the Irish being effectively worked to death. In India, the colonial government engaged in routine massacres, including the murder of 1,500 peaceful protesters in Amritsar. When Pakistan was created in 1947, it led to a wave of sectarian violence that left nearly half a million dead—but even these brutal mismanagements don't compare to the worst abuses.

During the Kenyan Mau Mau uprising, the colonial police beat, castrated, and burned prisoners alive. Rape of suspects, including with broken glass, was routine. In the Yemeni port of Aden, a secret torture center was operated for years, while authorities in Botswana drew up plans to test a batch of lethal toxic gas over the country. Basically, colonial Britain was nothing short of a one-stop murder factory—yet people insist on viewing it with a sort of misty-eyed nostalgia.

1 Iraq

It's now accepted that the Iraq War was nothing short of a total disaster: mass civilian casualties, no weapons of mass destruction found, and a coun-

try that remains a shattered ruin to this day. But hey, that's war, right? Civilian casualties are to be expected. Only these weren't just accidents: By almost every measure, they were war crimes.

From the murder of two journalists to the slaughter of surrendering insurgents, almost every record of the conflict shows a litany of horrific abuses. Prisoners handed over for torture; American "rape squads" stalking villages, abusing and murdering teenage girls; civilians gunned down at checkpoints; and helicopter "gun runs" over peaceful neighborhoods that saw the murder of dozens of innocent people. Almost none of these crimes have been accounted for, no apology given or compensation paid out. To this day, people describe the invasion as a "humanitarian mission" without a hint of irony.

TOP 10 Badass Gangs from History

by **Aaron Short**

10 Les Apaches

Les Apaches were a French street gang that operated in turn-of-the-century Paris before World War I. They were called Apaches because they were so ferocious during attacks that a policeman, upon hearing of their crimes, exclaimed that they were as vicious as Apache warriors.

They were stylishly dressed, with fancy, striped shirts and berets, creating their own distinct style that would catch on and end up becoming popular in Bohemian circles. But they weren't just fashion victims—they could actually fight. They practiced their own down-and-dirty martial art called *savate*. This was a fighting style that relied upon kicks and open-handed punches. A group of Apaches would mug Parisian gentlemen with a combination of *savate* and great numbers, creating such a fear in Paris that the upper classes also picked up on it to protect themselves from constant

Apache attacks. But it's not like the Apaches needed martial arts to protect themselves: They had a very specialized weapon that would make James Bond jealous. The Apache pistol also functioned as a knife and folded into a pair of brass knuckles. As you can see, the Apaches didn't just believe in overkill. They believed in over-overkill.

9 The Forty Elephants Gang

What distinguishes the Forty Elephants Gang from the other gangs on this list is that it was entirely female. Before feminism existed, these gals took advantage of the patronizing sexism of the age that meant women were afforded extreme levels of privacy while shopping. It only took a few of these ladies working together to practically strip a store clean of clothing, jewelry, and other loot during a shoplifting spree. The gang operated from some point after the late 1700s right up until the 1950s, mostly targeting areas around London. The most impressive thing about this gang is that men had a completely subservient role within their hierarchy. Their leader was a woman called Maggie Hill who was as deadly as she was pretty—she wore diamond-studded rings like brass knuckles in case things got messy and she had to start swinging her fists.

8 The Know-Nothings (aka The Bloody Tubs)

The Know-Nothings were a group of toughs from Civil War–era Baltimore who fought for something more terrifying than drugs or territory: politics. Working on behalf of nativists (politicians opposed to immigrants), they intimidated people into voting for the candidates they endorsed.

The Know-Nothings got their name from the politicians they supported, who always exclaimed "I know nothing!" when quizzed about the gang. They would block voting booths, stab voters with awls, beat people up, and dunk them into vats full of blood (which earned them their other name, "The Bloody Tubs"). They even rounded up voters and kept them in dank basements until they voted the way the Know-Nothings told them to. One of the voters unfortunate enough to receive this treatment was Edgar Allen Poe, who turned ill a few days later and died. They also fought with volunteer firefighters for control of fire hydrants during fires, causing bloody riots while houses burned to the ground. All in all, a nasty bunch.

7 Kabukimono

The Kabukimono ("crazy ones") are what became of lordless samurai who formed into drunken gangs of what can only be described as feudal Japanese glam rockers. They were mostly heavily armed, disenchanted teenagers who wore women's clothes and makeup and had their own slang and long hair—sometimes styled ridiculously. Just imagine roving gangs of them, trained to kill, armed with the sharpest swords ever invented.

Although they looked ridiculous, they were actually deadly—drunkenly dueling in the streets with their swords, committing petty crimes, and generally not caring about anything, having now become wandering gangs of hooligans. Their motto was "I have lived too long!" which paints a pretty clear picture of how much fear the Kabukimono had of the rule of law: zero.

6 The Vorovsky Mir

The Vorovsky Mir ("thieves in law") were formed in the gulags of Soviet Russia as collections of thieves, bandits, and murderers who banded together for mutual protection. They had little love for the short-sighted and brutal regime that created them, and in a kind of wacky echo of the Communist ideal, they created their own criminal code that they each vowed to uphold. If members broke this code, they were put on trial by the gang.

The Vorovsky Mir identified each other with elaborate tattoos, a tradition that still exists today in Russian organized crime. Because it was hard to get certain luxury items before the fall of the Berlin Wall, the Vorovsky Mir thrived on smuggling, bringing in clothes and food to Russia. They were so successful that they've survived to the present day—in a fashion— eventually evolving into the Russian Mafia.

5 Mohocks

Like Les Apaches, this London-based gang from the 18th century also modeled themselves after a Native American tribe and are the sort of gang you only expect to find in movies and nightmares. After a delegation of Native Americans arrived in London to visit the queen, they created such a stir that a youth gang was formed in their honor who called themselves "Mohocks." They assaulted people at night, slashing and disfiguring their faces, cutting their noses off with knives; they beat people up and even stuffed women into barrels and rolled them down hills.

This was all the more shocking to 18th-century London when rumors that the Mohocks were upper-class youth started going around. This caused moral panic among the lower classes (which mistrusted the gentrified rich folks of London) and plain old fear among the higher classes. And it's not surprising that people were scared. The Mohocks had a habit of getting drunk and creating huge riots. They would attack pedestrians willy-nilly, disfiguring their faces for no real reason, *Clockwork Orange*–style, gouging out people's eyes and stabbing them with swords.

4 The Five Points Gang

The Five Points Gang was a pre-Prohibition, Italian-American New York gang, operating from the mid-19th to the early-20th century from the Five Points district of Manhattan. Al Capone was a member at one point before he went on to bigger and more horrible things. In fact, he received the facial scar that gave him the nickname "Scarface" during a bar fight while serving in the Five Points Gang.

And although it was the Mafia who would later go on to popularize the image of the Italian gangster in an expensive designer suit, it was the Five Points Gang that was the first to require that all members dress sharply. They rose to prominence as the worst gang in New York, and possibly the whole of America, with even the Mafia poaching members from them.

3 Thuggee

The Thuggee of 1800s India were a gang of killers, robbers, and assassins who were as deadly and shadowy as ninjas. They left such an impact with their activities that the word "thug" literally derives from them, and they operated with such brutality that they put the Mafia to shame with a Guinness World Record for highest gang-death toll (yes there is a record for that, apparently). Every member gave the appearance of being a law-abiding citizen, even telling their wives that they were traveling tradesmen in order to explain their various murderous commutes.

Admission into the gang was hereditary. So, if your father was a Thuggee, you had to join the family business: murder. The Thuggee chose their victims almost at random, following certain signs that they believed were left by Kali, the goddess of death. They would then befriend the victim and travel with them until the time was right. One of them would say the code words "bring the tobacco" and the Thuggee would strangle their victim to death and rob them.

2 Live Oak Boys

The Live Oak Boys were a New Orleans group of nasties from the mid-19th century that managed to terrify a city that was already terrified enough. Around this time, cops would only travel in large groups—and even then only during the day and armed to the teeth. And it's little wonder why. The Live Oak Boys carried the oak clubs they were named after, which they used to spread pandemonium by attacking local bars and saloons and smashing them to pieces. If the proprietor was smart, he would disappear when he saw them coming; if he wasn't smart, he would likely soon be dead.

The Live Oak Boys would usually do this because a rival proprietor had paid them to put a competitor out of business. Of course, sometimes they did it just because they were bored. The leader of the gang was a man named Red Bill Wilson, whose beard was so manly that it was able hold a hidden knife in case of emergencies.

1 Scuttlers

"Scuttlers" is a collective term for the gangs of youths who terrorized Manchester, England, in the 19th century. Each subset came from a different area of the city, which subgroups of Scuttlers would name themselves after. Scuttlers usually fought among themselves for territory with bottles, knives, sticks, and iron bars, but not over money or drugs or anything else—just to control streets that were probably identical to the ones they already controlled.

They even looked like your average street gang with their own distinctive dress code: scarves and peaked caps on bald heads, shaved around bangs that came down over one's left eye. And in case you're thinking that they don't sound too bad—like average, yet rough teenagers—maybe you'll change your mind. They were so hooligan-ish that the term "hooligan" was essentially coined for them, and the Scuttlers absolutely went to war when they got worked up. And they did so in force, with up to 600 of them all fighting for control of a street, avenue, or corner while business owners and householders barricaded themselves inside in fear.

TOP 10 Horrible Historic Homicides

by Nene Adams

10 "A Wholesale Murder," August 1866

On a farm in Schleswig-Holstein, Germany, a house fire in the middle of the night brought neighbors from adjoining farms rushing to put out the conflagration. Inside, they discovered the charred and mutilated remains of eight people: seven members of the Thode family and an 18-year-old maidservant. It was clear from the wounds that the victims had been violently stabbed as well as struck with a hatchet. In particular, the eight-year-old daughter was so covered with deep cuts, investigators at first believed she'd been tortured.

Was the family killed by thieves looking for the father's hidden strongboxes full of silver? Twenty-three-year-old Timm Thode, the only survivor, fell under suspicion. He had constantly argued with his frugal, somewhat reclusive father over money. On the night of the fire, witnesses testified his clothing was bloodstained. Timm claimed he'd been awakened by the fire and fled to a neighbor's house, but under interrogation, he confessed to the murders. His motive? Greed, pure and simple.

Timm Thode was tried, condemned to death, and executed.

9 "God Accused of Breaking His Promise," May 1879

In Pocasset, Massachusetts, a farmer named Charles F. Freeman converted to a Christian sect, the Second Advent Congregation. Becoming inflamed with religious fervor at the revival meetings, he believed he'd received a communication directly from God ordering him to sacrifice his five-year-old daughter, Edith. The voice of God also promised a miracle—if Freeman obeyed, his dead child would be resurrected on Sunday.

Improvising an altar on the kitchen table, Freeman stabbed Edith to death with a knife on Thursday morning at dawn. Afterward, he called a meeting of his church and proudly showed the horrified congregation what he'd done before driving everyone out of the house and barricading the doors and windows to await a miracle that never came. After his arrest, he sang hymns and claimed to be a "second Abraham." Some followers of the church absolved Freeman of the crime, claiming God had broken the promise to resurrect the child.

Freeman was remanded to the State Lunatic Hospital in Danvers.

8 "Thrown into a Well," April 1868

James Killey, 33 years old and a small-time miner and farmer, lived with his wife, Esther, and five young daughters—aged from seven years to three

months old—on a farm near Foxdale on the Isle of Man. According to Esther, Killey was a hard worker, a decent provider, and a good father, which made it all the more puzzling when his behavior suddenly changed. He became sullen and depressed, and began to express violent and suicidal thoughts.

One morning after a sleepless night, Killey went outside where his children played in the yard. A little while later, hearing a scream, an alarmed Esther ran out into the yard with the baby in her arms to find her husband standing over the well, grasping one of the girls. There was no sign of the others. Killey dropped his daughter down the well, snatched the three-month-old from Esther, hurled the infant into the well, and finally jumped in himself.

Fortunately, a relative, Archibald Schimm, worked on the farm and came running to help. He managed to rescue two of the older girls. The rest were dead, including the father. All had drowned in the well. The inquest ruled Killey had committed the murders in a state of temporary insanity. His reason for killing his daughters remains unknown.

7 "Dreadful Barbarity," June 1871

At the Hall End Colliery (coal pit) in West Bromwich, England, the body of Joseph Marshall was discovered by an engine tender. The 50-year-old laborer lay on the ground in front of a roaring fire. Someone had covered the right side of his body with blazing-hot coals, possibly to prevent identification. His stockings were burned off his legs and his leather belt had been almost entirely consumed, but his head remained intact.

Investigators soon uncovered deep lacerations and holes in the victim's skull that pointed to murder. A search of the victim's nearby hovel revealed a pair of rakes and a hammer that had caused the awful head wounds. Witnesses pointed to John Higginson, another laborer who'd been seen drinking with the victim on the night of the murder. Higginson had also been spotted leaving the victim's hovel before the body was uncovered.

For some unknown reason, the jury found Higginson guilty of manslaughter and sentenced him to penal servitude for life. Why he killed Marshall remains a mystery.

6 "The Headless Horror," February 1896

Near Fort Thomas, Kentucky, a young boy walking to town found a woman laying facedown on the side of the road, her long skirt flipped over to cover her face. Assuming she was drunk or asleep, he continued on his way and alerted the authorities. The deputy sheriff went to the scene and discovered the woman was dead. When he turned over the body and pulled down the dress, he was shocked to find the victim's head missing.

The unknown victim's clothing was torn, her corset ripped off, and her underclothing cut and covered in bloody fingerprints. She had a defensive wound on her hand. However, the autopsy did not uncover any physical signs of rape. She'd been five months pregnant at the time of her death, which was judged to be due to manual strangulation based on the bruises on the stump of her neck. Her identity remained unknown until Fred Bryan of Greencastle, Indiana, brother of 22-year-old Pearl, came forward to report his sister missing.

The story became clearer to investigators. Impressionable, pretty Pearl had become the lover of Scott Jackson, a handsome ladies' man. He'd broken off the relationship with her earlier, but Pearl discovered their affair had left her pregnant. In a panic, she contacted him. He made promises he didn't keep. When she threatened to reveal his duplicity to her family, Jackson took Pearl to a field. After his strangulation attempt failed in her fight for her life, he cut her throat, decapitated her, and staged the scene to look like rape.

When he was arrested, Jackson's arm still bore the raw scratches made by Pearl's fingernails. His friend, Alonzo Walling, was accused of assisting Jackson in committing the murder. Both Jackson and Walling were hanged.

5 "The Splendid Darling," March 1886

Henri Jacques Pranzini, born in Alexandria, Egypt, was good looking, refined, and intelligent—a "splendid darling" according to the many women attracted to his charms. He worked as a translator, but also led a secret life as a gambler, thief, and professional liar who earned his real living conning money out of his female victims.

In Paris, Pranzini met Marie Regnault, an apparently depressed mother of an 11-year-old girl. She eagerly adopted his debauched lifestyle. While not rich, Regnault had a stash of jewelry, bonds, and other valuables. Pranzini wooed her for about a month before he struck. He was seen entering Marie's house with a carving knife. The following morning, the bodies of Marie, her child, and a servant were found dead at the blood-soaked scene, their throats cut.

Pranzini fled to Marseille, where he was caught with some of the victim's jewelry. He'd also boasted about the murder to a reporter, imparting knowledge only the killer could have known. After his arrest, he claimed he'd spent the night at a lady's house, but of course declined to name the woman in question. The jury sentenced him to death. He maintained his innocence, even as he was led up the steps of the guillotine. His body was supposedly flayed and the skin used to make a cigar case.

4 "Somnambulist Tragedy," October 1845

Twenty-one-year-old Maria "Mary" Bickford worked as a prostitute in brothels in Boston and New Bedford, Massachusetts. She was young, fashionable, and beautiful until she was found in her boardinghouse room, her throat savagely cut, blood splattered on the walls, and her bed on fire. The flames had destroyed her face and hair, but not the evidence her murderer had left behind: a bloody razor, men's clothing, and letters to Maria from an "A. J. T."

Albert Jackson Tirrell, 22 years old, had already scandalized the city by leaving his wife and children to live with Maria and squandering a fortune on her. The besotted man was under indictment for adultery. He was the last one to see Maria alive. More damning, he fled ahead of the authorities to Canada on his way to Liverpool, but bad weather forced the ship to dock in New York City. He was caught on his way to New Orleans.

Because he claimed to have no motive for murder, Tirrell and the legal team hired by his family attempted a groundbreaking defense. Tirrell was known to sleepwalk, so if he had done it—no admission of guilt intended—it wasn't his fault. After hearing Maria painted as a depraved Jezebel and a heartless seductress, the jury found Tirrell not guilty of murder.

3 "Shocking Discoveries," October 1892

In Australia, as in England and America at the time, the practice of "baby farming" was a legal, commercial practice—a mother (often unwed) who couldn't care for her infant would pay someone to take care of it for her, usually for a weekly fee. Promises of adoption were sometimes made. However, if a baby died, the fee might continue to be collected from the ignorant parent. Not all "professional child minders" committed murder, but...

The decomposing bodies of two babies wrapped in stinking clothing were found by a worker in a drain behind a house in a Sydney suburb. Authorities found five more infants buried on the property and tracked down the owner: John Makin, who lived with his wife, Sarah Jane, and four daughters. The Makins were baby farmers. When their new home was searched, more bodies were found buried, making 12 in all. Arrests were made immediately.

The trial played out to a packed courtroom. John and Sarah Makin stood accused of the murder of one of their charges, Horace Murray, whose mother, Amber, acted as the prosecution's star witness. The most damning evidence against the defendants came from their 16-year-old daughter, who testified against them. John and Sarah were given the death sentence. After exhausting all appeals, John met his end on the gallows. Sarah's sentence was commuted to life in prison with hard labor. She died after serving 19 years.

2 "Terrible Discovery in Bog," October 1849

Patrick Moore was a cruel man. Frequently drunk, he abused his wife, Catherine (née Thompson), the prettiest girl in Tolerton, a village in Ireland where they lived. She still had many admirers among the young men. Jealousy often sent her alcoholic husband into violent rages that turned physical. Eventually, she went to her mother's house, but her unhappiness continued to fester. A few weeks later, Patrick mysteriously disappeared.

His relatives heard he'd left for America, but why not take Catherine with him? She made excuses and departed for Liverpool the next Sunday, presumably to catch a boat to New York City and join her husband. However, no one heard from Patrick, which seemed unlike him. About a month later, a man's putrefying body was found in the isolated Rossmore bog.

The victim had not only been ravaged by dogs, but the killer had mutilated the face, gouging out the eyes and making such deep lacerations that his features were unrecognizable. The body fell apart when it was collected. A police inspector found someone willing to identify the remains as Patrick Moore, and Catherine was arrested when she returned from Liverpool. She confessed to Patrick's murder and named her mother, Brigit, as an accomplice.

Both women were found guilty of murder and sentenced to be hanged.

1 "What Child Is This?" March 1851

When Martha Clarke, 22 years old, let herself be seduced by the promises of a man who abandoned her, she was left alone, unmarried, and heavily pregnant. She entered a workhouse and gave birth to a son, Arthur, around Christmas 1850. It wasn't a joyous occasion. Destitute, her future ruined, she left the workhouse with her baby in March 1851.

The next night, Martha was seen in Suffolk, England, near Bury St. Edmonds, carrying her baby and a shovel. At eight o'clock, she arrived at her stepmother's house without Arthur. When questioned about the baby, her story kept changing. She said she'd sent him to live with her aunt, or sent him away to another family, or put him in school. Her stepmother was suspicious, but let Martha eat supper and go to bed.

Over breakfast the following morning, the stepmother expressed her opinion that Martha had murdered the baby. Martha calmly replied that she hadn't killed Arthur. She'd only buried him alive. The confession caused a panic. A local constable was summoned. The field was searched. At midnight, Arthur Clarke's lifeless little body was recovered from the grave Martha had carefully dug and concealed. She was arrested for suffocating her child.

Because she'd taken so much care to hide the body, her temporary insanity defense was rejected by the judge. The jury found Martha guilty, and she was sentenced to hang.

TOP 10 Mad and Murderous Victorians

by **James Fawcett**

10 The Cutthroat Killer

Born in Birkenhead, William Thomas was not your average farm laborer. From an early age, the young Mr. Thomas suffered from excruciating recurring headaches. Fearing for his health, his caring mother decided to admit him to a mental asylum. She told her son of her plans, believing it to be in his best interests. This act proved to be fatal.

Taking great offense at her decision, he waited until she was sleeping and then brutally cut her throat with a kitchen knife. After dismembering her corpse, he proceeded to bury her in the garden. His activities were noticed by a neighbor, who contacted the police. He was subsequently arrested and spent the rest of his life working as a cook and preparing meals for his fellow inmates in Broadmoor Hospital until his death in 1908.

9 A Murderous Mystery

On the morning of December 29, 1888, a grim discovery was made in the Yorkshire town of Bradford. The body of a young child was found inside an outhouse, mutilated almost beyond recognition. His arms and legs were roughly hacked off, his ears were removed, and his heart was torn out and cast aside on the ground nearby. The body was that of eight-year-old local boy, John Gill. At the time, the country was in the grip of the Jack the Ripper murders, and speculation at the time was that it was his work, although no evidence existed to support the theory. Shortly afterward, a local milkman was arrested on suspicion of killing the boy. The man was able to identify the body as that of Gill, because Gill used to accompany him on his rounds. However, the evidence presented was insufficient, and he was released. To this day, the true killer has not been identified.

8 Bacon the Butcher

Martha Bacon was from Lambeth, London. She had already done a stint in a mental hospital due to her erratic and sometimes violent behavior, but once she was deemed to be "treated," she was released back into society and the arms of her family. Sadly, her psychotic behavior was far from cured and, on December 29, 1856, she took a butcher's knife and brutally murdered her two young children, slashing at their throats almost to the point of decapitation.

After being questioned by police, she vehemently claimed that the murders were committed by a crazed intruder. The evidence did not back up her claims, and she was found guilty of murder by reason of insanity. She spent the rest of her life in a high-security mental hospital, using her spare time (of which she had plenty), to knit children's clothes and practice needlework.

7 The Killer Captain

George Johnston was the captain of the SS *Tory*, operating between Hong Kong and Liverpool in the 19th century. Maintaining trade routes between the locations was imperative at the time because both Liverpool and Hong Kong were major industrial locales, and Captain Johnston was entrusted with ensuring that operations ran smoothly and professionally. Unfortunately, he broke that trust when he attacked and killed a member of his crew with a saber during a drunken rage. He claimed his actions were to stop a mutiny, but the crew's testimony painted a far different story.

They claimed that the less-than-professional and profoundly insane Captain Johnston was in an almost constant state of alcohol-induced excitement, during which time he would have crew members shackled and then proceed to torture them by slicing their flesh with his razor-sharp saber. Although he was found not guilty on the grounds of insanity, he would spend the rest of his life in Broadmoor, haunted by delusions of persecution.

6 The Ghastly Grandfather

In April of 1900, four-year-old James Dawes ran to his mother in a flood of tears. The child had been badly cut around his face and neck. "Grandpa was drunk and tried to kill me!" he screamed. His mother, knowing young James to be a bit of a fantasist, dismissed his claims. However, far from being a typical, loving grandparent, Joseph Holden was a vicious and mean-spirited drunk who seemed to revel in making his family's life a misery.

After months of putting up with him, his daughter Mary, mother of James, told him that he should move out because of his negative influence on the children (which obviously made him pretty angry). Being a father of seven children, Holden believed that it was time he was looked after. In an act of revenge, he had indeed attempted to kill young James. Worse still, two weeks after the attack, he succeeded in killing Mary's older son, John. After stabbing the young child to death, he dumped his body in a ditch. When questioned about his motives, all he said was, "I did it to get even with her." He was hanged later that year at Strangeways Prison.

5 Killer Kate

On January 29, 1879, Julia Martha Thomas, a middle-aged former school-teacher, took on a servant by the name of Kate Webster. Unbeknownst to Mrs. Thomas, Miss Webster came from an extremely troubled background and held a rather lengthy criminal record. It had also been noted by authorities that she harbored an excitable and often aggressive attitude. The relationship started off well, but friction between the two soon developed.

In March of the following year, an argument broke out. Webster, in a fit of rage, pushed Thomas down the stairs. However, the severe impact was not sufficient to kill her. Still enraged, Webster ran to the bottom of the stairs and proceeded to throttle her to death. Determined to dispose of the corpse, Killer Kate dismembered the body, boiling and burning as much of it as possible inside a large copper kettle. She then discarded the body parts in various locations throughout the area. She was eventually caught following an attempt to sell the contents of her victim's house. Police searching the property discovered body parts and bloodstained items of clothing. Despite an extensive search, it would not be until 2010 that Julia Martha Thomas's head would be discovered on the grounds of the house.

4 Mary Ann Cotton

Mary Ann Cotton was arguably one of the most notorious serial killers England has ever seen. Born into a fiercely religious household to a young mother and a strict disciplinarian father, her childhood was turbulent, to say the least. In 1852, the 20-year-old Cotton married William Mowbray. They had five children. Sadly, four of them died from supposed gastric flu. The family moved to the north of England where they had three more children. However, as before, the three children (and Cotton's husband, this time) soon died of similar ailments.

She married again, only for her new husband to also die. Rumors of her possible involvement in the deaths began to circulate, and her trail of dead family members scattered around northern England was soon discovered. She was eventually arrested in 1873 and found guilty of murder. It is speculated that she killed at least 15 people, probably using arsenic to poison many of them. She was sentenced to death and hanged at HM Durham prison, County Durham, in the northeast of England.

3 The Jilted Willy

On September 22, 1888, Jane Beadmore headed out to buy some sweets. She never returned. A search was organized and her body was eventually found next to a railway line at Birtley Hill, Gateshead. Beadmore had been brutally slain. She had been stabbed in the chest three times, and even more alarmingly, her abdomen had been viciously torn open almost to the point of her being disemboweled. The murder was committed at the height of the Jack the Ripper slayings, so there was some speculation that the infamous killer had moved into the area, but it was eventually discovered that the young woman had in fact been killed by a local factory worker by the name of William (Willy) Waddell.

Waddell had been going out with Jane, but she had refused his sexual advances. On the evening she was killed, the pair had been arguing about Waddell's excessive drinking habits. Enraged, he killed her. Once the full realization of what he had done sank in, he attempted to cover his tracks by imitating the style of Jack the Ripper. He was arrested and later hanged for his heinous crime.

2 The Psychotic Artist

Prior to his murderous activities, Richard Dadd spent much of his time painting. He became noted primarily for his intricate depictions of fairies and other mythical beings. He would while away the hours sketching and taking inspiration from the serene countryside around him. However, his pursuits were soon to take a decidedly creepy and murderous turn. During a painting expedition to Egypt in 1882, he suffered a severe mental breakdown and his personality changed drastically. He became violent and aggressive and, more alarming, believed himself to be under the control of the Egyptian god Osiris.

Upon returning home, his behavior escalated. Believing his father was the devil incarnate, he stabbed him to death. During his attempt to flee the country, he slashed a tourist's throat, at which point he was caught and arrested. He continued to paint long after his imprisonment. His work can be viewed at the Tate Gallery in London.

1 The Chocolate Cream Poisoner

Christiana Edmunds, the Chocolate Cream Poisoner, was born in Margate in 1828. By all reports, Edmunds was an attractive young woman who suffered from an untreated mental illness, which only became known after her heinous crimes were revealed. In the late 1860s, while living in Brighton, Edmunds started an affair with a married doctor. When he attempted to end their relationship in 1870, she visited his house with a gift of chocolates for his wife, who became violently ill soon after eating them and did not recover for several weeks.

Several months later, still tortured by her lover's denial, Edmunds began buying chocolate creams and lacing them with strychnine. She then sold the toxic concoctions to unsuspecting members of the public. Many members of the local community became seriously ill; one, a young boy by the name of Albert Barker, died. Despite this, Edmunds escalated her campaign of hatred, sending the poisoned sweets to prominent people, including her initial victim, the doctor's wife.

By this time, the police had connected the poisonings to the chocolates, and it was only a matter of time before she was arrested. At Edmunds's trial in 1872, her mother testified that her family had a history of mental instability and that this was a contributing factor toward her actions. The Chocolate Cream Poisoner spent the last of her days in an asylum for the criminally insane.

TOP 10 Weird Stories about Famous People

by Simon Court

1 Charles Dickens

Charles Dickens was one of the most famous writers of the Victorian era, and anything that resembles his work has now been granted the honorable title "Dickensian." Although his stories usually have happy endings, his own story most certainly did not start happily. Dickens's early life was spent mostly in debtor's prison because his poor father couldn't pay off his debts so the whole family had to join him in jail, a fairly typical practice in Victorian England.

He eventually worked in a factory to help pay off the debts, and the terrible working conditions were a major inspiration for his writing. As an adult, Dickens appeared to be a more lighthearted guy, often playing practical jokes. He had a fake bookcase with books that were hilariously titled, including *Noah's Arkitechture* and a nine-volume set titled *Cat's Lives*.

9 Albert Einstein

Albert Einstein is the archetypal kooky scientist who was clearly more than a little bit crazy and yet was brilliant as brilliant could be. Einstein, although a seemingly friendly, intelligent guy, had quite a few skeletons in his closet. In 1901, Einstein and his first girlfriend, Mileva Maric, were on vacation in Italy. It ended when Mileva found herself pregnant and Einstein found himself with no money to support her and the new baby. The child, Lieserl, was born in 1902 and disappeared from Einstein's letters to Mileva around 1903. It's unknown what happened to the child, but she probably died of scarlet fever.

Einstein left Mileva in 1912 (and divorced her in 1919) and married his cousin Elsa Lowenthal soon after. In the latter marriage, Einstein had numerous affairs, which continued well after Elsa's death in 1936.

8 Robert Louis Stevenson

You probably know Robert Louis Stevenson for his novel *The Strange Case of Dr. Jekyll and Mr. Hyde*. What you probably don't know is that he wrote the novel on cocaine and then gave it to his wife for review. After his wife stated that the book was an allegory, and that he should write it as such, Stevenson burned it so that he could force himself to write it according to his wife's feedback. Speaking of his wife, Fanny Osbourne met Robert Louis Stevenson while she was in Paris—they fell in love, and she became his muse. When Fanny had to return home to America, Stevenson saved up for three years to see her again so that they could be together. That's one determined man.

7 Abraham Lincoln

Famous for his mighty beard, Abraham Lincoln was a curious figure. Though he wasn't actually born in a log cabin, he did have a relatively hard childhood. Hard labor was part of the daily regimen in the frontier where Lincoln grew up, and, at the age of nine, he lost his mother to milk sickness. As president, he would grow to be history's tallest president of the United States, standing proud at six-foot-four. Even after he died, his story didn't quite end. In 1876, a group of counterfeiters wanted to hold Lincoln's body for ransom, at the hefty fee of $200,000 in gold and the release of one of their accomplices. They were caught and sentenced to a year in jail.

6 King George III

King George III is thought to have begun to lose his marbles due to arsenic poisoning, since arsenic was spread around like fairy dust in everything from medicine to cosmetics in the early 19th century. Eventually confined to a straitjacket within his own palace, he died in 1820, blind and insane. He may have been a tyrant to the American colonists, but you can't help but feel a bit sorry for the guy.

5 Napoleon Bonaparte

Napoleon? Short dude with a complex that they eventually named after him, tried to take over Europe, etc. Well, he wasn't actually short. Napoleon was five-foot-seven, which was normal for the average Frenchman in his time. His childhood was a pitiful one—his father died of stomach cancer and left his family penniless due to his gambling. He was often made fun of in school for his studiousness and thick Corsican accent, but no one could have predicted Napoleon's rise to power. Strangely enough, Napoleon suffered from hemorrhoids and its rumored that his pain and illness prevented him from winning the Battle of Waterloo.

4 Theodore Roosevelt

Theodore Roosevelt's story is one of privilege, big personalities, and bigger sticks. Teddy Roosevelt was born to the wealthy Roosevelt family in New York City and was known to be sickly, asthmatic, and a (very) hyper child. He also took up boxing at a young age to combat his weak constitution. Roosevelt had an injury to the left eye caused by boxing while in office. He took many trips to Africa and South America, where he hunted and studied numerous exotic species.

His best story, perhaps, concerns a speech he gave in Milwaukee in 1912. During the speech, an assassin tried to kill Roosevelt with a gun, but the bullet was slowed down by the folded speech and eyeglass case in Roosevelt's pocket. Roosevelt promptly told the crowd he'd just been shot, continued giving his speech, and then headed over to the hospital to get it removed.

3 Peter the Great

If this were a list about strange monarchs, Peter the Great would top it. Peter the Great was the czar of Russia in the 18th century. Seeing how backward Russia was, he decided to tour western Europe in order to find ways to modernize his country.

Peter took the guise of an average merchant to avoid being discovered and came back to Russia with many ways to improve the empire. He set up new schools, created the mighty port of St. Petersburg, and ordered all Russian men to shave their beards or pay a tax. Yes, you read that right. Russians grow such poor beards that they had to pay to keep them.

He also had a museum of oddities ranging from deformed animal fetuses to animal parts to dispel superstition in his country. Now that's scientific curiosity.

2 Charlie Chaplin

Sir Charles "Charlie" Chaplin is perhaps best known for his comedic films of the Roaring Twenties, and he certainly has tales to tell. Chaplin's parents weren't exactly role models—his mother had two illegitimate children from affairs and his father left the family when he was young. His mother eventually died of liver issues after becoming psychotic due to syphilis and malnutrition.

His adult life was no less fascinating. Chaplin was once forced to pay child support for a child that wasn't even his. When a young woman claimed that her child was Chaplin's, blood tests determined that the child was not Chaplin's, but the judge refused to have the test admitted into court, so he made Chaplin pay a substantial sum. Even after death, his story didn't quite end. In 1977, Chaplin's body was stolen for ransom, but it was recovered about two months later.

1 Sir Richard Francis Burton

Spy, explorer, soldier—so many words to describe Sir Richard Burton, but his stories were perhaps the most amazing. In 1853, Burton convinced the Royal Geographic Society to give him a leave of absence from the army to travel to Mecca and disguise himself as a Muslim—even getting circumcised to keep up the illusion—to make it there. While exploring in Africa, he was impaled by a javelin in a foray with a group of Somali warriors, yet escaped alive. He spoke over 30 different languages and dialects and was a diplomat later in life. It seems likely that Sir Richard took plenty of tales to the grave.

TOP 10 Historically Significant Sites Destroyed for Awful Reasons

by Jeff Kelly

10 Everything Destroyed by MoMA

One would think that if anyone would be against destroying important pieces of culture and history, it would be a museum. When it comes to the Museum of Modern Art (MoMA) in New York City, however, that's completely wrong. Over the years, the MoMA has acquired and destroyed several historically significant sites in order to make room for expansion, and just recently added another to that list when it purchased the American Folk Art Museum and promptly announced plans to demolish it.

One of the other buildings the people at the MoMA have destroyed is an old brownstone home, which would likely be just another in a long line of traditional brownstones in the area but for the fact that it once belonged to John D. Rockefeller himself. Of course there is a catch to that one, as the MoMA was cofounded by Rockefeller's wife, and the family donated the home to the museum, which then tore down the house and turned it into a garden. However, several of the other houses were not donated and were at the center of an effort to preserve what remained of the neighborhood. It was an effort that ultimately failed, with many of the historic homes being razed, along with buildings like the Dorset Hotel and the City Athletic Club.

9 Civil Rights Site

Here is an entry that would almost be funny if it weren't so incredibly sad. George Elmore, owner of a small South Carolina store, had the audacity to put his name on a lawsuit calling for the end to all white primaries in the state. His participation in the lawsuit cost him his business and put him on the path toward financial ruin. For his part, however, he has been remembered as a civil rights pioneer and a historic marker was placed in front of his old storefront at a 2012 ceremony attended by city leaders and church members, praising Elmore for his bravery.

And then a week later the store was bulldozed, leaving that historic marker standing in front of a pile of rubble. Did we mention that church members were present at the ceremony honoring Elmore? Well this is the part where we tell you that it was the First Nazareth Baptist Church, which sat right next door, that had the building demolished despite the pleas of Elmore's son. Did we mention that Elmore won that lawsuit back in 1947? That's right, the people who tore down his store were the same people whom he helped achieve equality for 65 years earlier.

8 William Shakespeare's Home

Let's take our time machine back to jolly old 18th-century England — or rather, to not-so-jolly old England and the final home of the one and only William Shakespeare. The home, in the small town of Stratford-upon-Avon, was where Shakespeare is said to have written some of his later works, including *The Tempest*, and the site of his death in 1616. Fast forward to 1753, when a man named Reverend Francis Gastrell purchased the home. Six years later, he had it demolished.

Why would he have the home completely destroyed, you ask? Well, it boils down to bitterness and irritation. As is the case with famous homes, it turned out to be a pretty popular spot for tourists. People, after all, were curious to see Shakespeare's house. Think of it as the 18th-century version of a Hollywood star-homes tour. Gastrell quickly got so fed up with people constantly walking by and looking at his home that he decided to just tear the whole thing down. It was a move that, as you might guess, did not exactly endear him to the townsfolk, and he eventually moved out of town to escape the people's anger.

7 Ancient Chinese Grave Sites

Despite what Lara Croft may lead you to believe, tomb raiding is not cool. In fact, it is very much the opposite of cool, in that, while the likes of Lara Croft and even Indiana Jones may accidentally muck up some history while trying to preserve it, real-life tomb raiders do nothing but destroy history. Of course these grave robbers think only of financial gain, which is exactly why it has become a huge problem in China, with tomb raiders using dynamite and even bulldozers to blunder their way into ancient grave sites.

These thieves break into tombs and steal whatever looks valuable, selling the priceless valuables within days on the black market. Sadly, this means huge parts of history are being lost, and these ancient and historic burial grounds are being desecrated in the process. To put into perspective just how bad this problem has gotten, a team of archaeologists investigated 900 tombs, only to find that each and every one had been raided. Unfortunately for China, it's not just thieves doing their best to destroy ancient culture, as you'll see in the next entry...

6 Ancient Taoist Temple in Beijing

When Beijing hosted the Olympics in 2008, a lot of work needed to be done to prepare the city for the enormous event. That included building new, state-of-the-art stadiums and event centers, and in a city like Beijing, the land for such huge structures is difficult to come by. That's why the government gave no second thought to demolishing countless pieces of Chinese history, including a 680-year-old Taoist temple that had been named one of the most significant cultural sites in the entire country.

Historic homes and statues were bulldozed in order to make way for shopping malls and skyscrapers, with the government winding up spending more than $22 billion to almost completely redo the city for this one event. Despite the fact that the Olympics have the capability to generate an enormous amount of revenue for the host country, that is still an insane amount of money spent to renovate one of the world's most historic cities, and the real cost, as it turns out, was the loss of a huge part of Chinese culture.

5 ...And Most of China, Really

And unfortunately, as it turns out, there's a staggering lack of care for preserving Chinese history within the country. A survey revealed that thanks to continued land development, approximately 31,000 historical sites have been completely destroyed. The report comes from the State Administration for Cultural Heritage (SACH), from data collected over the past three decades.

Among some of the sites destroyed either in part or entirely, according to some reports, is a portion of the Great Wall of China. Illegal mining along the wall has led to the partial destruction of some segments. This all came about when the folks at the SACH set about trying to examine the hundreds of thousands of historical sites they had listed throughout the country, only to learn that tens of thousands had completely vanished thanks to the aggressive urbanization of the country. In one of the more ironic twists, included in the list historic sites that have been destroyed was the home of legendary architect I. M. Pei, which was demolished to make way for more modern architecture.

4 Buddha Statues

In the Hindu Kush Mountains in Afghanistan, there once stood 1,700-year-old Buddha statues of tremendous historical and cultural significance. We say "once stood" because in 2001, the Taliban decided that all non-Islamic statues should be destroyed, including those ancient Bamiyan Buddha statues. The United Nations begged the Taliban to spare these statues, but—shockingly—found it impossible to reason with a group of extremists.

And so the Taliban drilled holes into the Buddha statues, filled them with dynamite, and proceeded to blow them up and reduce them to rubble. The edict issued by the Taliban that all statues be destroyed did not allow for any to be removed and transported to another country, meaning every bit of non-Islam heritage fell as the Taliban attempted to wipe all pieces of evidence of other religions from Afghanistan. Not surprisingly, the destruction of all of these statues, particularly the Bamiyan Buddha statues, did little to endear the Taliban to the rest of the world.

3 A Mayan Pyramid

Imagine the embarrassment of a work crew when they've been tearing away at a big stone structure in order to create gravel to repair the roads, only to learn that they've just accidentally demolished a 2,300-year-old Mayan pyramid. Oops. Sadly, that's exactly what happened in 2013 in Belize when a construction company tore down the pyramid, which was actually part of the protected Noh Mul ceremonial center.

According to experts, the construction company absolutely should have known it was a Mayan pyramid, and the fact that the company has denied knowledge is almost laughable. To make matters worse, the maximum penalty is a $10,000 fine, which could never come remotely close to covering the damage since Mayan pyramids are priceless. Considering remnants of the lost Mayan civilization are relatively scarce, the fact that a piece of that ancient history was destroyed simply to fill in a few pot holes seems unfathomably stupid.

2 The Berlin Wall

Before you say anything, yes, I realize that the Berlin Wall was partially destroyed as a result of the end of the Cold War. I remember Reagan's famous words too. That's not the part I am talking about, however, because part of the wall remains and has become a cultural icon in the two decades following that historic event. Of course, now the rest of the wall will be torn down to make room for luxury apartments, a move that has angered many and led to thousands of Berliners protesting the decision.

Whether you think the wall should stay or go is irrelevant. At this point, it has indeed truly become a symbol and a place of historical significance. Heck, even David Hasselhoff flew to Germany to join in the protests. Unfortunately, developers have decided to move right on ahead with the demolition anyway.

1 Mecca

Mecca, for those who are unaware, is the holiest site in all of Islam. The city was the birthplace of the prophet Muhammad, the founder of the religion, and it is the place where Muhammad said that all Muslims would be equal. And now, today, it is slowly being transformed into the Middle Eastern version of Las Vegas. The holy city has become a victim of swift and progressive urbanization and capitalism, with its culture being paved away in favor of shopping centers, skyscrapers, and luxury hotels. Perhaps the saddest part is that much of the demolition has been ordered by the city's actual Wahhabi clerics, who believe that keeping the shrines equates to the sin of idolatry.

To a degree, the city has begun to look less like the holy land it once was and more like another Dubai. It has been argued that the city was in desperate need of at least some renovation and an improved infrastructure due to the massive number of pilgrims who make their way to Mecca each year, but the extent to which it has been changed and its culture buried has angered many historians and members of Islam, though few have spoken out for fear of losing access to the city and its remaining historical sites. One particularly egregious example is the fact that Muhammad's first wife's home has been demolished and turned into a public restroom. The symbolism in that alone speaks volumes about the current views these developers have on the city's heritage.

TOP 10 Dirty, Secret CIA Operations

by **Mike Floorwalker**

10 Operation PBSUCCESS

PBSUCCESS was the code name for a CIA-backed coup led against the democratically elected government of Jacobo Arbenz, the president of Guatemala, in 1954. It's one of the first in a long line of suspected or acknowledged CIA interventions in the governments of foreign countries, and it was indeed a tremendous success from the agency's point of view—the first indication that such a feat could be accomplished relatively smoothly.

Elected in 1950, Arbenz set about instituting reforms aimed at making his country self-sufficient by giving huge chunks of government land back to citizens. This rubbed the U.S. government the wrong way, as much of this land was "owned" by the United Fruit Company, a truly evil corporation with which the Eisenhower administration was snugly in bed at the time (CIA director Allen Dulles and his brother John, the secretary of state, both had strong ties to the company).

The CIA snidely referred to Arbenz's policies in internal memoranda as "an intensely nationalistic program of progress colored by the touchy, antiforeign inferiority complex of the 'Banana Republic.'" In other words, nondependence on the U.S. and its allies was not to be tolerated.

Four hundred and eighty CIA-trained mercenary soldiers, led by exiled Guatemalan military officer Colonel Carlos Castillo Armas forcibly wrested Guatemala from Arbenz's control. While he and his aides were able to flee the country, CIA documents show that "the option of assassination was still being considered" right up until the day he resigned on June 27, 1954.

9 Operation Mongoose

After the failed Bay of Pigs invasion of Cuba, the agency's public image was worse than ever. President Kennedy famously proclaimed that he would "splinter the CIA into a thousand pieces and scatter it to the winds." But to deal with Cuba, he turned to the only person he knew he could trust: his brother Robert, who organized Operation Mongoose. This operation was conducted by the Department of Defense in conjunction with the CIA, under Robert Kennedy's supervision. He told his team at its first briefing that deposing Castro was "the top priority of the U.S. government—all else is secondary—no time, money, effort, or manpower is to be spared."

Among the dozens of extremely silly methods of assassination proposed: infecting Castro's scuba gear with tuberculosis, planting exploding seashells at a favorite diving site, slipping him a poisoned fountain pen, and even poisoning or slipping a bomb into one of his cigars. Castro's bodyguard asserted that there were hundreds of CIA schemes on Castro's life—and they all ended in failure, a gigantic waste of time and money. Castro was Cuba's dictator for 49 years, stepping down in 2008 due to failing health and appointing his younger brother as his replacement.

8 CIA-Produced Pornography

President Sukarno ruled Indonesia from 1959 until 1966, when he was deposed by Suharto, one of his generals. Sukarno had been deemed pro-Communist by the CIA, which meant there would inevitably be an attempt to oust him or at least make him look bad—but the plot they actually came up with was truly laughable.

The CIA produced a porn film titled *Happy Days* and starring a Sukarno look-alike for distribution in Indonesia. Not that the culture generally frowns upon such things, but as the CIA understood it, "being tricked, deceived, or otherwise outsmarted by one of the creatures God has provided for man's pleasure cannot be condoned" in Indonesian culture, and "what we were saying was that a woman had gotten the better of Sukarno." The film went as far as production, and stills were made, but for some reason (perhaps commonsense) it was never deployed.

Bizarrely enough, this idea resurfaced shortly before the Second Gulf War, when the CIA suggested that a fake gay porno featuring Saddam Hussein or Osama bin Laden be produced in order to discredit these men in the eyes of their followers. This went nowhere—at least one official claimed that nobody would care. "Trying to mount such a campaign would show a total misunderstanding of the target. We always mistake our own taboos as universal when, in fact, they are just our taboos."

7 Pakistani Vaccine/DNA Collection Drive

The May 2011 raid that killed Osama bin Laden was the result of an insane amount of intelligence collection and planning; regardless of the target's crimes, conducting a U.S. military operation to kill a foreign national on Pakistani soil was bound to have myriad consequences. A courier had been tracked to an Abbottabad compound, where agents were pretty damn certain bin Laden was hiding. But before conducting the raid, they had to be absolutely sure—and one method of collecting this proof was shady in the extreme.

The CIA recruited a respected Pakistani doctor to organize a fake vaccination drive in the town and in the process they collected thousands of blood samples from children in the area—among them, as it turned out, bin Laden's children. Since theirs was a fairly upscale section of town, the campaign began in a poorer area to make it look more authentic, then moved on to the neighborhood housing the bin Laden compound a month later without even following up with the required second or third doses in the poor area. The whole thing worked—with consequences.

For one thing, the doctor involved, Dr. Shakil Afridi, has been convicted of treason by the Pakistani government and given a 33-year prison sentence ("Wouldn't any country detain people for working for a foreign spy service?" one Iranian official helpfully pointed out). For another, the campaign has caused irreparable damage to organizations that carry out legitimate vaccinations. There are deep-seated suspicions in many Middle Eastern regions about those who provide vaccinations, and this gambit to assist in finding bin Laden has only bolstered those suspicions—particularly in Nigeria, India, and of course Pakistan, where efforts to eradicate polio are ongoing.

6 Muammar al-Gaddafi

February 2011 saw the beginning of the Libyan Revolution, which would culminate in the August ousting of Libyan dictator Muammar al-Gaddafi, followed by his capture and killing in October. There was little mention at the time of any potential involvement by foreign interests—but about one year later, an incident occurred that shed a curious light on the entire Revolution.

On September 11, 2012, an American diplomatic mission in Benghazi came under attack by armed militants. The response came not from within the mission itself, but from half a dozen CIA agents deployed from a hidden base within the city. More reinforcements arrived from Tripoli, and diplomatic personnel were whisked by convoy to chartered aircraft, which carried them out of the country.

This betrayed a CIA presence in the city, which had hitherto been unknown. The agency was forced to admit that it had maintained a fairly strong presence in Libya since about February 2011—right around the time the Libyan Revolution began. The annex that had housed the secret base was scrubbed clean and abandoned after the incident at the mission.

5 Operation Mockingbird

Operation Mockingbird was a bit of a two-pronged approach to dealing with the media: On the one hand, journalists were routinely employed by the CIA to develop intelligence and gather information, or to report on certain events in a way that portrayed the U.S. favorably. On the other, there were actual plants within the media—paid off with bribes or even directly employed by the CIA—to feed propaganda to the American public.

Mostly, this program was meant to convince the public of how incredibly scary Communism was and to make sure that public opinion favored taking out the Red Menace at any expense. Even scarier was the fact that having major newspaper publishers and the heads of TV stations bought and paid for meant that significant overseas events could be excluded from coverage in the media—events like the aforementioned coup in Guatemala, which didn't see the light of the day in the American press at the time.

Congressional hearings in 1976 (the "Church Committee") revealed that the CIA had been bribing journalists and editors for years. Following the Church hearings, newly minted CIA director and future President George H. W. Bush announced, "Effective immediately, the CIA will not enter into any paid or contract relationship with any full-time or part-time news correspondent accredited by any U.S. news service, newspaper, periodical, radio or television network or station." Yet he added that the CIA would continue to welcome unpaid, voluntary support of said journalists.

4 Operation CHAOS

Protests against U.S. involvement in Vietnam were proving to be a giant pain in the backside for the government's plans in the mid 1960s. While Mockingbird was busily using the mainstream to try to shove the necessity of the war down the throats of the public, the "counterculture" couldn't be controlled so easily. Ever-mindful of the KGB's propensity for their own style of dirty tricks, the CIA attempted to weed out any foreign influence on the American antiwar movement by launching Operation CHAOS—and they didn't even bother to come up with an innocuous-sounding code name.

Since the FBI's COINTELPRO program of domestic surveillance wasn't quite producing the desired results, President Lyndon B. Johnson authorized the CIA to undertake its own program of spying on U.S. citizens. Their main task was to infiltrate student organizations—both radical and otherwise—in order to gather intelligence on potential foreign influences, and to subvert such groups from within. Famous groups such as "Students for a Democratic Society" and the Black Panthers were targeted; eventually, the program for some reason expanded to include women's liberation and certain Jewish groups.

There is strong evidence that this type of activity has never ceased, though CHAOS itself was shuttered after the Watergate scandal. In 2011, the agency came under fire for allegedly working with the New York Police Department to conduct surveillance of Muslim groups in the area, who had not done anything wrong and who are now suing in federal court.

3 Phoenix Program

Phoenix was a program headed by the CIA, in conjunction with U.S. Special Forces and Australian and South Vietnamese commandos, during the Vietnam War. Its purpose was simple: assassination. And although this was a military unit, their targets weren't military, but civilian.

From 1965–1972, Phoenix was involved in the kidnapping, torture, and murder of thousands upon thousands of citizens. People deemed critical to the infrastructure of the Vietcong, or thought to have knowledge of VC activities, were rounded up and taken to regional interrogation centers where they were subjected to: "rape, gang rape, rape using eels, snakes, or hard objects, and rape followed by murder; electric shock…rendered by attaching wires to the genitals or other sensitive parts of the body, like the tongue; the 'water treatment'; the 'airplane,' in which the prisoner's arms were tied behind the back, and the rope looped over a hook on the ceiling, suspending the prisoner in midair, after which he or she was beaten; beatings with rubber hoses and whips; the use of police dogs to maul prisoners…"

Phoenix was the subject of 1971 congressional hearings on abuse. Former members described it as a "sterile depersonalized murder program," and it was phased out after negative publicity, though the replacement program F-6 was quietly phased in to take its place.

2 Operation Ajax

The success of Operation Ajax paved the way for all future CIA operations of a similar nature. It resulted in the return to power of the shah in 1953 after a military coup planned by American and British intelligence.

The first democratically elected leader of Iran, Prime Minister Mohammad Mossadegh, was seen as a potential liability because of his plans to nationalize the oil industry. Fearful of having to compete with the Soviet Union for Iranian oil, the decision was made to install a leader who was partial to U.S. interests. You can probably see a theme developing here.

CIA agents Donald Wilber and Kermit Roosevelt, Jr. (the grandson of Theodore Roosevelt), carried out the campaign by bribing everyone who could be bribed in Iran: government officials, business leaders, and even street criminals. These recruits were asked to support the shah, in various ways, and to oppose Mossadegh.

It worked: An uprising was instigated, Mosaddegh was jailed, and pro-Western Iranian Army General Fazlollah Zahedi was installed in his place. Zahedi had been arrested by the British during World War II for attempting to establish a Nazi government, and he lived up to that legacy by appointing Bahram Shahrokh—a protégé of Joseph Goebbels—as his director of propaganda.

1 The Mujahideen

In 1978, Afghanistan became mired in civil war as two Communist parties seized control of the country. When it began to look like anti-Communist rebels were gaining a foothold, the Soviet Union invaded the country to lend support. And that's when the U.S., of course, decided to get involved.

The CIA set up camps to train the rebels, known as Mujahideen, in the necessary tactics for beating back the Soviets. Advanced weaponry was also part of the deal, including—importantly—Stinger surface-to-air anti-aircraft missiles. Soviet air strikes had driven hundreds of guerrillas out of the cities and into the surrounding hills, and mitigating the effectiveness of those strikes proved to be essential in prolonging the conflict, placing a great strain on Soviet resources.

The Soviet Union occupied Afghanistan almost until its collapse in the early 1990s, but the legacy of the Mujahideen lives on. The CIA are finding their own tactics and training turned against them by Mujahideen veterans who have begun their own training programs, producing highly trained and skilled terrorists who now make up the backbone of al-Qaeda and other radical groups. The U.S. discovered these ramifications the hard way after invading Afghanistan in 2001. The invasion led to a quagmire of an occupation, which—as of this writing—has dragged on for just as long as that of the Soviets.

TOP 10 Greatest Impostors of the 20th Century

by **Andrew Handley**

10 Cassie Chadwick

Our first entry begins in the final years of the 1800s and carries over to the leading decade of the 20th century. Cassie Chadwick was born Elizabeth

Bigsley in 1857, and it wasn't long before she embarked on a long and incredibly successful con career. It only took 14 years to lead to her first arrest—she was picked up after forging checks in Ontario under the claim they were inherited from a long-lost British uncle. The court released her shortly after, claiming she was insane—a dubious accomplishment for a 14 year old.

As the years progressed, so did Cassie's schemes. In 1882 she married her first husband, masquerading as a clairvoyant named Madame Lydia DeVere. The high-profile wedding, however, brought her past victims out of the woodwork and to her front door, demanding payment for the money she had stolen from them. The marriage lasted less than a year.

Fifteen years and three husbands later, Cassie Chadwick embarked on her most ambitious scam to date, and the one that turned her into a legend—she convinced the world that she was an illegitimate daughter of Andrew Carnegie, the ludicrously wealthy steel and railroad mogul. Over the next eight years, she scammed up to $20 million in bank loans under Carnegie's name—while the banks themselves were too afraid to ask Carnegie to vouch for the loans for fear of stirring up controversy over his "illegitimate daughter." The entire scheme collapsed around her in 1904 when she was arrested after one bank called her bluff. She was given 14 years in jail, but in 1907 she died due to heart complications.

9 Stanley Clifford Weyman

It's hard to fault a man for trying, no matter how devious his intentions may be. And it's hard to find a man who tried harder than Stanley Clifford Weyman. Unlike most impostors, Weyman wasn't in it for the money—he wanted the adventure, famously stating, "One man's life is a boring thing. I lived many lives. I'm never bored."

In between impersonating navy and military officials, journalists, and the actual U.S. secretary of state, he also masterminded a meeting between an Afghani princess and Warren Harding, the president of the U.S. In 1921, Afghanistan and Britain were in talks to negotiate a peace treaty, and Princess Fatima of Afghanistan was visiting the U.S. However, the American government wasn't acknowledging her official presence.

So what did Weyman do? He visited Princess Fatima under the guise of a liaison officer for the State Department and promised that he would arrange a meeting between her and President Harding. All he asked was that she supply $10,000 as a complimentary present to the State Department. But here, where most con men would have taken the money and run, Weyman actually followed through on his promise—he used the $10,000 for first-class transport and accommodations for the princess, then lied his way up through the chain of command at the White House until he got to the president himself. When the press released his photo beside the princess and the president, he was recognized and arrested. Why did he do it? Just to see if he could.

8 Ferdinand Waldo Demara, Jr.

It's rare that an impersonator will manage to make a positive impact on the world and save the lives of the people who come to depend on him. Most impostors are after money or, in the case of Stanley Weyman, excitement. For Ferdinand Demara, impersonation was about filling in gaps and picking up the pieces where a job was needed, whether he had the training for it or not.

Early in his "career," Demara was a soldier in the military. Not happy with where that was taking him, he decided to fake his own suicide in 1942 and assumed the name of Robert French, then began teaching college psychology at a Pennsylvania university. Every now and then he would move to a different university position under a variety of names. Eventually, though, he was caught and given jail time—not for impersonating anyone, but for deserting the army years earlier.

Out of jail and with the headlines of the Korean War plastered across newspapers, Demara decided to assume the name of an acquaintance, a surgeon named Joseph Cyr. Under his new identity he got a job on the Canadian destroyer HMCS *Cayuga* and was shipped off to Korea. Unfortunately, he turned out to be the only surgeon on the ship, and ended up performing more than 16 major surgeries—with no formal training. All of his patients recovered. In the biography of Demara's life, *The Great Impostor*, Demara claimed that he simply read a surgery textbook before operating.

7 George Dupre

George Dupre is an interesting case in that his only real impersonation was of himself. However, the history he actually had and the history he claimed to were so different that he inadvertently became one of the greatest Canadian war heroes in the years following World War II.

After the war ended, Dupre began traveling across Canada as a public speaker, describing his missions as a spy for the special operations executive, a legendary espionage organization sometimes referred to as the Ministry of Ungentlemanly Warfare. Dupre wove intricate tales of life behind enemy lines in occupied Paris, working with the underground resistance to overthrow the Nazi Gestapo. He described his harrowing experience as a prisoner of the Gestapo, undergoing weeks of physical and psychological torture yet refusing to divulge any information. His story became so widespread that a book was written about it, *The Man Who Wouldn't Talk*, and Dupre became an international sensation.

Except that none of it ever happened. With the fame from the book came testimonies from people who had actually served with Dupre in the war. The truth was Dupre spent the entire war behind a desk in London. It turned out that Dupre had just embellished a few stories for fun, and somehow the entire thing spiraled out of control. Aside from the fame though, Dupre never benefited from the book deal and the public talks—he donated all his proceeds to Scouts Canada. His biography was reclassified as fiction.

6 David Hampton

Most of the impostors on this list got their start at a young age—few of them achieved notoriety before the age of 20. David Hampton is now considered one of the youngest successful con artists and impersonators, and his story has since been adapted into the play and film *Six Degrees of Separation*. His gimmick: impersonating actor Sidney Poitier's son (Sidney Poitier actually has six daughters and zero sons).

In 1983, at the age of 19, David Hampton tried to get into a Manhattan night club with a friend. The bouncers refused to let them in, but when Hampton came back later and told them he was Sidney Poitier's son, they immediately showed him to the VIP section. Thus, an identity was born. Hammond took to showing up at first-class restaurants, claiming that he was meeting his "father." He would dine, then act disappointed when his father never arrived while simultaneously signing the check in Poitier's name.

Soon he began to target the wealthy citizens of Manhattan—including fashion designer Calvin Klein and actor Gary Sinise, among others. Hampton would introduce himself as David Poitier, then make up a story about how he had been mugged and needed a place to stay until his father arrived the next day. In one of these homes he stole an address book, and took to calling people first, claiming that he was a friend of their son or daughter from college.

After Hampton's story became famous in *Six Degrees* in 1990, he began traveling the country under various other personas ("David Poitier" wouldn't exactly fly anymore), playing the impersonation game until 1993, when he passed away from AIDS.

5 Christian Karl Gerhartsreiter

Christian Gerhartsreiter is a German who moved to the U.S. in 1979 in the hopes of getting a job as an actor. His plan worked—but not exactly in the normal sense. A mere 18 years old with no money, no connections, and no legal visa to be in the States, he decided that the best thing to do would be to get married and obtain a green card through his wife. So that's what he did. He found a young woman named Amy Duhnke and told her that if he were sent back to Germany, he'd be conscripted into the German army to fight the Russians (this was during the Cold War). She agreed to marry him, but the day after the wedding, Christian skipped out on the honeymoon and pointed his compass toward California, where his true calling lay.

His true calling, of course, was to become Clark Rockefeller, the faux multimillionaire social butterfly who spent the next two decades—from around 1985–2006—claiming to be a member of the illustrious Rockefeller family. The plan worked exceedingly well until his wife Sandra Boss (of 11 years, I should add), began to get suspicious that he was not, in fact, a Rockefeller. The married couple had been living exclusively on Sandra's income the entire time, while "Clark" pursued high-profile social connections.

And the rest, as they say, is history. Sandra Boss discovered the lie, filed for divorce in 2006, and left with their daughter. Two years later, Clark was arrested for kidnapping his daughter in Boston, sparking a whirlwind investigation into this mysterious German's true identity. As it turned out, he also killed a man.

4 Alan Conway

Stanley Kubrick is an American director who's something of a legend among movie buffs. The words "greatest director in history" have been thrown around, along with the words "not British" and "heavily bearded." Those last two are particularly important, because in the early '90s, the reclusive Kubrick began to show up in social clubs in London—only now, he was clean-shaven and decidedly English. The "new" Kubrick was actually a man named Alan Conway, who had taken to using the name for the social status it imparted.

Despite the changes in his physical appearance, and reportedly having next to no knowledge of any of Kubrick's films, Alan Conway (real name Eddie Alan Jablowsky) managed to keep the charade going. Since the real Kubrick hadn't been seen in public more than a handful of times in the past 15 years, it couldn't have been terribly difficult—and even people who had actually met Kubrick in real life were fooled by the act. The film critic Frank

Rich was famously convinced and, based on Conway's behavior, came to the conclusion that Kubrick was gay (which Conway was).

Unfortunately, this story would be hilarious if it wasn't quite so tragic. Conway was a violent alcoholic, according to his son, and his impersonations were closer to fanatical delusions than any carefully calculated plan. Conway passed away in 1998 from heart problems.

3 Anoushirvan D. Fakhran

In the past, masquerading as one of the captains of industry seemed to be the surest way to a quick million. These days, Hollywood faces are American royalty. In 1992, Tehran native Anoushirvan Fakhran came to the U.S. on a student visa and spent the next several years living a lavish lifestyle, sprinkled with privileges usually reserved for celebrities and visiting royalty. That's because no one knew him by the name of Anoushirvan— to everyone who knew him, he was Jonathan Taylor Spielberg, nephew of director Steven Spielberg.

In fact, he had even gone so far as to officially change his name to Spielberg in 1997. Then, in 1998, an anonymous woman placed a call to Paul VI High School in Fairfax, Virginia. She claimed to represent Steven Spielberg and said that his nephew would be filming a movie in the area and wanted to research high school life. So the school allowed "Jonathan" to attend free of tuition and gave him an official transfer from his previous school, the fictitious Beverly Hills Private School for Actors. Jonathan Spielberg was now a student.

During this time, Jonathan and his mother were living in a posh apartment in Fairfax Village and Jonathan drove a BMW to school, often parking in the school principal's reserved space. No one complained; he was related to a celebrity. Eventually though, the scheme backfired—Jonathan stopped attending classes and the school tried to reach Steven Spielberg to find out why. Jonathan was arrested and sentenced to 11 months in jail for forging documents.

2 Steven Jay Russell

Steven Russell is probably closer to an escape artist than an impostor, but the means through which he masterminded his many prison escapes are the stuff of legend. In 1990, Russell lost his job and, instead of searching for new work, faked an accident and sued the company. This landed him his first prison sentence, and his first chance to escape. In 1992, Russell impersonated a prison guard by changing his clothes and just walking right out of the prison.

On his second arrest, which was for embezzling nearly $1 million from a medical company, Russell was given a $950,000 bail—he couldn't pay it, so he simply called the courthouse, told them he was a judge, and reduced

the bail to $45,000, which he promptly paid. Unfortunately, he was quickly tracked down again once the error was discovered, and Russell found himself facing a 40-year sentence for the previous embezzlement charges.

So he escaped again—this time by coloring his prison uniform with several dozen green markers until it resembled surgical scrubs. Again, he walked right out the front door. And again, he was quickly found and arrested. So this time Russell typed up fake medical records on a typewriter in his cell, and, through judicious use of laxatives, convinced the prison guards he was dying of AIDS. Then he called the prison and said that he was a doctor looking for volunteers to test a new AIDS treatment. When the prison warden announced the news, Russell promptly volunteered.

The next time he was caught, he faked a heart attack and was taken to a hospital under guard of FBI agents. So he asked to use the phone—and called the very agents guarding him under the guise of an FBI detective to let them know that they no longer needed to guard him. Russell is currently back in prison, looking forward to his release date in the year 2140. The 2009 film *I Love You Phillip Morris* is based on his exploits.

1 Christophe Thierry Rocancourt

The Rockefellers just can't catch a break. Before the German Clark Rockefeller, there was Christophe Rocancourt, the "French Rockefeller." Christophe started his scams big, and kept the ball rolling his entire career—his first scam was faking a property deed in Paris and then selling that deed for $1.4 million.

With his wallet freshly stuffed, he then hopped the ocean to the United States and began fraternizing with the Hollywood fat cats, claiming to be a French relative of the Rockefellers. Through this alias (and others), he convinced multiple people to fund his fictitious projects. Most of the time, he never even had to make any concrete claims—he would just show up at a party and make a vague mention of his mother, who might happen to be an actress one week or a famous producer the next.

In 2006, he was interviewed by *Dateline* and claimed that he had, in total, scammed about $40 million in his lifetime. His modus operandi was to convince someone wealthy that he was working on a large investment, but needed some capital to get it off the ground. The person would give Rocancourt the money, and Rocancourt would disappear. He famously convinced action star Jean-Claude Van Damme to produce a movie of his.

He was arrested for fraud in 1998 but has continued his scams well into the 21st century. As of 2009 he was in jail in Vancouver, where he told reporters, "I never steal. Never. I lied, but I never stole."

CHAPTER 11

CRIME

1. Top 10 Evil Corporations You Buy from Every Day

2. Top 10 Instances of Violence Committed by Peace Movements

3. Top 10 Prison Break-Ins

4. Top 10 Gruesome Acts of Justice

5. Top 10 Monstrous Killer Babysitters

6. Top 10 Grotesque Examples of Male Genital Mutilation

7. Top 10 Female Serial Killers from around the World

8. Top 10 Serious Crimes Committed for Bizarre Reasons

9. Top 10 Criminals Caught Thanks to Their Own Stupidity

10. Top 10 Phantom Law Breakers

11. Top 10 Innocent People Sentenced to Death

12. Top 10 Terrorist Organizations Operating in the U.S.

13. Top 10 Terrifying Unsolved Serial Murders

TOP 10 Evil Corporations You Buy from Every Day

by **Andrew Handley**

10 Monsanto

Monsanto needs no introduction, but we'll do it quickly anyway: They're a pesticide manufacturer known for being the first company to geneti-cally modify a seed to be resistant to pesti-cides and herbicides. Their seeds are billed as "Roundup-Ready," meaning that it's the only thing that will stay alive in a field that's been sprayed with Roundup, Monsanto's main her-bicide product.

This led the movement toward genetically modified crops—food crops that are bigger, grow faster, and can be literally doused in chemicals and not die. Now, aside from the fact that GMO crops are largely untested except for this study where rats on an 11 percent genetically modified corn diet were six times more likely to die, Monsanto itself is, well, fairly unethical.

In 2002, Monsanto was convicted of dumping tens of thousands of pounds of polychlorinated biphenyls (PCBs) into the waterways of Annis-ton, Alabama, and then lying about it for years. This led to the highest concentrations of the toxic pollutant ever recorded in history. Monsanto's view on the situation is quoted as being, "We can't afford to lose a dollar of profit."

9 American Cyanamid Co.

In the four years between 1996 and 2000, companies in the U.S. exported a little over a billion pounds of chemical pesticides to third-world coun-tries. That's not really a big deal, but this is: Most of those pesticides were banned in the U.S. because they were known carcinogens—but through a loophole, it's still legal to manufacture and export them, as long as they're not being used in the country.

As a result, over 350 million agricultural workers in areas like Africa and Central America are put in contact with these chemicals, only, through another loophole, they're not told about the small fact that without the proper gear they have a very good chance of dying. So you end up with a situation like the plantation in Costa Rica that was sold a pesticide called Counter by American Cyanamid Co.

A quick fact about Counter: The chemical in it is an organophosphate—that's what they used to make nerve gas before World War II. Counter is only approved for handling if you're wearing gloves, a face mask, and eye protection. The uninformed Costa Rican farmers, on the other hand, worked shirtless and spread the pesticide with their bare hands. Some of them even used full bags of Counter as pillows at night. After a few days, the workers were literally vomiting blood and foaming at the mouth from the toxins that had gotten into their bodies.

And it's still happening every day. Companies like American Cyanamid and Chevron Chemical Co. export about ten million pounds of these chemicals each month to areas that provide approximately a quarter of the produce sold in America, freshly dusted with illegal pesticides.

8 Various Pharmaceutical Companies

In 2009, something strange was discovered in the water near Patancheru, India—high concentrations of over 21 different pharmaceutical drugs were mixed in with the town's water supply. As it turned out, these drugs were being dumped in the stream by the many factories in the region—factories owned by U.S. pharmaceutical companies. In particular, one factory was dumping 100 pounds of an antibiotic called ciprofloxacin into the stream every day. This is the town's only water source, providing everything from drinking water to a place to bathe.

Pharmaceutical waste like this has been discovered in the U.S. as well, and it's estimated that about 46 million Americans' tap water contains traces of pharmaceutical drugs in varying concentrations. Based on where the drugs have been found, EPA officials believe that it's coming from illegal dumping by nearby factories. How evil is this? Aside from its effect on wildlife (stunted growth), we don't really know what kind of effect small quantities of dozens of combined drugs will have on people. But it can't be that good.

7 Bayer

You may recognize Bayer as the maker of Aspirin. They're one of the top pharmaceutical companies in the world. In 1984, they discovered that one of the products they were selling, a medicine to induce blood clotting, was infecting people with HIV. So like any responsible company, they stopped marketing it and developed a safer medicine—right before exporting all of the contaminated medicine to Asia and Latin America, where it continued to be sold. They even continued making the HIV-infected medicine for another few months, because it was cheaper to produce than the new version. This was again sold straight to developing countries.

Six thousand people in the U.S. were known to have contracted HIV and AIDS from the medicine, but how many died from the tainted medicine overseas? At least 100,000 units of the medication made their way to Asia and Argentina after Bayer stopped selling it in America.

6 Rio Tinto

Rio Tinto is a mining company that operates mostly out of Africa. As the biggest private mining company in the world, they provide much of the world's raw aluminum and copper—along with ura-  nium, gold, and diamonds—and might have the worst track record for human rights violations ever.

It started in the 1970s, when Rio Tinto was dis- covered to have been running illegal uranium mines in Namibia and using the profits to support the apart- heid government in South Africa—in return, the gov- ernment allowed Rio Tinto to keep operating in the area. Additionally, Rio Tinto maintained its own pri- vate mercenary army to keep blacks from rising up against them and the government. Oh and also, the uranium mines used "brutal slave labor," in the words of the United Nations Council that dealt with the matter.

But far from getting shut down, Rio Tinto went on to bludgeon human- ity and the environment further at every turn. In 1981, it turned out that one of their Canadian uranium mines had been exposing workers for years to radiation levels more than seven times the legal limit. In Indonesia, they have tortured and killed opponents of their gold mines. And in 2000, an ex-security guard at their gold mine in Brazil revealed that security work- ers were urged to use violence to keep the miners complacent. It's basically modern-day slavery.

5 Siemens

Siemens is an electronics manufacturer that makes everything from car parts to vacuum cleaners—and, in times past, Nazi gas chambers. If you've ever wondered who was willing to take the job of building the group-sized hydrogen cyanide chambers used in Auschwitz, now you know. They were also immersed in building the infamous train system of Nazi-era Germany, the Reichsbahn, which transported Jews to the concentration camps.

And it's not as if they were on the fringe of the war—Siemens funded the Nazi Party during the 1930s and actively supported Hitler's regime once the war broke out. They had more than 400 factories operating throughout Germany by late 1944, many of which used Jewish labor.

But that's old news; these days, they've moved on to more modern endeavors like spearheading a worldwide electronics cartel, bribing government officials, and bribing the entire country of Greece.

4 Walmart

Walmart isn't exactly a poster-child for workers' rights. Besides running sweatshops in China and refusing to hire women, they've also been pegged with nearly 250 cases of hiring illegal workers to clean their stores, forcing them to work seven days a week and locking them in the stores at night.

And then there's the small matter of possible human trafficking. One of Walmart's supply partners is the Phatthana Seafood Company, a shrimp processing plant in Thailand. The workers paid recruitment agents large sums of money for the opportunity to work, after which their passports were taken from them until they had worked long enough to pay off the debt. In a legal sense, that's one of the criteria used to judge human trafficking cases.

The workers are paid $8.48 per day, but the factory only runs an average of 14 days a month, so many of them have to resort to catching snails and tadpoles just to eat.

3 James Hardie

We've known about the dangers of asbestos since the 1940s, even though it was still widely used as a building material until the late '70s when its use began to decline. One of the major downsides of asbestos is its tendency to cause mesothelioma, a type of malignant cancer that coats the internal organs. Fast forward to 1987 and you have James Hardie, an Australian manufacturing company, continuing to operate asbestos factories across Victoria, Queensland, and Western Australia.

James Hardie was the largest Australian producer of building materials at the time, and after thousands of cases of asbestos poisoning surfaced among its workers, an investigation was launched, which found that James Hardie was well aware of the dangers of asbestos, but continued to manufacture it anyway.

But James Hardie was prepared for the virtual avalanche of lawsuits that followed in the early 2000s. Here's how it worked: Their business structure was set up so that only subsidiaries of the James Hardie parent corporation were connected to the asbestos work. When the pressure got too heavy, James Hardie began cutting off ties to these subsidiaries, leaving them to take the brunt of the lawsuits even though they didn't have enough money to compensate all the victims. James Hardie then moved to the Netherlands, and is now denying the responsibility because "those other companies aren't part of James Hardie."

Basically, they had dodged most of the responsibility as of 2012, while over 12,000 people have been diagnosed with mesothelioma from their products.

2 Smithfield Foods

Smithfield Foods is a pig slaughterhouse—that's fine; plenty of people eat bacon and pork. They package about 6 billion pounds of pork annually, which means they need a lot of pigs. A lot of pigs produce a lot of waste—in the neighborhood of about 26 million pounds per year, as far as Smithfield is concerned.

But let's get visceral: Smithfield pigs are raised in barns that hold thousands of tightly packed hogs. The floors of these barns have slits that allow waste to fall through into a series of pipes that takes it to massive open-air holding ponds. The pigs are injected with a cocktail of antibiotics, sprayed with insecticides and dozens of chemicals that all end up in the holding ponds—ponds so toxic that if somebody falls in, they'll be dead before you can save them.

So how do they get rid of millions of pounds of liquid, chemical-infused pig waste? They spray it into the air in a mist so that it drifts off their property and becomes someone else's problem. A someone else's problem filled with hydrogen sulfide, ammonia, methane, and over a hundred other toxic gases that have given people in the surrounding areas conditions like bronchitis, asthma, and neurological damage.

1 Chiquita

In 1928, the United Fruit Company had a strike on its hands. The workers at their Colombian plantation wanted better working conditions, which United Fruit didn't want to give them. This resulted in the Colombian army setting up mounted machine guns around the strikers, and systematically mowing them down. Later, they changed their name to Chiquita, which is a word you can see on nearly every banana in the grocery store today. But wait, there's more.

In 1954, the Guatemalan president Jacobo Arbenz Guzman was implementing a revised labor code that would effectively take 40 percent of United Fruit Company's land away. At that time, Guatemala was basically United Fruit's playground, so rather than take the losses, they responded by initiating a coup d'etat that overthrew the entire government, dissolving the country into 36 years of civil war that had an estimated death toll of up to 250,000.

So by this time United Fruit has become Chiquita, and has washed their hands of Latin politics for good. Except, they haven't. In 2004, Chiquita was accused by the Justice Department of paying money to a right-wing terrorist group in Colombia to protect their plantations. And then they turned around and provided funding to the Revolutionary Armed Forces of Columbia, a leftist terrorist group that has in the past been involved in a plot to assassinate Hugo Chavez.

TOP 10 Instances of Violence Committed by Peace Movements

by **FlameHorse**

10 Glitter Bombs

Violent Act: Glitter Bombing

Glitter bombing cannot be blamed on any one group or organization. It has become a fad by which pro–gay rights activists protest anyone who speaks out against gay rights. The legality of throwing glitter on someone without warning falls in the gray area between assault and harmless prank. Those with an easy-going sense of humor have usually laughed it off, but it does rub plenty of people the wrong way, and former Arkansas Governor Mike Huckabee, among others, decries it as assault and battery, and possibly sexual harassment.

The latter definition he bases on the premise that some activists proclaim the victim gay upon being glitter bombed. It is, of course, an example of disturbing the peace, public humiliation, assault with intent to commit psychological harm, and perhaps invasion of privacy. Mitt Romney was glitter bombed twice during his presidential campaign and the second time, the assailant was dragged away by the Secret Service and pled guilty to disturbing the peace. He served no time.

9 PETA

Violent Act: PETA, Al Pieda, and the Biotic Baking Brigade

Al Pieda is pronounced as a rhyme with "al-Qaeda," and it is a self-described terrorist organization in the United States (with splinter cells across the world), that protests all things conservative, especially any supposed intolerance of gay rights. Their modus operandi is to throw a pie right in the face of the person they feel opposes their stance. The Biotic Baking Brigade is precisely the same organization, just a little more organized and official.

People for the Ethical Treatment of Animals (PETA) touts itself as a nonviolent protest organization, but has also engaged in pie throwing. The pieing of Bill Gates is rather famous across the Internet, but it doesn't count, since he was pied just for fun by a single prankster. But Ann Coulter and William Buckley have been pied for being conservative, and public opponents or supposed opponents of gay rights, feminism, and ecology (global warming). They also pied Fred Phelps of the Westboro Baptist Church, which, as deserving as it was, only galvanized his movement to be even more inflammatory. The pieing groups demand equal rights for homosexuals, animals, women, and more. Legally, pieing is assault, and quite a few members of these groups have been arrested and tried for it.

8 Greenpeace

Violent Act: Greenpeace Rams a Japanese Fishing Boat

Greenpeace is probably the most visible peace-championing organization in the world, present in over 40 countries. Their goal is to "ensure the ability of the Earth to nurture life in all its diversity." They are an environmental watch group that tries to stamp out nuclear weaponry, deforestation, reverse the trend toward global warming, and especially fight back against overfishing the oceans.

They make no secret of their contempt for commercial fishing, notably whaling, which still goes on legally around the world. Among commercial fishers, the Japanese have roused the ire of more than just Greenpeace by their wholesale slaughter of bottlenose dolphins, an intelligent and decidedly cute species of mammal, for human consumption, despite the well-established fact that dolphin meat is toxically high in mercury.

On January 8, 2006, the Greenpeace vessel *Arctic Sunrise* deliberately rammed the *Nisshin Maru*, a Japanese whaling ship attempting to avoid the *Sunrise* as best it could. Unfortunately, whaling ships are very large and do not maneuver very well. The much smaller *Sunrise* was given ample warning to get out of the way but continued directly into the side of the *Maru*. The video captured of the incident was filmed by Greenpeace and distributed under the explanation that the *Nisshin Maru* was the one that acted aggressively, and that the *Arctic Sunrise* simply refused to move.

7 Earth Liberation Front

Violent Act: The Earth Liberation Front Commits Arson

The Earth Liberation Front (ELF) states that they use "economic sabotage and guerrilla warfare to stop the exploitation and destruction of the environment." They have a presence in at least 17 nations worldwide, including the United States, almost all of Europe, parts of Asia, Australia, and New Zealand. They do not have actual offices or any headquarters, but are instead a covert, splinter-cell organization operating under the protection of anonymity.

Their actions require this secrecy, as the FBI has declared them the highest priority of domestic terror threats. They pride themselves on being animal liberationists, anarchists, anticapitalists, and ecofeminists.

ELF first came to prominent notoriety when they burned down a ski resort in Vail, Colorado, causing 12 million dollars in damage. They did this to stop clear-cut logging and protect the lynxes in the surrounding forests. They have burned down parts of the campus of the University of Washington, in Seattle, and have claimed responsibility for over 400 SUVs and Humvee vehicles being burned in dealership parking lots. They are probably responsible for the so-called "Street of Dreams" house fires on Echo Lake Road in Washington in 2008. Three mansions were razed to the ground, while a fourth was put out in time, causing $7 million in damage.

6 Suffragettes

Violent Act: The Suffragettes

The Suffragettes, as they dubbed themselves, were women who demanded the right to vote. Suffrage had been a long-ongoing affair. In the United States, women were not nationally given the right to vote until the 1920 presidential election. Protests for the right did not gain ground quickly until they became violent in England by 1912. There, women began burning mailboxes, chaining and handcuffing themselves to staircase banisters in courthouses and other municipal buildings, and even setting off explosives in public squares, streets, and post offices.

Some of these women were imprisoned and force-fed through tubes inserted down their throats into their stomachs when they refused to eat. The British government deliberately let some of them starve until too weak to participate in pickets and marches, then released them from prison. This was all because the British government did not approve of women voting.

On June 5, 1913, Suffragette Emily Davison went to the Epsom Derby, a horse-racing venue, and deliberately charged out onto the track during the middle of a race in order to slap a suffrage banner onto the rump of King

George V's personal horse, Anmer, as he galloped by. George was not riding him. Unfortunately for her, horses do not care if women have the right to vote, and the jockey was unable to rein him in or away from her in time. Anmer bashed into her, sending her flying onto her back, fracturing her skull and sending broken ribs into her left lung. She died four days later. Neither Anmer nor the jockey was injured, and they completed the race. The violence did help immeasurably, and British women were granted the right unconditionally in 1928.

5 Nelson Mandela

Violent Act: Nelson Mandela versus Apartheid
We all know Mandela was the primary driving influence for the anti-apartheid movement in South Africa. *Apartheid* is Afrikaans for segregated, and was the South African regime from 1948–1994, during which time, Afrikaners—white descendants of the Dutch, Germans, and French—ruled the nation and deprived blacks of many human rights.

Mandela began fighting back almost immediately upon apartheid's inception in 1948 and sternly advocated direct action, not merely passive nonviolence. He advised the other members of his organization, the African National Congress, to acquire weapons for their own defense, but never to attack anyone without provocation. He appeared to be conflicted about this, since he publicly advised a mode of nonviolent noncooperation in the style of Gandhi. By 1955, Mandela conceded that violent resistance was the only method that would work to end apartheid's civil rights violations.

Mandela is known to have fought back physically against the apartheid riot police at over three dozen different protests, marches, and parades. He founded Umkhonto we Sizwe, or Spear of the Nation, in 1961, and ordered its members to engage in sabotage, cutting communication lines and blowing up railways, to weaken the apartheid government. If this failed, he promised that "guerrilla warfare and terrorism" would be put into effect. On December 16, 1961, his organization bombed 57 separate businesses, law firms, courthouses, and vehicles. No one was killed, but people were wounded. Mandela was caught on August 5 of the next year, tried, and sentenced to life in prison. He spent 27 years in prison before being released in 1990.

4 Plowshares Movement

Violent Act: The Plowshares Movement Damages Nuclear Warheads
The Plowshares named themselves after Isaiah 2:3 and 4, the famous "beating swords into plowshares" passage of the Bible. This passage is meant to represent true world peace, and the movement considers itself a group of

Christian pacifists, although their actions said otherwise on September 9, 1980, when they broke into the General Electric nuclear missile and storage base outside King of Prussia, Pennsylvania.

The movement was founded by Daniel Berrigan with the sole intent to eradicate all nuclear weaponry from the planet. They claim utter nonviolence toward people, but violence toward property inasmuch as it will hinder a nation's nuclear weapon capabilities, and over 80 such violent actions have taken place on four continents to date. Their first act, on the Pennsylvania nuclear missile base, resulted in the demolition or damage of eight nuclear warhead nosecones. They had no idea whether their actions would trigger the devices, but luckily for many people in the area, the devices were designed with five safety measures and could not be detonated in the first place without first being armed, and they were not. They did, however, contain weapons-grade plutonium, which the Plowshares nearly exposed to open air. This would have killed every one of them and probably many more in the immediate area.

They also broke into two research offices and tore up classified documents, then poured cow blood over them and the furniture. They were arrested after breaking windows alerted guards who raised an alarm. The eight original members were all personally involved, and all spent ten years in prison before their appeal resulted in new sentences and they were paroled with time served.

3 Sea Shepherds

Violent Act: The Sea Shepherds Ram a Japanese Fishing Boat

The Sea Shepherd Conservation Society is similar in mission to Greenpeace. They are the basis for the Discovery Channel's *Whale Wars* reality show, which chronicles the SSCS's repeated aggravated harassment of Japanese whaling vessels, usually off the coast of Antarctica. Their avowed goal is to eradicate the practice of whaling by "direct action," a euphemism for violence.

One incident that took place on February 6, 2009, has become well known across the Internet. The SSCS vessel *Steve Irwin*, named after the late crocodile hunter, apparently sped up behind the *Yushin Maru 2* and swung its bow into the side of the *Maru*'s stern, quite like a police officer's pit maneuver against a fleeing car.

There were two whaling vessels involved, the other named the *Yushin Maru 1*, which was at the time hauling a dead whale into its slipway for butchering. The *Maru 2* had harpooned the whale. Paul Watson, founder and president of the SSCS, stated that the collision was the result of either reckless driving or a deliberate assault on the part of the *Maru 2*. The

Japanese have attested that they were simply doing their job when the *Irwin* arrived and rammed them deliberately. The Japanese attempted to drive the *Irwin* off by firing water cannons at them, and through the use of LRADs, which are very powerful, painfully loud sonic weapons that can perforate eardrums from half a mile. The collision nearly capsized the *Maru 2*.

The video of this incident has been incorrectly labeled as an attack by Greenpeace, but SSCS has proudly taken responsibility and maintains that it did nothing wrong.

2 Boston Tea Party

Violent Act: The Boston Tea Party
The original Tea Party was instigated by the British taxing the 13 American colonies to the point of usury. The colonies were founded by people attempting to get away from oppression in England, but the British had an all-powerful navy and were able to keep the colonies in check, first through peaceable means, during which time the British and Americans allied against the French and various Indian tribes, then through violent coercion. By the time of the American Revolution, the British had long since been treating the colonies as a money-making enterprise. Almost everything was taxed, to the point that the Americans simply had no money left for themselves.

The Sons of Liberty were founded to demand less taxation through the use of violence if necessary, and on December 16, 1773, anywhere from 30–130 Sons of Liberty, incited in part by Samuel Adams, boarded three British merchant vessels in Boston Harbor and spent three hours chopping into 342 large chests of tea and throwing them and their contents overboard. This tea had been shipped to America with an impossibly high tax levied on it. Every colony but Massachusetts bowed to the colonists' demand to return it. The incident infuriated the British and is marked as one of the specific instigations of the Revolution.

1 Temple of Solomon

Violent Act: Jesus Clears the Temple of Solomon
Think about this one in a new light. The Synoptic Gospels recount that Jesus entered Jerusalem triumphantly on what is now called Palm Sunday and immediately assaulted the men exchanging money and selling livestock in the temple. The people had been generally enthusiastic during his entrance based on the miracles he had performed and the fact that he had healed everyone who approached him with such a request.

He dismounted his donkey and in sight of the money changers and merchants, he flew into a rage, the only time in the Gospels when Jesus really loses his temper. The money changers' coins would have been stacked on the tables, and Jesus slapped the coins across the floor, threw the tables over, opened the bird cages, and threw the birds out to fly away, made a makeshift whip and drove all the livestock away, and probably took a few swings at the men themselves.

The Synoptic Gospels' placement of this event at the beginning of Jesus's final week of mortal life seems more likely than John's, which places it long earlier in Jesus's ministry. It is seen as one of the most imminent compulsions of the Jews' decision to kill him. He had already aggravated and frustrated them for three years by doing absolutely nothing for which they could arrest him, and yet he drew thousands to his ministry and expressly away from theirs.

His act of clearing the temple may be seen as what some organizations of the peace movement call "direct action." He did not actually harm anyone, but even modern societies would have viewed his action as assault and attempted to arrest him for it.

TOP 10 Prison Break-Ins

by **Michael Allison**

10 A Lawyer Breaks into Prison

Serhiy Vlasenko, the lawyer of former Ukrainian Prime Minister Yulia Tymoshenko, just wanted to see his client. When prison officials prevented Vlasenko from seeing her, he went one step further than most lawyers—and broke into prison.

While pop culture suggests intricate planning, months of physical preparation, and a team of suave ex-cons are required to pull this off, all Vlasenko needed to do was crawl under a fence when the guards were on a break.

9 A Woman Breaks into Jail Because She Wants to Be Arrested

In June 2012, Tiffany Hurd spent her morning baffling sheriffs in Butler County, Ohio, by trying to drunkenly scale a barbwire fence to get into jail.

Hurd's reason was refreshingly upfront: "I wanted to be arrested," she said. Sheriff Richard K. Jones granted that wish, and arrested her for disorderly conduct and trespassing.

8 A Cat Breaks into Prison

Outside Alagoas prison in Brazil, a suspicious-looking cat was arrested when agents felt "something about it seemed wrong."

After frisking the cat, the agents found it had been breaking into Alagoas with saw blades, drills, and fully-charged cell phones strapped to its body. While police officers were both surprised and impressed by the feline's abilities, it's currently unknown if it will be facing prison time.

7 A Man Dressed as Snoopy Breaks into Prison

In May 2010, a man dressed as Snoopy from the cartoon *Peanuts* attempted to break into England's Albany Prison armed only with a water pistol.

While his plan was to break in, grab a relative locked up inside, then break back out again while doing the Snoopy dance, it was later revealed he'd in fact broken into the wrong prison.

6 A Man Breaks into Prison to Reminisce

There are many places people go to reminisce and relive the best moments of their lives. Old schools, parks, and, in one particularly odd case, California's Folsom State Prison.

Martin Ussery, 48, was out on parole when he felt the need to visit his old stomping ground. He biked up to the fence, climbed over and was later found lying down quietly next to the facility's recycling center, presumably humming Johnny Cash's "Folsom Prison Blues."

5 Breaking into Prison for Drugs

In one unnamed prison in Yorkshire, England, drugs are so cheap that people on the outside have actually broken in to buy them. Officials have blamed the rock-bottom drug prices on supply and demand—there's just so much product available in this prison, it's practically being given away.

The Prison Officer's Association pointed out that when people break in, they often leave their ladders on the walls, giving prisoners the perfect opportunity to escape. But, as it turns out, prisoners are so comfortable on the inside that none of them have ever tried.

4 Breaking into Prison to Steal Cigarettes

When most people get a cigarette craving, they go down to their local store and buy a pack. These thieves, however, broke into England's Kirkham Prison to get their fix.

Once inside the walls, the thieves snuck into a storage area operated by courier company DHL. The area supplies not just Kirkham Prison, but several prisons across Lancashire, England. As the storage area was well stocked, the thieves didn't just grab two or three cigarette cartons, they ended up walking away with nearly $13,000 worth!

3 Breaking into Prison to Steal Tools

Perhaps bored of stealing from poorly guarded mom-and-pop stores, these criminals used tools to break into Sudbury Prison in England—to steal more tools.

Items taken included propane tanks, hoses, tools, and, to help with the getaway, a cart. When inmates at the prison were asked what they thought of the caper, they simply replied, "Hilarious."

2 Soccer Player Breaks into Prison

Mario Balotelli is considered one of the strangest men in soccer, so while the following reaches number two on our list of prison break-ins, it barely registers on his top-ten list of most bizarre moments.

Balotelli and his brother, much like a young couple inspecting a new home before putting in an offer, decided to take a casual stroll through a women's prison in Brescia, Italy.

When the bewildered guards caught and questioned him, Balotelli apologized, claimed the idea of a woman's prison intrigued him, and then headed off to find himself another embarrassing situation.

1 A Man Breaks into Prison for His Girlfriend

When a man's girlfriend was sentenced to prison on drug charges, he did what any young man in love would do—broke into prison to see her, night after night.

Though it was police dogs that finally caught him, other inmates in the prison were aware of his visits. They reported trouble sleeping when he was in the prison cell next to theirs. While being arrested, he yelled, "I love her. We're engaged!" He later discovered that when his girlfriend first entered prison, she wrote down another man's name as her partner.

TOP 10 Gruesome Acts of Justice

by **Karl Smallwood**

10 Agents Who Sent Condolence Letters to Terrorists' Families...Before Killing the Terrorists

When the Black September group executed 11 members of an Israeli athletic team, they poked a sleeping dragon. MOSSAD agents were basically given free rein to do whatever was needed to make them pay.

And boy did they make those terrorists pay. MOSSAD chased the men across the world, methodically killing as many of them as they could. But here's the stone-cold part: Hours before a terrorist was set to die, his family would receive flowers and a condolence card with a simple message: "We don't forgive and we don't forget."

9 The Jews Who Hunted Down Their Nazi Captors

After World War II ended, many Jewish people were left without a visible outlet to vent about the terrible injustice they'd been forced to suffer through. Some found this outlet by dedicating their lives to killing Nazis.

It's hard to say how many the avengers killed (yes, they were called the *Nokmim*, Hebrew for "avengers") because they made a lot of the deaths look like accidents, leading historians to assume that Nazis were clumsy as well as evil.

8 Davao City Punisher

Under the watchful eye of Mayor Rodrigo Duterte, the crime rate plummeted in Davao City in the Philippines. Why? Well, it almost certainly had something to do with the fact that the mayor really hates crime, and criminals had a tendency to drop dead while he was in power.

Though the mayor prefers to keep quiet about how his city operates, the fact remains that it has become a shining beacon of prosperity. *Time* magazine also once called him "The Punisher," making Duterte the most badass mayor in the history of world.

7 Russian Vigilantes Who Give Drug Dealers a Taste of Their Own Medicine

When heroin started gaining popularity in Russia, some concerned citizens took a shot of vodka and said, "*Nyet!*"

Though the tactics they use are questionable, you can't argue with the logic that stripping a drug dealer from the waist down and sticking used needles in his butt is going to send a message. That message being: Don't mess with Russia.

6 The Police Squad with a 99 Percent Arrest Rate

The Queens Violent Felony Squad in New York is the only item on this list that acts within the parameters of the law. They get featured not for their tactics, but for their results. TQVFS are the people you call when somebody absolutely needs to go to jail; they are the best of the best.

Nothing shows this better than the group's success rate: 99 percent of the jobs that land on their desks get done with ruthless efficiency. They may not pistol whip the criminals like others on this list, but gruesomely efficient is still gruesome.

5 The All-Female Gang That Beats Up Domestic Abusers

Domestic abuse is a big deal, and in rural India, where women's rights can be virtually nonexistent, it runs rampant. Someone needed to step up, and the Gulabi Gang did exactly that. Dressed in their trademark pink saris, the Gulabi Gang encourage men who hit their wives to see reason—by beating them with sticks.

Nowadays the Gulabi Gang is several thousand members strong, and they defend not only women but anyone who is being oppressed.

4 The Women Who All Killed Their Rapist

A serial rapist was standing in court, when out of nowhere, hundreds of women from the slums he'd terrorized ran in with the singular goal of seeing how many stab wounds his torso could take. During the ordeal, one of the women cut off his genitals while another threw chili powder in his face and wounds. After 15 minutes of frantic stabbing and punching, the man was dead. In court. In front of everyone.

Then, in an act of unbelievable solidarity, every woman present confessed to the murder, while the police looked on in disbelief.

3 The Town That Shot Its Bully

This isn't that uncommon; it's not even a recent trend. Consider the story of Ken Rex McElroy, a man who relentlessly bullied an entire town for a year. He stole, attacked, and raped with impunity, never once standing trial (because you can't arrest a man with a name that manly).

And then one day, he was shot. Though the shooting took place in front of 40 witnesses and with at least two different guns, no one saw a thing. Decades later, this murder still remains unsolved—because everyone in the sleepy town of Skidmore has kept their mouths shut. You may not respect this kind of vigilante justice, but you have to at least respect that kind of dedication.

2 The Disgusting Tale of Benito Mussolini's Body

Here's the short version. When Benito Mussolini was killed, hundreds if not thousands of people collectively decided to turn his body into raw meat. After killing the dictator, Italian partisans took his body to the place that had been used to kill 15 of their own men and put it on display for the public to use as a meaty piñata.

It was shot, spat on, and had rocks thrown at it by the public. The result? Just imagine what would happen if someone ran over a hot dog and put it in a suit.

1 The Concentration Camp
Victims Who Got Revenge

While some Jewish folks dedicated their lives to killing Nazis, some got their revenge a little quicker.

When concentration camps were liberated, the Allies were astounded and sickened at what they saw. Some former prisoners were given SS guards to dance for their amusement, while some were given guns, bayonets, and the freedom to exact whatever revenge they saw fit on their tormentors.

Even without the direct help of armed soldiers, during and after liberation many survivors found their revenge. As the Allied tanks approached, many German soldiers were captured by prisoners while fleeing. One story details how a particularly brutal guard was caught trying to climb over a window ledge. He was dragged by prisoners into an alleyway, where they silently tore him apart with their bare hands.

TOP 10 Monstrous Killer Babysitters

by **Simon Griffin**

10 Yoselyn Ortega

Yoselyn Ortega, 50, was hired by the Krim family to look after their three children. Their mother, Marina Krim, returned home after taking her three-year-old son to a swimming lesson to find the bodies of her other two children in a bath filled with bloody water. Six-year-old Lucia and one-year-old Leo had been stabbed to death by Ortega. As soon as Marina entered the room, Ortega slit her own wrists and began stabbing herself so violently that she pushed

the kitchen knife she was using out the other side of her neck. Ortega and the children were taken to hospital, where she was stabilized and they were pronounced dead. Their father, Kevin, was returning from a business trip and was met by police at the airport.

There is no clear motive for the killings, other than the stress Ortega was under trying to move her son from the Dominican Republic to the U.S. and her anger at failing to get a pay raise. She has not given a confession.

9 David McGreavy

Now nicknamed "The Monster of Worcester," David McGreavy was a young man staying with a family in Worcester, England, in 1973. One day in April, he was asked to take care of the family's three young children. Instead, he gruesomely murdered them before carrying the bodies outside to the garden railing, where they were impaled and put on display.

He was arrested that same day and sentenced to life in prison. In a controversial 2009 ruling, he was granted anonymity when his lawyers argued that it was his human right to have his identity kept a secret. McGreavy had already been assaulted by other prisoners twice, and lawyers argued that identifying him would result in further attacks. The anonymity order was later lifted, although McGreavy may be allowed to change his name in the future. He has unsuccessfully applied for parole many times.

8 Agnes Wong

In 2007, Agnes Wong was hired to look after 16-month-old Hugo Wang for a while. On January 25, Hugo was taken to a children's hospital in Manchester after incurring serious head trauma due to being swung around by his ankles. Wong had been abusing the child for the past few weeks, and by this point he was covered in bite marks, bruises, and burns, and had been severely beaten. Wong claimed she only disciplined the child when he was being naughty and that he got the burn marks from messing around with a hair dryer. Hugo died on January 26, and Wong was charged with his murder a few days later.

Wong was sentenced to five years in jail for the crime, but in a highly controversial decision, she only served two years, after which she was paid about $7,000 (£4,500) to go back to Malaysia. The logic behind this method of dealing with criminals is to save taxpayer money by getting the criminal out of the country and out of the system. The money given to the criminal is a sort of bribe to get them to waive their human rights so they don't try to appeal deportation and stay in Britain.

7 Karl McCluney

Karl McCluney was 15 years old when he was asked to look after 2-year-old Demi Leigh Mahon for an hour and a half while her mother ran some errands, including buying a birthday card for Karl. After going to the park, the kids returned to Demi's home, where Karl beat Demi, bit her, and shaved her head. When her mother returned, Karl was watching TV, while Demi was barely alive and was rushed to the hospital. Karl denied any wrongdoing, saying she had sustained her 69 injuries by falling in the park. The toddler was severely brain damaged and was taken off life support two days later. Karl eventually confessed to his psychiatrist, who said the boy had a low IQ and came from a broken home. Karl claimed that no one can punish him as much as he will himself, but he was still given 15 years for his crime, having been tried as a minor. The only apparent motive for this brutal infanticide is that Demi was annoying him.

6 Marquita Burch

In May 2012, when William Cunningham was just one year old, he was being looked after for a few weeks by Marquita Burch, a friend of his mother. On Friday May 25, Burch told police that the toddler had wandered off while they were in a park that night. While police, firefighters, and neighbors searched for over five hours, Burch's story started to unravel. She eventually confessed that the toddler was dead, hidden in the closet at her cousin's house. Burch claims she wasn't responsible for his death and that she just found him at the bottom of the stairs on May 23, having given him ibuprofen before putting him to bed the previous night. Upon finding him (still alive), instead of taking him to a hospital, she panicked, put him in a garbage bag, and stashed it. According to the coroner's report, by the time police found the child, he had been dead for at least 48 hours, having suffered an intracranial hemorrhage. Burch originally pleaded not guilty, but then changed her plea and was found guilty of endangering a child, involuntary manslaughter, and abusing a corpse. She was sentenced to 19.5 years in prison.

5 Frederick Mitchell

In March, 2013, Frederick Mitchell, a 21-year-old man from Cincinnati, was babysitting six-month-old Elliot Magrditchian, the son of one of Mitchell's housemates. At some point during the day, Mitchell threw the infant into a wall for reasons unknown. Elliot was taken to the hospital, where he died a few days later. Mitchell's mother, Angela, claims he suffers from blackouts and stresses that she firmly believes the tragedy was just an accident. Mitchell was initially charged with felonious assault and had his bond set at $1 million, but after the coroner ruled Elliot's death a homicide, the charges were increased to felonious assault and two counts of murder, for which Mitchell could spend life in prison. As of this writing, he is awaiting trial in the Hamilton County Justice Center.

4 Gabriela Gonzales

Twenty-five-year-old Gabriela Gonzales was smuggled illegally into the U.S. and forced into prostitution in 2002. She managed to leave that life behind and moved in with a number of people in Richmond, Virginia. In October 2011, one of the women she lived with went to Maryland in search of work, and Gonzales was left in charge of her two-year-old daughter, Kiery Nicole. Unfortunately, Kiery was suffering from a bad rash, and Gonzales couldn't get her to stop crying. Her frustration with the toddler grew until she snapped. Gonzales violently shook the two-year-old, and beat her head against either a bathtub or a toilet. The autopsy revealed both brain and spinal cord hemorrhages, as well as a severely fractured skull. Kiery was placed on life support, but died after three days.

Gonzales claimed that Kiery was injured after she fell while jumping on the bed, and even attempted to convince the police that she had accidentally strangled herself. Even during her hearing, she is said to have shown no remorse. Gonzales was given the maximum sentence of 20 years and is no longer allowed to see her own child.

3 Michael Plumadore

Aliahna Lemmon and her two sisters were being looked after by their neighbor, Plumadore, because their mother was sick and their father worked nights. On Friday, December 23, 2011, Aliahna went missing. Plumadore told police that he had just assumed she had left his trailer and gone back to her own. Christmas came and went without any sign of the missing girl. Then, the following Thursday, the FBI became involved in the case, and Plumadore admitted that he had beaten her on his front steps with a brick before working through the night with a hacksaw to dismember her body. He then separated the pieces, freezing her head, hands and feet for unknown reasons, and disposing of the rest of the body in a dumpster.

Plumadore never provided a motive for the killing, which is especially odd considering the other two girls were left unharmed. He was originally facing the death sentence for the crime, but upon pleading guilty, this was changed to life in prison without the possibility of parole.

2 William Howard Lail

William Howard Lail is being charged with one count of murder and two counts of child abuse after his girlfriend left her two children in his care. On a Saturday night, a panicked Lail ran out of the house looking for help, ran back in, and reemerged with 20-month-old Jaydon's body. Jaydon was dead, but paramedics came for his three-year-old sister, Kylie, who was with another neighbor by that point. This neighbor noticed that not only did Kylie have fresh marks from being scalded on her head, shoulders, and legs, she also had ones that were obviously there from a while back. She was taken to hospital and treated, while Lail was arrested.

The arrest warrant for Lail states that he had intentionally scalded Jaydon from the waist down, and when CPR was attempted on him that night, a large amount of water came out of the child. Although bail has been set at $100,000 for the charges of child abuse against Lail, the charge of murder means he can't get out. He is currently being held in Catawba County Jail, and was told while appearing in court that he faces either the death penalty or life imprisonment.

1 Elzbieta Plackowska

On October 30, 2012, Elzbieta Plackowska was looking after her friends' five-year-old daughter, Olivia, along with her own seven-year-old, Justin. That night, she stabbed her son 100 times and Olivia 50 times, killing them both.

After being arrested, Plackowska repeatedly changed her story. At first, she adamantly denied having murdered the children, saying someone had broken in and killed them while she was out smoking a cigarette. Soon after, she admitted to killing them because she thought they were possessed by the devil. Later, "the devil" was replaced by "the evil of society." She also claimed to have heard voices in her head and tried to use her father's recent passing as an excuse for her instability.

Finally, she admitted to murdering Justin in order to get revenge on her husband and to killing Olivia because she had witnessed the first murder. Artur Plackowska was a truck driver and consequently spent a lot of time away from home. Elzbieta said he took her for granted and ruined their marriage. Artur claims that this was not the case and that things were fine at home. The petty motive, the multiple confessions, and the fact that she apparently only murdered Olivia because she witnessed the other murder, even though she could have carried out the murder anywhere other than Olivia's house, all make it hard to know what to believe. In spite of her many confessions, Elzbieta pleaded not guilty in November 2012 and is undergoing psychiatric evaluation to determine if she can be deemed fit to stand trial.

TOP 10 Grotesque Examples of Male Genital Mutilation

by **FlameHorse**

10 Woman Defends Herself Against Rapist

On May 24, 2012, a woman in Bulawayo, Zimbabwe, was out walking with her two children, 11 and 9 years old, when a man named Mkhululi Ndubeko approached her near a bar and tried to stop her. She kept walking, but Ndubeko upped the ante by removing his pants and exposing himself to her in front of her children. She called for help just as he knocked her down and jumped on top of her. Fortunately, his attempt at sexual assault backfired. He was unable to remove her underwear before she grabbed both his testicles and squeezed them until they popped.

Passersby were drawn to the screaming and separated them. Ndubeko was dragged to a police station.

9 Amanda Monti vs. Geoffrey Jones

On May 30, 2004, Amanda Monti, who had had various fallings-out with her boyfriend, Geoffrey Jones, got into one final argument with him at a party and, in full view of dozens of witnesses, reached into his pants and ripped his left testicle completely off. Jones collapsed and Monti tried to swallow the testicle, but gagged and spat it out. A bystander picked it up and gave it back to Jones, saying simply, "That's yours."

Monti pleaded not guilty by reason of self-defense, but the judge disagreed based on her attempt to swallow the organ. She then told the court, "I am in no way a violent person."

8 Wife Tears off Husband's Testicles

Yes, both of them. The husband allowed only his first name, Howard, to be published. He lived in the Nicetown-Tioga neighborhood of Philadelphia, and during the night of May 17, 2006, he woke to excruciating agony in his groin. His wife, Monica, was yanking on his scrotum until she finally tore it open and ripped his testicles completely free from his body.

Monica claimed that her husband was cheating on her, while Howard claimed his wife was bipolar. After surgery, Howard was able to make a full recovery, but when asked how bad it hurt on a scale of one to ten, he replied, "30."

7 Geraldo Ramos Loses His Penis in His Sleep

Ramos, 64, was living in Santiago, Dominican Republic. He fell asleep one night toward the end of July 2013 and woke up bleeding profusely from his exposed groin and was missing his penis. He claims that he drank very heavily the night before and woke up at about 5 p.m. the next afternoon on the sidewalk in a pool of blood. One of his neighbors claimed to have seen him get attacked by a dog before passing out. Why that neighbor did nothing to help him is anyone's guess.

6 Woman Removes and Disposes of Husband's Penis

On April 29, 2013, in Garden Grove, California, a married couple going through a tough time got divorced the hard way when Catherine Kieu Becker slipped Ambien into her husband's soup, tied him up while he was asleep, amputated his penis with a kitchen knife, and ground the appendage up in the garbage disposal. Her husband has not been named publicly, but testified in court with tears in his eyes that he would never again have a sex life and is barely able to go to the bathroom without sitting down.

Kieu pleaded not guilty; citing emotional distress inflicted by her husband over the years. Her husband, though, had demanded that they get a divorce—which Kieu apparently refused. Kieu was convicted and faces life without parole, but her sentence has not been made public.

5 Man Corkscrews His Lover's Testicles

In January 2011, Renato Seabra bludgeoned his lover (the somewhat coincidentally named Carlos Castro) with a wine bottle, pulled down his pants, skewered his testicles with a wine corkscrew, ripped them completely out of his scrotum, and smeared the blood all over his own body. Seabra pleaded not guilty by reason of insanity, indicating a perceived "call from God to eliminate the homosexuality from his partner."

It is not clear whether Castro was still alive or conscious when Seabra mutilated his genitals. There is also no word as yet of Seabra's legal fate.

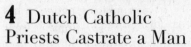

4 Dutch Catholic Priests Castrate a Man

Henk Heithius is the only named victim of ten teenagers who, in the 1950s, were accused by the Dutch Roman Catholic Church of homosexuality and punished with surgical castration. Heithuis claimed he was sexually abused by two priests. Though the priests were convicted, Heithius was sent to a psychiatric hospital against his will and, he claims, surgically castrated under the orders of Catholic priests. Heithuis died two years later in a car accident, and the investigation into whether the castrations were carried out against the teenager's will is ongoing.

3 Man's Dog Chews off One Testicle

On July 30, 2013, a 39-year-old paraplegic from Trumann, Arkansas, woke up to a severe "burning pain" in his abdomen. He looked down and saw blood all over the nose of his "small, white, fluffy stray dog" (which he had recently taken in off the street) and blood trickling from his groin. The man called an ambulance and was taken to a hospital. The dog, who had removed and eaten one of the man's testicles, was euthanized later that day.

The pain of a destroyed and severed testicle is not merely localized in the testicle, but spreads upward and outward into the abdomen (following the spermatic plexus), which is why paraplegics can feel it. The man is still able to have children.

2 Woman Kills Man by Crushing Both Testicles

If you've ever wondered if rupturing a man's testicles can kill him, the answer is yes. Regardless of blood loss, the intensity of the pain is so intolerable that the victim can go into shock and will die if not treated. This is what happened when an unnamed Chinese man got into an argument with a woman over a parking place in the Meilan District of Haikou City, Hainan, China. She parked her scooter and attacked the man when he began shouting at her to move. The first and only attack she employed was to grab his groin with both hands, squeeze, and yank. Witnesses heard her shout, "I'll squeeze it to death. You'll never have children again."

The man collapsed and could not be revived. A medical doctor testified that the level of pain resulting from crushing both of a man's testicles can give him a heart attack. The woman was arrested and faces the death penalty.

1 Pit Bulls Chew off Six-Month-Old's Testicles

On April 9, 2009, Carrie McKinney, a 22-year-old mother in Loma Linda, California, was visiting her boyfriend and put her six-month-old baby in a car seat on the apartment floor. She then left the room and the baby unattended in the company of two full-grown pit bulls, who promptly ripped the boy's diaper open and bit off his scrotum. Both dogs had blood on their muzzles when McKinney reentered the room and both were put down not long afterward. McKinney lost custody of her son and was charged with criminal negligence.

TOP 10 Female Serial Killers from around the World

by **Kate Morgan**

10 Beverley Allitt

Beverley Allitt was born in 1968 and started working as a pediatric nurse in 1991. During a period of 58 days, she murdered four children and attacked another nine who were lucky enough to survive. From an early age, she showed signs of Münchausen syndrome and later Münchausen by proxy, which may explain her actions. Münchausen is a mental disorder in which a person feigns illness or trauma to attract attention. She was finally arrested and tried at Nottingham Crown Court in the UK in 1993, pleading not guilty. She received 13 life sentences for murder and attempted murder.

9 Raya and Sakina

Sisters Raya and Sakina ran a drug and prostitution ring (along with their spouses) in Alexandria, Egypt. Being businesswomen, they saw great financial opportunity in killing and robbing women. Their victims were known to wear gold jewelry and carry large amounts of money. The sisters would lure the victim into a rented house where one of the husbands

would suffocate them. Afterward, the body was stripped of valuables and buried under the house. The disappearances didn't go unnoticed, and the investigations eventually led back to them. Both couples received death sentences. Raya and Sakina were the first women to be executed in modern Egypt.

8 Martha Needle

Born in 1863 in Morgan, South Australia, Martha Charles grew up in a poor and abusive family and showed signs of instability from an early age. In 1882, she married Henry Needle and had three children: Mabel, Elsie, and May. By 1891, she had poisoned all four of her family members, one by one. She then collected the insurance money, most of which she used for a family grave that she often visited.

A year later, she was hired as a housekeeper by two brothers, Otto and Louis Junken. She began an affair with Otto, but Louis opposed the engagement. He mysteriously fell ill and died a few months later. Otto's second brother, Herman, also fell ill after moving in with the couple. This time, the autopsy revealed the arsenic Martha was feeding Herman. An investigation began, and the bodies of her husband, children, and Louis were exhumed. All but Mabel tested positive for arsenic. Martha professed her innocence in court but was found guilty and sentenced to death. Surprisingly, Otto stuck by her side to the end.

7 Jeanne Weber

Jeanne Weber was born in 1874 and had three children, two of whom died in 1905. In March of that year, she murdered four children by strangulation, including her third (and last) son and two nieces. All of them showed visible signs of strangulation that were ignored by the physicians who examined the bodies. That April, Weber stayed home with her ten-year-old nephew while her two sisters-in-law went out shopping. When they came back early, they found Maurice gasping for air and Weber standing over him with a crazed expression on her face.

Eight murder charges were filed, including all three of her children and two others who died in her care. She was acquitted on February 1906 due to her brilliant lawyer and misguided jurors. She then started working as a babysitter, which resulted in two more deaths. In 1908, a father found her strangling his ten-year-old son and had to punch her three times to make her let go of the lifeless body. Weber was ultimately declared insane and spent two years in an asylum before hanging herself in 1910.

6 Juana Barraza

Juana Barraza was born in 1956. Her mother was an alcoholic who traded her own daughter to a man for three beers. That man repeatedly raped Barraza, who gave birth to four of his children. Experts believe that Barraza began her killings sometime around 1990. Her victims were always women over 60, typically those who lived alone. Posing as a government official, she would gain access to the victims' houses and then murder and rob them.

Witnesses led the police to believe the suspect was a male dressed in women's clothes due to Barraza's masculine features. Imagine their surprise when they arrested a woman who was trying to flee the house of the last victim. Fingerprints taken from Barraza linked her to ten murders, but at least 40 more were suspected.

Barraza confessed to four murders but denied involvement in all other cases. She was tried in 2008 and found guilty on 16 charges of murder and aggravated burglary and 11 separate counts of murder. She was sentenced to 759 years in prison.

5 Hélène Jegado

Hélène Jegado was born in 1803 and was trained as a domestic servant at an early age. Like most women killers of that time, Jegado poisoned her victims with arsenic. Her first suspected poisoning was in 1833. Seven people died over three months, including a priest and Jegado's own sister. Due to a recent cholera outburst in the area, no one suspected anything. In 1850, she poisoned several servants in another household. When the doctors requested an autopsy for one of the victims, Jegado declared her innocence out of the blue, before she was even suspected. She was arrested and tried in 1851 but was accused only of three murders, three attempted murders, and 11 thefts. Jegado denied all accusations but was found guilty, sentenced to death by guillotine, and executed in 1852.

4 Maria Swanenburg

Maria Swanenburg received the nickname Goede Mie (Good Me) because she loved to care for the children and ill people in her poor neighborhood. Over the course of three years, she poisoned every family she worked for, starting with her own parents. She would then collect the inheritance of the deceased, claiming she earned it for her services, and often left no money to pay for a burial. Some of her victims managed to escape death but sustained irreparable damage. The survivors eventually led to her discovery.

She was caught in 1883 and tried for 90 murders, but was found guilty of only three. She was sentenced to life in a correctional facility, where she died in 1915.

3 Amelia Sach and Annie Walters

Sach and Walters, better known as the Finchley Baby Farmers, also began their horrible operation in hopes of wealth. Sach owned two maternity homes in London around 1900. One day, she started advertising that babies "could be left" and cared for—for a fee, of course. The clients were mostly servant girls who couldn't keep both their children and their jobs. Parents were charged both for rent and for the adoption to a total amount of $40–$45.

After a baby was born, Walters would poison it with chlorodyne. They were caught after Walters raised the suspicion of her landlord, who was also a police officer. A total number of victims could not be determined. Sach and Walters were tried and sentenced to death by hanging in 1903.

2 Vera Renczi

Vera Renczi was born to a wealthy family in 1903. Renczi was beautiful, and she was known to be involved with older men from the age of 15. Early childhood friends described Renczi as possessive and jealous. Her first marriage was with a wealthy businessman, who fathered her son, Lorenzo. Renczi suspected him of cheating, so she poisoned his wine with arsenic, claiming he abandoned her to anyone who asked.

Her second husband disappeared the same way a few months later. Renczi decided she had enough of marriage—but not of men. Her boyfriends kept vanishing until she was reported to the police by an angry wife (she dated married men too). Searching her house, the police found a scene right out of an Edgar Allan Poe tale in her wine cellar: 32 male bodies in various stages of decomposition, each in his own coffin. She also murdered her son when he discovered her secret. Renczi confessed to all the murders and was sentenced to life in prison, where she died of a brain hemorrhage.

1 Magdalena Solis

Magdalena Solis (also known as the High Priestess of Blood) was a Mexican serial killer and cult member. She became a prostitute at a young age and is one of the few documented cases of female serial killers who had clear sexual motivations.

In 1963, Solis and her brother, Eleazar, were contacted by a pair of criminals, the Hernandez brothers. They tricked the poor and illiterate people of a small town into believing they were prophets of the Inca gods.

The villagers would pay economical and sexual taxes to the brothers after being promised that the gods would reward them with treasures.

After a few months, the villagers realized they weren't getting any richer, despite doing everything the "prophets" said. That's when the brothers claimed Magdalena was the reincarnation of a goddess—to restore faith. Magdalena demanded human sacrifice and devised a ritual that consisted of the brutal beating, burning, cutting, and maiming of the victim. The priests would drink the victim's blood after mixing it with chicken blood. In the last sacrifices, they reached the point of dissecting the heart of the victim while the victim was still alive.

In May 1963, a 14-year-old local accidentally witnessed one of those rituals. He immediately reported it to the police, and a detective escorted him back to the village. That was the last day either was seen alive, resulting in a further police investigation. The Solis siblings were arrested and the Hernandez brothers killed. Magdalena and Eleazar were sentenced to 50 years in prison for only two homicides (those of the boy and the detective) because the police were unable to confirm their participation in the other murders.

TOP 10 Serious Crimes Committed for Bizarre Reasons

by Mike Floorwalker

10 Attempted Murder

Reason: To cure a headache

We may all be guilty, at one time or another, of accusing our significant other of being a pain in the neck. Well, one Utah man was convinced that his girlfriend was a pain in the head. A literal pain in the head—he believed she was causing his crippling headache and that the only way to get rid of it was to shoot her.

So he did. Neighbors heard the gunshot and called police, who arrived to find the man hiding in a ditch, still clutching his 9-mm handgun. He readily admitted to shooting his companion; according to court documents, "He stated that his head began to hurt, whereupon he believed that the only way to ease the pain in his head was to shoot [her]...[he] believed that by shooting [her] she would die, and the pain in his head would cease."

The woman was hospitalized in critical condition, but survived. The man is awaiting trial at the time of this writing, and is hopefully still suffering from the headache.

9 Bank Robbery

Reason: Anger over bank bailouts

When Port Townsend, Washington, resident Michael Fenter was arrested for bank robbery in 2009, police could be forgiven for thinking they might have the wrong guy—even though he had been caught red-handed and was carrying an explosive device. Fenter had never been convicted of so much as a misdemeanor in his life.

A married father of three, he ran a farm with his wife; the family had even been recently profiled in a local paper. They were financially stable, and Michael was not a drug user, gambler, or involved in any illegal activities. Except, that is, for robbing banks. He had robbed four of them in recent months, and after his arrest, authorities couldn't account for any of the money he'd stolen.

The only clue to a motive came when Michael identified himself as "Patrick Henry," a famous revolutionary, upon his arrest. Interviews with bank employees yielded the fact that he had griped about government bailouts during the robberies; he eventually explained that he had done it because he was a so-called patriot. "What I am for is real justice, real truth, and real accountability within our system of government," he was quoted as saying in a local paper. "The money was used and is probably currently being used to get to the truth."

What truth that is was never made clear, but Michael Fenter's truth now involves a ten-year federal prison sentence. Fenter insists that the money is being used in a "peaceful" way, but considering that this is a man who threatened innocent bank employees with real explosives, authorities are probably not too comforted.

8 Assault with Deadly Weapon

Reason: Refusal to switch positions during threesome

Ashley Hunter and Orlando DeWitt were prison buddies who brought a girl home from a bar for some fun one night. Fortunately, this did not end as tragically as that sentence may lead you to believe.

It seems that (and we will tread delicately here) DeWitt began getting intimate with the woman on a couch in the living room, and Hunter decided he wanted in. Everything was going hunky-dory, when Hunter presumably rang a bell and shouted "switch!"

Orlando apparently refused, and it was at this point that Hunter produced a huge butcher knife from inside the couch (which as far as we can tell is not a normal place to keep a butcher knife). All hell broke loose: Hunter ended up stabbing DeWitt in the arm and was arrested for assault. The police report goes into (probably totally unnecessary) detail, but then "stabbing over dispute during threesome" is likely not something they get the chance to write up every day.

7 Faking Own Assault and Rape

Reason: To convince spouse to move to nicer neighborhood

Prison psychologist Laurie Martinez had a harrowing story for police when they arrived following her 911 call in April 2011. She had come home to find a "male black adult" in her home, who punched her unconscious and raped her while she was passed out defenseless. He robbed her home of some electronics and disappeared into the night—and it quickly became apparent that this was all a bunch of baloney.

In reality, the "stolen" belongings were at the home of her friend Nicole Snyder, whom Laurie had enlisted to help pull off this scam. She had split her own lip with a safety pin, had asked Nicole to punch her in the face a few times, sandpapered her own knuckles to make it look like there had been a scuffle, and—we're not joking—intentionally peed herself.

Perhaps it was the incredibly tired "a black guy did it" shtick that caused her story to unravel. Regardless, it turns out that it was all a plot to convince her husband that their neighborhood was unsafe, because she wanted to move to a nicer one. Unfortunately for Laurie, her husband didn't appreciate the gesture, and filed for divorce. Laurie got five years probation; she lost her job, her license to practice psychology, and the custody of her kids.

6 Aggravated Assault with Firearm

Reason: Clerk's refusal to honor $1 coupon

In March 2013, police responded to an incident involving a 61-year-old woman who had tried to use a one-dollar-off coupon at the local Walmart. This may not sound too threatening—but then, most elderly Walmart patrons don't start waving guns around when their coupons are rejected.

Mary Alday was told by a clerk that this particular store didn't accept coupons that were printed online, and the assistant manager didn't have much luck when she tried to explain the policy. Alday called her a five-letter word

rhyming with "witch," and hit her with a shopping cart. When the manager followed her out of the store, Alday produced the .38 from her car, threatening the manager and several employees with, "I have something for y'all!"

Fortunately, no shots were fired; Alday was pulled over a short time later by sheriff's deputies. She admitted to having a gun, refused to yield the gun, reached for something, and promptly got tasered. Four counts of aggravated assault with a deadly weapon later, Walmart still hasn't refunded her the dollar.

5 Attempted Murder

Reason: Request to leash dog

In another case of Walmart stores apparently inducing psychosis in certain people, a Walmart manager in Anchorage, Alaska, received an unexpected response to his request that a disabled patron leash his service dog.

Daniel Pirtle rode into the store on a motorized cart, his dog trotting alongside, and store manager Jason Mahi received him with the common (and totally understandable) request to please put it on a leash. Pirtle produced a gun and shot Mahi in the stomach. Amazingly, there does not seem to be much that happened in the period of time between these two incidents.

An off-duty police officer detained Pirtle while an army combat medic who happened to be in the store rendered aid. Mahi survived; Pirtle was charged with first-degree assault and weapons misconduct and is awaiting trial at the time of this writing. He has stated his intention was to defend himself.

4 Extortion, Criminal Threatening

Reason: Compensation for care of pet spider

Bryan Paul Smith, a resident of Leavenworth, Kansas, had a few surprises up his sleeve when he was contacted by police in July 2012. Nothing that could help him in any way, we should add, merely useless surprises, like the 14-year-old kid hiding in his closet.

While it's unclear which crime Smith was initially contacted for, it is known that he acted as a lookout for another man during a series of car burglaries. His strangest crime, however, was holding a spider hostage. Apparently, an acquaintance had given Smith the spider to take care of, but when Smith was asked to return it, he countered with a different offer: Give him a hundred dollars, or the spider gets it.

During the investigation it was revealed that he may have also threatened to shoot the spider-owner at some point, that he was in possession of a stolen Siberian husky, that he was involved in the burglaries, and—oh yeah—that there was a kid for some reason hiding in his closet. Smith was sentenced to five years in prison for these crimes of varying degrees of oddness.

3 Bank Robbery

Reason: To get away from overbearing wife

When Anthony Miller robbed an Ephrata, Pennsylvania, bank in 2007, tellers noticed something a little odd about him. He displayed a gun, but didn't threaten anybody—and he didn't seem very nervous. He kept asking them if they'd called the police yet, and after they'd given him the money he still loitered around for several minutes.

Similarly, when the police arrived, he didn't seem surprised and didn't put up a fight. He went along quietly, and in fact told them that he had wanted to be caught. He would gladly go to jail if it meant that he could get away from his wife.

When brought before a judge, Miller explained that his wife was very controlling, threatened suicide if he were to leave, and was often abusive—and the poor guy figured that jail was his only way out. Despite using an unloaded BB gun for the bank robbery, he was sentenced to three to six years in prison. But there was a silver lining: His wife filed for divorce. Miller's attorney told the local paper that he had met the wife when she had come to pick up the car after Miller's arrest. After about twenty minutes in her presence, said the attorney, "I was ready for jail too."

2 Contract Killing

Reason: Failing to return borrowed speakers

Kent Craig is a man who expects you to return his stuff when you borrow it. If you don't, then you will be made to pay. Oh, Kent won't do anything about it personally—such as ask for the stuff back, for example—but if you keep him waiting long enough, he just might take out a hit on you.

Craig Corle had the misfortune of having borrowed some stereo speakers from Craig. A friend of Craig's, Cesar Guzman, was also owed $100 by Corle, so they hatched a plan: Call him up and ask him politely to make good on his debts. Actually, scratch that—they instead hired a random thug to beat him up for 50 bucks.

At least, that's what Cesar thought was the plan. Supposedly unbeknownst to him, Kent gave their thug-for-hire the green light to kill Corle instead, which he did. Corle was shot ten times and his computer was stolen; the thug was arrested, and Guzman and Craig quickly followed. Guzman served 6 years for voluntary manslaughter for his part, and has been released; Craig got 26 years to life in prison—which wouldn't seem worth it, even if the speakers had been made of diamonds.

1 First-Degree Murder

Reason: Mother's failure to secure concert tickets

In March 2008, 39-year-old Robert Lyons savagely attacked and killed his mother in their condominium by bludgeoning her with a cognac bottle and stabbing her. At his trial, prosecutors said that he snapped; the two were prone to profane arguments on a fairly regular basis, and Robert had a lot of anger against his mother. But what had finally pushed him past his limit?

It turns out that it was his mother's failure to call a friend who had skybox-seating tickets to an upcoming concert Robert wanted to see.

We've all been disappointed when we couldn't see a much-anticipated show, but we can't imagine a more severe overreaction than this. What dark forces swirled inside this man? Who did he want to see so badly that his mother's failure to procure tickets could have driven him to a murderous, bloody rage? Slayer, perhaps? Cannibal Corpse? Napalm Death?

Nope. He had wanted to see Avril Lavigne. And although it would be more plausible that a middle-aged man would kill his own mother to avoid an Avril Lavigne concert, we stand by our sources.

TOP 10 Criminals Caught Thanks to Their Own Stupidity

by **Jeff Kelly**

10 Anthony Garcia

When a perpetrator actually gets away with a crime, he must have an overwhelming sense of relief and the urge for a bit of celebration. After all, he's just pulled off an illegal act and left no evidence behind that could tie him to the crime. Imagine the relief he must feel upon getting away with murder. And now imagine how dumb he'd need to be, after having gotten away clean with a murder, to have the crime scene permanently tattooed on his chest.

That's what happened with Anthony Garcia, a Los Angeles gang member who committed a murder during a liquor store robbery and got away with it for four years, until he was picked up for driving on a suspended license and the police noticed his unique tattoos when taking his mug shot.

It did not take them long to connect the dots, considering the crime scene was re-created in pretty exhausting detail.

9 Marque Moore

As far as crime goes, being a bicycle thief doesn't quite rank alongside murder, rape, or assault, but it's certainly not a victimless crime, and it can be a pretty lucrative career when you steal enough bikes. Marque Moore, a 57-year-old man from San Francisco, had decided it was the career path for him, and when police arrested him they found ten bikes and a number of bike wheels, seats, and frames.

So how did they track this master thief down? It was pretty easy. He tried to sell one of the stolen bikes back to the victim. The victim found his stolen bike in an online ad and arranged to purchase it, while alerting police to what was really going on. Moore was charged with possession of stolen property, probation violation, and felony possession of a firearm. Maybe next time he'll realize what the rest of us have known for years: Avoiding Craigslist is always a good idea.

8 Brittany Elder, Trent Blye, and Joseph Davis

It must be quite a shock, when you're at work doing business as usual and generally keeping to yourself, to discover that someone in the parking lot is attempting to steal the tires off of your car. But it would be even more shocking if, when you confront them, things go from bad to worse when they assault you and stuff you in the trunk.

In this situation, which actually happened in Louisville, Kentucky, Brittany Elder, Trent Blye, and Joseph Davis upgraded from simple theft to the full-on kidnapping of a gas station attendant. They then jumped into the attendant's car with him in the trunk and drove off. As luck would have it, however, the attendant's license plates had expired, and the car was pulled over by the police. Hearing the police outside, the attendant started shouting and banging on the inside of the trunk, and the cops quickly realized there was more going on than a simple case of lazy registration.

7 Hannah Sabata

You'd be forgiven if you thought that, by now, most people had figured out that crime and the Internet are not good bedfellows. Fortunately for our entertainment, this is not the case here. Usually it's a social-networking site like Facebook that alerts the authorities to something illegal, but in the case of Hannah Sabata, she must have thought the cops needed some help. She decided to make a video boasting about her crime and post it on YouTube for all the world to see.

This wasn't just some dumb 19-year-old girl bragging about vandalism or anything like that, either. No, this was some dumb 19-year-old girl bragging about robbing a bank and stealing a car. She was only too happy to go online and let everyone know how awesome she was at stealing things. What she is not awesome at, however, is covering up her crimes.

6 James Allan

There's a scene in the movie *Snatch* in which a pair of criminals attempts an armed robbery and are then unable to escape from the premises when they can't figure out if they should push or pull the door to open it. It's a comical scene, and one that no viewer would ever believe could actually happen. After all, who could possibly be that stupid?

Apparently the answer to that question is "James Allan," a 28-year-old man who attempted to rob a convenience store only to be foiled by, yes, pushing on the door rather than pulling. Not only that, but he was using a toy gun and actually removed his mask in full view of the security camera. The hits just kept on coming for Allan, as well, as he was a regular at the store and had actually robbed it only ten days earlier. It's fair to say that no one will ever accuse James Allan of being a master thief.

5 The Facebook Bandits

Facebook is usually not terrible to use. However, it can be dangerous since it has personal information and photos available for anyone to see. This is especially true if you go to an Internet café and fail to log off. What makes a situation like that even worse is when you then proceed to rob the Internet café at gunpoint.

That's exactly what happened in Calima, Colombia, when a pair of men stopped into the Internet café and sat down to use the computers. After surfing the web for a while, the duo produced handguns and robbed the place before escaping on a motorcycle. It was a clean getaway, and would have been a pretty solid crime if not for the fact that one of the men had failed to log out of his Facebook account, enabling the police to track him down since his home address was on display in his profile.

4 Richard Almaraoui

After someone has committed a crime and is released on parole or put on probation, they will often be given an electronic tag, generally an ankle bracelet, that tracks their movements so that the police can keep an eye on them and make sure they are behaving. Richard Almaraoui of Norfolk, England, was one such criminal.

But did that deter him from continuing to commit crime? Of course not. Instead of going about his business and enjoying not being locked in a jail cell, Almaraoui decided it would be a much better idea to break into a student's apartment to steal his laptop. It did not take long for the cops to track down the perpetrator, considering Almaraoui was a well-known repeat offender and, oh yeah, that whole movement-tracking ankle bracelet.

3 Ted Bundy

One of the most notorious murderers in history, Ted Bundy was known as "Lady Killer" because he would kidnap, rape, and violently assault and murder pretty young women. He was also one of the most deranged killers you could hope to come across, considering he was also a necrophile. Let's just say he liked to revisit his deceased victims from time to time.

It was in August of 1975 that Bundy was finally caught in Utah by Highway Patrol Sergeant Bob Hayward. And just how did Hayward manage to track down Bundy? It wasn't difficult. He spotted what he considered to be a suspicious-looking vehicle driving through his neighborhood at 2:30 a.m., and when he attempted to pull over the VW Beetle, Bundy took off in an effort to evade him. When Hayward finally caught up to Bundy, a look in the backseat revealed apparent burglary tools in plain sight.

2 Timothy McVeigh

In 1995, America saw an unprecedented act of domestic terrorism when the Federal Building in Oklahoma City was blown up via explosives planted in a truck. The attack killed 168 people and injured more than 800, and it was the most deadly terrorist attack to take place on American soil until 9/11. Through good investigative work, authorities were able to learn that Timothy McVeigh had been the one to rent the truck used in the explosion. But there was still the matter of finding and arresting him.

As it turns out, it was a routine traffic stop that did in McVeigh. Oklahoma State Trooper Charlie Hanger was on his way to the site of the bombing when he got a call to abort his trip to the city and stay in his area to patrol the highway. It was through this bit of fateful intervention that he happened to be in the right place at the right time. When he saw McVeigh's car driving without a registration tag, he pulled the car over to issue a citation. It wasn't until after he had already told McVeigh what he'd pulled him over for that he noticed a bulge under McVeigh's jacket, and moments later, he had a career-making arrest. The lesson, as always, is that if you're going to commit a crime, make sure the getaway vehicle has the appropriate tags.

1 David Berkowitz

David Berkowitz is one of the most infamous serial killers of all time, though he is more commonly referred to as the Son of Sam. In the 1970s, the Son of Sam terrorized the people of New York City, murdering six people and prompting a police operation known as Operation Omega, comprising 200 detectives trying to stop him before he could kill again.

So how did they finally catch the infamous murderer? A parking ticket. Berkowitz had parked his car in front of a fire hydrant before heading off to a murder, and a woman witnessed him tearing up the parking ticket and later reported it to the police. Just think about the fact that the Son of Sam may very well never have been caught were it not for his easily avoidable mistake of parking in front of a fire hydrant. Of course, given that Berkowitz claimed he was taking orders from his dog it makes sense. Dogs just can't resist fire hydrants.

TOP 10 Phantom Law Breakers

by **Nene Adams**

10 North Side Phantom

In 1945, in Pittsburgh, Pennsylvania, the "North Side Phantom" stole nearly $20,000 worth of jewelry in more than 40 burglaries over several months. Witnesses couldn't agree on a description. The thief was shot at, but never hit. Police investigations came no closer to identifying the elusive housebreaker until he was caught and arrested. The North Side Phantom was Vincent Donnelly, an 18-year-old escapee from the state's juvenile delinquent facility. After his escape, he slept in the cellars of unoccupied houses in the area and robbed others with the help of his accomplices, four other boys and a girl. To add insult to injury, he stored most of his loot in a basement storage locker belonging to a policeman.

9 Los Angeles Phantom Sniper

In 1951, Los Angeles women found themselves literally under fire by a "Phantom Sniper" armed with a rifle. The first victim was shot through the lung while making a call at a phone booth. Over the course of a year of public panic, six females were wounded, including a ten-year old girl; one woman was killed, and several others reported near hits. In April 1952, police arrested Evan Charles Thomas, a railroad switchman and father of two, who admitted to carrying a rifle in his car and shooting at women to fulfill an abnormal sexual urge. He readily confessed to the crimes, stating he was glad to be arrested. Thomas was only tried for the murder of Nina Marie Brice, whom he'd shot and killed at a hamburger stand. He was found guilty, sentenced to death, and executed in San Quentin's gas chamber in 1954.

8 Miami Phantom Rapist

In 1954, beginning in October, women in a Miami neighborhood were attacked and robbed by a "Phantom Rapist." The perpetrator entered some victims' houses between 2 and 3 a.m. by slitting a window screen or breaking a locked door. Victims said they woke with a towel or pillow over their faces and a knife at their throats. Some women were also ambushed walking home from the bus stop. Following the identification of William Henry, Jr., by a witness, a manhunt ensued that spread as far as Georgia and Alabama. Henry was eventually caught and arrested by deputies from the sheriff's office. He pleaded guilty to breaking and entering to commit grand larceny, but not to the attempted rapes. (Likely because victims were disinclined to testify in court, those charges were dropped.) He was found guilty of two counts of breaking and entering.

7 Pittsburgh Phantom Wreckers

Returning to Pittsburgh, Pennsylvania, this time in 1980, we find city officials puzzled by "Phantom Wreckers"—an unauthorized, illegal demolition crew razing condemned, unoccupied houses in broad daylight and taking off with loads of valuable resalable bricks and other materials. The Phantom Wreckers began in the North Side area in March, leaving nothing of the targeted house behind except a rusty metal staircase. By July, they'd stolen another house entirely and removed the brick facing from five others. At one address, the Phantom Wreckers were spotted by neighbors, who called the police. The men were arrested, but after receiving a call from a "Mrs. Brown," who lied and claimed they were authorized to tear down the residence, they were released. While a suit was later filed by the city against a construction company, because the police had no records of the men they'd arrested nor a phone number for the (fictional) Mrs. Brown, the case was dropped.

6 Texarkana Phantom Killer

Young couples in Texarkana, Texas, feared for their lives in 1946 as a murderer dubbed "The Phantom" went on a killing spree. The first murders occurred in March—a man and a woman, each shot in the head, were found in the backseat of a parked automobile. Another dead couple was discovered in April. The third couple was attacked in their home. In that instance, the husband was killed, his wife seriously injured. Here, the Phantom left his first clue: footprints in the mud. By May, the town's teenagers were setting themselves up as bait to try and catch the killer, while citizen vigilante groups patrolled the streets. The murders remain unsolved and the Phantom was never identified or caught.

5 Tokyo Phantom Arsonist

Beginning in November, 1976, the Shinjuku ward—the entertainment district filled with shops, clubs, restaurants, and bars—was terrorized by a "Phantom Arsonist" who set a fire in the early morning hours every Tuesday (hence his other nickname in the media, the "Tuesday Devil Arsonist"). Each blaze was started in a garbage can and spread to nearby buildings. Fortunately, no one was injured. Worried residents, well aware of Tokyo's long history of devastating fires, formed vigilante groups and volunteer motorcycle firefighting patrols. People began keeping flammable trash off the streets. By January 1977, the Phantom Arsonist had set 32 fires without being spotted by a single eyewitness. In February, police arrested a suspect, Shigeru Nagazawa, after he was seen setting a fire in a mailbox. He confessed to the crimes, saying he got a thrill from setting fires.

4 Phantom Burglar of Bel Air

In the years between 1934 and 1939, more than 60 homes of rich and famous film stars in the fashionable Los Angeles community of Bel Air received midnight visitations from the "Phantom Burglar of Bel Air," who stole jewelry, furs, bonds, silver, and collectibles worth millions. Despite extensive investigations, police weren't able to identify the man until the arrest of William Borton, aka Ralph Graham, in San Francisco in March 1939. Borton had been caught by plainclothes detectives while trying to fence $80,000 in stolen jewels. Following his arrest, Borton confessed to being the Phantom Burglar. More loot was found inside his home, although not all the stolen property was recovered. After pleading guilty, Borton was

sentenced to life in San Quentin due to his record as a habitual criminal—
he had served terms in three other states. He died in 1949 in a prison fight.

3 Halifax Phantom Slasher

For a week in November 1938, women in the town of Halifax, England,
were attacked by an unknown "Phantom Slasher" who snuck up on victims
at night while they walked on the street, grabbed them, slashed them with
a "gleaming instrument," and vanished into the darkness. The first victim, Mary Sutcliffe, suffered a second later attack. In all, 13 women were
wounded, though nonfatally. The Phantom Slasher was described as having
a flat nose "like a boxer" and blackened teeth. In response, churches, shops,
and movie theaters closed at dusk. Scotland Yard detectives organized a
volunteer citizen's watch with 5,000 members armed with sticks, Indian
clubs, and pokers to perform night patrols. Panic and hysteria spread to
four other towns. By December, five victims' reports were proven false. And
in January 1939, three young women were convicted of malicious mischief
and given a four-week sentence when they cut themselves and made a false
police report blaming the Phantom Slasher. The item is included on this
list because not all the victims' withdrew their testimony, and a chance
exists the elusive Halifax Phantom Slasher may not have been just a fig-
ment of the imagination.

2 Phantom Blockade Runner

During the American Civil War, U.S. Navy ships blockaded shipping lanes
to prevent supplies from reaching Confederate states. Blockade runners,
whether for patriotism or profit, snuck past or outran the opposing vessels
to bring their goods to market. One such blockade runner's ship was called
the *Phantom*, commanded by William Porter, brother of U.S. Navy Admiral
David Porter. The daredevil William Porter was well known for his reck-
lessness and nerve. In 1864, the *Phantom* was spotted off North Carolina.
A federal steamer, the *Connecticut*, set out in pursuit. Both ships battled
heavy seas as the chase continued for miles down the coast. Five more U.S.
Navy ships joined the pursuit and blocked the *Phantom's* progress. Faced
with overwhelming odds, Porter ran *Phantom* onto the beach, where he and
his crew set her on fire before escaping. After the war, Porter returned to
the merchant service.

1 Bel Air Phantom Fondler

This time, we're in Bel Air, Maryland. Beginning in July 1986 and continuing in waves until 1990, the "Phantom Fondler" broke into homes between
3 and 5 a.m. He stole nothing, nor was he violent. Instead, he watched a

female victim while she slept in her bed and touched her legs, feet, abdomen, and sometimes breasts. When the woman woke up, understandably alarmed by the stranger in her bedroom, he made his escape. The Phantom Fondler left fingerprints, but no other clues. Police investigations turned up nothing. Periods of frequent break-ins and fondling incidents followed by months of silence led investigators to suspect the suspect might have been jailed for unrelated crimes during those times. At last, police found a fingerprint match: Walter Porter, an area resident recently arrested for breaking and entering. When confronted, Porter confessed to being the Phantom Fondler.

TOP 10 Innocent People Sentenced to Death

by **Jeff Kelly**

10 Levon Junior "Bo" Jones

In 1987, someone robbed and murdered a North Carolina bootlegger named Leamon Grady. Levon Jones was later convicted of the crime and spent more than a decade on North Carolina's death row before finally being removed in 2006 and released from prison altogether in 2007. So why did Jones get convicted in the first place? Well, all evidence points to a jilted lover.

Lovely Lorden, a former lover of Jones, had been the star witness: She testified at the original trial that Jones had indeed been the murderer. But she later admitted that she had lied under oath, and had in fact collected $4,000 in reward money for providing clues toward Jones's arrest and conviction. Lorden lacked credibility to the point that a judge went so far as to chastise the defense attorneys who had originally worked on the Jones case, and removed the accused from death row while everything was sorted out. In 2007, the prosecution realized that they simply had no evidence and gave up trying to keep Jones on death row.

9 Glen Chapman

Glen Chapman was sentenced to death in 1994 and spent 15 years on death row before finally being released. Chapman had been convicted of the murders of Betty Jean Ramseur and Tenene Yvette Conley.

This was yet another case of the system being so hell-bent on getting a conviction that the authorities decided to take matters into their own hands. Chapman was given his new trial when it was discovered that detectives had actually concealed evidence that pointed to his innocence and that another detective had actually committed perjury while testifying at the trial. Chapman's defense attorneys were also so bad that the North Carolina State Bar disciplined one, while the other was removed from another death penalty case to get treatment for alcohol abuse.

8 Akabori Masao

We are not sure if there is a more heinous crime than the kidnapping, raping, and murdering of a small child. That's exactly the crime that Akabori Masao found himself accused of committing—and it's the crime which, in 1954, he confessed to carrying out. Of course, the fact is that he did not do any of those things, and it turns out that he admitted to them because of police torture. This was enough to get him convicted and sentenced to death anyway, despite his retraction of the confession.

Ultimately, Masao was exonerated and finally found himself a free man again in 1989, receiving compensation of just under $1 million from the Japanese government.

7 Paul House

In 1985, Paul House was convicted of raping and murdering his neighbor, Carolyn Muncey—and for the next 22 years he lived on death row in Tennessee. Eventually he was released into house arrest after being stricken with multiple sclerosis. In addition to this, new evidence had come to light that threw his guilt into question.

Of course, even after his exoneration in 2009, prosecutors remain unconvinced that he is not guilty of the crime. But multiple DNA tests have been conducted over the years, and none of the samples found under the fingernails of the victim matched House's DNA. This fact makes it pretty hard to fathom how he could possibly have raped Muncey, let alone killed her.

House had been set to be retried when this DNA evidence came to light, but the district attorney finally decided that there was enough reasonable doubt to keep him from being convicted.

6 John Thompson

In movies about people on death row, the final piece of evidence that will prove the innocence of a wrongfully convicted man always comes to light just before the executioner is about to throw the switch. But that can't possibly happen in real life, right?

As it turns out, that's pretty much exactly how things panned out for John Thompson in 1999. Though the evidence in question did not come to light mere minutes before his execution, it did come out only weeks before he was set to be executed in Louisiana. That's when it was discovered that prosecutors had withheld evidence that could have cleared Thompson of all charges.

Thompson was arrested for robbery and murder in 1985, and by 1987 he found himself on one of the most infamous death rows in the world, in Angola Prison. He was given six different execution dates over the period he spent on death row, but managed to delay them with appeals until, finally, a seventh execution date was apparently set in stone. But his lawyers had hired a private investigator who somehow managed to pull off a miracle: He found a report withheld by the prosecutors showing that Thompson's blood type did not match that of the perpetrator found at the scene of the crime. Because the robbery had been directly tied to the murder, he was taken off of death row. After receiving a new trial in 2003, it took the jury just 35 minutes to acquit him of all charges.

5 Ray Krone

In the U.S. over one hundred prisoners on death row have been exonerated; Ray Krone has the unique distinction of being the hundredth. He was convicted in 1992 of murdering a waitress at a bar in Arizona. To make matters worse, the authorities decided to slap kidnapping and sexual assault charges onto his "résumé" as well.

Amazingly, it took the jury only three-and-a-half hours to convict Krone, who had earned the nickname "The Snaggletooth Killer." But in 2001, a judge ordered a new DNA test on a piece of the victim's clothing, and it showed that there was no evidence that Krone had been present at the scene of the crime. The DNA did match that of another man, however, who was already in the system. Krone was released in 2002 after the other man—who was in prison for another sexual assault—admitted to the crime.

4 Juan Roberto Melendez-Colon

So we've just told you about the hundredth person released from death row in the U.S., and now you're probably wondering about the ninety-ninth, right? Well, Juan Roberto Melendez-Colon was released from Florida's death row just three months before Ray Krone—and apart from being the ninety-ninth prisoner in America to be exonerated from a death sentence, he was the twenty-ninth in the state of Florida alone.

Melendez-Colon was convicted of murder in 1983. As it turns out, he was convicted largely based on the testimony of two felons, one of whom was believed to have been coerced and threatened into implicating Melendez-Colon. There was no physical evidence tying him to the crime, yet the jury found the testimony of the two convicted criminals convincing enough, apparently, to sentence Melendez-Colon to death.

3 Kirk Bloodsworth

Since we've already told you about the ninety-ninth and the hundredth men who survived death row in the U.S., we may as well tell you about the first. Kirk Bloodsworth became the first man to have his death sentence overturned by DNA evidence. He was first convicted of murder in 1985 and sentenced to death. After the guilty verdict was overturned a year later, he was retried and convicted yet again shortly afterward. It wasn't until 1993 that he was finally granted his freedom.

Bloodsworth had been convicted of the rape and murder of a nine-year-old girl, and his initial guilty verdict and death sentence were only overturned when it was discovered that prosecutors had withheld crucial evidence from the defense. After his second trial, he was actually given two sentences of life imprisonment rather than being put back on death row—so it seems that there are small victories even when you've been wrongfully convicted.

The real murderer was apparently described as being a large, burly man, which also makes it almost laughable when the actual perpetrator turned out to be a mere five-foot-six, weighing only 160 pounds.

2 Gregorio Valero and Leon Sanchez

While most death row exonerations have taken place in more recent years—largely due to the fact that people used to be awfully gung ho about killing convicted felons—there are a few much earlier cases of innocent men being released from their death sentences. In 1910, for instance, two men in Spain were convicted of murdering a shepherd named Jose Maria Grimaldos Lopez and were prosecuted with the aim of securing the death penalty.

Those two men were Gregorio Valero and Leon Sanchez, and the gross miscarriages of justice that led to their conviction were to become infamous in Spain. Grimaldos Lopez disappeared without a trace in 1910, and despite there being no evidence of foul play, Valero and Sanchez were arrested and charged with murder. When the first trial failed to result in their conviction, the pair were tried again in 1913. This time, Valero and Sanchez were basically beaten into giving their confessions. In 1918, they were sentenced to prison time, though fortunately for them they did manage to narrowly avoid being sentenced to death, despite every effort made by the prosecution to see them killed for this crime they did not commit.

They were later exonerated when Grimaldos Lopez was discovered alive in a nearby town; apparently he had been living there the whole time. Oops.

1 Sakae Menda

No one would deny that 34 years is a very long time. And every one of those years must feel longer when you're on death row, waiting for that fateful day when the guards will enter your cell with their heads bowed. Yet that's exactly what Sakae Menda went through. He spent more than three decades on Japan's death row for a crime he did not commit.

Menda was arrested in 1948 for the murder of a priest and his wife who lived nearby. The police held him for three weeks without access to a lawyer, and they tortured him into a confession. He was convicted in 1951, and spent those long 34 years in a solitary cell with virtually no human interaction before finally being released.

Menda, now in his late eighties, currently works as an activist. In 2007 he delivered a speech against the death penalty to the World Congress. He has also lobbied the United Nations in the hope of abolishing capital punishment around the world.

TOP 10 Terrorist Organizations Operating in the U.S.

by Andrew Fitzgerald

10 Occupy Wall Street

While not an officially designated terrorist organization, the FBI is investigating the recently formed movement in such a manner. Members of Occupy Wall Street were appalled by the label, claiming they are a peaceful movement. While not nearly as violent as others on this list, the members of Occupy Wall Street are far from peaceful. Millions of dollars worth of property has been destroyed by the organization, including a fire in Fort Collins that damaged numerous homes and condominiums. Reports of assaults, rapes, rampant drug use, and murders emerge from nearly every Occupy Wall Street gathering, along with a lengthy list of property crimes, including stealing and vandalism. At numerous gatherings, self-appointed leaders have urged all who listen to lead a violent campaign toward economic freedom, while others have chanted for the execution of former President George W. Bush. Peaceful Organization? Far from it.

9 Phineas Priesthood

The Phineas Priesthood is a Christian-based terrorist organization that uses violence to promote its many hateful messages. Despite their supposed Christian roots, the Priesthood preaches hate to virtually everyone that is different from them. They protest interracial relationships, homosexuality, abortion, Judaism, multiculturalism, and taxation. They desire a Christian-only nation composed solely of whites. Members of the Priesthood have carried out attacks on abortion clinics and doctors in the past, and the group is labeled as a terrorist organization by the FBI.

8 Jewish Defense League

Another religious group using violence to promote its message, the Jewish Defense League states that it will stop at nothing to end anti-Semitism, while in the same breath criticizing acts of terrorism. The JDL was established in 1968, and gained notoriety for its harsh criticism of the Soviet Union. At its peak, the JDL had 15,000 members willing to fight for their cause. A 2004 FBI investigation noted at least 15 terrorist attacks were committed by the JDL in the 1980s alone. In 2001, the leader of the JDL, Irv Rubin, was arrested and charged with plotting to blow up a mosque in Los Angeles. In their desire to end terrorism, oppression, and poverty, the Jewish Defense League has turned into the type of organization they originally planned to fight against.

7 Earth Liberation Front

While prominent in the United States, this organization has cells in countries all throughout the Western world. "The Elves" as they call themselves utilize guerrilla warfare tactics in an attempt to halt the destruction of our ecosystem. These tactics include destroying expensive and important infrastructure, including power lines and businesses. Attacks in the U.S. often involve the use of fire; they've burned down ski resorts, logging camps, and park ranger offices. They've also attacked numerous fast food locations, most notably McDonald's. In their infinite wisdom, the Elves destroyed a laboratory at Michigan State University, claiming that the lab was being used to create genetically modified organisms funded by Monsanto, a large GMO company. In truth, Monsanto donated a meager $2,000 to send five African students to a conference on biotechnology. Despite the obvious mistake, the Elves maintain that what they did was justified.

6 Army of God

Much like the Phineas Priesthood, this terrorist organization spins religious texts to harm others. They often use violence to combat abortion and homosexual activity, as seen in their attacks on gay night clubs and abortion clinics. Their most notorious member, Eric Rudolph, planted a bomb at the 1996 Olympic Games in Atlanta, Georgia, killing 2 people and injuring 150. In 2005, Rudolph explained, without remorse, that the bombing was a necessary action carried out to criticize the government for its "abortion on demand" viewpoints. Rudolph has also confessed to the bombings of two abortion clinics and one gay nightclub.

5 Animal Liberation Front

The Animal Liberation Front, or ALF for short, views itself as a modern-day underground railroad for all creatures. Their attacks involve freeing animals from laboratories, farms, and factories. They claim to be nonviolent, and compare their actions to someone destroying gas chambers during the holocaust. In truth, these terrorists are causing millions of dollars worth of damage to innocent farmers and scientists, all while harming the animals they are attempting to save. Many of the animals they release simply cannot survive in the wild without proper care, and as such are left to die. Despite one's ideological views, animal testing is an important step in health care, specifically in the development of new treatment methods for diseases. Oftentimes these attacks disrupt this process, preventing the introduction of these treatments and costing these companies, and consumers, countless dollars.

4 Black Liberation Army

The Black Liberation Army was founded in 1970 in an attempt to promote equal rights for African Americans through violence. While its strength has since diminished greatly, the now-splintered BLA still has a number of followers who adhere to this original belief system. During its heyday, the BLA carried out brazen crimes, including bank robberies and the murders of at least 13 police officers. Their most notorious escapade involved the hijacking of a Delta Air Lines flight in 1972, demanding $1 million in ransom before diverting the flight to Algeria. While their goal is apparent, it is unclear as to how they believe their criminal actions will benefit African Americans and the United States as a whole.

3 Sovereign Citizens

This recently formed group follows a strange set of beliefs that promotes violence and anarchism amongst the populace. Sovereign Citizens believe that, although they reside in the United States, they are sovereign from the government. With such a mindset, they believe they do not need to pay taxes, acknowledge law enforcement officers, and, most alarmingly, abide by any government laws. In an attempt to "get back" at the government that oppresses them, they file thousands of frivolous law suits a month in an attempt to clog the court system. They threaten judges and politicians who they think will threaten their way of life. In some circumstances, Sovereign Citizens have shot at and killed law enforcement officers who have stopped them for minor violations, such as speeding. These people are truly frightening, and have no respect for any form of authority.

2 The Crips

Founded in the 1970s in Los Angeles, the Crips gang was originally formed to protect their neighborhood from outside threats. Since their inception, the Crips have grown to over 30,000 members across the United States and at military bases around the world. They hold no definite belief system and no agenda; they act only out of need and impulse, with no regard for anyone else. Murder is commonly used to scare both the public and rival gangs. The Crips are also to blame for the widespread use of PCP, crack cocaine, and amphetamines in the United States, as they are one of the top distributors in the world. The FBI acknowledges the Crips as ruthless and unpredictable, and their deadly ways continue over 40 years after their creation.

1 The Ku Klux Klan

By far the most notorious organization on this list, the Ku Klux Klan has been wreaking havoc since 1865 and the end of the United States Civil War. Founded by Confederate veterans, the group sought to restore white supremacy by assaulting freed slaves and those that aided them. They assassinated prominent African Americans, including politicians, religious figures, and community leaders.

Today, the Ku Klux Klan focuses on illegal immigrants, homosexuals, urban criminals, and African Americans. The Klan laid forth the groundwork for nearly every white supremacist group that exists today, and as such should be held accountable for their actions as well. This includes the murder and assault of thousands of individuals throughout their history and frequent property crimes against minority households.

TOP 10 Terrifying Unsolved Serial Murders

by **Mike Floorwalker**

10 February 9 Killer

On February 9, 2006, in a suburb of Salt Lake City, a Hispanic woman was attacked and murdered while alone in her apartment. Incredibly, the same thing happened again on February 9, 2008. And though at first the repeated circumstances were taken to be a grisly coincidence, DNA analysis of evidence collected at both scenes would later prove that the murders were committed by the same man, whom the media promptly dubbed the "February 9 Killer."

In the 2006 case, the victim, Sonia Mejia, was pregnant when she was assaulted and strangled. A few items were stolen from her apartment, but none of them ever turned up. In the 2008 case, Damiana Castillo was strangled in her apartment about a mile away from Mejia's place. In both cases, there was no sign of forced entry, and while the investigating agencies involved were and still are extremely reluctant to label the perpetrator a "serial killer," that certainly seems to be an apt description of a man who kills two women in a very similar fashion on the same date two years apart.

While police have a vague description of the killer, they're not saying how they arrived at it; and while they have a DNA profile, they don't have a match for that profile—meaning that unless the perpetrator is eventually made to surrender a DNA sample for some unrelated crime, he may never be caught.

9 The Phantom Killer

The twin cities of Texarkana, Texas, and Texarkana, Arkansas, have only had one reported case of serial murder, and it was a case that gripped the region in fear for several months in 1946. The attacks came at night roughly every few weekends for that period; in total, five people were killed and three more injured. The case so captured the public imagination that 30 years later, it inspired the 1976 horror film *The Town That Dreaded Sundown.*

Only the first victims, Mary Jeanne Larey and Jimmy Hollis, were able to give a description of their attacker—and it was more terrifying than it was helpful. They described a six-foot-tall man with a plain white sack over his head, which had holes cut out for the eyes and mouth. It isn't known whether or not the killer wore this mask during the other attacks; the only other survivor didn't get a look. The killer used a .32-caliber pistol, nearly always killed three weeks apart, and always carried out his murders in the dead of night.

After one of the murders, Sheriff William Presley exclaimed to the press, "This killer is the luckiest person I have ever known. No one sees him, hears him in time, or can identify him in any way." This led the press to dub him the Phantom Killer, and the killings themselves have become known as the Texarkana Moonlight Murders. One suspect, Youell Swinney, was imprisoned as a repeat car theft offender in 1947 and released in 1973; he was never charged with the crimes. Though some in law enforcement and the press have speculated that the murders may have been the early work of the Zodiac Killer, this has never been proven in any way.

8 The Doodler

In the 1970s, being gay in America was a very tricky and sometimes very scary thing. Even in relatively accepting communities, prejudice could rear its ugly head at any moment—and one predator of young gay men of the era seemed to understand this with terrifying clarity.

The "Doodler" or "Black Doodler," as he was frequently nicknamed by the press, was so-called because he carried out his murders in the following fashion: He would gain entrance to his victims' homes as a companion, then sketch them before stabbing them to death.

Between January 1974 and February 1975, no fewer than 14 young gay men were killed. Three more were attacked, but survived—yet the case remains unsolved because the survivors refused to out themselves by testifying against the prime suspect. Despite the fact that these killings occurred in San Francisco, which was one of the most accepting areas of the U.S. that existed at the time, these victims were more afraid of the ramifications of coming out than they were of the man who tried to murder them.

Two of these survivors were public figures—an entertainer and a U.S. diplomat. Harvey Milk, mayor of San Francisco at the time and a gay man himself, stated, "I can understand their position. I respect the pressure society has put on them…my feeling is that they don't want to be exposed." Shamefully, the police never named or arrested a suspect, and the case has long since gone cold.

7 West Mesa Bone Collector

In February 2009, a dog walker discovered a human bone on what's known as the West Mesa of Albuquerque, New Mexico. This discovery resulted in the largest crime scene, area-wise, in U.S. history—the dumping grounds of an unidentified killer, known to locals as the "Bone Collector."

The remains of 11 women, all prostitutes, were eventually excavated from the area; in the years since, not a single shred of promising evidence has been unearthed. No DNA, no potential murder weapons, no possible character descriptions—nothing has been found. Sex workers in the area still live in fear of the killer, even though no murders associated with him have been reported for years; some unscrupulous clients even gain the compliance of prostitutes by suggesting that they might be the killer. "He is their bogeyman," said the founder of Safe Sex Work, a local nonprofit.

Local police have stopped shrugging off reports of rapes and beatings of sex workers in the area, and a "Bad Date List"—a registry of local men who have mistreated prostitutes—is now regularly updated. Local sex workers have become exceedingly cautious, and while this may have played a part in foiling the killer's activities, his identity is still a complete mystery.

6 The Alphabet Murders

In the early 1970s, a series of brutal killings shook the area around Rochester, New York. The victims were all young girls—but that wasn't all they had in common. Carmen Colon, Wanda Walkowicz, and Michelle Maenza also happened to have alliterative initials, leading the press to initially refer to the incidents as the "Double Initial Killings," later revising this to the much punchier "Alphabet Murders."

Many people were questioned in relation to these crimes, and one suspect who killed himself shortly after the final murder was for a long time thought to be the most likely culprit—that is, until he was posthumously cleared in 2007 by DNA testing.

Likewise, an uncle of one of the victims was thought to be a prime suspect; he was never charged, and was subsequently cleared when DNA testing became available. Rochester native Kenneth Bianchi has long been under suspicion too. After moving to Los Angeles, he and his cousin committed the murders attributed to the "Hillside Strangler"—and while Bianchi has never officially been cleared of the Rochester killings, he has also never been charged, and still maintains his innocence.

Additionally, in 2011, 77-year-old New Yorker Joseph Naso was charged with murdering four women in California in the late 1970s. He probably wouldn't have been considered in relation to the Rochester case were it not for the names of his victims: Roxene Roggash, Pamela Parsons, Tracy Tofoya, and—incredibly—another Carmen Colon. But at the time of writing, Naso's trial has been repeatedly postponed in the California cases, nor has he been charged with the Rochester Alphabet Murders.

5 The Monster of Florence

Between 1968 and 1985, a monster stalked the streets of Florence, Italy. He (or she) wielded a .22-caliber pistol, murdering 16 people (and occasionally mutilating the genitals of female victims) before inexplicably vanishing. The killer almost always struck couples, and police have been utterly stymied in their attempts to definitively solve the case.

Over the course of the investigation, they interviewed more than one hundred thousand people; four different men have been convicted of the murders at four different times—and of course, they can't all be guilty of all the murders. Many others have been arrested in connection with the crimes, only to be released when the killer struck again using the same gun and modus operandi.

Independent investigations have arrived at the conclusion that Antonio Vinci, a relative of two other suspects in the murders, is a likely culprit; Vinci is still alive and free, and in 2008 maintained his innocence in a *Dateline* interview. Whoever the monster is—or was—a resolution seems highly unlikely nearly 30 years after the last murder occurred.

4 "Highway of Tears" Murders

Canada's highway 16, running for nearly 900 miles through the heart of British Columbia, has some of the most incredible scenery of any highway  in the world. Strange, then, that it should be known as the "Highway of Tears"—until you consider that it runs through many areas so isolated that nobody will be around to hear the screams when bad things happen. And they have indeed happened; over the last few decades, no fewer than 40 young women have disappeared while hitchhiking there.

For years, many blamed Canadian police for failing to make satisfactory investigations. Many of the victims were Inuit or nonwhite, and some say that the investigation only began in earnest when a white victim was killed in 2002.

Officials admit that the area is incredibly difficult to police effectively: Logging roads run for hundreds of miles and then reach dead ends; many stretches of the highway itself are deserted, with no towns for miles; and even mobile phone reception is patchy or nonexistent for long stretches.

Of course, there's a strong possibility that the disappearances are the work of more than one killer. A few suspects convicted of murders in the U.S. have fallen under suspicion in relation to some of the Canadian crimes, but nothing has ever been proven—and all of these suspects have been definitively ruled out in at least some of the Highway of Tears cases. As long as the highway continues to offer vast, isolated areas as hunting ground for predators, it seems likely that there will continue to be prey.

3 The Paturis Park Murders

The killer known as the "Rainbow Maniac" has for years been targeting gay men in the city of São Paulo, Brazil, home to one of the most vibrant gay communities in South America. The area is host to the largest annual gay pride march on the planet, and Paturis Park had become a popular "hookup" spot—until it became a stalking ground for a lunatic.

The park has been witness to the killings of 13 men since 2007. Police believe that the same murderer may also be responsible for three more deaths in nearby Osasco; they also have a hunch that their suspect may be a current or former police officer. Indeed, local papers were reporting in 2008 that retired officer Jairo Francisco Franco had been arrested and that police were sure they had their man. No charges or conviction were forthcoming, however, and the case remains unsolved to date.

2 Bible John

In the late 1960s, three young Scottish women met their end at the hands of a Scripture-quoting murderer who came to be known as "Bible John."

All of the victims were strangled with their own stockings. Additionally, they were all menstruating at the time of their murders—and this was evidently known to the killer, as pads or tampons were placed near the bodies of all of the victims.

Jean Puttock—sister of victim Helen Puttock—was able to provide the only known description of the killer after sharing a taxi with him, her doomed sister, and her own date for an hour. The man had identified himself as "John Templeton," and had extensively quoted from the Bible, and even referred to the types of dance halls in which he met his victims as "dens of iniquity." After Jean and her date exited the cab, Helen continued on with John only to be found dead the next morning. The man disappeared without a trace.

1 The Boston Strangler

One day in July 1962, the *Boston Herald* screamed from its front page, "Mad Strangler Kills Four Women in Boston!" It was a case that gripped the public's imagination—and its resolution may turn out to be no resolution at all.

Between 1962 and 1964, 13 women ranging in age from 19 to 85 were murdered in the Boston area. All were strangled with silk stockings, nearly all were sexually assaulted, and there was never any sign of forced entry into their homes. In October 1964, a man who had been arrested for raping a woman in her own house—Albert DeSalvo—confessed in detail to the killings and was convicted.

DeSalvo was able to describe details of the crime scenes that had not been made public, but inexplicably, he also got many of these details wrong. At the time of his confession, he was an inmate in a mental institution and was subsequently sentenced to life in prison. But the inconsistencies of his confession—inaccurate times of death, method of strangulation, and so on—were never addressed. More alarmingly, police had always been of the opinion that the murders were likely the work of more than one person, and indeed, DNA evidence has exonerated DeSalvo of one of the killings to which he had confessed.

John E. Douglas, an FBI agent who worked on the case and one of the first-ever criminal profilers, has stated that based on DeSalvo's profile he is unlikely to have committed the murders, but very likely to have wanted to claim credit for them. Which means that even though the murders are more than 40 years old, the possibility exists that one of the most notorious serial killers in history is still out there.

CHAPTER 12

RELIGION

TOP 10 Insane Facts about the Westboro Baptist Church

by **Mike Devlin**

10 They Rose to Fame through Tragedy

The Westboro Baptist Church was formed in 1955 by Fred Phelps, and its members languished in relative obscurity for decades, waving their signs at gay pride parades and the like. There are only a few dozen members at any given time, mostly extended family of the leaders.

They first received international exposure when they appeared at the funeral of Matthew Shepard, a 21-year-old University of Wyoming student who was beaten and tortured to death for being gay in 1998. During Shepard's funeral, they distributed leaflets that said, "It is too late to rescue Matthew Shepard from the life of sin and shame into which he was lured by the perverted, depraved, and decadent American society into which he was born. All who say, 'It's OK to be gay,' have the blood of Matthew Shepard on their hands."

9 They're Not Fond of Swedish Vacuum Cleaners

In 2005, the WBC—in what was perhaps their most ludicrous act—protested outside an appliance store in their native Topeka, Kansas, against the crime of selling Swedish vacuum cleaners. The protest was in response to Sweden's arrest of Åke Green, a Pentecostal Christian pastor who was arrested for hate speech against homosexuals. Green was sentenced to a month in prison, but was later acquitted. It's unclear whether he was touched by the WBC's support.

8 They're Hypocrites

When Apple co-founder Steve Jobs died in 2011, the WBC promised to protest his funeral. In an ironic twist, many of the church members—including Margie, daughter of founder Fred Phelps—sent their messages out via Twitter for iPhone. Margie posted, "Westboro will picket his funeral. He had a huge platform; gave God no glory & taught sin."

The WBC's promise proved hollow this time; they never made it to Jobs's funeral.

7 They're Musical

When Michael Jackson died in June 2009, the WBC quickly announced plans to picket his funeral, stating on their website, "We will be there to tell you to Thank God for the death of this filthy, adulterous, idolatrous, gender-confused, nationality-confused, unthankful brute beast." As part of their protest, they released a song called "God Hates the World," a takeoff of Jackson's charity hit "We Are the World."

6 Their Enemies Are Musical Too

Along with funerals, the WBC holds protests at dozens of public events, including local Kansas City Chiefs games, music concerts, and even Comic-Con (where they appeared to protest the comic book readers' worshipping of false superhero idols).

On September 16, 2011, they arrived in Kansas City, Missouri, to protest the concert of the rock band Foo Fighters. In one of the more awesome counterprotests ever, the band took the opportunity to arrive on a flatbed truck in homoerotic costumes and perform an impromptu version of their song "Keep It Clean," which contains heavy homosexual undertones. Dave Grohl, the Foo Fighters' lead singer, paused during the song to preach a message of equality.

5 The Supreme Court Ruled in Their Favor

After the WBC picketed the funeral of Marine Matthew Snyder in March 2006, the Snyder family sued them for invasion of privacy and defamation.

An initial ruling awarded the Snyder family $10.9 million in damages—but subsequent appearances in court began to diminish the settlement.

A federal appeals court eventually overturned the decision altogether, ruling that the WBC's picketing fell under constitutionally protected free speech. Moreover, the court ordered the Snyder family to pay the WBC's court costs of $16,000. An outpouring of public support paid the fees, but the battle raged on until March 2, 2011, when the Supreme Court again ruled in favor of the WBC, stating they were "entitled to 'special protection' under the First Amendment."

4 Canada and the UK Banned Them

In August 2008, 22-year-old Tim McLean was on a Greyhound bus bound for his hometown of Winnipeg, Manitoba, when he was brutally murdered. When the WBC announced plans to picket his funeral, the Canadian government acted swiftly, banning their entrance. Several church members were stopped as they tried to cross the border at Niagara Falls.

The UK took similar measures when the WBC claimed they would arrive to picket a production of *The Laramie Project* at Queen Mary's College, specifically banning the entrance of the Phelps family. *The Laramie Project* is a play about the plight of Matthew Shepard.

3 They Have Earned the Wrath of Hackers

Anonymous is a "hactivist" group, whose members could perhaps be described as Internet vigilantes. They are known to retaliate against anti-piracy laws, corruption, sex predators, and oppressive religions such as Scientology. Their power is vast; they have hacked into the websites of the FBI, the U.S. Department of Justice, major credit card companies, and other federal governments.

So when the Westboro Baptist Church threatened to picket the funerals of the Sandy Hook, Connecticut, school shooting victims, Anonymous responded with vengeance—hacking into the WBC's website, releasing the personal information of all its members, shutting the site down, and even hacking Fred Phelps's daughter's Twitter account. When they again threatened to picket at the Boston Marathon funerals, Anonymous released the statement, "If #WBC protests the Boston funerals, they will have to expect us." Soon afterward, they hacked the WBC website, posting such fare as inspirational pictures of Martin Luther King and photos of cute kittens.

2 They Have Cool Neighbors

In March 2013, the WBC got quite a shock when a house neighboring their property was treated to a glaring rainbow paint job. The Equality House, owned by Aaron Jackson, is only a small part of his organization, Planting Peace, which aims to build a better world by establishing orphanages, protecting the environment, and promoting tolerance.

According to the website, "The [Equality] House is a symbol of equality, peace, and positive change," and it will "serve as the resource center for all Planting Peace equality and anti-bullying initiatives." The organization recently recruited a surprise member, Fred Phelps's granddaughter Libby, who abandoned the hateful teachings of the WBC years ago.

1 Even the KKK Hates Them

Formed in the wake of the American Civil War, the Ku Klux Klan has been known for almost 150 years as one of the worst hate groups in the world. But even the reviled Klan is disgusted by the activities of the Westboro Church—especially their habit of picketing soldiers' funerals. Many of the KKK's members are veterans themselves, including "Imperial Wizard" Dennis LaBonte, and they have appeared at funerals in counterprotest to the WBC, generally keeping a low profile and handing out small American flags.

TOP 10 Popes Who Resigned

by **Jamie Frater**

10 Pope Gregory XII

Pope Gregory XII reigned between 1406 and 1415. During his papacy there were two antipopes. At the Council of Constance, in order to heal the schism in the church, Pope Gregory XII officially resigned along with antipope Benedict XIII. The remaining antipope, John XXIII, was deposed. All three were replaced by Pope Martin V two years later. Interestingly, Gregory XII was conditionally elected. The terms of his election (by a mere 15 cardinals) was such that he would be compelled to resign if Benedict XIII did.

9 Pope St. Celestine V

Pope St. Celestine V was the last pope not to be elected in a conclave (the gathering of cardinals together for the purpose of papal elections). He was pope from August–December 1294. As a Benedictine monk—from the age of 17—he lived as a hermit and was renowned for his spirituality. Because the cardinals could not decide on the right man to reign after Celestine's predecessor died, they agreed to elect someone who was a mere priest because of his well-known holiness. Reluctantly he agreed and he summoned the cardinals to him (rather than going to them in Rome). When they gathered together, Celestine V sat on a donkey in his humble dress and was led to Rome. The ropes guiding his donkey were held by two monarchs. Ultimately, he resigned because he felt he was unsuited for the role of the papacy. He returned to his humble beginnings and died in 1295. He was canonized as a saint in 1313 and his remains are still venerated to this day.

8 Pope Sylvester III

Pope Sylvester III had the shortest reign of all popes in this list. He was consecrated in 1045 and his pontificate lasted only 22 days before he was deposed and replaced by his predecessor, Benedict IX. His election occurred after Pope Benedict IX was driven from Rome under accusations of adultery and murder. Sylvester was excommunicated by Benedict while he was pope, and ultimately Benedict returned to the papacy in Rome and deposed Sylvester. Pope Sylvester III died in exile years later.

7 Pope Clement II

Pope Benedict V was pope for a mere 31 days. During his reign (May 22–June 23, 934) another man claimed to be Pope (antipope Leo VIII, later  Pope Leo VIII). Benedict's pontificate got off to a rough start as it began with his involvement in the deposition of his predecessor Pope John XII, who was a much-despised pontiff. When Benedict was elevated to the papacy, opposition members of the Church falsely elected Leo VIII pope (the election was invalid initially). Before Benedict had time to settle into his papal throne, Leo's men took Rome and the Romans handed Benedict over to them. Benedict gave in and resigned in favor of Pope Leo. He was stripped of his office as Bishop and reduced to the clerical state of Deacon. He lived the remainder of his life in relative calm in exile.

6 Pope Gregory VI

Pope Gregory VI was pope from May–December 1046. At the time of his election, Pope Benedict IX was reigning but he did not wish to be pope anymore and wanted to get married. He offered to sell the papacy to his godfather, Gregory VI, and his offer was accepted. Selling the papacy is never a good idea, and Gregory VI's reign was not a happy one. He was forced to abdicate and died in exile in 1048.

5 Pope St. Martin I

Pope St. Martin I, who reigned from 649–653, was the last pope to die a martyr. His election was not approved by the Byzantine emperor, who had Pope St. Martin kidnapped, taken to Constantinople, deposed, condemned, and exiled. Although his papacy was short, Martin I summoned a council that condemned certain acts that had the support of Emperor Constans II. It was this action which led Constans to demand his arrest. He died two years after his exile in southern Ukraine of ill treatment and neglect. His feast day is April 13.

4 Pope Benedict IX

Pope Benedict IX was one of the youngest popes and the only one to have sold the papacy. He is also the only pope to have reigned three separate times. His first term as pope was from 1032–1045, when he was deposed by Pope Sylvester III. Less than a month later, he was reinstated as pope only to resign after three weeks, selling the papacy to his godfather, Gregory VI. In 1047, he installed himself as pope for his third term, but less than a year later he was forced to retire to an abbey, where he repented of his sins, officially resigned as pope and spent the rest of his life doing penance. His papacy was—and is—one of the most shameful events in the history of the church.

3 Pope St. Silverius

Pope St. Silverius was the first pope to be deposed by force. He reigned from 536–537. In March 537, Byzantine Empress Theodora had him captured and exiled from Rome to the island of Palmaria, where he remained a prisoner until his death by starvation on November 11, 537. He was declared a saint by popular acclamation (as opposed to canonization) and is now the Patron Saint of Ponza, Italy.

2 Pope St. Pontian

Pope St. Pontian was the 18th pope, and he reigned from 230–235. He is best known as the first pope to abdicate. He abdicated because the Roman Emperor (Maximinus Thrax) reversed the Roman policy on tolerance to Christians and had him arrested. Pontian's only option was to abdicate so another pope—who was not imprisoned—could take the helm. Pope St. Pontian was martyred shortly after his abdication. His pontificate is notable not just for his abdication, but for the fact that he condemned Origen, a highly regarded, though heretical, theologian.

1 Pope Benedict XVI

Pope Benedict XVI is the first pope to resign in 600 years and he is the oldest of the ten. He is the 266th officially recognized pope—in other words, he is not regarded as an antipope. Pope Benedict XVI was elected in April 2005 after the death of his predecessor, Pope John Paul II. On February 11, 2013, he announced that he would resign the papacy at the end of the month. When he was elected in 2005 he had to manage a church rocked with scandals that had built up during the papacy of his predecessor. Scandals such as the child abuse cases that had gone under the slowly fading eye of John Paul II but started in the watch of his predecessor Pope Paul VI (Pope John Paul I didn't reign for long enough to be held accountable). The world now watches the Vatican, home of the papacy since the first pope, Saint Peter, reigned, to see who will be elected next. Curiously, in the "Prophesy of the Popes" by St. Malachi, Pope Benedict XVI is the second to last pope. His successor is listed as Peter the Roman—the last pope.

TOP 10 Things You Probably Don't Know about the Amish

by **Jamie Frater**

10 Bundling

Bundling is the rather odd practice of a young courting couple being bound in two separate blankets and laid together on a bed for intimacy that does not involve sexual contact. The practice has died out in most of the world (it was practiced by some non-Amish too) but it can still be found in the Pennsylvania Amish communities. In some cases in the past (though perhaps not now) the girl was tied into a sack and her potential husband would lie in bed with her. In modern times it is also not uncommon to see a bundling bed: a bed with a board in the middle to prevent touching.

9 Ordnung

The Ordnung (order) is the set of rules for each Amish community. It contains both religious and civil rules. Because the Amish believe in a strictly literal interpretation of the Bible, these rules are created in order to keep their members in line with the laws therein. Amish communities are not centrally governed, so each group comes up with their own version of the rules. There are two types of Ordnung—those determined in the early history of the religion by conferences (these are usually written-down rules) and those passed verbally within each group. The rules are mostly derived from the Bible, but those which aren't are justified by the fact that they will cause a person to ultimately become worldly and thus breach the Biblical laws.

8 Religion and Technology

The Amish believe in living a life separated from the non-Amish. They quote the Bible to justify this belief: "Be not unequally yoked with unbe-

lievers. For what do righteousness and wickedness have in common? Or what fellowship can light have with darkness?" (2 Corinthians 6:14). Each community has one bishop, two ministers, and a deacon, all of whom are male. Rather than worshipping in a church, the Amish take turns holding their services in the homes of the community members, and houses are built especially to accommodate large numbers of people. Funerals are held in the home of the dead, and coffins are plain, handmade by the community. Graves are dug by hand because the Amish believe that modern technology is a hindrance to family life; as a result, they shun electricity and machinery. In some cases, however, electricity is permitted to warm homes. This electricity is supplied by the community itself via simple devices such as windmills. Because of their other religious convictions, the Amish take no government benefits (and most don't have medical insurance), and they do not serve in the military.

7 Clothing

Belts, gloves, ties, sneakers: banned! The Amish have a very simplistic dress style in keeping with their overall life philosophy. Their clothes are handmade and are usually of a dark fabric. Coats and vests are fastened with hooks and eyes, but shirts have buttons (it is a myth that the Amish shun buttons). Men's trousers must not have creases or cuffs. Married men must grow their beards, while mustaches are forbidden. Amish women cannot wear patterned clothing or jewelry, and they are not permitted to cut their hair. The length of clothing, like dresses, is strictly governed by the Ordnung of the community.

6 Suborders

Not all the Amish are the same; as in most Protestant religions, there are divisions within the group, each following their own variations on the rules. The reasons for these divisions are, as usual, over matters of doctrinal disagreement. There are eight distinct divisions within the Amish as a whole, with the most conservative "Old Order" having split in the 1860s. Sometimes the divisions can be over very trivial matters; for example, the Troyer Amish split over a dispute about hat brims. These differences in beliefs can often lead to bizarre forms of violence.

5 Beard Cutting Attacks

Because men must grow their beards unrestricted and women their hair, it makes those two things prime targets for violence within or among differing Amish communities. The attacks involve cutting off the hair of the beard of the person to be punished. This is not a lawful form of punishment among the Amish, and even though the person being punished may not be guilty of anything in the eyes of his own community, the loss of hair causes great shame and shunning (not the excommunication type—just the social embarrassment type). Somewhat recently, an Amish sect leader Samuel Mullet coerced 15 of his followers to attack other Amish communities in this way. They were found guilty of the crimes; Mullet was sentenced to

15 years in jail for violation of hate crime laws, while his 15 followers were given shorter sentences.

4 Inbreeding

Because most Amish descend from the families of the 200 founders from the 18th century, they have a much higher rate of genetic disorders due to inbreeding, such as "maple syrup urine disease." They also have a high infant mortality rate, but this does not faze them. These disorders and childhood deaths are seen by the Amish as "Gottes Wille" (God's will). They refuse to undertake any form of genetic testing prior to marriage, which would ensure that they were sufficiently unrelated to their potential spouse.

3 Clean Health

If you are one of the lucky Amish who hasn't been born with a genetic mutation or disease (and you actually survived childbirth), you have the benefit of reduced rates of cancer, which may be attributed to their distinctive garb, which includes head coverings. It is also likely that their healthy lifestyle (which includes very little alcohol or tobacco) is a contributing factor. Furthermore, the Amish have suicide rates that are far lower (one-third) than the rate of non-religious people, and 50 percent lower than other religious people.

2 Rumspringa

Rumspringa or "the Amish get out of jail free card" is the Amish term for adolescence. During this time, young adults are most likely to be rebellious against their community, and consequently they are treated more leniently so as to not push the youths away. At the conclusion of rumspringa, the youth is expected to choose whether he wishes to stay with the community or leave it. If he stays, he is baptized and then held to a much higher behavioral standard. Adults who do not behave in a manner deemed fitting by the group are shunned. Most youths who undergo this process opt to stay with the Amish.

1 Meidung

Meidung (shunning) is the Amish form of excommunication. It is usually inflicted for breaches of the Ordnung or for other "crimes" such as marrying outside the faith. When an individual is shunned, they are expelled from the community and all ties are cut. This means that a shunned member cannot have any contact at all with other members of the group, including his immediate family or friends. Needless to say, this is the most serious punishment available to the Amish. Meidung lasts until death unless the sunned repents their crime before the community.

TOP 10 Biblical Figures Who Teach Outrageous Morals

by **Andrew Handley**

10 Elisha

Elisha was a prophet who is believed to have lived during the 9th century BC. When Elijah, who was Elisha's teacher, was called up to heaven, God commanded him to appoint Elisha as the new head prophet. He performed a good many miracles, such as conjuring water for the city of Jericho and bringing a woman's son back to life, but there's one "miracle" that really stands out. Sandwiched between various blessings and acts of kindness are two verses at the end of 2 Kings Chapter 2—verses 23–24—that seem so completely out of place you almost wonder if they were added as a joke. They weren't.

Here's what happened: Elisha was walking into the city of Bethel when a group of kids ran out and started making fun of his bald head. It's the only mention in the Bible that Elisha was bald, which is probably good, because the next thing Elisha did was curse the children to death. Immediately, two bears ran over and tore the kids to pieces. The most important—most Godly—prophet in the land brutally murdered 42 children because they laughed at him. He is now a venerated saint.

9 Jael

There's a good chance you've never heard of Jael—her only role in the Bible was to secure a man's trust before she killed him. Chapter 4 of Judges describes a battle between two generals: Barak, the general of the Israelite army, and Sisera, leader of the Canaanite army. The two armies met on a river bank and holy war was waged, 10,000 men fighting 10,000 men. As the tide of battle turned in favor of Barak, Sisera decided to cut his losses and fled into the desert alone. Back at the battlefield, the Israelites slaughtered every single Canaanite soldier ("and all the host of Sisera fell upon the edge of the sword; and there was not a man left").

So Sisera was alone in the desert, and he came across a tent belonging to an ally of his, a man named Heber the Kenite. The man's wife, Jael, ran out to greet Sisera and welcomed him into the tent, telling him he had nothing to be afraid of. She then hid him under a blanket (Barak was still chasing him), waited until he went to sleep, and then snuck up and hammered a tent spike directly through his forehead, nailing his head to the ground. And pretty much, through lies, deceit, and backstabbing, the hand of the children of Israel prospered.

8 David

King David is, arguably, the most righteous man in the Bible (even though he single-handedly killed and circumcised 200 men for a wife). When David's son Solomon sidestepped the path of holiness, God decided to lessen his punishment because he had loved David so much. But as several of these examples are going to show, brutality and mass genocide go hand in hand with righteousness, and it's usually the righteous man who leads the slaughter.

In 1 Samuel 27:8–11, David takes an army and invades several neighboring lands. The Bible doesn't give any reason for him to do this, other than a side note that the people he killed were "of old the inhabitants of the land," so it seems he was just wiping out the indigenous people. David's army killed all the men and women in the towns he defeated, then carried all the livestock back to their own land, leaving the towns in ruin.

Even the story of David and Goliath that's usually told to kids ends before it gets too violent—after David kills Goliath with a stone, he chops off the man's head and carries it around with him.

7 Samson

Samson was a man to whom God granted superhuman strength to help him destroy the evil Philistines (the Galactic Empire of the Bible). However, he would only have his strength as long as he didn't cut his hair. Even from the perspective of "a righteous hero that destroys the evil tyrant," Samson really just brings everything on himself, and then can only get himself out of trouble by killing more and more people, like a little white lie that won't go away. From any other perspective, he's a murderous psychopath.

In Judges 14:12–19, Samson makes a wager with 30 men that none of them will be able to guess his riddle; if they do, he'll give them 30 silk shirts. Lo and behold, they trick his wife into telling them the answer, so Samson, not one to shirk on a debt, takes the honorable route: He runs out and kills 30 men, steals their clothes, and pays them. He murdered 30 men; that's only 5 short of Ted Bundy status, and it doesn't even count the 1,000 he killed later with a donkey bone.

6 Elijah

We mentioned Elijah earlier; he was the prophet who appointed Elisha to take his place before God sent a flaming chariot to lift Elijah into heaven. Needless to say, he was fairly holy. During the time that he was a prophet in Israel, there came a period when many of the people began to worship Baal, a heathen god. Elijah was perturbed at this turn of events, and decided to prove himself to the Israelites.

In 1 Kings 18:19–40, he called together 450 of the prophets of Baal and gave them a challenge: Kill a bull and put it on an altar, then pray to Baal to light the altar for you. They prayed for hours but nothing happened, so Elijah took a turn. He killed a bull and set up an altar, then prayed to God to light it. Boom, instant fire. The Baal prophets immediately converted to believers, but Elijah wasn't satisfied. So he took them all down to a river and systematically executed every single one of them.

Elijah actually spent a lot of time proving how holy he was—in 2 Kings 1:9–14, 50 men were ordered to come bring Elijah to the king. Elijah said, "If I be a man of God, let fire come down from heaven and consume thee and thy fifty." So he killed them all, then did the same with the next hundred men who came for him.

5 Jephthah

Jephthah was the son of Gilead, a wealthy man, but his mother was a harlot (whore), which meant that he was doomed to be ostracized. True to form, Jephthah was kicked out of his home with no inheritance as a young man ("thou art the son of a strange woman"). After several years had passed, the Israelites went to war (or kept being at war—they were at war a lot). They sought out Jephthah and asked him to return to Gilead, and from there lead their armies into battle against the Ammonites. At this point, the king of Ammon asked Israel to just let them live peacefully, and the Israelites' reply pretty much summed up the reasoning behind every holy war up through the Crusades: "Whomsoever the Lord our God shall drive out from before us, them will we possess."

So Jephthah led the charge, but before the battle he made a bargain with God: Let us win, and I'll sacrifice the first thing that greets me at my home when I return. God kept his side of the deal, and when Jephthah returned home, his daughter ran out to meet him. And Jephthah kept his side of the bargain too—he performed a ritual sacrifice of his daughter, his only child, to pay back God.

4 Jehu

Jehu became the king of Israel after a violent coup overthrew the previous king, King Jehoram. In the aftermath of the battle, Jehu hunted down and killed all of Jehoram's royal family and had their heads—70 of them—piled outside the city gates. Then he ran over Jehoram's mother in his chariot. But wait until we get to the brutal part.

As the new king, anointed by the prophet Elisha, Jehu had some house cleaning to do. According to 2 Kings 10:18, Jehu put out a fake rumor that he was a Baal worshipper, and asked for all the Baal worshippers in the kingdom to come to a massive sacrifice in his honor. When the people came from throughout the kingdom they were ushered into the house of Baal; it doesn't say how many there were, but the house of Baal was "full from one end to another." With every single member of the religion safely clustered in the church, Jehu ordered his army to storm in and massacre them all. That's one of the literal definitions of genocide. God rewarded Jehu by granting his next four generations a guaranteed seat on the throne of Israel.

3 Joshua

The story of how Joshua destroyed the walls of Jericho with the blast of trumpets is the stuff of legend. Elvis can tell you all about it. But like most good Sunday school stories, the genocide comes later. Because once those walls came crumbling down, Joshua's army entered the city and killed the men, women, and children without distinction—"both man and woman, young and old, and ox, and sheep, and ass, with the edge of the sword."

What the story doesn't tell is that this an isolated battle; Joshua was on a zealous tirade all across Israel. Here are five meaningless words: Libnah, Lachish, Eglon, Hebron, Debir. Each one of those is a city filled with people, which, according to Joshua Chapter 10, the army of Joshua completely devastated. He "utterly destroyed all that breathed."

2 Moses

Moses is most famous for leading the Israelites out of Egypt; the book of Exodus covers the big stories—the ten plagues, the parting of the Red Sea, and receiving the Ten Commandments from God (thou shalt not kill, etc.). It's Numbers, however, that covers the 40 years in the wilderness (which was literally a punishment for not wanting to attack a city). And rather than wandering, the Israelites spent much of this time invading other cities.

After a victorious battle against the Midianites, Moses gave the following ludicrous order: "Now therefore kill every male among the little ones, and kill every woman that hath known man by lying with him. But all the women children, that have not known a man by lying with him, keep alive for yourselves." (Numbers 31:17–18). This is literally permission to rape all the little girls in the Midianite cities.

1 God

So far we've seen nearly a dozen cities completely ravaged and all the inhabitants put to death. We've seen commands for rape, religious genocide, the killing of children, and human sacrifice. What we haven't seen are the burning of whores, a ban on crippled people, or the killing of 70,000 men. There are 136 words in this paragraph, and if we linked a verse on every single word, it wouldn't even begin to scratch the surface of the acts committed either by God's hand or under his command that would be considered immoral—or blatantly insane—by today's standards. But that's the thing, right? Today's standards are held to a different moral code than the standards of the 800 years or so before the birth of Christ. But, then again, how does that make any sense?

TOP 10 Truly Bizarre or Unsettling Biblical Accounts

by Mike Williams

10 Devil Sender

Throughout the Bible, sorcery, invoking demons, and pretty much anything to do with magic is forbidden. However, the top-level offense of evoking evil spirits would appear to be an offense not so much because it is intrinsically forbidden, but rather because it is God's area of specialty when a leader does not respond. In the book of 1 Samuel, God's favor is not only withdrawn from King Saul, but "an evil spirit from the Lord" is sent forth upon Saul to "torment him," which makes him act like "an animal." In the book of Judges, Abimelech's dealings with the Sechemites turn dark when an evil spirit sent by God casts its influence. These Biblical passages are contrary to some views, and are sometimes ignored or reinterpreted to avoid the unsettling implications.

9 Allegorical Prostitution

No matter how you choose to interpret the Bible, it is pretty clear that when God wants to make a point, anything goes. Although the New Testament encourages believers "not to be unequally yoked" with infidels, for light has no kinship with darkness, in the days of the Israelites, God apparently had not quite gotten there yet. In the days of the prophet Hosea, God was concerned with unbelief, and instructed him to not only preach about the danger of corruption and waywardness, but to marry a prostitute as a symbol of Israel's unfaithfulness, coupled with his plan of redemption. Hosea was wed to Rahab under God's explicit blessing, and she proceeded to sell out on him in a predictable multitude of occurrences.

8 The Legend of Onan

According to Bible scholars touting their particular brand of moral values, ostensibly based on scripture, masturbation was condemned as a sinful activity. However, the issue is never mentioned directly in the Bible. The negative view stems from Genesis 38:9, in which Onan is commanded to provide a child for his deceased brother's wife to preserve the line, but "spilled his semen whenever he slept with her," as "he knew that the child would not be his" and did want to provide offspring for his brother. Onan is punished by God for "spilling his seed" and failing to continue the tribe, but for some reason, this passage has been taken by some as a condemnation of the masturbation itself required to "spill seed."

7 Dual Responsibility

In the book of 2 Samuel, King David is said to have been incited by "The Angel of the Lord" to take a census of Israel, against God's will, which triggered a massive wave of lethal retribution against the Israelites. While this seems like provocateurism, 1 Chronicles identifies Satan as the one who incited King David to take the census, casting him as one who can pit humans against God. A fascinating difference in reporting exists between the two accounts, and to this day, the Bible identifies both God and Satan as the cause of David's ill-fated actions. The apparent conflict has not only sparked debate, but it has led to some rather disturbing conspiracies and conceptions. Whatever the case, the identify of "The Angel of the Lord" remains shrouded in mystery.

6 The Nephilim Mystery

In many cases, popular interpretation of Biblical accounts may focus on allegorical interpretations that frequently present the universe as a place inhabited by man, other animals, and "angels." However, in a twist not unlike the themes of *Star Wars*, Earth may have been inhabited by another species of advanced being somewhat unlike man. This second species appears on Earth in a past time described in Genesis 6:5 and several other Old Testament passages, which tell how "the Nephilim were on the earth in those days, and also afterward, when the sons of God came in to the daughters of men, and they bore children to them." The Nephilim mystery has never been fully resolved, but many Biblical scholars have considered them to be angelic/human hybrids.

5 Underground Lion Hunting in the Snow

In one of the strangest and most seemingly random Biblical accounts, the warrior Jehoidah, the son of Benaniah, is described as "a valiant fighter from Kabzeel, who "engaged in great exploits."

Apart from taking on enemy tribes, he was known for "having gone out to a cave on snowy day, where he killed lion." In a more modern era, seeking out a wild animal in such a manner would be considered unethical, but he was valued as one of the king's mighty men. In a strange follow-on section that reads rather like a résumé, he "also defeated and killed a seven-foot Egyptian warrior" by taking his spear and using it against him. Following these events, one of the king's warriors apparently killed 300 men with his spear.

4 UFOs

The prophet Ezekiel offers one of the most fascinating accounts in the entire Old Testament, with an eerily modern description of flying vehicles. According to the writings in his namesake book, Ezekiel saw a craft descend through the Earth's atmosphere that contained "wheels within wheels." Beings with humanlike faces emerged from the craft, which had "legs with the appearance of bronze, and shining faces." Ezekiel's graphic description highlights the fact that the wheels rose up with the craft, and did not spin. The description is eerily similar to contemporary accounts of "flying saucers," and the strange creatures sound like an Earthling prophet's best efforts to describe something all too physical, and perhaps even robotic or alien, rather than a vision or spiritual concept.

3 Talking to the Dead

In the history of Judeo-Christian religious tradition, perspectives on ghosts have ranged widely from disbelief to partial acceptance and even attribution of ghosts to malevolent demon spirits. Letting the Bible speak for itself, 1 Samuel describes King Saul's visit to the now-famous "Witch of Endor," who proceeded to call forth the spirit of Samuel. The practice of necromancy was forbidden in the Bible for reasons still unknown, but it appears that Samuel really did come back as a ghost or spirit. The implications of this bizarre occurrence in the Bible are varied, but it did not end well for Saul, as his imminent death was predicted by Samuel's spirit. Most disturbingly, Samuel asks Saul "why he has disturbed him by bringing him up."

2 New Testament Slayings

A vast gulf exists between the prolific nature of Old Testament slayings by "The Angel of the Lord," versus the New Testament regime of peace, the commandment to "judge not," and the rise of benevolent spiritual forces. However, in the New Testament Book of Acts, Ananias and his wife Sapphira held back money for themselves following the sale of what was presumably church land, and were rebuked by the apostle Peter for "Lying to the Holy Spirit." After confessing, they were both promptly struck dead and "taken away by three young men." This New Testament terror is said to have spread great fear through the early church.

1 The Healing Serpent

In accounts from the book of Numbers, a plague of snakes beset the Israelites and were biting and killing many people in the desert. God instructed his prophet Moses to smelt a bronze serpent and place it in a pole in the ground in clear view. In a strange occurrence with almost magical overtones, people were instructed to look at the snake if bitten. Those who were attacked and looked at the likeness were reported to have recovered, while death followed those who failed to seek out the bronze serpent as a metaphysical antidote. The bronze snake might be seen as an amulet or charm, but it was intended more as a test of "faith."

TOP 10 Amazing Feats Performed by Saints

by Gregory Myers

10 Invulnerability to Poison

St. Benedict is known for both his skills at speaking and his general holiness and purity of heart. He is also known for surviving multiple attempts on his life by his enemies. According to the legends, some monks decided to poison him. The first time, they tried to poison his wine and the glass shattered into little pieces when he prayed over it. The next time, the monks decided to use food, since that can't shatter so easily. However, their plans were ruined when a bird flew away with the bread they had laced with poison. St. Benedict founded the most famous order of monks, the Benedictines, and placing a St. Benedict medal over the doors of your house is said to keep evil spirits away.

9 Super Strength

According to his life story, St. Boniface arrived in Germany and saw people worshipping a tree. He was angry at what he considered to be the worship of false idols and decided to destroy the tree. Supposedly with one blow of an axe, the tree was down and the Germans who saw this believed in his message. Some people claim that to satisfy the Germans' attachment to trees, Boniface invented the Christmas tree and told them to use it as a symbol of everlasting life.

8 Prophecy

There have been many saints who have supposedly had the gift of prophecy. One of the more interesting legends is that of St. Anthony Mary Claret. He asked a group of farmers to come to his mission; many explained they could not because they needed to tend to their fields. He told them that if they came, their fields would yield more, and if they did not come, their harvest would be completely ruined. According to the story, his prophecy did indeed come true. There is also the prophecy of St. Malachi. This prophecy of the popes predicts that the last pope will reign at the start of the end of the world. According to those who pay attention to the prophecy, our current pope (Francis) is supposed to be the last. The prophecy of the popes is suspected by some to be a forgery and—as with all post-apostolic prophecy—Catholics can freely choose to believe or disbelieve.

7 Out of Body Experience

Many Catholic saints through the ages have claimed to have something akin to an out of body experience. One of them, St. Theresa of Avila, claims that it felt like her soul was traveling to regions outside her body. Other saints to report this phenomenon include St. Pio of Pietrelcina and St. Frances Xavier. St. Theresa was said to gain this ability through long meditative states of prayer, eventually feeling as if she were going through a sort of "detachable death" and felt it took her much closer to God.

6 Invulnerability to Pain

The stories say that St. Andrew the Apostle was eventually captured for preaching the message of Christianity and was affixed to an X-shaped cross. His captors used this remarkably cruel means of execution because he seemed to feel no pain at all when they had previously tortured him. It is said that even though his execution was long and brutal, he felt no pain whatsoever. Some legends also say the specific type of cross was chosen because Andrew did not believe himself worthy to be killed using the same method Jesus had for his sacrifice—the same reason St. Peter chose to be crucified on a upside-down cross.

5 Incredible Tolerance to Heat

One of the oldest legends is that of St. Lawrence, who was a deacon stationed in Rome. He is said to have been in charge of taking care of the poor and was ordered by those in authority to give the Church's treasures. He brought the poor before the authorities and said that these were the true treasures of the church. In retaliation for his impudence, his execution was ordered. In order to make it as painful as possible, he was tied to a hot gridiron and slowly roasted to death. The story says that no matter how long it went on, it seemed not to bother him and he offered a quip near the end that he could be turned over as he was finished on one side.

4 Incorruptibility

Incorruptibility is when a corpse seems to not follow normal decomposition patterns and remains mostly fine. The skeptics argue that this is due to people secretly using different embalming techniques; however, some cases are harder to explain and there have been instances where it seems decomposition should have actually been going faster. Some of the more famous cases include that of Saints Catherine of Genoa or Francis Xavier. The bodies of St. Catherine of Laboure and St. Bernadette are also said to be incorruptible; after being examined thoroughly, it seems their bodies are in relatively the same shape as they were when they died.

3 Levitation

St. Joseph of Cupertino is the patron saint of astronauts, pilots, and most anything to do with flying. This is because he was known to have the ability to levitate. The stories say that his rapture in prayer was so great that he would get caught up during Mass and start levitating above the altar. Another legend says he was able to levitate while carrying an enormous cross as if it were basically weightless. It was believed among those who knew him that his incredible holiness gave him incredible abilities.

2 Stigmata

This one is perhaps the most well known but is also incredibly controversial. There are many who say the claims of stigmata (suffering mysteriously from the physical wounds Christ suffered on the cross) are simply untrue. Others believe in the stigmata, but argue over which cases are actually genuine and not faked. The most recent legend is that of Padre Pio, who is said to have received the stigmata. Padre Pio (now St. Pio of Pietrelcina) also allegedly had the ability to read the sins on a confessor's soul and to bi-locate.

1 Bi-Location

Bi-Location is one of the strangest paranormal phenomena. While many strange happenings are impossible to prove, some seem plausible. But how can you be in two places at once? Even if you could, it would seem a challenge to act in both places; your brain can only accomplish one task at a time. However, reports of this go back a long way. Among Catholic saints who have been seen in two places at once are St. Alphonsius Liguori and St. Gerard Majella. One of the strangest features of many of these stories is that we never hear any evidence that the saint in question was aware they were in two places at once. Some have then logically said that perhaps one of them was an apparition, but that would still make it quite a remarkable phenomenon.

TOP 10 Alternative Religions Based on Popular Culture

by **Fred Moutran**

10 The "Spock" Church

Worshipping Spock from the Star Trek franchise, this "religion" was officially created as a satire; however, many people seem to think it's legit. Some even follow the "church's" teachings despite the organization's status as a joke. It also ties into another entry on this list, lending it some credibility as an offshoot of a more serious religious movement.

The church's official title is the Church of Spock of Latter Day Science Officers. Embracing logic and eschewing emotion, the Spock, as it is known to many, seems to have derived few teachings from the "79 books of The

Original Testament and 6 books of The Motion Pictures." Among the eight teachings of Spock, one is that our inner eyelids can shield us from dangerous light.

It is a humorous diversion, yet some can easily argue the legitimacy of a religion admittedly created for satirical purposes, hence the number ten spot on this list. Do keep in mind, however, that more widely accepted religions were started on flimsier pretenses.

9 Cullenism

A religion based on the Twilight series of books and movies is bound to invoke groans of derision from many. There have been few franchises so divisive in popular culture. People either love the series or want to pluck out their own eyes at the mere mention of it. For the former group of rabid die-hard fans, it comes as no surprise that someone created a religious movement around their obsession with Edward Cullen.

The tenets of this religion essentially boil down to the stuff of bad fan-fiction. Edward is real, and if you are good, you get to spend eternity with him. Also, the Twilight books and movies along with their creator, Stephanie Meyer, are to be worshipped. That basically sums up the core belief system. Much like number ten, this "religion" is aimed at a rather specific audience. Most others will probably stock up on garlic and crosses after reading this.

8 The Sith

The villains of the *Star Wars* universe, the Dark Side of the Force—these are the things people think of when they hear the term "Sith." There appear to be many different groups online claiming to follow the teachings of the Sith lords. The premise behind all of these groups is the same.

They embrace the idea of crushing compassion in pursuit of power. Their philosophy claims that compassion and pity make one weak. It is basically Nietzsche's greatest dream realized. The Sith religion should recruit in philosophy departments across the country. Their numbers would likely skyrocket from all of the nihilists inhabiting the local Starbucks.

7 The Church of the Fonz

Many people reading this will realize it is a *Family Guy* reference. However, from the popularity of both *Family Guy* and the Fonz himself, there have been many who have sought to re-create Peter Griffin's vision of worshipping Arthur Fonzarelli from *Happy Days*. Given the efforts and commitment to making a fictional religion about a fictional character into a real religion about a fictional character, this entry deserves a slot on this list.

6 Cthulhu Worshippers

The works of H. P. Lovecraft have been among the more influential in modern literature. Among the most well known of those works are those within the Cthulhu mythos. These are the stories about the Great Old Ones, cosmic beings of indescribable horror who could drive men insane by merely being in their presence. In these stories, cults formed to worship these entities as gods.

Of course, as with anything cool and with even a hint of religious undertones, someone decided to base an actual religion around it. At least the old comparison between religion and slavery used by the more militant atheists would actually be appropriate here.

5 The Church of Ed Wood

Like the Church of Spock of Latter Day Science Officers, this was originally started in 1966 as a joke. However, after about a year in existence, it transformed into a serious religion. In 2009, the religion's founder, Reverend Steve Galindo, wrote a featured blog for the *Huffington Post* as an accompaniment to their documentary "Oh My God?"

The church believes in Ed Wood as their savior. Note that the previous line did not say "the" savior, but rather "their" savior. They make this distinction clear on their website. Ed Wood is the director of films such as *Plan 9 from Outer Space* and *Glen or Glenda*. In other words, he is known as the director of some of the most critically reviled films of all time. They preach total understanding and acceptance. That level of acceptance means respecting other religions as they would ask others to respect their own beliefs. They are critical of Christianity, but do not condemn it. Their message is actually among the more admirable seen within the religions on this list.

Also, unlike many of the religions presented here, they seem to provide more structure to their faith. They have a full list of holy days along with a very clearly presented doctrine. It is also one of the few churches on this list to have branched out with their own merchandise. To be fair, though, any Star Wars–, Star Trek–, or Twilight-inspired religious merchandise would probably be the target of a lawsuit on a Biblical scale.

4 Matrixism

Very few movies drum up debates on religion and the nature of reality quite like the Matrix trilogy. It should have been obvious that someone would come along to base an entire religion around the films themselves. Like some other entries on this list, Matrixism builds upon existing belief systems and puts a contemporary spin on them. They take elements of dystopian philosophy alongside the book *The Promulgation of Universal Peace* and meld that in with the message of the Matrix movies.

There are two Matrixist websites, an original and an updated version. The original has a "Frequently Asked Questions" section that has some information that does not seem to fit. For instance, one has to wonder how many people really asked if they would have to give up sports to join this religion. The more current site attempts to simplify and clarify things for those as confused by the original site (as many were by the second Matrix movie).

The core belief of Matrixism is the belief that society is, on some level, fake. They do not necessarily believe that we are in a computer simulation. The belief hinges on the subjective nature of perception, or a computer simulation. Okay, so they do not rule out the possibility of the Matrix being real. This is religion, and people have bought into crazier things. Of course, this kind of thought process is natural from a religion that may not require drug use but does accept it as a sacrament.

3 Star Trek

Listing one specific church here is difficult as there are individual groups with different takes on the religious aspect of the series. However, this differs from the Church of Spock of Latter Day Science Officers in that these people have been quite serious from the beginning and that they worship the series in and of itself and not one specific character.

The law of the United Federation of Planets is the law that many see as an ideal, and it is not hard to see why. The society presented in Star Trek is essentially an intergalactic utopia. Inhabitants of many different planets live in peace, achieving the ideal that modern organizations such as the United Nations strive for but continuously fall short of. There is still war and strife, but those always seem to come from outside sources. The federation stands strong. Plus, many adherents to this religious movement likely fantasize about being Captain Kirk and romancing alien women.

2 Dudeism

What do you get when you mix Taoism, a cult-classic movie, and copious amounts of white Russians? The answer is obviously Dudeism. Using the character of The Dude from the movie *The Big Lebowski* as a model for how to live an ideal life, Dudeism claims to be the "World's Slowest Growing Religion." With a philosophy that boils down to "take it easy," "live in the moment," and of course, "abide," it is not hard to see why this is a religion of choice for all the slackers and stoners out there. There is more to Dudeism, however, than drinking white Russians and slacking off. There is a legitimate ethos with real lessons that can apply to anyone.

With over 150,000 Dudeists worldwide, and numbers growing steadily, that is a whole lot of people taking it easy for all the sinners out there. There have been plenty of news stories and features on the success and growth of Dudeism, cementing the religion's status as being on the cusp of mainstream status.

Being one of the only religions on the list to have a method in place to ordain their own clergy, Dudeism has priests popping up everywhere. They are fully ordained clergy, which gives them the option to perform weddings and other religious services in many states in the U.S. and some other parts of the world as well. That is pretty well organized for a religion so laid-back.

1 Jediism

Of course, one could not mention alternative religions without mentioning the Jedi. These practitioners of the Light Side of the Force are the primary example given when people talk about alternative religions in census data. The Jedi are recognized in some places as being as mainstream as Wiccans. The Universal Life Church, one of the leading online ordainment destinations, will ordain official Jedi Knights alongside clergy from many other religions, and sells all of the gear necessary to be recognized as such by many governments.

Jediism is quite possibly the most mainstream alternative religion on the planet. If not, they definitely rank in the top five. The fact that the two "fictional" religions created by George Lucas for the Star Wars films became such big religious movements on their own merit really says something for the enduring legacy of the films and the philosophy they embody.

CHAPTER 13

FOOD

1. Top 10 Ways You Could Eat Feces Today

2. Top 10 Strange Facts about Hamburgers

3. Top 10 Truly Weird Food Tales

4. Top 10 Strange and Creepy Reasons Not to Eat Fast Food

5. Top 10 Food Facts and Fallacies

6. Top 10 Weird Foods Sold by Victorian Street Vendors

7. Top 10 Animals That People Eat Alive

8. Top 10 Strange Tales about Pizza

9. Top 10 Strange and Fascinating Fast Food Tales

10. Top 10 Fascinating Facts about Soda

11. Top 10 Disturbing Foods That Might Harm You

12. Top 10 Terrifying Things That Can Hide in Your Food

TOP 10 Ways You Could Eat Feces Today

by **Kelly R. Barkhausen-Rojahn**

10 Leafy Greens

Leafy greens are often grown using synthetic fertilizers rather than manure. However, even these crops can be invaded by various forms of fecal matter from nearby animals. According to research conducted by the Yuma Agricultural Center (YAC), fecal matter from cows can increase the possibility of contaminating crops with the bacteria E. coli. The research further indicates that feces from dogs, rabbits, birds, and other animals doesn't pose as high of a risk for contamination.

There have been a number of E. coli–related outbreaks linked to leafy greens such as spinach. The study conducted by the YAC determined that crops can become contaminated when the fecal matter containing the bacteria contaminates the irrigation system. The water used for the crops then spreads contamination. The study also indicates that furrow irrigation is the safest practice to avoid contaminating crops, though it can still occur even then.

9 Organic Food

Many people opt to pay for high-priced organic food, convinced that it is healthier than other conventional options. They purchase and consume the food because, understandably, they don't want to put pesticides or other chemicals in their bodies. However, studies have shown that organic food is at a greater risk for fecal contamination.

A study published in the *Annals of Internal Medicine* in 2012 revealed that 5 percent of organic lettuce was at a greater risk than non-organic lettuce for fecal contamination and 65 percent of organic pork was contaminated with E. coli. Another study conducted by the University of Minnesota found that 9.7 percent of their samples from organically grown produce were contaminated with E. coli, whereas only 1.6 percent of their conventionally grown samples contained the bacteria.

8 Candy and Chocolate

Children and adults alike enjoy a tasty piece of candy or a delectable chocolate treat from time to time. Many are drawn in by the smooth and flawless appearance of these foods and the enjoyable texture and flavors when they consume them. What many people aren't aware of is that certain types of candies and chocolates contain ingredients that are produced from insect feces.

Confectioner's glaze or resinous glazes are ingredients used to produce a smooth, shiny coating on certain types of candy and chocolates. These particular ingredients are produced by the female lac insect and derived from its feces. Tastes sweet, doesn't it?

7 Spices

There's nothing better than the aroma of a home-cooked meal that has been lovingly seasoned with a variety of carefully selected herbs and spices. These special ingredients add a delightful flavor to food, and certain herbs and spices have also been known to have health benefits. Oh, and of course they contain feces. Have health benefits ever tasted so good?

The FDA permits a certain level of contamination in food products before they take action, herbs and spices included. According to the FDA's website, "contamination of these products by animals usually results from either gnawing or defilement by excreta. Whole rodent pellets, bird droppings, and other pieces of animal dung are typically found." Who knew that insect and animal excrement could add such flavor?

6 Wheat

Bread, pizza dough, cakes, cookies, and an endless list of other products contain wheat as one of their main ingredients. Those who cook at home often use wheat flour in much of their baking. It's an ingredient that is widely consumed by a countless number of individuals. The fact that we eat so much of it doesn't matter—the FDA allows nine milligrams or more of rodent pellets per kilogram of wheat. In other words, a small percentage of rodent feces is tolerable in wheat and permitted to enter our food supply.

5 Imported Seafood

Americans consume a large quantity of seafood from overseas. For example, America received approximately 8 percent of its shrimp from Vietnam, some of its shellfish from Hong Kong, and some of its tilapia from Hong Kong. Although the FDA inspects these shipments, it is only able to do spot checks (about 3 percent of these imports).

A significant portion of the seafood imported to the United States from these countries has been raised on feces, including pig and geese feces because it is cheaper to use than commercially sold fish food. Some claim that the fish don't actually consume the feces, but rather the algae that is produced from using it. Either way, the idea of fish consuming and/or floating in swine feces isn't exactly appetizing.

4 Peanut Butter

Peanut butter can be a nutritious snack. Enjoyed with crackers or apple slices, it's a great treat to feed the kids and an excellent alternative to sugary snacks such as cookies or ice cream. Peanut butter also contains some extra ingredients that you won't find listed on the nutritional label, one of which is rodent feces.

As with other food items, the FDA finds that a certain amount (5 percent) of rodent feces or other rodent filth such as hair is permissible in peanut butter. As long as you get crunchy peanut butter, you probably won't know the difference. Right?

3 Ground Turkey

Ground turkey is often purchased as a healthier, leaner alternative to ground beef. But it's not an exception to the "must include some feces" rule this list is working on.

In a Consumer Reports study, 257 samples of ground turkey sold in the United States were tested. Of those, more than half were contaminated with bacteria from fecal matter. The study found that 69 percent of the samples contained enterococcus and 60 percent contained E. coli. In most cases, the bacteria discovered in the ground turkey can be destroyed by cooking thoroughly, but a fecal burger sounds decidedly less appetizing than a "turkey" burger.

2 Soda Fountain Machines

A small study conducted in the Roanoke Valley of Virginia found that soda fountain machines contained the bacteria coliform, which can, you guessed it, indicate fecal contamination. The U.S. Environmental Protection Agency (EPA) has even banned the bacteria from being present in drinking water because it may be a sign of contamination by feces.

Of the samples tested, 48 percent were contaminated with coliform, and 20 percent of the samples tested had a detectable amount of coliform that exceeded the limit allowed by the EPA. It is assumed that the contamination is not from the soda itself, but rather the machines. It seems the contamination occurs within the plastic tubing and is then deposited into the soda when patrons go to fill up their cups.

1 Human Feces Steak

Granted this is not a way you could eat feces today, but if you were one of the many to believe a tale that spread around the Internet, you certainly could have. A sensational hoax that just won't die is that of the steak created using human feces. According to Internet legend, a Japanese scientist developed the steak using human feces and a few other simple ingredients. He even taste tested the fecal steak and gave it his seal of approval.

Many legitimate news agencies reported the story as fact. But if they had done some digging, they would have discovered that the YouTube video that brought this poop steak to the Web was actually a hoax, with many subtle clues available in the video footage.

It's unlikely that humans will ever purchase human feces meat, but if they ever do, perhaps it would pair nicely with a side of shiitake mushrooms.

TOP 10 Strange Facts about Hamburgers

by **Mike Devlin**

10 The World's Most Expensive Burger

Hamburgers don't tend to be big-ticket items. You can typically get one with fries and a Coke for under $10 at a fast-food place. But some elite restaurants have turned the convention of a cheap burger on its head, using such ingredients as lobster tails, foie gras, and even barbecue sauce made with kopi luwak coffee beans (where the beans have first been eaten and then excreted by a civet).

While these establishments are constantly vying over who has the most expensive burger (some of which cost several hundred dollars), it is not likely anyone will soon be beating out the $10,000 defunct USocial.net anniversary burger. Nothing less than a culinary work of art, the burger, which was sold for charity, featured Wagyu beef, truffles, and 24-karat gold leaf. Arguably its most compelling element was sliced Spanish *jamón ibérico*, made from black Iberian pigs fed a specialty diet composed almost entirely of acorns.

9 The World's Worst Burger

Certainly, no one would classify hamburgers as a health food, and dietary wisdom dictates that a serving of meat should be about three ounces, or the size of a deck of cards. But one restaurant in Las Vegas, Nevada, shuns such conventions. Offering up what the founder calls "nutritional pornography," the Heart Attack Grill's menu includes such cardiovascularly destructive fare as butterfat milkshakes and fries cooked in pure lard. Their signature Quadruple Bypass Burger has been recognized by Guinness World Records as the world's most calorific burger. It consists of four half-pound hamburgers, three tablespoons of lard, 20 slices of bacon, eight slices of American cheese, 20 slices of caramelized onion baked in lard, eight tomato slices, one tablespoon of mayonnaise, two tablespoons of ketchup, one tablespoon of mustard, and a bun. It contains a staggering 9,982 calories.

The restaurant has a whole tongue-in-cheek hospital motif, with buxom, scantily clad "nurses" acting as waitresses. Diners who weigh more than 350 pounds eat for free. Should you fail to devour your burger in its entirety, the nurses will gleefully paddle your behind.

Unfortunately, patrons of the grill have actually succumbed to cardiac arrest, including unofficial spokesman John Alleman, a daily customer who died of a heart attack at a bus stop in front of the restaurant. Another spokesman, 29-year-old, six-foot-eight, 575-pound Blair River, died in 2011 of pneumonia, and his death was likely tied to his obesity. Despite these tragedies, the Heart Attack Grill continues to do incredible business in Sin City, and the restaurant has been featured on several food- and travel-related programs.

8 The Oprah Beef Scandal

Virtually no one without control of a standing army and a thermonuclear arsenal has held more sway over our culture than Oprah Winfrey. The so-called Oprah Effect has impacted entire industries. In 1996, when she began her Oprah's Book Club segment, every novel she chose instantly rocketed up the bestseller lists. But another show in 1996 brought her even more infamy.

During a segment about the beef industry, she claimed that she would never eat another hamburger. Beef prices immediately plunged, hitting a ten-year low after two weeks. A group of Texas cattle ranchers sued Winfrey for $10.3 million on the basis of a strange agriculture defamation precedent. In 2002, after four years of litigation, a U.S. district judge finally threw out all charges against the talk show maven. In an interview after the trial, she claimed that she was still "off burgers."

7 Monopoly Scandal

The largest purchaser of beef in the U.S., McDonald's is synonymous with the hamburger. Of course, the company's vast holdings are less a result of its delicious food than its marketing genius. One such scheme was their Monopoly game. Game pieces affixed to food and drink would either win customers items like free food or could be collected to win grand prizes like cars and cash. The contest was run by a third-party company called Simon Marketing, whose security chief, Jerome P. Jacobson, skimmed the game pieces for all the best prizes for years. The pieces were redeemed by a large group of associates who would split the proceeds among themselves. Twenty-one employees of Simon Marketing were indicted in 2001 for their role in the scam, which netted them some $24 million.

Perhaps the only good thing to come out of the Monopoly scandal was in 1995, when Jacobson sent a game piece worth $1 million to St. Jude's Children's Hospital. Likely realizing that whoever redeemed this prize would be subject to intense scrutiny, he passed it along. Although transferring game pieces was against the rules of the contest, McDonald's agreed to pay out the prize to the hospital, which treats children with cancer. When it was revealed years later that this was part of Simon Marketing's scheme, McDonald's told St. Jude's that they had no intention of asking for their money back.

While auditing procedures are likely far stricter these days, your chances of winning much more than a free burger playing the McDonald's Monopoly game are more dismal than you can imagine. According to the company's website, your odds of winning the $1 million grand prize are approximately 1 in 3,050,412,898.

6 The First Burger

The hamburger is actually a far more recent invention than most realize. While countless culinary innovators take credit for creating the burger, perhaps the most likely candidate was New Haven, Connecticut, lunch-cart operator Louis Lassen. As the story goes, in 1900, Lassen served a ground beef sandwich to a worker on the go, giving rise to the hamburger. The Lassen family is continuing the tradition 113 years later. At Louis' Lunch, the burgers are cooked in vertical cast-iron gas stoves and served on plain bread; the only condiments available are cheese spread, tomatoes, and onions. Ingredients such as ketchup, mustard, and mayonnaise are strictly forbidden. According to the owners, students from nearby Yale University are often caught trying to smuggle ketchup into the grill. They are politely asked to leave.

5 Veggie Burgers

Veggie burgers are readily available in fast-food franchises in many parts of the world, particularly places like India, which has large Hindu (who don't eat beef) and Muslim (who don't eat pork) populations. You can't even get a hamburger at a McDonald's in India.

Unfortunately, there is some evidence that veggie burgers aren't nearly as healthy an alternative to beef as they are made out to be. The soy that is used in veggie burgers is often made with hexane, an air pollutant that is the byproduct of refining gasoline. The hexane persists in the food, and it can be bad news. In 2010, a worker at an Apple factory died of hexane poisoning while using the substance to clean touchscreens.

4 Meat Cologne

Even when their fragrance aims to be appealing, perfumes can contain some pretty vile ingredients. Examples include ambergris, a waxy digestive secretion of the sperm whale; castoreum, which comes from a beaver's anal glands; and hyraceum, which is petrified rock hyrax poop. In 2008, fast-food giant Burger King unveiled their very own fragrance. Dubbed "Flame," it was marketed as "the scent of seduction with a hint of flame-broiled meat." The Flame cologne has its very own website, and is available for about $4. Strangely enough, Burger King is not the only restaurant in the cologne business. Pizza Hut also marketed a scent based on fresh-baked pizza dough and herbs.

3 Hundreds of Cows

Most people probably don't like to meditate extensively on where their meat comes from. Even the most humane butchering is pretty grotesque. The cow is first stunned (in the past, a sledge-hammer was used, but today processing plants generally use captive bolt pistols— the weapon used by Anton Chigurh in *No Country for Old Men*) and then suspended by its rear legs. Its throat is slashed and it is allowed to bleed out. Beef is too tough to eat  fresh and requires tenderizing, or, for the less genteel, controlled rotting.

While your steak probably comes from a single animal (although there are methods of "gluing" even the most prime cuts together), the ground beef used in hamburgers comes from the toughest and least appetizing portions of the cow. These are mixed communally so that the average four-ounce hamburger you get at a fast-food franchise has, according to one study done in 1998, at least 55 different cows mixed into it. They discovered samples with over 1,000 different cows mixed into a single hamburger. This is particularly concerning because such a cross section of animals vastly increases your chances of contracting a food-borne illness like E. coli.

2 Test-Tube Meat

Many vegetarians make their decision not to eat meat based solely on ethics rather than any disdain for the flavor. The growing of meat in laboratories would certainly alleviate these concerns, but the benefits extend beyond morals. The keeping of animals for meat is an enormous strain on the environment, and with the global population skyrocketing, the demand continues to grow. According to a report published by Stanford University, livestock production occupies more than one-fourth of Earth's land and contributes to 18 percent of greenhouse gas emissions attacking the atmosphere. Recent experiments using stem cells from pigs and cows, cultured in a nutrient-rich bath that allows them to grow, have shown much promise.

The burger program is headed up by Dr. Mark Post at Maastricht University in the Netherlands. He has cultivated beef in a laboratory, using thousands of strands and layers stacked together to form a five-ounce burger. Post uses Velcro to flex and "exercise" each strand of muscle to prevent it from wasting away. Although the meat doesn't contain any fat (which gives beef much of its flavor), Post claims that it "tastes reasonably good." Of course, the implications of this technology far exceed usage in food. One day, it might soon be possible to grow healthy organs or even replacement limbs in laboratories. However, perfecting this technology is sure to be an uphill climb; as with the use of human stem cells, a great deal of fundamentalists will surely call foul in "playing God."

1 Immortal Burgers

A frequent "experiment" conducted by fast-food critics involves taking a plain hamburger and allowing it to sit out in the open. Astonishingly, even after weeks, the burger doesn't rot and looks much the same as the day it was cooked. The ostensible conclusion is that the burgers are riddled with such excessive preservatives that they cannot decompose. Surely, anything potent enough to prevent decay for months at a time must have horrifying effects on human organs.

The truth is a little more pedestrian (and certainly friendlier to your liver). Burgers under a certain weight will dehydrate before they can begin to rot or grow mold. Larger burgers, such as McDonald's Quarter Pounder, generally begin to exhibit a fur of mold before they fully dry out. This experiment can be easily duplicated at home using a control group of home-made burgers, though a collection of mummified sandwiches might turn off houseguests.

TOP 10 Truly Weird Food Tales

by **Mike Devlin**

10 Canadian Maple Syrup Heist

Maple syrup is one of the most expensive things you can pour on your pancakes. A bottle generally retails for well over $20. Part of the expense involved in the syrup is the great inefficiency in producing it. It requires anywhere from 5 to 13 gallons of maple sap to make just one quart of syrup. To make sure that it has enough to meet the international demand, the Canadian province of Quebec maintains a Global Strategic Maple Syrup Reserve. In 2012, during an audit, it was discovered that six million pounds of the syrup (worth about $18 million wholesale) had been stolen in a daring heist. This was not some smash-and-grab  theft; it would have taken dozens of trucks to move so many barrels. In the subsequent months, several arrests were made, and some two-thirds of the missing syrup was recovered.

9 Most Stolen Food

Asked to guess the most frequently stolen food on the planet, some might guess candy or alcohol or even steak. But according to multiple studies, up to 4 percent of the cheese put up for sale ends up pilfered. Next time you're in the market, pay attention to the way the store displays cheese, particularly the valuable imported kinds. Generally, it is centrally located and well lit to keep thieves from scampering off. The phenomenon is not completely understood, though researchers indicate that cheese is relatively expensive, easy to conceal, and can be resold to other stores or restaurants. Black market cheese is big business.

8 Eggs

American and Canadian tourists traveling outside their respective countries are often astonished to see eggs sitting out at room temperature. They would probably be even more shocked to find out that in the countries of the

European Union, the eggs they are getting are straight from the chicken—they have not be sanitized or washed in any fashion. A chicken actually imparts a liquid coating around its egg called a cuticle, which protects against contamination. The layer is mostly removed by cleaning, which involves washing the egg with water of at least 90 degrees and an odorless detergent. The washing actually makes the egg more porous and susceptible to contamination, so it must be kept in a refrigerator. The counterproductivity and expense of this process is astonishing, but American shoppers do not seem soon to relent.

7 Ice Cream

With dozens and dozens of ice creams available on the market, a distinctive taste sets a company apart from its competitors. The largest producer of ice cream in the United States is Dreyer's (which includes Edy's and Häagen-Dazs), due in no small part to their official taste tester, John Harrison. Harrison travels throughout the country to different Dreyer's plants to impart his expertise. He uses a gold spoon, which does not impart any flavor to the ice cream. His taste buds are insured for $1 million. He helped create several different popular flavors of ice cream, including the Oreo-based cookies and cream.

Other ice cream makers use different philosophies. Using fresh, local ingredients, Vermont's Ben & Jerry's is a crowd favorite. Their ice cream is noted for large chunks of things like brownies and fruit, added in response to cofounder Ben Cohen's anosmia (he cannot smell and can barely taste anything). Since Cohen couldn't really taste what he was eating, he tended to add more stuff to satisfy a need for texture.

6 Mushrooms

People are rarely ambivalent about mushrooms; they are generally a food that is either loved or despised. Regardless of one's opinion on their taste, they are marvelously interesting organisms. Some, like the awesomely named Western North American Destroying Angel, can be deadly, and others, like the psilocybes "magic mushrooms," result in profound psychedelic experiences. There are 71 known species of mushrooms that glow in the dark, and there is even a type called the Laetiporus that is said to taste like chicken. Most recently, scientists have discovered that running electricity through mushrooms can more than double their production, a fact that has been known to Japanese farmers for generations. Lightning hitting fields of shiitake mushrooms send voltage buzzing through the soil, thus increasing the farmer's yield. The scientists are not entirely sure what causes this phenomenon, but it is most likely a kind of defense mechanism, amping up reproductive capabilities in the face of a hazard.

5 Gatorade

Gatorade was invented in 1965 by University of Florida professor and nephrologist (kidney specialist) Robert Cade and staff to help keep football players hydrated. While today's product line features a veritable rainbow of flavors, the early stuff was pretty much water, sugar, salt, and some lemon juice for taste. When Cade unveiled his beverage to the Gators team, tackle Larry Gagner tried some, announced "This stuff tastes like piss," and dumped the rest of the cup onto his head. The staff was intrigued at the comparison. According to Cade, "None of us had tasted urine...We wee-weed in a cup and dabbed a finger. You know what? There's a significant difference in flavor."

4 Sushi

Prior to the explosion in popularity of sushi, many fish such as the bluefin tuna were so plentiful that they were used as cat food. Today, the bluefin

 is one of the most highly valued creatures in the world, with exceptional specimens costing hundreds of thousands of dollars. With the expense rising and the ocean's population falling, many sushi restaurants take advantage of most peoples' inability to distinguish between types of fish, often substituting cheaper species. In the United States, many establishments selling "tuna" are actually pushing escolar, also known as the oilfish or snake mackerel. Escolar has a staggering oil content known to have a laxative effect in many people. Many countries throughout the world consider escolar toxic; it's sale has been banned in Japan since 1977, but many American diners still (unwittingly) consume it each day.

3 Ancient Snack

Woolly mammoths lived beside early man, but the vast majority became extinct around 10,000 years ago. The last isolated populations died out around the time the Great Pyramid of Giza was built. We know so much about these magnificent creatures because many of them roamed in areas like the Siberian tundra, where they were frozen and quite well preserved after death. So well preserved that modern humans have eaten thawed mammoth meat. There are many stories of feasts of these ancient elephant ancestors, and while many are dubious, some are quite well verified. Not surprisingly, descriptions of the meat range from "awful" to "rotten." Zoology professor Dale Guthrie offers a remarkably generous explanation of the flavor; he and his team cooked some mammoth from a 36,000-year-old carcass found near Fairbanks, Alaska, into a stew. He wrote "the meat was well aged but still a little tough, and it gave the stew a strong Pleistocene aroma." Whatever that means.

2 Cannibalism

Despite being seen by most modern humans as "the ultimate taboo," cannibalism has been practiced in every part of the world and is still more frequent than most of us would like to believe. Many of the civil conflicts in central Africa, particularly in the Congo, have resulted in cannibalism, and primordial tribes like New Guinea's Korowai sometimes indulge in the consumption of human flesh. That said, the natural although somewhat macabre question most people would ask is, "What does it taste like?"

Accounts vary somewhat, but a rather concise explanation comes from William Buehler Seabrook, a reporter who received a chunk of flesh from a hospital intern at the Sorbonne in Paris. Seabrook cooked it, later writing, "It was like good, fully developed veal, not young, but not yet beef. It was very definitely like that, and it was not like any other meat I had ever tasted. It was so nearly like good, fully developed veal that I think no person with a palate of ordinary, normal sensitiveness could distinguish it from veal."

1 Perfect Food

You would be hard pressed to find someone who doesn't like the taste of ketchup, and for good reason. Unlike nearly every food on the planet, ketchup, particularly the Heinz brand, satisfies the entire palate. Simultaneously salty, sweet, sour, bitter, and umami (savory, the flavor profile created by adding MSG), the ketchup created by Heinz is very carefully mixed so that no one part of its recipe overwhelms the taste buds. Lesser ketchups are not so neatly balanced and tend to have a note that you can focus on, like that of vinegar or the sweetness of the tomatoes. This is why, over 100 years since it first hit shelves, the ketchup created by Heinz remains so popular, selling some 650 million bottles annually. Unlike many other foods, you will rarely encounter "new and improved" ketchup. It's already perfect.

TOP 10 Strange and Creepy Reasons Not to Eat Fast Food

by **Pauli Poisuo**

10 Chick-fil-A Gets Homophobic

For most fast-food joints, a customer is a customer. As long as they're not buck-naked or drunk out of their minds, they're welcome to stuff their faces with greasy deliciousness. A fast-food restaurant is a neutral zone—political views or sexual orientation rarely play a part.

Unless you go to a Chick-fil-A. These days, many view the mere act of eating there as a political statement.

In June 2012, it was revealed that the chicken-sandwich chain had made significant contributions to organizations that opposed the LGBT (Lesbian, Gay, Bisexual, and Transgender) community. The CEO of Chick-fil-A then made a number of statements that made it obvious that he (and, by extension, his company) was very much against same-sex marriages. This caused an immediate outrage and boycott from the LGBT folks. This, in turn, caused a backlash from conservatives, who went as far as inventing a Chick-fil-A Appreciation Day to salute the restaurant's political stance.

The company soon stated that they would leave political conversations to politicians and later ceased all donations to anti-LGBT organizations. Yet the scandal has made its mark. To this day, few pro-LGBT people frequent the restaurant if they have any other options.

9 Ajisen Ramen Soup Base Scandal

Most successful fast-food companies have a signature dish (such as McDonald's Big Mac) or a secret sauce (such as, well, McDonald's Secret Sauce)

that is meant to set them apart from their competition. For Ajisen Ramen, a famous Chinese fast-food chain, that dish was their soup stock. Ajisen Ramen's menu was based around noodle soup, and their secret was that the stock used for every soup came from "a broth of pork bones simmered to perfection." That broth was their secret recipe, the entire selling point their empire rested on.

Imagine their embarrassment in 2011, when the media found that their precious soup base was made from concentrates and flavoring powders instead of actual pork bone stock. Their stock (market, not soup) plummeted and customers were revolted.

What's worse, the company had always claimed that their soups were extremely nutritious, containing "four times the calcium content of milk and 10 times that of meat." The test sample mentioned in the report was taken from the concentrate instead of actual soup.

Ajisen Ramen is still in operation, but their reputation will probably never be the same.

8 Burger King's Horse Burgers

When we dine in a hamburger joint, our biggest fear is that a disgruntled employee spits in our burger. However, sometimes the foreign and unwanted substances in our meal don't need help—because they're already there.

When the 2013 horse meat scandal swept through Europe, U.S.-based fast-food companies were left relatively unscathed, save for one or two. Findus (the food company whose beef lasagna served as Patient Zero for the scandal) took the biggest blows. However, Burger King was the company that suffered the biggest embarrassment. The company quickly and aggressively declared Burger King restaurants in outbreak areas to be 100 percent horse meat free. However, despite their claims, testing soon found horse DNA in Burger King hamburger patties that were supposed to be pure beef.

What saved Burger King was their quick reaction: They immediately severed all ties with the meat company that provided the "beef" patties. Then, they gave the public a heartfelt apology and continued business as usual. Although this got them out of trouble, some people feel it was not enough. The company gave very little information to the public, and apparently offered no compensation to the numerous people whose burgers they accidentally horsed up.

7 Domino's YouTube Scandal

Sometimes, all it takes to send a company into a crisis is hiring the wrong people. Domino's Pizza learned this the hard way in 2009, when some of its employees shot a video in which one of them stuck raw ingredients in his nose, and then put them in the food they were preparing for a customer. They put the video on YouTube, where it became an instant Internet hit.

Domino's quickly located, fired, and sued the responsible parties. Other than that, the restaurant chain chose a very poor way to handle a social media crisis: They decided to shut up about the incident completely. The lack of positive media visibility (and the impact of the gross video) soon tore their carefully built brand image to pieces in a matter of days. Although the company took to Twitter and embraced social media soon afterward, some say the damage still hasn't quite healed.

6 Pizza Hut Delivery

In 2011, a Pizza Hut delivery driver from Iowa briefly became the world's least favorite person to handle food. When the customer he was delivering to didn't have enough money for a tip, he decided to leave a little tip of his own and urinated on her front door.

Unfortunately for the driver (and Pizza Hut), the customer was less than pleased with the yellow pool by her front door and decided to go public. Her apartment manager provided a local news channel with surveillance footage of the incident, and it became a popular news story.

Luckily for Pizza Hut, the manager of the restaurant did all the right things. He was very cooperative from the start, actually visiting the customer and viewing the surveillance tapes. He then immediately fired the driver. Later, the driver himself (who was probably feeling very guilty and embarrassed at that point) came to apologize to the customer and clean the mess he had made.

5 Starbucks Coffee

In Starbucks, everything starts with water. You can't make coffee (or any other beverage) without it, so it's extremely important that it's clean.

At least, that's what you'd think. A Starbucks manager in the business district of Hong Kong had a very different attitude. The water he brewed his coffee with came from a tap in a nearby bathroom.

Although the tap itself had been kept relatively clean, the fact that it had been in a dirty restroom immediately created a scandal. Even in many other parts of the world, Starbucks-related Google searches are beginning to turn up unsavory suggestions such as "Starbucks Toilet Coffee Lawsuit."

4 Subway "Footlongs"

Fast food may be unhealthy. It may sometimes be prepared in unsanitary conditions. But there is one golden rule that must never be broken: There needs to be lots of it. After all, this is the industry that introduced the concept of "super-sizing" meals. At the very least, people expect their food to be as big as the restaurant advertises. A quarter-pounder with a patty that weighs any less would be a tragedy.

Still, some companies see things differently. When an Australian Subway customer decided to measure his "foot-long" sandwich, he found it was quite a lot shorter than the advertised length of one foot. Subway Australia tried to explain this as an individual manufacturing error, before finally stated that the "Footlong" is just a name and not a measurement. This was interesting, because the company had always specifically stated the exact opposite.

Meanwhile, an American newspaper found that many stateside Subways were also quietly shrinking their subs. It wasn't just about the length, either: They were reducing the size of their cold cuts by up to 25 percent too.

Subway responded to the international criticism by sticking to their guns and claiming that the "Footlong" really is just a descriptive name. Then, they just stopped all communication and started hoping for the crisis to go away. How well this tactic will serve them in the long run remains to be seen.

3 Arby's Finger Sandwich

In 2012, an unfortunate Michigan teenager got a taste experience he's not going to forget in a hurry. He was enjoying a delicious roast beef sandwich at a local Arby's when he bit into something strange and rubbery. As the boy removed the foreign object from his mouth, he found to his horror it was human flesh. A restaurant worker had accidentally sliced off part of his finger and left his station without telling anyone. The human meat had then somehow ended up in a sandwich that was served to a customer.

Although Arby's was quick to apologize what it accurately called "an unfortunate incident," the restaurant's reputation took a blow.

2 McDonald's and Children

Children are the future, and the future is looking larger than ever. Childhood obesity in first-world countries is higher than it's ever been. In the United States alone, one-third of children are obese and the situation (along with the health issues that come with it) is not getting any better.

All fast-food companies are happy to serve children, but McDonald's in particular is a master of targeting children in its advertising. Their Happy Meal (a simple hamburger meal with a toy included) is possibly the best-known kid's meal there is. McDonald's is estimated to give away over 15 billion toys per year as part of their cross-promotions with popular toy lines, thus giving the children an early taste of the fast-food nation they will grow up into.

The strange thing is that McDonald's refuses to admit they're doing it— seemingly even to their own shareholders. Their shareholders have asked that the company take responsibility of its (presumably not insignificant) part in America's childhood obesity problem. Yet the McDonald's board has dismissed the issue, because associating the company with childhood obesity issues would be "unnecessary."

To be fair, McDonald's has made some changes to their Happy Meals to make them healthier. They now come with complimentary apple slices and a milk drink instead of a soda.

1 Taco Bell

Taco Bell's history is spotted with embarrassing events that range from slightly awkward to truly terrifying. Their taco shells have been recalled because they were made with genetically modified corn. Their meat has been revealed to be just 36 percent actual beef (the rest is tasteless fiber filler and various seasonings). The company has been linked to multiple food-borne disease outbreaks, including an E. coli outbreak that killed three people and gave 200 more customers the stomach bug of a lifetime.

With the advent of social media, it looks like the company (together with many of its competitors) is heading for even more hot water. In June 2013, a picture of a Taco Bell employee licking a stack of taco shells was posted on the company's own Facebook page, to the disgust of loyal Taco Bell fans everywhere.

TOP 10 Food Facts and Fallacies

by **Jamie Frater**

10 Diets

Fallacy: Diet X, Y, or Z is the best!

No magical combination of foods, avoidance of foods, increase in the intake of certain foods, or special diet plans (no matter how bizarre) will make you lose weight. The only way you can lose weight is to eat fewer calories than you burn in your daily activities. If you burn 1,700 calories a day, you need to eat 1,700 calories to maintain your weight. If you want to lose weight, eat 250 less (give or take) a day and you have it. It doesn't matter whether your daily calories come from chocolate, salad, fat, sugar, or beans. The reason that fad diets work so well is that the people subscribing to them are initially motivated and ultimately eat fewer calories than they are burning. Diets like Atkins (in which you cut out carbohydrates) work in the same way: Cream and high-fat meats are so rich you can only eat so much, so you eat less. The best diet (which should be your diet for life) is to moderate the amount of food you eat. It doesn't matter what you eat— just don't eat too much.

Did you know: Robert Atkins, inventor of the Atkins Diet, died after sustaining head injuries when he slipped on some ice after a snowstorm in New York. He was 72 years old.

9 Cooking Off Alcohol

Fallacy: Cooking or flaming removes most alcohol.

From time to time we have a special event or family occasion that requires some fancy cooking. These are, for the average home cook, the times we like to cook extravagant recipes that sometimes require large quantities of alcohol. And that is fine for a family meal because the cooking removes the alcohol, making it safe for the alcoholics and children among us. Or at least that is what we have all been led to think.

In reality, it is actually quite difficult to remove alcohol from food by cooking. Setting fire to alcohol in the pan (which seems to be the most extreme way to burn off the booze) actually reduces the total alcohol percentage by a mere 25 percent. In other words, when you add one cup of brandy to a pan and set it alight, once the flames go out, you still have the equivalent of three-fourths of a cup of brandy left behind with the alcohol intact. If you want to reduce the alcohol to 0 percent, good luck. Cooking alcohol for two-and-a-half hours with other liquids and ingredients still leaves 5 percent alcohol behind. That certainly explains some of the more unusual episodes of Julia Child's cooking show.

Did you know: Alcohol in high doses has been known to cause increased rates of "regrettable" sexual encounters in humans.

8 Salt Kills

Fallacy: Salt kills.

Salt is a naturally occurring substance that, when added to low-salt food, enhances and deepens flavor. The human body contains around 1 percent salt, and this is constantly removed through natural processes like urination and sweating. The salt is essential to our health, so we need to replace it through our diet. Excess salt does not cause a high salt percentage; our bodies are smart enough to handle it. If you eat too much salt, you just pee it out. There may be some negative impacts on the body through extremely high consumption of salt in those with blood or heart disorders, but the average healthy human can quite happily overconsume the substance without ill effect. To kill yourself with salt, you need to consume about one gram per two pounds of body weight. In other words, if you weigh 130 pounds you need to eat around three-and-a-half tablespoons of salt, an immense amount, and you would probably vomit before you could finish it (because salt is an emetic).

Did you know: Before Biblical Judaism ceased to exist, salt was mixed with animal sacrifices. This originated from Moses in Leviticus 2:13, which states: "Whatsoever sacrifice thou offerest, thou shalt season it with salt, neither shalt thou take away the salt of the covenant of thy God from thy sacrifice. In all thy oblations, thou shalt offer salt." The salt was a symbol of wisdom and discretion.

7 Grill Death

Fallacy: Grilled meat is bad for you.

When rats are fed high doses of nicely browned grilled meat, they have a statistically higher chance of getting cancer. But that is rats. So far, no study of humans has found the same result. Despite that, the U.S. National Toxicology Program says that these chemicals (heterocyclic amines) are "reasonably anticipated" to be carcinogens in humans. Why? No one is really sure. Tripterygium wilfordii is deadly to rats but is consumed by humans as an oral contraceptive with no negative impact. A recent study of humans consuming grilled meat found no association between that and cancer. Let's face it: For thousands of years humans have cooked meat and evolved (some might say) to tolerate it. When was the last time you saw a rat cooking at a barbecue? Humans are not rats, and what is deadly to a rat is not always deadly to a human.

Did you know: Potato chips, breakfast cereals, crusty bread, and the like are all crunchy because of the same chemicals as those that produce the nice browned effect on grilled meat. Furthermore, these chemicals are known to be antioxidants that suppress the bacteria that causes peptic ulcers. Speaking of that delicious crust around a good steak...

6 Raw Pork

Fallacy: Pork and poultry should be cooked to high temperatures to make them safe for eating.

Trichinella spiralis, a type of roundworm, is the main culprit behind the huge campaign for cooking pork to 160°F (beyond well-done). For decades, governments around the world have been promoting cooking at that level as the only safe way to eat pork. Sadly, this is another case of science and government's failure to be able to backtrack when they are wrong. Between 1997 and 2001, eight cases of roundworm infection attributed to pork occurred in the U.S. This is from a total consumption of 70 billion pounds of pork. Trichinella spiralis infection is one of the rarest diseases known to modern medicine. When it does occur, it is neither fatal nor serious and is easily treated. Sadly, to prevent such a minuscule amount of infections, virtually all pork eaten is destroyed in the cooking. Pork can be safely consumed at temperatures as low as 136°F, which results in a moist, pink cut of meat. The same is also true of chicken, which can be safely eaten rare (cooked to 136°F). At this temperature both trichinella spiralis and salmonella are destroyed.

Did you know: Raw chicken sashimi (*toriwasa*) is popular in Japan; it is served with a mirin-and-soy dipping sauce and a little ginger. Along with the raw chicken flesh, raw chicken gizzards and hearts are also consumed.

5 Vegetarian

Fallacy: Man is a vegetarian.

This is nonsense most regularly spewed by vegans and some vegetarians.

The lengths people will go to disprove man's meat-eating disposition are, at times, ludicrous: from posters of Jesus denouncing the consumption of meat (contrary to the fact that Christ's most significant act in the Bible—second to his death—was the last supper, which was a big roast lamb dinner) to statements from Gandhi denouncing the practice as evil. In reality, at least two million years ago, our ancestors were eating cooked foods, and a UC Berkeley anthropologist specializing in diet has gone so far as to say that we would not have evolved into humans were it not for meat in our diet. According to said evolutionary dietitian Katharine Milton, "It's unlikely that protohumans could have secured enough energy and nutrition from the plants available in their African environment at that time to evolve into the active, sociable, intelligent creatures they became. Receding forests would have deprived them of the more nutritious leaves and fruits that forest-dwelling primates survive on." Her thesis complements the discovery by UC Berkeley professor Tim White and others that early human species were butchering and eating animal meat as long ago as 2.5 million years.

Did you know: Veganism (not just the refusal to eat meat but the complete abstention from all animal products) was a concept invented in the

1940s by Englishman Donald Watson, an avowed vegetarian who decided to take his diet to fanatical levels in all areas of his life.

4 Organic Produce

Fact: Organic foods are potentially more toxic than non-organic.

Plants left in the wild naturally develop complex methods to self-manage pests. Often this is in the form of mild toxins. These toxins can repel pests but in high doses can be harmful to humans. In organic farming, many plants are left untreated and this allows those toxins to increase more than in pesticide-treated produce. In other cases, natural pesticides are used in place of man-made, pesticides such as nicotine infusions. Nicotine is known to be deadly to humans when consumed (even in small doses) yet the majority of "unnatural" pesticides have been rigorously tested for human safety. There are many loopholes in the rules around organic produce that allow other deadly products such as pyrethrum and rotenone to be used in organic farming—both of these chemicals have been linked to Parkinson's disease. Also many things labeled as organic contain non-organic matter: "organic muffins" are leavened with baking soda, which is inorganic (not a product of a living thing) and it is purified through a chemical process. Other ingredients are also allowed despite non-organic origins: table salt, for example, which is heavily chemically processed for purification. Most of the higher-quality products bearing the label "organic" are not of a superior standard because they are organic—they are superior because they come from small farms where greater personal care goes into the farming. Unfortunately, most organic produce these days is mass produced by conglomerates jumping on the latest bandwagon. Thus the quality of organic produce is usually no better than non-organic and can be potentially more harmful.

Did you know: No study exists to prove that man-made agricultural chemicals cause harm to people who buy and eat non-organic fruits, vegetables, or meats.

3 Fiber Benefits

Fallacy: High fiber reduces cancer risk.

Thanks to Dr. Denis Burkitt who spent some years in Kenya and Uganda studying the diet of the natives, most of the Western world has been fooled into thinking a high fiber intake helps prevent cancer. Unfortunately for us poor bewildered masses, he was wrong. Dr. Burkitt noticed during his tenure in those countries that colorectal cancer was rare there. Alas, the poor doctor fell for the common logical error of post hoc ergo propter hoc (also known as coincidental correlation). The native Kenyan and Ugandans ate lots of fiber and, according to Burkitt, consequently suffered low incidences of the cancer, which ultimately took his name: Burkitt's lymphoma. His "research" was groundbreaking, and realizing the huge financial benefits, the Seventh-Day Adventist company Kellogs, among others, began to tout the benefits of an excessively high-fiber diet. But what does science say? Unfortunately a lot of "science" is reliant on donations from such companies as the aforementioned, so it tends to say little or nothing at all. But the few studies that have been undertaken (and oftentimes buried shortly thereafter) show no benefit to a high-fiber diet. In fact, horrifyingly for those of us who have been persuaded by these multinationals that excess fiber is good for us, one observational study by the Women's Health Initiative showed an 8 percent higher risk of invasive cancer of the colon or rectum in a low-fat/high-fiber diet. Food for thought.

Did you know: When studies began to show that Burkitt was probably wrong with his link between fiber and cancer, new studies from the previously mentioned conglomerates showed that a high-fiber diet reduces risk of heart disease and diabetes. These new "findings" also lack any credible scientific backing. But they are definitely helping the Seventh-Day Adventists maintain a roaring trade in the "health" food business.

2 Chinese Restaurant Syndrome.

Fact: You eat MSG every day

Look back over your food consumption today. Did you eat any of the following:

- Processed snack food (for example, chips, Cheetos, etc.)
- Meat
- Any non-meat protein (for example, beans)
- Mushrooms
- Tomatoes
- Soy sauce
- Cheese (especially hard cheeses)
- Wheat-based products (for example, bread)

Every one of the above foods—plus many, many more—contain high concentrations of MSG. Some (the processed foods) have MSG added, but the rest are all natural. Chinese Restaurant Syndrome (an alleged reaction some people claim to suffer after eating MSG with symptoms of headaches, sweating, numbness, and fatigue) is a huge fraud unintentionally (maybe) perpetrated by well-meaning people, but, alas, there are still millions of people who think MSG is the cause of all their woes. There are huge websites dedicated to helping "MSG-sensitive" people avoid the dreaded chemical in their daily lives. Let us get this straight once and for all: MSG occurs naturally in most foods, and no single study ever has been able to give even the slightest hint of evidence that MSG (naturally occurring or extracted from naturally occurring sources) is harmful in any way. Parmesan cheese has the second highest concentration of MSG, with sun-dried tomatoes and tomato paste also having massive doses. So why, as food critic Jeffrey Steingarten put it, have we "never heard of a Parmesan Headache or Tomato-Paste Syndrome"? Incidentally, KFC chicken coating is not made of 11 secret herbs and spices—it's flour, salt, pepper, paprika, and MSG. Now you know why it is "finger-licking good."

Did you know: Europeans and Americans consume an average of one gram of MSG from natural food sources every day of their lives.

1 Forbidden Fats

Fallacy: Fat kills.

Much of this fallacy revolves around the role of cholesterol in heart disease. HDL ("good" cholesterol) and LDL ("bad" cholesterol) are actually lipoproteins that contain exactly the same cholesterol; HDL (high-density lipoproteins) are merely the mechanisms used to transport cholesterol from bodily tissue to the liver, thereby reducing the amount of cholesterol in the blood stream. LDL (low-density lipoproteins) deliver cholesterol to places in the body that need it. The failure to properly differentiate between these lipoproteins has led to many erroneous studies on the dangers of cholesterol and fat in our diets. Studies have shown that a high-fat diet causes an increase in overall cholesterol in the blood stream. Consequently, people have the idea that high fat means high cholesterol, which means high risk of heart disease. In reality, more nuanced studies show that a high fat intake actually causes a dramatically higher ratio of "good" cholesterol to bad. This, according to the commonly held views of scientists, should actually result in a decrease of heart disease risk—but no one will admit it. Three randomized controlled clinical trials discovered that a reduced total fat or saturated fat diet over several years results in no lowering of heart disease, stroke, or other cardiovascular disease. In other words, a high-fat diet probably has no bad impact on your health.

Did you know: Due to government guidelines and what can only be called antifat propaganda from the 1970s until now, fat consumption has been reduced by over 10 percent per person on average per year. Coincidentally (maybe) obesity rates have increased at the same time by around 10 percent. It is highly possible that a strict low-fat diet can prevent a person from feeling satiated and consequently overeat "low-fat" but high-calorie foods.

TOP 10 Weird Foods Sold by Victorian Street Vendors

by **Nene Adams**

10 Sheep's Trotters

Sheep's trotters were sold either cold or hot. These delicacies were typically bought cheap by vendors from the slaughterhouses, skinned and parboiled at their home, and then sold on the street. Customers would purchase a whole trotter, and suck the sticky meat and fat off the bones. If you were lucky, the vendor cleaned the nasty, dingy-looking stuff from between the toes of the hoof before he cooked it—or at least before you ate it.

9 Hot Eels

Eels were imported from Holland, cut into pieces, and boiled. The juices were thickened with flour and parsley, and the whole thing was seasoned with pepper and kept hot for sale. A portion of meat was served in a cup; the liquor came separately. Customers could add vinegar if they chose. A scrape of butter cost extra. A customer had to eat his snack quickly, since the vendor needed the cup returned. If you were lucky, the vendor would dip the cup in a bucket of dirty water before service. Most of the time, he didn't bother.

8 Saloop

Saloop had been popular since the 1600s. It was a hot and supposedly nutritious, heavily sweetened drink made from ground orchid roots. Toward the latter part of the 19th century, the base of the drink changed to sassafras bark flavored with milk and sugar. Regardless, saloop was considered a delicious and starchy way to start or finish the day. If you were lucky, the beverage was made with the real roots or bark, and not something like used tea leaves picked from the garbage pile.

7 Plum Duff

Basically a carbohydrate bomb, plum duff was a British-style boiled "pudding" or dessert resembling a damp dough. The "plum" part of the name comes from the raisins sprinkled throughout. It made for a somewhat gluey experience, yet it was loved by working-class children and adults more concerned with filling their bellies than having a nutritious meal. Adding a trickle of treacle (molasses) cost extra. If you were lucky, the raisins were dried fruit rather than mouse droppings.

6 Pickled Oysters and Sea Snails

Most types of shellfish could be bought for practically nothing in the Victorian era. Of course, shellfish has a distressing tendency to go bad quickly, hence the popularity of pickling to preserve the goods as long as possible. When shellfish was sold fresh, about half of the customers preferred to eat it raw and still alive as opposed to boiled. If you were lucky, the oysters, whelks, and such were relatively fresh when they went into the pickling solution.

5 Donkey's Milk

Regular cow's milk was available in summer from vendors who had the animals on the street, udders ready to deliver. They also purchased skim milk from dairies for resale, carrying pails or milk cans in yokes across their shoulders. However, some customers preferred richer, more exotic beverages such as donkey's or mule's milk. A few women believed drinking this milk—or eating curds and whey (cottage cheese)—made them appear more youthful. If you were lucky, you got actual dairy, rather than a mixture of chalk and water.

4 Bloaters

A bloater was a salted herring, cold-smoked whole: head, eyeballs, guts, and all. Hence the bloating. Vendors would impale the fish on a long fork and "toast" it over a flame to cook it before selling it to customers who consumed the whole gamy, soft, flabby thing.

If you were lucky, the fish had roe in its belly cavity. If you were really lucky, the fish fell off the fork, a stray cat stole it, and you didn't have to eat it.

3 Ginger Beer

The original ginger beer was a mildly alcoholic beverage made by boiling water with ginger and sugar, adding yeast, and flavoring it with citric acid and cloves. It was generally bottled and sold within a couple of days. Mild fermentation could be achieved in as little as 12 hours, in a pinch. The cheaper "playhouse ginger beer" was sweetened with molasses. Vendors made the drink at home, where if you were lucky, they brewed it in something other than the washtub used by their wife for boiling the baby's dirty diapers.

2 Rice Milk

Rice "milk" was made by boiling rice in skim milk. A cupful was served hot with a spoonful of sugar and a sprinkle of allspice. The dish resembled a very thin, watery rice pudding. Cheap to produce, it was often sold by female vendors from a metal basin over a charcoal fire. Once again, customers consumed the portion while standing in the street. If you were lucky, the vendor wiped off the spoon before you ate with it.

1 Blood

Though technically not a street food, I had to include this one on the list. Tuberculosis, then called consumption, was rampant at the time. It was believed that the fresh, hot blood of a slaughtered animal would build up the sick person's constitution, alleviating the disease. Consumptives would line up in the slaughterhouse with cups ready to catch the blood, which was swallowed right away. If you were lucky, the animal was dead when the collection began.

TOP 10 Animals That People Eat Alive

by **Simon Griffin**

10 Sannakji

Sannakji is a dish served in Korea and probably the most well-known item on this list because of videos that have circulated online. Usually seasoned with sesame seeds and sesame oil, the main component of *sannakji* is *nakji*, a small octopus. The tentacles are usually cut from the live octopus and brought straight out to the customer, although sometimes it is served whole.

The main "appeal" of this dish is that when chewed, the tentacles are still wriggling. But because of this, the suction cups on the tentacles are also still active, and they can become stuck in the throat of whoever's eating them.

9 Sea Urchins

Going into the sea to collect your own sea urchins and eating them right away has become a popular practice in Italy, where they call them *ricci di mare.* Since the edible part—the roe—is on the inside of the sea urchin, there is a special tool to open them up, though it can also be done with scissors.

They can be eaten with a spoon, although many people prefer to lick them out with their tongues. But given the extremely spiky nature of sea urchins, you'd want to be careful when eating them.

8 Odori Ebi

Odori ebi is a type of sashimi that contains a baby shrimp. The shrimp has its shell removed, and sometimes its head as well. These can be deep-fried and served alongside the rest of the shrimp, which is still moving its legs and antennae while being eaten. The shrimp can be dipped in the alcoholic drink sake to intoxicate it and make it easier to eat. It only dies, finally, when being chewed. *Odori ebi* is quite expensive to order in a restaurant, because to serve the shrimp alive, it must be prepared quickly and skillfully.

7 Drunken Shrimp

Drunken shrimp is similar to number eight, but with a few differences. First, it comes from China, not Japan, and is not always served live. But when it is, it is always served in a bowl of *baijiu*, a drink with about 40–60 sixty percent alcohol content.

Another main difference is the size of the portions: This recipe involves full-grown shrimp, rather than babies. Furthermore, there are usually around ten of them served, making this more of a main course, as opposed to *odori ebi*, of which many people would eat just one piece.

By far the biggest difference is that the shrimp are far more active. They jump around, trying to escape, and the consumer has to catch them and stuff them in his mouth before they get away. They can even keep moving after being swallowed—provided you haven't chewed them to death. Charming.

6 Noma Salad

Noma, based primarily in Copenhagen (although it has recently become a pop-up restaurant across the globe), has ranked as the best restaurant in the world for three years now, so it's not all that surprising to find that they have some innovative ideas.

Unfortunately, one of these ideas is their salad—their ant salad. The restaurant serves a salad crawling with ants, chilled so that they move slower, and that are supposed to taste like lemongrass. Chilled or not, the fact remains that there are ants crawling all over your lettuce leaves.

Plenty of cultures consume insects, true, but not many of these cultures charge over $300 for an insect salad.

If, for some reason, you want to try this, I'd suggest that you simply pour some sugar in the backyard. Much more cost effective.

5 Casu Marzu

Casu marzu is a traditional Sardinian cheese made from sheep's milk. Now obviously milk isn't an animal, so you must be wondering what this is eaten with. Well, the answer is, perhaps, the most disgusting one so far: maggots.

The cheese is brought to a stage that some consider decomposition. Larvae of the cheese fly (Piophila casei) are brought to the cheese to help break down its fat. They eat through the cheese, softening it, and seep a liquid known as *lagrima* (teardrop). While some people remove the maggots before consumption, many people consume the cheese maggots and all. When doing so, people are advised to cover their eyes, as the maggots can leap out in an attempt to escape.

4 Frog Sashimi

This one is relatively famous, as the video of it being made caused quite a stir last summer. For this dish, a frog is kept in the kitchen until someone orders the frog sashimi, at which point it is taken out and sliced open on a cold platter. The sashimi bits are taken off, and then the rest of the frog is simmered to make a soup.

Presumably, if you're ordering this dish, you have no qualms about watching a frog be disemboweled alive in front of you and then cooked for your culinary pleasure—but as disturbing as that would be for most people, it doesn't end there. For the dish contains, of all things, the frog's still-beating heart.

3 Ikizukuri

Also a type of sashimi, *ikizukuri* is a fish dish whose name means "prepared alive." Generally, as with lobster, there is a large tank in the restaurant where patrons can go to choose the fish they want to eat. That alone is objectionable enough for many people, but *ikizukuri* goes a lot further than lobster in the cruelty department.

When the fish is selected, the chef will gut it and serve it almost immediately. What sets it apart from other entries in this list is that the point of *ikizukuri* is for the chef to slice off a few pieces of fish, but leave the whole thing largely intact. Not only that, but the bits that are cut off are to be done in such a way that the person eating it can see the fish's heart beating and mouth moving while they eat it.

It's almost as if this is a secret conspiracy to try and guilt-trip people into becoming vegetarians.

2 Yin Yang Yu

Meaning "dead and alive fish," this is pretty similar to the last dish—with one major difference. While *ikizukuri* is gutted, chopped up, and served alive, *yin yang yu* is completely deep-fried, except for the still-attached head.

It is served with sweet and sour sauce, with the fish still completely alive and the head still moving. It is prepared extremely quickly, with care not to damage the internal organs, so that the fish can remain alive for a full 30 minutes. The reason these live dishes became so popular was so restaurants could boast about how fresh their food was. In more recent years, this dish has caused a lot of controversy, but it is still quite popular among some people.

1 Oysters

Most people who eat oysters don't even realize that they're alive at the time (to be fair, it's often difficult to tell).

Oysters are generally served live because they deteriorate much faster than most other animals when dead. When their shells are cracked open, they can survive for a significant amount of time. It is only when the flesh is actually separated from the shells that they begin to die; this is why oysters are almost always sucked directly out of their shells. So while this is much less extreme than most of the other entries in this list, it is a lot more common.

TOP 10 Strange Tales about Pizza

by **Mike Devlin**

10 Contaminants

It's one of the most popular food items in the world, so you'd think the government would keep a careful eye on the pizza trade. Except that if you ever saw a list of the contamination levels the United States Food and Drug Administration (FDA) found acceptable, you might go on a hunger strike. Tomato paste and pizza sauce can be pretty funky, with an allowance of 30 fly eggs per 100 grams, or 15 or more fly eggs and one or more maggots per

100 grams. When you consider the crust and toppings, you'll most certainly be tasting mold, mildew, insect fragments, aphids, rodent hair, and what the FDA politely calls "mammalian excreta."

9 The Moon

As mentioned in a previous list, Pizza Hut is no stranger to wild marketing stunts. In 1998, they had the idea to burn their logo into the surface of the moon with high-powered lasers. Luckily, common sense prevailed. Upon consulting experts, they learned that the necessary technology was still some years off. Moreover, for earthlings to be able to see the logo with the naked eye, it would have had to be the size of Texas. In the years since, Pizza Hut has made several deals with the cash-strapped Russian space program, including emblazoning their logo on a rocket and delivering a pizza to the international space station.

8 Nguyen Ngoc Loan

On February 1, 1968, perhaps the most enduring image of the Vietnam conflict was captured when photographer Eddie Adams snapped a shot of South Vietnamese National Police Commander Nguyen Ngoc Loan executing an unidentified Vietcong prisoner on the streets of Saigon. The photo (which would later go on to earn Adams the Pulitzer Prize in 1969) is an unflinching study on the horrors of war—the bullet from Loan's pistol can actually be seen exiting the man's skull. While the Vietnam War was hardly popular, this incident in particular helped fuel antiwar sentiments. Three months after the incident, Loan was wounded in action (he would eventually lose his right leg). Originally transported to Australia, he was so reviled there that he was moved to the U.S. Although there was talk of deporting Nguyen back to South Vietnam as a war criminal, he and his family were allowed to stay in the U.S.

After the war, he opened up a pizzeria in a Virginia suburb of Washington, D.C. He operated the restaurant, called Les Trois Continents for some 15 years, until he was identified. Business fell off, and Loan reportedly found threatening graffiti in the bathroom. He was forced out of business in 1991. Loan died of cancer on July 14, 1998, aged 67.

7 Bulletproof

In 1969, former Marine Richard Davis was delivering pizzas in Detroit when he was held up. In the ensuing shootout, he wounded two of his attackers, but he was shot twice. While recovering, Davis came up with the idea for a bulletproof vest. Bullet-resistant vests have been in use at least since the 1500s, but up until about 45 years ago, they were bulky and ineffective, composed of heavy sheets of metal. Davis sought to create a vest that could be concealed beneath clothing. He designed a vest made from nylon and called his body armor Second Chance. Davis so believed in his product that he marketed it by bringing his vests to individual police stations, putting one on, and allowing an officer to shoot him in the chest with a sidearm. By the mid 1970s, the nylon was replaced with Kevlar, a synthetic fiber originally developed for use in tires. It is estimated that bulletproof vests have saved the lives of over 2,000 police officers in the United States alone.

6 Danger

Richard Davis survived his brush with muggers because he was an armed ex-marine. Other drivers aren't nearly as fortunate. Although it might seem like an innocuous profession often performed by teenagers, delivering pizza can be extremely dangerous. Robberies and beatings occur on a weekly basis. Drivers are often lured with fake orders and addresses into places where they can be attacked. In the most extreme cases, drivers have even been raped and murdered. Worse still, the major pizza chains do not allow their drivers to carry concealed weapons. In 2004, when a Pizza Hut driver shot and killed a robber while on the job, he was fired.

5 30 Minutes or Less

Domino's Pizza got its start in the University of Michigan college town of Ann Arbor in 1960. Today, this multibillion-dollar company is controlled by the controversial Bain Capital (cofounded by former U.S. Presidential hopeful Mitt Romney). Domino's has largely stuck to more orthodox advertising strategies than its competitor Pizza Hut. In fact, the company's greatest claim to fame was their guarantee to deliver in 30 minutes or less, or the pizza would be free.

Unfortunately, the policy put them in some pretty damning legal crosshairs when their drivers got into accidents. Lawsuits alleged that the drivers were forced to drive recklessly to meet their deadlines. In 1992, Domino's paid $2.8 million to the family of an Illinois woman whose van was struck by a vehicle delivering pizza. But then in 1993, a court awarded $78,750,000 to a Missouri woman for injuries she'd received in a 1989 crash. They settled out of court for a sum believed to have been approximately $15 million, but the under-30-minute policy was scrapped.

4 The Noid

As advertising icons go, Domino's Noid was particularly unappealing—a monosyllabic gremlinlike character in a red rabbit suit meant to manifest the difficulties in delivering a pizza in the 30-minute deadline. The Noid would do anything in his power to make the driver late, including shooting the pizzas with a gun that turned them ice cold. Much like the Trix rabbit, the Noid was constantly foiled. The gimmick was popular enough to roll it into its own video games for computers and Nintendo.

The story of the Noid took a truly bizarre turn on January 30, 1989, when a deranged customer named Kenneth Lamar Noid burst into a Domino's in Atlanta, Georgia, taking a pair of employees hostage. Kenneth Noid actually believed the ads were an attack on him. The siege lasted five hours, with Noid making outlandish demands for $100,000 and a getaway car, among other things. He forced the employees to make him pizza during the ordeal. After they escaped, Noid turned himself over to police. He was charged with a laundry list of felonies, but he was found not guilty by reason of insanity.

3 Philip Workman

While binging on cocaine, Workman robbed a Wendy's. An employee triggered a silent alarm, and Workman fled when the police arrived. What happened next remains contested to this day. Workman alleged that he fled, but when the officers caught up with him, he attempted to relinquish his firearm, and it accidentally discharged when they hit him with a flashlight. The police returned fire, wounding Workman.

In the melee, Lieutenant Ronald Oliver was killed. The trial, which many regard as a sham, eventually condemned Workman to death. There was some evidence that Lt. Oliver died from friendly fire, and Workman was briefly granted a stay of execution, but a judge ruled that the evidence did not warrant a new trial.

Perhaps as some kind of last-minute act of martyrdom, Workman requested that a vegetarian pizza be delivered to any homeless person living near the prison in lieu of his last meal. His request was denied. When the story went public, there was an outpouring of support for the cause, and hundreds of pizzas were delivered to homeless shelters throughout the country.

2 OJ Simpson

In America, the day of the year when the most pizzas are sold is Superbowl Sunday. But remarkably enough, some other odd events have caused spikes and drops in pizza sales. One such phenomenon was the OJ Simpson saga; on June 17, 1994, the nation was glued to their television sets, watching as the former football hero fled from police with friend Al Cowlings in a low-speed chase. Domino's reported a huge increase in sales as the white Bronco crept down the highway.

Several months later, the pizza chain would notice another bizarre trend when sales skyrocketed in the moments leading up to the verdict in the case. According to company spokesman Tim McIntyre, things slowed down considerably a little after noon, when the decision was finally read out. McIntyre said, "We could barely believe it, but not a single pizza was ordered in the United States for five minutes between 1 o'clock and 1:05."

1 The Pizza Bomber

The case of the pizza bomber is one of the most bizarre crimes in American history. On August 28, 2003, pizza delivery man Brian Wells burst into a bank in Erie, Pennsylvania. He was armed with a shotgun and had a bomb attached to his neck. Wells requested $250,000, but he received only $8,702 and was intercepted by the police in the parking lot. From there, he proceeded to tell a weird story—that he was delivering pizza when some men forced him to put on the bomb. Unless he pulled off the robbery for them, it would explode and kill him. While negotiating with the police, and minutes before the bomb squad arrived to disarm the device, it detonated, killing Wells.

The case remained a mystery for years, but was solved in 2007, when several people were indicted for the conspiracy. It is believed that Wells was in on it the entire time, but did not know that a live bomb was going to be used. When he found out the bomb was real, his coconspirators forced him to strap it on at gunpoint. The money from the robbery was to be used to hire a hit man for prostitute Marjorie Diehl-Armstrong, who wished to kill her father, whom she believed to be wealthy. Diehl-Armstrong was sentenced to life plus 30 years, and another man involved in the plot, Kenneth Barnes, received 45 years.

The story would go on to be used as the plot point in several television shows, as well as the basis for the largely forgettable comedy *30 Minutes or Less*. In his review of the film, critic Roger Ebert said, "Moral of the story: If you occupy the demographic that this film is aimed at, Hollywood doesn't have a very high opinion of you."

TOP 10 Strange and Fascinating Fast Food Tales

by **Mike Devlin**

10 Burger King

Burger King is no stranger to weird marketing stunts, such as the dreadful 2004 Coq Roq campaign, wherein faux nu metal rockers with chicken masks on thrashed to music filled with double entendres. Their mascot—a towering, creepy king with unmoving features—was mercifully retired in 2011. But perhaps the worst idea in company history was their 2009 Facebook "Whopper Sacrifice" campaign. The premise was simple: Use the Burger King application to unfriend ten people on Facebook, and you would get a coupon for a free Whopper. Normally, there is no notification involved in unfriending someone, but in this instance, Burger King would send the friend a message informing them that their friendship was less important to you than a free sandwich. The campaign was promptly dropped, but not before people leapt at the opportunity, abandoning almost 234,000 friends in the process (that's more than 23,000 Whoppers).

9 Taco Bell

Taco Bell is perhaps best known for its Chihuahua ad campaign, which was often derided as racist. The ads, starring Gidget the Chihuahua, were stopped in 2000. Gidget didn't remain unemployed for long; she found several other roles, including a spot in *Legally Blonde 2: Red, White, and Blonde*. Taco Bell didn't fare so well—they'd stolen the Chihuahua idea from two Michigan men, Joseph Shields and Thomas Rinks. The pair pitched the idea to Taco Bell in the 1990s, but they were rejected. Shortly thereafter, the restaurant chain's new ad agency began using the concept. The men took Taco Bell to court, and in 2003, a jury awarded them $30 million. The judge promptly added on $12 million. Shields and Rinks walked away with $42 million for their troubles.

A subsidiary of Yum! Brands, Inc. (which also owns KFC and Pizza Hut), Taco Bell enjoys considerable popularity worldwide, and has locations selling its Mexican fare in several countries throughout the world. A notable exception: Mexico. They made two attempts to crack the Mexican market, in 1992 and 2007, but both times folded due to lack of patronage.

8 Wendy's

Wendy's is best known for its simple commercials starring earnest, plain-spoken founder Dave Thomas. Thomas was working as a head cook in a restaurant in Fort Wayne, Indiana, when Kentucky Fried Chicken owner Colonel Harland Sanders came calling, selling franchises. Thomas, as well as the family for he worked for, bought in. In doing so, Dave worked closely with the Colonel on marketing ideas. It was Dave Thomas who suggested the idea of buckets of chicken, which help keep the product crisp. He also suggested Sanders appear in his own commercials.

The response was phenomenal, and Dave Thomas was later able to sell his share in the restaurants back to Sanders for $1.5 million, thus giving him the capital to open Wendy's. He'd later use this advertising formula to great effect in his own restaurants, appearing in over 800 commercials.

Despite its feel-good American dream origins, Wendy's is not immune from the bizarre. In 2005, an employee named Steve LeMay and a coworker were caught robbing the safe from the Manchester, New Hampshire, store where they worked. The coworker's name? Ronald MacDonald.

7 KFC

KFC is extremely popular on Christmas Eve in Japan, with lines snaking out the door. While business thrives in America, you aren't likely to see that kind of rush the next time you stop in for a bucket of chicken. Unless you'd happened by in early May of 2009. None other than Oprah Winfrey advertised on her show that a coupon could be downloaded on her website for a free grilled chicken meal at KFC. According to a KFC press release, they received "unprecedented and overwhelming response," which is the politically correct way of saying that the campaign turned into a complete circus. Millions of coupons were printed, the website couldn't handle the traffic, and hordes of people descended on the restaurants, which quickly ran out of food. By the time KFC axed the program, an astonishing 10.5 million coupons were printed, which were eventually honored with rain checks.

6 McDonald's

Whenever the subject of the frivolity of lawsuits comes up, the 1992 McDonald's coffee case always pops into the conversation. While on its surface, it sounds ridiculous that someone should be able to sue a restaurant for burning themselves with a beverage that by its very nature is supposed to be hot, there are several less obvious elements at play. First, McDonald's served its coffee extremely hot—in excess of 180°F (your home coffeemaker will generally clock in around 140°F), and Stella Liebeck suffered horrifying third-degree burns right down to the bone. There are pictures available online, but I don't suggest you look for them unless you have a strong stomach.

Second, Liebeck did not sue McDonald's hoping to reap a fortune. Initially, the 79-year-old only wanted a settlement to cover her medical expenses, which were in excess of $10,000. McDonald's offered a mere $800.

Liebeck retained an attorney, and much legal wrangling followed. McDonald's staunchly refused to settle despite multiple attempts to mediate the case before trial. During the court hearing, it came to light that the restaurant had fielded hundreds of complaints about burns from their coffee, and had settled many claims in the past, some for as much as $500,000. This was pretty much the kiss of death for McDonald's; the jury awarded Stella Liebeck $2.86 million. The judge reduced the settlement, and both McDonald's and Liebeck appealed. Before further legal proceedings occurred, both parties settled out of court for an undisclosed sum.

5 Tim Hortons

Tim Hortons is a Canadian donut chain with some presence in the United States and some scattered stores in the United Arab Emirates and Oman. Unlike a lot of restaurants, Tim Hortons was named for a real person—professional NHL defenseman Miles Gilbert "Tim" Horton, who played for several teams, including the Toronto Maple Leafs and the Buffalo Sabres. On February 21, 1974, Horton was driving home from a hockey game in Toronto in his De Tomaso Pantera sports car. When police attempted to pull him over, he fled, reaching speeds over 100 m.p.h. When rounding a curve, he lost control of the car and hit a concrete culvert. Horton, who was not wearing a seatbelt, was killed instantly. It was discovered that his blood alcohol level was twice the legal limit. Horton's business partner promptly paid his widow $1 million for her shares in the restaurant chain. Today, the company's revenue exceeds $2.5 billion.

4 Pizza Hut

Most would agree that their neighborhood pizzeria serves far better fare than Pizza Hut, whose formulaic, prepackaged recipes do very little to stimulate the palate. But the local joint will only deliver in a five-mile radius. Pizza Hut delivered to space. In April of 2001, the company paid the Russian space program approximately $1 million to take a pizza aboard a rocket sent to resupply the international space station orbiting Earth. Rolled into the price was a photo op with cosmonaut Yuri Usachov, who offered a thumbs-up after receiving his snack. Since it is difficult to taste things in zero gravity, the vacuum-sealed salami pie they delivered was heavily spiced.

3 Arby's

Rahm Emanuel isn't exactly a household name, but he has maintained a distinguished career in American politics, serving in multiple advisory positions to Presidents Clinton and Obama, most notably as White House Chief of Staff. He is currently the mayor of Chicago. In high school, Emanuel worked part time at an Arby's restaurant, a chain known for its roast beef sandwiches. One day, while operating the meat slicer, he severely cut his right middle finger. Being a teenager, he eschewed getting stitches and decided to go for a swim in Lake Michigan. Infection set in, and doctors were forced to amputate the top of his finger.

As an interesting aside, one of Rahm's brothers is Hollywood super-agent Ari Emanuel, the person on whom the character Ari Gold is based on in the show *Entourage*.

2 Dairy Queen

Mark Cuban is one of the world's richest men, a dot-com billionaire who owns the NBA's Dallas Mavericks and is regularly featured on the NBC show *Shark Tank*, investing in startup businesses. In 2002, the outspoken Cuban lashed out at Ed Rush, the NBA's head of officiating, claiming that he wouldn't hire Rush to manage a Dairy Queen. He was fined half a million dollars by the NBA for his big mouth. The popular ice cream chain took offense at Cuban's insult, inviting him to manage a Dairy Queen for a day if he thought it was so easy. He accepted, good-naturedly serving cones and signing autographs at a store in Coppell, Texas. The event was a media circus, with lines over an hour long. Cuban had considerable trouble mastering the swirl of a soft-serve cone, telling customers, "Be patient with me, please. I'm new at this. It might not be pretty, but it works."

1 Subway

Subway is the world's largest restaurant chain; as of this writing, there are 39,517 Subways operating around the globe, in 102 countries and territories. The most exclusive location? Inside one World Trade Center. The restaurant sits inside a trailerlike "pod" that is lifted up level by level as the construction of the skyscraper progresses, from the ground all the way up to the planned 105th floor. The restaurant was opened to cater to union workers, who only have half-hour lunch breaks and thus couldn't leave the premises for food, since leaving required waiting for a hoist to bring them back to ground level.

TOP 10 Fascinating Facts about Soda

by **Mike Devlin**

10 Brands

If you were to survey the refrigerated section in your local convenience store, you might figure there are at most a few hundred different kinds of soda. However, Coca-Cola alone has some 3,500 different soft drinks in its international arsenal; if you were to try one every day, it would take nine years to sample them all (by which time there would surely be more). There are many exotic sodas to be found worldwide, particularly in Japan, which seems to have an affinity for novel beverages. Soda flavors in the land of the rising sun include yogurt, green tea, octopus, wasabi, kimchi, cheese, cucumber, and eel, among others.

9 7UP and Lithium

Lithium citrate is a mood-stabilizing drug used to treat depression and bipolar disorders, sold under trade names Litarex and Demalit. Today it requires a prescription, but years ago it was a common ingredient in many medicated beverages, including "Bib-Label Lithiated Lemon Soda." Today, we know it as 7UP (it's interesting to note that no one really knows where that name came from). It contained lithium until 1948.

8 Dr Pepper

One of the greatest culinary mysteries of all time, the 23 ingredients that make up Dr Pepper have been speculated upon for decades. One of the ugly rumors spread about the soda is that it contains prune juice. While this is not in fact one of the components, the others are up for debate, but most probably include cola, vanilla, cherry, orange, caramel, and lemon, among others. On the company's website, the question of flavor is answered rather cryptically: "Dr Pepper is a unique blend of 23 flavors. The exact formula for Dr Pepper? That's top-secret proprietary stuff."

7 Grossest Soda

Taste is extraordinarily subjective, but there is one soda that has acquired a reputation as one of the most vile in the world. Manufactured for the Italian market by the Coca-Cola Company, Beverly is described as a nonalcoholic aperitif. It is available in the United States at the World of Coca-Cola museums in Atlanta and Las Vegas, and those who have deigned to try it are almost universally shocked by its bitter, astringent flavor. YouTube abounds with amusing videos of those enjoying a taste test.

6 Passover Coke

During the weeklong Jewish festival of Passover, which celebrates the exodus from slavery in Egypt, Jews are forbidden from the consumption of leavened bread. Ashkenazic Jews (those from Eastern Europe) are also forbidden from eating corn, beans, and rice during this time (Sephardic Jews are allowed). Because Coca-Cola is sweetened with high-fructose corn syrup, at least in the U.S., it is not considered kosher. However, kosher Coke is produced in March and April to coincide with the Passover season. It is sweetened with pure cane sugar and can be identified by a yellow cap. Many non-Jews also enjoy the subtle change in flavor, and during the short period of time it is available, it is heavily stockpiled.

5 Variable-Price Coke Machines

In the late 1990s, Coca-Cola got the bright idea to install vending machines whose price was dependent on the temperature. That is, as the mercury rose, the price of a soda would become exponentially higher, raised via a computerized temperature sensor within the machine. The proposal was a public relations nightmare; people hailed it as a perfect example of price gouging and corporate greed, and Coca-Cola quickly backpedaled.

4 Magican

In 1990, as part of its "Magic Summer" promotion, Coca-Cola began its Magican program. Relying on the desire for instant gratification, they installed spring-loaded mechanisms in special cans that contained prizes, such as cash and concert tickets. To keep people from detecting the prize-winning cans without buying them, they installed chambers filled with chlorinated water. Unfortunately, the mechanisms that released the prizes weren't always reliable, and sometimes people drank the water instead. It wasn't poisonous, but it was foul, and it resulted in at least one trip to the hospital for an unsuspecting family. Coca-Cola printed advertisements warning consumers to "take a good look" at their cans before drinking, but the disastrous campaign ultimately folded after just three weeks.

3 Pepsi Points

Another short-sighted promotion took place in 1996, when Pepsi unveiled its "points" program. The premise was simple: buying Pepsi products would earn you a number of points that could be redeemed for merchandise like T-shirts and hats. When they released a commercial to unveil the concept, they included a tongue-in-cheek climax that featured a Harrier military jump jet, available for seven million points. That would be more Pepsi than you could drink in 50 lifetimes, but business student John Leonard noticed a loophole: You could purchase Pepsi points from the company for ten cents apiece. At this price, the $33.8 million Harrier jet could be had for the bargain basement price of $700,000. He gathered a group of investors and turned over a check for his jet. Pepsi refused, and the case was brought to court. In 1999, it was settled when a judge ruled that "no reasonable" person could have expected the prize.

2 Diet Soda Cocktails

Recent research conducted by Northern Kentucky University indicates that drinking cocktails made with diet soda versus regular can get you 18 percent drunker. Participants in the study were given equal amounts of vodka, some mixed with Squirt (an unfortunately named citrus soda) and some mixed with diet Squirt. After 40 minutes, those who had consumed the diet cocktails registered much higher blood alcohol concentrations. The science here is really quite simple: The body views the sugar present in regular soda as food, and thus slows the absorption of alcohol into the bloodstream. This study is especially important to women, who are more likely to order diet cocktails and whose bodies react to the potency in alcohol more than men's.

1 Nazi Fanta

When trade embargoes against Nazi Germany separated Coca-Cola Deutschland from headquarters in Atlanta, the ingredients to produce Coke in Germany quickly dissipated. German-born Max Keith, in charge of operations, developed a soda that could be made with the limited ingredients they had at their disposal. The result was "Fanta," a play on the German word *fantasie*. It was made with odds and ends: beet sugar, orange juice, leftover apple fiber, and even whey byproduct from cheese production. The recipe has since been updated (the original would probably taste something like laundry water to modern palates). It is noteworthy to add that despite governmental pressures, Keith never joined the Nazi party and remained loyal to Coca-Cola.

TOP 10 Disturbing Foods That Might Harm You

by **Christian Marlberg**

10 Hakarl

While Greenland sharks are physically dangerous to humans, including Inuit hunters who may be turned over in their kayaks, they also pose a more subtle risk—to your palate and health. Greenland sharks lack the ability to urinate, causing massive amounts of ammonia and trimethyl oxide to instead be processed through the tissues of these sharks. The ever-enterprising Greenland natives have devised a traditional meal known as *Hakarl*, which is basically aged shark flesh. Not only is the smell of the shark flesh nearly unbearable, but the consumer faces potential organ strain, intoxication, and sickness from the poisons still present in the flesh.

9 Kiviaq

Kiviaq is an extremely stomach-straining and, in fact, dangerous food that completely tops any other bird-based dish. The Icelandic heritage food known as *kiviaq* consists of the fermented (some might say decomposed) corpses of gulls and murres, small marine birds related to puffins. The birds are captured with hunting nets and sewn into aged sealskins before being buried underground for up to three years. The birds slowly marinate in seal oil in the cold arctic tundra. The resulting meal, when finally dug up, is not only somewhat repulsive, but may be deadly due to the potential for botulism. A famous research biologist's last meal was *kiviaq*.

8 African Poison Bullfrog

The African bullfrog is disturbing to consider, but it is classified as a delicacy in the African country of Namibia. However, bullfrog flesh is infused with the potent toxin known as *oshiketakata*, which may lead to kidney failure, muscle damage, and even death. Recommendations for processing the fickle frog meal include lining a pot with special wooden planks that supposedly "neutralize" the toxin. The poison levels are reputed to be lower at certain times of year, which makes the food acceptable to the brave, or maybe foolhardy, if combined with the wood planks. We can't guarantee that the consumer won't croak.

7 Stewed Asian Bat

There are some foods that simply defy the imagination, and possibly the most counterintuitive food is Asian bat soup, which contains an entire bat placed in a soup bowl after being boiled with chicken broth. The bat is dissected with a knife and fork, and the broth is then eaten with a spoon, along with the bat's innards. The dish includes hair, along with the membranes of the bat's wings. The bats are capable of carrying a number of human-transmissible diseases, and the practice is considered unsustainable by many conservation organizations.

6 Star Fruit (Carambola)

Star fruit is the most seductive and innocent-looking food on this list. While other dishes may be complex or disturbing, star fruit is simply beautiful.

The Asian plant contains five huge ridges that form perfect stars when the plant is served sliced crossways. But after eating it, you may begin to see stars in your head due to the neurotoxins contained in the "fruit." Star fruit also contains massive quantities of oxalic acid, the same poison found in rhubarb leaves. Star fruit may therefore strike down those with weak kidneys, leading to death in some notable cases.

5 Octopus Tentacles

A number of exotic Japanese and Korean restaurants, including those seeking to appeal to Western tourists, are offering sushi that is not only raw, but partially alive. Miniature octopuses are brought into the sushi bars alive and are quickly chopped in two pieces, leaving the writhing, reflex-operated tentacles to be served on a plate with soy sauce. Because the animal is an invertebrate with a partially decentralized nervous system, the tentacles continue to grasp, coil, and squeeze as they are consumed. In several unfortunate and eerie cases, death has resulted from the disembodied tentacles conspiring to block the airways of diners.

4 Gastropod Eggs

The sturgeon eggs known as caviar are a popular dish in Russia, while escargot, or snails are a popular French dish. Extreme delicacy entrepreneurs are popularizing a new dish known as "snail caviar," which consists of the raw eggs of land snails themselves. The eggs are placed on hard-boiled quail eggs, or served alongside roasted vegetables and exotic salads. Coming neatly packaged in little tins, this marvelous condiment, which carries the taste of fresh Earth has a catch: The eggs cannot be cooked, and deaths have been documented from the consumption of raw snails infected with brain parasites.

3 Serpent Burger

In southwestern U.S., rattlesnakes are not only feared, but they are raised as food by specialty suppliers. Proponents of "rattler rations" note that snake flesh is biologically similar to chicken due to the reptilian ancestry of birds. It is a surprisingly Southwestern dish that makes a trip to the desert very....authentic. In southeast Asia, eateries are actively marketing their own snake snacks in the form of actual snake burgers, made from cobras and other snakes. Because snakes are venomous, rather than poisonous, it is perfectly safe to eat snake flesh itself, as the toxin is not distributed through the tissues. After filleting and frying, you would never know you were not eating beef or chicken.

2 Inside Job

The insides of the digestive, reproductive, and nervous systems of certain animals form the basis of some grotesque but surprisingly popular dishes. A number of dishes feature the stomach linings, intestinal sections, and even testicles of cows and sheep. The "trimmings" must be carefully cleaned due to the sometimes-questionable body parts involved, but can be surprisingly flavorful to the strong-stomached diner. Lamb testicles are among the most popular and are served breaded, while bull testes come marinated in sauce. In Europe, a most distressing food known as "chitterlings" may be served. The content is nothing less than pig intestines. Sheep's heads and fish eyes also appear on "nose to tail" menus. Risks of deadly parasite infections have led to stronger regulations on the consumption of entrails and sheep heads.

1 Crow Pie

Telling someone to "eat crow" is not exactly far-fetched, or even insulting if you are in Lithuania. Crow pie is a traditional bird-based dish derived from the meat of carrion crows. The birds are hunted at a fairly young age and cooked at a high heat in oil before being served on a plate of roasted vegetables. The meat is rumored to act as an aphrodisiac, and ostensibly is used to "manage" crow numbers. Crows are a traditional component of Lithuanian food, but consumption declined sharply during Soviet occupation of the country. Crow hunters are pleased to revitalize the dish and have driven hundreds of miles in pursuit of crow flocks. Concerns have been raised over the possibility of contracting diseases from these scavengers, and crow is not considered kosher or halal for these reasons.

TOP 10 Terrifying Things That Can Hide in Your Food

by **Pauli Poisuo**

10 Teeth

If there's one thing that you'd never expect to find in your food, it's what you eat it with: teeth. Even so, biting into a meal that has teeth of its own has  been known to happen. All it really takes is one freak accident at some point in the manufacturing process. Maybe a packing line employee gets hit in the jaw by a piece of malfunctioning equipment. Maybe someone's dental hygiene is so bad that their teeth just keep falling out. Whatever the reason, the results are scary. Human teeth have been found in canned food, sausages, and ice cream. An Australian man nearly choked on a gold tooth in his Mars bar.

And the people who just found human teeth are the lucky ones. One man sued Kraft Foods in 2006 for making him physically and mentally ill. He said his symptoms started when he bit into a large rodent tooth that was in hiding in his Planter's peanuts.

9 Human Blood

Technically speaking, blood is not a particularly bad food item. Everyone who has ever ordered a rare steak is familiar with the taste. Still, the very idea of eating the blood of another human being is nauseating. Even if you forget the moral questions (eating someone's blood would technically make you a cannibal), the disease risks alone make it a very, very bad idea.

Even so, human blood in food is more common than we'd like to think. Chefs and fast-food employees spend their days using knives and cutting equipment, so cuts happen. Sometimes they don't notice the wound (or just ignore it), and spatters of blood can end up in the food. Even if they tend to the wound, it may not help. If the bandage falls off during a busy hour, the customer's food might include a latex surprise.

And sometimes things get weird beyond comprehension. Just ask the tourist who claims to have found a used tampon in her steak and spinach at the Waldorf Astoria Hotel.

8 Rotting Frogs

Eating frogs can sound unappetizing. But as any fan of classic French or Cantonese cuisine can testify, eating frogs, especially their legs, can be extremely rewarding. However, drinking frogs is a very different experience.

In 2009, a man opened a can of Diet Pepsi and took a sip. Instead of the familiar cola taste, his mouth filled with a strange liquid that tasted so awful he could not even describe it properly. When he poured away the undrinkable liquid, he found out why: A small, partially molten creature was slowly decomposing inside the can.

The Food and Drug Administration office examined the can and said that the thing inside was probably a frog or a toad. It was difficult to say because its internal organs were completely melted. Strangely, the FDA said the situation was not Pepsi's fault in any way—they inspected their bottling plant but found no association with the problem. Officially, the frog creature in a Pepsi can remains a mystery.

7 Glass Shards

In popular culture, lacing a person's meals with finely ground glass is often portrayed as an effective way to slowly kill someone. While this is not true (the intended victim would easily notice the glass, unless it was so finely ground that it would not cause lethal internal damage), eating glass is still a very bad idea that can cause serious internal injuries.

Glass has a nasty habit of finding its way into our food. Nestlé has been forced to recall a large batch of ravioli products because they had somehow been contaminated with glass shards (and in an earlier scandal, pieces of plastic). A Texas school cafeteria accidentally served beans in glass shard sauce because a badly constructed glass barrier near the food was literally chipping away.

Even small babies aren't safe from glass in their food. In 1986, Gerber was found to distribute glass-contaminated baby food. Before the situation was brought under control, toddlers across the nation accidentally consumed pieces of glass that ranged from tiny, harmless specks to lacerating shards the size of a dime.

6 Mice

Although mice generally avoid humans, they're never far away. Since our pantries and garbage provide good eating for the tiny critters, there's always an unhealthy amount of them living in every population center. Mice are literally everywhere, and sadly, that sometimes includes our food.

Deep-fried mice are a delicacy in China, but their consumption tends to be accidental in Western countries. Mice get caught in food production lines, ending up deep-fried and salted in bags of potato chips.

A less crisp, but infinitely more disgusting variation of mouse food happens when one gets caught in a bakery line. A large British food company was once fined because a customer bought a loaf of bread and found a mangled mouse baked in the crust.

5 Condoms

A condom is probably one of the most disgusting things you can find in your food, even if it's a bacon-flavored one. A customer of a California seafood restaurant experienced this the hard way when she found a rolled-up condom in her clam chowder. Despite an investigation and lawsuit, the reason for this was never discovered (although the woman suspected it was a prank by a rude waiter). It was also not certain whether the condom had been used.

A student at a Chinese university wasn't as lucky. His cafeteria meal came with a clearly used condom in it. When he tried to complain to the kitchen staff, the cafeteria chef brushed him off and claimed it was just a sausage skin.

4 Live Bullets

In 2004, a California woman literally bit the bullet. In fact, she bit two—and they both came from the same hot dog. She was eating a hot dog from a local Costco when she suddenly found herself chewing metal. At first, she thought her braces had come loose, but a closer inspection revealed a live 9mm bullet hiding inside the hot dog. This was not a good thing, considering that live bullets can sometimes explode from such impact.

And it gets worse: When she later visited a doctor for stomach pains, an X-ray revealed a second live round that she had swallowed without noticing. Luckily, doctors said she was in no danger and the bullet would just come out the usual way.

Perhaps the strangest thing about the incident is that no one knows how the bullets got there. The police investigated all the other hot dogs at the food court but found no further contaminations. Even the CEO of Costco said the incident is "regrettable, but difficult to understand."

3 Spiders

Spiders have a tendency to get almost everywhere—up to and very much including our dinner tables. In some cultures, they are actually a very welcome source of protein; when correctly prepared, spiders are said to taste quite nice. But very few people want to find an unwanted eight-legged surprise in their groceries.

Still, it's fairly common. Spiders are often found crawling inside shipments of fruit. These spiders are usually as exotic as the fruit itself, and they can often survive the trip to the grocery store. Some of these world-traveling arachnids can be quite large and even dangerous. They are also extremely good at hiding in the fruit section, especially in bunched fruit such as bananas. A person can buy a bunch of grapes and never notice the massive, heavily pregnant wolf spider hiding in it until it starts crawling around the house. A part of this is because some companies actually use spiders (usually deadly black widows) instead of pesticides to combat crop-destroying insects.

But even if you never shop for fruit, you're not safe from a nasty spider surprise. Just ask the woman who bought a can of Chef Boyardee ravioli—only to bite into a spider the size of a quarter that was stuffed inside one of the pasta pillows.

2 Razor Blades

Biting into a razor blade in the middle of your meal sounds like a scene from a bad horror movie. It's a very real danger, though: Many people have experienced this horrible situation. Razor blades are occasionally found hiding in fast-food meals. McDonald's, Burger King, and (allegedly) Chipotle have all faced situations where their customers have been served razors.

This is not because some psychopath is deliberately slipping razor blades into people's food. Some fast-food companies actually use razor blades for cleaning purposes, as they're handy for scraping difficult corners clean. These blades are not always stored properly and sometimes loose blades are left in the food preparation area. This puts them at risk of ending up in the worst possible place—a customer's meal.

1 A Tongue-Eating Louse

A Belfast man had the shock of his life when preparing his fish dinner. As he was cleaning the fish and shaking it upside down, its mouth opened. A strange, disgusting creature popped out like the tongue of the monster from *Alien*. However, the creature inside the fish was no alien. It was something even more frightening.

Cymothoa exigua (commonly known as the tongue-eating louse) is one of the worst nightmare creatures nature has to offer. It's a small but frightening parasite that crawls into the gills of a fish and devours its tongue from within. To complete its horrifying task, it then attaches itself to the stub, effectively becoming a new tongue. The fish can use the louse in the exact same way it used its real tongue. It may never realize it now has a terrifying crustacean living in its mouth. Meanwhile, the tongue-eating louse has an easy life. All it has to do is wait for the fish to eat and then grab the best bites as they enter the mouth.

Although fish companies know to look for these parasites, sometimes they slip through the control system and end up in supermarket fish counters. So next time you buy a fish, remember to check its mouth beforehand. Be careful, though: If the fish is so fresh that the parasite is still alive, it can actually bite you—just like the *Alien* monster's tongue.

CHAPTER 14

ANIMALS

TOP 10 Strange Animal Freaks of Nature

by **Ron Harlan**

10 Blood from a Stone

Tunicates are just plain weird. Although extremely primitive and almost entirely immobile, these inorganic-looking entities are, in fact, animals. They are not conventional invertebrates, either. Belonging to a subphylum of the chordates, they are actually related to vertebrates. Pyura chilensis is one of the more shockingly bizarre tunicates, and seems to disprove the popular wisdom that you cannot get "blood from a stone." The creature looks for all the world like an ancient, craggy rock, but inside it has bright, red flesh. These South American "sea tomatoes" are a popular delicacy in Chile, a large part of their limited native range.

9 Long-Horned Orb Weaver

Most orb weavers epitomize the stereotypical, ordinary garden spider. However, a small subsection in the genus Macracantha bend the outer limits of human comprehension. These tiny web builders measure less than half an inch, but instead of looking like a normal arachnid, they resemble a giant, albeit stiletto-thin, cow skull. On each side of the orb weaver's abdomen, long, decurved, and solid horns extend from a sort of rear carapace. Horns on a spider are pretty weird, but even weirder is their sheer size—each horn is up to four times the arachnid's length. The horns are not known to serve any specific purpose, but comparison with other animals suggests that the ornaments could serve as sexual symbols, or even as "badges" to show dominance.

8 Three-Wattled Bellbird

Central America is home to what can only be described as a real-life avian version of the Davy Jones character from *Pirates of the Caribbean*. While many songbirds are renowned for their beauty and sweet singing, the primitive three-wattled bellbird has a shockingly loud voice and downright creepy appearance. The robin-sized bird sports dangling, fleshy wattles growing from its facial area, where the beak joins. Wattle tissue also extends around the eyeball.

The three wattles are limp and soft to the touch and would seem to be something of an impediment to the bird. Its handsome plumage is apparently not sufficient to impress, as truly outrageous wattles, coupled with an extremely loud voice, are very attractive to female birds. Like many bizarre creatures, it is unfortunately an endangered species. The three-wattled bellbird is migratory, but unlike most bird species, which go south outside of the breeding season, this odd creature travels down from the mountains to warmer lowland regions every year.

7 African Shoebill

The monstrous and awesome shoebill is possibly the most bizarre bird on the African continent. Standing over almost five feet in height, and weighing over 15 pounds, the massive gray bird resembles a cross between a whale and a heron. While precision bills define most birds, the shoebill sports an enormously broad and shockingly massive bill, measuring up to ten inches. It looks like an oversized Dutch shoe, but with a truly wicked hook on the end. The shoebill will take on almost anything it can catch, including monitor lizards, catfish, and young crocodiles. The bird gained some notoriety after pictures circulated of a shoebill with a duck in its beak (it was presumably just moving it, though the shoebill does eat waterfowl). Most incredible is one unconfirmed report of a shoebill that ate a baby antelope.

6 California Sheephead

The clear waters off California contain lush, otherworldly forests of kelp. And in these kelp forests, wild, toothy beasts can be found lurking. The California sheephead is a freakish fish, with huge teeth more commonly expected in a mammal. In order to effectively crush shellfish, the sheephead uses enormous, almost human or doglike teeth, within immensely powerful jaws. These shell-crushing fangs are equally suited to crushing bones, should a human hand get in the way, and can deliver serious bite wounds. The giant fish also sport showy pinkish and black scales. Oddly, all sheephead are born female. Social and environmental factors determine whether an individual fish will remain female or become a male.

5 Long-Wattled Umbrellabird

This bizarre, all-black songbird is a certain jaw-dropper when spotted. The creature sports a long, feather-covered appendage dangling from its chest, which assumes a perfectly rod-shaped form. The "ludicrous" bird looks as if it were mounted on a post. The giant wattle may be expanded during courtship routines and contracted while the bird hunts lizards and collects fruits, seeds, and palm nuts. Unfortunately, this endangered bird is restricted to a tiny area of Ecuador and Columbia, and is increasingly threatened by hunting and land use changes.

4 Saiga Antelope

Mongolia's rare Saiga antelope is a bizarre animal with a truly preposterous, yet purposeful, proboscis. This novel nasal apparatus means the antelope looks at first glance to be all nose, or a real-life version of Alf. The bizarre snout is thought to warm air before it is inhaled and also filters dust from its bleak surroundings. This living relic once roamed throughout North America and much of Eurasia, instead of its limited current range in the central Asian steppes. The amazing creature is, unfortunately, critically endangered due to high levels of poaching. The Saiga Conservation Alliance is spearheading efforts to restore populations and welcomes public support.

3 Blind Mole Rat

Blind mole rats are strange Eurasian mammals that burrow through the ground, largely devoid of sight. In a truly bizarre example of recent evolutionary change, their eyes remain functional, but are covered by a layer of skin, rendering the animals nearly sightless. The covered eyes still allow the mole rats to perceive light and darkness, while the layer of skin seems to protect them from the constant dirt exposure and abrasion. Interestingly, researchers discovered notable physical differences between mole rats living in the same areas. This is thought to have stemmed from lifestyle-based segregation of specific populations.

2 Water-Holding Frog

Frogs, like most amphibians, need large amounts of water due to their porous, respiring skin. The water-holding frog is no exception, but it still manages to survive in the dry, sandy deserts of the Australian outback. How does any amphibian manage such a feat? By carrying its water with it! During dry periods, the frog burrows deep into the ground and produces a mucus-filled cocoon, incorporating shed skin, which encases its entire body. The cocoon lets the frog retain massive quantities of water, allowing it to hibernate for up to two years until the rains come again. Aboriginal Australians have learned to gently squeeze the frog and drink some of its retained water, before releasing the animal unharmed.

1 Standard-Winged Nightjar

The irrationally plumaged standard-winged nightjar is anything but standard in the typical sense of the word. In fact, this bird is named for its truly bizarre giant pair of wing feathers, which can extend over 14 inches. These giant, stalked feathers are actually longer than the bird's entire body. The strange plumage accessories fly in the face of sensible aerodynamics and are therefore molted out when they are not needed to impress females during the breeding season. The birds put on a rather spectacular group mating display and still manage to fly reasonably well despite the extra baggage. At first glance, the nightjar in flight looks like a group of three different birds.

TOP 10 Surreal and Twisted Fish

by Jonathan Wojcik

10 The Blind Waterfall-Climbing Loach

Inhabiting deep subterranean environments in Thailand, Cryptotora thamicola is a troglobite and has lost all traces of eyes and pigmentation in its pitch-black home. What makes this particular cave fish especially unique, however, is its preference for fast-moving currents and even vertical surfaces. The rough, clingy undersides of its four large fins allow it to tightly grip smooth rocks without getting swept away and even allow it to climb the rocky walls behind waterfalls.

9 The Tripod Fish

This deep-sea weirdo is one of the few known examples of a stationary, suspension-feeding fish—meaning that like corals, sponges, anemones, and many other sea creatures, it simply stands in place waiting for plankton to drift into its grasp. Three of its fins extend into long, thin poles, allowing it to prop itself up in the muck of the abyssal floor and remain there for days at a time. It moves only when necessary and uses its two front fins to help catch bits of food and sweep them into its mouth.

Since they don't need to chase their food, tripod fish are very nearly blind, and since they may not encounter one another very often, they're simultaneous hermaphrodites—meaning any chance encounter between two adults can impregnate them both.

8 The Stargazer

The Uranoscopidae, or "stargazers," are a group of stealth predators whose upturned, puglike faces allow them to hide almost their entire bulk under sand or mud until another tasty fish wanders too close. Popping open its jaws, the stargazer turns itself into a killer sinkhole, capable of swallowing fish almost its own size.

Some species of stargazer are even capable of luring prey with a long, wormlike tongue. Others possess a pair of highly venomous spurs just behind the head, and many also boast an electrical organ between the eyes, capable of paralyzing small prey and delivering a painful shock to the unwary human wader. It's like a grab bag of fish powers, all rolled into one meat-eating, underwater bear trap.

7 The Land Catfish

The rarely seen and poorly studied order Phreatobius are said to be the only fish that live exclusively out of the water, slithering around in wet leaf litter along the banks of streams. Pink, slimy, wormlike, and seemingly blind, it's possible that these creatures spend most of their time deep beneath the soil. Everything else about them is completely unknown.

6 The Tonguewhale

The Pleuronectiformes, or "flatfish," are already some of the world's oddest vertebrates. Though they are born relatively ordinary, their skulls gradually deform as they mature until both eyeballs are on the same side of the body, allowing the animal to lie flat on one side and camouflage itself like a carnivorous bathroom rug.

The tonguewhales, also called tonguefish or tongue soles, are even further specialized, having totally lost their pectoral fins and evolved a smooth, teardrop body shape. In many species, an elongated lip or snout wraps around the front of the jaws, giving the mouth the appearance of a toothed hole clear through their two-dimensional bodies. This odd arrangement assists them in trapping small, soft-bodied prey on all sides at once.

5 The Wolftrap Fish

The Thaumatichthyidae, or wolftrap anglerfish, may boast the most absurd overbites in the animal kingdom. Though the upper jaw is often several times larger than the lower one, it is also capable of folding in half lengthwise, forming a cage for the wolftrap fish's prey, and allowing it to suck a meal down its throat. In every member of Thaumatichthyidae, a bioluminescent lure even dangles directly from the roof of the mouth.

Like other deep-sea anglerfish, they have a parasitic mating ritual: The male fuses himself to the female's flesh before shedding every extraneous body part.

4 The Mudskippers

We've looked at one rare and obscure fish that slithers about on land, but the most famous amphibious fish is the mudskipper. Mudskippers are a kind of goby that spend more time crawling about on muddy shores than they do submerged—they can even move faster on land than they can swim. Their large gill chambers are capable of holding a supply of water for extended periods of time, and as long as they keep moist, they can also breathe directly through their thin skin.

Male mudskippers are highly territorial and battle one another for dominance in ridiculous displays of flailing and chomping.

3 The Whipnose Anglerfish

We already know how strange the deep-sea anglerfish can get, but members of the Gigantactinidae, or whipnose seadevils, stand out in two perplexing ways. First, their natural fishing lures grow to extraordinary lengths, sometimes more than ten times that of the animal's entire body. Stranger still, all living examples of these creatures have been observed swimming upside-down. Why? No one knows.

2 The Walking Batfish

Resembling the offspring of a toad and a chicken carcass, members of the Ogcocephalidae family are so adapted to the seafloor that their fins are structured more like legs, allowing them to walk through the sand in pursuit of bottom-dwelling prey. Yet another group related to the anglerfish, they often have a retractable lure just above the mouth, sometimes situated in a noselike protrusion.

1 The Tube-Eye

Also known as a thread-tail, Stylephorus chordatus is a rare deep-sea fish so unusual, the single species is alone in an entire taxonomic order. To put this in perspective, all the world's cats, dogs, bears, raccoons, ferrets, and their relatives belong to one order, the Carnivora. Imagine if none of those existed except for one rare species of weasel in all the world, and you have a situation much like the tube-eye's.

Despite its name, the strangest thing about this animal is probably its mouth. Except for one tiny, tubular opening, its jaws are fused together by an expandable bag of skin, functioning exactly like a set of bellows, or an accordion. By expanding the bag, it creates a powerful suction through that tiny, tubular opening to slurp up minute, planktonic crustaceans. This same maneuver also bugs out its eyeballs and twists them forward, like a set of binoculars, focusing in on its incredibly small prey.

TOP 10 Genetically Modified Animals You Can Buy

by Lisa J.

10 Designer Babies

The first batch of genetically modified babies was created in 2001. Out of the 30 babies that were born, 15 were found to have DNA from three different adults. Although having DNA from more than two sources can occur naturally (as in the cases of microchimerism and tetragametic chimerism), these 15 babies were created with a method called "cytoplasmic transfer," which had been banned by the FDA. The method was initially developed to save female eggs that had been difficult to fertilize and was showing much promise—until tracking the growth of the genetically modified babies revealed that one of the babies had been diagnosed with pervasive developmental disorder, a classification of developmental disorders that includes autism.

9 Featherless Chicken

In the name of economy and KFC-loving humans, scientists in Israel have created a prototype of a breed of featherless chickens that can save time on plucking, are more environmentally friendly, and in general significantly reduce the cost of raising and processing than traditional chickens. The scientists claim that featherless chickens are extremely safe because they are created by breeding a regular broiler chicken with a Naked Neck.

Despite the number of benefits featherless chickens will provide, there are some serious drawbacks to consider. Mother Nature wouldn't give chickens feathers if she thought they were useless. The feathers on the chicken are there to protect them from parasites, harsh weather conditions, and overzealous cocks that can hurt the hen's skin when mating.

8 Hypoallergenic Pets

What can you do when you are a cat or dog lover but are extremely allergic to them? I guess you could accept your less-than-perfect immune system and settle with having a goldfish—or you could purchase a hypoallergenic pet. A company called Lifestyle Pets claims that they are able to breed hypoallergenic pets by selecting cats and dogs that have "naturally occurring genetic divergences" for breeding. This group of cats and dogs doesn't produce the types of pet allergens (a total of four in cats and six in dogs) responsible for allergic reactions in humans. But with prices starting at $6,950, you might find you prefer owning a goldfish anyway.

It's interesting to note that before Lifestyle Pets found the proper pets to breed, they actually turned to gene modification to produce their first batch of hypoallergenic animals. The scientists isolated the protein responsible for producing the allergens in cats and destroyed it with a method called "gene silencing." As the name suggests, it can be a very torturous experience for the animal—and perhaps an unjust one, considering the pet owner could just vacuum more often and maybe take some antihistamines now and again.

7 Mostly Male Tilapia

Tilapia have been genetically modified to drastically reduce the time it takes for the fish to reach maturity, to make them larger, and to help them survive with less food. That's all standard stuff for genetically modified animals, but there's one tweak that's largely unique to their species: Tilapia farmers want their fish to be primarily male.

The reason has to do with their reproduction. Female tilapia protect their eggs through a tactic called "mouthbrooding" that involves holding the eggs in their mouth for an extended period of time. To avoid swallowing its own eggs, the female tilapias will not consume anything during this period, which obviously negatively impacts their size. For this reason, tilapia farmers prefer males.

6 Glittering Gold Seahorses

Forget about gold-encrusted phones, gold-sprinkled bacon, or gold-plated cars: If you really have the cash to throw around, you can now buy yourself a glittery gold seahorse.

These creatures are created by Vietnamese scientists and are the first ever genetically modified animal from Vietnam. Gold dust was mixed with jellyfish proteins, then inserted into seahorse's eggs by using the "gene shooting method," which has incredible potential uses. With more research and trials, gene shooting can potentially treat incurable human diseases, like diabetes, by replacing problematic DNA in the patient's body.

5 Pharmaceutical Camels

Dubai scientists believe that the best way to cure genetic diseases is by modifying animals to produce curative proteins in their milk. But not just any animals—so far, the experiments have focused on camels. Why camels? Because they're cheap: They are disease-resistant, able to adapt to many climates, easily maintained, and have an efficient food-conversion ratio.

4 Sudden-Death Mosquitoes

Each year, one million deaths are caused by malaria, and another 300 million people are infected—so it stands to reason that scientists should  develop ways to end the fight against this disease. With the inspiration of fighting fire with fire, scientists have come up with malaria-fighting mosquitoes. These types of mosquitoes have been genetically modified to develop resistance against the plasmodium parasite—making it near impossible to infect the host mosquito. But past experiences have shown that plasmodium parasites are able to quickly evolve and develop an immunity to anything that threatens to destroy them. So would it be better if scientists just killed all mosquitoes?

Funny you should mention that: A team of scientists have banded together to create a type of mosquito that is supposed to pass on a "sudden death" gene to their offspring, which will cause those baby mosquitoes to die of old age before they reach sexual maturity. However, the devastating ecological effect must be taken into consideration; if mosquitoes were eradicated, organisms like bats, which depend on mosquitoes for food, would quickly face extinction as well.

3 Super Cows

Herman the Bull, the first genetically modified bovine, was created in 1990 to humanize his calves' milk—but we've come a long way since him. We now have cows that are less horny and resistant to mad cow disease and udder infections. We can even determine their sex or turn out a Belgian Blue.

Although the Belgian Blue was not created through genetic modifications, you can be forgiven for thinking otherwise. The Belgian Blue is a breed that has a defective myostatin gene (the gene responsible for muscle inhibition) that results in double muscling. Belgian Blues are said to have more lean meat and reduced fat content, which leads to significantly more health risks (and inbreeding) than other breeds and puts a premium price on these steaks.

2 Popeye Pigs

Bacon generally has a bad reputation in the health food community. But now might be the time for those health fanatics to take back their own words: Scientists in Japan have genetically modified pigs that are both meat and vegetable!

Dubbed "Popeye Pigs," these pigs have been inserted with a spinach gene that converts saturated fat into unsaturated fat (linoleic acid). Although the pigs have been cleared of any health complications, the announcement was met with public outcry, with many people wondering why shoppers aren't happy eating vegetables instead of trying to mutate pigs into something they're not.

1 Glow-in-the-Dark Cats, Sheep, and Worms

It seems like once the scientists figured out how to make glow-in-the-dark animals, they wasted no time in making everything within reach into a Halloween decoration. Although the cool factor is probably enough to start someone experimenting (one rabbit was created solely for art's sake), there are actually other, nobler reasons for these strange-looking creatures.

For example, cats injected with the glow-in-the-dark gene are more resistant to feline HIV, which affects 500 million cats around the world. Scientists have also injected fish with glow-in-the-dark genes in order to track their migration. If you couldn't care less about cats or the environment (what kind of monster are you?), then perhaps knowing that scientists are also using glow-in-the-dark animals to learn more about debilitating diseases, such as Parkinson's and Alzheimer's, will change your mind.

With all these noble causes, there will always be the odd one out, and in this case, it's the glowing silkworm. Some were infused with glow power by Japanese scientists in order to create exotic silk for expensive dresses.

TOP 10 Truly Terrible Species Invasions

by **Alexandre Thompson**

10 Crown-of-Thorns Starfish

Resembling an alien invader, the crown-of-thorns starfish presents as the echinoderm of nightmares. Growing over 13 inches in diameter and pos-

sessing up to 21 arms, the animal is covered in razor-sharp spines that protect it from most predators as it feeds on coral polyps. Unlike introduced invaders, the starfish has become a problem in its native range due to environmental changes. With a voracious appetite and rapid rate of reproduction, each starfish in a "herd" may consume up to 64 square feet of coral reefs per year, destroying massive reef sections. Scientists believe the outbreaks stem from human-induced changes in the ocean ecosystem, primarily increases in nutrient pollution. As a result, population control programs to inject the starfish with lethal toxins have been implemented in some areas.

9 European Starling

The European starling was established on the North American continent by American nostalgic and Shakespeare devotee Eugene Schieffelin, a man with a self-styled mission to introduce every bird mentioned in the works of Shakespeare to North America. Schieffelin's 60 birds were released in Central Park and proceeded to take over the continent, from Alaska to Central America. The birds invaded cities and neighborhoods, destroyed crops, and were responsible for massive declines and local extinctions of many treasured native songbirds, including woodpeckers, bluebirds, and swallows. Swarms of starlings threaten aircraft, and 62 people died when an American airliner sucked birds into its engine. Despite massive control programs, the European starling population currently sits at around 150 million birds in North America.

8 Giant Canada Goose

Although Canada has no official national bird, the vast majority of wildlife admirers would name the Canada goose as the country's most representative avian species. However, Canada is large enough to support several different subspecies of Canada goose, with somewhat different ways of life. In an avian equivalent to a civil, rather than foreign invasion, resident Canada geese subspecies from Canada's interior regions are damaging estuaries along the Georgia Basin, a globally significant stopover for thousands of migratory birds and a core salmon habitat that in turn supports humans and endangered orca populations.

Former federal wildlife scientist Neil K. Dawe has conducted field studies on a series of estuaries and published findings that suggested the geese are destroying the habitat and causing the food chain to crumble.

7 Burmese Python

Many invasive species are rather small, but the Burmese python is an enormous and potentially deadly giant. First introduced to the Florida Everglades, a world-famous wetland region, these monster constrictors are among the largest snakes on the planet, growing to lengths over 16 feet and weighing up to 200 pounds. The snakes are believed to number in the thousands in this habitat far from their original range in southern Asia. The jaws contain powerful, razor-sharp teeth. The giant pythons threaten to devastate the wetlands as they devour native species with their massive strength, even preying on the usually invulnerable American alligators. The snakes have been flagged as a priority for removal by state wildlife management authorities, but control efforts have been rather ineffective to date.

6 Cane Toad

The cane toad is living proof that introducing a second species to control an existing invader may lead to an even worse disaster. Originally native to Central and South America, the huge, toxic amphibian (which can weigh nearly four-and-a-half pounds and grow up to nine inches in length) was released in the early 20th century to control sugar cane beetles on various tropical island plantations. Instead, the toads spread through a wide range of habitats, pushing native fauna into decline, including predatory lizards, marsupial mammals, and songbirds, and even the fierce, man-eating saltwater crocodile may have its nests threatened by cane toads.

Like many invasive species, cane toad populations remain artificially high in their new environment due to the absence of predators adapted to feeding on them and tolerating their defensive toxins. Proposals to control cane toads with a virus were met with concern that this would perpetuate a chain reaction by harming native species. In a strange twist, the toad's natural toxin is being used to lure tadpoles for extermination.

5 Brown Tree Snake

When a predator is introduced to an island, native species are ill-equipped to handle a threat they never evolved to resist, while an absence of suitable predators sparks a population explosion (an effect amplified in the restricted space). When the brown tree snake arrived on the island of Guam after World War II, likely as a stowaway in a ship's cargo hold, the reptile triggered what may have been the single largest ecological catastrophe attributable to one introduced species. The mildly venomous snakes proceeded to wipe out most of the native forest-dwelling vertebrate animals and were responsible for painful bites and power outages when they invaded human settlements. Airdropping of dead mice laced with drugs has been used to control the reptiles, which have grown up to ten feet long due to the unnaturally large food supply.

4 Oceanic Rat and Mouse Plague

Ships do not only carry humans, but they often carry some of man's greatest enemies: the Norway rat and the house mouse. The invasive, sometimes disease-carrying rodents also deliver a death sentence for entire populations of seabirds when they disembark at island ports, where they subsequently devour eggs, young, and even adult petrels, auklets, and other waterbirds that rely on nesting grounds free of terrestrial predators. Worldwide, the presence of invasive rats is contributing to a global seabird extinction crisis that has seen predation rates rise to extremes of up to 25,000 chicks per year in the case of the endangered Henderson petrel. Equally dangerous are the invasive house mice, threatening species such as the critically endangered Tristan albatross, and even eating chicks alive.

3 Worldwide Feral Cat Invasion

Cats may be man's second-best friend, but they have also proven themselves a scourge of invasive potential as they stalk through foreign environments and decimate the native fauna. With man's direct and indirect assistance, feral cats have caused the deaths of millions of continental songbirds ill-equipped to handle the stealthy attacks of the burgeoning predators. Impacts to island birds are especially catastrophic. In an unprecedented occurrence, one individual cat is believed to have caused the extinction of an entire species of New Zealand bird, the Stephens Island wren. Numerous islands and continents have experienced serious declines in populations of nesting seabirds and native mammals following cat infestations. However, there is a flip side. Some scientists believe that cats may actually save some individuals by exerting top-down control on smaller predators such as rats.

2 Crab-Eating Macaque Monkey

Humans are often flagged by concerned conservationists as a primary invasive species on the planet, but we seldom imagine a monkey as an invasive species. However, the crab-eating macaque actually made the International Union for Conservation of Nature's 100 Worst Invasive Species list. Crab-eating macaques are prolific primates that have proven capable of invading a range of island environments following human introduction.

Like many land-based invaders, the intelligent primates threaten globally significant tropical bird breeding sites and are believed by some to be responsible for pushing endangered bird species toward extinction. Macaques may behave aggressively towards humans. The monkeys carry a potentially fatal endemic strain of the herpes virus that also infects humans. Symptoms resemble herpes simplex, but brain damage and death may follow without proper treatment.

1 Brown-Headed Cowbird Invasion

Terrestrial animal invasions may also result where human-induced changes in land use provide a species with increased opportunities to prey on its vic-

tims or, in the case of the brown-headed cowbird, to parasitize its nests. Brown-headed cowbirds originally evolved on the plains of North America, where they followed the buffalo to pick up disturbed insects. Buffalo chasing prevented the birds from building a nest and raising young. A strategy evolved where the eggs would be placed in another bird's nest for them to incubate as the cowbirds moved on. In the evolutionary arms race, many species developed methods of removing or failing to incubate the planted eggs.

However, growing fragmentation of forests into small patches allowed cowbirds to spread across thousands of square miles of woodland territory, where they contributed to the decline of numerous forest-dwelling songbirds who were not prepared to remove the eggs, resulting in the starvation of their own (true) young. In order to compensate for cowbird invasions, conservationists sometimes shoot this "native invasive" in songbird protection programs. Cowbirds even succeeded in driving the rare Kirtland's warbler to the highest levels of endangerment.

TOP 10 Sadistic Killers
of the Natural World

by **Victor Evans**

10 The Praying Mantis

The mantis is famous because the female often eats the male during intercourse, the latter being easily overpowered by his mate but hardwired to proceed with the mating process. The sadistic part is that mantises do not bother to kill their prey before eating them: As soon as the female embraces her hapless lover, she begins to consume him alive. Although we tend to be less sympathetic toward invertebrates, the brutality of mantis eating habits is noteworthy, and the creature is viewed as a remorseless killer by many cultures around the world.

9 The Photuris Firefly

The male mantis may get eaten during the mating process, but at least he passes on his genes in the process. Another femme fatale of the insect kingdom employs a more cunning approach to get a meal, and this time the male loses it all: its life and the chance to procreate. The Photuris firefly imitates the light signals of females belonging to other firefly species in order to lure the lustful males toward her. Before he has a chance to realize his mistake, the male is devoured.

8 Grass Snakes

Grass snakes are considered the most harmless type of snake, even though many humans still fear them. Only venomous and large constrictor snakes pose a danger to humans. Nevertheless, when it comes to killing methods, venomous snakes and constrictors are quite humane when subduing their prey. On the other hand, grass snakes kill their victims in a particularly cruel manner: swallowing it alive. While the frogs, mice, lizards, and insects that make up the diet of these species are spared the horrible fate of being dismembered, they slowly suffocate inside the snake.

7 The Black-Footed Ferret

The members of the Mustelidae family are notorious for their ferocity, often managing to bring down animals several times their size. The black-footed ferret is no exception— just look at the way it kills its favorite prey, prairie dogs. The ferret sneaks into the prairie dogs' mazelike den during the night and uses its paw to hit them in the head. The strike wakes up the prairie dog, which raises its head in surprise and exposes its vulnerable throat to the assassin. Although the victim dies a quick death, it is ambushed in its sleep in the "safety" of its own home.

6 The Sea Lamprey

Leeches are disgusting creatures; no one's arguing that. Now, imagine a three-foot-long leech that feeds on the blood of larger prey. Congratulations, you've imagined the sea lamprey, a primitive vertebrate that resembles an enormous leech. The sea lamprey is considered a pest in the Great Lakes of North America, because it often kills the fish it attaches itself to. The reason the lamprey is so nightmarish a killer is that its victims have no limbs to fight it off and must wait for their attacker to gorge itself on their blood.

5 The Candiru

The candiru is a fish that has swum into the urethras of people who have urinated while swimming. Such cases are, of course, accidents, as the fish can easily mistake the human urethra for the gills of the fish it preys upon. The candiru inserts itself into the gills of Amazonian fish and sucks their blood. In humans, this would be like a worm swimming directly into your lungs and sucking your blood until you die.

4 Komodo Dragons

The Komodo dragon is known as one of the largest and most dangerous lizards. Their mouths are full of a toxic mixture of bacteria that causes gangrene in the wounds of their prey. Venom acts quickly, whereas the gangrene inflicted by the Komodo dragon's saliva means prolonged pain and agony for the animal targeted by the reptile. Many people believe this means that they have no venom, but this is untrue. A recent scientific study discovered that Komodo dragons have venom as potent as the most venomous snake in the world.

A Komodo bite is a double whammy of poison and infection that is very difficult to survive.

3 Carnivorous Plants

Speaking of prolonged agony, carnivorous plants are experts in that department. The hapless insects that are unfortunate enough to fall prey to these rather beautiful organisms are digested alive for several hours of pure agony. Pitcher plants trap their prey in vessels that have slippery edges. The insect struggles in vain to climb out of the plant, inevitably falling into the digestive soup found at the bottom of the pitcher. Venus fly traps immobilize their prey using a vicelike trap that doesn't kill it, and then the digestion begins. Sundews employ a flypaper-catching method. Nevertheless, all the species dissolve their pray alive, which is far from a pleasant way to go.

2 Parasitic Wasps

Parasitic wasps are so horrifying and terrible that Charles Darwin used them as an argument against the existence of a benevolent God. The wasps use a variety of host organisms, such as spiders, caterpillars, or the larvae of other insects. The wasp stings its prey and lays its eggs in it. After the eggs hatch, the wasp larvae slowly consume the victim from inside out, leading to a slow, painful death.

1 Mind-Control Worms

The number one on this list goes to parasites that manage to rewire their host's behavior to help them survive—which, of course, means that the hosts must commit suicide in order to ensure the parasite's survival and reproduction.

Dicrocoelium dendriticum is a tiny fluke that, in one stage of its life cycle, can be found in the bodies of certain species of ant. The infected ants are controlled by the parasite, and during the night, they leave the anthill, climb up grass straws, and simply wait. This leads to them getting eaten accidentally by sheep and other herbivores, inside which the parasite can continue its life cycle. Strangely enough, the ant returns to the colony during the day and proceeds with its usual activities.

Horsehair worms enter other insects and make them drown themselves once the worm gets the urge to reproduce, which can only happen in water. The fascinating ability to control the mind of the host seems ripped from a science-fiction movie.

TOP 10 Bizarre Animal Facts

by **Mike Devlin**

10 Armadillo Leprosy

Leprosy is a horrible, disfiguring disease largely confined to more ancient times. It is extremely rare in the United States, with just 150–250 yearly cases reported, mostly among those who have traveled to third-world countries. But there is another bizarre carrier for leprosy: the armadillo. The elusive, armored creature is native to the American South, where it is most likely to be seen as roadkill. But even in this age of fast food and frozen pizza, some people still eat armadillos, mostly in Louisiana and Texas. They're taking their lives in their hands. While leprosy is treatable if caught early, often the damage is done before symptoms manifest. Humans and armadillos are the only two animals in the world known to have the disease.

9 Crocodile Plane Crash

Crocodiles are some of the most fearsome creatures on the planet, responsible for many human deaths throughout the world. They are even formidable enough to feast on adult lions who wander too close to the water's edge. But few could ever imagine such a beast terrorizing them while flying in a plane thousands of feet from the Earth's surface. Unfortunately, that is exactly what happened in 2010 on a flight in the Democratic Republic of the Congo.

The small passenger plane was flying its customary route between the capital city of Kinsasha and the Bandundu airport when the crocodile, which was being smuggled inside a passenger's bag, broke loose. The stewardess fled toward the safety of the cockpit, with the passengers in tow. The commotion caused a catastrophic load imbalance on the plane that the pilots were unable to correct. The aircraft crashed into a house, killing the crew and 19 passengers. The crocodile survived. It was killed later with a machete blow to the head.

8 China Owns Pandas

There are few creatures on the planet as cute as the giant panda. But you may have noticed that your local zoo doesn't have any, and for good reason. The critically endangered panda is native only to a tiny section of China. They do not breed well in captivity, and there are only a couple hundred in zoos, with another 1,500–3,000 potentially living in the wild. All of the pandas in the world currently belong to China. Years ago, the country exercised what was called "panda diplomacy," giving pandas as gifts to powerful allies such as the United States and Great Britain as a sign of good faith. Since 1984, however, the Chinese government will only lease the animals, at a cost of up to $1 million a year. This fee, along with the enormous cost of maintaining the panda's diet (it

costs about five times more to feed a panda than it does an elephant) make it almost impossible for all but the largest and most profitable zoos to keep them.

7 Robot Camel Racing

Although it lacks some of the high-speed excitement found at the Kentucky Derby, camel racing has been popular in the Middle East for hundreds of years. In the past, jockeys were typically children (some barely older than toddlers), whose light weight allowed the camels to run faster. Today, robot jockeys are taking over. The robots are remote controlled; in one arm, they hold a whip, and the other arm controls the reins. Unfortunately, it has been reported that some racers use more devious methods to spur on their camels, such as electric shocks.

6 Bloodthirsty Deer

The Isle of Rum, off the west coast of Scotland, is home to only about 20 people. And some bloodthirsty deer. The diet of the Scottish Red Deer is the stuff of nightmares; they dine on the heads and limbs of baby seabirds. For some time, it was a mystery what was mutilating the Manx shearwater chicks of Rum, until the deer were observed chewing on them. It is believed this chilling adaptation has been adopted by the deer to make up for a mineral deficiency in their diet, and the bones of the birds likely give them some desperately needed calcium. The phenomenon remains under investigation.

5 Sea Otter Rape

The sea otter is another adorable creature, known to bob on its back in the ocean, clutching the hands of family members to keep them from floating away. They prey primarily on shellfish, using rocks to break them open. But like many animals, the sea otter has a dark side. The males have been known to confront baby harbor seals and attack them—biting into their faces, drowning them, and raping the bodies. Indeed, the otter mating ritual is among the most brutal in the animal kingdom, with many females losing their lives each year.

4 Grolar Bears

Global warming is a very real concern, with some environmentalists pointing toward some obviously imminent ecological disasters. Some effects are more unpredictable, such as the recent appearance of "grolar bears" in the wild. In years past, the climate kept polar bears and brown bears somewhat separated; the polar bears kept far north, where they could hunt for seals from ice floes, while brown bears remained farther south. But as winters have become markedly shorter and less cold, the polar bears have been forced farther and farther from their original habitat in the pursuit of food. This has caused them to come into contact with brown bears and actually mate. Scientists have asserted that these aren't "chance encounters," as both varieties of bear have an extended courtship ritual. In 2006, the first known wild grolar bear was shot in the Canadian Arctic. It is very difficult to determine how many such beasts might exist, but the continuing trend toward rising temperatures indicates many more will soon be born.

3 Michael Vick's Dogs

In 2007, NFL quarterback Michael Vick's Bad Newz Kennels were raided, and dozens of pit bull terrier fighting dogs were seized. Evidence of incredible cruelty too depressing to recount was found on the scene. Both PETA and the Humane Society campaigned to have the dogs put to sleep. A public outpouring of support saved them, and a curious thing happened: When the killer Vick dogs were approached, most of them were found to be incredibly friendly. As their breed standard describes, fighting dogs love people. Of the 51 dogs rescued from Vick's kennel, only one was destroyed for being too aggressive. Several are kept at sanctuaries or with experienced handlers to work through behavior issues, mostly fear due to minimal socialization. But then there are the success stories: Six have earned Canine Good Citizen Awards, and some are even therapy dogs that visit cancer patients and help children practice their reading skills. Sadly enough, once Vick's probation expired, he was able to get another dog.

2 Snapping Turtles

India's Ganges River is sacred to those of the Hindu faith, with worshippers often bathing in its purifying waters. The problem is the Ganges is actually one of the most foul and disgusting rivers in the world. In addition to industrial pollutants, it is used to dump human corpses as somewhat of a portal to heaven. Although the bodies are supposed to be burned, often the fami-

lies do not have the means to properly cremate their loved ones, and partially burned carcasses are a common sight along the river's banks. Each year, thousands of carnivorous turtles are released in the Ganges to help combat the problem. The turtles are born in captivity, and for their first year, they are fed a diet of nothing but dead flesh. This keeps them from attacking live bathers and only going after the bodies. It is estimated that a full-grown turtle eats about a pound of meat a day.

1 Rats of Tehran

Nearly every big city in the world has its issue with rats, but the monsters that run the streets of Tehran are another thing entirely. The city is under siege from enormous sewer rats, some of which weigh over ten pounds. According to city council environment adviser Ismail Kahram, the rats are the result of a genetic mutation stemming from exposure to radiation. He says, "They are now bigger and look different. These are changes that normally take millions of years of evolution. They have jumped from 60 grams to five kilos, and cats are now smaller than them," Some experts disagree, but no concise explanation has been given to just where the monster rats came from. The Iranian government has grown so desperate for a solution that they have employed snipers to roam the streets at night, picking off the giant vermin.

TOP 10 Amazing and Creepy Corpse Fauna

by Jonathan Wojcik

10 Dermestid Beetles

When other scavengers are done picking soft tissues from a carcass, all that's eventually left are the "dry" remains: the bones, hair, and leathery scraps of skin. These materials are edible to both larval and adult dermestid beetles, found worldwide, and sometimes even in our homes where they consume organic fibers in clothing, carpeting, and furniture. Museums and taxidermists even employ thousands of these creatures at a time to clean skeletons for display but must be careful to retrieve them before the bone itself gets nibbled on.

9 Burying Beetles

Burying beetles, or Nicrophoridae, are one of the two main groups of carrion beetle. These Halloween-colored creatures usually mate for life atop the body of a small, dead bird or rodent, then spend all night working the entire corpse into a small ball and burying it underground. The devoted mother is buried alive with the body, spending the rest of her days chewing up the rotten flesh for her larvae, while the male, if he didn't join her, stays on guard above ground.

8 Vulture Bees

Related to ants and wasps, bees come in a massive variety of forms through-out the world, but all feed at least partially on plant matter (especially nectar and pollen) with the exception of three bizarre species in the genus Trigona. These stingless social bees raise their larvae almost exclusively on decaying meat, which they chew and regurgitate into a liquid form the same way other bees make honey, filling their egg chambers with a thick, sticky slurry of rotten flesh.

7 Striped Hyena

Most hyenas are primarily hunters, but the species Hyaena hyaena fits their scavenging reputation to a T. Feeding almost entirely off the kills of other predators—including their fellow hyenas—they are even specially adapted to easily digest whole bones, even consuming so much bone that it turns their droppings chalky and white.

6 Marabou Stork

Storks are usually wetland predators, feeding primarily on small fish and frogs. Leptoptilos crumeniferus, however, also known as the "undertaker bird," takes a cue from vultures and feeds frequently on decaying meat, even sporting a completely bald head for reaching deep into wet, festering body cavities. Due to these unusual dietary habits, it's just as at home in dry, arid plains as it is in muddy marshland and is possibly the largest scavenging bird in the world.

5 King Vulture

Living up to its title, Sarcoramphus papa is one of the largest of all true vul-tures, by far the most extravagantly colored, and dominates over all carrion birds but the even larger Andean condor. Though it usually lives alone, it will follow flocks of other, smaller vulture species to more easily locate food, and these vultures in turn often depend upon the "king's" stronger beak to make the first tear in a large, tough carcass. Preferring to eat the skin, cartilage, and other tough tissues, it leaves much of the meat and entrails to the lesser subjects.

4 Carrion Beetle Mites

Many species of mite live in symbiosis with the carrion beetles we've already talked about, using the beetles as transportation from one corpse to the next. It's not the putrid meat these arachnids are after, but rather the eggs and larvae of flies. It's one of the most ghoulish mutual partnerships in the insect world; the mites devour the maggots, and the beetle's larvae get all that decayed flesh to themselves.

3 Hagfish

In the ocean, the dead often become a free-for-all buffet, scavenged by sharks, crabs, starfish, worms, and innumerable other opportunists. The bizarre hagfishes, however, exhibit special adaptations for deep-sea scavenging. Survivors of an ancient, jawless vertebrate lineage, they wield a rasping, tooth-covered plate to shave flesh into their throats, and stranger still, are able to absorb nutrients directly through their skin as they writhe through decaying innards, similar to the feeding mechanism of a tapeworm. They are particularly renowned for the thick, sticky slime they can secrete in copious amounts, which assists them in slipping through the orifices of the dead and suffocates any sea creature foolish enough to attack them. These maggots of the water are usually the dominant scavengers at whale carcasses, swarming over the sunken giants until only the bones remain.

2 Bone Worms

Hagfish may be the sea's leading connoisseurs of rotten meat, but there's still a lot of nutrients locked deep within a skeleton once the flesh-eaters have had their fill. This is the domain of the Osedax worms, also affectionately referred to by some researchers as "zombie worms" and "snot flowers." More plantlike than wormlike in anatomical structure, these otherworldly creatures drill into bare bones with a network of corrosive "roots," breathe through pink, flowerlike gills, and rely on symbiotic bacteria to metabolize the lipids in bone tissue. At least, the females do, anyhow. Male Osedax are virtually microscopic, and live inside the females by the hundreds, continuously fertilizing thousands of tiny eggs. Like fungal spores, these eggs are released to drift in the water, hatching only when they come into contact with a suitable skeleton.

1 Maggots

Flies are notorious for carrying disease, and their larvae are regarded as truly repulsive by much of the human race, but our world would overall be far filthier without them.

Every aspect of a maggot's biology is exactly what the little creatures need to strip away dead tissues with maximum possible speed and efficiency; their tapered, limbless bodies, ringed with bands of rough pustules, function as the perfect organic drill as they undulate and twist into their food source. A set of hooks, like the tusks of a walrus, give them a firm grip as they feed, regurgitating digestive enzymes and slurping the remains into their soft, jawless throats. Thanks to a pair of breathing pores near their anus, they can bury themselves in their food and eat continuously without coming up for air, "snorkeling" through their butts.

All this may sound nauseating to our tastes, but these garbage men of the insect world are the most ubiquitous, efficient, and ecologically important of all scavengers on the Earth's surface, eliminating more animal waste than virtually all other processes combined. If they looked or moved too differently, maggots would not be the perfect recycling system that they are. They're Mother Nature's all-purpose deep-cleaning solvent, even getting those tricky squirrel stains out of asphalt.

Next time you see these little guys inching around your trash, just be glad we're not the ones who were given such a dirty job, and consider that maybe, just maybe, animals like maggots, snot flowers, and bone beetles can have as much beauty and character as any fluffy grass-eater or majestic hunter.

TOP 10 Strangest Defense Mechanisms in Nature

by **Caleb Compton**

10 Flying Fish

There are many creatures with the power of flight, but this feature is generally not attributed to fish. Flying fish are able to jump out of the water and fly or glide for long distances. This is used as a defense mechanism to escape from predators.

The flying fish has a streamlined, torpedo-shaped body that helps it gain enough energy to break through the surface of the water. To get out of the water, the fish swims at speeds of up to 37 miles per hour. The fish's pectoral fins have evolved into large wings that allow it to become airborne. Once out of the water, it can fly for up to 656 feet (200 meters), using its tail fin as a sort of propeller. In 2008 in Japan, a flying fish was observed gliding for a record 45 seconds.

9 Hagfish

The hagfish is an ancient organism that has existed for 300 million years and is the only animal with a skull and no vertebrae. When disturbed, it expels a disgusting, slimy substance at predators. As it mixes with water, the slime expands and there can be up to five gallons produced. This creates a distraction as the attacker tries to get out of the mess. It also creates a knot in the fish's body and this, along with the slime, allows the hagfish to escape the predator's clutches. The slime can choke fish as it accumulates in the gills. The tiny threads that make up the hagfish's slime are ten times stronger than nylon; this is of great interest to scientists, who believe it can be used to make clothes.

8 Potato Beetle

The potato beetle has developed a strange way to avoid being eaten by larger insects. The larvae cover themselves in their own feces. The dung is poisonous and the foul smell wards off predators.

The beetle eats from nightshade plants and it reuses the toxic substances produced by the plants in its feces. This defense is called a fecal shield. Feces is guided onto the beetles' backs through a series of muscle contractions in the abdomen, and it forms the shield over time.

7 Boxer Crab

When it detects a significant threat, the boxer crab will pack a powerful punch using sea anemones attached to its claws. They look like pom-poms, but they can be deadly to other sea creatures and they have a strong sting. When disturbed, the crab waves his claws around to ward off danger.

There is a mutual agreement between the two organisms, as they both benefit from the arrangement. The boxer crab gains an awesome defense mechanism that would put most other animals to shame, and the anemone becomes mobile and is able to obtain more food. The crab also uses sponges and corals in place of the anemone.

6 Eurasian Roller

Similar to the potato beetle, the Eurasian roller's offspring will cover themselves in their own body fluid to avoid becoming food for a hungry animal. This time however, it is vomit that forms the shield. The vomit-covered baby birds look and smell horrible so they are less likely to be eaten. The parents will smell the vomit too and they quickly fly back to the nest to ward off the threat, which is usually a bird of prey or snake. This is the only bird observed to use vomit as a form of communication.

5 Sea Cucumber

Nature's most disgusting defense mechanism is that of the sea cucumber. Once disturbed, it will eject its sticky intestines and other organs out of its anus at the attacker, entangling it. This dazzles and distracts the enemy. In some species, the intestines are poisonous, containing a toxic chemical called holothurin. The sea cucumber's body contracts violently to squeeze out the insides.

The creature doesn't seem to mind this process, and the organs are restored quickly. It takes about six weeks for the missing body parts to be regenerated.

4 Turkey Vulture

When the turkey vulture is approached by a hungry predator, it will regurgitate the entire contents of its stomach. This is used as either an offering of food or to make the predator flee. The vulture's vomit is utterly disgusting, and the smell completely puts off most predators. The vulture can then run away at a quicker pace as it is a lot lighter, although by this point, a lot of predators would have left already. Some starving animals will actually resort to eating the vomit, even though it is very acidic and can burn.

3 Japetella Heathi Octopus

This octopus is found in the oceans at depths of 1,900–3,200 feet. The japetella heathi octopus has had to adapt to evade two types of deadly predators—those that hunt by looking for silhouettes created by the lighter waters above and those that use their own light from bioluminescence. To avoid creating a silhouette, the octopus is almost completely transparent, except for its eyes and guts. However, these have become reflective, reducing their shadow. This allows light to pass through the creature, reducing its visibility to predators.

However, this is a disadvantage against predators with bioluminescence, such as the angler fish, as the octopus reflects the light, allowing the fish to easily locate it. To avoid becoming food for the angler fish, when the octopus detects their light, it activates skin pigments. These pigments allow the octopus to change its color to red in less than a second, greatly reducing its reflectivity. This effectively makes the octopus invisible to angler fish and other headlight fish. When the threat is gone and the light is no longer present, japetella heathi reverts to transparency.

2 Iberian Ribbed Newt

When under threat, this newt, found on the Iberian Peninsula and Morocco, will push its ribs through its skin and out the tubercles on the side of its body. These ribs act as weapons to ward off attackers. Despite the rupturing of skin, the process causes the newt no pain.

In order to do this, it moves its ribs away from its spine, increasing their angle by up to 50 degrees. The skin is stretched and the bones rip through. At the same time, a poisonous substance is secreted through pores on the skin. The spiky ribs puncture the attacker's skin and then the poison enters. This can even cause death. The newt's defense proves to be very effective.

1 Malaysian Exploding Ant

Although the Iberian ribbed newt is unaffected by its defense mechanism, the same cannot be said about the Malaysian exploding ant. The ant defends the colony from attackers by blowing itself up. Two large glands full of a poisonous chemical are located all across the ant's body, and when attacked, it will violently contract its muscles. This causes the fluid-filled glands to burst, releasing the sticky, poisonous substance from the head at the target. This substance not only entangles the attackers, but also causes extreme irritation and corrosion. This restrains the creature and can kill.

TOP 10 Extreme Insect Species

by **Victor Pintilie**

10 Largest Insect: Little Barrier Island Giant Weta

The giant weta native to the Little Barrier Island of New Zealand (Deinacrida heteracantha) proudly bears the honor of being the heaviest and largest adult insect in the world; the record size for one is 2.5 ounces in weight and over 3.4 inches in length. A relative of the grasshopper and of the common house cricket, the giant weta is now a vulnerable species.

9 Smallest Insect: Dicopomorpha echmepterygis

Fairyflies are tiny members of the wasp family and the smallest family of insects known to science. Dicopomorpha echmepterygis is a fairyfly native to Costa Rica. The males of the species are no more than 0.14 mm in length, about the same size—if not smaller—than the single-celled paramecium normally found in lake waters. This species feeds on the eggs of other insects.

8 Most Venomous Insect: Harvester Ant

The harvester ant (Pogonomyrmex maricopa) is the world's most venomous insect—however, it does not pose any threat to humans at all. Its venom is roughly 25 times stronger than that of the honey bee, but it is delivered in small doses, therefore rendering the harvester ant quite inoffensive. You may have expected the Japanese giant hornet, the African killer bee, or the bullet ant of South America as contenders to this title; surprisingly enough, the winner turns out to be in your very backyard— members of these species are generally found throughout the U.S.

7 Longest Insect Migration: Globe Skimmer

The globe skimmer (Pantala flavescens) has recently been found to have the longest migration of all insects, its journey dwarfing that of the famous monarch butterfly. During the monsoon season, these dragonflies travel from India to eastern and southern Africa and back again, which adds up to between 8,700 and 11,200 miles. Furthermore, the long migration of these insects renders them an accessible food source for migratory birds, which means that if anything  happens to this species, many species of birds would find it very difficult, if not impossible, to perform their annual migrations.

6 Fastest Flying Insect: Southern Giant Darner

This species of dragonfly (Austrophlebia costalis) has been clocked at a speed of 35 miles per hour, which makes it the fastest insect in the world in terms of flight speed. Although there are previous claims that it would top 60 miles per hour, most experts disagree on their veracity. Nevertheless, there are many who consider that the title of fastest insect remains disputed among dragonflies, hawk moths, and horseflies, with various unverified measurements circulating about each of these species.

5 Most Feared Insect: Migratory Locust

Locusta migratoria, or the migratory locust, is arguably the most feared species of insect known to humankind. Although the mosquito is responsible for the most human deaths, the locust is the one insect that has made men cry in horror throughout history. Although locust swarms are rare nowadays, locust plagues still occur in some parts of the world, as was the case in Madagascar in 2012, or the 2004 locust outbreak that affected several countries in west and north Africa that resulted in losses of around $2.5 billion in terms of agricultural devastation.

4 Most Resilient Insect: German Cockroach

I suppose few people will be surprised by this entry. I mean, everyone knows the allegations that cockroaches are capable of surviving nuclear fallout. Therefore, in hopes of raising at least a few eyebrows, I would like to mention a case in which a German cockroach nymph (Blattaria germanica) managed to live inside another very hostile environment: a human colon. The cockroach probably arrived there after having been inadvertently swallowed by the 52-year-old woman while she was eating, and somehow managed to survive her stomach's digestive enzymes.

3 Rarest Insect: Lord Howe Island Stick Insect

This rather large member of the stick insect family lives on the Lord Howe Island found between Australia and New Zealand. It is also an example of what biologists refer to as the Lazarus effect, or when a species is thought to be extinct, but it is then found again. The current population of wild Dryococelus australis is thought to consist of less than 50 individuals (24 at the moment of their rediscovery); with so small a population, however, the species remains critically endangered. Nevertheless, there are efforts to breed the Lord Howe Island stick insect; the Melbourne Zoo of Australia has managed to breed over 9,000 individuals in their specially designated breeding program.

2 Loudest Insect: Water Boatman

A species of cicada, the water boatman (Micronecta scholtzi) is the loudest animal on Earth for its size. Although the entire cicada family is famous for their volume (with some species managing to sing in almost 120 decibels), the water boatman, at only two millimeters in length, manages to make a noise 99.2 decibels loud, which is similar to standing in the front row of a loud orchestra or listening to a jackhammer from 50 feet away.

1 Biggest Insect Colony: Argentine Ants

Argentine ants (Linepithema humile) have recently been found to be the insects with the largest colony in the entire world, whose domination may rival that of humans! Scientists have discovered that the members of the species living across America, Europe, and Japan actually belong to the same colonies, as they will refuse to fight one another. Furthermore, a series of experiments hinted that these super colonies might actually be one worldwide ant colony, as their members did not exhibit hostile behavior toward one another and recognized their familiar pheromone scent, despite being separated by thousands of miles. Furthermore, this unusual phenomenon seems to have been created by humans, who inadvertently introduced them to all continents from South America.

TOP 10 Aberrant Avian Hunting and Feeding Methods

by Alexandre Thompson

10 Black Heron

Herons are stealthy hunters that normally patrol the shallows of coastal marshes, inching forward to get in stabbing range of surprisingly large fish. However, the black heron of the central African wetlands has forgone the stalking in favor of a deadly invitation. In a scene that would rival an Aesop's fable, the heron spreads its wings in a circle that creates a shaded silhouette, perhaps resembling a reed palm over the sun-bathed waters. Tetras and other small fish seek out what they think is a cool, safe resting spot, but it will be their last. As the fish settle down, the heron's bill plunges down from the "canopy," spearing the fish. The black heron will set itself up at several different locations throughout the day.

9 Black Skimmer

Related to gulls and terns, but resembling a sea-going toucan, these incredible gull-like skimmers are the only bird species with a lower bill longer than the top. Extending up to three inches past the top mandible, the bizarre jaw allows the skimmer to pursue an even stranger feeding technique. Flying at speeds of over 25 miles per hour, the skimmer drags its grooved lower mandible in the water, snapping it shut and swooping upward whenever a small fish is encountered. Black skimmers often hunt in pairs and must maneuver constantly to avoid obstacles in the water. The bird's-eye view in this case would resemble the most extreme action film. Danger does exist; on occasion, a skimmer's lowered bill may strike submerged driftwood, resulting in serious injury.

8 Antipodes Island Parakeet

Of all the parrots that could truly be associated with piracy, the Antipodes Island parakeet might be the most fitting. Endemic to New Zealand's Antipodes Islands, the 12-inch relative of the pet budgerigar looks like the quintessential green parrot, but this true bandit hides a dark secret behind its façade of normalcy. On the Archipelago, grey storm petrels, robin-sized relatives of shearwaters and albatrosses, nest in burrows excavated along the shoreline. Searching the coast, the parakeets dig apart the storm petrels' burrows and proceeds to kill them with their sharply hooked parrot bills before devouring them. The green parakeet presents an incongruous image as a predator, but it is also a scavenger of meat and will feed on any dead seabirds it finds along the shore. As a true parrot, the bird still eats fruits and seeds.

7 Fish Owl

When we think of an owl, we immediately imagine a secretive, nocturnal forest-dwelling predator that emerges from the darkness to hunt rabbits, skunks, and mice. However, the Blakiston's fish owl swoops down under the cover of darkness to hunt in the water, targeting fish in wetlands and forested rivers. With a six-foot wingspan and a weight of over ten pounds, it is the world's largest owl, specially equipped to hunt fish through spikes protruding from its foot pads. The spines quickly sink into the fish as the well-insulated owl swoops down and lifts its prey out of the water. Unfortunately, needless removal of trees along river banks both degrades the fish habitat and removes vital roosting sites, threatening these rare predators.

6 Golden Eagle

The true king of birds, golden eagles are featured on many national emblems and occupy an ecological role in the avian world equivalent to that of a lion. With a wingspan of up to nine feet, the 15–20 pound eagle ranges across the entire Northern Hemisphere, inhabiting the mountains and foothills, where it may take a territory of up to 37 square miles. Where most raptors hunt prey smaller than themselves such as rabbits and ducks, golden eagles combine their incredible strength, size, and agility to bring down large mammals. Diving down a mountainside, the raptor extends its massive talons to seize a mountain sheep or ibex, carrying it a short while before hurling it off a cliff to kill it. When cliffs are not available, the hunters may descend into a forest and simply squeeze a deer to death. Threats to livestock are minimal, however.

5 Japanese Hooded Crow

Some birds have bizarre foraging strategies that do not result from a specific adaptation, but rather their incredible intelligence and ability to adapt to human presence in the world. Among these fortunate species, the Japanese hooded crow used to experienced great difficulty in feeding on ornamental tree nuts, which have a hard shell, but lack sufficient weight to break by dropping. The clever corvids came to the ingenious solution of waiting for a red light and then walking into the crosswalk to place the nuts in the path of car tires. When the cars roll forward, the nuts are crushed, allowing the crows to retrieve their meal when the light turns red again. The amount of forethought and consideration is incredible, and continues to suggest that crows, not parrots, may in fact be the smartest of all birds.

4 Bat Falcon

In Mexico and Central America, prehistoric-looking limestone caverns appear to pour forth clouds of black smoke every evening. Massive flocks of Mexican free-tailed bats emerge to hunt forest midges, but nature abhors a vacuum, allowing the hunters to become the hunted. The bat falcon is a tiny but ferocious raptor that has given up the typical falcon mainstay of small birds and instead focuses on winged mammals. With specially adapted night vision, the falcon tears through flocks of bats, snatching one by the wing on each feeding pass and carrying it to its perch, where it is carefully dismembered. When bats are in short supply, the falcon may also capture insects and finches. As birds, the falcons are also immune to the risk of rabies.

3 Ivory Gull

Gulls are known as scavengers of dead crabs, beached fish, and detached mussels that wash up on the shore, but one species takes scavenging to its logical extreme. Inhabiting the far northern regions of the Canadian and Russian Arctic, the ivory gull patrols the frozen ice sheets in the land of the midnight sun, and during the winter, the midday moon. Lacking any reliable source of normal food, this avian equivalent of the dung beetle feeds upon seal and fox excrement, and even the afterbirth of mammals. This bizarre diet provides much-needed protein to the paradoxically beautiful little seabird, which has become endangered by introduced predators. The gull's powerful gastric juices mitigate the risk of bacteria and parasite contamination that would harm most birds.

2 Pied Oystercatcher

Most members of the sandpiper suborder use their sharp bills to poke in the sand for shrimps, snails, and mudworms. The Haemetopedia, or oyster-catchers, are an oddly adapted shorebird that takes an entirely different approach to foraging. Possessing a razor-sharp, solid-red bill, the black oystercatcher, the most aggressive species, prowls rocky shorelines for mussels, clams, and oysters, and inserts its bill sideways through the shells, cutting through the shell's holding muscle. Interestingly, certain populations of oystercatchers seem unaware of how to sever the muscles. Instead, these even stranger birds use brute force to smash through the shells. Oystercatchers then use their strawlike bill to suck out the insides.

1 Great Black Backed Gull

Unlike most of the 45 gull species, the great black backed gull has adaptations of size, ferocity, and maneuvering skills that make it more akin to a raptor than a gull. With a wingspan of six feet, Larus marinus, translating literally to "sea gull," is the world's largest gull species and by far the most ferocious. Lacking talons, the great black backed gull screams through jet fighter–like spiral dives in pursuit of such unlikely prey as puffins, ducks, or even other gulls, which are seized by the massive bill  and then swallowed nearly whole. If the prey evades the first pass, the enormous, dark seabird may pull an aircraftlike inside loop and return. No other bird has the maneuvering powers of this unlikely predator, and few predatory birds are quite so aggressive.

TOP 10 Unusual Animal Senses

by LordZB

10 Electrical Bill

When the platypus was first reported to scientists in Europe, the description of a mammal with a bill like a duck and that lays eggs was considered to be a hoax. Just what is the purpose of the absurd-looking bill? The platypus hunts for small invertebrates at the bottom of rivers and ponds. While diving, its eyes, nostrils, and ears close against the water. The platypus's bill is packed with sensory cells able to detect the weak electrical fields put out by animals as they move. The bill also contains cells sensitive to disturbances in the water. Together, these two senses, electroreception and mechanoreception, enable the platypus to locate their prey with stunning accuracy.

9 Echolocation

While bats are proverbially said to be blind, the real animals do have sight. If bats' eyes are small and rather less powerful than other predatory animals, it is because some have developed the ability to hunt using sound. Echolocation in bats is the use of high-pitched sound pulses and listening for the return of that pulse to judge the distance and direction of objects in their environment. They judge their target not just on the length of time it takes the pulse to return but also the Doppler shift of the sound, which reveals speed. Being nocturnal and hunting mostly for small insects, bats need a sense that does not rely on light. Humans have a very rudimentary form of this sense (we can judge where a sound comes from), but some individuals have developed it into true echolocation.

8 Infrared

When police chase criminals at night or rescuers search for people trapped under rubble, they often turn to infrared imaging devices. Most of the thermal radiation emitted by objects near room temperature is in the form of infrared, so detecting this can be used to judge surroundings on the basis of heat. Several groups of snakes that hunt for warm-blooded prey have pits on their heads that can detect infrared light. Even snakes that have been blinded can still hunt accurately using just their ability to sense infrared. Interestingly, the molecular basis of infrared detection in snakes is completely different from their sensing of visible light and must have evolved separately.

7 Ultraviolet

Most people agree that flowers are pretty. While they are mere adornments to us, they are vital to the plants themselves and to the insects that feed from them. The flowers are there to encourage pollination by insects, so it makes sense that they should stand out in some way to help insects find them. In the case of flowers pollinated by bees, there is far more to their appearance than meets the (human) eye. Such flowers viewed in the ultraviolet spectrum often reveal patterns designed to draw in the bees. Bees do not see the world as we do. They have a different range of visible light (blue and green) than humans do and have a set of cells specifically for the detection of ultraviolet.

6 Magnetism

Bees have a second sensory trick up their furry little sleeves. For a bee, finding the hive again after a busy day of flying around is a matter of life or death. For the hive, it is important for a bee to remember where a source of food can be found. Bees may be many things, but they are not blessed with an overabundance of brains. To navigate they must use a variety of information, and one of those sources seems to rest inside their abdomen. A small ring of magnetite particles, magnetic granules of iron, inside the bee can detect the Earth's magnetic field and help a bee define its location.

5 Polarization

Light can oscillate in many directions, but when all light is moving on the same plane, we call it polarized. Humans cannot detect the polarization of light without equipment to help. This is because the detection cells in our eyes are randomly positioned. In octopuses, the cells are regimented and so they will see polarized light as most bright when their cells line up with the direction of oscillation of the light. How does this help octopuses hunt? One of the best forms of disguise is to be transparent, and a number of animals are nearly invisible to visible light in water. However, underwater light has a polarized component that some octopuses can detect. When this light travels through the body of a transparent animal, its polarization will be changed and the octopus can see that and capture the prey.

4 Sensitive Armor

Humans can feel all over their body because the skin has touch-sensitive cells distributed all over it. If you clad us in a suit of armor, however, we would lose much of that sensitivity. That would not be much more than an inconvenience to us, but to a hunting spider it would be disastrous. Spiders, like other arthropods, have a tough exoskeleton that protects their bodies. But how are they to sense what they are touching, how much it is moving, or what the stress is on their legs? They have small slits in the exoskeleton that allow for stress to be measured by the deformation of the slit by force. This allows spiders to get a much better sense of their world than would otherwise be possible.

3 Tasteful

In most societies, it is polite to keep one's tongue inside your mouth. Unfortunately for catfish, this is impossible because their entire body is covered in taste-sensitive cells. Using up to 175,000 of them, catfish can taste in all directions from the water flowing over them. Their amazing sense of taste gives them the ability to detect the presence of prey from far away, as well as to locate their position when close by in the muddy waters they typically live in.

2 Blind Light

Many animals that have evolved in dark environments have either only rudimentary, vestigial eyes or have lost their eyes entirely. In the very near pitch-black of a cave, there is no advantage to species in maintaining organs of sight. The cave fish Astyanax mexicanus has entirely lost the use of its eyes and yet has developed a method of sensing the very small decrease in light given by being under a rock. When young, this ability allows them to flee predators and hide. The pineal gland in animals responds to light to govern their sense of day and night. In these fish, their translucent body allows light to reach the pineal gland directly, and they use this to find shelter.

1 Dot Matrix Eye

There are a huge variety of eye forms to be found in nature. This makes the evolution of eyes surprisingly easy to understand, despite creationists raving about its impossibility. Most eyes are composed of a lens, to focus light, and a patch of sensitive cells onto which the image of the world is projected. To focus the image, the lens can change shape, as in humans, or move back and forth, as in octopuses, or in a variety of other ways. So while sight is common, there is a type of crustacean, Copilia quadrata, that has a novel solution to imaging the world around them. Their eyes use two fixed lenses and a mobile sensitive spot. By moving the detector cells, the Copilia builds up an image with a series of dots as it measures light levels in a number of positions.

CHAPTER 15

TECHNOLOGY AND SPACE

TOP 10 Bizarre Scientific Stories

by **Shelby Hoebee**

10 The CIA Created the Unabomber

The Unabomber, also known as Ted Kaczynski, is a man currently serving a life sentence in prison for killing 3 people and injuring 23 others with a series of bombings. What many people don't know is that before his attacks, Kaczynski was mainly recognized for his incredible genius.

As a child, Kaczynski skipped both 6th and 11th grades and began studying as an undergraduate at Harvard when he was only 16. He was the subject of much bullying when he was younger due to his lack of social skills, but many of his colleagues realized his mathematical intelligence was unlike anything they'd ever seen. As an undergraduate, Kaczynski took part in a psychologically damaging experiment done by the CIA as part of the behavioral engineering project MKULTRA. The study was run by Dr. Henry Murray, who had each of his 22 subjects write an essay detailing their dreams and aspirations. The students were then taken to a room where electrodes were attached to them to monitor their vitals as they were subjected to extremely personal, stressful, and brutal critiques about the essays they had written.

Following the psychological attacks, the participants were forced to watch the videos of themselves being verbally and psychologically assaulted multiple times. Kaczynski is claimed to have had the worst physiological reaction to being interrogated. These experiments, paired with his lack of social skills and memories of being bullied as a child, caused Kaczynski to suffer from horrible nightmares that eventually drove him to move into isolation outside Lincoln, Montana.

In Lincoln, Kaczynski built his own cabin and began living simply, without electricity or running water. He set out to become self-sufficient and create primitive technologies by hand. He found his work was limited by the development and industry that was destroying the environment around him. After he found his favorite spot in the wilderness destroyed by industrialization, Kaczynski had reached his breaking point.

He began to believe that technology was evil and so were those promoting it. Many believe Kaczynski's participation in the Harvard study is what later influenced him to send letter bombs to multiple establishments, including airports and universities, in an attempt to get the public's attention. Kaczynski became a big target for the FBI after his 18-year reign of terror over those whom he believed were promoting antihuman technology that was destroying the world. In 1995, Kaczynski demanded that newspapers publish his 50-page manifesto called "Industrial Society and Its Future." He eventually became known as the Unabomber.

9 LSD French Hysteria

The town of Pont-Saint Esprit in France isn't known for much—aside from an odd and widespread outbreak of psychosis on August 15, 1951. Many believe this outbreak (involving over 500 people) to be the result of an experiment carried out by the CIA's own program, MKULTRA.

Supposedly, a report issued in 1949 had been found regarding the United States' experimentation with the newly discovered drug, LSD. These mass hallucinations ranged from people believing they were being eaten by snakes to people jumping out of windows because they thought they were airplanes. At the time, the U.S. believed it could harness the power of LSD to cause mass hallucinations in their enemies, damaging their ability to respond to attacks.

The hysteria ended with the death of five people and the suicide of at least two others, with no apparent explanation. The hallucination was deemed to be widespread ergot poison by the Sandoz Chemical Company near Pont-Saint Esprit. It is believed, however, that the chemical company had been working alongside the CIA to produce mass amounts of LSD for their experimentation.

Regardless of the cause, the massive hallucinogenic outbreak that occurred in this little French town is mired in unanswered questions.

8 Beauty and Brains

Hedy Lamarr is most known for her beauty on the silver screen as an actress during the golden age of MGM, but few know that her immense beauty was matched by her equally immense brains.

In the midst of her acting career in the 1940s, Lamarr teamed up with George Antheil with the idea to create a secret communication system. Lamarr was a talented mathematician and, with the help of Antheil, she was able to create and patent an early version of frequency hopping using piano players. She hoped her invention could be used by the military to make radio-guided torpedoes less detectable and harder to jam. Despite securing a patent and pitching the idea to the U.S. Navy, few men of the day took Lamarr or her ingenious idea seriously because of her reputation as an actress.

The idea of frequency hopping that she had developed using a piano roll to change between 88 frequencies was finally picked up by the Navy in 1962. By then, the patent had expired, along with Lamarr's hope for getting any recognition. Today, Lamarr's invention is widely used as a basis for things such as Bluetooth and Wi-Fi—but she received little credit for her idea until 1997.

7 Suicide Song

What if there was a song so depressing, it could cause you to commit suicide? According to many believers, there is: "Gloomy Sunday" was composed by Rezso Seress in 1933. Laszlo Javor wrote the lyrics and it was first recorded by Pal Kalmar in 1935.

While it was being written, the United States was in the grip of the Great Depression with a Fascist government coming to power in Seress's native country of Hungary. His lyrics reflect his loss of faith in man and the injustices that were being committed. The song is an unusually sad prayer to God to have mercy on the bad people in the world, which is why Seress had a difficult time finding someone willing to publish it. Laszlo Javor, who had just broken up with his fiancée, later published the song with music and lyrics. Nineteen suicides in Hungary and the United States have been linked to this song in some way or another, including Seress's own failed attempt to throw himself out a window (though he later succeeded in choking himself with a wire in the hospital).

The creepily melancholy song had been banned from Hungarian (and American) radio stations for worsening the wartime morale. The links between the deaths include suicides right after listening to the song, references to it in suicide notes, corpses holding the sheet music, or having it played on their gramophones.

6 Haber's Rule

Most know Fritz Haber for his Nobel Prize–winning development of synthesized ammonia for fertilizers and explosives, but few know about his evil work for Germany during World War I. Many scientists of the day saw World War I as not only a war between countries, but between the chemists that represented them when it came to developing new and deadly techniques for chemical warfare. Also known as the "father of chemical warfare," Haber played a major role in developing chemical weapons. He was able to develop uses for deadly chlorine gas that, because of its density, would settle in  the enemies' trenches, choking and burning them to death. He also discovered that long exposure to low concentrations of deadly gases had the same effects as short periods with high exposure. He was able to calculate the relationship between exposure and time, calling the equation "The Haber Rule."

Haber was proud to serve for Germany and was even promoted to captain by the Kaiser for his work in chemical warfare. Haber believed gas warfare was humane, claiming that death is death regardless of the means by which it is caused. But his wife, Clara Immerwahr (the first female chemist to ever achieve a PhD at the University of Breslau), strongly opposed his involvement in gas warfare. She eventually committed suicide after witnessing the horrid effects the chlorine gas had at the Battle of Ypres.

As World War II began, the Nazis approached Haber, a Jew, offering him funding to continue his chemical weaponry research. Haber declined and fled to Cambridge, England, with his assistant. While he was there, it was said that Ernest Rutherford refused to shake Haber's hand for what he had done in the field of chemical warfare. During the 1920s, researchers at Haber's institutes continued developing several forms of deadly chemical warfare, including the cyanide formula Zyklon A, which was later developed into Zyklon B for gas chambers at Nazi concentration camps.

5 Missing Cosmonauts

Most think that Yuri Gagarin was the first man in space, but is that true? As the space race boomed between the United States and the Soviet Union during the Cold War, both countries were going to great lengths to be the first to cross that great boundary. Many attempts made by both the United States and Soviet Union ended in failure, and because of this, most of those stories have been destroyed. It's believed that prior to Gagarin's successful attempt, two or more cosmonauts had been sent into space—never to return.

In order to avoid the bad publicity, most information on any "lost" cosmonauts has been covered up. However, the Torre Bert listening station in Italy has captured several recordings of the almost mythical figures. The first was of a very frightened and confused woman talking about her craft failing upon re-entry; she is believed to be saying, "Isn't this dangerous? Talk to me! Our transmission begins now. I feel hot. I can see a flame. Am I going to crash? Yes. I feel hot, I will re-enter—" and then the transmission cuts out. (Some believe this to be a hoax because radio signals cannot be transmitted during re-entry). Another recording picked up sounds of heavy breathing and other noises that lead some to believe Sputnik 7 was a manned flight and that the pilot, Gennady Mikhailov, died of heart failure during orbit.

The Torre Bert heard three more signals, one from a couple aboard Lunik affirming that "everything is satisfactory, we are orbiting the Earth" at regular intervals until an abrupt shift to garbled and frantic communication on February 24, a description of something very large outside their ship, and then silence. The next transmission came in as an SOS signal that seemed to be fading as the cosmonaut drifted farther and farther from Earth. The final transmission received is believed to be from Alexey Belokonev frantically radioing "conditions growing worse—why don't you answer? We are going slower. The world will never know about us."

Whether or not the Soviets ever covered up a lost astronaut, it was certainly within their capabilities. For proof, look no further than the case of Grigori Nelyubov, a man dismissed from the Soviet space program only to have all documentation about him destroyed (including his removal from a series of pictures documenting his membership in the program).

4 Killed by Kindness

George Price was a chemist and geneticist who moved to London in 1967 to do some work in theoretical biology. With no formal training in the fields of population genetics or statistics, Price was still able to formulate an equation that mathematically disproved the idea of true altruism. No theory had ever had the sheer number of applications in evolution, biology, and mathematics that Price's theory on kin selection did. In a nutshell, his theory stated that people are most likely to show altruism to an organism whose genetic makeup is most similar to their own (like a parent or child perhaps) because in doing so, their genetic heritage would be most likely to live on.

Price also theorized that, in the same way an organism would "sacrifice" itself to further its genetic line, it would also sacrifice itself to eliminate others closely related to it if that meant that the organism's genes would better propagate. The implication is that kindness is never truly selfless if it's actually a survival adaptation.

As mind-blowing as that is, the more interesting part of the story is what the theory did to its creator: Price could not emotionally handle the idea that he belonged to an exclusively selfish species. He began partaking in increasingly random acts of kindness toward both strangers and the homeless, only to have his hopeful altruism continuously disproven by his own theory. He gave up all of his belongings and allowed homeless people to live in his house. Eventually, people began stealing his things until he himself was both homeless and sick with depression.

In the end, he lost everything in his effort to disprove his own theory. George Price committed suicide in January of 1975.

3 Weighing the Soul

In 1901, a doctor by the name of Duncan MacDougall made a discovery that he thought would revolutionize science—a way to measure the mass of the human soul. While it may seem crazy, the loss of mass that was experienced by his patients is documented as real.

MacDougall began by recruiting participants who were in their last few days of dying from tuberculosis. He took his six participants, laid their beds on a large scale, and closely monitored their weight before and immediately following their passing. What he discovered was astonishing: The subjects lost, on average, 0.75 ounces in body weight when they died. With no other possible explanation, MacDougall concluded that this must be the exact weight of the human soul.

He claims that the weight drop couldn't be a result of evaporation, sweat, or loss of bowels because of how rapidly the drop occurred. He also claimed that it could not have been loss of air in the lungs, because when he attempted to force air back into the patients, the scale didn't change. His colleague and critic, Augustus Clarke, believed the weight change to be caused by the sudden rise in body temperature as the blood stops being cooled and circulated, but Dr. MacDougall maintained his theory, testing it on dogs as well as other animals and finding no weight drop as he did in humans. MacDougall believed that his hypothesis should be put up to more testing due to his small sample size, but his research ended when he abruptly died in 1920.

2 Living Digestion

Scientific discoveries often stem from the sacrifice of others, and the discovery of human digestion is no different. William Beaumont was a surgeon for the United States Army during the 1800s. He came across a man by the name of Alexis St. Martin who had been injured while working for a fur company. St. Martin was shot in the stomach by a buckshot-loaded shotgun, which ripped a large hole right through his skin but let his organs remarkably intact. Despite Beaumont's belief that St. Martin was going to die from his injuries, he survived—albeit with a gaping hole that gave a clear view into his stomach.

Beaumont knew St. Martin could no longer work at the fur company, so he hired him as a handyman. As Beaumont examined St. Martin's odd injury, he did as most scientists would and snatched up the opportunity to see human digestion in action. Beaumont ran digestion experiments on St. Martin for years by extracting his stomach juices and even lowering pieces of food into the hole tied on a string. Beaumont was able to discover that stomach acids, and not just the movement of the stomach, play a huge role in the process of digestion.

Understandably, St. Martin grew tired of being Beaumont's science project and left for Canada. Their paths crossed yet again in 1826 when St. Martin was again ordered to be Beaumont's handyman. The experiments increased in their intensity as Beaumont put digestion up against the effects of temperature, exercise, and emotion. Beaumont was able to publish a book on his findings, though the two men eventually parted ways for the last time later that year.

1 The Death Diary

Since the beginning of time, humans have been fascinated by death—what it feels like, when it occurs, what we think about as we're dying—yet to this day many of these questions are still unanswered. On the evening of November 25, 1936, Dr. Edwin Katskee, with the use of cocaine, set out to document this last stage of life by injecting a powerful and lethal dose into himself. He planned to document his thoughts and feelings at each stage on a wall that has come to be known as his death diary.

There had been a note scribbled on the wall stating he did not intend to kill himself, as well as detailed instructions on how to use a pulmotor to revive him, but they were found too late. The rest of his notes are so erratic and illegible that the only way to discern their order is by tracking a visible decrease in legibility over time. Some of the earlier notes included, "Eyes mildly dilated. Vision excellent," "Partial recovery. Smoked cigarette." But as the drug began to take its toll, Katskee began suffering from seizures and paralysis in waves. High on the wall there was a note that said "Now able to stand up," and another that read "After depression is terrible. Advise all inquisitive MDs to lay off this stuff."

One of the more difficult-to-read notes says, "Clinical course over about 12 minutes." Katskee was fascinated by his "staggering gait" and noted that his voice was "apparently OK" despite the fact that no sound came out when he spoke. His final note was only one word, "paralysis," which tapered off into a wavy line down to the floor. An antidote was found with him, but it was never used.

While there is some evidence Dr. Katskee wanted to commit suicide, it is more likely that he meant to document as many stages of death as possible and then ring for help at the last moment, and he tragically underestimated how impaired he would become.

Though many of Dr. Katskee's scribbles are ultimately illegible and useless, his tragically fatal experiment stands as a testament to the dedication, bravery, and madness of history's greatest scientific minds.

TOP 10 Orwellian Technologies That Exist Today

by S. Grant

10 Implantable Memories

Most of us realize anything we say, do, or look at online is subject to monitoring by a third party. Combine that fact with camera drones, facial-recognition software, and in-house spies (game consoles and TVs), and it appears the only truly private place left in the world is our brains. But is it really? It seems not, since even going off the grid or taking a vow of silence can't protect our minds from being hijacked by implantable memories. Yes, thanks to the work of MIT scientists, you soon might not know whether your thoughts are truly your own or were artificially implanted.

The scientists have already successfully inserted false memories into mice by using optogenetics to turn individual brain cells "on and off." Essentially, light is fed into the hippocampus, where it triggers specific cells known to relate to particular thoughts. The researchers can then tweak those memories to make the mouse believe something happened when it didn't. For instance, they can cause a mouse to think a room is dangerous even though the rodent has never had a negative experience in the room.

While toying with the memories of mice is one thing, what happens when the technology inevitably expands to humans? Could someone make you believe you committed a crime when you hadn't? What about education—one day, will everyone be implanted with the same, homogeneous knowledge and belief systems?

9 Power to See Through Walls

Apparently the scientists at MIT have a fascination with Orwellian technology, because in addition to figuring out how to manipulate memories, they've also designed a way to "see" through walls.

The technology, nicknamed "Wi-Vi," interacts with the radio waves of Wi-Fi signals to detect movement on the other side of a wall. Similar to sonar or radar, it works by sending out wireless signals and using the ping, or bounce-back, to get an impression of the nonvisible. To differentiate between stationary objects and humans, the Wi-Vi sends out two signals that cancel each other out unless they hit a moving target. Thus inanimate objects such as furniture are ignored while human movements are easily tracked on the Wi-Vi monitor.

Currently, Wi-Vi only shows moving blobs, not silhouettes or other details, but it can still give someone a glimpse of what's happening behind closed doors. The technology is relatively inexpensive, and the Wi-Vi team hopes one day to see their product in smartphones, where it could be used for home security and baby monitoring. On the flip side, we can easily envision it as every stalker's favorite new toy.

8 Filter Bubbles

On first consideration, filter bubbles seem benign, if not downright helpful. Google and other search engines use them to filter search results based on your past Internet activity. In other words, you and a buddy can perform a search using the exact same terms and get entirely different results. The search listings you are given are based on what Google thinks you will like.

So, what's the problem? Well, instead of giving you the most relevant results, search engines put you in "information bubbles" that feed you content you tend to agree with. This can lead to people getting news only from like-minded sources and entirely missing competing arguments.

Consequently, the Internet—which is supposed to be the world's largest source of information—becomes incredibly limiting. Those who aren't careful can wind up filtering out all important issues and existing strictly in a world of content "junk food" consisting entirely of celebrity baby news and porn. Of course, Big Brother is happy to oblige, since the unaware usually don't make waves.

7 Televisions That Watch You

Earlier this year, Chinese manufacturer TCL introduced an HDTV that uses voice and video recognition to detect who is watching. The technology uses the Google TV platform and is intended to offer customized programming and advertisements based on the viewer. Other companies are producing similar TVs that connect to your whole home network and can, for example, suggest products or ads on your computer related to what you're watching on TV.

As if that weren't enough of an intrusion, some camera-enabled TVs are even capable of peering into your home and monitoring your habits and facial reactions to what's on the screen. So much for slumping over a bowl of ice cream while watching TV in your underwear.

Fearing the implications these televisions could have on a person's privacy, Massachusetts Representative Michael Capuano submitted the "We Are Watching You" bill, which requires companies to get permission from a consumer before their TV, DVR, or cable box can collect information. If passed, it will also force companies to post the message "We are watching you" any time information is being gathered.

It seems as though today's world has two Big Brothers—the government and big business.

6 Internet Scrubbing

While filter bubbles can serve as a passive method of keeping people uninformed, or at least isolated from alternative thinkers, Internet scrubbing is a blatant way to suppress the free distribution of information. If you think there's no way to hold back the massive tide of content on the Internet, just take a look at what's happening in China, where Internet scrubbing is big business.

Since around 2007, "Internet crisis public relations companies" in China have been removing negative or controversial articles about their clients from the net. The services aren't cheap—blocking a search term can cost $160,000—but desperate companies and public figures are willing to pay the price to maintain their reputations and keep the truth away from citizens. Law enforcement is trying to crack down on such services, which is somewhat ironic considering that the Chinese government also tampers with the Internet. For instance, nothing online reaches the Chinese people without first going through the country's "Great Firewall."

Although such extreme censorship is not seen in other places around the world, some believe it's only a matter of time before it spreads, calling China a kind of Orwellian testing ground where autocrats can see what does and doesn't work.

5 Hackable Cars

What's scarier than being in a car that's constantly followed? Having a vehicle that will violently turn on you without notice. No, we're not talking about that weird episode of *Knight Rider* when we met KITT's evil twin, KARR. We're referring to all the modern vehicles on the road with built-in software.

According to a recent report, today's "connected" cars have software fixed into all onboard systems, such as brakes, powertrain, and throttle. Many also have built-in navigation systems and smartphone integration. While these features offer convenience and the promise of added safety, what they really do is make a car susceptible to theft, spying, and cyber attacks while they're being driven. Essentially, someone with the right skills and resources can hack into a car and take over the controls.

While many fear the power this puts in the hands of terrorists and hackers, conspiracy theorists claim government intelligence agencies are already using these tools for evil and recently assassinated journalist Michael Hastings by causing his Mercedes to crash into a tree.

4 License Plate Scanners

If you drive an automobile, there's a pretty good chance there's a file somewhere filled with photos of your car along with its location on the day each picture was taken. Thanks to lowered costs, local and state police departments everywhere are adopting license plate scanners and accumulating millions of digital records of vehicles and plates. These scanners are mounted all over the place, including on police cars, buildings, bridges, and traffic lights. They indiscriminately capture the image of every automobile that passes by and send the information to a police database.

While the purpose of the scanners is to deter serious crimes such as drug trafficking and child abduction, so far the most common crime people are being busted for is driving on revoked or suspended registrations. In the U.S., the Supreme Court made it illegal for police to use GPS to track an individual without first getting a judge's approval, but there is no such restriction on using a network of scanners to follow a person's movements.

With the eyes of the scanners always on, as one reporter put it, "You can drive, but you can't hide."

3 Kinect

Not to be outdone by the privacy-infringing smart TVs, Microsoft has its own Orwellian device—the Kinect. The Kinect has been the silent observer in many people's living rooms for several years, and with the release of Xbox One in the fall of 2013, its creepy factor is going up. That's because the new Kinect is required to always be on. There's no unplugging it or throwing a towel over it when you're feeling a little shy, as the Kinect must stay at the ready for voice or hand commands even when the Xbox is off.

So, if a lot of your entertainment revolves around the Xbox, be prepared to have your actions, voice, and heart rate constantly recorded. Microsoft says they don't transmit data back to their servers without user consent, and they swear they'll never divulge your information to the NSA. However, Skype—now owned by Microsoft—promised the same thing, and we all saw how that turned out.

2 Brain-Fingerprinting

In a form of brain scanning, forensic scientists have discovered how to use electroencephalography (EEG) to discover what information you're hiding in your brain. It works by presenting you with images or words and measuring your electrical brainwaves. Currently it can perceive whether you have knowledge about something as well as pick up on your emotional state.

In 2008, an Israel-based security company announced plans to fine-tune the technology for airport security by integrating it with infrared devices, flashing subliminal messages, and remote sensors. The idea is that instead of having to search your luggage or shoes, they can simply analyze your brain to gauge your intent. In other words, if you appear stressed or are reacting to subliminal images of bombs, you're probably not going for a plane ride.

If that idea seems like a stretch, consider the fact that brain fingerprinting is admissible in court and has already been used to challenge the murder conviction of Terry Harrington. In fact, brain fingerprinting has huge potential as a law-enforcement tool, as it can be used tell whether or not a person remembers an event. With a less than 1 percent error rate, it's a shoo-in to replace traditional lie detector machines. However, when we consider that memories are now controllable, brain-fingerprinting might not be as foolproof as originally thought.

1 Implantable Body Sensors

Scientists in both the U.S. and Britain are developing implantable biochips with the ability to monitor your vital signs and behaviors and wirelessly transmit the data to medical staff. These biochips are implanted in the body and can detect fluctuations in blood pressure, blood glucose levels, and heart rate. They also notice changes in behavior that could indicate a health issue, such as a difference in posture or whether you have taken prescribed medication.

VeriChip—now branded as PositiveID—paved the way for such technology with its implantable identity chips, which electronically linked people with their medical records. VeriChip earned United States FDA approval back in 2004 and was the first to market a biochip to the public, but in 2010 the product was discontinued because of poor sales. Not surprisingly, people weren't too keen on having a scannable microchip capable of divulging personal information embedded in their skin.

Still, the newest biochips being created have a better chance of success, as they are targeted specifically at people in dangerous professions, such as the military, and those with serious medical conditions. Such individuals are more likely to accept a loss of privacy for the reassurance that comes with constant medical supervision.

The Orwellian fear about these chips is that, were they to become mainstream, it could be a slippery slope leading to employers or insurance agencies requiring us to get a biochip so they could oversee our health and lifestyle habits. Thus, like everything in this list, biochips are a double-edged sword—they have the potential to do so much good, yet could easily be manipulated to work against us.

TOP 10 Unexplained Mysteries of the Stars

by Michael Thomas

10 The Star That Shouldn't Exist

The star in question is called SDSS J102915 +172927. For the record, I much prefer stars with simple names as opposed to those named like this one. The odd names do serve a purpose though, as they are typically coordinates for where the star can be found in the sky.

In 2011, a team of European astronomers discovered this star in the constellation Leo. It is a small star—only about 80 percent the size of our sun—and is believed to be around 13 billion years old. Since the universe as we know it is thought to be around 13.7 billion years old, this is considered one of the oldest surviving stars. Nothing is particularly unusual about this star, except that according to all of our theories, it shouldn't even exist. The star is made up of 99.99993 percent hydrogen and helium, elements that are too light to condense and form a star on their own. When these figures are put into any star formation supercomputer simulation, the result always comes back that such a star is not possible. Astronomers are puzzled as to how such a star could have formed without the aid of heavier elements. Research is ongoing.

9 The Star Surrounded by Spirals

Located 400 light-years from Earth in the constellation Lupus, SAO 206462 gained the attention of astronomers in 2011. What surprised them was not the star itself, but what surrounded it: It seemed to have spiral arms rotating around it. Now, spirals are no strangers to space, being one of the common formations for galaxies; but scientists have never observed one rotating around a star before. The cause? It's still a mystery, although a widely accepted theory is that gravity from planets, forming in the dust that orbits the star, is responsible for the features. However, there is not enough evidence to support this theory; until planets are actually detected, it is likely to remain a mystery.

8 The Eternally Youthful Star

Messier 4 is a globular cluster, about 7,200 light-years away from Earth. If galaxies had human life cycles, this one would be an old-timer at 12.2 billion years. For any who are unfamiliar with astronomy, it is believed that

all galaxies eventually become globular clusters once all the gas and dust used for star formation has been depleted. This means all the stars are expected to be very old stars in the late stages of their lifespan. While looking at stars in this particular galaxy in September 2012, a team in Chile found a star rich with a material called lithium.

Although lithium is not an uncommon element for a star, it is a compound that burns off typically within the first few billion years of a star's lifecycle. As most of the surviving stars in this cluster are around ten billion years old, finding a star with this element was like finding a needle in a haystack. It is like a teenager living in a nursing home—it just doesn't seem to fit. Scientists think the star may have found a way to actually replenish its lithium supplies, which in a way keep the star from aging. Many have nicknamed it "the fountain of youth star." Exactly how it replenished lithium supplies is a complete mystery, which still puzzles astronomers today.

7 The Stars That Escaped a Black Hole

This mystery deals with probably several million stars rather than just one. At only 2.5 million light-years away, the Andromeda Galaxy is the closest spiral galaxy to our own. Anyone with an Apple computer running Lion should have a good idea of what this galaxy looks like. In the center of the galaxy is a supermassive black hole, like one enormous vacuum cleaner, so strong that even light cannot escape.

In 2005, the Hubble space telescope zoomed in on the galaxy's core and discovered a blue pancake-shaped disk rotating dangerously close to the black hole. Further analysis showed that this was not just hot dust: The glow was coming from millions of young blue stars. These stars are zipping around the black hole at more than 2.3 million miles per hour. That is fast enough to circle the Earth at the equator in only 40 seconds. The thing about this disk is that—given what we believe we know about the tidal forces around black holes—it should not exist. The gas that formed it, and the stars themselves, should have been torn apart by the black hole's immense gravity. How they were able to remain intact in such a close orbit remains a mystery.

6 The Siamese Star?

Swift J1822.3-1606 is a special type of star known as a neutron star located about 20,000 light-years away in the constellation of Ophiuchus. (There are generally three ways a star can end its life: as a white dwarf, for smaller stars like our sun; as a neutron star, for much larger stars; or as a black hole, for the largest. The latter two are formed following the largest explosions known in the universe: supernovas.)

There are a number of different types of neutron stars, including a magnetar, with the strongest magnetic fields in the universe; and a pulsar, which shoots beams of electromagnetic radiation from its poles (somewhat like a lighthouse). For years, everything we knew about these stars told us that they could only become one or the other class, never both. But in 2011, Swift was discovered to have the properties of both. It is only the second star ever found to have such qualities, after a discovery of another a few months before.

The mystery? Astronomers have no idea how a star can possibly exhibit properties of both stars. While the fact that we have discovered two in recent years means that they are more numerous than once thought, we are still no closer to discovering the secret behind them.

5 The Planet That Should Have Been Swallowed

Wasp-18 is 330 light-years away in the Phoenix constellation and about 25 percent more massive than our sun. This is another entry where not the star itself, but what orbits it, is the real mystery.

In 2009, Coel Hellier of Keele University in the UK discovered that Wasp-18 had a planet. Dubbed Wasp-8b, the planet is slightly bigger than Jupiter but has about ten times its mass. This is just below the mass that would make it a brown dwarf, which is a star that failed to initialize. What puzzles astrophysicists is that the planet orbits less than two million miles from its parent star. By comparison, Mercury is nearly 36 million miles from our sun.

Wasp-18 is so close to its parent that it completes its orbit in less than 23 hours, and its surface temperature is around 4,000°F. Being so close, the planet should eventually fall into its sun, yet it has survived already for about 680 million years. Given the mass of the star it orbits, this planet should have been consumed long ago. How a planet was able to form and remain in a location where planets were thought unable to exist is a question that continues to perplex astronomers.

4 The Stardust That Found Its Way Home

Since PSR B1257 +12 is a remnant of a supernova explosion, scientists never expected to find planets anywhere near it. But they found an entire solar system. A total of three planets and one dwarf planet orbit this pulsar. Thinking they must be common, scientists began looking at other pulsars for planets; however, only one other pulsar was confirmed to have a single planet orbiting it, showing that they are indeed extremely rare.

The process by which such planets are able to form is still not well understood. The most accepted theory is that the planets formed a little like our own: from a planetary disk that originally surrounded the star. However, any planet-making material and dust should have been thrown billions of miles out into space by the supernova explosion. How the gas and dust were able to return to the remaining pulsar, become tidally locked, and contain enough material for the formation of a whopping four planets remains a mystery.

3 The Disco Star

V838 Monocerotis is located in the constellation Monoceros, which is about 20,000 light-years from Earth and was at one point considered one of the largest stars in the universe.

In 2002, the brightness of the star shot up suddenly. It was thought to be a simple nova, which is what happens when the remaining core of a dead star (known as a white dwarf) accumulates too much hydrogen gas from a neighboring star, causing a fantastic explosion. The star dimmed after a couple weeks, as expected, and scientists put it in the record books as a nova.

But less than a month later, the star burst into light again. Since the time period between the explosions was too short to be caused as two sep-

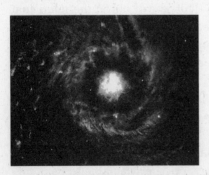

arate novas, astronomers were puzzled and took a closer look. It was then they discovered their problem: There was no white dwarf. The star had simply erupted by itself, and it repeated this process of brightening and dimming several times over the next few months. During its brightest eruption, the star became a million times brighter than the sun and one of the brightest lights in the sky.

Typically, stars brighten slightly before their death, but measurements indicated that the star was only a few million years old, a mere toddler in star years. When the Hubble telescope captured an image of the star after the eruptions, a large cloud of gas and debris was seen accelerating away from the star. One theory is that the star had collided with something unseen, such another star or planet, but scientists are still puzzled by this now decade-old mystery.

2 The Rogue Planet

CFBDSIR 2149–0403 is classified as a brown dwarf. These have failed to initialize nuclear fusion in their cores and develop into real, burning stars. While characterized as an AB Doradus star, due to its size and mass, many others characterize it as a gas giant. This would make it a planet without a parent star, which has been theorized but only rarely observed.

Only four possible candidates for the title of "rogue planet" are known to exist, the one in question being the closest to Earth at an estimated 130 light-years. Without a large star to orbit, the motion of the plant is influenced by other stars in the AB Doradus star group. This doesn't mean that it travels through space in any sort of straight line, a common misconception about rouge planets. But just how a planet is able to go rogue remains a mystery.

1 The Vanishing Stardust

TYC 8241 2652 is located 450 light-years away in the constellation Centaurs. It is believed to be around the same size as our sun but a mere child, at ten million years old, compared to our 4.5-billion-year-old star. From 1983–2008, astronomers searched a bright ring of dust around the star for possible planet formation, believing they were getting some insight into how our own solar system formed. But when the star was due for a checkup in early 2009, astronomers were astonished: When they looked through their telescopes, they saw nothing but the star itself. The once-visible, glowing disk of dust was gone. It did not leave behind any planets or any signs as to where it had gone; it had quite simply vanished. Scientists were baffled. When asked about it, astronomer Carl Melis simply stated, "We don't have a really satisfactory explanation to address what happened around this star."

TOP 10 Crazy Things You Should Know about Our Solar System

by **Jaime Trosper**

10 The Crazy Surface of Mars

Mars is seriously misunderstood. Most of time—in the media—astronomers are discussing the possibility of Mars once being home to oceans of liquid water or ancient forms of bacteria. Recently it was revealed that the most primordial forms of Earth microbes likely originated on Mars before they were transferred to Earth via asteroid impacts.

Rarely do we see some of the mind-blowing images of the most bizarre surface features Mars has to offer, which is a shame, since most of these images would reinvigorate interest in Mars, a planet with an exciting past. Since the Mars Reconnaissance Orbiter began orbiting the Red Planet in 2006, its HiRISE camera has unveiled some of these incredible regions.

One of the most amazing of these depicts trails left by massive dust devils, the Martian equivalent of tornadoes. They carry away the outermost layer of iron oxide (the agent responsible for the soil's reddish hue), revealing the dark gray color of the basalt located just underneath.

9 The Missing Planet

Astronomers have long seen a discrepancy in the orbits of the outermost gas giants, particularly since they seemingly contradict most of our models that depict the early years after our solar system's formation. The idea is that, at one point, our solar system was home to a rather large planet containing the mass of more than a dozen Earths.

The planet in question, sometimes called Tycho, was likely flung out of our solar system and into interstellar space billions of years ago, where it will roam the celestial ether until the end of time.

This theoretical planet would have been located billions of miles beyond Pluto in a region that receives little illumination from the sun. Its orbit around the sun would also have been highly elliptical, taking millions of years to complete one full orbit. Taken together, these factors could partially explain why such a planet has never been detected.

8 Diamond Rain on Neptune and Uranus

Other than the mystery surrounding their eccentric orbits, the planets also have magnetic poles that are misaligned by as much as 60 degrees from their geological poles. One explanation for this is that the planets once collided with—or consumed—an unknown planet, but another, more logical, theory suggests something much cooler.

Based on the information about their strange inclinations and their large concentration of carbon, astronomers believe that Neptune and Uranus are home to enormous oceans of liquid carbon with solid diamond icebergs floating on top. Tiny diamond bits could also fall on these planets like rain.

7 Earth Is Shrouded by a Halo of Dark Matter

Dark matter is one of the most profound mysteries of modern cosmology. Astronomers know that we're missing the key calculations needed to decipher its exact properties, but it's known to make up a huge fraction of the overall mass of the universe.

Currently, we do know some of its behaviors. Particularly, dark matter acts as an anchor to keep galaxies and solar systems from flying apart. As such, dark matter also plays a role in the inner workings of our solar system, which is particularly noticeable when observing its effects on space-based technologies.

One keen observation, known as the flyby anomaly, notes that some of our spacecraft and satellites inexplicably change orbital speeds when traveling to or away from Earth. The theory for this discrepancy says that Earth itself is enshrouded by a huge halo of dark matter. If it were visible at optical wavelengths, it would appear similar in size to Jupiter!

6 On Titan, You Could Strap on Wings and Fly

Titan, a moon of Saturn, is one of the most fascinating places in our solar system. Not only does it rain a gasolinelike substance, but the moon also has large concentrations of liquid methane and ethane that can be seen on its surface.

But there's one bit of information that should convince you to spend a day exploring Titan—thanks to a combination of low surface gravity and the low atmospheric pressure, if humans visited Titan equipped with an artificial set of wings, we would be able to take flight. Granted, you'd still die without the proper equipment, but what's breathing compared to flying anyway?

5 Our Solar System Has a Tail

In August 2013, NASA revealed that one of its missions had successfully mapped the tail of our solar system, discovering it looked similar to a four-leaf clover.

The tail, dubbed the heliotail, is composed of neutral particles that can't be seen through traditional means. As such, specialized instruments were needed to properly image the particles before scientists subsequently pieced the separate images together to produce a coherent picture.

This picture revealed that the heliotail extended more than 8 billion miles beyond the outermost planets, with fierce winds causing the material to stream in every direction traveling at more than one million miles per hour.

4 The Sun's Magnetic Field Is about to Flip

The sun is actually pretty predictable. It goes through a continuous 11-year cycles in which solar activity peaks before declining again, culminating in the sun's magnetic field flipping its polarity. According to NASA, all signs point to this event occurring very soon. The North Pole has already begun its changes.

When this happens, don't expect fiery doom to rain from the sky. The flip just signals the second half of solar maximum, when the sun sees an increase in sunspot activity.

3 We're Surrounded by Black Holes

Black holes come in several varieties. First, there are stellar-mass black holes, the most common type, which form when massive stars collapse. This occurs when a star no longer has the necessary hydrogen for nuclear fusion, causing it to resort to burning helium. This causes the star to become unstable, resulting in one of two scenarios: contraction into a neutron star or collapse into a black hole.

Eventually, many of these black holes merge, combining to form a supermassive black hole, and our galaxy—like millions of others—orbits a central supermassive black hole.

Another type of black hole, called a micro black hole, might bombard Earth constantly. These tiny, atomlike singularities can theoretically be produced in particle accelerator collisions when proton beams are slammed together at near light speed.

There's no need to worry though. In most cases, they evaporate immediately without doing any damage. Even if they didn't, it would still take a significantly longer time than the universe's current age for a micro black hole to consume a single atom of matter, let alone an object with as much mass as Earth.

2 The Sun Could Fit in Jupiter's Magnetosphere

Jupiter is the king of our solar system, with enough room to accommodate approximately 1,400 Earths. The only thing larger than Jupiter is the sun.

Jupiter's magnetosphere (magnetic field of influence) is the largest and most powerful magnetosphere in our solar system, even stronger than the sun's. Jupiter's magnetosphere could easily engulf the sun itself with some room to spare, including the entirety of the sun's visible corona.

To make that a bit more accessible, if we could see the magnetosphere here on Earth, it would look bigger than the full moon in our sky. Furthermore, some parts of the magnetosphere have temperatures hotter than the surface of the sun.

1 Weird Life Could Exist on Gas Giants

Once upon a time, our list of key components needed for life to form were much more stringent. These days, we know things aren't that simple, especially upon the discovery of certain bacterium thriving in deep geothermal vents on the ocean floor, where the temperatures can exceed boiling.

Regardless, when you think of life, Jupiter likely isn't the first place that comes to mind. It's essentially a giant cloud of gas, right? There's just no way life could develop—let alone thrive—there.

As it turns out, that could be wrong. An experiment done in the early 1950s, known as the Miller-Urey experiment, demonstrated that we can generate organic compounds, a prerequisite to life, with little more than lightning and the right chemical compounds. Considering this information and the fact that Jupiter already meets several requirements, such as having water (Jupiter may even have the largest ocean of water in our solar system), methane, molecular hydrogen, and ammonia, it's possible the gas giant could foster life.

That said, Jupiter has the highest atmospheric pressure of any planet in our solar system. It also has strong winds that could hypothetically help circulate the appropriate compounds. All of this indicates that life would have a hard time getting the necessary foothold, but many have suggested that certain ammonia-based life-forms could thrive in the cloud deck that makes up the upper atmosphere, the region in which the temperature and pressure would allow for a layer of liquid water to remain.

While it's still outside of the realm of theoretical astrobiology, Carl Sagan was a huge proponent of this idea, not ruling out the possibility of extreme life-forms based on our limited knowledge. In his view, the life-forms living in Jupiter's atmosphere would be diverse. There would be sinkers, floaters, hunters, and scavengers, each playing a necessary role in their own Jovian food chain.

TOP 10 Strangest Things in Space

by Jeffrey Sieminski

10 Hypervelocity Stars

Everyone knows that shooting stars are just meteors entering the atmosphere, right? What some people don't know, however, is that real shooting stars exist as well; they're called hypervelocity stars. These are big, fiery balls of gas rocketing through space at millions of miles per hour.

When a binary star system is gobbled down by the supermassive black hole (that's the scientific term, by the way) at the center of a galaxy, one of the two partners is consumed, while the other is ejected at high speed. Just try to imagine a huge ball of gas, four times the size of our sun, hurtling out from our galaxy.

9 The Planet from Hell

Gliese 581 c wants to kill you. Seriously. Scientists have determined that this hell of a planet is the most likely candidate for future colonization, despite the fact the entire planet is out to get you.

This planet orbits a red dwarf star, many times smaller than our sun, with a luminosity of only 1.3 percent of our sun. This means that the planet is far closer to its star than we are to ours. Because of this, it is stuck in a state of tidal locking, meaning that one side of the planet is always facing the star, and one side is always facing away—just like our moon's relationship with Earth.

The tidal locking of the planet alone results in some pretty odd features. Stepping out onto the planet's star side of would immediately melt your face off, whereas standing on the opposite side of the planet, where there is no sun, would freeze you instantly. However, in between these two extremes is a small belt where life could theoretically exist.

Living on Gliese 581 c would have its challenges, though. The star it orbits is a red dwarf, which means that it is at the lower frequency end of our visible spectrum, bathing the entire sky of Gliese 581 c in a hellish red color. Another side effect of this is the fact that photosynthesizing plants would have to adapt to the constant bombardment of infrared radiation, rendering them a deep black color. That Greek salad wouldn't seem so appetizing any more...

8 The Castor System

As if one or two giant, fiery balls of gas weren't enough, here we have the Castor System. As one of the two bright stars from the Gemini constellation in our night sky, it has some serious luminosity. This is because the Castor System isn't one, or two, but six stars, all orbiting around a common central mass.

Three binary star systems orbit each other here, with two hot and bright A-type stars being stuck in the system, as well as four M-type red dwarves. All together, though, these six stars put out roughly 52.4 times more luminosity than that of our sun.

7 Space Raspberries and Rum

For the last few years, scientists have been studying a dust cloud near the center of our Milky Way galaxy. If there's a God out there, it seems that he decided to get creative—this dust cloud, named Sagittarius B2, smells of rum and tastes like raspberries.

The gas cloud in question consists largely of ethyl formate, which is known to give raspberries their taste and rum its distinctive smell. This large cloud is said to contain a billion, billion, billion liters of the stuff—which would be great, if it weren't rendered undrinkable by pesky particles like propyl cyanide.

The creation and distribution of these more complex molecules is still a mystery to scientists, however, so we won't be opening up an intergalactic pub anytime soon.

6 A Planet of Burning Ice

Do you remember Gliese? That hell-hole of a star that we visited earlier? We're heading back to the same solar system for this one. As if one murderous planet weren't enough, Gliese supports a planet made almost entirely out of ice—at 804°F.

Gliese 436 b is, quite simply, a burning ice cube. Imagine Hoth from *Star Wars*—except that it's on fire. The only reason this ice stays solid is because of the huge amount of water present on the planet; the gravity pulls it all in toward the core, keeping the water molecules so densely packed that they cannot evaporate.

5 The Diamond Planet

Finally: a planet fit for Oprah, or perhaps even Bill Gates. 55 Cancri e—made entirely out of crystallized diamond—would be priced at 26.9 nonillion dollars. That's the kind of stuff that even the Sultan of Brunei dreams about at night.

The huge diamond planet was once a star in a binary system until its partner began to cannibalize it. However, the star was not able to pull its carbon core away, and carbon is just a ton of heat and pressure away from being a diamond—so at a surface temperature of 2998°F, the conditions are almost perfect.

One-third of the planet's mass is said to be pure diamond, and whereas Earth is covered in water and abundant in oxygen, this planet is made mainly of graphite, diamond, and a few other silicates.

The huge gemstone is two times the size of Earth, and has eight times the mass, making it a "super-Earth."

4 The Himiko Cloud

If there has ever been any object that has shown us the origins of a primordial galaxy, this is it. The Himiko Cloud is the most massive object ever found in the early universe, and it dates to only 800 million years after the Big Bang. The Himiko Cloud astounds scientists with its sheer size, roughly half that of our Milky Way galaxy.

Himiko belongs to what is known as the "reionization epoch," or the period from around 200 million–1 billion years after the Big Bang—and it's the first glimpse scientists have managed to get of the early formation of galaxies. To make it even cooler, it has been introduced as the "Giant Mystery Blob Discovered Near the Dawn of Time" by Space.com.

3 The Universe's Largest Water Reservoir

Twelve billion light-years away, the universe's largest water reservoir resides in the heart of a quasar. Containing 140 trillion times the amount of water in Earth's oceans, and found near the colossal black hole at the center of the quasar, the water unfortunately manifests itself in the form of a massive cloud of gas, several hundred light-years in diameter—our dreams of the universe's most kick-ass water slide have been destroyed!

But the kicker is that this black hole, 20 billion times the size of our sun, is constantly spewing out huge amounts of energy—equivalent to what would be produced by 1,000 trillion suns.

2 The Universe's Largest Electrical Current

Only a few years ago, scientists stumbled upon an electrical current of cosmic proportions: 10^{18} amps, or roughly one trillion lightning bolts. With that kind of power, you could even use that pesky seven-blade electric razor you have lying around!

The lightning is thought to originate from an enormous black hole in the center of the galaxy, which has a core that is supposedly a "huge cosmic jet." Apparently, the black hole's enormous magnetic field allows it to fire up this lightning bolt through gas and dust to a distance of over 150,000 light-years away. And we thought that our galaxy was big—this single lightning bolt is one and a half times the size of it.

1 The LQG

So yeah, the Himiko Cloud is pretty big—like, half the size of our galaxy. Big whoop, right? Well, what about a structure in space so enormous that it breaks the conventional laws for modern astronomy? This structure, my friends, is the LQG—the Large Quasar Group.

Our galaxy, the Milky Way, is only 100,000 light-years across. Think about that for a moment; if something happens on the far side of the galaxy, it would take 100,000 years for the light to reach the opposite end. That means that when we watch an event take place at the other end of our galaxy, it actually occurred when the human species was just beginning to form.

Now, take that length of time and multiply it by 40,000. That's right—the Large Quasar Group is four billion light-years across. The cluster of 74 quasars actually breaks the rules of standard astrophysics, since the maximum size of any cosmic structure should be only 1.2 billion light-years across.

Scientists have absolutely no idea how this huge structure formed, since they had previously only been aware of other clusters of perhaps several hundred million light-years across. The gargantuan structure absolutely spits on a certain physical law, which states that when viewed from a distance, the universe would look relatively uniform. This is exactly the type of condescending cosmic structure that looks over at our galaxy and, with a smirk, says "cute."

TOP 10 Mind-Blowing Sci-Fi Technologies That Really Exist

by **Andrew Handley**

10 Automated Driverless Cars

The 2002 film *Minority Report* was futuristic sci-fi at its sleekest. One of the major technological components was the automatic car: Set it on autopilot, and it seamlessly moves along with traffic. We saw it again in *I, Robot*, and this is one real-world technology that we've been waiting a long time for.

The Google Driverless Car was the first real-world attempt that gained widespread public recognition, even after those videos of it running over traffic cones. Google claims that its small fleet has now driven more than 300,000 miles unassisted by human control, and usually has at least 12 cars out on the road at all times.

Not to be left behind, Volvo has recently tested its own "platooning technology" in which a string of driverless vehicles follows behind a lead car, stopping, turning, and accelerating in unison. In essence, they're being electronically towed by the lead car, allowing the driver to "spend their time doing other things while driving," which is something everybody does anyway.

9 Invisible Bike Helmets

We don't remember this being in any sci-fi movies, but it totally should have been. The device is a mobile airbag that will supposedly replace all those unstylish bicycle helmets. It's contained in a scarf that is worn around your neck, and at the moment of impact it inflates and forms a protective cushion around your head. The Invisible Bike Helmet was created by Hovding, a Swedish technology company.

8 Shark Repellent

The Batman franchise is rarely viewed as science fiction, but on closer inspection, that's exactly what it is. The gadgets, the vehicles, the supervillains—all the elements point towards the sci-fi genre. The 1966 film *Batman* introduced us to one of the greatest gadgets of all time: shark repellent. In the movie, Batman, upon being attacked by a shark, reaches into his utility belt for a spray can of shark repellent. It was awesome, but not something anyone ever expected to see in real life. Until now, that is.

Chemist Eric Stroud has developed a device that effectively repels sharks and sends them swimming in the other direction. It's based on magnetism (unfortunately, there are no spray cans involved), which overwhelms the sensors known as ampullae of Lorenzini that sharks use to hunt and feed. Biologists think that sharks use Earth's magnetic field to navigate, and a spinning magnet overloads those sensors, effectively shooing the shark toward calmer waters.

In the future this magnetic shark repellent could be used to keep sharks out of fishing nets, or to "fence" off swimming areas. And yes, Stroud is also working on a few chemical shark repellents. Fingers crossed that they'll go into an aerosol can.

7 Data That Lasts Forever

In the 2002 movie *The Time Machine*, Alexander Hartdegen (played by Guy Pierce) creates a time machine and accidentally propels himself to the year 802,701 AD. While there (then?), he discovers the ruins of a building that contain a hologram from 800,000 years ago, and thousands of moviegoers collectively rolled their eyes at the idea that any type of data storage could last that long.

Or can it? The Japanese company Hitachi has recently developed a data storage medium that can hold onto data—wait for it—forever. The square quartz glass sliver is a mere .08 inch thick and just .8 inch on each side. The chip stores binary data, up to 40 megabytes worth, in the form of tiny dots that can be read by a device as simple as a microscope (or any machine that understands binary, which is every machine).

Furthermore, quartz glass is waterproof, chemical and radio wave resistant, and is able to last for two hours at 1,832°F. In other words, it's like the Terminator of data storage compared to hard drives, compact disks, books, and literally every other storage device we currently have. It's extremely close to indestructible, meaning that it can withstand even the disasters that will eventually destroy the building it was made in. And hey, speaking of Terminators…

6 Androids

Androids are a staple in sci-fi, and although we've been able to create some incredibly intricate robots, the mechanics of creating a creature that's able to walk upright on two feet are just downright difficult. Not only is balance an issue, but for the robot to be practical it has to have the ability to avoid obstacles, navigate on its own, traverse difficult terrain—everything that we humans take for granted, but which present enormous challenges at even the most basic processing level in robotics. It's the age-old question: Do I walk around the kitten or trip over it?

Well according to DARPA, the answer is probably "DESTROY ON SIGHT." Their Pet-Proto robot is a walking robot capable of autonomous decision making. Not only can it walk over obstacles, but it has reflexes; if it loses its balance, it actually reaches out and steadies itself with its robot arms.

And relatively speaking, that's old news. DARPA's Robotics Challenge allowed contestants to pit their own androids against similar obstacles. The goal of the challenge was to create robots that will be able to enter dangerous areas and utilize human tools and vehicles. The challenge's finals are to be held in December 2014.

5 Nanodrones

What's more terrifying than a human-shaped robot? How about nanodrones: flying drones as small as mosquitoes that can take pictures, record audio, and take DNA samples from you without your knowledge.

Unmanned aerial vehicles (UAVs)—and the government's use of them—have been attracting widespread public attention for several years now. You've probably seen stories about the Predator drones on the news.

Evidence for micro aerial vehicles (MAVs), on the other hand, hasn't been provided quite so publicly, although some people claim that the government has been using them as domestic surveillance tools for years. It's not as far-fetched as it might sound: An MAV with a wingspan of only three centimeters (just over one inch) was unveiled at the 2007 International Conference on Intelligent Robots and Systems, and eyewitness reports of dragonfly-shaped MAVs came in from an antiwar rally that same year.

An image of a mosquito drone with the ability to inject viruses through skin has been circulating for a while, but the existence of that specific drone is still unverified.

4 A Conversation with a Man in a Coma

Science fiction authors have been fascinated with the human mind for centuries. As much as we know about the human body, the mind is still largely unmapped territory. In the medical world, comatose patients have always been a subject of intensive study. What are their minds doing? Do they dream? Can they hear you talk? According to Professor Adrian Owen of the Brain and Mind Institute, they cannot only hear you—they can talk back:

Meet Scott Rouley, a 39-year-old man who was involved in a car accident that left him in a coma for more than 12 years. Through the use of fMRI, a brainwave imaging technology, he has been able to respond to questions by forming thoughts that lit up specific areas of his brain.

This result was first achieved in 2010 by Professor Owen in a study where comatose patients were asked to imagine themselves playing tennis, which caused activity in one part of the brain, and walking around their home, which caused activity in a different part of the brain. One of these activities represented "yes" and the other stood for "no." When asked questions, 5 out of the 54 patients were able to respond correctly. Remember, these are people in comas with absolutely no motor function. They're not writing books yet, but it can't be far off.

3 Immortality

Transplanting a human brain into a robot: It doesn't just sound like science fiction; it sounds like bad science fiction. But that's what Russian Dmitry Itskov claims to be working toward. Granted, this isn't a technology that is currently available, but Itskov plans to have it running in the next ten years, well before all those billionaire baby boomers punch their final ticket.

The process would upload the person's consciousness like a computer program into the robot's mechanical "brain." The project, creatively dubbed "Avatar," envisions lifelike humanoid robots by 2015 and full consciousness transplants by 2020.

DARPA is taking a similar approach to thought transference by setting aside $7 million to a project that would allow soldiers to remotely operate robots on the battlefield through mind control.

2 A Supervirus That Can Kill Everyone

Nothing is more terrifying than a supervirus with the potential to wipe out billions of people, but fortunately that's the kind of stuff left to James Bond villains and shadowy corporations in movies. Or at least it was, until Ron Fouchier, a Dutch virologist, announced that he had created that exact virus in 2011.

The virus is a genetically altered version of the H5N1 virus, otherwise known as the avian virus or avian flu, which is deadly among birds but has only accounted for around 500 human infections since 2002 (for comparison, the regular flu kills about 3,000 people per year).

With a few minor tweaks to the virus, Fouchier and his team made it simultaneously more deadly and much, much more contagious, to the point that it killed approximately 50 percent of the ferrets used for testing. Ferrets are commonly used to test viruses because their bodies behave much like humans'.

In the tests, the virus was first transmitted between the ferrets manually, but after ten generations it became airborne and easily reached the entire population. And remember, this is a working model for how it would affect humans. Just imagine if that was released to bioterrorists. Oh wait, people already have—this has become one of the biggest controversies in the virology community, since Fouchier wanted to publish his entire method for the public.

1 Face Scanners

Out of all the science fiction premises, the most frightening has got to be the government that can spy on every one all the time. Cameras at every street corner, a massive database matching every face to a stored record, nowhere safe to hide. California law enforcement looked at that scenario, shrugged, and said, "Yeah, let's do that." The result? A San Diego police department is using facial recognition technology that can instantly take any picture or any video feed and compare it against four million possible matches every second.

The technology was developed by FaceFirst, and even in a crowd you can't escape their watchful eye: FaceFirst can track each individual face on a camera feed and run matches at the same time, and all of this happens live. According to Joseph Rosenkrantz, the CEO of FaceFirst, "Within just a couple of seconds, whoever needs to know receives an e-mail containing all the evidence and stats about the person identified, along with the video clip of them passing the camera so they may be approached then and there."

So here's the scenario: You walk in front of a traffic camera. Five seconds later, your face and a detailed history of your past are sitting in someone's inbox. A minute later, a police officer pulls you aside and places you under arrest for that candy bar you stole when you were 12.

You know, maybe we're better off without all this technology.

TOP 10 Mind-Bending Discoveries in Physics

by MJ Alba

10 Time Stops at the Speed of Light

According to Einstein's Theory of Special Relativity, the speed of light can never change—it's always stuck at approximately 300,000,000 meters/second, no matter who's observing it. This in itself is incredible enough, given that nothing can move faster than light, but it's still very theoretical. The really cool part of Special Relativity is an idea called time dilation, which states that the faster you go, the slower time passes for you relative to your surroundings. Seriously—if you go take a ride in your car for an hour, you will have aged ever-so-slightly less than if you had just sat at home on the computer. The extra nanoseconds you get out of it might not be worth the price of gas, but hey, it's an option.

Of course, time can only slow down so much, and the formula works out so that if you're moving at the speed of light, time isn't moving at all. Now, before you go out and try some get-immortal-quick scheme, just note that moving at the speed of light isn't actually possible unless you happen to be made of light. Technically speaking, moving that fast would require an infinite amount of energy.

9 Quantum Entanglement

While it's technically still true, at least in theory, that nothing can move faster than the speed of light, it turns out that there's a loophole to be found in the mind-blowing branch of physics known as quantum mechanics.

Quantum mechanics, in essence, is the study of physics at a microscopic scale, such as the behavior of subatomic particles. These types of particles are impossibly small, but very important, as they form the building blocks for everything in the universe. I'll leave the technical details aside for now (it gets pretty complicated), but you can picture them as tiny, spinning, electrically charged marbles.

So say we have two electrons (a subatomic particle with a negative charge). Quantum entanglement is a special process that involves pairing up these particles in such a way that they become identical (marbles with the same spin and charge). When this happens, things get weird, because from now on, these electrons stay identical. This means that if you change one of them—say, spin it in the other direction—its twin reacts in exactly the same way. Instantly. No matter where it is. Without you even touching it. The implications of this process are huge—it means that information (in this case, the direction of spin) can essentially be teleported anywhere in the universe.

8 Light Is Affected by Gravity

But let's get back to light for a minute and talk about the Theory of General Relativity (also by Einstein). This one involves an idea called light deflection, which is exactly what it sounds like—the path of a beam of light is not entirely straight.

Strange as that sounds, it's been proved repeatedly (Einstein even got a parade thrown in his honor for properly predicting it). What it means is that even though light doesn't have any mass, its path is affected by things that do—such as the sun. So if a beam of light from, say, a far-off star passes close enough to the sun, it will actually bend slightly around it. The effect on an observer, such as us, is that we see the star in a different spot of sky than it's actually located (much like fish in a lake are never in the spot they appear to be). Remember that the next time you look up at the stars—it could all just be a trick of the light.

7 Dark Matter

Thanks to some of the theories we've already discussed (plus a whole lot we haven't), physicists have some pretty accurate ways of measuring the total mass present in the universe. They also have some pretty accurate ways of measuring the total mass we can observe, and here's the twist—the two numbers don't match up.

In fact, the amount of total mass in the universe is vastly greater than the total mass we can actually account for. Physicists were forced to come up with an explanation for this, and the leading theory right now involves dark matter, a mysterious substance that emits no light and accounts for approximately 95 percent of the mass in the universe. While it hasn't been formally proven to exist (because we can't see it), dark matter is supported by a lot of evidence and has to exist in some form or another in order to explain the universe.

6 Our Universe Is Rapidly Expanding

Here's where things get a little trippy, and to understand why, we have to go back to the big bang theory. Before it was a TV show, the big bang theory was an important explanation for the origin of our universe. In the simplest analogy possible, it worked kind of like this: The universe started as an explosion. Debris (planets, stars, and so on) was flung around in all directions, driven by the enormous energy of the blast. Because all of this debris is so heavy, and thus affected by the gravity of everything behind it, we would expect this explosion to slow down after a while.

It doesn't. In fact, the expansion of our universe is actually getting faster over time, which is as crazy as if you threw a baseball that kept getting faster and faster instead of falling back to the ground (though don't try that at home). This means, in effect, that space is always growing. The only way to explain this is with dark matter, or, more accurately, dark energy, which is the driving force behind this cosmic acceleration. So what in the world is dark energy, you ask? Well, that's another interesting thing...

5 All Matter Is Just Energy

It's true: Matter and energy are just two sides of the same coin. In fact, you've known this your whole life, if you've ever heard of the formula $E = mc^2$. The "E" is for energy, and the "m" represents mass. The amount of energy contained in a particular amount of mass is determined by the conversion factor, "c," squared, where "c" represents the speed of light.

The explanation for this phenomenon is really quite fascinating, and it has to do with the fact that the mass of an object increases as it approaches the speed of light (even as time is slowing down). It is, however, quite complicated, so for the purposes of this article, I'll simply assure you that it's true. For proof (unfortunately), look no further than atomic bombs, which convert very small amounts of matter into very large amounts of energy.

4 Wave-Particle Duality

At first glance, particles (such as electrons) and waves (such as light) couldn't be more different. One is a solid chunk of matter, and the other is a radiating beam of energy, kind of. It's apples and oranges. But as it turns out, things like light and electrons can't really be confined to one state of existence—they act as both particles and waves, depending on who's looking.

No, seriously. I know that sounds ridiculous (and it'll sound even crazier when we get to number one on this list), but there's concrete evidence that proves light is a wave, and other concrete evidence that proves light is a particle (ditto for electrons). It's just both. At the same time. Not some sort of intermediary state between the two, mind you—physically both, in the sense that it can be either. Don't worry if that doesn't make a lot of sense, because we're back in the realm of quantum mechanics, and at that level, the universe doesn't like to be made sense of anyway.

3 All Objects Fall at the Same Speed

Let's calm things down for a second, because modern physics is a lot to take in at once. That's okay—classical physics proved some pretty cool concepts too.

You would be forgiven for assuming that heavier objects fall faster than lighter ones—it sounds like common sense, and besides, you know for a fact that a bowling ball drops more quickly than a feather. And this is true, but it has nothing to do with gravity—the only reason this occurs is because the earth's atmosphere provides resistance. In reality, as Galileo first realized about 400 years ago, gravity works the same on all objects, regardless of their mass. What this means is that if you repeated the feather/bowling ball experiment on the moon (which has no atmosphere), they would hit the ground at the exact same time.

2 Quantum Foam

The thing about empty space, you'd think, is that it's empty. That sounds like a pretty safe assumption—it's in the name, after all. But the universe, it happens, is too restless to put up with that, which is why particles are constantly popping into and out of existence all over the place. They're called virtual particles, but make no mistake—they're real, and proven. They exist for only a fraction of a second, which is long enough to break some fundamental laws of physics but quick enough that this doesn't actually matter (like if you stole something from a store, but put it back on the shelf half a second later). Scientists have called this phenomenon "quantum foam," because apparently it reminded them of the shifting bubbles in the head of a soft drink.

1 The Double Slit Experiment

So remember a few entries ago, when I said everything was both a wave and a particle at the same time? Of course you do, you've been following along meticulously. But here's the other thing: You know from experience that things have definite forms—an apple in your hand is an apple, not some weird apple-wave thing. So what, then, causes something to definitively become a particle or a wave? As it turns out, we do.

The double slit experiment is the most insane thing you'll read about all day, and it works like this: Scientists set up a screen with two slits in front of a wall and shot a beam of light through the slits so they could see where it hit on the wall. Traditionally, with light being a wave, it would exhibit something called a diffraction pattern, and you would see a band of light spread across the wall. That's the default—if you set up the experiment right now, that's what you would see.

But that's not how particles would react to a double slit—they would just go straight through to create two lines on the wall that match up with the slits. And if light is a particle, why doesn't it exhibit this property instead of a diffraction pattern? The answer is that it does—but only if we want it to. See, as a wave, light travels through both slits at the same time, but as a particle, it can only travel through one. So if we want it to act like a particle, all we have to do is set up a tool to measure exactly which slit each bit of light (called a photon) goes through. Think of it like a camera—if it takes a picture of each photon as it passes through a single slit, then that photon can't have passed through both slits, and thus it can't be a wave. As a result, the interference pattern on the wall won't appear—the two lines will instead. Light will have acted as a particle merely because we put a camera in front of it. We physically change the outcome just by measuring it.

It's called the Observer Effect, generally speaking, and though it's a good way to end this list, it doesn't even scratch the surface of crazy things to be found in physics. For example, there are a bunch of variations of the double slit experiment that are even more insane than the one discussed here.

TOP 10 Weird and Fascinating Facts about Space Travel

by **Mike Devlin**

10 Nixon's Speech

Traveling to space remains an inexact science; incidents like the *Challenger* and *Columbia* disasters prove we have yet to perfect the procedure. But in 1969, the program was truly in its infancy, and the Apollo 11 mission was the epitome of human innovation. And bravery. No one truly knew what would happen upon landing on the moon. To that end, then-President Richard Nixon commissioned a speech written by William Safire to give to the nation in the event that the astronauts became stranded.

It began, "Fate has ordained that the men who went to the moon to explore in peace will stay on the moon to rest in peace. These brave men, Neil Armstrong and Edwin Aldrin, know that there is no hope for their recovery. But they also know that there is hope for mankind in their sacrifice. These two men are laying down their lives in mankind's most noble goal: The search for truth and understanding."

9 Free Corvette

Although astronauts have been comparatively well paid, none could be described as "rich." According to the NASA website, civilian astronauts earn a yearly salary between $64,724 and $141,715. There have been, however, certain perks to the job. When Alan Shephard showed up for space training in 1959, he was driving a 1957 Corvette. Quickly realizing what a boon having astronauts drive their vehicles could be, General Motors offered "special" (practically free) lease terms to them. Although NASA certainly did not officially endorse Corvettes, the vast majority of astronauts drove them. An exception was John Glenn, the first American to orbit the earth. Glenn had a family and drove a much more practical station wagon.

8 Cosmonauts Clog

The International Space Station, a multinational project, is divided into two parts: an American section and Russian section. In 1998, when the venture began, it was reported that the Americans and Russians got along famously, sharing resources such as food and exercise equipment. Unfortunately, squabbles began after the first few years. One of the biggest tiffs between them has been the use of bathroom facilities. In the past, the astronauts/cosmonauts used whichever bathroom was closest, but the Russians, whose meals include such rich fare as jellied fish and borscht, have a tendency to clog the toilets and the Americans have banned them from using their facilities.

7 Autograph Life Insurance

Perhaps the most shameful part of the Apollo 11 mission to the moon was the United States government's failure to insure the lives of its astronauts. No life insurance company in the world would sign on to what was very likely to be a suicide mission. Hoping to provide some kind of legacy to their families, the astronauts signed a series of autographs, which could be sold if they indeed perished on their miracle mission. Luckily, this would not prove necessary, and the men returned safe. Some of the emergency autographs have since emerged and have sold at auction for tens of thousands of dollars.

6 Income Taxes

It is often said that nothing is certain but death and taxes, and that holds true for everyone, including astronauts. Apollo 13 Command Module Pilot Jack Swigert (best known for informing Houston of a "problem" with the electrical circuits), had another problem at the beginning of the mission. He'd forgotten to file his income taxes. When he reported this, mission control found it hilarious, and fellow astronaut Jim Lovell joked that Swigert's income tax return was going to be used to buy fuel for the shuttle. Swigert was serious though and didn't drop the subject until he was told he'd be granted an extension. Fast forward 33 years, and Russian cosmonaut Pavel Vinogradov, former commander on the International Space Station, used the Internet to become the first person to pay their taxes from space.

5 Smell of Space

If asked to guess what outer space smelled like, the majority of us would be tempted to say that it smelled like ozone, like nothingness. But astronauts claim that is not in fact the case. After going on space walks, most report a hot "meaty-metallic" scent, others assert that there is a fruity note of raspberry and rum, or an acrid odor like welding fumes. No truly conclusive description has ever been created, and NASA's attempts to re-create the "indescribable" scent have generally met with failure.

4 Food

In museums and NASA gift shops, "astronaut food" is readily available. These freeze-dried meals were prepared on space shuttles with the addition of water. The most famous was a little slab of Neapolitan ice cream. It doesn't taste all that great, but in zero gravity, one's senses are often severely compromised. Without gravity to moor things in place, food does not settle on taste buds in the way we are accustomed. Moreover, the fluids rise and coalesce in sinuses, leaving astronauts with a feeling rather like the congestion of a bad cold. The lack of taste leads those in space to favor foods with rather strong flavors, like Tabasco sauce. However, space programs continue to try appealing to the astronauts' palates; in describing the need for a traditional meal during the holidays, NASA's website claims, "Should a crew member wish to have a typical American holiday feast, there would be no problem. Smoked turkey, dehydrated mashed potatoes, and thermostabilized cranberry sauce are on the list of acceptable menu choices."

3 Diarrhea

The Apollo 8 mission was meant as a precursor of the eventual moon landing of the Apollo 11, gathering reconnaissance. It was commanded by Frank Borman and piloted by James Lovell and William Anders. There were several setbacks on the mission, but none more vile than when Borman woke from a nap with an upset stomach. He vomited and had diarrhea, the globules of which floated all over the inside of the ship in zero gravity. The men cleaned it, and Borman insisted his sickness not be relayed back to mission control, but Lovell and Anders forced him to report it. After taking some medication, he seemed to recover.

2 Explosion Survival

On January 28, 1986, an unimaginable tragedy occurred when the space shuttle *Challenger* disintegrated shortly after launch. The initial fireball made it seem as though the crew died instantly, but there is evidence to suggest several survived until the remains of the ship plunged into the Atlantic Ocean (going just over 200 miles per hour, an unsurvivable speed). Just how many of the astronauts made it, or how long they remained conscious as the shuttle fell back down to Earth, is debatable. For some time immediately after the incident, NASA denied that anyone could have lived through the initial blast. But at least three emergency air tanks had been turned on, and eventually they conceded that some of the astronauts probably survived. The real issue at hand was whether the cabin of the shuttle depressurized after the explosion. If it lost pressure, death would have been relatively quick and painless. If not, they could have been conscious the entire two-and-a-half minutes it took the ship to plummet into the ocean.

1 Lunar Pathogens

When Neil Armstrong and Buzz Aldrin returned victorious from their moon landing, they were not immediately hoisted on the shoulders of their countrymen and treated to a ticker tape parade. In fact, the fear that they might have acquired some kind of "lunar pathogen" during their trip to the moon led them to be quarantined in a converted Airstream trailer for 21 days. Only after it could be determined that they were healthy and not bringing back some kind of space plague, were they allowed to begin the celebration, by being featured in several parades and visiting 25 foreign countries, including a meeting with Queen Elizabeth II. This procedure was followed for the next three missions, until after the Apollo 14 mission when it was finally determined that the moon was devoid of life.

CHAPTER 16

GRAB BAG

TOP 10 Ridiculous Cold War Government Projects

by Mike Floorwalker

10 Real Flying Saucer

Before the development of the Intercontinental Ballistic Missile and the real threat of total nuclear destruction, people projected their atomic fears onto all kinds of weird things. In the 1950s, flying saucers were all the rage. Little green men were the go-to villains of movies and television, and sightings of flying saucers exploded to such a degree that the U.S. Air Force was essentially forced to take them seriously.

At some point, someone undoubtedly suggested that perhaps the saucers had a more sinister origin: a Russian origin. And by God, if there was any chance that the Russians had a flying saucer, the U.S. was damn well going to have one too.

U.S. Air Force project 1794, as described in an official document from 1956, was an effort to create a vertical takeoff and landing real-life flying saucer that would just beat the crap out of anything else in the sky, including the USAF's own fighter jets. This machine, built by Canadian aerospace firm Avro at the behest of the United States government, was projected to be capable of reaching altitudes of 100,000 feet while traveling at Mach 4.

Its performance fell somewhat short of expectations. That is to say, it began to wobble uncontrollably any higher than three feet off the ground, never got beyond blistering speeds of 35 m.p.h., and proved completely aerodynamically unsound in wind tunnel tests. We're not sure if "aerospace" means something else in Canada, but then it should have been obvious to everyone involved from the beginning that the very idea of a flying saucer is just wildly unscientific.

9 Green Run

The Hanford Site, a decades-old government complex in Washington State, is the site of the first working plutonium-producing nuclear reactor. Plutonium manufactured there was used in the very first atomic bomb test and also in Fat Man—the bomb that destroyed Nagasaki and ended World War II.

Residents of the nearby town of Hanford were subjected to many small releases of radioactive iodine between 1944 and '47 as batches of spent fuel that were allowed to decay for a shorter time than normal were released as clouds into the atmosphere. While there is little documentation or detail about these exposures, the "Green Run" of 1949 is slightly more well-documented—and terrifying.

A batch of fuel of the type that was usually allowed to cool for up to 101 days underwent only a 16-day cooling period, making the exhaust from the plant much, much more radioactive than normal. The resulting cloud was released over a populated area, its movement tracked by the air force.

The likely purpose of the experiment was to get an idea of the pattern with which such a cloud could spread so that similar patterns could be detected via reconnaissance in the USSR and their plutonium production facilities could be located and kept track of. But that's kind of the scary thing—even that is only an educated guess on the part of one of the scientists who helped run the experiment. Even they weren't told for sure.

8 PROFUNC

And in the Refusing to Learn From History department, we have this decades-long Canadian program designed to keep tabs on Communists and Communist sympathizers throughout America's neighbor to the north. The 1946 Gouzenko Affair, in which Canadian spies were accused of passing secrets to the Soviets in one of the first North American trials of its kind, helped to jump-start the Cold War and was the beginning of a (not so) healthy Red Paranoia that was soon to sweep the continent.

Part of the project—the part that was implemented—involved collecting names, and lots of them; 16,000 suspected Communists and 50,000 potential "sympathizers" had made PROFUNC's list by the time all was said and done. The really insane part of this plan was its provision for "M-Day," which would have been implemented in the event of a "national security crisis"; which, if you think about it, could cover a lot of things.

Short for "mobilization day," this would have involved literally rounding up everyone on the list and sticking them into internment camps— you know, like the ones the American government had employed to detain Japanese Americans during World War II and eventually had to apologize profusely and pay reparations for. These camps were in place all across Canada, ready to house thousands of suspected Commies should a "crisis" arise.

The very detailed plan helpfully provided for a course of action should anyone try to escape one of these hypothetical camps in this purely "what if" scenario: They would be shot dead. Hypothetically.

7 Amazonian Indian Tests

By the 1960s, the Atomic Energy Commission was funding all kinds of horrifying experiments, the worst of which we'll get to shortly. They thought they could find answers to a couple of their burning questions—how does radiation affect a completely unspoiled population, and how would disease spread after the outbreak of nuclear war—by studying the Yanomami Indian tribe of Venezuela. After doing unbelievably terrible things to them.

While intentional exposure to radiation did occur, probably the single most harmful aspect of this incursion into the Amazonian rainforest was the introduction of a measles "vaccine," Edmonson B, that was known to essentially cause measles, which was unknown in the indigenous population. Introduction of the vaccine kicked off an epidemic of the disease that killed at least hundreds, and maybe thousands, of Yanomami.

Geneticist James Neel, who ran the experiment, explicitly ordered his research team to refrain from offering medical assistance or aid of any kind as the epidemic spread, as they were only there as observers—probably the most ironic sentiment in the history of science. All of this was funded by the United States Atomic Energy Commission, and if you find that to be shocking, just wait.

6 Chemical Weapons Tests on U.S. Soldiers

For nearly 20 years, from the early 1950s–the early '70s, Colonel James Ketchum ran hundreds of experiments at the Edgewood Arsenal outside of Baltimore, Maryland. The Edgewood experiments overlapped with a number of other shady government operations—they were said to be a subset of the CIA's notorious MKULTRA program, and it has become known that eight German (see: ex-Nazi) scientists worked there for a time under Project Paperclip. Colonel Ketchum was of the belief that chemical warfare was a "humane" alternative to conventional warfare with bullets and grenades, and he spent years at Edgewood developing these "humane" weapons by testing them on hundreds of healthy U.S. soldiers.

None of them gave informed consent or were told what they were being given, and no effort was made after the fact to track the progress or health of anyone who had unwittingly taken part. Substances tested ranged from the predictable (hallucinogens like the everpopular LSD) to the insane (nerve gases like VX and sarin), and to this day no one has been prosecuted or even disciplined.

Ketchum, for that matter, is still alive and continues to defend not only his experiments, but the use of chemical and biological agents in warfare. One must assume that he never volunteered himself as a test subject. The Edgewood facility, part of Aberdeen Proving Ground, was shut down, and all chemical weapons stockpiled there were destroyed as of 2006.

5 Biological Weapons Tests on U.S. Cities

There have been numerous instances of U.S. cities being used as testing grounds for chemical or biological agents—most of these tests have taken place using inert, nonharmful chemicals in order to examine spreading patterns and determine how such weapons would be deployed. Of course, the use of such weapons in war was outlawed by the Geneva Protocol of 1929, making the intent behind such experiments rather questionable—but a couple in particular veered straight into the deplorable.

Of the many tests conducted with zinc cadmium sulfide, a fine fluorescent powder, the two that took place a decade apart in St. Louis in the mid-1950s and '60s stand out for their irresponsibility. Motorized blowers were placed on top of low-income housing projects, schools, and in the backs of vans to disperse the chemical over underprivileged areas of St. Louis in both cases. The army told the city that it was a test of experimental "smoke-screens" to shield the city from some undefined Soviet offensive—but in reality, St. Louis was chosen because of its similarity in layout to several Russian cities that the U.S. thought it may want to someday attack with illegal biological weapons. Research undertaken by a St. Louis area college professor has recently suggested that radioactive particles may have been mixed in with the chemical, research spurred by abnormally high rates of cancer in the area.

A 1955 CIA experiment in the Tampa, Florida, area makes this look borderline ethical. Whooping cough virus obtained from an army biological warfare center was released over the area to see how it would spread—live, deadly whooping cough. Cases of the disease in that state tripled, and 12 people in the Tampa area died as a direct result of the "test."

4 Project SUNSHINE

Following the somewhat standard protocol of giving innocuous-sounding names to shamefully unethical projects, SUNSHINE was part of an effort by the Atomic Energy Commission to determine the long-term effects of radiation exposure on the human gene pool. Specifically, it had become known that above-ground nuclear tests were kind of damaging human genetics on a planet-wide scale, and the AEC wanted to know just how much was too much. The easiest way to do this was to examine the bones and teeth of those who had been exposed.

How to acquire these? Why, by grave robbing, of course. Preferably infant graves, as they were particularly interested in examining the under-developed bones of infants who had been exposed. This is not an exaggeration: AEC Commissioner Willard Libby said in 1953, "So human samples are of prime importance and if anybody knows how to do a good job of body snatching, they will really be serving their country."

Body snatching: literally stealing human remains with no notice given to or consent sought from the families of the deceased. Later in the decade, much the same data was gathered in a far more responsible manner—by collecting and examining hundreds of thousands of baby teeth, which one notably does not have to be dead to surrender.

3 Swiss Network of Fallout Shelters

While most European countries spent this era with their heads down, trying to pretend there wasn't gigantic, America-baiting target directly to the east, Switzerland had other plans. The famously neutral Swiss came up with a purely practical solution to the threat of nuclear war and then proceeded to take that solution to the craziest extreme of any nation on Earth.

Switzerland has enough fallout shelters to house its entire population. They're mandated by Swiss law—property owners must have "a protected place that can be reached quickly from his place of residence" and "apartment block owners are required to construct and fit out shelters in all new dwellings." Some other European nations, like Finland and Norway, had similar laws that were repealed decades ago, but the Swiss laws remain active to this day.

It turns out there's a reason the Swiss are so famously neutral in international disputes, and it's not because they're just really relaxed. It's because of an enormous sense of self-preservation. Service in the Swiss army is mandatory for all male citizens (and that army is surprisingly formidable), because it turns out that being armed to the teeth and teaching the entire population to fight is a pretty effective way to remain neutral.

2 Strategic Defense Initiative

In 1983, at the height of the saber-rattling between the U.S. and USSR, there was a pervasive, underlying uneasiness that permeated American culture. It actually seemed like a possibility that mushroom clouds might appear in the horizon at any moment, that we might actually destroy ourselves; and in response to this surreal scenario, President Ronald Reagan proposed a solution straight out of science fiction.

The "Strategic Defense Initiative" or SDI, colloquially referred to as "Star Wars," proposed a series of space-based laser weapons that would shoot down incoming Soviet ICBMs. Billions of dollars were spent on the project between 1983 and 1993, as SDI became a subdivision of the Department of Defense.

The problem isn't that it didn't work—it's that such a system was never even shown to be possible. Criticism rang far and wide despite the president's enthusiasm for the project simply because on the surface it appeared to be exactly what it was—obviously and transparently unscientific.

A 1987 study concluded that it would take at least ten more years of research, not to make SDI work, but to determine if it were even feasible. This was, of course, six years *before* the plug was finally pulled on space-based laser defense.

1 Human Radiation Experiments

And now for something truly horrifying. Beginning at the very dawn of the Atomic Age in the 1940s (when at least an argument could be made that science simply didn't know any better) and continuing well into the '70s (at which point said argument would be laughable), the Atomic Energy Commission in conjunction with other government agencies performed dozens of tests at many locations on hundreds of unwitting subjects to study the effects of radiation on the human body. Details of these experiments were kept under wraps until 1993, when *Albuquerque Tribune* reporter Eileen Welsome began publishing a series of reports entitled "The Plutonium Experiment," for which she eventually won the Pulitzer Prize.

In the reports, she meticulously laid out information she had begun collecting while sifting through Kirtland Air Force Base documents nearly a decade earlier describing the experiments, each more horrible than the last: hundreds of expectant mothers were given radioactive "vitamin drinks" to see how quickly the radioisotope crossed the placenta; patients at Billings Hospital in Chicago were literally injected with plutonium (one subject was given the highest dose ever measured in a human); and disabled schoolchildren were spoon-fed radioactive oatmeal after being told they were part of a "science club."

President Clinton, by executive order, created a committee to look into just how extensive the government's human-irradiating activities had been. The committee's thousand-page report was released in October 1995, and contained many, many more tidbits on the long, terrible history of the "Human Radiation Experiments":

Dozens of patients—usually elderly, black, or disabled patients—at several hospitals were injected with or fed radioactive material. Planes were ordered to fly through radiation clouds from bomb tests just to see how it would affect the crew. Subjects were made to dirty up their hands with radioactive soil to see what, if any, cleaning agents could remove the contamination, and on and on.

A 1986 report by the staff of Massachusetts Congressman Ed Markey titled "American Nuclear Guinea Pigs," which had been buried at the time of its release by the Reagan administration, was cited at length by the Committee—especially its helpful recommendation that, "It seems appropriate to urge the Department of Energy to make every practicable effort to identify the persons who served as subjects for the experiments described below, to examine the long term histories of subjects for an increased incidence of radiation associated diseases, and to compensate these human guinea pigs for damages they have suffered."

Appropriate? Yes, that would have been very appropriate. Was it ever done? No, no it was not.

TOP 10 People Who Exposed U.S. Government Secrets and Lies

by S. Grant

10 Gary Webb: The Dark Alliance

In 1996, Gary Webb, a writer for the *San Jose Mercury News*, published a series of articles known as "Dark Alliance." The articles detailed how the CIA turned a blind eye as Nicaraguan drug traffickers sold and distributed crack cocaine in Los Angeles throughout the 1980s. It also described how the Reagan administration protected drug dealers from prosecution.

According to Webb, the CIA allowed the traffickers to ship large amounts of drugs into the country because the profits were being used to fund the Reagan-supported Contras (a rebel group opposing the Socialist Sandinista government in Nicaragua).

Naturally, insinuating the crack cocaine epidemic of the '80s was partially caused by the government was a controversial stance—especially when the Reagan administration was already tainted by the Iran-Contra affair. Because of this, Webb's articles were initially viewed with contempt by the government and his fellow journalists. Speaking out caused him to lose his position at the *San Jose Mercury News* and he was never able to find a job writing daily news again.

In 2004, he was found dead, with two gunshot wounds to the head. Although Webb's family is confident that his depression and inability to find a job drove him to suicide—and that is the official cause of death—there are many who believe he was murdered.

Unfortunately, Webb was not vindicated until after his death, as recent internal investigations and declassified documents have affirmed his Dark Alliance reports.

9 Mark Felt: Watergate

Arguably the most famous whistleblower in U.S. history, FBI agent Mark Felt was responsible for feeding sensitive details about the Watergate scandal to *Washington Post* reporter Bob Woodward, which ultimately led to the resignation of President Richard Nixon. Felt was an anonymous source who went by the nickname "Deep Throat," and he didn't reveal himself as the informant until 2005—officially ending a public 30-year guessing game.

Felt told Woodward about the Nixon administration's illegal attempts to spy on political opponents at the Watergate Hotel, as well as a widespread spying and sabotage ring meant to help Nixon re-election. Felt also believed he was passed over as director of the FBI (following the death of J. Edgar Hoover) because Nixon wanted a man in charge who was easier to control.

There were many players involved in uncovering Watergate, and Woodward and his partner, Carl Bernstein, later admitted they were surprised people became so captivated by Deep Throat—he'd mostly just confirmed info they'd gotten from other sources. Nevertheless, receiving confirmation from the second in command at the FBI was just what they needed to legitimize their stories.

In 2008, Felt died peacefully in his home at the age of 95.

8 Daniel Ellsberg: The Pentagon Papers

In 1971, Daniel Ellsberg disclosed the Pentagon Papers and confirmed what many U.S. citizens had suspected for decades: The government lied about its actions and involvement in the Vietnam War through four consecutive presidential administrations.

Secretary of Defense Robert McNamara originally commissioned the papers in 1967 in an effort to create a history of the Vietnam War and a sort of "what not to do" account for future administrations. However, as the research grew more extensive, those involved realized the government had repeatedly lied to its people. Daniel Ellsberg, a military analyst, worked on the study and became fed up with the dishonesty, subterfuge, and seemingly endless war. So Ellsberg leaked the top-secret papers to the *New York Times*, which published a series of articles on the report's shocking findings.

Some of the worst evidence found in the papers included:
- The administration had strong intelligence that Vietnam was a war they could not win, but they joined anyway.

- The U.S. had no real interest in helping South Vietnam and entered the war only for political maneuvers.
- Leaving the war before a pro-American government was installed was never considered.
- The Kennedy administration had plans to overthrow South Vietnamese leader Ngo Dinh Diem.
- On the campaign trail, President Johnson promised to scale back the war even though he had specific plans to bomb North Vietnam.
- The U.S. expanded the war and conducted bombings and raids without informing the American people.

The list goes on and on, but it boils down to Eisenhower, Kennedy, Johnson, and Nixon all lying about Vietnam.

Ellsberg's whistle-blowing earned him and Russo a front row seat in front of a Los Angeles grand jury. They were charged with espionage, conspiracy, and theft, but the case was declared a mistrial when it was discovered the government illegally tapped Ellsberg's communications.

7 Thomas Drake: Trailblazer

How did Thomas Drake, a former senior executive at the National Security Agency (NSA), end up working retail at an Apple store? By doing such dastardly things as trying to protect the 4th amendment and eliminate wasteful spending. Yes, a man who was once privy to the nation's greatest secrets and technological strategies found himself showing people how to use the latest apps on their iPhone.

In reality, the gig at the Apple store was likely a relief for Drake, considering he was once being prosecuted under the Espionage Act of 1917 and facing 35 years in prison. He came into the government's crosshairs after disclosing unclassified information about Trailblazer, a $1.2 billion NSA program that infringed on people's right to privacy.

The government initially designed Trailblazer as a method of sifting through the increasing amounts of electronic communications created by the Internet, cell phones, and elsewhere. While having a program to fill such a need is understandable, there was an alternative program (known as Thinthread) that was more efficient, only cost $3 million, and didn't violate the privacy of ordinary citizens. Although Drake continually advocated using Thinthread, the bloated and unlawful Trailblazer system was adopted instead.

In 2011, the NSA's case against Drake collapsed and all felony charges against him were dropped. He never spent a day in jail and was only charged with the misdemeanor of "exceeding the authorized use of a computer."

6 Bunnatine (Bunny) Greenhouse: U.S. Army Corps of Engineers/Halliburton

The U.S. government's cozy relationship with the oilfield services company Halliburton has frequently aroused suspicion. Things looked even worse in 2003 when Bunny Greenhouse, the chief contracting officer at the U.S. Army Corp of Engineers, came forward saying the government showed favoritism to Halliburton and granted them a contract to rebuild the oilfield facilities in Iraq.

So, what was the problem with the contract? It was a no-bid arrangement, which means no other company had the opportunity to offer a price for the work. The Halliburton subsidiary Kellogg, Brown, and Root (KBR) was simply pushed through the usually cumbersome bureaucratic channels with no competition and given a $7 billion five-year contract. It was Greenhouse's job to monitor and approve such contracts, and she argued through the whole process that the arrangement was unjust. How was she rewarded for doing her job and trying to save the U.S. money? She received poor performance reviews, was demoted, and was stripped of her top-secret clearance.

After feeling discouraged and increasingly harassed, Greenhouse went public with the information while also revealing that Halliburton frequently overcharged the Pentagon and that Donald Rumsfeld's office controlled all aspects of the shady arrangement.

Greenhouse eventually filed a lawsuit against the U.S. Army Corp of Engineers for her treatment. In 2011, her employers settled the case for $970,000, which reflected full restitution for lost wages, compensatory damages, and attorney fees.

5 Coleen Rowley: FBI

Immediately after the September 11 tragedy, Americans were dumbfounded and wondering how a primitive group of terrorists could unleash an attack on U.S. soil without drawing suspicion from any of the country's intelligence agencies. It seemed impossible, and it was.

While government agencies feigned utter surprise, FBI Special Agent Coleen Rowley immediately came forward explaining that her Minneapolis field office knew Zacarias Moussaoui (one of the 9/11 conspirators) had paid $8,000 in cash for Boeing 747 flying lessons and was planning a suicide hijacking. However, her requests to search Moussaoui's room and computer were denied by her superiors.

Frustrated by the mishandling of information before and after the attacks, Rowley wrote a 13-page memorandum and hand-delivered copies to FBI Director Robert Mueller and two members of the Senate Intelligence Committee. Among other things, the letter claims the bureau deliberately thwarted efforts that may have stopped the 9/11 tragedy. *Time* magazine printed full details of the memo in its June 3, 2002, edition titled "The Bombshell Memo."

Rowley also testified in front of the 9/11 Commission about the debacle and wasn't shy in saying the deadly attacks could have been delayed or completely avoided if her office had been allowed to properly investigate the suspected terrorist.

Rowley retired from the FBI in 2004 and was named one of *Time*'s "Persons of the Year" in 2002.

4 Bradley Manning: United States Army

U.S. Army Private Bradley Manning is responsible for what some have called the biggest leak of secret military data ever. His actions also helped put WikiLeaks on the map, as he provided the organization with hundreds of thousands of classified documents.

Because Manning was a known disgruntled and often bullied worker, there is some debate regarding his intentions for the leak. Was he really trying to inform the public about crimes, brutality, and corruption within the government, or was he simply seeking revenge on his military associates, whom he described as a "bunch of hyper-masculine, trigger happy, ignorant rednecks"? Two of his superiors even advised not sending Manning to Iraq (where he eventually accessed the secret documents) because he was considered a "risk to himself and possibly others." However, Manning was one of the few qualified intelligence analysts available, and evidently the army thought his skills were worth the risk. Obviously, their gamble didn't pay off.

Among the things Manning revealed were:

- A secret video, nicknamed "collateral murder" that showed a U.S. air crew laughing after killing dozens of people (including reporters and civilians) in an air strike.
- Detailed records of the civilian death toll in Iraq (even though the military repeatedly said there was no record). Out of 109,000 deaths logged in a six-year period, 66,081 were unarmed civilians.
- U.S. soldiers committed horrific acts of torture on Iraqi prisoners, and despite hundreds of filed complaints, authorities never investigated.
- U.S. defense contractor DynCorp was involved in child trafficking.

Currently Manning is being imprisoned by the military and is facing 21 charges, including "aiding the enemy," which comes with a life sentence.

Yes, Manning is in jail for exposing the U.S. government for paying a company that sold child slaves.

3 Russell Tice: National Security Agency/ Defense Intelligence Agency

Does the NSA really care about the phone conversation you had with your grandma or the embarrassing pics you messaged your significant other? Apparently so.

According to Russell Tice, an ex-NSA intelligence officer, "The National Security Agency had access to all Americans' communications—faxes, phone calls, and their computer communications. It didn't matter whether you were in Kansas, in the middle of the country, and you never made foreign communications at all. They monitored all communications."

Besides illegally wiretapping and eavesdropping on ordinary citizens, it seems U.S. intelligence agencies are especially curious about the goings-on of journalists. Tice says he personally witnessed communication channels of journalists being recorded 24/7, and, although he's not sure what they did with the info, he's confident it's digitized and in a database somewhere.

In June 2013, Tice also divulged that the NSA even conducted unconstitutional domestic spying on judges, military officials, members of Congress, and more. Perhaps most shocking was the revelation that, back in 2004, his office was given the task of wiretapping a "40-something-year-old wannabe senator" from Illinois. Five years later the wannabe senator became president of the United States.

Tice was labeled "paranoid" by the NSA, demoted, and finally fired. He continues to tell his story to the media, Congress, and anyone who will listen.

2 Edward Snowden: National Security Agency

Edward Snowden worked as a technical contractor for the NSA and is currently making headlines for disclosing info on warrantless mass surveillance programs conducted by the U.S. and British governments. Essentially he is whistle-blowing about the same types of things Russ Tice did in 2005, but for whatever reason, it's woken the sleeping masses this time around. People everywhere are wondering why and to what extent the government is intruding into their private lives.

Some of the most shocking info Snowden has leaked is:
- An order from the Foreign Intelligence Surveillance Court to Verizon instructing them to hand over all metadata for all U.S. customer phone calls. Note: that is all phone calls made by U.S. citizens. Every phone call every minute of every day. Did you just talk to your mom? The NSA now has a record of that. Oh—and if you're not in America,

they are listening to you too if you spoke to an American or had any phone conversation with anyone in the world that passed through the U.S. phone system.

- The NSA program PRISM, which allows the NSA to monitor people's e-mail, Web searches, and overall Internet use (meaning they have direct access to Google, Facebook, and Apple).
- The NSA's record of hacking into China's computers, universities, and mobile phone companies.

At the time of publication, Snowden is staying in Russia and trying to find a safe haven to avoid extradition. If brought back to the U.S., he will face multiple charges, two of which fall under the Espionage Act: unauthorized communication of national defense information and willful communications of classified intelligence with an unauthorized person.

Although some on the left regard him as a traitor, most view Snowden's disclosures as the most important in American history. Even Daniel Ellsberg said there has never been a more crucial leak (including his own Pentagon Papers). On his blog he wrote, "Snowden's whistle-blowing gives us the possibility to roll back a key part of what has amounted to an 'executive coup' against the U.S. constitution." Change we can believe in? Well it sure is a change from the days when every U.S. citizen wasn't spied on by their government.

1 Peter Buxtun: The Tuskegee Syphilis Experiment

Today, we get our feathers ruffled when we learn the government is secretly spying on ordinary citizens. However, that injustice pales in comparison to what happened between 1932 and 1972 when the U.S. Public Health Service tricked people who were already down on their luck into becoming human lab rats.

It began when the U.S. Public Health Service teamed up with the Tuskegee Institute to study the long-term effects of syphilis on the human body. They contacted a group of 600 poor, African-American men (399 of whom had syphilis) and offered to give them free health care. However, this "health care" never involved treating the men for syphilis or even informing them they had the disease. Instead, the clinicians told the men they had "bad blood," an ambiguous and unscientific term for a variety of illnesses. Making matters worse, by the 1940s, penicillin was a proven cure for syphilis—yet none of the men received it.

Thanks to Peter Buxton, a 27-year-old employee of the U.S. Public Health Service, the 40-year study was put to an end in 1972 when Buxton revealed information about the experiment to the *Washington Star*. He went public with the details after filing multiple complaints within his organization and didn't receive a response. Unfortunately, dozens of men had died and many of their wives and children were infected by that time.

In 1997, President Clinton offered an official apology for the racist and inhumane study, but it seems the damage was already done.

TOP 10 Lesser Known Amazing Facts about the Human Body

by Mike Williams

10 Allergies as Cancer Prevention

Airborne allergies such as hay fever are among the worst allergies one can experience. While foods that trigger allergies may be readily avoided and many chemical exposures can be reduced, avoiding grass, dust, pollen, and mold may be exceedingly difficult. However, scientific research indicates that there may be a bright side to the scourge of spring and summer. Exposure to airborne allergens appears to tinker with the immune system in such a way that the risk of cancer is mitigated in allergy suffers. Preliminary research suggests statistically significant reductions in cancer among human study samples suffering from hay fever due to an immune stimulation effect similar to inoculation.

9 Syphilis: A KTI

Sexually transmitted infections are a scourge of modern society originating in behavioral, socioeconomic, and medical education shortcomings. Syphilis is a mutilating and eventually fatal disease if not treated, and it is often flagged as prime example of the STI problem. Believed to have originated from ancient human deviance with animals or unsafe consumption, syphilis is widely seen as a sexually transmitted illness. However, the illness is also transmissible through mere kissing as a Kissing Transmissible Infection (KTI). Spirochete bacterial infection manifests in the form of oral sores, and even boils on the hands and face. The first manifestation during the infectious stage is a small canker sore in the mouth. If the patient kisses another human, they may become infected with the diseases in certain cases.

8 Sense and Synesthesia

Humans frequently consider the possibility of a sixth sense. However, humans possess far more than five distinct senses. Vision is actually a combination of senses for light and color, while evidence shows that humans share some of the avian ability to detect magnetic fields. Humans also have the ability to detect their relative position, which is known as proprioception. The diversity of human sensory experience becomes even more complicated in the disorder known as synesthesia, where sounds may be associated with particular colors, or colors may be attributed to the descriptions of letters. Human senses are surprisingly subjective and may become highly confused as the brain interprets raw data collected through the body's many sensory systems.

7 Allergic to Work—Literally

Accusing someone of being "allergic to work" is a frequently used method of encouraging industry or taking laziness to task. But for those with exercise-induced anaphylaxis, being allergic to work is no joking matter. In fact, it may be a disabling reality that can be life-threatening at worst. Sufferers break out in hives upon exercise, often in concert with exposure to an aggravating food. The exact mechanism of the reaction is unknown, but a related condition known as cholinergic urticaria triggers allergic symptoms upon exposure to heat. It is thought that production of stress chemicals and changes in metabolism associated with exercise set the stage for the anaphylactic reactions to occur. Without treatment, complications can lead to potentially fatal shock.

6 Eye & Breast Tissue Discrepancies

Humans, like many other animals, display a startling degree of symmetry among body parts. Surprisingly, a small number of humans may be born with heterochromia iridum, or dual eye coloration. One eye may be blue, and the other brown or hazel. Causes of eye color discrepancies may stem from genetic mutations, or combinations of distinct cells. Although most people with this "condition" are born with it, rare cases of medication-induced heterochromia have been reported. A more common discrepancy is in breast size. Human females tend to have a slightly larger left breast than the mammary gland on the right. Additionally, the vestigial breast tissues in males may display the same discrepancy.

5 Herpes Keratitis Blindness

In developed countries, up to 60 percent of the population caries the herpes simplex virus, responsible for the distressing skin lesions euphemistically referred to as "cold sores." While this viral disease is seen by many people as an unappealing nuisance, cold sores are in fact potentially dangerous and rank as a leading cause of blindness worldwide. Herpes simplex resides in the facial nerves, and emerges into the skin causing lesions during active phase. However, the virus may also inhabit the optic and trigeminal nerves. During the active phase, virulent herpes can then form lesions on the cornea of the eye. Complications of the outbreaks may lead to blindness through keratosis and subsequent scarring, or even necrosis of eye tissues.

4 Organ Transplant Cell Memory

Traditional Western models of psychology and physiology tend to view the brain as the center of human intelligence where thoughts are formed and memories are stored. However, numerous reports from organ donation recipients claiming changes in personality have sparked interest in some researchers who believe that memories and thoughts that do not appear to be their own may originate from a more systemic consciousness that features cell memory. Cases where food preferences and even sexual orientation have switched have been reported, and in one especially eerie case, the recipient of a heart from a murder victim led police to the killer. It is unknown whether these changes could be purely stress related or if something much more mysterious is at work when human body parts are merged.

3 Optical Inversion

When we look at the world around us, we must remember that the veil of human perception means things are not always what they seem. When you glance at an object, the image received actually appears inverted on the retina. Our eyes in fact see everything upside down, but incredibly, our brain compensates by default, allowing us to perceive the world right-side up. The brain's ability to be misled in this regard presents an eerie insight into the potential for manipulation of human experience. In a series of experiments, volunteers wore lenses to turn the world upside down. This reversal caused the brains of the subjects to stop compensating for the retinal inversion in order to see upright. When the lenses were removed, the participants saw upside down for a time.

2 Extra Ribs

Humans are normally equipped with 24 symmetrical ribs to protect the vital organs, but around 1 in 500 people are born with an extra rib extending from the neck and shoulder section, known as the thoracic outlet. The cervical rib, or in even rarer cases, extra pair, may interfere with the blood supply to the arm, causing a loss of pulse when the arm is moved in certain directions. The vestigial rib is believed to be connected with genes that suppress cancer risks, but the nature of this effect is unknown. In some cases, complications include numbness, tingling, coldness in the hands, and, most disturbingly, a protruding sensation in the arm. The ribs are useful in other mammals, but are vestigial in humans.

1 Born with Teeth

Human babies are certainly not as precocious as many other mammal species such as ungulates (hooved mammals) that are born ready to walk on their own. Teeth in humans normally start to appear after six months, but around 1 in 2,000 infants are born with neonatal teeth appearing through the gumline. Although mildly startling, newborns with teeth are often perfectly healthy, as the condition may not be associated with harmful genetic mutations. The often loose teeth may form a choking hazard, and are known to be capable of inflicting rather painful bites if the infant is allowed to nurse. Normally, only one or two teeth appear in cases of neonatal dentition development.

TOP 10 Fascinating Scientific and Psychological Effects

by **Andy Martin**

10 Allee Effect

The Allee effect is a biological phenomenon where the per capita population growth of a species (or a population within that species) drops when the total number of members of the species drops. Stated differently, each female gives birth to more offspring when density is higher within a population. Named after American zoologist Walter Clyde Allee, the effect changed the common understanding of population growth.

At the time of his studies, it was believed that populations would, in fact, thrive at a certain lower population, because more resources would be available to those fewer specimens. In other words, population growth would slow with higher numbers, and grow with smaller numbers. However, the work of Allee (and others) demonstrated that as population drops, so does the number of available mates—and the amount of group protection—and thus, the population growth slows. Conversely, the more members of a population there are, the faster growth occurs.

9 Audience Effect & Drive Theory

The audience effect is the effect an audience has on a person or a group of people who are attempting to perform a certain task while being watched. First studied by psychologists in the 1930s, the audience effect primarily shows up in two opposite extremes: many performers (athletes in particular) will actually raise their level of play when a large crowd is watching, while others will succumb to stress and self-consciousness and end up performing worse than their true talent level.

In 1965, social psychologist Ribert Zajonc suggested that the drive theory could account for the audience effect. Zajonc postulated that what determines whether a passive audience causes a positive or a negative effect on the performer depends upon the relative "easiness" of the task being performed. If the performer believes that she should win a fight, for instance, the audience effect will tend to motivate her to perform at a high level. If she is unsure to begin with, the audience effect may facilitate a loss due to lower self-esteem.

8 Pygmalion Effect

Related to the audience and drive effects is the Pygmalion effect, which connects the positive expectations placed upon a performer to the resulting high quality of that performance. Named after the classic George Bernard Shaw play *Pygmalion* (upon which the film *My Fair Lady* is based), and sometimes called the "Rosenthal effect," the effect is essentially a type of self-fulfilling prophecy. The opposite of the Pygmalion effect, which states that lower expectations may lead to lower performance levels and success, is known as the "golem effect."

The effects of Pygmalion have been studied at length in the world of athletics, business, and especially education. In business, the effect is seen most often in the way managers get results based on their expectations of their own employees; as former business professor J. Sterling Livingston noted in his studies of the effect, "The way managers treat their subordinates is subtly influenced by what they expect of them." Similarly, the research conducted by Robert Rosenthal and Lenore Jacobson on the Pygmalion effect in the classroom suggests that when teachers expect higher performance from certain students, those students deliver more likely than not.

7 Bruce Effect

When pregnant female rodents detect the smell of an unknown male, they will occasionally terminate their own pregnancy. This effect, first studied by British zoologist Hilda Bruce, has also been observed in certain mice, voles, lemmings, gelada monkeys, and perhaps even lions. Thought for some time to be restricted to animals in captivity, the effect was observed and studied in the wild for the first time by Uni-

versity of Michigan researcher Eila Roberts. The burning question, in all cases, is: Why would a mother abort her own child?

Roberts spent five years studying geladas in Ethiopia and collected data from 110 females from 21 different groups. After analyzing fecal samples for hormones that would give her hard pregnancy data, Roberts discovered that in groups where a male gelada had asserted his dominance—effectively "taking over" the group—a significant number of females experienced early termination of their pregnancies. Groups without a male takeover, on the other hand, saw far, far higher birthrates. The answer to the $64,000 question hinges on the tendency for dominant males to kill infant geladas; they do this because females are only fertile after they stop raising their young, and the males get impatient. As to why the mothers terminate their unborn babies, it's speculated that knowing the babies will be killed anyway, it will save the mothers wasted time, effort, and resources.

6 Leidenfrost Effect

If you've ever sprayed droplets of water on a very hot pan and seen those droplets skitter around like crazy, then you've observed the Leidenfrost effect. Named after German doctor Johann Gottlob Leidenfrost way back in 1796, the Leidenfrost effect is the physical phenomenon of what happens when a liquid comes extremely close to a surface that is much hotter than the liquid's boiling point. Under these conditions, the liquid creates a protective layer of vapor that surrounds itself and prevents rapid boiling. In the case of water droplets zooming around on a hot pan, the water does eventually boil and evaporate, but much more slowly than if the pan had been between the boiling point and the Leidenfrost point.

This effect allows water, under certain conditions, to travel uphill. It's also the reason you can stick a wet finger into liquid nitrogen without damage or even safely hold liquid nitrogen in your mouth. But seriously, don't try either of those. They're extremely dangerous.

5 Diorama Effect

The diorama effect—also known as "miniature faking" and the "diorama illusion"—describes when a photograph of a real-life, life-size subject is manipulated in such a way that it ends up looking like a miniature scale model. It's also sometimes described as the "tilt-shift" effect, though for the sake of accuracy it should be noted that tilt-shifting is a photographic technique that often results in a fake-miniature photograph. One can apply tilt-shift effects to a digital photograph taken normally to give the impression one has actually used a tilt-shift lens.

There are a number of steps involved in creating a fake-miniature photograph. In effect, it boils down to a few keys elements:

- Shoot the photo from above.
- Use heavy blurring around the edges of the photo.
- Boost the color saturation.

There can be a lot more to it, of course. Check out online tutorials for a step-by-step guide.

4 Overview Effect

Of all the psychological effects ever named, observed, and studied, the overview effect has to be in the running for the least common—only 534 people have ever experienced the conditions that lead to it. When astronauts in orbit or on the surface of the moon first see the Earth in its entirety, many report feeling a deep sense of scale and perspective that has come to be called the overview effect. Coined by writer Frank White, the effect can be deeply moving, confusing, inspiring, and emotionally challenging, as a view of the entire Earth changes one's perspective in a profound way. Astronauts have returned home with a renewed sense of the way we're all connected, of the relative meaninglessness of cultural boundaries, and a desire to take care of the Earth's environment.

3 Pratfall Effect

Let's say you have a crush on someone, and this person seems talented, kind, and graceful. Then let's say you see her trip on the sidewalk and take a giant spill, falling flat on her face. For various reasons, the intensity of your crush increases, and you find yourself even more attracted to her as a result of her clumsiness.

Studied especially in the world of sports, business, and politics, this is a psychological phenomenon known as the "pratfall effect." Originally described and named by researcher Elliot Aronson in 1966, the pratfall effect carries with it certain implications. Research on the subject suggests that people tend to like others who are imperfect, who make mistakes, and who admit errors. The effect has been dissected and refined—for instance, it's been found that it affects the attractiveness of clumsy women to men more than vice versa—but the fundamental principle of someone becoming more likable as they display imperfections remains.

2 Sleeper Effect

The sleeper effect is an oft-studied, controversial psychological effect that has to do with the way people's opinions are affected by messages they receive. In general, when a viewer sees an advertisement with a positive message, that viewer will create a positive association with the message (and the product). Over time, however, that positive association fades, and eventually there may have been no net positive to the ad at all. Under certain conditions, however, if the initial message comes with a "discounting cue," the positive associations may actually remain for a longer period of time.

A "discounting cue" usually comes in the form of a source that's not considered reliable or trustworthy, when the message comes with a disclaimer, or when you hear something from an unusual source. For instance, if you see a negative political ad paid for by the opponent of the ad's subject, you may initially be suspicious of the ad's credibility; over time, however, you may start to believe the message. Research has suggested that the sleeper effect is real but very difficult to pull off in reality, and that in order to be truly effective, it must follow a strict set of guidelines.

1 Tamagotchi Effect

Ah, the Tamagotchi. If you lived through the 1990s, you probably owned one, knew someone who did, or at the very least knew about them. As of 2010, over 76 million of the little electronic critters have been sold worldwide. A Tamagotchi, for those of you scratching your heads, is a small, hand-held "digital pet" invented in 1996 in Japan. A Tamagotchi's owner is responsible for, among other tasks, feeding, administering medicine, disciplining, and cleaning up after it.

The Tamagochi effect is the psychological phenomenon of owners becoming emotionally attached to a robot or other digital object. A person may come to see their relationship with a Tamagotchi, a cell phone, a robot, or even a piece of software as a viable emotional relationship. Research suggests that the Tamagotchi effect is seen in all ages and has both positive and negative psychological implications for a person's mental health.

TOP 10 Astonishing Near-Death Experiences

by **Shawn W. Larson**

10 Veronika-Ulrike Barthel

Veronika Barthel says that, after being struck by lightning while driving her car one day in 1981, she was instantly transported into hell, where she found demons escorting her into a big waiting room.

The creatures that I saw there were more terrifying than anything I even saw in a horror movie. Today I know that they were demons. As soldiers they were marching past me, and in the middle of them were people that were screaming with pain. It was very difficult to breathe down there, because of the terrible smell of this place. I saw a lake, which looked like the inner part of a volcano, where people were cursing because of great pain.

She says that she saw people being thrown into caves, which were guarded by demons who threw spears at them as they screamed. She also recalled there being snakes all over the ground to frighten and intimidate the people in hell.

After her experience, Veronika found herself transported back into her car, where for a moment, she saw her own burning hands gripping the steering wheel.

9 Howard Storm

Once a self-described "double atheist" and "know-it-all college professor," Howard Storm was leading a three-week European art tour with his students when he retired to his hotel room in France on the last day of the trip. Without warning, he suddenly screamed and dropped to the floor, prompting his wife to call for help. At the hospital, the news was grim: Howard had a perforated stomach that required surgery, and if he didn't get it soon, he would die.

The wait for a doctor to arrive at the hospital was lengthy—so much so that Howard turned to his wife at one point and said his final farewell to her, insisting that he was moments from death. That's when he recalled finding himself standing next to his own body (which was still on the hospital bed) and feeling more alive than ever, with no more stomach pain. Soon after, he heard unfamiliar voices calling to him.

"Come with us," they said. "Hurry up, let's go. We've been waiting for you."

After calling out to his wife and getting no response, he began to follow the voices, which led him out of the room and down a long, dark hallway. He followed them for so long and became so increasingly terrified that he told the voices he wasn't going any farther. Then they attacked him.

"We had a big fight and the fight turned into them annihilating me, which they did slowly and with much relish," he says. "Mostly they were biting and tearing at me. This went on for a long time. They did other things to humiliate and violate me which I don't talk about."

Collapsed on the ground, Howard began reciting the Lord's Prayer after hearing a soft voice tell him to "pray to God." After saying a few other prayers, he said that Jesus personally saved him from the demons and sent him back to Earth, telling him to live his life differently. Storm's book, *My Descent Into Death*, was published in 2000.

8 Dr. Mary Neal

During a kayaking trip in 1999, Dr. Mary Neal became pinned under the water when her kayak capsized, making it impossible for her to breathe for anywhere between 15 and 25 minutes. That's when she says she experienced a near-death experience that brought her into the presence of God, Jesus, and angels.

During the experience, God told her that her family would be facing an upcoming tragedy and would need her to help them through. Specifically, her nine-year-old son Willie was going to die—but she wasn't told when, where, or how. Ten years later, at age 19, Willie was killed in a car accident in Maine by a driver who was on his cell phone.

Mary is convinced Jesus helped her under the water, making it possible for rescue workers to revive her following the kayaking accident. She awoke with two broken legs and lung complications, and spent a month in the hospital, followed by six weeks in a wheelchair. She wrote a book called *To Heaven and Back*, which was published in May 2012.

7 Ben Breedlove

When 18-year-old Ben Breedlove of Austin, Texas, began posting a series of videos on YouTube telling the world about his rare heart condition, they instantly went viral, attracting millions of viewers. In one of them, he tells the story of being wheeled down a dark hall by nurses to the surgery room and seeing a bright, peaceful light near the ceiling. He was four at the time it happened.

Through a series of index cards in the video, he wrote: "There were no lights on in this hall. I couldn't take my eyes off it, and I couldn't help but smile. I had no worries at all, like nothing else in the world mattered." He talks of different times when he "cheated death," including an incident when he fainted in the hallway at school.

> While I was still unconscious, I was in this white room; no walls, it just went on and on. There was no sound, but that same peaceful feeling I had when I was four. I was wearing a really nice suit, and so was my favorite rapper, Kid Cudi. I then looked at myself in the mirror—I was proud of myself, of my entire life, everything

I have done. It was the best feeling. I didn't want to leave that place. I wish I never woke up.

Ben's videos attracted the attention of rapper Kid Cudi, who apparently "broke down" after viewing them. He responded, "I broke down, I am to tears [sic] because I hate how life is so unfair. This has really touched my heart in a way I can't describe, this is why I do what I do. Why I write my life, and why I love you all so much."

On Christmas Day 2011, one week after posting the videos, Ben Breedlove suffered a heart attack and died. A family friend stated, "There are times that [the family is] overwhelmed by the pain and the loss of Ben, but then it's replaced with knowing that he was at peace with what was going to happen." The final index cards in Ben's last video stated, "Do you believe in angels or God? I do."

6 Colton Burpo

Colton Burpo wasn't quite four years old when his appendix burst, landing him in a hospital for emergency surgery. When he awoke two hours later, he had an amazing story to tell. He said he had been to heaven, where he met Jesus, John the Baptist, God, and even family members who had passed away previously—including a baby sister that his mother had lost due to a miscarriage. Neither of his parents had ever mentioned the miscarriage to him.

He also met an old man he called "Pop," whom he had seen as a young man. Later, he was able to identify Pop in a family photograph as the man he had seen in heaven. It was his paternal grandfather. And Colton told his father that while the surgery was taking place he had seen him in another room, where he had gone to pray.

His father, Todd Burpo, said, "We knew he wasn't making it up, because he was able to tell us what we were doing in another part of the hospital. Not even Sonja had seen me in that little room, having my meltdown with God."

Todd wrote a book called *Heaven Is for Real* that recounts the entire story of his son's incredible experience in detail. Colton Burpo now travels the country with his parents, sharing his story with others.

5 Betty J. Eadie

In November 1973, Betty Eadie underwent a partial hysterectomy, after which she says she floated out of her body and passed through a tunnel to heaven. She said she was guided by three hooded, monklike figures who claimed to have always been her guardian angels and informed her that she had died prematurely.

In an excerpt from her book, *Embraced by the Light*, she recalls:

I saw a pinpoint of light in the distance. The black mass around me began to take on more of the shape of a tunnel, and I felt myself traveling through it at an even greater speed, rushing toward the light. I was instinctively attracted to it, although again, I felt that others might not be. As I approached it, I noticed the figure of a man standing in it, with the light radiating all around him. There was no questioning who he was; I knew that he was my savior, and friend, and God. He was Jesus Christ, who had always loved me, even when I thought he hated me.

Following its publication in September 1994, her book became a number-one bestseller and remains in print today.

4 Don Piper

Following a pastor's conference in January 1989, Don Piper was driving over a bridge when a Texas Department of Corrections tractor-trailer truck crossed the centerline and ran into him head-on. He said he was "instantly transported to heaven," where he found himself surrounded by dead relatives and friends, and a large pearl gate.

"The gate of heaven was a magnificent edifice, the one that I saw. It looked no less like a giant gate that had been sculpted from mother-of-pearl," he said. "Behind that portal was such a light that I don't conceive of how you could see it in an earthly body. It could only be envisioned in a heavenly body because it was too bright."

As he lay there crushed in his vehicle on the bridge, a pastor came by who prayed over him. The EMS staff had told him that Don was deceased. After the pastor prayed, Don instantly found himself back in his vehicle, staring up at a tarp that had been draped over him. At the hospital, it was revealed that, although he suffered no major head trauma, nearly every bone in his body had been broken or shattered. Don wrote a book called *90 Minutes in Heaven* after his recovery.

3 Bill Wiese

In his book *23 Minutes in Hell*, author Bill Wiese tells the story of laying in bed at 3 a.m. and being suddenly thrown into the depths of hell, where he was tormented by demons. He said he was placed in a small cell with vicious "beasts" who looked like reptiles. He recalls understanding that they had been assigned to torment him, which they did, throwing him against the walls and piercing his flesh with their claws. The pain became so bad that he wished for death but was not obliged. He said that he heard the cries of millions, who were either burning in hell or being tortured as he was.

2 Crystal McVea

Following a simple medical procedure for pancreatitis in 2009, Crystal McVea of Oklahoma went into full respiratory arrest on the operating table. She says that when that happened, she experienced a trip to heaven that renewed her faith in God, whom she met in person. She described him as "an immense brightness," one that she could "feel, taste, touch, hear, and smell," and recalled having 500 senses while in heaven, as opposed to the traditional human five.

"I had angels, I had God, and I fell to my knees in front of him," she said, adding that she'd always been a doubter prior to the experience. When she was asked twice by God if she'd like to return to Earth, she chose to stay both times. But despite her insistence, God sent her back—though not before relieving her of her guilt and shame.

McVea released a book about her experience called *Waking Up in Heaven* in April 2013.

1 Ian McCormack

While diving for lobster one day on the island of Mauritius, Ian McCormack was stung on the arm by a box jellyfish. He says that by the time the ambulance arrived he already felt completely paralyzed and necrosis had begun to set in. As he lay dying, McCormack saw a vision of his mother praying for him, and after he made it to the hospital, he was clinically dead for a period of 15–20 minutes. That's when he found himself in a very dark place and began to hear people screaming.

> From the darkness I began to hear men's voices screaming at me telling me to "shut up"—that I "deserved to be there"—that I was "in Hell." I couldn't believe it, but as I stood there a radiant beam of light shone through the darkness and immediately began to lift me upward. I found myself being translated up into an incredibly brilliant beam of pure white light—it seemed to be emanating from a circular opening far above me (I felt like a speck of dust being drawn up into a beam of sunlight).

As he walked toward the light, Ian says he could feel it giving off a "living emotion," and that God then spoke to him. McCormack hasn't written a book but has shared his story with several news outlets and talk shows.

TOP 10 Ridiculously Cool Natural Phenomena

by **MJ Alba**

10 Volcanic Lightning

If someone asked you to name the two coolest things you could ever see in nature, your answer would be "volcanoes and lightning." Or possibly "lightning and volcanoes," I guess, but those are the only two options—it's just a fact. But nature, it seems, is constantly looking for new ways to impress us, which is why it went ahead and made volcanic lightning a reality.

And yes, it's exactly what it sounds like: a lightning storm that takes place in the middle of a volcanic eruption. Scientists aren't 100 percent sure why this happens, but the primary theory goes that when a volcano erupts, it projects positively charged debris into the atmosphere. These charges then react with negative charges already present, which results in a bolt of lightning and a really cool picture.

9 Brinicles

When the surface of the sea freezes—such as around the North and South Poles—it does so in a way that forces pockets of especially cold and salty seawater to gather on the underside of the ice. This mixture of brine is denser than the seawater below it, and as a result it tends to slowly sink to the bottom. Now, because it's so cold, the fresher water below the brine actually freezes around it as it falls, which results in a giant icicle under the surface. The technical name for this sort of thing is "ice stalactite," but what kind of boring title is that for such a breathtaking phenomenon? Hence the need for their cool nickname, "brinicles." Regular English didn't have a good enough word, so we had to come up with a whole new one (or, more accurately, sloppily mash together two old ones).

8 Penitentes

Here's another cool ice formation about as far away from underwater as you can get—high in the mountains. These spiky fields of ice are called penitentes, and each individual shard can be up to a whopping 13 feet high. These intimidating snow structures are formed in high-altitude areas with low humidity, such as the glaciers of the Andes Mountains. If the conditions are right, the sun's rays are so hot that they can actually sublimate fields of snow, meaning that the frozen water vaporizes without ever becoming a liquid. This leads to slight pockets in the ice, which—thanks to their shape—actually end up attracting even more heat. The sharp spikes, then, are just the lucky parts of the snowfield that the sun didn't target for complete and utter annihilation.

7 Supercells

If Superman is basically a stronger, more flight-enabled version of a regular man, then a supercell is basically a stronger, more tornado-enabled version of a regular storm cell. This is because, much like tornadoes, supercells have the tendency to spin around a lot, but also—and more importantly— because they can actually create tornadoes. If you remember one thing after reading this article, let it be this: Stay the hell away from things that can do that.

In case it needed to be mentioned, supercells are the most dangerous of the four major storm types, in addition to being the scariest to look at. Thankfully, they're also the rarest, and tend to be confined to the central United States during the springtime. If you ever happen to come across one, wherever you are, just remember the advice you got before: Move in the other direction.

6 Fire Rainbows

These colorful offshoots can often be seen during the summers of middle-latitude areas, such as most of the United States. What they actually are is a large halo of refracted light, and despite their nickname, they have nothing to do with either fire or rainbows. They only occur when the sun is at least 58 degrees above the horizon, when there are cirrus clouds in the sky that are filled with plate-shaped ice crystals. The refraction of light is always parallel to the horizon, and because the arcs are so big, only sections of them are ever commonly seen—which is why it can look like certain patches of cloud are on fire. The proper name for these, in case you ever need to impress a scientist, is "circumhorizontal arc."

5 Sun Dogs

Here's another phenomenon that has to do with ice crystals in the atmosphere. Like fire rainbows, sun dogs are massive halos in the sky as a result of light refraction, though in this case, they appear to actually encircle the sun. Sun dogs can be recognized by the two distinctive bright spots on either side of the halo; if these blips are bright enough, it can even look like there are three suns in the sky, all side by side. And the good news is that this happens all the time, all over the world, so you'll be able to start seeing them if you look closely enough (especially when the sun is low in the sky). Just remember that if you look closely enough at the sun for too long, you won't be able to see much of anything. Ever. So be careful.

4 Waterspouts

Waterspouts are exactly as awesome as they sound: They're tornadoes that form over water. Because of this, they don't pose a major threat unless you happen to be in a boat—but if you are, then watch out, because these things can achieve speeds of up to 190 miles per hour. In fact, it's been speculated that many mysterious shipwrecks—such as those within the Bermuda Triangle—are simply a result of bad luck with waterspouts. They can occur anywhere over water, but are especially prevalent in the Florida Keys, where there can be 400 or 500 waterspouts a year.

3 Snow Donuts

You know how when you were a kid, and it snowed outside, the first thing you did was roll up a nice big snowball? You either threw it at somebody's face or made a snowman with it (depending on what type of kid you were), but that's not the important part of the memory right now. The important thing—the fantastic thing—is that nature has its own way of rolling snowballs: snow donuts. These rare shapes are formed—only under perfect temperature conditions—when a mass of snow either falls or is blown by the wind. If it manages to catch on to some other snow, and gravity or the wind is in its favor, then the new snowball will roll itself in the exact same way kids do. In this case, though, the middles tend to collapse to create a donut shape, which can end up as tall as 26 inches.

2 Columnar Basalt

Admittedly, on the surface this doesn't seem all that impressive—columns aren't traditionally very exciting—but when put together into a sprawling honeycomb, this type of basalt is a sight to behold. The unique formations are a result of lava flows cracking as they cool, in a perpendicular direction to the original flow. Columnar basalt clusters can be found all over the world—and then, naturally, climbed.

1 Frost Flowers

Frost flowers are buildups of ice particles around the base of certain plants and types of wood. When the temperature outside the plant is below freezing and the temperature within them is not, then water is pulled to the surface in a process similar to transpiration. This leads to a fragile chain of ice being pushed outward, which ends up forming sprawling, delicate formations. So they're not exactly flowers—more like leaves, if anything—but they're just as pretty to look at, and at least twice as cool.

TOP 10 People Who Survived Your Worst Nightmares

by **Mike Floorwalker**

10 Joan Murray: Fell 14,500 Feet onto a Mound of Fire Ants

In September of 1999, 47-year-old Joan Murray experienced failure of her main parachute during a skydive from over 14,500 feet. By the time she got her reserve chute to deploy, she was less than 1,000 feet from the ground. She spun out of control, her reserve chute lost most of its air volume, and she smacked into the ground traveling at 80 miles per hour, landing directly on a large fire ant mound.

Murray broke most of the bones in her entire right side, and fillings shot from her teeth upon impact; yet she somehow was alive, though unconscious. The whole situation didn't go over well with the fire ants. Joan was bitten over 200 times before paramedics were able to assist her. Incredibly, her doctors (one of whom scrawled "miracle" on her chart) think the ant bites may have aided in Joan's survival by causing an extreme adrenaline response. Several years, and more than 20 reconstructive surgeries and countless physical therapy sessions later, Murray returned to work, life, and skydiving—taking her 37th dive in 2002.

9 Louis Nell: Attacked by Two Pit Bulls

At first, it was just a dog owner's worst nightmare: Louis Nell's golden retriever, Chrissy, was being attacked in their home by two aggressive pit bulls that had come out of nowhere. Then Louis made an attempt to defend his dog, and it quickly turned into a situation that could have spelled the end for Louis himself.

The pit bulls, the dogs of one of Louis's neighbors, had burst in through their screen door and set upon Chrissy before anyone knew what was happening. His wife, Linda, frantically dialed police as Louis fought with the animals "for a good five to ten minutes," sustaining a profusely bleeding bite on one hand after he toppled over while trying to pin one of the dogs beneath a chair.

Fortunately, police arrived quickly and shot one of the dogs dead on the scene (the other was later euthanized). Chrissy was killed in the attack.

"They tore her throat completely open," said Linda. But if not for Louis's bravery and the quick police response, it could have turned out much, much worse.

8 Geary and Suzan Whaley: Picked Up by a Tornado

In late May 2013, a series of tornadoes rocked the central United States; Oklahoma, it could be argued, took the worst of it. On May 20, a twister that devastated the town of Moore killed 24 people. By May 31, nine more had died as multiple twisters tore across central Oklahoma. One of these tornadoes, an E4—the second-most powerful rating, was sighted near the town of Shawnee by husband and wife Geary and Suzan Whaley as they were heading home on the highway. They don't remember much else about the rest of the day, but investigators think they tried to pull under an overpass (bad idea), where the twister met them, picking up their truck and sucking them both right out the windows.

Suzan had been shooting video of the twister on her cell phone when it struck, and it continued shooting through the entire incident. She says she can barely remember waking up on the ground, cell phone still in hand, her husband missing. She found him over 50 feet away, with about a dozen broken bones but somehow still alive. They now know that the structure of an underpass can amplify a tornado's winds, but hopefully it's knowledge they won't need to use again. Amazingly, their dog Rocky was also with them at the time and went missing afterward, until he was found four days later, trapped under some debris and also alive.

7 Theresa Christian: Locked in a Freezer for Five Days

Yes, twisters are to be avoided at all costs...well, almost. For the claustrophobic among us, here's an example of how some methods of protecting yourself from a tornado can potentially turn even scarier than the tornado itself. Investigators believe Theresa Christian, 59 at the time, was attempting to take shelter in a deep freezer when she accidentally locked herself inside. And she remained there for five days.

Unbelievably, her sons dropped by on day four and turned over the apartment, calling their mother's name, to no avail. On Wednesday, they and an apartment maintenance crew returned. This time, Theresa's son Stewart heard a very faint cry for help. They discovered her sitting upright, conscious, inside the deep freezer—which was itself inside a closet. The lid was cracked, but she was unable to move. She had severe frostbite on her legs and was hospitalized in serious condition. Oddly, no inclement weather was forecasted for the area at the time—it's just the only explanation authorities could come up with, and Theresa wasn't talking.

6 Janis Ollson: Cut in Half for Cancer Treatment

A diagnosis of cancer is never good, but Janis Ollson's diagnosis was of the type that would make most people simply crumble. There was cancerous bone tissue in the middle of her pelvis, and doctors told her that her only option was essentially to be disassembled to get at the problem area, then put back together again like a puzzle. She would lose her left leg, and her right would have to be totally detached during the procedure. And they weren't sure if they would be able to reattach it.

Basically, the surgery involved cutting Janis Ollson in two, and it was her only hope. Despite the procedure never having been attempted on a living patient, doctors at the Mayo Clinic in Rochester, Minnesota, were willing to give it a shot. Since the treatment would leave "no bony continuity between her torso and her remaining leg" (in the words of Dr. Michael Yaszemski, who originated the treatment), bone from her amputated left leg was used to reattach the right, closer to her spine in the center of her body. Over two surgeries of 28 hours, with 240 staples used to piece Janis together, the groundbreaking procedure was done—and it was successful. Obviously, there was incredibly demanding rehabilitation, and lots of it, required. And Janis requires a bit of hardware to get around, but she isn't complaining. Since her lifesaving treatment, it has been attempted on three other patients, two of whom died.

5 Rita Chretien: Stranded in the Wilderness for Seven Weeks

Rita Chretien and her husband, Albert, set out for Las Vegas from their home in British Columbia in their van in March 2011. She would later tell journalists that the couple had little experience on such a trip, and they were relying on their GPS to guide them accurately. On March 20, their van became bogged down in the snowy Nevada wilderness, unable to go any farther. There it remained until May 6, when it was found by hunters on ATVs. The  search had been on since March 30, when they had been expected home by their children. May 6 was the very day, Rita said, that she felt the last of her energy slipping away after surviving on a small amount of trail mix and hard candy for the past 49 days. When she heard the hunters' engines, she had just laid down to prepare to die.

Albert had set out for help two days after the van became stuck, but he unfortunately did not get anywhere near it—he was over five miles from the nearest town when his frozen body was finally found in late September 2012. He had, however, made it roughly the same distance from the van, a valiant effort in unforgiving conditions. Sheriff's Deputy David Prall said, "Once he [Albert] lost the ability to use that GPS, due to the snow drifts, he couldn't tell where the road was. He did a lot of unnecessary climbing. He was heading literally for the summit of the mountain...where he made it to was far beyond what he was equipped for...this man had tremendous courage and inner strength to get where he was."

4 Randal McCloy, Jr.: Trapped by Sago Mine Explosion

On January 2, 2006, an explosion at the Sago Mine in West Virginia trapped 13 miners for two days. According to Randal McCloy, Jr.—the only one of them to make it out alive—at least four of the miners' emergency breathing devices failed. And that was only the nail in their coffin, as many oversights were eventually found to have contributed to the blast.

For one, McCloy also reported after his rescue that about three weeks prior to the incident, he and a coworker had come upon a pocket of methane—which, for the record, is explosive—while drilling in the roof of the mine. After reporting this, they found the next day that the leak they had reported had been plugged up with glue used for sealing bolts in the mine walls. And that was the last they heard of it.

McCloy came very close to the same fate as all of his coworkers—death by carbon monoxide poisoning. Even with all of the emergency breathing devices functioning, his survival would have been improbable. They provide an hour's worth of oxygen, and help did not arrive until 41 hours after the explosion. Unbelievably, some news outlets erroneously reported during the incident that one miner had died and twelve had been rescued, prompting relief from a dozen families whose hearts were broken when the numbers were reversed just hours later.

3 Regan Martin: Abducted by a Serial Killer

David Alan Gore was a rapist and serial killer who was active in the late 1970s and early '80s in the United States. He was executed for his crimes in 2012, and his accomplice Fred Waterfield was sentenced to consecutive life sentences in prison. In all, Gore killed six women. He and Waterfield abducted their final two victims on July 26, 1983. They were 14-year-old

Regan Martin and 17-year-old Lynn Elliott, and it's a day Regan will never forget: She's the only one of Gore's victims to survive.

It began when Gore and Waterfield picked the girls up at the beach, planning to bring any who were willing to go back to Gore's parents house (they were out of town) and rape them. After getting Martin and Elliott in the car, the glove box popped open, revealing a .22 pistol, which Gore used to threaten Martin. At first taking it for a joke, it quickly became apparent that it was not. They were taken to the house, where both were sexually assaulted.

In all likelihood, Elliott saved Martin's life—and sacrificed her own—by attempting to escape. While Gore was assaulting Martin, Elliott slipped out of the house, naked and handcuffed, and was running down the driveway when Gore spotted her, having heard the door. He shot Elliott in the head in full view of a child witness, and it was her murder that he was convicted of and sentenced to die for in 1984. The witness called police, who were able to arrive in time to rescue Martin.

2 Anna Hjelle: Attacked by a Mountain Lion

Mountain lions are notoriously territorial animals. The one that attacked 30-year-old ex-marine Anna Hjelle in 2007 had killed before—in fact, it had killed another victim earlier that day—and it was going for seconds. Anna had been mountain biking in the wrong place, and if not for the quick thinking and immense bravery of her friend Debby Nicholls, she would likely not be here to tell her story.

Debby refused to let go of Anna's legs as the giant cat was attempting to drag Anna by her face into the wilderness. Anna remained conscious throughout, and distinctly remembers thinking that she should really just die. "You think about the fact that your face is ripped off," she said. And roughly half of it was. Two more bikers heard screaming and came to help, fending off the lion with rocks while Debby held on. The lion eventually acquiesced, and the men carried Anna up the trailhead while continuing to be stalked by the lion.

Police shot the big cat as it was hovering near the body of Mark Reynolds, whom it had killed and partially eaten earlier in the day. Anna was airlifted to an Orange County hospital, where she received some 2,000 stitches over five hours of surgery.

1 Eugene Han and Kirstin Davis: Shot in Colorado Movie Theater Massacre

Finally, we have a couple who picked the worst possible time and place to go to a movie: They were present at the notorious theater massacre carried out by James Holmes in July 2012. A dozen people died in the Aurora, Colorado, mass shooting. Eugene and Kirstin were among 70 who were injured but survived the massacre, but their story is unique for one awesome reason.

The couple was attending the midnight screening after Eugene's 12-hour shift at work, and as such, he fell asleep during the previews. As he woke, Holmes entered through the exit door, a mere ten feet or so away. Eugene saw the outline of his gun against the movie screen, and knew there was about to be big trouble. Then the tear gas canister came, and the shooting started.

Eugene, of course, pushed Kirstin under the chairs and wedged himself between her and the wildly firing gunman. He watched as bullets sprayed about; he says he saw "pieces of flesh fly," and then he took one in the hip and another in the knee. Then he heard the gun click and figured this was their chance to make a run for it. They dragged themselves out the door as Holmes reloaded, locking eyes with Eugene briefly as he did. The bullet in Eugene's hip was too dangerous to remove, and it took months of physical therapy for him to regain use of his leg, but the couple was able to turn one of the most harrowing experiences imaginable into a positive. Eugene proposed in April 2013, and they were married on July 20—a year to the day after the shooting.

TOP 10 Strangest Places People Actually Lived

by Caroline Coupe

10 In a Stranger's Closet

A 57-year-old man in Fukuoka, Japan, was mystified when food kept disappearing from his kitchen. He rigged a surveillance camera that sent pictures to his mobile phone of an intruder in his apartment. When police arrived and searched the residence, they discovered 58-year-old Tatsuka Horikawa hiding in the upper compartment of a storage closet.

She moved a futon into the space and even took showers while the owner was out. The woman said she had nowhere else to live and first snuck into the residence a year before because the owner had left it unlocked. She was charged with trespassing.

9 With a Dead Body

A woman in Michigan lived with her dead roommate's body for up to 18 months because she was lonely. Charles Zigler was 67 years old and suffering from emphysema when he passed away. Instead of reporting his death, Zigler's 72-year-old friend Linda Chase, with whom he'd lived for ten years, propped his body up in a chair in front of the television.

She kept the body clean and dressed and talked to the mummified remains while watching NASCAR. Chase was investigated for social security fraud for continuing to cash Zigler's checks after his death, but that doesn't appear to be the motive for keeping her friend's corpse. When asked why she had done such a thing, Chase said "I didn't want to be alone. He was the only guy who was ever nice to me."

8 In a Shopping Mall

In 2003, Michael Townsend and several of his artist friends took over an unused space in a Rhode Island shopping mall. They managed to sneak two tons of construction materials into the mall to create their studio apartment, which was hidden from view by a wall of cinder blocks. The room had electricity and was fully furnished, though they used the mall bathrooms. They managed to go unnoticed—living in the space for up to three weeks at a time—for four years.

Townsend had plans to improve the space, but the group walked in one day and was greeted by security guards. Townsend said he was inspired by a holiday ad that said how great it would be to live at the mall. He claimed the apartment was an art project, and his goal was to "understand the mall and life as a shopper." He was sentenced to six months probation for the stunt after pleading guilty to criminal trespassing.

7 In a Cave

A 56-year-old man in New Mexico was found living in a cave on property that belonged to the Department of Energy. Roy Moore's makeshift abode was equipped with a bed, front door, wood-burning stove, solar panels, and satellite radio. He'd been living in the cave for four years without being detected. Smoke from the stove finally drew the attention of the authorities, who also discovered marijuana plants on the property. Moore and his belongings were removed, and he was charged with misdemeanor drug offenses.

6 In an Ex-Girlfriend's Attic

When a South Carolina woman heard noises coming from her attic, and nails began dropping from the ceiling, she had a feeling that "somethin' just ain't right." When her grown sons investigated, they discovered their mother's ex-boyfriend sleeping in a heating unit full of coats.

He'd been released from prison two weeks prior and had lived in the attic ever since. Not only was the woman unaware that he had been released, the couple's relationship had ended 12 years before. Adding to the creepiness factor, cups from a fast-food restaurant filled with human waste were found nearby. The man had also rigged the ceiling vents so that he could peer into his ex-girlfriend's bedroom.

5 In the Jungle

An eight-year-old Cambodian girl who disappeared with her sister while tending buffalo was found living in the wild after 19 years. A villager saw Roshom P'ngieng emerge naked from the jungle and attempt to steal his rice. He described her as "half human and half animal." According to police, she had no intelligible speech. The villager and his friends caught the woman, whose father identified her by the scars on her arms.

Attempts to reintegrate the woman failed; she was unable to learn the local language, preferred to crawl rather than walk, and refused to wear clothing. She eventually fled back into the forest. Some are skeptical about whether this woman truly was Roshom P'ngieng. They believe it unlikely that an eight-year-old girl could have survived such harsh conditions on her own, and her father has refused a DNA test.

4 In a Mini Apartment

A 50-year-old man in Paris was found living in a small room with a slanted ceiling, which had only 17 square feet of inhabitable space. There was barely enough room to stand, and the man had lived there for 15 years. The rent for this minuscule living space was about $442 a month. When asked how he coped with the accommodations, he told a French radio station, "I come home, I go to bed." The landlord found himself in hot water because French law says apartments in Paris need to be at least 97 square feet and must include a shower.

3 In Underground Tunnels

While investigating copper thefts at a nearby grain mill, police in Kansas City, Missouri, discovered an elaborate series of underground tunnels where some of the city's homeless had taken up residence. The tunnels were dug in a wooded area and ventilated with PVC pipe; the entrances were disguised by brush and other debris. One tunnel was as deep as 25 feet and led to a room with bedding and candles. A pile of diapers nearby led to concerns that there were children living down there. The tunnels were cleared out and shut down because the living conditions were unsafe, and the incident sparked debate about the city's homeless situation.

2 In a School Bus

A postal worker in Texas became concerned when she kept seeing two unkempt children on her route and contacted child welfare. The girl and boy, ages 11 and 5, were living alone on an abandoned school bus parked in a garbage-strewn lot. Their parents were in prison for taking part in a conspiracy to embezzle money from victims of Hurricane Ike. The bus had electricity, running water, an air conditioner, and bathroom facilities, but the children were essentially on their own.

An aunt was supposed to be looking after them, but she was working 12-hour shifts and overwhelmed, leaving the children unsupervised. They weren't enrolled in school, had little food, and were dirty. They were taken into custody by child welfare. Once released from prison, the parents regained custody of the children and were reportedly working hard to improve the living conditions on the bus.

1 With No Contact

In 1978, a team of geologists in Siberia was stunned to discover a family of six living on a mountainside, miles from the nearest civilization. The Lykov family fled religious persecution in 1936 and lived in the wild for the next 40 years. The two youngest children had never seen a human being that wasn't a member of their own family, but they were aware of their existence. Their language was distorted due to the isolation, and they had never seen bread.

In a single room, the family survived on a diet of potatoes, ground rye, and hemp seeds and hadn't eaten meat until the late '50s when the younger boy taught himself to trap. Their shoes were made of bark, and their only reading materials were prayer books and a family Bible. In 1961, cold weather destroyed the family's crops, reducing them to eating bark and shoe leather. Their mother died of starvation during this time, making sure her children had enough to eat. After their discovery, the Lykovs remained in their remote home, accepting only a few useful items.

Three years later, three of the Lykov children died within days of each other. Their father died in 1988, leaving Agafia, the only remaining child, alone on the mountain, where she has chosen to stay for another 25 years.

PHOTO CREDITS

Page 13: Mayan ruin © Zakharova Natalia

Page 16: desert © tobkatrina

Page 19: sunken ship © Andrew Jalbert

Page 24: witch hazel tree © Matjoe

Page 28: Ouija board © siouxsinner

Page 37: Superstition Mountains © Danette Carnahan

Page 44: Tiwanaku © Yolka

Page 45: Giza Plateau © WitR

Page 57: sheep © tomocam

Page 68: game controller © pixbox77

Page 73: computer © Hywit Dimyadi

Page 75: crying baby © Olesya Feketa

Page 78: old radio © jannoon028

Page 85: old liquor bottles © alfocome

Page 94: satellite © qingqing

Page 100: aircraft bombs © Straight 8 Photography

Page 102: cow © Eric Isselee

Page 103: Jimson weed © Melinda Fawver

Page 105: Antarctica snow © Volodymyr Goinyk

Page 109: Pearl Harbor memorial ©Donald R. Swartz

Page 110: Hollywood star © byggarn.se

Page 113: Confederate flag © Graeme Dawes

Page 117: Abraham Lincoln © KarSol

Page 121: World Trade Center © robert paul van beets

Page 126: ampoules and syringe © urfin

Page 128: moon © David Woods

Page 130: astronaut © Peter Hansen.tif

Page 134: nuclear explosion © curraheeshutter

Page 135: Pompeii body © Vacclav

Page 141: Doberman Pinscher © Eric Isselee

Page 147: skull © Ivancovlad

Page 151: old mirror © Kladej

Page 159: old dental tools © fotografos

Page 163: bat on cloudy background © javarman

Page 166: clown shoes © Szasz-Fabian Ilka Erika

Page 167: clown © Kalmatsuy Tatyana

Page 174: milk gallons © L Barnwell

Page 179: arrowhead © trekandshoot

Page 180: leech on skin © Sergey Lukyanov

Page 182: marionette dolls © PerseoMedusa

Page 187: guitar © MariusdeGraf

Page 189: crucifix © Michael Bann

Page 191: stiletto heels © stockbyMH

Page 194: katana © michelaubryphoto

Page 195: bucket of fried chicken © michelaubryphoto

Page 198: Earth © Loskutnikov

Page 200: toilet papers © Multiart

Page 203: fish pedicure © Maridav

Page 205: accupuncture needles © Bork

Page 206: segway © Sergiy Kuzmin

Page 208: angry cat © Oliver Hoffmann

Page 208: hot dog © Anastasia Tveretinova

Page 213: cereal in bowl © Oliver Hoffmann

Page 216: Spartan helmet © Dmitrijs Mihejevs

Page 218: caryatid © Dimitrios

Page 219: Saint Basil's Cathedral © Art Konovalov

Page 221: White House © Orhan Cam

Page 223: Great Wall of China © Hung Chung Chih

Page 223: swastika © Jim Vallee

Page 227: beer mug © Picsfive

Page 230: cat with mouse © smart.art

Page 232: serval cat © Four Oaks

Page 235: police dog © alterfalter

Page 237: dog panting © Victoria Rak

Page 242: binoculars © Yalik

Page 249: computer keyboard © David Lee

Page 249: baseball with glove and bat © Sergey Nivens

Page 250: bunny © Tsekhmister

Page 258: old letter © Brooke Becker

Page 259: spotlight © MANDY GODBEHEAR

Page 260: deck of cards © Tatiana Popova

Page 261: brain © Marc Bruxelle

Page 263: medical pack © Abel Tumik

Page 265: bullets © George W. Bailey

Page 266: cockroach © Somchai Som

Page 268: small television © Aaron Amat

Page 271: yo-yo © joppo

Page 272: roller skates © Stefano Pareschi

Page 274: cap gun © Hurst Photo

Page 275: pouring soda © kazoka

Page 278: pills © Brian Goodman

Page 280: Cheerios © Natalia Ganelin

Page 281: cigarette tray © wavebreakmedia

Page 286: police car lights © Ilya Andriyanov

Page 288: hundred dollar bills © evka119

Page 294: gerbil © Camilo Torres

Page 300: carved pumpkin © Yellowj

Page 302: knitting © Erlo Brown

Page 303: disco ball © Olga Selyutina

Page 304: telephone © Steve Collender

Page 308: underwear © Lucy Liu

Page 310: balloons © Ivonne Wierink

Page 312: puppies running © Orientgold

Page 314: kangaroo © Volodymyr Burdiak

Page 316: flyswatter © Ispace

Page 318: boxing gloves © imagedb.com

Page 321: Mount Fuji © Twonix Studio
Page 322: radiation sign © J.D.S
Page 326: cow tongue © Bernd Schmidt
Page 327: surgery procedure © Burlingham
Page 330: Lake Baikal © Konstantin Shishkin
Page 333: spoon © Igor Kovalchuk
Page 335: stack of CDs © imagedb.com
Page 341: marijuana joint © Eldad Carin
Page 342: ants © Nathalie Speliers Ufermann
Page 344: heroin and syringe © Evdokimov Maxim
Page 357: pigeons © pryzmat
Page 366: flea © Cosmin Manci
Page 373: dice © Vladimir Kim
Page 376: wooden shoes © Neirfy
Page 379: noose © Mega Pixel
Page 381: oranges and lemons © Nattika
Page 387: birch tree © Larisa Koshkina
Page 389: sparrow © Eric Isselee
Page 392: rose bush © YanaG
Page 393: lily pad © Olena Tur
Page 394: Hamburg chicken © Eric Isselee
Page 403: pig © Tsekhmister
Page 405: wild rabbit © Tom Reichner
Page 407: myrtle tree © Moolkum
Page 410: ring © schankz
Page 415: gallows © Zack Frank
Page 419: black cat in tree © Gunta Klavina
Page 428: solar eclipse © Suppakij1017
Page 433: comet © Krasowit
Page 436: statue of Stalin © Alfredo Ragazzoni
Page 438: American soldiers © Adam Ziaja
Page 443: old well © creativei images
Page 451: paintbrush © Karramba Production
Page 457: bulldozer © Smileus
Page 466: checkbook © plasid
Page 471: jail bars © Diego Schtutman
Page 474: pesticide canisters © Jiggo_thekop
Page 476: uranium © Kletr
Page 480: dolphins © Gerald Marella
Page 485: handcuffs © DenisNata
Page 488: white flowers © LiliGraphie
Page 491: bath tub © SasPartout
Page 497: corkscrew © windu
Page 498: gold jewelry © Elnur
Page 502: handgun © Peteri
Page 504: coupons © Jim Barber
Page 505: tarantula © Hyde Peranitti
Page 508: bicycle © Horiyan
Page 511: parking ticket on windshield © Chuck Wagner
Page 513: footprint in mud © Stephen Rees
Page 523: moon over dark forest © Tom Reichner
Page 526: scenic highway © Robert Crum
Page 531: judge hammer © Africa Studio
Page 534: Vatican plaza © Banauke
Page 536: old windmill © Kenneth Keifer

Page 541: bull's head © Roberto Cerruti
Page 545: lion in snow © davemhuntphotography
Page 547: broken wine glass © Africa Studio
Page 553: white Russian drink © Wollertz
Page 556: chocolate © kaband
Page 559: hamburger © Sukharevskyy Dmytro (nevodka)
Page 561: beef patties © atm2003
Page 563: syrup on pancakes © Brenda Carson
Page 565: sushi © nakamasa
Page 567: ramen © gori910
Page 571: taco shells © paintings
Page 573: grilled meat © Joe Gough
Page 574: vegetables © Ana Blazic Pavlovic
Page 578: eel © geniuscook_com
Page 580: small octopus © Madlen
Page 583: fresh oysters © kreatorex
Page 585: pepperoni pizza © Joshua Resnick
Page 588: Chihuahua © Eric Isselee
Page 590: coffee cup © Fotofermer
Page 594: glass of soda © chevanon
Page 596: star fruit © Viktar Malyshchyts
Page 598: tooth © schankz
Page 601: spider © Henrik Larsson
Page 605: African Shoebill © Jearu
Page 609: mudskipper © WICHAN KONGCHAN
Page 612: mosquito © claffra
Page 614: giant starfish © Ethan Daniels
Page 617: Brown-Headed Cowbird © gregg williams
Page 619: Komodo dragon © Anna Kucherova
Page 621: panda © leungchopan
Page 623: snapping turtle © Darko Zeljkovic
Page 626: maggots © Dario Lo Presti
Page 629: sea cucumber © e2dan
Page 631: dragonfly © Jessica Kuras
Page 636: seagull © Christian Musat
Page 637: bat © Kirsanov Valeriy Vladimirovich
Page 643: gas fumes © nikkytok
Page 651: licesnse plates © tobkatrina
Page 654: star cluster © Wolfgang Kloehr
Page 656: erupting star © Vadim Sadovski
Page 661: Jupiter © MarcelClemens
Page 666: shark © Joe Belanger
Page 678: space shuttle liftoff © Joe Stone
Page 697: rat © Oleg Kozlov
Page 702: kayak © Vereshchagin Dmitry
Page 707: supercell cloud © Minerva Studio
Page 710: tornado © Minerva Studio
Page 711: trail mix © picturepartners
Page 713: mountain lion © Wild At Art

ACKNOWLEDGMENTS

I would like to acknowledge the following people for their tireless efforts working for Listverse in one capacity or another. Without this amazing team, Listverse.com and this book would not be possible.

First I want to thank every person who has sent in a list to Listverse for consideration and especially those whose work has ended up on the site or in our books. Listverse is built on your contributions.

I must also thank Judy Richardson, our senior moderator, for her vigorous and fair monitoring of the commenters on Listverse. Thanks also to our other moderators, Aimee Counts, Caleb Compton, and Patrick Weidinger, who manage to find the time to ceaselessly read, moderate, and comment every day.

I wish to also thank our chief editor, Micah Duke, and our editorial team. Editing such a diverse range of topics is hard work and the whole team manages to do it with ease.

A very special thank-you is also owed to my wonderful partner, Soni Nguyen, who worked day and night on this project making sure we met the deadlines.

And finally I must thank my parents, Adam and Lois Frater, family, and friends who never get sick of my constant outbursts of trivia and myth busting.

ABOUT THE AUTHOR

Jamie Frater was born and raised in New Zealand. After a stint in the seminary he undertook postgraduate studies at the Royal College of Music in London. Deciding against a career in music he combined his thirst for knowledge and obscure trivia with his passion for computers and launched Listverse. He has been a guest speaker on numerous national radio and television stations in the United States, Canada, and Great Britain and has been featured in numerous national newspapers. He has also compiled two previous tomes of trivia, *The Ultimate Book of Top Ten Lists* and *Listverse. com's Ultimate Book of Bizarre Lists*.